"Erudite . . . The author balances the academic strength of a scholar with the pastoral sensitivity of a rabbi. Readers will be intrigued by the dizzying array of references to Jewish teachers across the centuries, as well as philosophers, Christian theologians, and others, and he approaches topics such as family relations with practicality and nuance. A highly literate, thought-provoking, persuasive argument for the centrality of love in the Jewish faith."
—*Kirkus Reviews* (starred review)

"[A] paradigm-shifting study . . . Held avoids dogmatism and is never anything less than transparent . . . Held draws profound meaning from Judaism and its promise that 'we are capable of living lives animated by love, mercy, compassion, and generosity.' This has the power to reshape Jews' views of their faith." —*Publishers Weekly* (starred review)

"A deeper reflection of what spirituality and love are . . . A relevant and useful title that's perfect for readers interested in Judaism, theology, religious ethics, or social justice." —John Jaeger, *Library Journal*

"In this provocative book, Shai Held challenges the widely held view that Judaism is mainly about justice and law while Christianity is mainly about love. Through a learned but beautifully accessible interpretation of biblical and Talmudic texts, Held shows that Jewish ethics and theology are fundamentally about love—the love expressed in God's creation of the world, and the love of the neighbor, of the stranger, of humanity, and of God that the Torah commands. This book will prompt readers, religious and secular alike, to rethink the ethical teachings of Judaism and Christianity and to reflect anew on the meaning of a good life."

—Michael J. Sandel, author of *The Tyranny of Merit: Can We Find the Common Good?*

"This is a truly magnificent book, necessary for our troubled times. Shai Held, one of Judaism's leading scholars and thinkers, rebuts facile stereotypes of Judaism that contrast Jewish law with Christian love, and demonstrates the centrality of love, imagination, and compassion in the Jewish tradition. Held's discussion is nuanced: love of strangers is an unequivocal mandate; concerning the love of enemies, however, there are goals, but no easy answers. Nonetheless, Judaism commands, in all of the traumatic situations of our lives, an exacting self-development of emotions and imagination, so that we can hope to live together well with others, as strangers and fellows, in this difficult world. *Judaism Is About Love* should be required reading for Jews and non-Jews alike."

—Martha C. Nussbaum, Distinguished Service Professor of Philosophy and Law, University of Chicago

"Destined to be a classic of Jewish thought, this is a text to be read, studied, and savored—not only by individuals but, perhaps most fittingly, *b'hevruta*, in dialogue among beloved learning companions."

—Rabbi Sharon Cohen Anisfeld, president, Hebrew College

"Held is known for his ability to . . . seamlessly navigate between the head and the heart. *Judaism Is About Love* is a master class in negotiating these two aims . . . Few recent books of theology will leave readers feeling as knowledgeable, inspired, or moved."

—Marc Katz, Jewish Book Council

"This will probably be the most important Jewish book to publish this year or even in the last few. Its message is essential, important for a Christian-centric world that seems to perceive the Christian tradition as all about love, while considering Judaism to be about law and justice . . . [Held] is one of the most articulate rabbis and scholars in North America today."

—Jon M. Sweeney, *Spirituality & Practice*

"One of the most highly regarded voices in the American Jewish community, Rabbi Shai Held frames the teachings of Judaism not only around issues of justice and law, but also around love, compassion and emotion. In this original, provocative work, he writes about God, theology and faith in ways that are deep yet also accessible. Engaging with a wide range of thinkers both sacred and secular, Held shows the potential of love to transform individuals—and the world—for the better."

—Sandee Brawarsky, *Hadassah Magazine*

"This magnificent book combines prodigious learning, theological depth, ethical insight, and spiritual inspiration—all on terms that are edifying to scholars and non-experts alike. If, after centuries of ignorance and contempt, we Christians are finally to learn the depth and coherence of Jewish traditions of biblical interpretation, practice, and prayer, *Judaism Is About Love* is our best chance in this generation."

—Ellen F. Davis, Amos Ragan Kearns Distinguished
Professor of Bible and Practical Theology,
Duke Divinity School

"Immensely learned, genuinely accessible, and overwhelmingly moving, *Judaism Is About Love* is destined to exert a massive and enduring influence upon Jewish life and thought; I would go so far as to predict that people will still be reading it centuries from now. Jewish and non-Jewish readers alike will be enlightened and inspired by this theological magnum opus!"

—Rabbi David Ellenson, chancellor emeritus,
Hebrew Union College, Jewish Institute of Religion

"For a long time the world has needed a Jewish thinker as treasured and respected by both Jews and Christians as Rabbi Abraham Joshua Heschel once was. It has also needed truly significant books that make Judaism accessible, compelling, and believable to a mass audience. Shai Held is that thinker and *Judaism Is About Love* is that book. Held's portrayal of Judaism as a humane, compassionate, and generous religion of love will bring Jews closer to Judaism and will enable Christians to see Judaism in a radically new light. This book is written with genuine intellectual honesty and a captivating style that will appeal to a wide range of readers."

—Rabbi Irving (Yitz) Greenberg, theologian and
author of *The Jewish Way*

"There are good thinkers, there are great thinkers, and then there are once-in-a-generation thinkers like Rabbi Shai Held. His astounding and contagious knowledge of his faith, mixed with his endlessly curious dives into and dialogue with other religious and philosophical traditions, makes him an utterly unique figure in religion and philosophy. As a Christian, my first and enduring thought as I finished reading *Judaism Is About Love* was simple and said out loud: 'I have met the Jewish Rowan Williams.' Christians who teach and preach your faith or who have ever wondered what Jews really believe: read this book, more than once if possible. It's that good and that important."

—Reverend Dr. Patricia Lyons, Virginia Theological Seminary

"In this magisterial work, Rabbi Shai Held clearly demonstrates from the Hebrew Bible, Talmud, and other authoritative Jewish sources that Judaism is about love. This work is an indispensable contribution to Jewish ethics, to be sure, but really to all ethical reflection. In this bloody, hateful era, how desperately we need this nuanced exposition of the theological ethics of love."

—Reverend Dr. David P. Gushee, Distinguished University Professor of Christian Ethics, Mercer University

"Shai Held's powerful, learned, and passionate book makes it clear that Judaism has always placed love at the center, and eloquently urges its readers to do the same. *Judaism Is About Love* cites texts and thinkers from the Bible to the present day, ranges widely over Christian thought and secular philosophy, and brings telling lessons from Held's personal experience—all of them marshaled to make the point that God loves the human beings created in God's image, and wants each of us to become vehicles through which God's love, grace, and compassion flow to others. One leaves the book inspired by the author's wisdom and grateful for his tradition's counsel on how to spend our time on earth well."

—Arnold M. Eisen, chancellor emeritus, Jewish Theological Seminary of America

SHAI HELD

· · ·

JUDAISM
IS
ABOUT
LOVE

Shai Held—theologian, rabbi, educator, author—is the president and dean of the Hadar Institute in New York City. He is the author of *Abraham Joshua Heschel: The Call of Transcendence* and *The Heart of Torah*, a collection of essays on the Torah in two volumes. He lives in White Plains, New York.

ALSO BY SHAI HELD

Abraham Joshua Heschel:
The Call of Transcendence

The Heart of Torah, Volume 1:
Essays on the Weekly Torah Portion: Genesis and Exodus

The Heart of Torah, Volume 2:
Essays on the Weekly Torah Portion: Leviticus, Numbers,
and Deuteronomy

JUDAISM IS ABOUT LOVE

JUDAISM

IS

ABOUT

LOVE

Recovering the Heart of Jewish Life

SHAI HELD

Picador
Farrar, Straus and Giroux
New York

Picador
120 Broadway, New York 10271

The Library of Congress has cataloged the Farrar, Straus and Giroux
hardcover edition as follows:
Names: Held, Shai, 1971– author.
Title: Judaism is about love : recovering the heart of Jewish life / Shai Held.
Description: First edition. | New York : Farrar, Straus and Giroux, 2024. |
    Includes bibliographical references and index.
Identifiers: LCCN 2023040928 | ISBN 9780374192440 (hardcover)
Subjects: LCSH: God (Judaism)—Love. | God (Judaism)—Worship and love
Classification: LCC BM610 .H452 2024 | DDC 296.3/11—dc23/eng/20231002
LC record available at https://lccn.loc.gov/2023040928

Paperback ISBN: 978-1-250-37179-9

Designed by Patrice Sheridan

To

Lev Moshe,

Maya Aviva,

and

Yaakov (Coby) Carmel Tzvi

באהבה רבה ובאהבת עולם

With love abundant and abiding

• • •

CONTENTS

PART III:

HESED: BRINGING GOD'S LOVE TO OTHER PEOPLE

PART IV:

THEOLOGY OF A LOVING GOD

JUDAISM IS ABOUT LOVE

INTRODUCTION

JUDAISM IS NOT what you think it is.

Judaism is about love. The Jewish tradition tells the story of a God of love who creates us in love and enjoins us, in turn, to live lives of love. We are commanded to love God, the neighbor, the stranger—and all of humanity—and we are told that the highest achievement of which we are capable is to live with compassion. This is considered nothing less than walking in God's own ways.

If this seems new or surprising to you, this is likely because centuries of Christian anti-Judaism have profoundly distorted the way Judaism is seen and understood, even, tragically, by many—probably most—Jews.

The journey that led to this book began more than two decades ago. Speaking to a classroom full of senior students at one of America's major rabbinical seminaries, I remarked in passing that "Judaism is built on the idea that God loves us and beckons us to love God back." Seemingly bewildered by what I'd said, one of the students declared: "I'm sorry, but that sounds like Christianity to me." I was perturbed, even somewhat distraught, by how he'd responded, and I explained that I'd been thinking of Judaism's daily liturgy: in the twice-daily recitation of the Shema we first declare that God loves us, and then recite Deuteronomy's command: "And you shall love the Lord your God with all your heart, and with all your being, and with all your might" (Deuteronomy 6:5). How, I wondered, could something so foundational to Judaism have come to seem so foreign that even an advanced rabbinical student could react in this way?

We have all heard it a thousand times. Christianity is about love, we are told, but Judaism is about . . . something else, like law, or justice, or whatever. In the past, such ideas were propagated by Christian thinkers who created a "theological discourse about the supersession of a love-less Judaism by a loving Christianity."[1] But strangely—and tragically—many Jews, including many rabbis and teachers, have accepted, and in some cases even embraced, this legacy of Christian anti-Judaism. And so generations of American Jewish children have been taught that Judaism is about something other than love.

In a similar vein, we often hear that whereas Christianity cares about how you feel and what you believe, Judaism cares only about what you do. Judaism is a religion of action, we've been taught, not emotion; a religion of deeds, of rote rituals, not inwardness.

Along the same lines, we are told that whereas the God of the New Testament is a God of love and mercy and grace, the God of what Christians refer to as "the Old Testament"—that is, the Hebrew Bible—is angry, vindictive, and bloodthirsty. This idea, an enduring legacy of anti-Judaism, tends to be treated as an unquestioned commonplace in our culture.

This is all hopelessly misguided. Judaism is a religion of love *and* law, of action *and* emotion; indeed, Jewish liturgy reminds us daily that Jewish law is itself a manifestation of divine love, not a contrast or an alternative to it.

Jewish texts push us to love both more deeply and more widely. They help us understand what intimate relationships and families and communities require of us—and what they make possible for us. They push us to love our neighbors—to want them to flourish and to con-tribute in meaningful ways to making that happen. They teach us to see the world with eyes of love and generosity of spirit. They prod us to love the stranger, the outsider, who is so often ignored, or cast out, or even demonized. They invite us to cultivate compassion so that we can be present with others when they are hurting and suffering.

Jewish theology, spirituality, and ethics thus contrast sharply with popular conceptions of them.

Centuries of Christian anti-Judaic polemics are not the only source of such distortions and misapprehensions. They are also part of a broader phenomenon in American Jewish life: perhaps because of anxiety about assimilation, American Jews long ago began to define Judaism as whatever they thought Christianity was *not*. So because Christianity was about love, Judaism was, well, *not* about love. Because Christianity placed such great emphasis on feeling, Judaism was necessarily not about feeling, but about action and ritual; because Christians were so focused on belief, the centrality of faith and belief in Judaism was dramatically downplayed.

Another crucial example: because Christianity stressed divine grace, many Jews held that Judaism did not really have a notion of grace. I have been asked countless times by educated and religiously observant Jews whether grace is a Jewish idea; each time I am surprised afresh at how something so essential to Judaism can seem so alien to it.[2] Yet grace (*hein/hesed*) is foundational to Jewish theology and spirituality. The gift of life is grace—the existence of the world is not something that anyone earned. God's love for us is grace—it is not something we earn but something we strive to live up to. And the revelation of Torah is grace—it is a divine gift given to us through no merit of our own.

Some of these misperceptions are also rooted in long-standing internal Jewish debate. Judaism does underscore the centrality of concrete action; after all, genuine emotions express themselves in concrete actions. Compassion without acts of kindness, for example, is arguably not really compassion at all. But as the medieval sage Rabbi Bahya Ibn Paquda (eleventh century) already lamented, there have been times in the history of Judaism when "duties of the heart" (*hovot ha-levavot*) were underemphasized in favor of "duties of the limbs." Always, Jewish thinkers emerged who sought to steer Judaism back to its proper path, one of both emotion and action, of deep-seated integration of the internal and the external worlds. They understood, and sought to remind us, that the apparent dichotomy between emotion and action is ultimately artificial and unhelpful. Judaism is about both the heart *and* the deed, not one *or* the other.

This book is, to a significant extent, an act of recovery. My aim is to tell the story of Jewish theology, ethics, and spirituality through the lens of love, and thereby to restore the heart—in both senses of the word—of Judaism to its rightful place.

CHOOSING LOVE

The world is a complicated place, suffused with both beauty and barbarism. Any given day can make us dance with joy and recoil in horror. We shudder at the depths of human depravity and marvel at the extent of human goodness; we see signs of moral progress in one corner and symptoms of decay in another. We encounter some who revel in killing innocents, and others who risk life and limb to save perfect strangers. The dignity of one group is finally affirmed even as the humanity of another is brutally denied. One page of the newspaper bolsters our faith in humanity while the next all but destroys it.

We as individuals are also excruciatingly complicated. We are capable of unbridled cruelty and dreadful selfishness—and also of great kindness and immense generosity. We are capable of trampling on the poor and ignoring the weak—and also of fighting for justice and siding with the oppressed. We are capable of reveling in our own prejudice and xenophobia—and also of welcoming the outsider. We are capable of murderous hate—and also of prodigious love. As the Scottish philosopher David Hume memorably puts it, we human beings have "some particle of the dove, kneaded into our frame, along with the elements of the wolf and serpent."[3]

We are complex beings with contradictory natures, struggling to make our way through an often bewildering world. In the face of all this, Jewish tradition makes a simple but audacious claim: our conflicting impulses notwithstanding, we remain capable of choosing the good—and the height of the good is love. Embracing Torah and its teachings can help us make that choice—not once and for all, but again and again, multiple times each day.

Judaism is not naive or Pollyannaish about who and what we are; it knows how often we go astray, embracing the expedient and the self-serving instead of the right and the good, choosing hate or indifference over love. The Jewish tradition is not optimistic about human nature but it is stubbornly, insistently possibilistic.[4] Its deeply held conviction is not that we *will* choose the good but that we *can* do so. Although we so often fail, it teaches, we are capable of succeeding. We can choose love.

LOVE: FIRST IN TIME, AND FIRST IN VALUE

Jewish ethics champion an array of character traits and virtues. To take just a few examples, honesty and integrity, loyalty and faithfulness, and a passion for justice are all held up as ideals toward which to strive. But one virtue, I think, stands above all the rest: love. Judaism is about many things, but above all else Judaism is about love.

Why is love preeminent among Judaism's values? Isn't justice, say, just as important? Justice is undoubtedly essential to Jewish theology and ethics, but it is love that makes a concern with justice possible in the first place.

None of us ever did anything—none of us *could* ever have done anything—to earn the gifts of life and consciousness. The creation of the world, and of human beings within it, is an act of grace—something we did not earn, *could not have earned*. As Maimonides (Rambam, 1138–1204) puts it, "This reality as a whole—I mean, that God has brought it into being—is grace."[5]

For Judaism, grace is closely entwined with love. God creates the world, we are taught, as an act of grace, benevolence, and love.[6] As a

modern sage puts it, "God's whole involvement in creation and bringing into being was in order to do good for creatures."[7] But God doesn't
just want to bestow benevolence; Judaism's startling claim is that God
wants to love[8] and be loved. God wants relationships, and for that,
God has to create a world that is other than God and human beings
within it who are also other than God. (I realize that these are difficult
claims for many modern readers to embrace. More on that below.)

Without God's prior, love-inspired act of creation, there would be
no creatures to care about justice in the first place. Divine love makes
the human pursuit of justice possible.

What is true of the world as a whole is equally true of each of us as individuals. In order for us to grow into adults who care about justice—or
anything else, for that matter—we first need the kind of parental love
and nurturance that (ideally at least) gives no thought to justice, or even
reciprocity. It is our experience of being loved that enables us to become moral agents at all. More generally, "to live as a creature is to live
through the nurture of others."[9] In our individual lives as in the world
as a whole, love comes first.[10]

All of this suggests that love is first in time, but is it also first in
value?

A midrash imagines that when God was about to create Adam, the
angels split into factions and began to argue. "Kindness said, 'Let him
be created, since he will perform acts of lovingkindness'; Truth said,
'Let him not be created, since he is all lies.'" How does God respond
to the debate? "God took truth and cast it to the earth."[11] Faced with
a choice between love and other competing values, God embraces the
former and rebuffs the latter. As Rabbi Zalman Sorotzkin (1881–1966)
explains, the key point is that "essence of the creation of the human
being is because they perform acts of lovingkindness."[12] God risks a
lot, and puts up with a lot, all in the name of love—both the love God
has for us and the love God hopes that we will embody and bring into
the world.

God creates us *with* love, *for* love. The source of our godliness, an
array of Jewish sages teaches, is our capacity for kindness and generos-

ity. Accordingly, our greatest desire should be to do good for others.[13] As Rabbi Aharon Kotler (1892–1962) puts it, "The whole purpose of creation is love (*hesed*), and a person is obligated to conduct themselves accordingly."[14]

WHAT IS LOVE? EMOTION AND ACTION

What kind of love are we talking about? Is love an emotion or an action? And how do we go about placing it at the very center of our lives?

The kind of love Judaism speaks about is not an emotion *or* an action; it's an emotion *and* an action. It's an existential posture, a life orientation, a way of holding ourselves in the world; it's a way of life. Love is not (only) an emotion, since love, to be coherently considered love, persists over time in a way that many ordinary emotions do not. For comparison, we can say, "I was angry at you for five minutes," but we can't really say, "I loved you for five minutes."[15] So although love obviously has emotional dimensions, I'm not sure it makes sense to define it as an emotion. It's more accurate to understand love as a disposition, "a property of persons that is distinct from its manifestations."[16] What I mean when I speak of love as an existential posture or a life orientation is, in part, that it is a disposition to feel certain things and act in certain ways.

You might have thought that emotion and action were two separate domains. After all, I can feel one thing and do another. In our society, we tend to talk that way: emotions are seen as fundamentally private and internal, whereas actions are more public and external. But for the Bible, emotions are not really separable from the actions to which they lead. The very idea of an emotional realm that is wholly distinct from the realm of action is foreign to the ancient world.[17]

In general in the Hebrew Bible, words like "love," "hate," and "fear" are not limited to the internal states we tend to refer to as emotions; they also include actions, ritual performances, and physical experiences.[18] Love, our central concern, is both an emotion that leads to action and, equally, a commitment to action that elicits emotion.[19] Thus, when we ask whether "love" in the Bible is an emotion or an action, the answer is simply "yes," it is both, and more.

THE THREE (OR FIVE) LOVE COMMANDS

The Torah issues three dramatic love commands. We are charged to love our neighbor, a fellow member of the covenant between God and Israel, in both emotion and action; to love the stranger, someone who lives among us despite not being part of our kin group and who is therefore vulnerable to exploitation, in both emotion and action; and to love God, who created the world, redeemed us from slavery, and gave us the Torah as an act of love and commitment, in both emotion and action. Later Jewish sources clarify that we have an additional obligation to love all human beings, who were created in the image of God and who are part of the same single human family as we are, in both emotion and action. Rabbinic* tradition adds the challenge to "walk in God's ways," to respond to other people's suffering with both compassionate feeling and compassionate action.[20] In each instance, what we are asked for is a combination—or more accurately, an integration—of emotion and action. Each of these charges will be the subject of one or more of the chapters that follow.

Human beings are complex, and ambivalent by nature. When I speak of integrating emotion and action, I don't mean that we come to feel love and nothing else, or compassion and nothing else—though that may happen sometimes—but rather that when different feelings come to the surface we choose to embrace and identify with the loving and compassionate ones.

These five obligations, all of which involve an integration of emotion and action to varying degrees, are so salient and central to Jewish life that in my view they form the very heart of the Jewish tradition; everything else grows out of and revolves around them.

---

* As is common, I use "Rabbinic" in referring to the Rabbis of the Talmud and "rabbinic" in referring to rabbis from later periods.

JUDAISM AND THE HEART

Jewish thinkers seek to bolster the intuition that *how* we give to others matters as much as—and sometimes more than—*what* we give them. As the Talmudic sage Rabbi Elazar declares, "The reward for charity (tzedakah) depends entirely upon the extent of the kindness (*hesed*) in it."[21] In the same vein, a modern rabbinic figure writes that "the essence of acts of *hesed* (lovingkindness) is the heart that is put into the deed."[22] Judaism is about *what* you do, *why* you do it, and *how* you do it. Jewish ethics ask for deeds of love done from love.

A similar logic applies in the ritual realm. Someone who observes Shabbat because she wants to acknowledge God for the wondrous gift of creation, or for the fact that she is free, or even because she just wants to do what she believes God wants, is very different from someone who observes it because she hopes God will reward her for it. Someone who keeps kosher out of a yearning to be connected to God is very different from someone who does so because he fears that otherwise God will smite him. Similarly, observing Shabbat or keeping kosher because "that's what my community does" or "that's what Jews have always done" is very different from observing them as part of a disciplined commitment to serving God. Their lives and their patterns of observance may seem externally similar but they diverge internally. And since the heart matters for religious life, they are in a deep sense living profoundly disparate religious lives.

On the surface, at least, one can keep the commandments without giving a thought to God (one can be outwardly observant without being inwardly religious in any way). Or one can live the commandments as an expression of, and a path to deepening, love of God. A significant gulf separates these two ways of engaging with Torah* and mitzvot (commandments); this gulf matters. If God wants to be loved with the

---

* I use "the Torah" when referring to the Pentateuch and "Torah" when referring to Jewish teaching more generally and expansively.

whole of our hearts, then whether and in what way we involve our hearts in our religious lives is pivotal.

It is not bad to care for a friend because it is our duty to do so. In fact, it's good, but it's less than ideal, and it would be better to act from love or compassion.[23] It's not bad to observe Shabbat because we feel attached to a Shabbat-observant community. It's just less than ideal, and it would be better to act from a desire to acknowledge God as Creator. It is not as if there are only two possibilities: perfect integration of our inner world and our external actions, on the one hand, or abject failure, on the other. Ideals are just that. We all fall short of them some of the time; many of us fall short of them almost all the time. But an ideal is something to strive for. To live a spiritual life is to seek to grow in love and kindness—and to persevere even when love as a perfect integration of emotion and action seems daunting or out of reach.

The Talmudic sages understood the complexity of our inner lives and saw that our motivations are often mixed. They counseled observing the commandments even for imperfect reasons, yet they held out hope that through observing the commandments for imperfect reasons we would eventually come to observe them for more perfect ones.[24] We should not lose sight of the ideal: a life in which emotion and action are deeply integrated and intertwined. And at the same time, we should remember that even at its best, human love as a posture is an asymptotic ideal:[25] We strive to get closer and closer to it, but we never fully arrive because only God loves wholly and perfectly.

The heart matters. As one of the most frequently cited Talmudic teachings has it, "The Blessed Holy One desires the heart."[26]

LOVE AS AN UMBRELLA TERM

But aren't love and compassion, for example, separate things? Yes and no. In Jewish thought, these modes of engagement with the world bleed into each other. In Aramaic, the language of the Talmud, love and compassion are deeply intertwined. The root that means "mercy" or "compassion" in Aramaic is r-h-m. And the root that means "love"? Also r-h-m. In other words, Aramaic knows no way to distinguish mercy or compassion, on the one hand, from love, on the other. It's the same word. The Talmud frequently refers to God as Rahamana, which translators conventionally render as "the Merciful One." But it would be just as correct to render God's name as "the Loving One" or "the Tender One."[27] Perhaps not surprisingly, then, some philosophers categorize compassion as "a form of love."[28]

As translations of the all-important biblical word *hesed* indicate, love and kindness also belong together. *Hesed* can be translated and defined in a variety of ways, and its precise definition is a subject of scholarly debate. In his search for an accurate way to render *hesed* in English, the Bible translator Myles Coverdale (1488–1569) coined the neologism "lovingkindness." As he understood *hesed*, love and kindness could not very easily be teased apart. Perhaps tellingly, the word *hesed* has been rendered over time as "love," "kindness," "lovingkindness," "mercy," "faithfulness," and more. The fact that one Hebrew word has been taken to refer to all these suggests that they are so interwoven with one another that we can't fully explore one (love) without investigating the others as well. As the philosopher Robert Roberts helpfully points out, "Although love is a matter of emotions, it is not right to identify it with any particular emotion. Instead, it is the caring or passion that may be expressed by any number of possible emotions."[29]

This "slippage" among these terms is part of why I am neither bold nor foolhardy enough to attempt a rigorous definition of love.[30] In any case, I am not sure a singular definition is all that helpful, since we should avoid reducing the inherent complexity and diversity of what love is. It's probably better to see love as an integral part of many of the ways we interact with and feel bound to one another, to the rest of creation, and to God. At bottom, love as a posture values and pursues the flourishing of others.

JUDAISM IS NOT CHRISTIANITY

As religions of love, Judaism and Christianity have much in common. But it's crucial to emphasize: Judaism is not Christianity avant la lettre. There are obviously foundational theological disagreements between the two traditions. To encapsulate two thousand years of theological debate in one sentence, Jews reject the idea that God is a trinity and the notion that God became incarnate in a human being; and, living in a thoroughly unredeemed world, Jews insist that the Messiah has not yet come. But even where love itself is concerned, there are essential differences between Judaism and Christianity.

To take just a few examples: I've already mentioned Judaism's "possibilism" about human nature, its conviction that we can choose the good even if we often don't. Although we should always be careful about painting religions in overly broad strokes—no religion is a monolith—I think it's fair to say that Christianity takes a darker, dimmer view of human nature than Judaism does. Put simply, Jewish theology assumes that we are capable of keeping the commandments; Christianity, especially in its Protestant forms, usually does not. Accordingly, as we'll see in chapter 14, Jewish thinkers traditionally see the law as a divine gift, a site where God's love and our own meet. The dichotomizing between law and love, so prevalent in some Christian quarters, is utterly alien, and even antithetical, to Judaism.

Jews and Christians also tend to diverge in how they think about and prioritize the particular and the universal. As we'll see in chapter 6, some Christian thinkers highlight universal love at the expense of particular loves, placing little emphasis on the affections and loyalties that make up much of our day-to-day lives. I think it's fair to say that the Jewish tradition is less ambivalent about the religious significance of family, friends, and community; our more local loves are the stuff out of which broader, more universal commitments may emerge. For Jewish thought, if not always for Christian, the path to universal love always runs through the particular.

In chapter 9, we'll consider what is often considered to be one of the key divides between Jewish and Christian ethics: whether or not there is a mandate to love our enemies. Although I'll show that the disagreement is not as stark as is often suggested—both traditions are more nuanced and variegated than we might at first think—it remains fair to say that Christianity places greater weight on love of enemies than Judaism does. The Jewish tradition's ambivalence on this point arguably stems from a more "realistic" approach both to the world as a whole and to our place—and our capacities and responsibilities—as human beings living within it.

CARING ABOUT THE QUESTIONS

Over the course of this book, I make a series of robust theological claims. I speak freely about a God who relates to us, loves us, and has expectations of us. I talk about what I think it means to worship God and to love God. But I make no assumptions about what you believe, or even about what you want to believe. I simply invite you to join me on this journey of uncovering and recovering the love that I believe lies at the heart of Judaism, and of probing how taking this love seriously has the potential to transform our lives and our world for the better.

Not long ago, an interviewer who considers himself an atheist asked me what I thought about people finding my interpretations of the Jewish tradition compelling but not subscribing to my theological assumptions or commitments. I responded by saying that although such reinterpretations would not likely ever be my own, I respect the fact that we live in a world that is fundamentally ambiguous, and that we can have no absolute certainty about how the world ultimately is. In my view, there are good reasons for belief and good reasons for unbelief. If readers who do not believe, or who believe differently, can find nourishment or inspiration in what I've written, if they can feel challenged or prodded by the interpretations that I offer, I will feel only gratitude.

Let me take this one step further. I do not think of believers and nonbelievers as "us" and "them." Belief and nonbelief are both part of us, and to be totally honest, they are both part of me. When I talk about a God who loves and cares about the dignity of every human being, I am aware that there are readers who will wonder, How on earth can anyone still believe that? I am aware not least because I too hear those voices, both in my heart and in my head. In this day and age, I think, a theologian has to be able to imagine secularity from the inside. In ways I sometimes wish that I didn't, I imagine that secularity every day.

How can I write theology when I am beset with doubt? I often think of a wonderful story told about the Hasidic master Rabbi Menahem Mendel of Kotzk (1787–1859). A student approaches the rebbe and says, "Rebbe, I am not sure there is a God," to which the rebbe responds, "What do you care?" Perplexed, the student replies, "What do you mean, what do I care? If there is no God, then the Torah doesn't matter." The Kotzker replies, again: "What do you care?" Frustrated, indignant, the student begins to yell: "If there is no God and the Torah doesn't matter, then I have no idea what the purpose of my life is! *Of course I care!*" To which the Kotzker responds, "You care that much? You are a kosher Jew." I wrestle with and write about theology because I care about it to the depths of my being, because questions about who and what God is, and about what it means to be a Jew and a human being in the twenty-first century matter to me like almost nothing else does. I care—I want God to be.[31] And for me faith is at least as much about possibility as it is about certainty.

I care, and given that you've found your way to this book, I assume that you do too. I assume that you care about God, or about love, or simply about what it means to live a good life. In the pages that follow, we'll explore that together.

QUOTING AND INTERPRETING: WHAT JEWS DO

As readers of this book will quickly discover (or be reminded), Jewish thought is inherently commentative. When traditional Jews explore a subject, whether a small point of Jewish law or a vast issue of theology, our first impulse is to consider what earlier texts and thinkers have said. Quoting those who came before us helps us escape solipsism,[32] but more than that, it roots us in both history and community.[33] "To speak as a Jew is to quote . . . [and] to quote is to see the present through the prism of tradition."[34] At its best and most vital, Judaism is a conversation across centuries and millennia. Later generations expound, elaborate upon, and sometimes subvert the teachings of their predecessors. As the Jewish philosopher Simon Rawidowicz (1897–1957) writes, the Jewish people are "a people of commentators, all postbiblical Jewish literature being a chain of commentaries on the 'text' and commentaries to the commentaries."[35] This book is a small link in that endless and infinitely precious chain.

The Jewish tradition is staggeringly vast; it contains a breathtaking array of voices within it. The project of this book is not to survey everything any Jewish thinker has ever said about love. That task would be impossible, and frankly rather tedious too. Instead, I seek to mine the vast resources of Jewish tradition in order to say something—or, really, many things—both deeply human and genuinely Jewish about love. I aim not merely to report on Jewish sources but to think with them.

The tradition is also immensely variegated. It contains divergent perspectives on just about everything.[36] To inherit a tradition is to make decisions, whether conscious or not, about which texts and ideas to place at the center, and which to treat as more marginal. If someone wanted to, they could presumably write a book entitled *Judaism Is About Hate*, and marshal an abundance of sources to bolster their case. And yet as we'll see in chapters 5 and 7, it is surely significant that when two of the most influential Talmudic sages seek to identify a core principle of the Torah, they settle on love (Rabbi Akiva), on the one hand, and on human dignity and solidarity (Ben Azzai), on the other. In privileging love and responsibility as I do in this book, I am standing on the shoulders of giants of the Jewish tradition.

To put it somewhat colloquially, as inheritors of traditions we must necessarily decide what to read in light of what. Standing inside a tradition prevents us from rejecting classical sources, but it allows us—and arguably invites or even requires us—to interpret and reinterpret them. Accordingly, I read the Jewish tradition as a story about a God of love who loves humanity and the Jewish people and who bids us to lead lives of love. As I understand it, everything else about the tradition revolves around that fundamental claim.

Traditions do not interpret themselves. Jewish religious writing—or at least Jewish religious writing worth taking seriously—emerges from the encounter among the thinker, the texts with which they engage, and whatever wisdom life has managed to impart to them. I am thus under no illusions that what I have produced is the—or even a—definitive statement on Judaism and love. What I offer, rather, is a meditation—or series of meditations—on love, grounded in the immense resources of the Jewish tradition.

Readers who wish to dive deep into the world of Jewish theology, biblical studies, and moral philosophy will find abundant textual references and amplifications in the notes. Because some of the arguments that I make upend conventional ways of understanding and presenting the Jewish tradition, I have been especially careful to include relevant sources and references. But I want to emphasize that the book and its ideas can be fruitfully engaged without consulting the notes. They are intended as a resource, not a burden or an obstacle.

Readers of both the text and the notes will undoubtedly notice how deeply I have engaged with a range of modern Christian thinkers and writers. I want to underscore, though, that this is not because Christianity or its texts have a monopoly on love; they decidedly do not. But a wide range of contemporary Christian thinkers have thought long and hard about the place of love in theology, spirituality, and ethics. So I engage with them, sometimes learning from them, sometimes dissenting from them, and sometimes merely noting how the two traditions answer similar questions similarly or differently. At all times, I have been guided by the principle Maimonides lays out: learn the truth from whoever says it.[37]

GROWING IN LOVE

The word "love" is abused incessantly. It's invoked as an empty cliché or, worse, as a marketing slogan. Worse still, it's used to refer to a kind of saccharine sentimentality that doesn't actually ask anything of us. Unconscionably, some speak of love while engaging in acts of barbarism (it's crushing to consider how many innocents have been killed in the name of other people's "love of God"). The novelist Walker Percy long ago aptly warned: "Beware of people who go around talking about loving and caring." The word "love," he insisted, had been utterly "polluted."[38]

But we still need the word, and we need it urgently. The best response to people using the word "love" poorly is not to use it less but to use it better.

Restoring love to its proper and authentic place in Jewish understanding is urgently necessary. If you're a Jewish reader, I aim to provide you with a critically important lens on Torah and the Jewish tradition. Whether you're a relative newcomer to Jewish learning or whether you've been studying Jewish texts your whole life, I trust that you'll come away with something new, and that you'll be challenged to grow ethically, spiritually, and theologically. I hope you'll be inspired to grow in love.

But *Judaism Is About Love* isn't intended only for Jews. If you're a Christian reader who seeks to discover what a living, breathing, thriving Jewish spirituality looks like, I hope you'll find sustenance in *Judaism Is About Love*. I hope you'll also be moved to reconsider and reimagine the relationship between Judaism and Christianity. Most importantly, I hope that like Jewish readers, you'll be stirred to grow in love.

If you're a reader from another religious tradition, or just a curious general reader, I hope you'll have your eyes opened to the depth and riches of Jewish ethical and spiritual thinking and that you'll be motivated to think in new ways about major questions of ethics, politics, and spirituality. I hope that you too will be moved to grow in love.

Ultimately, I hope enriching your understanding of Judaism will change your perception of what's possible and required in living a good life. I hope you'll encounter ideas and interpretations that will prod you to become a better parent, spouse, friend, and community member; I hope you'll feel challenged to become a better, more engaged citizen of your country and the world; and I hope you'll gain insights that can help you negotiate the complex and often ethically confusing world of life in the twenty-first century.

This book is, at bottom, an invitation to love.

PART I

THE SELF FACING
A LOVING GOD

1

WE ARE LOVED

WE ARE LOVED. We are loved, Judaism teaches, because God loves us. Not because of anything we have done or accomplished, but simply because we are created in God's image. As the Talmudic sage Rabbi Akiva puts it, "Beloved is the human being, for he was created in the image of God."[1]

God's love is not something we earn but rather something we (ought to) strive to live up to. This is a good definition of Judaism's vision of the spiritual life: the attempt to live up to God's love.

R. Akiva adds: "Even more beloved is [the human being], for it was made known to him that he was created in the image of God, as Scripture says, 'For in God's image did God make the human being' (Genesis 9:6)." In other words, God did not just create us in God's image and leave it at that. Instead, in the book of Genesis, God told us that God did so. God wants us to know that God created us in God's image.[2] Having this truth made known to us, Maimonides explains, is an additional act of kindness over and above the fact of having been created in God's image. "Sometimes one does good for someone out of pity for them and, because one disrespects them, one doesn't [bother to] inform them of what one did." Here, in contrast, God makes God's gift known—an obvious sign of respect, Maimonides suggests.[3]

Some Jewish thinkers go further. When you love someone, says

Rabbi Judah Loew of Prague (Maharal, 1525?–1609), you don't tell them unless you want to enter into relationship with them. God makes it known to us that God loves us because God hopes that we in turn will reciprocate that love.[4] This is the core structure of the twice-daily recitation of the Shema in Jewish prayer: we attest to God's vast love for us, and then take upon ourselves the charge to reciprocate that love.[5]

Portraying God's love for the Jewish people along the same lines, the prophet Hosea presents God as a parent[6] filled with love for his or her children: "When Israel was a child, I loved him, and out of Egypt I called [him?] My son" (Hosea 11:1)."[7] With these few words, Hosea makes two subtle but essential points. First, he teaches that God loves the people before God asks or demands anything of them. Second, Hosea does not attribute God's love to this attribute of the people or that. God's love for Israel is a function of divine grace rather than human merit. In other words, Israel does not earn God's love; it receives it as a gift from God. "Love comes first. Before anything else happens, God loves Israel. No reasons are given why God should feel that way about Israel. It is simply stated as a fact. Everything else flows from that basic statement of feeling."[8] The Jewish people are called upon not to earn God's love but to live up to it.

To be sure, divine love comes with expectations, and love does not preclude disappointment. The fact that God loves us no matter what does not mean that God is indifferent to the decisions we make and the paths we take. (I have often wondered whether the Bible would be more aptly named *The Book of Divine Disappointment*.) On the contrary, as any parent can understand, because God loves us so deeply, the choices we make matter profoundly. But even when we fail, God does not stop loving us.

Many of us struggle with ambivalence and uncertainty about ourselves, about our worth and lovability. God doesn't share our ambivalence; God loves us more than we love ourselves.[9] This is part of why self-loathing is so religiously problematic: we ought not hate what God loves.

God's love is a gift, but it is also an invitation. God loves in the hopes that we ourselves will become lovers too. We are called to love God, but also to love one another—the neighbor, the stranger, and, at moments at least, all of humanity and creation.

We are created *with* love, *for* love.

WE ARE INFINITELY VALUABLE

We matter, and matter ultimately.

According to my teacher Rabbi Irving "Yitz" Greenberg, all human beings are endowed with three "intrinsic dignities": infinite worth, equality, and uniqueness.[10]

A mishnah* wonders why God chose to begin by creating one human being—why not a dozen, or a hundred?[11] "Therefore was Adam created singly [, it declares]: 'to teach you that if anyone destroys a single life, Scripture charges him as though he had destroyed an entire world, and if anyone saves a single life, Scripture credits him as though he had saved an entire world.'"[12] In its original context, the meaning of this statement was that in killing a human being, we not only bring her life to an end, we also prevent countless of her would-be descendants from coming into being.[13] In killing (or saving) a single human being, then, we kill (or save) an entire world. But over the past half century, R. Greenberg has used the mishnah to make a different, more radical claim. Since all human beings on earth are images of God, we are each infinitely valuable in and of ourselves. To extinguish a single life is therefore akin to destroying an entire world. The value of human life is utterly incalculable; from a theological perspective, the very thought of placing a number on a human life is an abomination.

Many years ago, a close friend of mine, a promising young rabbinical student named Matthew Eisenfeld, was murdered in a terrorist attack in Jerusalem. His parents eventually sued the Iranian government, which had funded Hamas, the terrorist organization that had

---

* I use "Mishnah" to refer to the authoritative collection of oral teachings from early Rabbinic sages and "mishnah" to refer to an individual unit of instruction found therein.

carried out the killing. To his credit, the judge in the case insisted on hearing from Matt's friends about his life and the kind of person he was. I will never forget the shock I felt when I entered the courtroom. An actuary had constructed an elaborate chart spelling out in great detail just how much Matt was likely to have earned over the course of a career as a rabbi—and there it was, intended to be exact down to dollars and cents, a number attached to my friend's life. Appended to that number were punitive damages so steep that they effectively rendered that first estimate irrelevant. But all these years later the horror of that first number still startles and repels me. A human being is not a commodity. What it means to have dignity—what it means to be a *person*, in other words—is to be "exalted above any price."[14] Now, on one level, it may well be that in a less-than-perfect world, where bloodshed is rampant and human life is frequently debased, such calculations are necessary. But on a deeper level, the very idea of attaching a number to a human life is a sacrilege. What may be legally unavoidable nevertheless remains theologically unbearable.[15]

A single person, we are taught, is worth as much as an entire world. But maybe we'll tell ourselves, whether consciously or not, "Okay, fine, every human being is infinitely valuable, but let's be honest: I'm a little more infinitely valuable than anyone else. After all, I'm me." It is perhaps understandable that people so often fall into this trap: because we perceive and experience the world through our own consciousness, we can easily come to believe that our consciousness is the center of the universe. (Few of us would defend this as a truth about the way the world really is, but many of us live much of the time as if it were true; it becomes a psychological-experiential truth for us.) I find it striking that so many different religious traditions work to expose this sense that "I am the center of the universe" as a dangerous illusion. My consciousness is no more the center of the universe than yours is, and reminding myself of that is a first step toward remembering that you matter no less than I do.

We matter, but so too does everybody else—without exception.

WE ALL COME FROM THE SAME PLACE

The mishnah continues: "And [Adam was created singly] for the sake of peace in the human race, so that no one might say to his fellow, 'My ancestor was greater than your ancestor.'" Push far enough up our respective family trees, the mishnah says, and you and I will discover that, lo and behold, we're family.[16] Discrimination based on origins is thus not just reprehensible, it's also incoherent. The history of humanity is overrun by examples of people appealing to racial or ethnic origins to bolster their feelings of superiority—and worse, to legitimate horrific abuse and degradation of others. The mishnah seeks to nip this possibility in the bud.

Building on the mishnah, R. Greenberg notes that every image of God has the dignity of equality.[17] There is no preferred image of God; to claim that one "image of God" is superior to another, he insists, is to succumb to the temptation of idolatry.

The mishnah then adds what might at first appear to be a non sequitur: "And [Adam was created singly] so that the heretics should not say, 'There are many powers in heaven.'" In this context, I think, the text is less interested in mounting a metaphysical defense of monotheism than in spelling out what it takes to be the moral and political consequences of monotheism: since every human being is created by the same God (in the mishnah's language, there is only one power in heaven), we must avoid the trap of insisting that some people ("us") are the children of light, while others ("them") are the children of darkness. This may sound outlandish to some modern readers, but there have been many moments in history when such distinctions were common: not only are we biologically superior to others, some claimed, but we are also ontologically different (and better) than they are.[18] (This raises potentially thorny questions about what the chosenness of the Jewish people does—and doesn't—means in Jewish thought, an issue we'll consider at length in chapter 14.) The mishnah therefore reminds us that we are—all of us, every last one of us—children of the same one God. With apologies for using highly gendered theological language, the sages insist that arguments for the superiority of some over others fail both because we are descended from the same father (Adam) and because we were created by the same Father (God).

To be absolutely clear: what the mishnah is presenting is not an empirical history of what religion has all too often been, but rather a theological argument about what it ought to be. The argument is not that religious people are never racists—we know, sadly, how false that is—but that at the deepest levels religion and racism are mutually incompatible. At its core, racism is a denial of God. According to the mishnah's logic, to believe in one God who brings all of humanity into being is to affirm that we all come from the same place and that on some level we are therefore all equal.

There is another version of this text in which a crucial word is added. The variant of our text reads: "If anyone destroys a single life *from Israel*, Scripture charges him as though he had destroyed an entire world, and if anyone saves a single life *from Israel*, Scripture credits him as though he had saved an entire world." In other words, according to this version, it is Jews in particular, and not human beings in general, who are the subjects of this Rabbinic exploration of human value. Jewish life is infinitely valuable; human life is simply not the subject at hand. Two things ought to be kept in mind in considering these two very different versions of our text. First, historically speaking, scholars have shown that the original version does not include the words "from Israel"—this is a text about human dignity and value, not (just) Jewish dignity and value.[19] But even without historical evidence, the internal logic of the mishnah makes it obvious that we are talking about human beings rather than just Jews. Adam, after all, is the father of humanity as a whole, not (just) of the Jewish people. In other words, there are two paths the mishnah could have taken. One path is the one we've been discussing: "Therefore was Adam created singly: to teach you that if anyone destroys a single life, Scripture charges him as though he had destroyed an entire world, and if anyone saves a single life, Scripture credits him as though he had saved an entire world." An alternative path would have been: "Therefore was Abraham elected (or chosen) singly: to teach you that if anyone destroys a single life from Israel, Scripture charges him as though he had destroyed an entire world, and if anyone saves a single life from Israel, Scripture credits him as though he had saved an entire world." But appealing to the creation of Adam, who was not Jewish, to derive a lesson about the value of Jewish life in particular would have made no sense. This foundational Jewish text, then, is a dramatic affirmation of the value of all (and each) human life.[20]

WE MATTER IN ALL OUR UNIQUENESS

Sometimes people assume that equality somehow effaces difference. If we're all equal, we must all be the same. The mishnah disagrees: "And [Adam was created singly] to proclaim the greatness of the Blessed Holy One, for a human being stamps many coins with one die and they are all alike one with the other, but the King of the kings of kings, the Blessed Holy One, has stamped all of humanity with the die of the first man, and yet not one of them is like his fellow." The mishnah's message is startlingly powerful: never before in the history of the cosmos has there ever been, and never again in the history of the cosmos will there ever be, another human being just like you. And that simple fact testifies to the glory of God. As R. Greenberg observes, not only are we all absolutely valuable, we are all also distinctive and unique; that fact, the mishnah reminds us, is to be cherished and celebrated.

According to Jewish theology, then, some of our most primal emotional experiences actually tap into elemental truths about the universe. When a parent looks at their child and thinks, "Nothing could possibly be more precious than you," they are not just expressing the depths of their own love; they are giving voice to the profound Jewish conviction that the child in front of them, like every child everywhere, is infinitely valuable. And when a grieving parent wails, insisting that "nothing can ever make up for the loss of this child," the unspeakable pain they convey actually discloses something that Judaism considers a foundational truth: because each and every life is genuinely unique, each and every life is utterly irreplaceable. With the death of a human being, something inestimably valuable is gone forever.

We do not matter, in other words, simply because we are examples of a privileged species. We matter, rather, in all our singularity and uniqueness. Before God, we are never anonymous or faceless.

TRUE SELF-WORTH

The mishnah ends on a somewhat surprising, and, for many, even a jarring note: "Therefore each and every person is obligated to say, 'For my sake was the world created.'" When I teach this text, there are usually at least a few students who are troubled, and even offended, by this conclusion. Why, they demand to know, would the text end by asking us to say something that seems so narcissistic, and thus so antithetical to everything we have just been taught? Doesn't a teaching like this really just surrender to the impulse to place our consciousness at the center of the universe? The question becomes even stronger when we note that the mishnah does not just *permit* us to say these words; it actively *requires* us to do so.[21]

The mandate to say—and by implication, to think and feel—that the world was created for my sake is not a license to affirm my own superiority to other people, a possibility the mishnah explicitly rules out ("that no one might say . . ."). Affirming our significance is decidedly not the same thing as asserting our superiority over others. Our text may actually want to jolt us, to prod us to think more deeply about what a true sense of self-worth looks like. If I am willing to reflect upon *why* I am obligated to affirm my own value, I quickly realize that the basis of my self-affirmation actively requires me to affirm others—*all* others—as well, since we are all infinitely valuable images of God. I matter, and so do you—and for precisely the same reason.

To return to where we started: the mishnah subtly makes the revolutionary claim that our ultimate worth as human beings is a function not of what we achieve in the world, but of the simple fact that we have been created by God. This radical insight turns many of our conventional assumptions about self-worth on their head. As I've said, our worth is not something that we earn, but something that we strive to live up to. We matter, and matter ultimately, not because of what we *do*, but because of what we (always already) *are*: creatures created in the image of God.[22] To sit with this stark claim can at first seem frightening—it is not easy to let go of the illusion that our worth is something we work for—but it is also potentially extraordinarily liberating: we no longer have to compete with others in order to gain the confidence that we matter.

Imagine I am walking down the street, mired in a pit of self-loathing; I feel worthless and unloved. Or maybe, less dramatically, I am alternating, as so many of us do, between telling myself I'm wonderful and wondering whether I'm worthless. But then I start to look around, and I think to myself, "Well, I may be worthless, but I am smarter than she is, better-looking than he is, more successful than that other guy," and so on.[23] Depending on just how badly I am feeling about myself and how desperate I am to build myself up, I can go on like this all day—or my whole life, for that matter. In the face of all this, Jewish theology insists that genuine self-worth is never competitive or comparative, never purchased at the expense of others. The source of my value, and theirs, is ultimately one and the same: we are all created in the image of God.[24]

The sad truth is that comparison with other people offers only fool's gold. After all, the rich sometimes get poorer, the beautiful inevitably get older, and the smart often encounter people they suspect are just a little bit smarter (this is why the culture of academia can so often be so utterly competitive and brutal).[25] So our sense of self-worth feels shaky and tenuous. The more threatened our sense of ourselves becomes, of course, the more ferocious our need to put others down becomes.[26] Comparing ourselves with others doesn't heal our insecurities, it merely papers over them. Worse, it frequently amplifies and exacerbates them.

Even more damaging, our lives become animated by schadenfreude, pleasure derived from other people's failures or misfortunes: if my sense of self depends on my being richer, smarter, more attractive, or more successful than you, then your rising must entail my falling, and almost inevitably, I grow invested in your failure. At a certain point, I cease to see *you* at all—your successes and failures matter only because of how they reflect on me. Needless to say, this is not a prescription for emotional health and interpersonal connection. If I am truly going to love others, it helps a lot to feel confident that I, too, am loved; if I am going to affirm the worth of others, it helps to feel sure that I, too, have worth. Judaism understands this and teaches us: we are always already loved and always already "worthful."[27] If we can internalize this, we can love and honor others more fully and deeply.[28]

Over the course of my career, I have counseled countless students whose lives were poisoned to one extent or another by a frantic, desperate pursuit of the sense that they were valuable. The culture of competition and ranking that so pervades our schools only intensified their desperation. (How deep does this pathology run? Not long ago a friend reported to me of visiting a preschool where the head of school boasted that her school was "a feeder for the Ivy League." Really.) Offering us a theological antidote to all this, the sages invite us to stop chasing our worth and to know—to really know, emotionally and existentially, not just cognitively—that we already have it.

HUMILITY: WHAT IT IS AND WHAT IT ISN'T

There is something surprising in all of this. On the one hand, Jewish sources tell us that humility lies at the very core of the religious life. Moses is singled out in the Bible for this trait above all others (Numbers 12:3), and Maimonides insists that where humility is concerned, the golden mean, to which he is otherwise committed, does not apply: one should be as humble as one possibly can.[29] And yet, at the very same time, our mishnah requires us to declare that the whole world was created for our sakes. Is there not a contradiction here? Can we humbly declare our infinite worth?

Jewish tradition insists not only that we can but that we must do precisely that. Knowing that we matter, Jewish theology insists, is not pride; pride would be the insistence that we have earned all of the worth we have, or the pretension that we matter while others do not. Knowing our worth is not vanity; vanity would be the insistence that our worth is something we ourselves have achieved, or that we are worth more than others. In a similar vein, knowing our talents and abilities is not arrogance but self-awareness.[30]

Being humble does not entail feeling incompetent or inferior to others. Jewish sources are clear: it is actively forbidden to bear a negative view of ourselves. Humility has nothing at all in common with self-hatred or self-loathing. To see ourselves as wretched and worthless, Jewish teachers warn, is to grant ourselves license to behave in vulgar and abject ways. As Maimonides memorably puts it, "If one has a base view of oneself, one will readily do base things."[31] Conversely, if we internalize our own nobility as human beings, we will be far less likely to behave in abject ways.[32] We are thus obligated to affirm our own worth.[33] "Just as a person believes in God," the Hasidic master Rabbi Zadok Ha-Kohen of Lublin (1823–1900) teaches, "one must also[34] believe in oneself."[35] How we see ourselves profoundly shapes who and what we become. "The more one knows his own worth, the greater his worth in truth."[36]

The desire to change and be better depends on a robust sense of self-worth. Many people who engage in introspection assume that what it means to work on ourselves is to dwell incessantly on our flaws. But to probe our shortcomings, the Musar master Rabbi Shlomo Wolbe (1914–2005) insists, is only half of what is required—and to be conscious *only* of our shortcomings is a prescription for failure and despondency. "The beginning of all individual work," he writes, "is specifically the experience of a human being's exaltedness. Anyone who has never focused on the human being's exaltedness from his very creation, and whose only self-work is to know more and more about the bad sides of himself and to make himself suffer as a result—that person will sink deeper and deeper into despair, and in the end will make peace with the bad out of sheer lack of hope of ever changing it." In order to grow, R. Wolbe argues, we first have to appreciate—not just cognitively, but experientially as well—the fact of human greatness.[37] R. Wolbe cites his teacher, Rabbi Yeruham Levovitz (1873–1936): "Woe to a person who is unaware of their shortcomings, because they will not know what to work on. But even greater woe to a person who is unaware of their virtues, because they don't even know what they have to work with."[38] No sense of self-worth, it seems, no spiritual growth.[39]

What all of this points to is the realization that "arrogance and high self-esteem have little in common." On the contrary, arrogance has much more in common with low self-esteem than with high: "Both arrogance and low self-esteem are forms of self-reference which lead a person to evaluate life experiences predominantly in terms of their impact on self."[40] Whether we think too much of ourselves or too little, we all too frequently end up thinking *only* of ourselves. The irony is that "the self-condemnation often associated with an inferiority complex can be just as self-centered as selfish pride. Both involve obsession with self."[41] Perhaps paradoxically, then, a healthy sense of self-worth liberates us from having to spend all our time thinking about ourselves. Real humility makes self-transcendence possible (that is, it enables us to think and care about things other than ourselves), and that frees us from the abyss of self-absorption.[42] As William Temple, the Archbishop of Canterbury (1881–1944), wonderfully puts it, "Humility does not mean thinking less of yourself than of other people, nor does it mean having a low opinion of your own gifts. It means freedom from thinking about yourself at all."[43]

Imagine taking all of this to heart: By virtue of the fact that we are created in the image of God, we are infinitely valuable, and we are loved. We do not need to earn our worth, and we do not need to earn God's love. The spiritual life is a response to the fact that God loves us and we matter.

There is another vital implication in all this: Just as no human being can confer God's love upon us, so also can no human being take it away. And just as no human being can bestow our worth upon us, no human being can ultimately take it away. We can be attacked or assaulted, humiliated or betrayed—and those crimes can leave intense scars, both physical and psychological—but no abusive parent or teacher, no political power, no torturer or interrogator, can ever strip us of our worth.[44] No matter what happens to us, regardless of what we accomplish or are forced to endure, we matter, and we are loved.[45]

MISSION AND PURPOSE

Every year, as we move into the final hours of Yom Kippur, Jews read the story of the prophet Jonah. People usually assume that the story is read when it is because it is a simple but powerful story about the power of repentance. Threatened with obliteration for their many sins, the people of Nineveh heed Jonah's warning: they repent and change their ways, and thus avert the divine decree (Jonah 3:5–10). The book of Jonah, so the argument goes, is intended as a goad and an inspiration, a call to remember that profound change is not only necessary but also possible. If people as corrupt as the Ninevites could change, then so, presumably, can we.

But this isn't the only reason we read about the ambivalent prophet. Jonah is a man called by God, given a mission to accomplish in the world—and yet he refuses, fleeing, as one modern translation has it, "from the Lord's service" (Jonah 1:3).[46] It is only reluctantly, kicking and screaming, that he finally responds to the summons to fulfill God's word. Jews traditionally read the story of Jonah on Yom Kippur, I'd like to suggest, because to one extent or another, *we are all Jonah.*[47] Each of us has things, often deeply consequential things, we're called upon to do that we'd simply rather not. And so, like Jonah, we run away from our calling. On Yom Kippur, we acknowledge that painful reality, both to God and to ourselves, and stand ready to respond to God's call.

There is a stunning scene near the beginning of the book of Exodus. (It is so familiar that we often miss just how remarkable it is.) God hears the moans of the Israelites suffering in Egyptian bondage, remembers God's covenant with their ancestors, and resolves to liberate them. God, it seems, is finally ready to charge into history and put an end to the horrific oppression of God's people. And then God reveals the concrete divine plan. Addressing Moses, God says: "Come, therefore, I will send you to Pharaoh, and you shall free My people, the Israelites, from Egypt" (Exodus 3:10). God intends to free the Israelites and radically alter the course of Jewish, and human, history. How will God accomplish God's goals? By summoning a homeless shepherd and enlisting him to be God's emissary.[48] As a modern Bible scholar explains, "In one brief utterance, the grand intention of God has become a specific human responsibility, human obligation, and human vocation . . . After the massive intrusion of God, the exodus has suddenly become a human enterprise."[49] The book of Exodus here brings a key aspect of Jewish theology to light: for the accomplishment of divine aims, God chooses to need people. "God's dream," Rabbi Abraham Joshua Heschel (1907– 1972) writes, "is not to be alone, to have mankind as a partner in the drama of continuous creation."[50]

Rabbi Joseph Soloveitchik (1903–1993) boldly insists that in this amazing encounter, Moses serves as a paradigm for what is true of every human being: to be created in the image of God is to be assigned a specific task by God.[51] Playing with the Jewish legal idea that "an agent is likened to the sender,"[52] R. Soloveitchik argues that one who is similar to his sender thereby becomes his agent—in other words, being created in the image of God entails becoming God's agent and emissary.[53]

According to R. Soloveitchik, each of us is given a distinctive mission, and the moment into which we are born is reflective of the assignment God has in mind for us: "The fact that someone lives in a particular time and a particular place, and not in some other time, under different circumstances, can only be understood if we accept the idea of the human being having a distinctive mission. Providence knows how and where each individual, with her capacities and weaknesses, can best fulfill her mission,"[54] and we are created accordingly. (A question I am not at all sure how to answer: Can one hold this as an existential orientation without affirming it as a metaphysical truth? I think so, but I am honestly not sure.) It is crucial to understand, R. Soloveitchik adds, that, normatively at least, we are not free to accept or decline our mission. Sometimes we are called to a task that is overwhelming or exhausting, or that seems like a fool's errand—and yet we are not free to walk away.[55] This, I am suggesting, is the lesson Jonah found it so difficult to learn. We read his story because to some extent it is also our own.

But we are not prophets, and in some ways, that makes our task even harder: unlike Moses, we first have to discern our mission, and then decide whether to heed the call. And yet we do sometimes feel a call. If all this sounds too daunting or grandiose to contemplate, think about a moment in your life when you knew—we can bracket the question of precisely *how* you knew; sometimes you just know—you had to fulfill a particular task in the world. Perhaps you didn't want to—maybe it would have cost you socially, or professionally, or economically; or maybe you were just feeling lazy—and you ran away, pretending not to hear, obfuscating matters until you rationalized your way out of performing the unwanted task. Reading Jonah on Yom Kippur, we remind ourselves that although we have the ability to turn away, religiously speaking we do not have the right to do so.

R. Soloveitchik captures this insight beautifully by suggesting that this is why both human beings and angels can be referred to in biblical Hebrew as *mal'akhim*, which we usually take to mean "angels," but which in fact refers to messengers more broadly. What is the difference, according to classical Jewish sources, between an earthly messenger and a heavenly one? Whereas the latter has no choice but to fulfill the divine mission, the former is free to disobey.[56] Again and again, we are asked: Are you Jonah? And are you willing to start being something else?

IN WHAT SENSE WAS THE WORLD CREATED FOR ME?

I mentioned earlier that some of my students were troubled by the idea of declaring—of being *required* to declare—that the world was created for their sake. I confess that for years I shared their unease—the last thing the world needs, I thought, is for religion to bolster our already overdeveloped sense of entitlement—until one day it occurred to me that perhaps our unease said more about our culture than it does about the text itself. We hear the phrase "for my sake was the world created" and immediately assume that those words must be a statement of privilege, an affirmation of what we are entitled to. But what if the text means something else entirely? Our mishnah teaches that each of us is obligated to believe that the world was created for our sake because there is some distinct way that each of us is called upon to serve. The world being created for me isn't a statement of how much I'm entitled to, but rather a declaration of how much is asked and expected of me.[57] One of the many ways the kind of self-worth we have been exploring differs from many pop-psychological approaches is in its insistence that self-worth is bound up with expectation and obligation.

Rabbi Abraham Isaac Kook (1865–1935) weaves this idea—about each of us having a task (or tasks) that we all too often resist—into his interpretation of the Yom Kippur liturgy. At the end of the Amidah prayer on Yom Kippur, we declare, "My God, before I was formed, I was of no worth, and now that I have been formed, I am as if I had not been formed."[58] On the surface, the prayer reads like a declaration of our ongoing worthlessness. As it goes on to say, "I am but dust in my life, all the more so after I die." But R. Kook spins the text around, yielding something radically different:

> "Before I was created, I was of no worth." Before I was born, in that unlimited expanse from the beginning of time until I was created, there was nothing in this world that needed me. Because if I had been needed for some purpose or completion, I would have been created then. But since I was not created until this time, that is a sign that at that time, I was "of no worth" [or: it would not have been worthwhile to create me]. There was no need of me. But now, at this very moment that I have been created, the time has come when I need to participate in some aspect of completing the world.
>
> Were I to dedicate my life toward fulfilling the purpose for which I was created, I would indeed now be worthy. But since my actions are not in accordance with my true goal, I am not accomplishing my life's mission, and I am still not worthy. Things have changed; I am now needed. And yet I go on living as if nothing had changed and I were not needed.[59]

What we confess on Yom Kippur, says R. Kook, is not our lack of worth, but precisely the opposite: we take responsibility for the fact that we insist on living as if we were worthless, and as if the hour did not need us. I often recommend to students who are willing to engage in the deep spiritual work of ceasing to be Jonah that they alter the Yom Kippur liturgy just a little bit. During the first four Amidah prayers of

Yom Kippur, we ought to recite the traditional text: "My God, before I was formed, I was of no worth, and now that I have been formed, I am as if I had not been formed." But in the last Amidah prayer, during what is known as the Ne'ilah service, as the day wanes after long hours of introspection and recommitment, I suggest that we say, borrowing words from the prophet Isaiah: "My God, before I was formed, I was of no worth, and now that I have been formed, here I am, send me."[60]

There are thus two questions we ought to ask about our lives: First, what can I *give*? And second, what can *I* give? In other words, when we think about serving—and to live well is necessarily to think long and hard about service—we have the privilege/responsibility to ask not just how we can serve as human beings in general, but also how we can serve as human beings in particular. It is not some generic abstraction called "human" that God calls into action, but concrete, flesh-and-blood people with unique biographical narratives and distinctive talents and abilities, passions and proclivities—and also with particular weaknesses and shortcomings. I am called to serve, in other words, not as a member of a species but as me, an utterly unique and wholly irreplaceable person, created in the image of God.[61]

God's love and bestowal of worth upon us are invitations to us to become lovers who discern and affirm the worth of others[62]—all others. God's love is grace—we don't earn it, but we do have to learn to accept and receive it. And we have to live in its light. God's love and our worth are blessings, and as we shall see in the next chapter, God's blessings are meant to be passed on to others.

2

THE GIFTS OF GOD
FLOW THROUGH YOU

Grace, Gratitude, and Generosity

THE RELIGIOUS LIFE begins with the simple awareness that "we did not create ourselves."[1] None of us ever did anything, none of us *could* ever have done anything, to earn the gifts of life and consciousness.

Everything we are, and everything we have, is a gift. The world is a gift, and my life is a gift; my life in the world is a gift within a gift.[2] In other words, life is grace—something we were given even though we did nothing to earn or deserve it.[3]

The gift of life is unlike any other gift. Ordinarily, in human life, A gives a gift, X, to B. Nathan gives a new book to Dinah, for example. But the gift of life is different. In this situation, A (God) brings B (us) into being as part of the act of giving. B does not just receive A's gift; she is constituted by it. We do not exist until God confers the gift of life upon us. The gift of life, then, is not something we *get*, but something we *are*.[4] The very fact that we are is grace.

In theological terms, God's grace is interlaced with God's love. As Rabbi Joseph Soloveitchik explains, God creates the world—an act of grace—"in order to care, to sustain, and to love."[5] We are, all of us, products of grace and love.

And yet most of the time we simply take life for granted. The pace of our lives is so fast, the routines we settle into so familiar, that the sheer wonder of being alive gets crowded out of consciousness. And sometimes, too, the pain of living makes being alive feel like less than a blessing. Occasionally, though, we remember: we did nothing to earn all this. "We have no claim on life, reality, or continuity, not even for an instant—but there they are."[6]

GRATITUDE FOR THE GIFT OF LIFE

One of the central tasks of religion is to help us remember that life is grace—and to prod us to wrestle with the implications of that simple but startling perception. When religion works, instead of taking life *for* granted, we begin to experience it *as* granted.[7] Instead of feeling entitled, we feel blessed. More than that, rather than thinking of life as having been bestowed once and for all, we experience it as a gift received again and again from moment to moment.

There is a Rabbinic teaching that has become more and more important and helpful to me the older I've gotten. The Talmudic sage Rabbi Hanina declares: "For every single breath that a person breathes, she must praise the Creator."[8] I readily admit that when I first encountered these words, I was put off by them: I am not capable of praising God with every breath, I thought, so these words offer nothing more than a prescription for guilt. But over time I have come to hear R. Hanina's dictum very differently. On one level, R. Hanina lays down a daunting challenge: Can we maintain a sense of gratitude at all times? Can we remember that each moment we are alive is another unearned gift? Yet on another level, he provides wise and gentle counsel. If we have trouble with gratitude—perhaps we've suffered so deeply that the depth of our hurt threatens to crowd out the possibility of gratitude; perhaps the pace of our lives is so overwhelming that we can't seem to slow down enough to touch into gratitude—there is a resource perpetually available to us: we can take a breath and ask, Who made that? A simple inhalation is a portable and perpetually available reminder of the gift we are given at each moment. Every breath, R. Hanina reminds us, is both a summons and an opportunity to be grateful.

Traditionally, Jews begin each day with three simple words: "*Modeh/Modah Ani Lefanecha*," grateful am I before You.[9] As we all know well, ritual can easily become rote, mechanical actions replacing heartfelt gestures. But think about what it would mean to take this practice seriously: as we awaken each morning, the very first word we say is "grateful." In uttering that single word, we take a major step toward setting an orientation for our lives. We recognize that life is a gift, that each day is a gift, that consciousness is a gift, and we commit to cultivating and expressing appreciation for that wondrous fact.

Crucially, we do not say "*Ani Modeh*" (I am grateful), but rather "*Modeh Ani*" (grateful am I). Were we to wake up each morning and have the first word we speak be "I," we would be reproducing an awful lot of what ails us as a society, both morally and spiritually. In saying "grateful" first and "I" only second, we articulate something profound about what it truly means to be a human being. It is common, especially in modern times, to think of oneself first and foremost as an "I," an isolated self. First I am a self, and then I decide whether and with whom I want to enter into relationship. At bottom, I am detached, independent, and totally autonomous. But what if that's not the way life works—or at least not the way it ought to? By saying "grateful" and only then saying "I," I remind myself that, from a Jewish perspective, there is no self without gratitude, and that I exist in relationship even before I exist as a self. Before I ever make or do anything in the world, I first receive. It is only possible for me to become a maker or doer precisely because I am first, and always, a receiver. I am grateful, and only then am I a self. Grateful am I: "I thank, therefore I am."[10]

Ultimately, gratitude for the gifts of life and consciousness can form a baseline from which a more pervasive sense of gratitude can grow and expand. We respond gratefully to this kindness or that, but even more fundamentally, gratitude comes to "color our entire outlook." When this happens, gratitude becomes "the salient characteristic, the dominant mood or theme of a total way of life."[11] Gratitude becomes a way of being in the world.

None of this should paper over the fact that aspects of our life can be profoundly disappointing. A sense of life as a gift is a crucial starting point for religion, but it is not the only one—which is a good thing, because life can be excruciatingly painful, and it is sometimes immensely difficult to see it as grace. As we'll see in the next chapter, sometimes religion begins elsewhere, with an insistent protest: life and the world are meant to be radically different than they are. One of the challenges of the spiritual life is to become capacious enough to hold gratitude and disappointment—or gratitude and protest—at the same time.[12]

GRATITUDE AS AN EXISTENTIAL POSTURE

The kind of gratitude I am speaking of here is not primarily a feeling, but an "existential posture," a way of holding oneself in the world.

Why not focus exclusively on gratitude as a feeling? To begin with, it isn't possible to have an overflowing feeling of gratitude at every moment. After all, we can't maintain *any* feeling at each and every moment. Feelings are, by their nature, ephemeral; they often disappear as quickly as they come, frequently for reasons that completely elude our conscious awareness. We all know what this is like. Feelings have their own mysterious rhythms. But while it may not be possible to feel grateful at every second, it is still possible to be oriented toward gratitude. An orientation does not depend on what we happen to be feeling at this moment or that, or with what intensity we happen to be feeling it.

When I say that I love my wife, what do I mean? At bottom, of course, the love of another person is not—or, in any case, is certainly not only—a fleeting feeling, a purely subjective experience that constantly ebbs and flows. When I say that I love my wife, part of what I am declaring is an existential commitment to act lovingly even in those moments when the depth of emotion and the intensity of passion elude me. If I come home and my wife is sick and in need of care, I can't say, "Sorry, sweetie, but I'm not feeling the love tonight. You'll just have to take care of yourself." Whatever I might be feeling at that particular moment is secondary to a more fundamental commitment I have made. To be sure, a relationship from which passion has permanently faded is a tragedy, but so, equally, is a relationship that threatens to dissipate with every diminution of ardor. We can witness the tides of consciousness without being slaves to them. Gratitude is similar: I can be—and Judaism insists that I *should* be—oriented toward gratitude and committed to grateful living regardless of what is happening at the surface of my consciousness at any particular instant.

Our focus is on gratitude as a trait rather than a state.[13] Feelings do matter, of course: gratitude utterly devoid of feeling would be unrecognizable as gratitude. Having the trait is conducive to experiencing the state,[14] and experiencing the state in turn bolsters the trait, forming a kind of virtuous circle. But the key point is that we can have the trait even at moments when the state is elusive.

THE IMPLICATIONS OF GRATITUDE

Where does gratitude to God lead?

According to many Jewish philosophers, gratitude is the basis of our obligation to worship and serve God.[15] Yet they are quick to emphasize that being ungrateful doesn't constitute an exemption. There is, these philosophers insist, a *natural obligation* to be grateful. Ingratitude, they argue, constitutes both a moral failure and a failure of reason.[16] Reason compels us to be grateful, and our gratitude, in turn, gives rise to a willingness—and ideally, an eagerness—to worship the One who gives us life and consciousness. These thinkers suggest that gratitude to God is a duty. On their account, that is not *all* that gratitude is, but it is certainly *part* of what it is.

It is easy to misunderstand this dynamic by thinking of it in purely legalistic terms, as a divine-human barter of sorts, on the order of, "I, God, give you life, now you give me worship." This makes God's granting us life look less like a gift and more like a bloodless business transaction. But this is not Judaism's approach (though there are texts that sound this way). Ideally, gratitude is also something we willingly, even joyfully, embrace. Jewish thinking consistently resists the easy dichotomization of duty and delight. Duties can be the source of extraordinary delight. Think of the joy parents take—at least some of the time—in doing what they know they have to for their children.

The Talmudic sage Rabbi Yohanan teaches that Torah is given to the world as a gift.[17] And Torah is not just any gift: "In God's giving the Torah to Israel, part of the Giver is given with the gift."[18] As a midrash beautifully explains, when we buy an item at a store, we take home the item, but we obviously don't acquire its owner. Yet Torah is different—Israel acquires it, and God announces, "You are getting Me too, as it were!"[19] So far from its being a burden, Jews traditionally think of God's gift of Torah as a delight, so much so that a midrash imagines King David declaring, "'O, how I love Your Torah' (Psalm 119:97). It is always with me—I walk, and it is with me; I sleep, and it is with me. I have not neglected it at all. And because I have not neglected it, it has become not a burden to me, but a song."[20] Related, perhaps, is the Talmudic sage Rabbi Shefatiah's condemnation of one who studies Torah without a melody, or Mishnah without a tune.[21] It goes without saying that people who think of Torah as a song and a delight hardly experience it as a burden.

For Judaism, the relationship between divine grace and divine commandments is not a gift followed by a burdensome duty, but rather a series of gifts upon gifts. In Judaism, the giving of the Torah is also a manifestation of divine grace; it is a gift that the Jewish people did not earn. Already blessed by the marvelous gifts of life and consciousness, already freed from slavery in Egypt, we are blessed further with Torah. Already blessed with the world itself, we are blessed further with a path for making our way through it—and, tradition teaches, with a God who accompanies us along the way. Gratitude is compounded of both duty and desire.[22]

GRATITUDE AND GENEROSITY

Yet gratitude yields more than an obligation or an urge to worship. It also elicits an urge to pay forward what we have received. Think of a moment in your life when you were filled with an overwhelming sense of gratitude to God or to another person. Perhaps you really wanted or needed something—a kind word, a smile, a home-cooked meal—but you had no expectations of receiving it, and no right to demand it. And yet someone conferred it upon you as a gift.[23] When you remember a moment like that and allow yourself to fully inhabit it, one of the things you may notice is that when you are truly grateful, you want others, too, to have what you've received. Gratitude opens your heart, and you want to meet kindness with kindness.

This is the nexus of grace, gratitude, and generosity: an awareness of grace elicits a profound sense of gratitude. And a fully blossomed sense of gratitude, in turn, contains an impulse to generosity within it. By its very nature, a grateful heart overflows.

In paying gifts forward, gratitude both reflects and perpetuates the generosity received.[24] Both gratitude and generosity, in turn, embody what one philosopher calls an "ethic of grace," an approach to life that "especially values voluntary, nonobligatory expressions of concern for others' well-being, joy, and pleasure and the relief of their distresses, unhappiness, and deprivations."[25]

The point I am making is wonderfully—if also subtly—conveyed by the biblical law of the thanksgiving offering (*korban todah*), described in the book of Leviticus.[26] The thanksgiving offering is one of several sacrifices referred to as "sacrifices of well-being" (*zevah ha-shelamim*). In general, such sacrifices may be eaten until the third day after they are placed upon the altar, but the thanksgiving offering is different. The Torah mandates that "the flesh of [the] thanksgiving sacrifice of well-being shall be eaten on the day that it is offered; none of it shall be set aside until the morning" (Leviticus 7:15). Whatever is left over until the following morning must be burned.

The Torah implicitly requires a person who brings a thanksgiving offering to invite others to dine with him. Why? The laws around the consumption of the thanksgiving offering are intended to inculcate and express a core religious value: when we have been the beneficiaries of God's kindness, we are expected to bestow kindness ourselves. The gifts

of God are meant to be shared, not hoarded. Authentic gratitude is antithetical to possessiveness and acquisitiveness; the impulse of a grateful
person is to give rather than grasp.[27] Leftovers unshared are thus a sign
of ingratitude.[28]

This biblical lesson ought to have contemporary reverberations. To
take one example, many families customarily set aside money for tzedakah (alms for the poor) immediately before lighting candles to welcome
Shabbat. It's as if we can't quite enter Shabbat, when we rest in the fullness of God's creation and savor what God has made, without first ensuring that others too can partake of the good that life has to offer. More
broadly, Jewish law requires that we invite the neediest members of the
community into our homes for holiday meals so that they can share in
our bounty,[29] and we take up collections to help provide for holiday
needs of those who may be hesitant to ask for hospitality.[30] Holidays are
times when we are filled with gratitude; not surprisingly, it is precisely
then that we intensify our commitment to sharing.

We can understand this both prescriptively and descriptively. On
the one hand, the Torah insists that if we are grateful, we *must* share;
yet on the other, it suggests that if we are grateful, we will *want to* share,
because the urge to share is a significant part of what it means to be
grateful. This is arguably what distinguishes being *grateful* for something from merely being glad or pleased about it: when I am grateful, I
"want to favor another because [I have] been favored [myself]."[31] Here
again, duty and desire are interwoven.

Gratitude is thus the bridge between the realization of how much
we have been given and the commitment to being givers ourselves. This
insight-impulse lies at the very heart of the spiritual life: we have been
given, and therefore we, too, seek to give.

By its nature, *hesed* (generous giving) reproduces itself; *hesed* begets
hesed. An act of *hesed* is, as Rabbi Yitzhak Hutner (1906–1980) writes,
"the planting of a seed that cannot but bring forth fruit similar to itself."
When someone performs an act of *hesed* for us, "a seed of *hesed* is planted
in our world," and when both we and the world function "healthily,"
that seed cannot but bring forth more *hesed* in its wake. The process

is both legal and organic. On one level, receiving a gift from someone obligates me to behave similarly. Yet on another level, if allowed to flourish the gift will naturally take root and reproduce itself.[32] This insight suggests an important spiritual practice: we should ask ourselves where and how the flowering of *hesed* in us gets blocked and what we could do to heal and overcome those blockages.

R. Judah Loew (Maharal) imagines the flow of goodness that comes from God as a river. We are intended to keep the river flowing rather than stopping it up, because waters that are dammed or diverted ultimately spoil. For Maharal, to hoard, to stop the flow of divine blessing, is to declare oneself far removed from God, since to cleave to a giving God is to become a giver oneself.[33] Maharal's description anticipates the way the cultural critic Lewis Hyde portrays gift economies in general: "The only essential is this: *the gift must always move*"—that is, people must keep passing it on. To treat a gift correctly is thus to "allow [ourselves] to become a channel for its current."[34]

In other words, we are not only "beneficiaries" of God's gifts, but also "intermediaries."[35] God gives not alone *to* us but also *through* us. (How would our lives change if we really took this idea to heart?) To serve God is, in large part, to keep God's gifts in circulation. This is, ideally, a joy rather than a burden: "The opportunity to give is a part of the gift."[36]

The gifts of God flow through us, but these gifts do not flow only *through* us; they also flow *to* us. To reverse what I've said above, we are not only intermediaries, we are also beneficiaries. We are permitted—and arguably required—to enjoy God's world, and even to delight in life's manifold gifts.[37] What we are absolutely forbidden to do is to hoard them. Judaism without generosity is a hollow shell.

As we've seen, according to Rabbinic tradition God does not love us as anonymous members of a species but as unique individuals, with distinctive talents, abilities, and callings, as well as shortcomings and flaws. That we should be grateful for the gift of life is universal; how we should act, what we should do to manifest that gratitude in the world, will depend on who we are in particular. On the one hand, traditional Jewish spirituality assumes that all Jews are required to obey God's commandments as expressed in halakha (Jewish law). But on the other hand, how best to keep *hesed* flowing in the world—where we give our time and our money, to whom we show love and generosity, whom to welcome into our home—in this domain there is abundant room for freedom and individuality.

The freedom to respond as we see fit underscores a pivotal point in Jewish theology (to which we shall return): God's grace makes us not debased and powerless slaves but dignified and creative agents. God gives in the hopes that we, too, will become givers.[38] As we'll see again and again over the course of the book, Judaism is concerned not only with *what we do* but also with *who we are*. In the words of a classic rabbinic text, just as God gives free gifts (*matnot hinam*), so should we.[39] Having been endowed by God's gifts with a sense of self-worth, we are able to "envision [ourselves] as givers too," and we feel confident that we "have something worth giving."[40] Rabbi Eliyahu Dessler (1892–1953) says it very simply: giving is among the highest powers God has—God gives us without receiving anything in return—and in creating us in God's image, God gives us some of that same power and potential to bestow goodness upon others.[41] Implicit in R. Dessler's words is the claim that *we are made to give.* "We are givers because we were made that way, and if we don't give, we are at odds with ourselves."[42] For Jewish theology, giving is integral to being alive.[43]

If the gift of life is grace, then we should respond with gratitude. But how ought we to respond when the world seems impossibly, unbearably broken?

3

SACRED INDIGNATION

On Protest

THE WORLD IS a gift, but it sometimes seems like an inferno; life is a gift, but it can sometimes be unbearably painful. Authentic spiritual life requires us to live with our eyes open and to refuse to lie about what we see, either to God or to ourselves. So although gratitude is fundamental to the spiritual life, it cannot be the whole story. Side by side with gratitude lives protest, a deep and unabashed conviction that the world as it is is a very far cry from the world as it should be, and a demand that the gap between them begin to be closed.

In December 1987, during my junior year of high school, I had the privilege of traveling to what was then the Soviet Union to visit refuseniks, Soviet Jews who had sought and been refused permission to immigrate to the state of Israel. Many had not merely been forced to stay; they had had their lives destroyed by Soviet authorities. Hour after hour, day after day, a few friends and I sat in often sparsely appointed apartments hearing appalling stories of abuse and humiliation. One man we met had spent decades as a renowned chemist, but since applying for permission to move to Israel, he had been forced to work as a chimney sweep instead. A woman we visited had been told by a snickering Soviet bureaucrat: "Tell you what, we'll let your husband and son go, and you can go to prison and be the next Anatoly Shcharansky." Although I had been raised on stories of the Shoah, and on reports of seemingly countless relatives who had been slaughtered by the Nazis, this was a new and frankly shattering experience for me: I was being brought face-to-face with gratuitous, merciless cruelty. Suddenly terms like "oppression" and "dehumanization" had a human face.

Sitting with Boris and Yelena and many others like them, I knew in my bones that I had to speak up on their behalf. Although in those days I didn't yet have the words to explain why, I understood that the suffering of the refuseniks I was meeting made a claim on me. Witnessing their mistreatment, I was called to protest against it, summoned to do my small part in helping bring it to an end.

Boris and Yelena and many others I met refused to be cowed into submission. They wrote letters to Soviet authorities and made phone calls to diplomats and activists around the world, all at great risk to themselves and their loved ones. I remember asking Yelena how she found the wherewithal to keep struggling and fighting, even in the face of such hostility and brutality. "I love my son and want him to have a different life than mine," she said. In that moment, I learned two powerful lessons from her, lessons that have stayed with me ever since: first, that protesting oppression and injustice is a mitzvah, a moral and religious responsibility that we are not permitted to shirk; and second, that protest can be a potent demonstration of love. In risking life and limb to insist that she and her fellow Jews did not deserve the degradation to which they had been subjected, Yelena showed great love for her son, her husband, and her broader community. But whether or not she would have put it this way, I remember thinking that she also displayed immense love for the world because, although she had been given ample reason to give up on it, she refused to do so. She cared so much about the world that she was willing to fight for it. Yelena's deep love was bound up with insistent hope, the belief that present circumstances can be overturned, that they need not—that they *must* not—have the final word.

From refuseniks like Yelena and Boris, I learned that to be a Jew is to cry out, even when silence would be safer, easier, and more convenient.

As Jewish tradition demonstrates, protest comes in many forms. We can remonstrate with God—about the state of the world, or about what we see as God's complicity in and responsibility for it; about suffering in general, or about our own personal afflictions or the agonies of those dear to us. If we can protest heavenly authorities, then we can surely protest earthly ones: we can forcefully object to interpersonal brutality and challenge oppressive political regimes. Sometimes it's not even clear whom we mean to summon with our cries. We cry because we hurt, and the very act of voicing our pain helps restore our dignity.

THE WORLD IN FLAMES

Protest can be a manifestation of deep faith, and sometimes, an audacious midrash suggests, it can be the very path through which the possibility of faith is discovered.[1]

The book of Genesis never tells us why God singled out Abraham. Jewish tradition has often sought to fill in the blanks, to tell us something about the patriarch that would explain God's embrace of him and his descendants. Surely, at least some of the Talmudic sages seem to have thought, Abraham must have done *something* to earn God's affection? The most famous answer is that Abraham fearlessly destroyed his father's idols, exposing the theological bankruptcy of idolatry.[2] So celebrated and widespread is this story that many people are shocked to learn that it is not found in the Bible itself.

But there is another, less well-known midrash that is worth reading closely. As it has often been translated, the midrash reads as follows:

> The Lord said to Abraham, "Go forth from your land" (Gen. 12:1) . . . Rabbi Isaac said: To what may this be compared? To a man who was traveling from place to place when he saw a palace full of light (*doleket*). He wondered, "Is it possible that this palace has no one who looks after it?" The owner of the building looked out at him and said, "I am the owner of the palace." Similarly, because

Abraham our father wondered, "Is it possible that this world has no one who looks after it?" the Blessed Holy One looked at him and said, "I am the owner of the world."[3]

According to this story, Abraham intuits or infers a divine Creator from the fact that the universe is lit up. One imagines Abraham thunderstruck by the sheer beauty of creation, perhaps even sensing a pervasive meaningfulness in the cosmos. A commentary attributed to the great medieval sage Rashi (1040–1105) interprets the story as an early form of what philosophers call "the teleological argument" for the existence of God, or "the argument from design": Abraham "saw heaven and earth—he saw the sun by day and the moon by night, and stars shining. He thought, 'Is it possible that such a great thing could be without its having a guide?' Whereupon God looked out at him and announced, 'I am the owner of the world.'"[4]

But as beautiful as this interpretation undeniably is, it is beset by a major linguistic difficulty: in Rabbinic Hebrew, *mu'eret* would have been the word to use to describe the world as "lit up" or "full of light," whereas the word actually used in the midrash, *doleket*, means "in flames." This seemingly small philological point yields a dramatic theological difference:

The Lord said to Abraham, "Go forth from your land" (Gen. 12:1) . . . R. Isaac said: To what may this be compared? To a man who was traveling from place to place when he saw a palace in flames (*doleket*). He wondered, "Is it possible that this palace has no one who looks after it?" The owner of the building looked out at him and said, "I am the owner of the palace."

It is one thing to behold order, beauty, or meaning and be led to an awareness of God. But to behold a "palace in flames" and *thereby* be led to God? What are we to make of this bold and disturbing story?

So far from wonder, Abraham here discovers God from the very midst of moral and existential anguish. What kind of world is this, a contemporary Abraham might ask, where the poor are degraded and the weak exploited, where the powerless are crushed underfoot, and where tyrants and despots murder and destroy lives without a second thought? What kind of world is this, where the fate of Yelena and her family, who only want the right to live where they choose, is left to the whims of bureaucrats devoid of mercy or decency? Reading our story, Rabbi David Luria (Radal, 1798–1855) explains that "when Abraham saw that the wicked were setting the world on fire, he began to doubt in his heart: perhaps there is no one who looks after this world. Immediately, God appeared to him and said, 'I am the owner of the world.'"[5]

What happens here, exactly, for Abraham, for God, and between Abraham and God? This text does not tell us most of what we want to know. And yet perhaps that is part of its richness: it asks us to do the work of imagining Abraham in his moment of consternation and bewilderment, and to speculate about how that very state led him to God. In asking that question about Abraham, it also asks us a question about God. What is it about Abraham's state of agitation that elicits God's self-revelation?

Abraham refuses to look away. Confronted with the abyss of meaninglessness, he will not avert his eyes. But not only does Abraham refuse to turn away, he cares: "Is it possible that this world has no one who looks after it?!" Whatever faith Abraham finds, it will not be easy. It will be the faith of a man who has considered the very real possibility that chaos and bloodshed are simply all there is. That possibility shakes Abraham to the very core of his being. According to this story, the founding father of the Jewish people is someone who will not hide from the reality of human suffering.

This refusal to hide or look away is, I think, a manifestation of deep love. Faced with a world afire, Abraham will not grow calloused or indifferent. He continues to care, even when it hurts. And so he cries out.

If Abraham's question is, at heart, really a protest—he is not simply confused by the state of the world, he is aghast, and he gives voice to his horror—then that very protest itself can be said to reveal a deep and abiding sense that *things are meant to be otherwise*. Abraham does not cry out simply because he doesn't like the way the world presently looks; he objects, rather, because the empirical reality he sees fails to measure up to a transcendent standard he intuits. The insistence that the world as he encounters it is not yet the world as it must be, as it is in some ultimate way *intended* to be, is itself a manifestation of faith.[6] When God peers at Abraham and announces that "I am the owner of the world," then, God is only making explicit what is already implicit in Abraham's anguished cry.[7]

The Christian theologian Miroslav Volf writes of his urge to protest in the face of natural disasters:

> Why are we disturbed about the brute and blind force of tsunamis that snuff out people's lives? . . . If the world is all there is, and the world with moving tectonic plates is a world in which we happen to live, what's there to complain about? We can mourn—we've lost something terribly dear. But we can't really complain, and we certainly can't legitimately protest. The expectation that the world should be a hospitable place . . . is tied to the belief that the world ought to be constituted in a certain way. And that belief—as distinct from the belief that the world just is what it is—is itself tied to the notion of a creator.[8]

What Volf says about natural disasters can be extended to humanly inflicted devastation as well. The overwhelming certainty that this— a world of crushing poverty, degrading oppression, and murderous hatred—is not how things are meant to be testifies to the possibility of something different, and perhaps also to the Source of Life, who, Jewish theology insists, wants something different and summons us to help build it.[9]

It seems clear that the midrash is not offering an argument for God's existence. Instead, it evokes something like a primal religious awareness. As Volf insightfully writes of protest more generally: "God is both the ground of the protest and its target . . . I protest, and therefore I believe."[10]

Rabbi Jonathan Sacks (1948–2020) takes this midrashic story and the moral protest that underlies it as the very starting point of Jewish faith. Judaism, he insists, "begins not in wonder that the world is, but in protest that the world is not as it ought to be. It is in that cry, that sacred discontent, that Abraham's journey begins."[11]

This seems only partly right to me. Protest and indignation are central, but wonder at the beauty of the universe and gratitude to its Creator constitute the other, no-less-crucial pole of Jewish faith. Rabbi Zev Wolf Einhorn (d. 1862) expresses this well. Abraham, he writes, is like a person who sees a beautiful building and realizes that it must have had both a wise architect and a devoted owner. But since it is being left to burn, he imagines it to have been abandoned.[12] In other words, Abraham senses order and beauty and confronts chaos at the very same time. Like many of us, he discerns powerful reasons to believe and powerful reasons not to. And it is precisely this honesty that leads God to embrace him as a covenantal partner.

"The faith of Abraham," R. Sacks writes, "begins in the refusal to accept either answer, for both contain a truth, and between them there is a contradiction . . . The first says that if evil exists, God does not exist. The second says that if God exists, evil does not exist. But supposing both exist? Supposing there are both the palace and the flames?"[13] There is a magnificent palace, and yet it is in flames. Abraham, the paradigmatic Jew, is simultaneously grateful and indignant.

We are grateful for a world saturated with so much beauty, and we are indignant at a world suffused with so much suffering and injustice. As the Catholic essayist G. K. Chesterton wonderfully puts it, "What we need is not the cold acceptance of the world as a compromise, but some way in which we can heartily hate and heartily love it. We do not want joy and anger to neutralize each other . . . We have to feel the universe at once to be an ogre's castle, to be stormed, and yet as our own cottage, to which we can return at evening."[14] It is Abraham's achievement to have stormed the castle and made it home.

A GOD WHO SOLICITS PROTEST

This midrashic story shows that docility is far from a religious ideal. God reveals Godself to Abraham in the very midst of, and precisely because of, Abraham's willingness to protest. But the text of the Bible itself is in a sense even more radical: it tells of a God who actively teaches Abraham to remonstrate with God.

In one of the most remarkable stories in the Torah, God is moved to respond to the rampant corruption and lawlessness of Sodom and Gomorrah. But before taking action, God makes a choice to consult with Abraham. Alarmed at the prospect of God acting unjustly, Abraham protests, demanding to know whether God will "sweep away the innocent along with the guilty" and asking indignantly, "Shall not the Judge of all the earth deal justly?" "Far be it from You," Abraham twice boldly admonishes God (Genesis 18:23, 25).

There is much that is striking, even captivating, about this story: a God who has so much respect for human beings (or at least for the prophets among us) that God will not act without consulting with them; a man who has so much confidence in his moral intuitions that he insists that God live up to them; and a God who listens to and engages with this bold, presumptuous covenantal partner.

God does not merely tolerate Abraham's argument, God actively seeks it out: "Now the Lord had said, 'Shall I hide from Abraham what I am about to do?'" (18:17). Why should God share God's plans with this mere mortal? "For I have singled him out, that he may instruct his children and his posterity to keep the way of the Lord by doing what is just and right, in order that the Lord may bring about for Abraham what [the Lord] has promised him" (18:19). God wants Abraham to train his descendants to do what is just and right, but Abraham cannot teach what he himself has not yet learned. Abraham needs to learn how to stand up for justice and how to plead for mercy, so God places him in a situation in which he can do just that. God wants a leader and a prophet who will not always acquiesce and submit. The God of the Bible actively wants protest.[15]

In deciding to consult with Abraham, God recalls that "all the nations of the earth are to be blessed through him"[16] (18:18), a promise God had made to Abraham during their initial encounter, when God had also instructed Abraham to "be a blessing"[17] (12:2–3). It is possible, I think, that God's deliberations in Genesis 18 make clear what had been left somewhat vague in Genesis 12: *How* is Abraham to be a blessing to the other nations? The Bible scholar Joel Kaminsky wonders whether "calling God to account in an attempt to protect potentially innocent civilians is one way in which Abraham, and later Israel, become a blessing for the nations."[18] To protest, then, is part of what it means to be a blessing.

NO INNOCENT BYSTANDERS

Why is all this so important? It is not just prophets who must step forward; what is true of Abraham ought to be true of us as well. Even "the children of prophets"[19] must argue for justice and plead for mercy. If, following Abraham's example, Jews are asked to argue with God, how much more so are we called to speak up in the face of human injustice. As the Talmud startlingly puts it:

> Whoever is able to protest against the transgressions of his own family and does not do so is held responsible for the transgressions of his family. Whoever is able to protest against the transgressions of the people of his community and does not do so is held responsible for the transgressions of his community. Whoever is able to protest against the transgressions of the entire world and does not do so is held responsible for the transgressions of the entire world.[20]

This passage is daunting, and I believe that it is meant to be. Judaism worries about how easy it is for us to swim with the tide, to go along to get along. Faced with injustice, or oppression, or interpersonal brutality, it is almost always easier to keep quiet. Why is the one who remains silent held accountable? Because, Rabbi Menahem Ha-Meiri (1249–1316) explains, if we don't protest an injustice, it is as if we ourselves committed it.[21] I think often about a powerful statement made by the medieval sage Rabbi Abraham Ibn Ezra (1089–1167): "The legal status of the one who oppresses and of the one who witnesses the oppression but keeps quiet is the same."[22] In Jewish ethics, there is no such thing as an innocent bystander.[23]

BETWEEN PROTEST AND SUBMISSION: (MIS)READING THE BINDING OF ISAAC

Whenever I teach about Abraham as Judaism's paragon of protest, one student or another inevitably objects. What about the Akedah (the binding of Isaac, Genesis 22), they demand to know. When God threatens to obliterate Sodom, Abraham speaks up, but when God instructs him to offer up his son as a sacrifice, he simply acquiesces. Doesn't the latter disqualify him as a model of protest in the face of injustice?

I don't think it does.

Many modern commentators interpret Abraham in the shadow of the Danish philosopher Søren Kierkegaard (1813–1855) and his immensely influential interpretation of the Akedah, according to which Abraham's actions should be understood as a "teleological suspension of the ethical." On Kierkegaard's retelling of the story, in *Fear and Trembling*, Abraham has moral obligations toward his son Isaac, but as a "knight of faith" he sets them aside and obeys God's command.[24]

If Kierkegaard's interpretation is correct, then Abraham is at best an erratic exemplar of protesting injustice. With the Akedah in mind, one could just as easily portray him, as some of my students suggest, as the epitome of conformity, as someone who surrenders in the face of injustice.

But I think this line of interpretation is misguided. For all the power of Kierkegaard's reading, it is not what the biblical text intends. Strange and disturbing as it sounds, child sacrifice was common, even widespread, in the ancient Near East. As the Bible scholar Rabbi Robert Gordis (1908–1992) explains, "To be sure, offering up one's child was an infinitely more painful gift than sacrificing the first-born of one's cattle or the tithing of one's crops. Yet it took place time and time again" in the ancient world. In other words, child sacrifice was often seen as (very) different in degree, but not necessarily in kind, from other forms of sacrifice.[25]

The Bible does rule out child sacrifice in general, and the prophets lambaste those who engage in it.[26] Yet as Bible scholars have noted, the donation of the firstborn son to God appears to be somewhat different: at one point, the Torah seems to require it,[27] and at others, it presents rituals in which a substitute for the firstborn son is offered—for example, the paschal sacrifice of a lamb on the evening when the Israelite firstborn sons are spared, and the redemption of the firstborn, in which money is paid to the Levites in place of firstborn children.[28] All of this makes clear that the idea of giving one's firstborn to God was common in ancient Israel.[29]

On the logic of the biblical text itself, Abraham does not protest the immorality of God's command because . . . *he does not see it as immoral.* God's command to sacrifice his son is undoubtedly excruciating for Abraham, but he does not see it as a moral violation—as he does God's plans for Sodom. So he protests in the latter case and complies in the former.

An interpretation like this, which I believe to be historically accurate, is not without costs. On the one hand, we gain a more stable, coherent picture of Abraham, and we undercut the temptation to use the Akedah as a justification for acquiescence and surrender in the face of religious commands that seem to contradict morality. Yet on the other hand, we run the risk of opening a vast moral gap between the Bible and us, because although Abraham did not see God's command to bind his son upon the altar as immoral, many of us today will—and will thus feel the need to grapple with the distance between the sacred text and our own most deeply held moral intuitions.

This is obviously a significant issue, but for our purposes the essential point is that from a biblical perspective, Abraham's obeying God's command to bind his son upon the altar does not contradict my portrayal of him as the paragon of protest. When Abraham perceives a situation as unjust, he makes himself heard—even when his "opponent" is God.

To be clear, submission and even surrender do play pivotal roles in Jewish spirituality. We may wish to eat whatever we please, but we subdue that impulse when the food in question is prohibited to us by Jewish law; we may wish to tinker with our taxes so that we can keep more of our income for ourselves and our family, but we do not (in part) because doing so would constitute a violation of God's will; we may feel pulled in inappropriate ways by lust, but we resist the urge because there are few things more appalling and sinful than to violate a marital bond; we may even harbor professional aspirations that we relinquish because we find them incompatible with an observant Jewish life. All of this involves sacrifice. But it is crucial to understand: God's commandments "come to tame the id, not to override the superego."[30] When "the notion of sacrifice moves beyond the giving up of desires, instincts, and goals" and demands "the sacrifice of moral conscience" too,[31] then we are on extremely treacherous ground: human history is littered with the corpses of victims of such theologies.[32] Kierkegaard notwithstanding, Abraham does not subdue his superego, and neither may we. Not only are we not *required*, we are not *permitted* to do so!

MOSES AS HEIR TO ABRAHAM

The Bible portrays Moses as a worthy heir to Abraham. As soon as Moses grows up, the book of Exodus tells us, he immediately intervenes in three scenes of interpersonal brutality. Witnessing an Egyptian taskmaster beating an Israelite slave, Moses steps in and kills the abuser;[33] seeing two Israelite men scuffling, he tries to separate them and admonishes the offender. Having been forced to flee Egypt, Moses arrives in Midian and observes a group of male shepherds mistreating young Midianite women at a well; without hesitating, he drives the shepherds off and waters the women's flocks (2:11–17). Three things are worth noticing about this narrative. First, when Moses sees injustice, looking the other way is simply not an option for him: he notices, and he acts. Second, when injustice is at issue, the identity of the victim does not matter: Moses stands up for an Israelite against an Egyptian oppressor, for an Israelite against a fellow Israelite, and for a Midianite against other Midianites (and for women against men).[34] Finally, in biblical narrative the first thing a character says reveals something significant about his character. Moses's first words are a direct challenge to a man who is abusing another: "Why do you strike your fellow?" (2:13). Tellingly, the first words spoken by the leader of the Israelites are "an attempt to impose a standard of justice."[35] Moses cannot tolerate interpersonal wrongdoing. Where many of us would be tempted to look away, would immediately begin offering rationalizations for why we should "mind our own business," Moses chooses a different path. Not for naught is it this person (and this *type* of person) who is entrusted with helping Abraham's family become a nation. If Abraham's children are to do "the just and the right," they need a man like Moses to lead them, and to model for them a courageous commitment to justice.[36]

Exodus describes Moses as "saving" the Midianite woman (*vayoshi'an*). In the very next chapter, we learn that God, too, is about to serve as a rescuer (Exodus 3:18). Soon enough, the text will tell us that "the Lord saved (*va-yosha*) Israel that day from the Egyptians" (14:30). Moses's actions on behalf of the Midianites are described with the same word as God's actions on behalf of the Israelites. The point is subtle but unmistakable: in siding with the oppressed and resisting injustice, we emulate God. Just as God rebels against injustice and embraces the stranger, so too must the divinely appointed leader—and so, too, must we.[37] As one contemporary philosopher puts it, the "spirit of protest coincides with the belief in God. Faith cannot sit idly by while others suffer."[38] A Jew who finds injustice tolerable is a contradiction in terms.

CRYING OUT IN EGYPT

But it is not just Moses. What gets the ball rolling in the book of Exodus? "The Israelites were groaning under the bondage and cried out, and their plea for help from the bondage rose up to God. God heard their moaning, and God remembered [God's] covenant with Abraham and Isaac and Jacob. God looked upon the Israelites and God took notice of them" (2:23–25). In an attempt to convey that the people's agony is "intense, continuous, and pervasive," the Torah piles on four differ-ent terms for crying: "groan," "cry," "plea," and "moan."[39] The people's moans are "the catalyst for the entire Exodus story; it is the cry that evokes God's care."[40] No cries, it seems, no Exodus.

Now surely God was aware of Israel's suffering before they cried out. Yet God waits to intervene until the people themselves begin to declare their afflictions intolerable. We can ask the obvious questions of theo-dicy here—*why* does God allow Israel to be abused for so long?—but I think the text's own focus is elsewhere: the first step in the liberation of the people consists in their knowing and insisting that what they are enduring is intolerable and unacceptable.[41] As the Hasidic master Rabbi Yehudah Leib Alter of Ger (1847–1905) notes, the slaves "had been so deeply submerged in exile that they did not even notice that they were in exile." It is only when they begin to shake off their numbness and groan that redemption becomes a possibility.[42]

The act of crying out, even wordlessly, is a "bold act of self-assertion":[43] despite the ways the slaves are abused, they are not cogs in a machine but human beings with feelings, experiences, and needs.[44] More than that, the groans of the downtrodden represent the first glimmers of re-sistance. "In the moment of crying out, of letting pain become public and audible, the slaves [break] with the definitions of reality imposed by the policies and values of the [Egyptian] empire."[45] With their cries, they announce, however inchoately, that reality as the oppressor con-structs it need not have the final word; another, very different reality is possible. In that moment of questioning the inevitability of present circumstances, hope for a different future is born.[46]

When the people begin to moan, it is not even clear to whom their cries are directed.[47] Perhaps they have forgotten God, or perhaps their uninterrupted suffering has convinced them that *God* has forgotten *them*. Yet key to the story, and to Jewish theology more broadly, is the insistence that God hears the cries of the slaves, takes them seriously, and, as the following chapters of Exodus will show, responds to them. The Bible scholar Walter Brueggemann characterizes this story as show-ing both that Israel has "a bold voice for hurt" and that God has "an attentive ear for hurt." The voice of pain becomes the story's "mode of linking heaven and earth."[48]

GOD AND HUMAN PROTEST

The story is powerful—but for modern readers, also quite challenging. Exodus 2 presents a story of slaves who begin to protest, but also of a God who dramatically intervenes to interrupt and overturn the unjust status quo. There is something enormously compelling about this picture of God, but the reality described in the story is a far cry from our own. We can understand lament as (often desperately needed) self-assertion, can be energized by the ways that tears can generate hope—but many of us find it harder to relate to the idea that such lament will elicit divine response of the kind described in Exodus.[49] And so we are left to struggle with what kind of God it is to whom *we* cry out.

This is part of why the idea of God's transcendence is so crucial to Jewish theology. If God and God alone is ultimate, then every earthly status quo—every form of social, economic, or political arrangement—is (or ought to be) relativized[50]—and this is so even if God does not (any longer) split seas. It is one of the central thrusts of the book of Exodus: despite Pharaoh's grandiose pretenses, God, and not Pharaoh, is God. God is eternal; present-day political arrangements are not. Thus Pharaoh's rule can be overthrown—from a biblical perspective, *must be overthrown*. To retell the Exodus each day, then, is also to engage in a robust act of protest-hope in the face of oppression and tyranny. Despots in the past who had seemed invincible ultimately went down in ignominious defeat; what happened then can and must happen again.

But even from a less explicitly theological perspective, there is something powerful about what the moment of Israel's crying out sets in motion. Brueggeman makes the provocative suggestion that "publicly processed pain unleashes new social imagination . . . Pain, loss, grief, failure, discontinuity, publicly processed through the arts, liturgy, speech, pain honestly shared, spoken to neighbor, submitted so that it can be heard and received, enables us to move on where there seems no moving on."[51] In protesting their ongoing abuse at the hands of the Egyptian empire, in effectively declaring it intolerable and unsustainable, the slaves plant the seeds of a different kind of society. This is, as we'll see in chapter 8, a significant part of what biblical law is: an attempt to create a radical alternative to Egypt. Crying out creates social hope and new ways of imagining how people might live together.

CRYING OUT WITH THE PSALMISTS

Like the Israelite slaves, the psalmists cry out *to* God, but like Abraham, they also cry out *against* God.

Say the word "psalms" and most people conjure up hymns of thanksgiving (the Hebrew title for the book is Tehillim, which means "praises"), but in fact there are more laments than songs of praise in the book of Psalms. Individuals cry out over their personal circumstances, and the people as a whole lament their national humiliation. "All the multifarious forms of human affliction, oppression, anxiety, pain, and peril are given voice in the lament."[52]

The power of the psalms stems, in part, from the fact that the psalmists are human beings, not disembodied spirits. They appeal to God to help them with illness, or social isolation, or having been falsely accused of one crime or another. They care about, and complain about, the sufferings of real people in real life—and, when they sense that God has mistreated them, they refuse to let God off the hook. The psalmists accuse God of abandoning them (e.g., Psalm 22:2); they charge God with murder (22:16); they lament that God has humiliated them (44:14); and they arraign God for falling asleep on the job (44:24).

In contrast to Abraham, who protests what he perceives as God's injustice at Sodom but also apologizes for his temerity in doing so (Genesis 18:27, 30–32), the psalmists do not back down. There is no sense in the psalms that complaining to God, and even holding God accountable, are somehow religiously inappropriate. On the contrary, "there is not a single line [in the Bible] which would forbid lamentation or which would express the idea that lamentation ha[s] no place in a healthy and good relationship with God."[53] For a certain kind of piety, expressions of anger, frustration, and disappointment are unacceptable, even blasphemous. But that is not the spirituality of the psalms. For them, anger, frustration, and disappointment are a natural and integral part of genuine relationship—and if the psalmists care about one thing, it is the genuineness of their relationship with God. They simply assume that a relationship with God should involve the whole person, and should be honest. More than that, they seem to maintain a steadfast faith that God loves them enough to hear their cries.

Both as a child and as a young adult, I spent years studying in fairly traditional religious institutions. In those schools, these psalms of lament were never mentioned, let alone studied—let alone prayed! (I literally did not know that they existed until I was an adult.) We were taught a different kind of piety, one that counseled placing our trust in God and enduring our sufferings patiently; it almost went without saying that we were not permitted to question God, let alone cry out in anger or disappointment. When good things happened, we were to praise God; when bad things happened, we were to maintain silence, or affirm that according to some deeper accounting available only to God, what seemed like an unbearable tragedy was in fact for the ultimate good. We were taught to venerate the Talmudic sage who, "whatever befell him, would declare, 'This also is for the best' (*gam zu le-tovah*)."[54] Given that approach, it's really no wonder that these psalms were all but totally erased. After all, by refusing to suppress pain in the name of some purportedly higher piety, they explode conventional assumptions about what faith ought to look like.

My father died suddenly of a brain aneurysm when I was twelve years old. Having internalized some truly poisonous ideas about how boys should be "strong" and not express their feelings, I decided that I would go about my business in school without letting on that anything at all was amiss in my life. For months on end, I made no mention of the desolating loss I had just experienced and said nothing about my grief and desolation. Then one day, a small chink appeared in my armor. During a short morning class about Jewish law, my classmates and I were learning about the blessing traditionally recited upon hearing sad news, "Blessed is the True Judge." Haltingly, I raised my hand and asked the teacher, "But what happens when you hear something so bad and so painful that you just can't bring yourself to say that?"

Now imagine for a moment how you'd have responded to a question like that, asked earnestly by a grieving child. Here's what my teacher said: "For a true believer, that is *not* a question." I was devastated by his response. I remember feeling an overwhelming urge to crawl into the tiles on our classroom floor. For years after that, I moved in and out of belief, and in and out of religious observance. If religion could crush a wounded child in that way, I wanted no part of it.

Except that religion does not have to be like that, and for the psalmists it isn't like that at all. "Dogmatism insists on the repression of pain,"[55] but the psalms decidedly do not. On the contrary, they recognize that genuine relationship with God needs to make space for the expression of pain and disappointment.

My teacher's dogmatism likely stemmed not from arrogance but from fear. All these years later I wonder whether he responded as he did because he was anxious about the meaning-world he had constructed for himself. When you let the questions in, you risk destabilizing your world. Your faith might be refined, but it might also be defeated.

The Bible is bold enough to take that risk.

As I've gotten older, I've come to spend more and more time studying and teaching biblical texts. One of the key reasons for this is the sheer power of the Bible's often searing honesty. It affirms that God created the world by subduing chaos and enabling life to thrive—yet it boldly admits and laments the fact that chaos often seems to rule the day.[56] It teaches that the Creator of heaven and earth has entered into a covenant with Israel—yet at times it almost brazenly insists that God has failed to live up to God's commitments. It avers that God is on the side of the downtrodden—yet it frankly acknowledges that the weak and vulnerable are often shamelessly exploited, even as the heavens remain silent. Heroically, the Bible refuses to simply accept all this; instead, it wails and it shrieks about it. There is something profoundly liberating about these texts and their (faith-ful!) refusal to sweep human suffering under the rug. Propriety is not allowed to trump pain. The psalms are guided by the (sometimes tortured) faith that our pain matters to God.

PROTEST AS A MANIFESTATION OF FAITH

If faith is about life—about real life, and not some spiritualized ideal thereof—then there has to be room for anguish. As long as life contains both joy and sadness, weal and woe, liturgy must contain both praise and lament. If all we are ever allowed to do is praise, then what do we do with our sorrows, our hurts, and our disappointments? If all we do with our pain is silence it, then we run the very real risk that our religion will depend on developing a "false self," one that does not mean what it says and is afraid to say what it means.[57] It's vital that we grasp this point: being honest with God, even when life hurts, is not a *rebellion* against faith but a *manifestation* of it.[58]

This can be clearly seen in the book of Job, in which the protagonist protests against the immense suffering God has inflicted upon him while his "friends" offer explanations and justifications of his pain. The book is enormously complex and its ultimate message is elusive, but in this context one key moment is worth keeping in mind: it is Job, who protests against God, and not his friends, who defend God, about whom God says that he has "spoken truth about Me" (Job 42:7).[59] Job's speech is not true because he offers a convincing set of metaphysical propositions or a neat solution to the problem of evil; he doesn't. Job's speech is true because he speaks honestly and with an integrity that he will not compromise.[60]

How can God censure Job's friends when they have offered what is seemingly a genuine "biblical perspective" on suffering, that God is just and therefore God rewards the righteous and punishes the wicked? If Job is being punished, then surely he is unrighteous! The problem with Job's friends is that they invoke dogma to silence pain. So God instructs them: Job, who gave utterance to his suffering, has spoken more truly than you, who have tried to override it.[61] (Think again of my teacher's response to a twelve-year-old child beset by grief.) One can thus see how a psalm of lament can be truer speech than an untroubled declaration of faith.[62]

I've suggested above that if Abraham is willing to question God, then all the more so will he be willing to challenge human leaders. Conversely, Brueggemann argues that where laments are ruled out, so too, eventually, are "questions of justice in terms of social goods, social access, and social power." If lament keeps questions about justice "visible and legitimate," discarding lament would render them invisible and illegitimate.[63] As Brueggemann writes:

> A community of faith which negates laments soon concludes that the hard issues of justice are improper questions to pose at the throne, because the throne seems to be only a place of praise. I believe that . . . if justice questions are improper questions at the throne . . . they soon appear to be improper questions in public places, in schools, in hospitals, with the government, and eventually even in the courts. Justice questions disappear into civility and docility.[64]

Neither Abraham nor the psalmists will permit a culture of civility and docility, let alone require it. Staring injustice in the face, a Jew cries out.

IS PROTEST INHERENTLY REDEMPTIVE?

For many modern readers (and, frankly, for me too), all this no doubt raises an array of difficult questions: What kind of God do we need to believe in, and what notion, if any, of divine providence do we need to have, in order to utter these psalms with integrity? If we don't believe that God actively runs the world, can the psalms of lament still have a place in our religious lives? I am honestly not sure of the answer to these questions, but I *am* certain that the psalms of lament teach us something critical: for our religion to be vital and alive, for it to feel authentic in and to the kind of world we find ourselves in, we must bring our suffering into the sanctuary.[65] Better a suffering religion than a sanitized one.

The psalmists cry out to God because they believe that God can relieve their suffering; they don't just want to be heard, they want to be *answered*—and saved by a God who cares about their suffering. The primary purpose of lament in biblical times was not catharsis but salvation. This leads some Bible scholars to assert that "prayers of sorrow and complaint that expect no concrete answer have no point of contact with biblical lament."[66]

I am not so sure that they are right. In lament, regardless of response, "suffering is given the dignity of language."[67] Suffering can render us passive, voiceless, mute. As Rabbi Soloveitchik teaches, there is something inherently redemptive about finding words for our pain. "A mute life is identical with bondage," he writes; "a speech-endowed life is a free life."[68] Even before they are saved by God—or even, for that matter, in situations when they are not saved at all—the psalmists, like the slaves in Egypt, accomplish something transformative simply by giving voice to their afflictions.

What I am describing here may in part be a psychological process, but it is primarily a relational one. It is not just that the psalmists speak; it is that they speak *to someone*—and not just to anyone, but to the One who created them, affirms their dignity, and hears their cries.[69] In protesting, the psalmists reach out to a God who loves them. Returning to the themes of chapter 1, even in the midst of their suffering, on some level the psalmists are confident that they matter and that they are loved—or perhaps we can say that in the very process of lament, they *rediscover* that they matter and are loved.

In our own time, many of us are more often confident of God's solidarity than we are of God's salvation; in other words, we believe that God is with us even if we don't think that God will dramatically intervene to save us. That may indeed represent a vast gap, or even a chasm, between us and our biblical forebears. And yet they have bequeathed us something precious and potentially transformational: the insistence that we need not lie about our suffering, the awareness that honesty is never a sacrilege, the courage to cry out, and the confidence that injustice is to be resisted rather than accepted.

PROTEST AND ANGER

After King David engages in adultery with Bathsheba and then has her husband murdered in an attempt to hide his crime, the prophet Nathan approaches him with a parable: There were two men in a city, one rich and one poor. The rich man had an abundance of flocks and herds, whereas the poor one had only one little lamb that he had bought and that he treated with great tenderness, so much so that "it was like a daughter to him." One day, a traveler came to visit the rich man but the latter did not want to give up one of his own animals to prepare a meal for the wayfarer, so he took the poor man's lamb and served it instead. Hearing this story (the fact that it is a parable seems to elude him), David flies into a rage; the rich man's crime is so egregious, he insists, that he "deserves to die! He shall pay for the lamb four times over, because he did such a thing and showed no pity." Nathan informs David that he has incriminated himself: "That man is you!" and tells him of the divine punishment that awaits him (2 Samuel 12:1–12).

Nathan is unafraid to speak the truth and protest injustice, no matter how powerful the culprit. But for our purposes, it's essential that we notice something else: the prophet counts on the fact that David will be incensed when he hears of such a travesty of justice. Given the gravity of what the rich man has done, the king's sense of indignation is entirely appropriate, even commendable. The prophets count on us to be appalled by injustice.

When we see people suffering from mistreatment, we *ought to feel anger* toward the sources of their suffering;[70] to confront injustice and oppression and *not* to get angry is a moral failure. "An individual absent of all moral anger and indignation must be indifferent to the existence of moral evil, must be absent of all moral sensitivity."[71] Anger, then, is a sign of being morally sensate.

When we respect other people, when we take them seriously, we believe they ought to be accountable for their actions. But what does holding them accountable look like? We know that it has a cognitive dimension—we judge their behavior negatively, and we know that in many cases it has a behavioral dimension—we cause them to suffer the consequences of their actions. But a good case can be made that holding people accountable also has an emotional dimension. As the philosopher Peter Strawson argues, "Holding someone accountable for doing something is in the first instance a matter of having a negative attitude from the anger family toward that person."[72] Sometimes we get angry at people precisely because we respect them; our anger is in fact a manifestation of our respect.

But it's not just respect for the culprit that requires us to get angry; it's first and foremost respect for the victim. "When we value someone as a person, we see him or her as *commanding* respect." This means not only that we are obligated to treat the person with respect, but that we expect others to do so as well. Truly valuing people in this way "entails resentment or indignation when they are abused." In other words, respect for the victim requires us to become angry at the victimizer.[73]

What is true with regard to respect for others is true for self-respect as well. If we believe that we are entitled to be treated with respect—and anyone who believes that they are created in the image of God *must* believe this—then when we are disrespected, we ought to get angry. Not to be angry at how we are treated in certain situations suggests that we lack adequate self-respect.[74] In a political context, moral anger allows the oppressed to preserve their self-respect even as the powerful treat them with contempt.[75] To get angry at being mistreated is to declare without equivocation that we deserve to be treated otherwise. Thus, for oppressed groups, although there may be costs to being angry, there are also costs to *not* being angry.[76]

Anger can serve as an antidote to feelings of impotence. As the Christian theologian Beverly Harrison writes, "Where anger rises, there the energy to act is present."[77] Moral anger is, quite plainly, a source of energy;[78] passion precludes passivity. If you try to mitigate anger in every circumstance you may end up bolstering, intentionally or not, apathy and accommodation in the face of injustice.[79] Despite its perils, I am not sure that anger is a greater threat to the human future than apathy.

Counterintuitive as it may seem, anger in the face of injustice can actually be a manifestation of deep love. Expanding on Hannah Arendt's notion of *amor mundi* (love of the world), the theologian John Kiess writes that "our love for the world is measured by the anger we express in response to the injustices that happen within it, the outrage we feel at the occurrence of systemic murder or the subjection of individuals to inhumane conditions, the indignation we feel at the moral detachment of perpetrators who participate in such crimes or the complicity of wider society."[80] So far from closing us off or shutting us down, anger can—note: can, but does not necessarily—in turn stem from and deepen our care and concern for the world and its well-being.

And yet we know that anger can be dangerous. It can and often does lead to dramatic overreaction. In Genesis, when Jacob's daughter Dinah is raped, two of her brothers react by *slaughtering an entire city* (Genesis 34); not surprisingly, their father forcefully condemns them for their explosive rage (49:5–7).[81] The Talmudic sages worry about the ways anger can overpower us and cause us to spin out of control. As one of them puts it, whereas God masters God's anger, "a human being is mastered by his anger."[82] Responsible anger requires a high degree of emotional maturity and self-control.[83]

On another level, injustice is so pervasive in the world around us that if we deem anger in the face of injustice appropriate, we risk being angry all the time.[84] And this, needless to say, can have profoundly negative consequences for our peace of mind and our overall well-being.[85] As Mark Twain is reputed to have said, "Anger is an acid that can do more harm to the vessel in which it is stored than to anything on which it is poured." So moral anger needs to be balanced—with love, and laughter, and small acts of gentle kindness.

A life animated by faith and love requires us to respond to the sufferings of the oppressed but also to work to bring an end to their oppression. (Compassion is sometimes unavoidably political.) This means that while love can and must express itself as kindness, and compassion, and generosity, there are also times when it can and must manifest itself in indignation and protest.

Judaism asks us to love the world so acutely that we are prepared to fight for it; it beckons us to love human beings so deeply that we are primed to side with them in the face of oppression and injustice. When we see a palace in flames, we may not remain silent. Judaism summons us to love God so profoundly that God's desire for a just society becomes our desire as well. As the Christian ethicist Timothy Jackson writes, "Love takes responsibility for the world . . . Rather than resignedly accepting the evils of the world, love confronts and seeks to overcome them."[86] Love is demanding, both of ourselves and of others; it is decidedly not "limp acquiescence to cultural norms that maintain an unjust status quo."[87] Love is not always "nice" or "civil"; in a world as broken as ours, "anger is sometimes the most loving response."[88]

THE NEED FOR BOTH PROTEST AND GRATITUDE

I argued at the outset of this chapter that a religious life cannot consist of gratitude alone; that just isn't the kind of world we live in. For Judaism, grace is not a prescription for passivity. On the contrary, one of the unearned gifts that God gives us is our capacity for agency, our ability to build and shape worlds. Conscience, and the commands that it issues, are also gifts from God. So there is an important place for protest, for lament in the face of a horribly fractured world.

But neither can protest be the whole picture, because protest alone is potentially dangerous and deeply destructive. To protest against injustice without also expressing gratitude for the gifts of life, and consciousness, and Torah, is to develop a religion that is all anger and indignation. To be all anger and indignation is to lose the capacity for softness, and humor, and the simple delights of daily living—themselves not to be taken for granted in a world in which they are not equally available.

People who are always protesting can forget how to listen. After all, when you're indignant all the time, it can be hard to stop talking (or screaming). Yet when it's time to move from protest to policy, the ability (the eagerness, really) to listen is critically important, because once we've established, say, that tens of millions of people living in poverty in the wealthiest nation in the history of the world is a moral and theological scandal, we still need to ask how to lift them out of destitution. And that requires thoughtful, reasoned analysis and debate—and, for that matter, respect for disagreement, and an ability to tolerate uncertainty.

Even beyond all this, protest against God carries significant theological risk. Protest has its place, but if the entirety of our relationship with God is about outcry and lament, then we will end up experiencing God as cruel or abusive.[89] Another way of saying this is that protest can be a compelling *practice*, but when it hardens into a full-blown "theology of protest," it can render faith incoherent, or destructive, or both.[90] What grounds theological protest and gives it life and coherence is precisely faith in God's love and ultimate goodness.

No gratitude without protest, but equally, no protest without gratitude. We live in a complex, multivalent world, and so an honest religious life needs both. That's what Chesterton means when he invites us both to storm the castle and to make it home.

PART II

WIDENING CIRCLES:
WHOM SHOULD WE LOVE?

4

LEARNING TO LOVE
AND BE LOVED

The Family

GOD LOVES US, but God's love is mediated and experienced, at least initially, through the love shown to us by human caregivers. We sense the possibility of God's love only because we experience human love—most commonly at home, in families.

God creates us with love in the hopes that we, too, will become lovers, but for that to happen we need families to serve as "schools of love" where kindness, compassion, gratitude, and generosity can be learned and internalized.

God seeks us out as partners in creating a more just and loving world but in order for us to be able to step into that role, to have a healthy sense of agency, to muster the courage to think for ourselves and to act even when doing so seems unpopular or even dangerous, we need parents and caregivers to bolster our sense of dignity and self-worth.

If we are to live out the Jewish ideals we've been exploring in these opening chapters, we need families, and we need the love that families ideally embody.

BEING TOGETHER IN OUR SEPARATENESS:
ADAM AND EVE

After God creates Adam, God faces a problem. Although God has looked at the creation as a whole and declared it "very good" (Genesis 1:31), God soon realizes that there is something about the world that is not in fact good: "The Lord God said, 'It is not good for man to be alone; I will make a fitting helper for him'" (2:18).[1] Crucially, the text makes clear, it is not God who will be Adam's partner; that role will be played by a creature rather than a god.[2] As it turns out, not just any creature will do: for a fitting helper, Adam needs another human being, so God provides him with just that (2:19–24). Adam is delighted with Eve and the two form a couple.

Genesis declares: "Hence a man leaves his father and mother and cleaves to his wife, so that they become one flesh" (2:24). From the perspective of this text, human love and companionship are a blessing, not a concession to weakness. We are social animals all the way down, meant to live in relationship with others.

Scholars have detected an array of meanings in this highly evocative verse. One approach has it that whereas "cleaving" to one's partner suggests that "both passion and permanence should characterize marriage," "becoming one flesh" implies that spouses form a kinship relation; when two people marry they become *family*.[3] According to another interpretation, although the patriarchs Abraham and Jacob had multiple wives, the ideal expressed by this verse is "God's intention that marriage be monogamous."[4]

Some interpreters identify a tension in the verse between the notion of "cleaving," which expresses the idea of "two distinct entities becoming attached to one another while preserving their separate identities," and the concept of "becoming one flesh," which can be taken to suggest a deeper unity of identities.[5] That tension, I think, gives voice to one of the deepest truths of human relatedness. For some people, the idea of "being in love" is bound up with the illusion that lovers somehow merge and become "one person." Yet marriage is a covenant, and a covenant is a relation—and a relation always implies that two parties rather than merely one are involved. As the philosopher Ilham Dilman explains, a certain separateness between two people, "far from being a gulf between [them], unless [they] make it so, is in fact a necessary condition of friendship, love and human give and take." Even more strongly, Dilman writes, "I cannot really love someone with whom I have identified myself to the extent that I do not feel her to have an identity apart from mine."[6] In other words, in order for us to be in a relationship, you have to be you and I have to be me. Friendship, intimacy, and marriage—not to mention covenant with God—all depend on human separateness, from God and from one another.

Separateness need not imply separation; separateness is what makes genuine relatedness possible. As Dilman puts it, "It is only when one cannot accept the other person's separateness, give him or her space in which he or she can be himself or herself, that this separateness turns into something that separates."[7] When we are driven by the fantasy that another person will complete us or make us whole, we find separation intolerable, but if we see ourselves as whole—or at least understand that wholeness cannot be a gift that another person bestows upon us[8]—then we can embrace separateness as the only viable path to intimacy and the covenant of marriage.

Among Jewish thinkers, this idea is most forcefully emphasized by Martin Buber (1878–1965), who places great weight on the "otherness" of the person to whom I relate. "I wish his otherness to exist," Buber writes, "because I wish his particular being to exist." In other words, it is precisely the other person's otherness, his not being me, that enables me to enter into relation with him. This is, Buber says, "the basic principle of marriage," and it is the reason that marriage is in some sense the paradigmatic human relationship, what Buber calls "the exemplary bond."[9]

When we love, we don't just acknowledge the other's separateness; we also embrace and celebrate their uniqueness. In this sense, our love reflects God's. In creating us, God allows us—*wants* us—to be other than God. And, as we saw in chapter 1, God loves us not as generic examples of the human species but as unique, distinctive individuals. In loving others in all their uniqueness, then, we take a step toward loving as God loves.

To love someone is to be together ("one flesh") in our separateness ("cleaving"). It also requires learning to be present while making space.

BEING PRESENT AND MAKING SPACE

If God is everywhere, the Kabbalist Rabbi Isaac Luria (known as the ARI, 1534–1572) wondered, how can the world exist?[10] If God is infinite, how can there be anything that is *not* God? His answer was enormously influential in the later Kabbalah: the existence of the world is made possible by an act of contraction or withdrawal on God's part. God recoils or withdraws into Godself, leaving a space that is not God. This process of divine self-contraction, which R. Luria called *tzimtzum*, is what makes the existence of the world, of everything that is not God, possible.

Yet the origins of the term *tzimtzum* are very different. In the book of Exodus, God directs Moses to "tell the Israelite people to bring Me gifts . . . And let them make Me a sanctuary (*mikdash*) that I may dwell among them" (Exodus 25:2, 8). A midrash imagines Moses's bewilderment at God's instructions: "When God said to Moses, 'Let them make Me a sanctuary,' Moses responded, 'Master of the Universe, the highest heavens cannot contain You, and yet You say, Let them make Me a sanctuary?!'" Seeking to reassure Moses, God replies, "Moses, not as you think. Rather, twenty boards to the north, twenty boards to the south, and eight to the west—and I will descend and contract (*metzamtzem*, from the same root as *tzimtzum*) My presence (*shekhinah*) among you below."[11] For the sages, then, *tzimtzum* explains how a vast and uncontainable God can dwell in a finite space.

Notice just how different these two conceptions are. They begin with disparate questions: R. Luria wonders how a world can exist apart from God, while the sages want to know how God can be intensely present in one place within the world. Not surprisingly, they arrive at divergent conclusions. According to R. Luria, *tzimtzum* means that God moves *out from* the world; for the sages, it means that God moves profoundly *into* it—or into one part of it. For Luria, in other words, *tzimtzum* yields divine absence; for the sages, in contrast, it yields intensified presence.

On one level, these ideas are starkly contradictory. Luria seems to take the Rabbinic idea and "st[and] it on its head."[12] And yet there is something powerful, I think, about holding the two conflicting images in mind at the same time. The idea of God's retreat, on the one hand, and God's intensified presence, on the other, tells us something important about who God is in relation to the world, and also about who we ought to be in relation to each other. Taken together, these Rabbinic and Lurianic notions of *tzimtzum* convey the importance of being present while making space.

These twin notions of *tzimtzum* suggest that God is radically present while still making space for us. Since we are commanded to "walk in God's ways," this paradox can teach us about the kind of human relationships to which we should aspire: we must be present while making space; we must make space while remaining present. So often in life, we are tempted to seize one pole at the expense of the other—to be present in a demanding or domineering way that we leave no space for the other or to allow so much space that we cease to be present at all. Our goal, then, should be to steer a course between narcissism and abandonment.

One of the core challenges of loving a friend, a spouse, or a child as they mature is to learn to be completely present—available, attentive, loving, and nurturing—while also making space for the other to be who they are, independent of us. Perhaps another way of saying this is that in loving other people, we are always there for them even as we respect their freedom and remember that, close as we are, we are not the same person. God contracts God's presence so that we can exist, and so that we can exercise our agency and act in the world without being suffocated or coerced by a power other than our own. Just as God makes space for a world that is other than God, we make space for a spouse or a friend who is other than ourself.

In his classic *I and Thou*, Buber writes that "in the beginning is the relation."[13] Who and what we are is constituted in the moment of relating to another. But in his later writings, Buber emphasizes that in order for genuine relation to be possible, something else has to happen first.

Buber argues that "the principle of human life is not simple but two-fold." It begins with what he calls the "primal setting at a distance" and continues with "entering into relation." That first step—recognizing and affirming that the other is not me, and allowing her to be genuinely and fully other than me—is a precondition for the second, and makes it possible, since "one can enter into relation only with a being that has been set at a distance or, more precisely, has become an independent opposite."[14]

Honoring separateness is also fundamental to sexual love, which is always about two separate people coming together in moments of intense physical intimacy. Sex can be treated as a mere biological need—on one level it *is* that—but it can also be an expression of profound emotional closeness and connection. Remarkably, Imma Shalom, the wife of the Talmudic sage Rabbi Eliezer, speaks of sexual relations using the euphemism "conversing" (*mesaper*) (BT, Nedarim 20a–20b). Sexual intimacy is "a kind of dialogue (an *intercourse*) in which two people speak to one another and with one another";[15] in making love, they tell a story about themselves and about the depth of their passion and care for one another.

Marriage is not between ethereal souls or disembodied spirits but between real, flesh-and-blood human beings. Although there are voices in the Jewish tradition that express ambivalence about, and at times even revulsion at, human embodiedness and sexuality,[16] there are also many voices that celebrate our carnality and physicality and that see marital lovemaking as a blessing to be enjoyed and savored.[17] As Rabbi Joseph Soloveitchik writes:

> A covenantal marriage is a . . . pleasure-oriented community. Judaism did not overlook or underestimate the physical aspects of marriage . . . The two partners owe each other not only fidelity, but also full gratification of their sexual needs . . . The marriage must not be converted into an exclusively spiritual fellowship. Marriage without

carnal enjoyment and erotic love is contrary to human nature and is to be dissolved.[18]

From a Jewish perspective, committed sexual relationships are a genuine good, not a concession to human weakness.

All relationships can devolve into their destructive opposites. As the Talmudic sage R. Akiva puts it, "If a man and a woman merit, the divine presence rests between them. But if they do not merit, fire consumes them."[19] Sexual partners can objectify or even dehumanize one another. Sanctified sex involves seeing the other in their otherness, recognizing and responding to their individual wants and needs (emotional, physical, etc.). This may be what a midrash has in mind in declaring that, unlike most animals, human beings can and often do have sex face-to-face.[20]

LOVE ABUNDANT AND ABIDING

There is a subtle variation in how the morning and evening liturgies in many traditions describe God's love for Israel: In the benediction immediately preceding the recitation of the Shema in the morning we speak of God's "abounding love" (*ahavah rabbah*), whereas in the evening we speak of God's "everlasting love" (*ahavat olam*). Seeking to shed light on the shift, the Hasidic master Rabbi Zadok Ha-Kohen of Lublin explains that morning and evening evoke very different moods and thus differently textured love. Morning is a time of passionate hope and open-ended possibility. Accordingly, R. Zadok writes, "When the light of the day shines forth and enters the hearts of the Children of Israel, their hearts become enflamed with abounding love for God. Because God's love is parallel to Israel's love, we say, 'You have loved us with abounding love.'" Evening, in contrast, is a time of anxiety and apprehension. In the evening, consequently, we speak of "everlasting love," the kind of love that remains "indestructible even during the night and the darkness of troubles."[21]

The logic of R. Zadok's argument about the mutual love between God and the Jewish people is equally applicable to the love between human partners. R. Zadok maintains that covenantal love must be both abundant and abiding. It must have its share of "mornings"—that is, times of great passion and feeling—but it must also be durable enough to endure "evenings"—that is, times of crisis or weakened ardor—because every life and every relationship faces its share of evenings. ("Love is not love," Shakespeare wrote, "which alters when it alteration finds / Or bends with the remover to remove. / O no! it is an ever-fixed mark / That looks on tempests and is never shaken.)[22] I am not sure love can be truly "everlasting" if it does not have moments, at least, of being "abounding." But no love is "abounding" at all times; the emotional intensity of love, like all emotional intensity, inevitably ebbs and flows. Covenantal love remains steady even when passion has temporarily subsided, either because of life circumstances or because of the natural—and inescapable—rhythms of emotional life. It is this covenantal love that R. Zadok has in mind when he writes that "in reality, love is required whether one is in a good mood or a troubled one."[23] Covenantal love is above all a commitment and an orientation. It includes passion and emotion but is not limited to them. We can and must love one another regardless of what kind of love we happen to feel at any particular moment, regardless even of whether we feel *any* kind of love at all at that particular moment. I would argue that a commitment to remain steadfast in moments when passion is attenuated or diluted is a significant part of what constitutes the covenant of marriage.

We should not be naive: finding an appropriate partner is difficult—so difficult, in fact, that one midrash imagines that only God can successfully pair people off, and even God finds it as difficult as splitting the Sea of Reeds.[24] For those who enter marriages, abiding love can be enormously difficult to achieve. Tradition is only too keenly aware that marriages can sour over time; in a particularly poignant Talmudic passage, the sages quote a man who declares of his wife, "When our love was strong, we could have slept on a bed that was the width of a sword. Now that our love is not strong, a bed of sixty cubits is not sufficient for us."[25] Some marriages fail because despite the best efforts of one or both partners, the love the partners share(d) simply dissipates over time; some fail because one or both partners betray the trust that makes lasting marriage possible. And some marriages become abusive, degrading, and even violent; religious leaders need to be cautious lest they romanticize fidelity in situations when it is no longer appropriate (or sometimes even safe). The Talmudic sage Rabbi Elazar declares that even the Temple altar sheds tears when a first marriage ends in divorce[26]—divorce may be painful but it is sometimes also necessary.

MARITAL LOVE BETWEEN CREATION AND REDEMPTION

There are seven special blessings that form the heart of the Jewish wedding ceremony (*sheva berakhot*). These blessings tell the story of the universe from its beginning in creation to its culmination in the redemption of Jerusalem. Reciting (or hearing) these blessings, one cannot help but wonder: What is all this doing here? Why not simply thank God for the precious love between the two partners committing their lives to one another under the bridal canopy (huppah)?

In reciting these blessings at a wedding, we make the bold and dramatic claim that this wedding matters, and matters ultimately. It has a vital role to play in bringing the world closer to redemption. Through the blessings we implicitly declare that the love between these two people has cosmic implications. A wedding is never just a private affair between lovers; it is a sacred coming together that adds more love to the world and thus helps move us closer to the world God envisions.

This interpretation of the wedding is decidedly not an invitation to grandiosity on the part of newlyweds. We saw in chapter 1 that a person who comes to understand that God loves her simply because she is a human being created in God's image must immediately realize that what is true of her is true of every other human being in the world too: God's love is not exclusive to any one of us. In a similar vein, two people who grasp that the love they share has potentially redemptive implications for their community and the broader world must also recognize that what is true of them is true of other couples too: The manifestation of God's love is not exclusive to any one couple. The love between two people who stand together under the huppah is a momentous but nonexclusive midpoint between creation and redemption.

It is easy for couples to forget that their marriage is intended to have broader redemptive impact upon the world. We have all met couples whose love seems totally insular. Having found each other, they live as if there were no reality, no one else who really existed, outside their own little bubble. The narcissism of two is no better than the narcissism of one; the love between married couples is meant to radiate outward.

It is in part for this reason that Jews traditionally marry under a canopy (huppah) with no walls: the structure is intimate in that it brings the couple together in their symbolic first home, while its lack of walls serves as a dramatic declaration of openness to the world. There is an obvious tension here. On the one hand, the huppah establishes a home, which is at least to some extent an intimate and private space; Rabbi Abraham ben Natan (b. twelfth century) writes that without a huppah it would be as if the marriage were taking place "in the market," which would smack of "licentiousness."[27] Yet on the other hand, that intimate and private space refuses to close in on itself.[28] The huppah reminds us of Abraham and Sarah's tent, which the Talmudic sages describe as having been open at both sides so that they could hurry out to greet passersby and welcome them into their home.[29] In the spirit of Abraham, the Talmudic sage Yosi ben Yohanah instructs, "Let your house be wide open," and, pushing us harder, "Let the poor be members of your household."[30]

It's worth pausing here to note that in biblical times families were thought of and experienced in more expansive ways than many modern families are.[31] Living under the same roof might be a father, a mother, their children—some of whom might themselves already be married—an unmarried or widowed aunt or uncle, a sojourner (ger), and perhaps some hired hands as well. Biblical households were thus fuller than many of ours tend to be, and "family" often included people who were not related by blood. There was a much more wide-ranging sense of connection and obligation.[32]

For all the power of a close nuclear family, something is obviously lost when the boundaries of family are drawn too tightly. A sense of being connected beyond the nuclear family is potentially a built-in first step toward a more extensive and inclusive sense of who belongs, and who matters.[33] Of course, clans can be selfish too, so this is no guarantee, but it does open the door to a more wide-ranging sense of connection and obligation.

BECOMING MORE FULLY HUMAN

In light of what we've seen, I think we can say that marriage is, at its best, both an intrinsic good and an instrumental one. It is an intrinsic good because love, faithfulness, and nurturing attentiveness to the well-being of another person are an inherent good; it is an instrumental good because "marital love is a training ground for the exercise of care in the world."[34] Ideally, marriage reminds us that our hungry ego is not the center of the universe: it teaches us how to attend to others, instructs us in the art of granting and receiving forgiveness, and deepens our capacity for listening and caring. In other words, marriage changes who we are and thus enables us to be more fully present, more loving, more compassionate, and more generous in the rest of our lives too.

I have often been struck by the fact that as part of the seven blessings, we acknowledge God as "Creator of the human being." It has always seemed odd to me that these words are proclaimed at a wedding rather than a circumcision or some other event celebrating the birth of a child (and their entry into the covenant). Reciting this blessing at a wedding is a subtle reminder that committed relationships, and their paradigm, the covenant of marriage, represent unique opportunities to grow in our capacity for abundant and abiding love, and thus to become more fully human. To be clear: marriage is no guarantee that we will grow in love—some people become only more brittle, or hostile, or indifferent as their marriage grows stale and lifeless, or insular. And many people grow in love without being married. The point, simply, is that marriage is a challenge and an opportunity. We learn to love one another and those to whom we are responsible more and more deeply, and we allow our love to flow to ever-widening circles of community, people, humanity, world.

LOVING CHILDREN

As we saw in chapter 1, according to Jewish theology God creates us so that God can love us. If that is the case, then having children can be a form of *imitatio Dei* (the imitation of God): we bring new lives into the world so that we can love them. Like God, we create with the hope of showering love and bestowing blessings upon our children.[35]

In chapter 1, we discussed R. Akiva's claim that every human being is loved simply by dint of being created in God's image. We don't have to earn God's love; God always already loves us.

But there's the rub. The only way for young children to internalize the sense that they matter, and that God loves them, is if parents and teachers mediate that love for them.[36] Try telling an adolescent who has been assailed time and again by an abusive parent that he matters because God loves him and you will not get very far (at least not at first, and not without deep work dedicated to healing what the parent has broken). Low self-worth in children is of course not necessarily an indication of parental failure. The world is a complicated and often brutal place, and the human heart and mind are profoundly fragile. But as parents, in doing our best to love our children unconditionally we strive to emulate and reflect God's love.

Every few weeks, before I put my children to bed, I tell them some version of the following: "I love you so much. You really can't even imagine how much I love you; I barely even understand it myself. But there's something else I want you to know: as much as I love you, God loves you so much more than that. I can't even begin to fathom how much God loves you." I say this to them in part because I am only too keenly aware of my own shortcomings: I have no doubt that there will be moments when I will communicate to them, whether I mean to or not, that my love for them is conditional, that they have to earn (or worse, buy) my love.[37] And I want them to know in those moments that no matter how bad I make them feel or how deeply I hurt them, they are loved by an inexhaustible Source of Love who loves them more profoundly and more unconditionally than I, as a human being, ever could.[38]

We reflect God's love for our children, but because we are human, we do so imperfectly, and sometimes downright badly. I want my children to know that whether or not they matter, and whether or not they are loved, does not ultimately depend on me.

(UN)CONDITIONAL LOVE

The Mishnah teaches that "any love that is dependent on something—when the thing ceases, the love also ceases. But a love that is not dependent on anything never ceases."[39]

Ideally at least, parental love would be unconditional. We would love our children in much the same way that God loves us: with expectations, but without conditions.[40] Parents often get tripped up by conflating expectations with conditions. Whether we mean to or not, we make our children feel either that our love depends on their meeting our expectations, or, no less insidiously, that because we love them unconditionally, we don't have any real expectations of them.[41] Except in abusive families, the conditions are not usually expressed explicitly: we don't actually say, "Do this, achieve that, or I'll stop loving you." But our children sometimes hear that message between the lines. A lack of genuine expectations on our part is also easy for them to discern, and the consequences are poisonous. Parental love should prepare our children to live decent, just, and love-filled lives; it should not—*must* not—instill complacency or self-satisfaction in them.

We are not always conscious of the conditions we place upon our love. *Of course* we love our children unconditionally, we want to say; we're offended at the suggestion that it (or we) would be any other way. And yet there are often moments when it becomes clear to our children that our love is more conditional than they thought (or we intended). As the philosopher Robert Roberts explains, "The strings may be invisible to us; we think that we love our friends, our neighbors, and our children 'unconditionally,' but when the condition on which our love hangs begins to go unsatisfied, it becomes apparent that it hung on that condition all along." That doesn't mean that we don't actually love our children, but it does mean that our love is "a compromised, imperfect kind of love."[42]

I'm not sure that human beings are actually capable of unconditional love—and in any case, we can't ever be sure that our love is truly unconditional. Our children could change in ways that undermine the steadfastness of our love, whether or not we want them to. To take an example from the philosopher Christopher Cordner, they "could become . . . drug addict[s] dedicated to feeding their addiction[s] at any cost, including deceiving [their] parents, stealing from them, attacking them physically, expressing apparently relentless anger and hostility towards them and others." It's hard to be confident that our love would not waver under such circumstances. And we too could change: corrosive forces like "serious illness or hardship, betrayal of friends, loss of reputation, [and] being taken over by envy and resentment," to take just a few examples, could severely compromise our ability to love.[43] Tellingly, as we'll see in chapter 13, the prophet Hosea suggests that part of what makes God God and not a human being is the fact that God cannot, will not, give up on God's children no matter what (Hosea 11:8–9); the implication is that God's love, and only God's love, is truly unconditional.

Yet even if we cannot fully achieve it, unconditional love can still serve as an aspirational ideal against which we measure ourselves and toward which we seek to grow. Asymptotic though the ideal may be, we can regard our actual loving as "answerable" to the requirements of unconditional love.[44]

THE UNIQUENESS OF EACH CHILD

Our goal as parents is to love children unconditionally but also to love them individually, in all their distinctiveness. Good parenting requires constant attunement to the uniqueness of each child—a much taller order than it might appear at first glance.[45] The Talmud emphasizes that every one of us has a distinctive face and voice. God sees each of us as unique, and as we saw in chapter 1, God glories in that uniqueness.[46] To model our parenting on divine love is to do likewise.

The Jewish theologian Mara Benjamin captures this point beautifully: "Children's needs and abilities can be plotted in the abstract," she writes, "but the distinctive needs of any given child determines the command she issues. The specific command can only be heard in the immediacy of one's particular child at a particular moment." As Benjamin observes, it is not any baby (or child) that makes a claim on me, but this baby (or child) in particular. "Every child," she notes, "issues his or her own law."[47] This is reflective of a much broader and more basic point about life with others: ethics is about responding not to human beings in general but to human beings in particular—and in all their particularity.[48]

This all means that we often fail. What one child finds funny the other finds hurtful; what the same child is entertained by one day she is irritated by the next. What is required of parents is not perfection but attention, a willingness to learn and relearn, repeatedly—what each child individually needs, and needs *from us*, in order to blossom and thrive.

An oft-cited verse from the book of Proverbs teaches: "Train a child on the way he should go" (Proverbs 22:6). The Hebrew has often been read to suggest an emphasis on the singular pronoun: "Train a child in the way that *he* should go," or even, "Train a child in his own way." The path that each individual must follow is unique to her. According to Rabbi Samson Raphael Hirsch (1808–1888), "The verse demands a totally individualized education." The ideal of a life guided by Torah and God's commandments is universal, he explains, but the paths that get each young person there are different. They depend on the child's distinctive inclinations and capacities. As a result, R. Hirsch observes, "no one educational approach is appropriate to each and every child."[49] In the same vein, Rabbi Meir Leibush Weiser (Malbim, 1809–1879) points out that the verse actually commands two things: first, that we actively guide our children and train them in good actions, attributes, and ways of thinking ("train the child"), and second, that we pay careful attention to their unique interests, yearnings, and predilections, and guide them accordingly ("in his own way").[50] There are no cookie-cutter human beings; accordingly, there can be no generic education.

(HEALTHY) PARENTAL LOVE BUILDS US UP

We know from decades of psychological research just how pivotal children's earliest relationships are in forming their very selves. According to object-relations theory, which, in contrast to Freudian approaches to development, focuses on early relationships rather than drives, "the self is formed by the internalization of its relationships. As internalized objects, relationships become the basic ingredients from which a sense of self is shaped."[51] In a more biological vein, neuroscientists are increasingly confident that the brain structures that facilitate empathy and socio-emotional learning and affect regulation are in vital ways "experience-dependent." The healthy functioning of these structures depends upon "healthy attachment interactions between the infant and her primary caregiver." Conversely, unhealthy attachment can contribute to a variety of psychopathologies and difficulties in loving, trusting, and being vulnerable.[52]

In fundamental ways, our parents' love helps create us as who we are. We learn from our parents how to love—and how to mourn loss; how to form real and enduring relationships; how to live peacefully with others; and how to learn and grow from our experiences. Hence "healthy, loving, and supportive families are crucial to nurture compassionate, ethical persons and create sane and just societies." The converse is true too: if love and nurture build us up, neglect and abuse tear us down. We are, all of us, extremely vulnerable: while good care can help us mature into loving people, poor, indifferent, or abusive care can damage or stunt us in countless ways. "The fragility of their earliest existence makes children easily broken."[53] Children's early interactions and relationships reverberate for the rest of their lives.

This idea, that parental love helps create who we are, ought to be fundamental to any religious vision of the family. Commenting on

Søren Kierkegaard's declaration that "love forms the heart,"[54] the philosopher Natalia Marandiuc writes: "It is not the case that the human self gives rise to love," but rather that "the love that comes from others gives rise to the self."[55] On one level, of course, we come alive simply by virtue of breath and a beating heart. Yet on another level, we come fully alive through love.[56] Parents can both give love and withhold it, and can thus give life or thwart it (and in extreme cases, snuff it out entirely).

There is no more effective way to prepare children for lives animated by love than to provide them with a loving childhood. Although the world is a complicated place and there are no guarantees—good kids can come from bad homes and problematic kids can come from good ones—as a rule, loving children teaches them love, while neglecting or abusing them trains them in neglect and abuse.

We can't educate our children without loving them first. A Talmud sage reports that when Moses set out to build the *mishkan* (tabernacle), he wanted to build the ark and the vessels first and only then construct the tabernacle itself. But Bezalel, his prime builder, demurred: "You say, 'Make me an ark and vessels and a tabernacle.' Where shall I put the vessels that I am to make?!"[57] The child's feeling of being loved is like the tabernacle, and education the ark and the vessels that are contained within it. Unless we establish a foundation of love between us and our children, they will have no real self that can internalize what we wish to teach them. To teach without first establishing a firm grounding in love, a contemporary Jewish educator argues, is like pouring water from a pitcher with no cup to receive it.[58]

Children learn who and what they can be in the world by observing who and what their parents are. Asked when a person should start educating his child, Rabbi Hayyim of Volozhin (1749–1821), one of the most prominent modern Eastern European rabbis and Talmudists, is reported to have replied, "Twenty years before they are born."[59] When it comes to raising children, our character really does matter, especially since as parents, "the majority of what we teach, and how we teach, lies below the surface of cognition."[60] Who we are and what we have made of ourselves—I mean this in terms of character rather than profession—affects our children at every turn. If we want to raise children who embody the cluster of emotions and postures I have associated with love—compassion, care, empathy, kindness, etc.—then we have to manifest them ourselves. "Children do not practice what their parents only preach."[61] There are no shortcuts: we have to embody the love we seek to impart.

This applies to both women and men. In most of the world, it is simply assumed that women will perform the bulk of care work, especially where raising children is concerned. But a world in which the burdens of caregiving are distributed unevenly by gender is, to put it simply, an unjust one. Fathers too can wash dishes, change diapers, and cook dinners. No less importantly, in a world in which mothers alone engage in emotional forms of caregiving, boys are likely to undervalue and even repress their capacities for caring, empathy, and forging deep emotional ties. A world in which "a caring man is a contradiction in terms, or at least a highly ambiguous figure"[62] is a world in which boys are robbed of the fullness of their humanity. The converse of all this is borne out by empirical research: An array of studies shows that "boys whose fathers engage in caregiving show a greater capacity for sympathy and compassion . . . and are generally more caring toward others."[63] Assigning care exclusively to women and girls does a profound disservice *both to women and to men*. In addition, we'll see in chapter 10 that "walking in God's ways," or being present with other people in their suffering, is Judaism's highest human ideal; it is an ideal not for women alone but for Jews (and human beings) of any gender, and we should raise our children accordingly.

PREPARING CHILDREN FOR LIFE

A significant part of parental love is preparing children to make a life of their own.

The Talmudic sages enumerate a father's obligations to his son: "A father is obligated with regard to his son to circumcise him, to redeem him, to teach him Torah, to marry him to a woman, and to teach him a trade.[64] And some say: a father is also obligated to teach his son how to swim."[65] The Talmudic list speaks of fathers and their obligations toward their sons. Reading in an egalitarian spirit, I will ask what we can learn from the text about parents of any gender and their obligations to their children of any gender.[66] Let's consider what values and aspirations underlie the sages' list.[67]

Circumcision is a concrete act that is expressive of something much deeper and more fundamental: parents are obligated to enter their children into the covenant, to bring them into intense, intimate, and enduring relationship with God,[68] with Torah, and with the Jewish people. Covenantal living is intergenerational living—it is to know oneself as the descendant of ancestors and the ancestor of descendants, all sharing a dream of a world in which human dignity is real and the presence of God is manifest (more on this dream in chapter 12).

Redemption of the firstborn child, a ritual in which a firstborn child is "redeemed" through payment to a *kohen*, or priest, introduces the child into the foundational story of the Jewish people: in the simple words of the Passover Haggadah, "We were slaves to Pharaoh in the land of Egypt but now we are free." The story of Egypt and Exodus teaches us that we are a people shaped by the memory of suffering, called to lives of empathy and service of God.[69] Indeed, the God whom we are called to worship champions widows and orphans and loves the stranger.[70] In teaching our children to remember the Exodus and to make the story their own, we help them see themselves as anything but orphans in history; they are part of a story and a covenant community that have persisted for thousands of years. We can't know what the story will mean to them or how they will interpret its contemporary implications, but we can root them in it and thereby ground them in something far larger and more enduring than themselves. As Rabbi David Hartman (1931–2013) nicely puts it, "The mother's and father's task is not to decide how the child will use his memories. Their obligation is to see to it that the child does not enter into the future without a past."[71]

To teach a child Torah is to welcome them into the intellectual and spiritual treasures of the Jewish people. Jews read texts, and through texts we ask every conceivable human question, from the most quotidian—at what time is it permissible to say the evening prayers? If I damage your property how do I compensate you? What blessing do I recite before drinking a glass of water?—to the most sublime: Why is there something rather than nothing? What kind of human beings does God want us to be? What kind of society does God want us to build? Parents are tasked with enabling their children to participate, both cognitively and emotionally, in the inexhaustible conversation that is Judaism. To learn Torah is to be reminded in countless ways every day that we have responsibilities and therefore obligations. Through Torah we teach our children to orient their lives not only around what they want but also around what their community and the broader world need from them—and we help them discover the joy of being obligated and commanded.

The obligation to prepare children for marriage can be understood in part as teaching them how to love in deep and abiding ways—to prepare them for the covenantal relationships we have already explored. This duty, R. Hartman explains, "indicates the importance of creating family conditions which foster the psychological capacity to love."[72]

At the end of each meal, during the Grace After Meals (*Birkat Ha-Mazon*), Jews traditionally ask God not to make us "dependent on the gifts and loans of other people." Accordingly, to teach a child a trade is to prepare them to help them achieve economic dignity and independence,[73] and to enable them to support a family.[74]

To teach children to swim is to teach them resilience.[75] As R. Hartman notes, this last obligation "in some way implies that part of the role of the parent is to teach and help the child to cope with unpredictable circumstances and events."[76] Recent psychological research suggests that resilient people have what psychologists call an "internal locus of control": "They believe that they, and not their circumstances, affect their achievements." They see themselves, in other words, as "orchestrators of their own fates." Part of good parenting is about helping children develop a sense of their ability to shape their own lives, to maintain their sense of agency even in extraordinarily difficult circumstances.[77] Thrown into the deep, as it were, they know how to swim.

But is all this—teaching a child a trade, teaching them to swim—really about love, or is it about obligation? The answer, I think, is that it is about both, and that is precisely the point. In Jewish thought, love and obligation go hand in hand. Much of what parents do for their children stems not from love *or* obligation but from love *and* obligation. Love and obligation are so intertwined that love itself is sometimes an obligation.

Implicit in the Talmudic list of parental obligations is another critical lesson about love. To want the good for our child and to commit to bringing it about are inextricably linked.[78] This is true by extension for other loves too—though, to be sure, sometimes less intensely. For tepid "well-wishing" to become genuine love, wanting flows over into doing and making happen. We want our child to flourish in the world, and so we help equip them to do so. As we've seen and will see again, love involves both emotion and action; in its ideal version, it involves an internal state concretely expressed in tangible deed.

OUR CHILDREN ARE DIFFERENT FROM US

To raise children well requires us not only to embrace the ways that they differ from one another, but also to acknowledge and accept the ways that they differ from us.

Consider again R. Hartman's claim that the parents' task is "not to decide how the child will use his memories." This is part of a harder and more fundamental truth about love: Our children are different than we are. It is a crucial implication of a theology that celebrates human uniqueness: our children are not, and should not be, carbon copies of ourselves.

Hard as it can sometimes be, as parents we need to let our children become who *they are*, not who *we have decided they should be*. That's what it means to allow other people "a separate, non-slave life."[79] Recall what we've seen: without genuine otherness and separateness there can be no authentic relationship. Our children are not extensions of our will, and they do not exist to repair or redeem what is broken in our own life stories. Loving our children as who we wish them to be is not really loving *them* at all. It is loving a fantasy, a projection of ourselves—of our hopes, our dreams, our insecurities, and so on.[80] We sometimes convince ourselves that we are animated by love when in fact we are driven by a need for power or control.[81] Good parenting therefore requires a steadfast commitment to self-awareness.

Ideally, we don't just *tolerate* our children being different from us; we actively *want* them to be different. After all, we want them to be *them*, and not *us*. The poet C. Day-Lewis evocatively declares that "selfhood begins with a walking away. And love is proved in the letting go."[82] This type of letting go is necessary, no matter how sad and painful it can sometimes be.[83]

DON'T ROMANTICIZE PARENTHOOD

We should not romanticize parenthood. Raising children can enchant us one day and disenchant us the next; it can fill us with awe one moment and dread the next. Life with children can set us on a roller coaster, joy, delight, and pride alternating with anxiety, resentment, and even despair. The philosopher Sara Ruddick declares with good reason that "ambivalence is a hallmark of mothering . . . Mothers' feelings toward their children vary from hour to hour, year to year. A single, typical day can encompass fury, infatuation, boredom, and simple dislike."[84] In the same vein, for the poet Adrienne Rich parenthood is marked by an "interpenetration of pain and pleasure, frustration and fulfillment."[85] If we romanticize parenthood, if we describe it in purely idyllic terms, we condemn real, flesh-and-blood parents to an endless flood of self-doubt and self-castigation.

Parenting is enlivening but it is also exhausting; for parents it can be difficult to disentangle exhilaration from enervation. I think often of a wonderful little poem from Ogden Nash: "As a father of two there is a respectful question which I wish to ask of fathers of five: How do you happen to be still alive?" After an hours-long bedtime that comes on the heels of an already long day, no parent wants to hear about the wondrous glories of parenthood; they just want some sleep, or some time for themselves.

AMBIVALENCE AND CONSTANCY

The fact of parental ambivalence returns us to a point we have encountered before and will return to again: the love we have for our children is not dependent on what we happen to feel (or not feel) at this particular moment or that. Parental love is a commitment (or set of commitments), an orientation, a way of holding and conducting ourselves with our children. The emotion(s) of love are part of love but they do not exhaust its meaning: we can love our children even if at this particular moment our primary feeling is fatigue or frustration. To repeat (and perhaps belabor) the point: loving our children does manifest in emotion—few emotions are more powerful than moments of tender love for a child snuggled in our arms, for example—but no feeling endures perpetually, without moments, or even extended periods, of abating.

Parental love, in other words, is about constancy, about a commitment that remains steady even as the parents' feelings ebb and flow, and even as children's needs evolve and change.[86] Remarkably, in biblical Hebrew the words for fidelity and faithfulness, on the one hand, and for the act of rearing or nursing a child on the other, share the same root ('-m-n). In other words, in ancient Israel the constancy of a parent—and specifically a mother—"came to function as a signifier of faithfulness." It is even possible that the term for "constancy" ('-m-n) is related to the Hebrew word for "mother" ('m).[87] Although the possible linguistic connection between faithfulness and child-rearing was less often noticed over time[88]—mothers becoming invisible is not rare in the history of culture—the point is still striking: parental constancy is, in a sense, the paradigmatic instance of human faithfulness and commitment. In all genuine relationships meant to endure over time, faithfulness constitutes the essential baseline. Whatever we happen to be feeling at a particular time, we remain committed—and defined by our commitments.

"SOME MOTHER'S CHILD"

Many people understandably dedicate a great deal of time, energy, and resources to caring for their families. Yet as we saw above, the huppah is open-walled. Our responsibilities may begin at home but they decidedly do not end there; the love we give and receive at home is meant to radiate outward. Parents need to know this themselves, and they must also instill a similar awareness in their children, teaching it by word and modeling it by deed: it is a mitzvah for family love to flow outward. The fact is that families can serve as incubators of social responsibility but they can also become bastions of self-indulgence. So we should remind ourselves regularly that family commitments are no excuse for blindness (or worse, indifference) to the world around us.[89]

Think for a moment about the love and attention that good parents devote to their children—how protective we are of their safety; how dedicated we are to their flourishing; and how committed we are to teaching them right from wrong. We are ever conscious of their vulnerability, dependence, and need. In her work on the moral implications of human dependency, the philosopher Eva Kittay writes about the realization that everyone is "some mother's child." Just as my child is dependent and in need of care and concern, so too is yours. Just as my mother (or some other caring figure) nurtured me, so too did someone nurture the person (whether they be friend or stranger) in front of me. An awareness of my own child's dependency awakens me to the dependence of others and even, according to Kittay, to a sense of equality rooted in dependence and interconnection.[90]

Building on Kittay's insight, Mara Benjamin observes the ways that loving a child can be a double-edged sword. On the one hand, loving a child can severely limit our moral horizon; we come to behave as if our child were the center of the whole world, rather than just the center of ours. But there is another possibility that parenthood presents. Reveling in the wonder of one's own child can expand our vistas so that we see all people, and not just the child entrusted to our care, as "manifesting the divine and issuing a command." This vision awakens a sense of "obligation and responsibility" that extends far beyond our family. We can come to see other people as "wonder[s] of creation" just as our child is.[91] In other words, being a parent can narrow our world but it can also expand it.

FILLING CHILDREN WITH LOVE

In a venerable Jewish tradition, when the *kohanim* (priests) bless the community with the priestly benediction (Numbers 6:24–26) during prayer services, they do so responsively: The prayer leader recites each word of the blessing and the *kohanim* repeat it.[92] On the face of it, this ritual is extremely strange. Do the *kohanim* really need to be reminded, word by word, of a set of verses most no doubt know by heart? Rabbi Shlomo Ephraim Luntschitz (1550–1619) explains that the prayer leader is not, in fact, prompting the *kohanim* by reminding them of the words, but rather mediating God's blessing for them so that they can in turn bless others. In the image R. Luntschitz invokes, the prayer leader channels blessing from above and pours it forth upon the *kohanim*. The leader fills the *kohanim* with blessing so that they are like "vessels full to overflowing with God's blessing." They are now so filled with blessing that they can channel it to others. Otherwise, the scene would be tragic, empty vessels being poured out onto other empty vessels.[93]

The priestly blessing is about love. Just before they bless the people, the *kohanim* recite a blessing acknowledging that they have been "commanded to bless the people with love." R. Luntschitz's interpretation is stunning, and it provides a magnificent insight into parenting. Parents with children are like prayer leaders with *kohanim*. Our children need to be filled with love so that they in turn can love others. If they are not loved, they enter the world as empty vessels, devoid of the one thing that matters most: the capacity to love others.

I spoke in chapter 2 about how the spiritual life involves becoming a vessel through which God's blessings flow. When it comes to love, we are neither the starting nor the ending point: we are loved by others in no small degree so that we can love others in turn. Recall the idea that bringing children into the world so that we can love them is an act of *imitatio Dei*. The imitation of God actually runs deeper, since our hopes for our children mirror God's hopes for us: we bring children into the world so that we can love them *and so that they can become lovers themselves*.

Like marital love, love of parents for our children is both an intrinsic good and an instrumental one. It's an intrinsic good because loving relationships are elemental to how we imagine what a good life looks like; and it's an instrumental good because it is in families that we (generally) learn to love and be loved, to care and be cared for. Family love is thus not just a personal good but a social good as well. In a more particularist perspective, families are also where we learn to be part of a people with a millennia-long relationship with both God and Torah. Ideally, at least, we learn to be both loving human beings and passionate Jews at home.

5

LOVING OUR NEIGHBOR

Judaism's "Great Principle," but What Does It Mean?

NO WORDS IN the Torah are better known or more frequently cited than "love your neighbor as yourself" (Leviticus 19:18), and no words are generally seen as more significant. The Talmudic sage R. Akiva goes so far as to declare that the mandate to love our neighbor is "the great principle of the Torah"[1] and prominent modern scholars consider it the "apex"[2] or "epicenter"[3] of the book of Leviticus. And yet for all its manifest centrality in Jewish spirituality and ethics, the precise meaning of the verse is difficult to pin down. There is something wonderfully, almost quintessentially Jewish about this: we all agree that the command is crucial but we disagree about precisely what it requires.

WHAT DOES "LOVE YOUR NEIGHBOR" MEAN?

Each component of the verse raises an array of difficult questions:

Love (*ve-ahavta*). In mandating that we love our neighbor, is the Torah making a claim on our emotions, our actions, or some combination of the two? If, as the surface meaning of the word "love" suggests, the Torah is focused on emotions, then we have to ask: Can emotions be commanded? In order to be commanded, emotions would need to be subject to our control,[4] but are they?

If the Torah is in fact concerned with the emotion of love, what kind of love is it asking for? Surely we aren't asked to love the person who lives down the street (or in some faraway place) in the same way as we love our spouse or our children. So what kind of love *is* the Torah talking about?

More technically, in Hebrew the verse reads oddly. The Hebrew does not say *ve-ahavta* et *rei'akha kamokha*, "love your neighbor as yourself," as we might expect, but rather *ve-ahavta* le-*rei'akha kamokha*, which, translated hyperliterally, would seem to mean "love *for* your neighbor as yourself." Where the Hebrew verb *ahav*, "love," usually takes a direct object, here it takes an indirect one. What is the difference between loving our neighbor, on the one hand, and loving *for* our neighbor, on the other?

Your Neighbor (*le-rei'akha*). Who is the neighbor whom we are commanded to love? Are Jews obligated to love one another or to love all human beings? Assuming that at minimum, all Jews are included, are there any exceptions—that is, are there some Jews whom we are not supposed to love or even some whom we are supposed to hate? (We will explore the troubling question of religiously mandated hate in chapter 9.)

As Yourself (*kamokha*). Let's assume for the moment that the commandment makes a claim on our emotional lives: we are obligated to feel love for others. It may be possible for us to love others, but can we really love them as much as or in the same way as we do ourselves? Moreover, even if it were possible, would it be desirable for us to do so?

Even more fundamentally, does the mandate to love our neighbor as ourselves suggest or assume that we are obligated to love ourselves? Is self-love a good thing, an essential prerequisite for living a good and God-connected life, or is it a bad thing, the root of selfishness and indifference to the legitimate needs of other people?[5]

CAN LOVE BE COMMANDED?

Talk of a commandment to love may strike some readers as odd. Can love really be commanded?

Many thinkers, both Jewish and non-Jewish, have thought not. We can't control our feelings, they assume, and therefore we can't be obligated to feel anything. Immanuel Kant, for example, denying that we can will ourselves to feel love, distinguishes between the passion of love (what he calls "pathological love," meaning an active feeling of liking for the other), on the one hand, and "practical love," on the other.[6] Since "there can be no obligation to have feelings," he writes, "love must be thought of practically."[7] The duty of love, then, is really a duty to act beneficently. We may not be able to decide to like other people at will, but we are capable of acting kindly and beneficently toward them—regardless of what feelings we have (or don't have) toward them.

This is true as far as it goes: we can act kindly toward someone even if we have no feelings of kindness for them. In fact, as we've seen, according to Jewish ethics we are obligated to behave kindly even when we are not feeling kindly at all. But Judaism's ideal is different. Ideally we act lovingly out of feelings of love, and kindly out of feelings of kindness.

The beneficence Kant speaks of may be a value, in other words, but beneficence is not love.[8] We can be beneficent reluctantly, or even begrudgingly; we can be beneficent toward others without actually caring about them. Yet we obviously can't love someone if we don't care about them. As the philosopher James Kellenberger reminds us, "Religious love, and all love in some degree, has both an interior and an exterior dimension." Love without an affective dimension, he points out, is not really love at all.[9]

But again, can love and kindness really be commanded? Are emotions really subject to our control?

The assumption that we cannot control our emotions is almost a truism in our culture. And yet this belief is no less mistaken for being so widespread. In fact, we have far more agency over our feelings than we are usually willing to admit.

We regularly hold people responsible for their emotions. Consider an example: a worker who had sought a promotion that a colleague has just received instead. The first is so filled with envy and fury that he can barely see straight. Even if he never acts on his negative feelings, most of us would regard their very presence within him as morally problematic. Or imagine someone who is so frustrated by her poor grades in school that she comes to actively loathe fellow students who perform better than she does. Her external behavior is totally proper—she is never less than polite and respectful in her interactions with others—but internally she is overrun with envy and hatred. In this case, too, most of us would judge her inner state as morally blameworthy.

We also hold people responsible for what they *don't* feel. Imagine you tell a friend about a mutual acquaintance whose spouse has abruptly left him after decades of marriage, leaving him utterly desolated. Your friend responds callously: "He'll get over it." Your friend's lack of compassion, his refusal to care, is, most of us would agree, morally blameworthy.

Everyday examples like these indicate that most of us do believe that people are at least to some degree responsible for their emotions.[10] We regularly hold people accountable for their feelings, and not just for their actions. It's not just that we judge the emotion itself as good or bad; we also blame the person for having the negative emotions and admire them for having the positive ones.[11]

We don't deem emotions morally relevant only because they have the potential to have an impact on our behaviors—though they surely do. Rather, we take such emotions as morally significant in their own right.[12]

How is it that we are responsible for (at least some of) our emotions?

Emotions don't just happen to us. Explaining that as human beings we have what she calls "emotional agency," the philosopher Nancy Sherman argues that "many popular and traditional views of emotions as devoid of all agency are simply misguided." A vast body of research in developmental psychology shows that "from earliest infancy, we regulate and manage many of our emotions in a way that gives credence to the notion of emotional agency." To be sure, emotions are different from actions and they are not subject to our will in quite the same way, yet we do play an active role in having and shaping them.[13]

Obviously, not all emotions are the same.

We can no doubt recall experiences in our own lives where an emotion seemed to just come upon us—perhaps an old trauma manifested itself as overpowering anxiety in a very different situation that unconsciously triggered memories of the past. Yet we can also recall times when we chose to care for someone, or when we chose to let go of anger. "There is a continuum between agency and passivity, between willing and being affected. Agency comes in degrees . . . To conceive of emotional experience as fully on the side of passivity is to misconstrue what it is like to have and live with emotions."[14] If you have ever taken a deep breath in order to calm your anxiety, then on some level you do believe (and have likely experienced) that we have some degree of control over our emotions.[15]

When we consider romantic love, we sometimes speak of "falling in love," which sounds awfully passive. Yet even here, we have more agency than we (or the movies we see) tend to acknowledge. Whom we choose to spend time with, which qualities in a person we come to value, and what kinds of physical responses to another person we regard as necessary for romance all play a part in the experience of falling in love. We surely cannot simply decide that "today I will fall in love with you," but decisions we make, thoughts we entertain, and feelings we nurture all play a part in bringing love about.

What is true about loving another person romantically applies even more so to caring for our neighbor. We can't simply decide to feel love or compassion—or, for that matter, to feel hatred or anger—toward another person. Approach someone on the street and decide to love them on the spot, and you'll quickly discover that emotions just aren't subject to our will in that way. And yet, as Aristotle maintains, "We may not be able to choose how we will emotionally react to something at a given desired moment, but . . . we indirectly contribute, through previous actions and habits, to our emotional dispositions."[16] In other words, although we can't just decide to feel emotional care for the person in front of us, countless decisions large and small that we have made in the past significantly impact upon our present response to them. If that is correct, then it makes sense to maintain that we are, at least to some significant extent, responsible for our emotions.

The essential point, as Rabbi Louis Jacobs (1920–2006) puts it, is that although "emotions cannot be turned on like a tap," they can nevertheless be "cultivated" so that they "become second-nature."[17] We can't always (or even often) control our emotions in a direct way, but we can nurture and cultivate them in more indirect ways. To take just one example, we can learn to feel compassion or concern for the plight of an ethnic group others around us disdain "through efforts at imaginative transport and empathy—efforts at conceiving of what it would be like to be them, standing in their shoes, facing [their] struggles, living [their] battles."[18] In other words, whether or not we see members of a targeted minority in all their humanity depends in no small measure on decisions and commitments we have made, or failed to make.

Since emotions can be cultivated and dispositions can be acquired, they can be—and according to Judaism they are—commanded.[19] An example: in commanding us to respond with compassion to people who are poor, Deuteronomy does not merely obligate us to give loans with an open hand; rather, it insists that we do so with an open heart: "Be neither hard-hearted nor tight-fisted" (Deuteronomy 15:7), it memorably tells us. This means, explains a medieval Jewish thinker, that we are exhorted by the Torah "to remove hard-heartedness from within us and to supplant it with . . . compassion and true lovingkindness."[20] Ideally, giving and caring will be inextricably intertwined—and mutually reinforcing.

There is another related challenge we need to consider. Having dealt with the question of whether love can coherently be commanded, we now have to ask whether it's still love if it's commanded. After all, don't many—perhaps most—of us think of love as "spontaneous and free"? I share the philosopher Stephen Evans's worry that our culture can sometimes seem "dominated by a cult of spontaneity." Spontaneity is fine, and is sometimes even a value, but so too is commitment. Love does not become less genuine because we have worked to nurture and cultivate it; one could argue that the opposite is the case. And commanded love may actually be freer than spontaneous love. God's command, coupled with our commitment, frees us to love our neighbor whatever we happen to be feeling at this moment or that; "such a commanded love can be ours in a deeper sense than is possible for an emotion that is rooted in what is momentary."[21] Commanded love is also more stable and reliable than spontaneous love because it is not conditional on the other person's response. As Kierkegaard puts it, "Only when it is a duty to love, only then is love eternally secured."[22]

WHAT DOES LOVE MEAN? WHAT WE SHOULDN'T DO

Some traditional Jewish thinkers worry that the commandment to love our neighbor as ourselves can't quite mean what it seems to. In the first place, they are uneasy about the idea that an emotion can be commanded.[23] But they have an additional concern as well. Loving our neighbor is hard enough, but the Torah seems to go much further, asking us to love our neighbor *as much as we love ourselves*. Is such love possible? And even if it were possible, would such love be desirable?

In an oft-cited passage, the Talmud presents a case of two people who are traveling on a journey far from civilization. One of them has a pitcher of water. If they share the water, they will both die; if only one of them drinks, however, he will be able to reach civilization. Although one sage teaches that it is better for both to die than for either to be forced to witness the death of the other, R. Akiva insists that the life of the one who possesses the water takes precedence. In other words, when my life and the life of another are at risk, I may give precedence to saving my own life.[24] Since that is the case, some Jewish thinkers conclude, it is manifestly not the case that we are required to love our neighbor as much as we love ourselves.[25]

In light of all this, a minimalist school of interpretation emerges. "Love your neighbor as yourself," some interpreters say, refers not to emotions, but to actions. And not to a positive duty to help others, but only to a negative duty, not to harm them. A classic Talmudic story tells of a Gentile who approaches the sage Hillel asking to be converted to Judaism on condition that the latter teach him the entirety of Torah while he stands on one foot. Hillel responds: "That which is hateful to you do not do to your neighbor. All the rest is commentary; go and learn."[26] Interpreters who insist that "love your neighbor as yourself" is a warning not to hurt people maintain that the biblical verse and Hillel's teaching are one and the same. As a traditional translation of the Torah renders our verse, "Love your fellow, for what is hateful to you yourself, do not do to him."[27]

If we never did anything to others that we would not want them to do to us, the world we live in would be a far healthier, more just place. And yet this approach to the commandment seems too deflationary: "Love" is taken to refer to action rather than emotion, and what is presented as a positive obligation is transformed into a mere prohibition.[28] Can this really be all "the great principle of the Torah" asks of us?[29]

WHAT DOES LOVE MEAN? WHAT WE SHOULD DO

A second school agrees that the verse is focused on actions but insists that it has positive duties in mind. Thus, for example, in his great legal code Maimonides includes such kindnesses as visiting the sick, comforting mourners, preparing a body for a funeral, and preparing a bride for her wedding under the umbrella of "love your neighbor as yourself." As Maimonides explains, the principle underlying the commandment is that "all the things you would want others to do for you, you do for your brother in Torah and the commandments."[30] On Maimonides's interpretation, "as yourself" means not "as much as you love yourself" but "as you yourself would want to be loved."[31] Note that there is no mention of emotions here, just the commitment to doing concrete good for others.

But wait. In declaring that the mandate to "love your neighbor as yourself" obligates us to do "all the things [we] would want others to do for [us]," hasn't Maimonides opened the door to untenable (and even preposterous) demands and expectations? If I would like my neighbor to hand over his life savings to me, am I obligated to turn over mine to him? If I would like my neighbor to clean my house twice a week, does my wish obligate me to provide that service to him? The answer would obviously seem to be no, but how can we refine Maimonides's principle so that it seems more plausible?

A prominent nineteenth-century Bible commentator, Rabbi Yaakov Tzvi Mecklenburg (1785–1865), offers a nuanced alternative. We are (obviously) not obligated to do for our neighbor every last thing we could imagine wanting her to do for us; rather, we are obligated to do those things that we are convinced that she *ought* to do for us. Perhaps we could even say that we are obligated to do those things that we would be disappointed in our neighbor's failing to do for us. Writ large, says R. Mecklenburg, we want our neighbor to be "a faithful friend in all things," so we ourselves are obligated to be faithful friends.[32]

R. Mecklenburg offers a series of examples of what he has in mind. We would expect our friend (1) to sincerely love us; (2) to treat us with respect; (3) to always seek our well-being; (4) to share in our sorrow; (5) to welcome us warmly when we visit her home; (6) to judge us favorably in all matters; (7) to gladly go through a little trouble for our sake; (8) to help us with a little money when we need a loan or a small gift; and (9) not to act haughtily toward us. Noting that we can think of "many more such things," R. Mecklenburg makes clear that the list is intended to be illustrative rather than exhaustive. Crucially, he says, the examples given are all "reasonable"; we wouldn't think that our neighbor needs to hand over all her wealth to us, since this is plainly unreasonable. The meaning of the commandment, in other words, is that we must love our neighbor in the same ways we ourselves would want *and expect* to be loved by her. The "as yourself" (*kamokha*) in "love your neighbor as yourself," R. Mecklenburg concludes, does not mean that we are obligated to love others *as much as* we love ourselves, but rather in *the same concrete ways* that we ourselves would want and expect to be loved.

It's worth noticing that R. Mecklenburg does not focus *exclusively* on actions—he lists "loving" as the first obligation of friendship (which in context sounds like emotional love), and includes things like "sharing in our sorrow" and "judging us favorably" among his illustrations—but he does focus *primarily* on actions. In commanding us to love our neighbor, the Torah's primary intention is for us to act lovingly toward her. Yet the slippage between action and emotion in R. Mecklenburg's presentation is instructive. The actions love requires are most often bound up with emotions: they are elicited and sustained by emotions and they draw forth and strengthen emotions in turn.

For all its power, there is also something problematic—or at least limited—about R. Mecklenburg's approach. He maintains that the best way to determine what I am obligated to do for another is to ask what I would want and expect him to do for me and then to do the same for him. Yet people are different from one another, and we frequently have disparate wants and needs. Ethics requires us to embrace and respond to those differences. It can be dangerous to assume that my needs and yours are identical and thus interchangeable. When you are ill, you may want visitors whereas I might wish for privacy. When you are unhappy, you may wish your friends would reach out multiple times a day whereas I might just want to know that they are available when I need them. Often the best way to know how best to treat another person is to *ask them*. As a friend recently observed, the first step to acting on the mitzvah of loving our neighbor is to be open to learning and understanding their own individual needs.[33] To put the matter differently, the commandment is not to treat others as *we* would wish to be treated but as *they* would. Or, if you prefer, we could say that the guiding principle of ethics is not "Do unto others as you would have them do unto you," but rather "Do unto others as they would have you do unto them."

WHAT DOES LOVE MEAN? EMOTION

Taking "love" more literally, a third school of interpretation maintains that the love we are obligated in is about emotion, and not just action.[34]

Nahmanides (Ramban, 1194–1270) writes that the commandment to "love your neighbor as yourself" is obviously "hyperbolic," because "the human heart is not capable of accepting" such a demand. And in any event, R. Akiva's insistence that the person in the desert who possesses the water should drink it shows that the law does not require loving others to the same extent as we love ourselves. So what then *does* it require?

Some people genuinely wish others well, but with certain caveats (such caveats are, I think, far more common than most of us would want to admit). Perhaps we want a friend or an acquaintance to have everything we do, but less of it. I want you to be wealthy, we think, as long as it's clear that I'm a little wealthier; I'm happy for you to be smart, as long as it's clear that I'm a little smarter; and so on. Or, perhaps we're happy for others to have as much as we do, except in the one domain we are most invested in. I'm happy for you to be as wealthy as I am, we might feel, as long as it's clear that I'm smarter; I'm happy for you to be smart, as long as it's clear that I'm better-looking; and so on. The worm of comparison and competition eats away at our capacity for generosity of spirit. Others can be good, but we need to be better; others can have a lot but we need to have more.

For Nahmanides, the mandate to love our neighbor is a challenge to let go of this mode of thinking and feeling. Loving our neighbor requires us to be truly generous and openhearted, to wish for our friend to have whatever we have to the same extent as we do.[35]

Picking up on the fact that the verse seems to instruct us to "love *for* our neighbor as we love for ourselves," Nahmanides argues that our obligation is to wish for others the same as we wish for ourselves—in all matters. Nahmanides rejects the idea that loving our neighbor entails literally loving others as we love ourselves, but on his interpretation, our text still demands an awful lot: that we truly and unambivalently desire for others what we desire for ourselves. As a modern commentator aptly observes, on Nahmanides's approach "the Torah is not demanding the impossible—only the overwhelmingly difficult."[36] But note the crucial point: for Nahmanides, as long as something is possible, it can be commanded. The fact that an obligation is difficult does not count against it; on the contrary, to live in light of the Torah is to strive to grow into it.

In enumerating Judaism's 613 commandments, Maimonides writes in the same spirit that "we are commanded to love one another even as we love ourselves; my love and compassion for my brother should be like my love and compassion for myself, in regard to my money, my person, and whatever I possess or desire. Whatever I wish for myself, I should wish the same for him; and whatever I do not wish for myself or for those close to me, I should not wish it for him."[37] On this account, too, love of neighbor is fulfilled in the heart. I wish the same for me and for her.

LOVE AS DISPOSITION TO ACTION AND EMOTION

Notice that we've now seen two passages from Maimonides. Whereas the first holds that "love your neighbor" refers to concrete kindnesses we perform for others, the second maintains that its concern is with what we wish for others. In one place, then, Maimonides seems to belong to the (positive) action school, but in the other he appears to belong to the emotion school.

Which one is it? Does he think "love your neighbor" refers to emotions or to actions? My sense is that he thinks it refers to both. For Maimonides, love is a disposition, a quality of character, and as such it has both emotional and actional dimensions. I want only good for my neighbor and I act accordingly.[38] As the Bible scholar Samuel Balentine comments on our verse, "One must not only feel love, but also act in ways that translate love into concrete deeds."[39]

Elsewhere, Maimonides makes this integration of emotion and action more or less explicit: "Each person is commanded to love each and every Israelite as he does himself, as it is said, 'Love your neighbor as yourself.' Therefore, one must speak the praises [of the other] and be considerate of his property, just as one is considerate with one's own property and protective of his own reputation."[40] To make this starker and more concrete: If I truly care about a person and want the best for her, I can't but act concretely as a manifestation of that care. Hence the "therefore" in Maimonides's formulation: I love someone and therefore I act with their good in mind.

As we've seen before, it is almost always a mistake to ask whether Judaism asks for emotion *or* action; it asks for emotion *and* action,[41] and it believes that emotion and action can be mutually reinforcing. A feeling of love leads us to act lovingly, and loving acts, in turn, elicit (or reinforce) feelings of love, thus creating a virtuous circle.

Let's dig deeper in considering what loving our neighbor requires of us.

A "GOOD EYE"

When a prominent sage instructs his disciples to "go and see what is the right path to which a person should cleave," one of them returns with the answer: "a good eye."[42] What, exactly, is that? According to some thinkers, it's "contentment" and "rejoicing in what one has."[43] The more content we are with what we have, obviously, the less likely we are to begrudge others their successes; on the contrary, we are able to delight in other people's happiness and success. A "good eye," in other words, yields generosity of spirit.

Israelis have a slang word *lefargen*, which means, roughly, not to begrudge something to someone. This derives from the Yiddish *ferginen*, which means "to relate to another without envy."[44] For Nahmanides, as we saw, to fulfill the mandate to love our neighbor entails *firgun*, relating to the other without envy.[45]

Some thinkers go further, and interpret a "good eye" as suggesting openhandedness, a willingness to share of one's own bounty.[46] Beyond renouncing envy, we are challenged to embrace liberality. The biblical verse that introduces the notion of a good eye appears to support this interpretation: "The generous person [literally 'good-eyed,' *tov ayin*] is blessed, for he shares his bread with the poor" (Proverbs 22:9). A good eye manifests in a willingness, and even an eagerness, to give.

AGAINST ENVY

A good eye is the antithesis of an envious[47] one. Envy is the feeling that we lack something someone else has, want it for ourselves, and resent them for having it when we do not. Because she feels threatened, even belittled, by other people's successes, the envious person cannot truly wish the best for them; accordingly, she has what tradition labels a "bad eye"[48] or a "narrow eye"—that is, an envious, ungenerous one.[49] Envy is thus a major obstacle to fulfilling the commandment to love our neighbor.

Envy is toxic, both for the envious person and for those around her. The book of Proverbs says that "a heart at peace gives life to the body, but envy rots the bones" (Proverbs 14:30).[50] Tellingly, traditional commentators disagree about the meaning of the verse: whereas some take it to suggest that envy wounds everyone with whom the envious person interacts, others take it to mean that envy ravages the envier herself.[51] (The political theorist John Rawls makes much the same point: envy, he says, is "a form of rancor that tends to harm both its object and its subject."[52]) Her inability to tolerate other people's happinesses and successes metaphorically "rots her bones"—or, as we might say, it eats her alive. In the same spirit, a Talmudic sage teaches that "envy, lust, and the pursuit of honor drive a person out of the world."[53] Fundamentally, persistent envy disconnects us from others and leads us to resent them, thus fracturing real human connection and "driving [us] out of the world."

From a religious perspective, envy is so problematic because it stems from a "perverse conception of value."[54] That conception assumes that self-worth is something we need to achieve, most often by comparing ourselves with others.[55] Accordingly, what we lack in comparison with others we believe (or fear) is due to our own inferiority.[56] As the philosopher Rebecca DeYoung nicely puts it, "The bottom line for the envious is how they stack up against others, because they measure their self-worth comparatively, and because the comparison reveals not only their lack of that particular good but also their consequent lack of worth." In other words, envy "signals defeat in the competition for self-esteem," which is part of why "the envier typically tries to suppress both tell-tale signs of his own envy and his own awareness of being envious."[57]

Almost inevitably, then, envy is, at one and the same time, demeaning of ourselves, distrustful of God, and hostile to others. It is demeaning of ourselves because our envy "embodies a standard of self-assessment that demeans [us] as persons [and] violates [our] dignity."[58] Created in the image of God, we are infinitely valuable; no invidious comparison should be able to take that away from us. More than that, to make our worth dependent on some merely human standard is to fall into the trap of idolatry. God, and not earthly success, is the source and guarantor of our worth.

Envy arguably reflects distrust in God, since it suggests that we do not really believe that God loves us or that we are genuinely and intrinsically valuable.[59] We pursue a sense of our worth, often with no small degree of desperation. But as we saw at length in chapter 1, according to Judaism we don't need to do that; worth is something we always already have. Our frenzy to achieve "comparative success" suggests that our awareness of God's love and our own value has become attenuated at best.

Most crucially for our exploration of loving the neighbor, envy is hostile to others because it interprets their success as our failure, their accomplishment as our defeat. If our sense of self-worth depends on competition with others, then we become invested in their failure (at least in comparison to us).[60] Our insecurity means that we either dwell on our purported superiority or stew in our ostensible inferiority—or, as is often the case, we shuttle back and forth between the two. To put this very simply, lack of a stable sense of self-worth means that we are perpetually envious, which in turn means that we can't truly wish others well—and that, recalling Nahmanides, means that we cannot fulfill the commandment to love our neighbor as ourselves.

Significantly, envy is a violation of friendship even when it is not manifested in deeds. As the philosopher Robert Roberts explains, "A person can be attitudinally, [and not just] behaviorally, misused." Imagine a case where we are envious of a friend because she receives a promotion that we had been hoping for; "becom[ing] smaller in our own sight for [her] becoming larger," we develop hostile, even belligerent feelings. Yet "it is a feature of our ordinary moral concepts of friendship that of our friends we not only demand that they *behave* toward us like friends, but also that they *think of* us and *feel toward* us in ways appropriate to friendship." No matter how internally contained, therefore, our envy is "destructive of friendship."[61]

When we find ourselves stewing in envy, it's usually because there is some hole within us, some need that we cannot seem to fill (and often cannot even bring ourselves to admit is there in the first place). The bigger and deeper the hole is, the more desperate and insistent our begrudging attitude to others becomes. All of this makes clear that the best prophylactic for envy is a healthy sense of self. Recall where we began in chapter 1—with the insistence that each and every human being is created by God and is therefore intrinsically and irreducibly valuable. Although we frequently feel that status is a zero-sum proposition,[62] such that someone else's rising entails my falling, from a theological perspective the very opposite is the case: I have value for the same reasons that you do. In some ultimate sense, therefore, we rise and fall together. Unless we really know this—not just cognitively but also emotionally, not just in our mind but also in our heart and in our belly, we will never truly love our neighbor.

JUDGING OTHERS FAVORABLY

Since love involves seeing others with a generous eye, we are also obligated to evaluate other people and their behaviors favorably (*le-khaf zekhut*, literally "on the scale of merit").[63] This, suggests Rabbi Abraham Saba (1440–1508), is the very meaning of loving our neighbor as ourselves.[64] Judging people favorably requires us, Maimonides explains, "always to put a good and charitable interpretation on other people's deeds and words."[65] Many Jewish thinkers see judging others favorably as key to the fulfillment of all interpersonal obligations more broadly. As a medieval sage puts it, judging others favorably is what makes "peace and friendship [possible] among people."[66] Constantly casting others in the worst possible light, on the other hand, makes strife inevitable: we project the darkness of our own heart onto others and ceaselessly discover (or invent) grounds for struggle and conflict.[67] When all is said and done, "the way we treat others is determined by how we look at them."[68] Love is a way of being, but it is also a way of *seeing*.[69]

Love and generous perception are mutually reinforcing. Adopting a posture of love toward others leads us to see them positively; as the book of Proverbs puts it, "Hatred stirs up strife, but love covers up all faults" (Proverbs 10:12). (If the idea that love—or its absence—profoundly impacts how we see others seems abstract, think about how you would evaluate someone you love and someone you don't for doing the very same thing.) Conversely, seeing people positively makes it much easier to love them. This logic is implicit in the Mishnah, which teaches: "Make for yourself a teacher, acquire for yourself a friend, and judge every person favorably."[70] What enables us to have genuine teachers and friends is our willingness to see people favorably, not to constantly find faults in everyone we meet; and, on the flip side, part of what makes it possible for us to judge others favorably is the experience of feeling connected to and loved by others.

Sometimes people hurt or disappoint us to such an extent that it becomes impossible—or even dangerous[71]—for us to judge their actions favorably. For such circumstances, the Mishnah offers another piece of advice: "Do not judge your fellow until you have been in his place."[72] When someone behaves poorly, we can usually be certain *that* they have done so, but we should hesitate before assuming that we know *why* they have done so. In the moment when a friend refuses to loan us money despite the crisis we are in, we may be tempted to assume that we know exactly why she has rebuffed us ("she refused because she's a horrible person"), but in many cases we don't know that at all (perhaps, unbeknownst to us, she is in financial straits herself). Even when a person's actions are unambiguously problematic, or even egregious, we should hesitate before reaching sweeping conclusions about her character. Empathy may offer an alternative to unequivocal condemnation.

Why work so hard to see others through generous eyes? Let's look at the entirety of the verse in which we are commanded to love our neighbor: "You shall not take vengeance or bear a grudge against your countrymen. Love your neighbor as yourself, I am the Lord" (Leviticus 19:18). When someone lets us down, says Rabbi Israel Meir Kagan (The Hafetz Hayyim, 1838–1933), we may find ourselves wondering how we could possibly not harbor bitterness toward them. The answer, he suggests, is implied in the ending of the verse, "I am the Lord." It's as if God is saying, "I, God, love the sinner, and since you, Israel, are my children, you are capable of loving her as I do."[73] This, then, is the deepest fulfillment of the mandate to love the neighbor: to strive to see others through God's (merciful, loving) eyes.[74]

Seeing others through the eyes of love includes a commitment to seeing them as capable of love themselves. It is sometimes tempting to write people off altogether, to imagine them as beyond hope or redemption. When we find someone difficult to like, let alone love, we may be inclined to see them as loveless (even though it is we who are struggling to love). As a rule, though, as Kierkegaard explains, one of love's works is "the strange duty to presuppose love in others." Instead of dismissing them, "we are duty bound to presuppose an essential ability to love in everyone, not only in people we feel simpatico toward but also those whom we cut across the street to avoid."[75] If the capacity to love is part of what it means to be human, then to assume that someone is incapable of love is to see them as less than human; and conversely, to see them as capable of love is to affirm their humanity (even as their behavior may well be less than admirable).

As any teacher of small children can attest, the way we see others shapes who they are (and can become) in very real ways. View a child as nothing more than a problem and her self-esteem will suffer, and so, too, will her prospects in life; see in her an infinitely precious image of God with all that she has the capacity to become and she is far more likely to blossom and flourish. When you judge someone favorably, the Hasidic master Rebbe Nahman of Bratzlav (1772–1810) teaches, you elevate them and bring out the best that they are capable of being.[76] Conversely, the philosopher Charles Taylor observes, "[A] person or group of people can suffer real damage, real distortion, if the people or society around them mirror back to them a confining or demeaning or contemptible picture of themselves. [It] can be a form of oppression, imprisoning someone in a false, distorted or reduced mode of being."[77] To no small degree we create people—or maim them—with how we view them.[78]

And yet all of this said, Jewish ethics refuses to be Pollyannaish. When it would be plausible to construe someone's actions positively or negatively, we should strive to interpret them in the best possible light. But when someone has a pattern of appalling behavior, says Rabbi Obadiah of Bertinoro (c. 1445–c. 1515), one may cast their behavior in a negative light. After all, the Talmud warns us only against "suspecting the innocent";[79] there is no prohibition against "suspecting the wicked."[80] This is especially important to keep in mind in dealing with sexual predators and domestic abusers, for example. If we encourage innocent victims to judge perpetrators favorably, we run the very real risk of setting them up for persistent, and potentially worsening, abuse.[81] In general, I think, Judaism gives expression to a profound tension. On the one hand, making our way through the world with a posture of love entails viewing others positively, and generously; on the other hand, being cognizant of human nature in all its complexity means that we sometimes have to be careful, even cautious, about trusting too easily and interpreting too naively. As a somewhat surprising rabbinic dictum has it, "Every person should be a thief in your eyes."[82] Hyperbolic statements such as this one should not be overplayed or given more weight than they deserve. But they do serve to remind us: be loving, be generous, be kind—but don't be oblivious or gullible, and don't ignore what victims of abuse tell you.

People are complicated. Some of us condemn others easily but have no trouble rationalizing similar behaviors in ourselves. (When *you* speak harshly to your employees, it's because you are a cruel person; when *I* speak harshly to mine, you have to understand, it's justified because of my traumatic past.) Just as we manage to love ourselves despite our shortcomings, we should find ways to love others despite theirs.[83] It's worth noting, though, that for some of us the reverse is true. We condemn ourselves for behaviors we'd readily find ways to rationalize in others. Sometimes learning to judge ourselves favorably is an obligation too.

FORGIVENESS AND EXPANDING OUR VISION

Love as a way of seeing is also pivotal to the process of interpersonal forgiveness.

In describing the dynamics of forgiveness in his classic code of Jewish law, Maimonides discusses three intertwined obligations. First, one who wounds another person must apologize and conciliate them.[84] Second, the one who was hurt must not be obdurate or cruel toward the offender but should forgive him when he apologizes. Third, Maimonides emphasizes the mitzvah of rebuke: "When a person sins against another, the injured party should not hate the offender and keep silent . . . Rather, it is his duty to inform the offender and ask him, 'Why did you do this to me? Why did you sin against me in this manner?'"[85]

For many years I heard the words that Maimonides places in the offended party's mouth as sharp and severe, as if the victim were asking a rhetorical question: Why did you do this to me?! Or even: How could you do this to me?! But as I've gotten older, I've come to hear the suggested words very differently. Perhaps Maimonides's guidance to the wounded party is to ask the wrongdoer an earnest, openhearted question: What made you act in the way you did? The latter is, obviously, a very different question than the former. It is aimed not at expressing judgment but at arriving at understanding.

Understanding is neither necessary nor sufficient for forgiveness. It's not necessary in that, for example, we can forgive someone who repents wholeheartedly even if they don't offer an explanation for why they behaved as they did (and in any case what motivated them may sometimes be hidden even from them); and it's not sufficient in that, on occasion, coming to understand why a wrongdoer acted as they did only deepens the hurt we feel.[86] But sometimes, at least, understanding what lay behind someone's behavior does help us see them and their actions differently—with compassion rather than resentment. And that shift of perspective makes forgiveness easier.

More generally, when we're angry at someone who has hurt us, we tend to see them as "alien" and distant from ourselves, as "bad" and "unworthy." But sometimes—perhaps not always, but certainly sometimes—another path is available to us: we can see the person who has hurt us "in terms of [their] damage, weakness, suffering, inadequacy."[87] I don't mean that we come to see someone as defined exclusively by their frailty and limitations, in which case we'd be more likely to excuse than forgive them, but that we see them with empathy, as a person with weaknesses and shortcomings rather than as a villain. They thus start to appear less alien and more . . . human.

Rabbi Natan Gestetner (1932–2010) finds this idea in the mandate to "judge every person favorably." Noting that the words usually rendered as "every person" (*kol ha-adam*) can also mean "the entirety of the person," R. Gestetner suggests that we expand our vision to include more of the person who has wounded us. Don't judge on the basis of this specific action they took, he advises, but instead look at their broader life story and situation, understand what drove them to act as they did—and the way you see them may well change.[88]

If we're willing to take the next step, we remember that in being flawed, the person who has wounded us is . . . like us. We too are human, so we too have failings, and we too have undoubtedly hurt and disappointed others. (We may well have different failings, possibly even less severe ones, but we too have our share of imperfections.) In more traditional religious language, we are not saints who forgive sinners but sinners who forgive one another.

In recognizing that the person who wronged us is not, in the end, so different from us, we stop seeing them as defined by their transgressions. For R. Gestetner, this is another aspect of viewing the entirety of the person. Looking at a fuller range of who they are in the world, we can get (or restore) a fuller, less monochromatic picture of them, which enables us to see them as more than their limitations. Surely the wrongdoer has virtues as well as vices, R. Gestetner writes, perhaps even more of the former than the latter.[89]

To forgive someone, I am suggesting, is at least in part to see them from a more expansive, loving perspective.

If we return again to the mitzvah of rebuke, we discover another powerful dimension of seeing others favorably. Years ago, early in my rabbinic career, I was telling my mentor Dr. Bernie Steinberg about a hurtful experience I'd recently had with a colleague. "Maybe I should give him the benefit of the doubt and just forget it," I said, to which Bernie responded with words I have never forgotten: "Actually, maybe you should give him the benefit of the doubt and assume he'll be able to hear you if you tell him how he hurt you." So perhaps this is another manifestation of judging people favorably: seeing them, where appropriate, in the best possible light, and knowing that this includes a capacity for genuine remorse and genuine growth. We've already seen how the explanation that someone who wronged us offers can (sometimes) lead us to see them through a more forgiving, compassionate lens; but even before that happens, the very fact of asking for the explanation is already an act of love and respect.

CARING FOR AND CARING ABOUT

Wanting others to have what we do is closely entwined with the simple idea of caring about them. When a loved one suffers, we feel concern and work to ameliorate their pain; when they flourish, we share in their joy and celebrate with them. But how many people can we really care for? Caring for all of humanity seems impossible; time and energy, both physical and emotional, are far too limited for that.

Caring-*for* may be impossible, but caring-*about* need not be.

In her classic book *Caring*, the philosopher Nel Noddings disparages the idea of caring-about as "too easy." "I can 'care about' the starving children of Cambodia," she writes, "send five dollars to hunger relief, and feel somewhat satisfied. I do not even know if my money went for food, or guns, or a new Cadillac for some politician." Caring-about, Noddings concludes, is "a poor second-cousin to caring"; after all, she says, "'Caring about' always involves a certain benign neglect. One is attentive just so far."[90]

For Noddings, it seems, there are those whom I care for and then there is everybody else. The former group is obviously tiny in comparison with the latter.

But if the only possible caring is caring-for, then we can care for very few people. What's more, our ethical horizons will remain rather limited.

In later writings, Noddings retreats from her dismissal of caring-about. For the later Noddings, caring-for is still primary but caring-about also plays a significant role in ethics. "Caring-about moves us," she writes, "from the face-to-face world into the wider public realm." Learning of the suffering of others, even distant others, "we are moved by compassion for their suffering, we regret it when they do not experience the fruits of care, and we feel outrage when they are exploited. Often we wish that we could care [for] directly, but because that is impossible, we express our care in charitable gifts, in social groups we support, and in our voting. These are not," Noddings observes, "insignificant ways of responding."[91] When we are *about* others, in other words, we seek to ensure that they can be cared *for* too. Caring-about is not caring-for's poor second cousin but rather its partner and enabler.[92]

What I am suggesting—somewhat tentatively, I admit—is that perhaps universal love should be understood as caring-about.[93] We can care for only some, but we can aspire to, and by working to care about more and more, grow asymptotically toward caring about all.

Like judging people favorably and cultivating a "generous eye" toward them, caring for and about people is obviously noble and virtuous. But what would it mean to truly treat caring and loving as "the great principle of the Torah"?

The Israeli Rabbi Elimelekh Bar-Shaul (1913–1964) offers an interpretation that I find particularly helpful. Life is made up, R. Bar-Shaul writes, of a seemingly endless array of details that sometimes distract us from the overarching purpose that underlies them. When we get caught up exclusively in the nuts and bolts of a project, we can become bereft of vision and lose our way. This is true of the interpersonal realm, too, where a million and one daily interactions can lead us to forget the ideal that ought to underlie all of our relationships. We find ourselves just getting through the day as best we can; perhaps we even want to do the right thing, but we lose sight of what it is that ought to animate and guide our every interpersonal encounter.

Keeping the great principle of loving our neighbor at heart and in mind, R. Bar-Shaul says, helps prevent us from losing our way. As we move through the world, we are called to "maintain direct and continuous nourishment from the central principle"; "it must serve as background and framework, as guiding light above [the details of our interactions], and soul-force within them."[94] In daily encounters large and small, we are challenged to remember that our animating commitment is to love others, and that our personal mandate is to grow in love.

WHO IS MY NEIGHBOR?

Who is the neighbor whom we are commanded to love?

In context, the Bible seems clearly to be mandating that Israelites love their fellow Israelites—or, in a more contemporary idiom, that Jews love their fellow Jews. Let's look closely at the verses: "You shall not hate your kinsfolk in your heart. Reprove your kinsman but incur no guilt because of him. You shall not take vengeance or bear a grudge against your countrymen [but] love your neighbor as yourself." The concern of these verses is with relationships among "kinfolk" (*ahim*), "kinsmen" (*amitim*), and "countrymen" (*benei am*). All three of these terms refer unambiguously to members of one's people, fellow participants in Israel's covenant with God. It stands to reason that the fourth term, "neighbor" (*rei'a*) does too. So the contextual meaning of the verse is: "Love your fellow Israelite (or Jew) as yourself."[95]

In order to understand what's at stake here, it's worth making several observations. First, loving Jews decidedly doesn't mean hating everyone else. Quite the contrary: I suspect that the mandate here is to love your fellow Jews and respect everyone else.[96] I'll have more to say about the relationship between love and respect in chapter 7, but for now we can say that although we owe more to members of our community, we owe *something* (again, precisely what will be discussed later) to everyone. Love of neighbor and universal human solidarity need not—ought not—be in conflict.

Second, although some readers will feel uneasy about the particularism the verse embraces, I'm not sure they should. Almost everyone assumes that we owe more to our family and friends than we do to others; this is considered a normal and healthy part of moral and psychological life (though some philosophers disagree—I will discuss this extensively in the next chapter).[97] Since Jews have traditionally understood themselves as members of an extended family, we have seen ourselves as having more intense obligations to our fellow Jews than to others. Again, though, to return to the first point, having a more demanding set of obligations to our family emphatically doesn't mean that we have no obligations to others.

Third, the vision of Leviticus 19 is in fact quite complex. Just a few verses after we encounter the commandment to love the neighbor, we are taught that "when a stranger resides with you in your land, you shall not wrong him. The stranger who resides with you in your land shall be to you as one of your native born; you shall love him as yourself, for you were strangers in the land of Egypt: I the Lord am your God" (Leviticus 19:33–34). The revolutionary mandate to love the stranger, which we will explore at length in chapter 8, expands upon and pushes beyond the boundaries of the earlier love command. It is not only the fellow Israelite whom we must love but also the vulnerable stranger.[98]

Taking the stranger as a kind of stand-in for the non-Israelite more broadly, some interpreters assume that the biblical text effectively mandates love for all humanity.[99] Sympathetic as I am to the urge to read the text in this way, I do not think the leap is warranted. Including *the stranger* in the commandment is a bold and radical move but it is not equivalent to including *everyone* in it. As the Bible scholar Jon Levenson notes, the Hebrew word used here to convey love (*a-h-v*) has "connotations of preference . . . or special favor that are too easily missed . . . For that reason, it does not readily lend itself to conveying the concept of universal benevolence."[100] Levenson suggests that God's special concern for the stranger, which we are meant to emulate (Deuteronomy 10:18–19), is rooted in God's special concern for vulnerable people more generally; as a psalm that forms part of the daily liturgy puts it, God "secures justice for the oppressed, gives food to the hungry . . . sets prisoners free, restores sight to the blind . . . makes those who are bent stand straight . . . watches over the stranger . . . [and] gives courage to the orphan and widow" (Psalm 146:7–9). In other words, the command to love the stranger "is not an act of universalization but rather a response to a particular condition of vulnerability."[101] According to the Torah, then, we are not commanded to love Israel and everyone else; rather, we are commanded to love Israel and everyone else *who is vulnerable*.

This is a breathtaking claim about God—and, by extension, it places a radical demand upon us. Those who are vulnerable have a special place in God's heart; accordingly, they must have a special place in ours too—whether or not they are fellow Jews. To return to a point I have already made repeatedly, this is not a matter of mere sentimentality. The mandate to love someone includes a commitment to respond to their concrete needs. As Deuteronomy tells us, God loves the stranger and manifests that love by providing him with food and clothing (Deuteronomy 10:18).

Fourth and finally, some medieval Bible commentators argue against too narrow a reading of biblical laws governing our interactions with our "neighbors" and "fellows." Describing the character traits of one worthy of dwelling with God, Psalm 15 speaks of one "who does no wrong to his neighbor, and casts no slur upon his fellow" (Psalm 15:3). Interpreting the verse, Rabbi David Kimhi (Radak, 1160–1235) insists that the terms "neighbor" and "fellow" refer to "anyone with whom he has regular dealings or one who lives in his vicinity." Crucially, he emphasizes, when Scripture characterizes the upright person as doing no wrong to his fellow, "it does not imply that he does evil to others. Scripture alludes, rather, to the ordinary case." In other words, we may not mistreat our neighbor—*or anyone else*. Similarly, Radak argues, when the Torah instructs us not to wrong our fellow (Leviticus 25:17) or bear false witness against our neighbor (Exodus 20:16), this does not mean that we are permitted to wrong a non-Jew or bear witness against her. The terms "neighbor" and "fellow" are used here, Radak repeats, because Scripture talks about those with whom we are most likely—or our ancestors were most likely—to come into contact. We may not bear witness against, or otherwise wrong, anyone.[102]

Applying the same logic to the commandment to love our neighbor, some modern Jewish thinkers argue that the book of Leviticus lays down laws for a society in which there simply are no non-Israelites, save for the stranger who emigrates from another land and comes to dwell with the Israelites.[103] In mandating love for both the neighbor and the stranger, they maintain, Leviticus effectively mandates love for everyone. "Though the term *rei'a* [neighbor] refers to an Israelite," Rabbi Louis Jacobs writes, "this is not because of any intention to exclude the non-Israelite but simply because the society spoken of is one in which there are no non-Israelites." Consequently, according to R. Jacobs, "In a different society where Israelites lived together with non-Israelites the implications of the general rule would be extended to include the latter."[104]

Yet R. Jacobs's suggestion suffers from the same weakness as those of the other universalistic interpretations we've seen: It doesn't grapple with the ways that *ahavah*, the word for love in the Bible, refers to special relations, not to universal benevolence. Biblically speaking, at least, we can't simply move from "Israelites" to "everyone."

LOVING JEWS . . . AND EVERYONE ELSE TOO

For the Bible, then, as for much of later Jewish tradition, love of neighbor refers to love of fellow Jews. Does this mean that Judaism recognizes no obligation to love non-Jews (even if it does recognize an obligation to respect them)?

Not quite. If we love God, says the renowned Talmudist Rabbi Jacob Emden (Yaavetz, 1697–1776), then we have to love those whom God creates. Detesting someone's *actions* is one thing; detesting *them* is another altogether. Where the former may sometimes be necessary, he says, the latter is always prohibited. Rather, R. Emden insists, "One must love every person steadfastly."[105] It's crucial to note, though, that R. Emden does not consider the obligation to love non-Jews part of the obligation to love our neighbor;[106] rather, one must love non-Jews because they, like Jews, are created by God.

It's worth dwelling on R. Emden's point for a moment. Imagine that you're a parent and someone tells you, "I love you, but as for your children—I find them utterly insufferable"; or, in a different register, imagine that you're an artist and someone tells you, "I love you, but I find your work atrocious." You'd more than likely respond ambivalently (at best) to their professions of love. "If you love me but hate my children," you'd be inclined to say, "then I'm not sure I want anything to do with your love." Or, put more positively, when someone claims to love us, we usually want them to love those we love, let alone those we helped create.[107]

The implications of this are clear: We can't love God and hate God's creatures. If we want to love God, we have to love those whom God loves—and makes. That's the moral and emotional logic underlying R. Emden's point: Whether or not the non-Jew is technically our "neighbor," she is our fellow creature and that means that we are obligated to love her.

Unfortunately, R. Emden doesn't work through the implications of all this. Jews are obligated to love everyone but they also have a special obligation to love their fellow Jews—more? Differently? He doesn't say.

R. Emden is not alone in insisting that we are obligated in universal love.[108] There may be a special obligation to love other Jews, but many traditional voices do not leave it at that, seemingly *cannot* leave it at that, because they sense that a person of character will not rest content with loving only one's own people.

A virtuous person, says the great Kabbalist Rabbi Hayyim Vital (1542–1620), loves every person, Jew and non-Jew alike.[109] Much more expansively, Rabbi Abraham Isaac Kook (1865–1935), first chief rabbi of Palestine, assumes that the heart's basic posture toward all creation is love. According to R. Kook, for one who loves God, "it is impossible not to be filled with love for every creature, for the abundance of God's light shines in all of them, and all of them are revelations of God's sweetness." Indeed, the love in the souls of truly righteous people "embraces all creatures," even those who seem detestable. Warning against the impulse to see everything outside one's own nation "only as ugliness and impurity," R. Kook writes that such "narrowness of vision" (*tzarut ha-ayin*) is "one of the most terrible sources of darkness, which brings destruction upon every aspect of the positive spiritual development whose light sensitive souls await." Love of humanity needs to be kept alive in the human heart and soul, says R. Kook, and this requires serious effort and cultivation.[110]

So which one is it? Is the mandate to love particular (love your fellow Jews) or is it universal (love all human beings)?

The dialectic we've encountered here demonstrates an essential point about Jewish ethics. Faced with the complexity of human experience, Judaism doesn't try to simplify it so much as *embrace and express* it. If we ask whether Jewish ethics is particularistic or universalistic, the answer is that it is emphatically both. At its best, it tries to make room for the sense that we owe those closest to us more than we owe to others, as well as for the conviction that we have real and deep obligations to everyone (much more on this in chapter 6). To put this differently, Judaism gives voice both to the urge (and obligation) to love one's people and to the impulse (and obligation) to love all of humanity.[111] It refuses to choose one pole and deny the other; it includes and even celebrates both.

6

LOVING OUR OWN, AND EVERYONE ELSE TOO

Judaism's Particularist Universalism

IN THE PREVIOUS chapter, we saw that Jewish thought embraces a dialectical vision of love. Jewish ethics allows us—indeed, it *requires* us—to prioritize concern for those near and dear to us over concern for others who are more distant, whether relationally or geographically. But at the same time, Jewish ethics demands that we not stop there: family first is decidedly not—*must not be allowed to devolve into*—family only. We saw further that, on the one hand, the mandate to love our neighbor refers to love of fellow Jews; yet on the other hand, the fact that all human beings are created by God in God's own image means that Jews are also obligated to love all humanity. The summons is clear, if also more than a little bit daunting: love for the near *and* the distant; love for one's own people *and* love for humanity as a whole.

PRINCIPLES OF PRECEDENCE:
EXPANDING CONCENTRIC CIRCLES

The book of Exodus teaches: "If you lend money to My people, to the poor among you, do not act toward them as a creditor; exact no interest from them" (Exodus 22:24). Commenting on the verse, a Talmudic sage articulates priorities in loan-giving. If a Jew ("My people") and a non-Jew both ask for a loan, he says, the Jew "takes precedence" (*kodem*); a poor person ("the poor") and a rich person, the poor person takes precedence; a poor relative and another poor person from your city, the poor relative ("among you") takes precedence; a poor person from your city and a poor person from another city, the poor person from your city takes precedence.[1]

The Talmudic commentator R. Menahem Ha-Meiri observes that implicit in the claim that our obligations to x "take precedence" over our obligations to y is the fact that we have obligations *both to x and to y*. We prioritize our poor relative, for example, but we are still obligated to assist another destitute person from our city. Especially important to R. Ha-Meiri is to note that although the Jewish poor take precedence over the non-Jewish poor, it is unequivocally a mitzvah and a moral requirement to give to both.[2]

In Jewish ethics, the laws of loan-giving are closely entwined with the laws of tzedakah; in general, the same principles of precedence apply to both. Thus a midrash presents guidance for tzedakah:

> If a person has abundant provisions in his house and wishes to set some aside for the sustenance of the needy, what order is he to follow in providing for them? First he should take care of his father and his mother. If he has some provisions left, he should take care of his brother and his sister. If he still has some provisions left, he should take care of the members of his household. If he again has some provisions left, he should take care of the people of his family. Then, if he has some left, he should take care of the people in his immediate neighborhood. Next, if he has some left, he should take

care of the people on his street. And finally, [with what remains], he
should provide charity freely throughout Israel.[3]

All of this is established Jewish law in the realms both of loan-giving
and of almsgiving.[4]

The priorities reflected in these laws are part of a broader Jewish
ethos: we (ideally) spread our love and concern in expanding concentric
circles.[5] We saw in chapter 5 how Rabbi Jacob Emden speaks both of a
special obligation to love our fellow Jews and of a more general obligation to love all human beings. Before turning to love of neighbor, however, he says something else: "A person is obligated to love his neighbors
and his relatives, his spouse and children . . . he should love those closest
to him the most, with a more personal and magnanimous love."[6] R. Emden's is an ethics at once insistently local and utterly global: family and
friends first, but also the whole of one's people; all of one's people, but
also, ultimately, all of humanity.

There are a great many questions one could ask about these principles of precedence. For example, everything we've just seen would seem
to apply when the parties in question are equally in need, but what do
we do when, say, a fellow resident of our city is in much more urgent
need than a member of our family? And if a person in a distant land is
in desperate need while a member of our local community is in moderate need, does the faraway person take precedence? After all, a midrash
states that "the one who is most in need takes precedence."[7] This, in
turn, raises more questions. How, for example, is need to be measured?
And how do personal relationships play into all this—if we have a dear
friend to whom we feel closer than we do to a distant sibling, may we
give precedence to the friend? *Must* we do so? If we take inspiration from
the book of Proverbs, which teaches that "a close neighbor is better than
a distant brother" (Proverbs 27:10), then perhaps so.[8] Does someone
who lives across the street from us but whom we have never met take
precedence over someone with whom we are cordial (but hardly close)
who lives two towns over? Once we get into the fine-grained details of
the choices we face in giving tzedakah, the questions become harder

and definitive answers grow more elusive. What is clear in theory is far messier in practice.

Yet difficult as such questions are, the general thrust of the texts remains clear. Jewish law clearly embraces an ethic of widening circles of concern. We start at home and move further and further out from there.

Maimonides emphasizes that giving precedence to one's relatives is a manifestation of virtue rather than a concession to human nature—or, as some might see it, human weakness. The Torah, he tells us, "safeguards and fortifies the moral quality . . . of taking care of relatives and protecting them." In general, Maimonides says, "One ought to take care of his relatives and grant very strong preference to the bond of the womb."[9]

Some might be tempted to criticize passages like these for their seemingly narrow focus. Others might be inclined to defend (or at least explain) them as a function of "the insular parochialism of a persecuted people":[10] in a world in which no one else looks out for you, you learn to take care of your own first. But it would be more constructive, I think, to take a different approach, one that eschews both condemnation, on the one side, and apologetics, on the other. We should ask instead: What values are expressed by passages like these? What vision of the moral life do they put forward?

THE INTERPERSONAL ENCOUNTER AS THE PARADIGM OF GIVING

In explaining the obligation to give tzedakah and support the poor, Maimonides cites two biblical phrases: first, from Deuteronomy, "You must surely open your hand [to him, i.e., the poor person]" (Deuteronomy 15:8), and second, from Leviticus, "You shall sustain him, even though he were [as] a stranger or a sojourner, let him live by your side . . . Let your kinsman live by your side" (Leviticus 25:35–36).[11] Rabbi Ozer Glickman (d. 2018) points out that both of the verses cited "emphasize the relationship between the donor and the beneficiary." Legally speaking, "the obligation is defined by the characteristics of each party to the relationship. The beneficiary is entitled to tzedaka according to his or her need; the donor is only obligated to give what he or she can afford."[12] In other words, the laws of tzedakah underscore the interpersonal dimension of giving. The paradigmatic case of almsgiving is an interpersonal encounter, in which a person with the means to do so responds to a person in need of assistance.[13]

There is a powerful lesson here: the central ethical moment, the paradigm for all others, is when one person attends to another, cares for her, and acts to ameliorate her suffering. Recall our discussion of "caring-for" and "caring-about" from the previous chapter.[14] The philosopher Nel Noddings notes that it is sometimes tempting for "big-picture" thinkers to dismiss caring-for as "too immediate, personal, parochial, or emotional to be widely effective." Who has time for local solutions when the world is in flames? We can readily concede that caring-for is inadequate to the tasks of ending injustice and healing suffering around the world—injustice is too entrenched and suffering too pervasive for that—but at the same time we should insist, with Noddings, that "there is no adequate substitute for caring-for (direct caring) . . . Caring-about is empty if it does not culminate in caring relations." Sincere, thoughtful caring-about is crucial but its main contribution, Noddings writes, is in "suggest[ing] ways to extend caring-for to many more recipients."[15] In the same vein, I think, the laws of tzedakah enshrine the primacy of caring-for.[16]

PARTIALITY: OBVIOUS TO SOME, INTOLERABLE TO OTHERS

Yet there is another key point here too, one that seems obvious to most people but that is a source of perpetual controversy among moral philosophers. As people situated in place and time, embedded in a web of personal and communal relationships, we have greater obligations to some people than we do to others. I may be obligated to respond to your children when they are in need, but I have a greater obligation to respond to my own children when *they* are. In any case, Jewish law—and most people's moral intuitions—insists that my obligations to my own children take precedence over my obligations to yours.[17]

Why might some be troubled by this?

Morality, it is commonly held, is meant to be free of bias or prejudice; under most circumstances, "playing favorites" is considered immoral. Accordingly, some philosophers argue (or assume) that taking an impartial perspective is constitutive of moral thinking; they "identify the moral view with lack of personal involvement."[18] As one such thinker puts it, "The moral point of view . . . [is] . . . that of an independent, unbiased, impartial, dispassionate, disinterested, objective observer."[19] Strict impartialists ask us to disregard our personalities and our circumstances, our loves and our passions, our interests and our commitments in making moral choices; they claim that "feelings, personal relationships, and peculiarly individual aspirations" carry no moral weight.[20]

Let's take perhaps the most extreme example I know of this approach. Borrowing a key term from the economist and philosopher Adam Smith,[21] the Princeton philosopher Peter Singer holds that ethics requires us to take the standpoint of "the impartial spectator or ideal observer." To approach a problem morally, Singer maintains, we can't prioritize our needs or the needs of our loved ones; on the contrary, since everyone counts equally, thinking ethically requires us to weigh up all the interests of all people affected by our decision and "to adopt the course of action most likely to maximize the interests of [all] those affected."[22] Just how far is Singer, a radical utilitarian if ever there was one, prepared to go? While admitting that vanishingly few—if any—parents would give away their last bowl of rice while their own child was starving, Singer is nevertheless unsure whether such an action would be wrong.[23] After all, he maintains, no morally admissible argument would legitimate prioritizing my child's needs over another's.[24]

Partialists—myself included—reject this kind of thinking out of hand, allowing that "it is (not merely psychologically understandable but) morally correct to favor one's own," those with whom we have personal ties of some kind.[25] A significant part of what it means to have relationships with particular people is precisely to be partial toward them.

Parents, for example, are obligated to be partial; if they refuse to favor their own children, they are derelict in the duties of parenthood. For the sake of contrast, compare Singer's wondering whether giving the last bowl of rice to one's child is morally defensible with the philosopher John Cottingham's insistence that granting priority to one's own child in an emergency is obviously "the morally correct course—it is precisely what a good parent *ought* to do." A parent who abandons his child, on the grounds, say, that "someone else whose future contribution to the general welfare promises to be greater," is also in need, "is not a hero; he is (rightly) an object of moral contempt, a moral leper."[26] On Cottingham's account, in such circumstances it is not partiality but *impartiality* that is morally unjustifiable.

Let's dig a little deeper here, so that we can better understand what's at stake in this discussion, and so that we can more clearly see why Jewish ethics chooses a partialist path.

PRIORITIES AND PERSONAL "PROJECTS"

Every person has her own distinctive set of desires, concerns, or, as the philosopher Bernard Williams calls them, "projects." These projects, Williams notes, help make us who we are; having personal projects and commitments is what gives us a reason for living at all. It just can't be the case, Williams argues, that we are forbidden to give priority to the things that give us reason to value our lives in the first place. As Williams puts it, we can't be expected to give up the things that are conditions for our "having any interest in being around in the world at all."[27] Were we obligated to do so, we would cease to be (or have) individual selves at all.[28]

Personal relationships are a key example of what Williams means by "projects." To be a human being is to have interpersonal loyalties and commitments. It is unreasonable to demand that these be shunted aside in the name of impartialistic moral reasoning. Williams gives the example of a man who sees his wife and another person drowning and knows he can only save one of them. As most people in this situation no doubt would, the man chooses to save his wife—which, to be clear, means letting the other person drown. Most people (though not all) would agree that he was *permitted* to act in this way; some would even insist that he was *obligated* to do so. Some impartialists would concede that he did the right thing; a utilitarian, for example, might argue that in situations like this one, it is best for each person to look after their own.[29] But Williams maintains that there is something strange and inappropriate about making arguments to justify saving our spouse. This is, as he controversially puts it, having "one thought too many." As he explains, "It might have been hoped by some (for instance, by his wife) that his motivating thought, fully spelled out, would be the thought that this is his wife, not that it was his wife and that in situations of this kind it is permissible to save one's wife." The key point is that in any life there will be situations when our deep personal attachments express themselves in our behavior, regardless of whether or not they conform to a moral standard. Without commitments and loyalties, Williams argues, "there will not be enough substance or conviction in a [person's] life to compel his allegiance to life itself."[30] A lack of personal projects and personal relationships means no self and no reason for living.

THE MORAL WEIGHT OF PARTICULARITY

Williams is arguing that in certain situations and in light of certain relationships, there will be times when we will make choices *whether or not they are morally justifiable.* If my wife were drowning, the question of whether moral standards would permit my giving priority to saving her simply wouldn't interest me; it would be, to return to Williams's phrasing, "one thought too many." Other values, like love, would take precedence over asking moral questions.[31]

According to Williams, then, being partial to a spouse, a child, or a friend is important, whether or not it always conforms to the standards of morality. But I'm inclined to defend partiality as integral to morality itself.[32] Partiality, after all, is not just integral to being a self; it's also fundamental to living a good life. If love is essential to the good life—and it hardly needs arguing that it is—and part of what it means to love someone is to be partial toward them,[33] then some degree of special concern for those we love seems permissible and even required. Cottingham eloquently spells out the implications of this: "If I give no extra weight to the fact that this is *my* lover, *my* friend, *my* spouse, *my* child, if I assess these people's needs purely on their merits (in such a way as an impartial observer might do), then that special concern which constitutes the essence of love and friendship will be eliminated. Partiality to loved ones is justified because it is an essential ingredient in one of the highest of human goods."[34] To ask people not to show partiality toward those they love is thus to deprive them of one of life's most essential goods. Even more fundamentally, a world without partiality would be one "where much of what gives human life preciousness and significance had disappeared."[35] It seems implausible to believe that morality mandates our living in what would be an arid, loveless world.[36]

To get at this from a more theological angle: strict impartiality would undermine my individuality—and the individuality of those dear to me. Having family and friends to whom we are partial is part of what makes us individuals rather than abstract, generic members of a species. Recall the mishnah's insistence that the irreducible uniqueness of each human being redounds to the glory of God.[37] This means that we can't all just be "inter-substitutable," to borrow a rather inelegant term from Williams.[38] To insist that moral thinking requires us to strip away whatever it is that makes me *me* rather than someone else is to run afoul of one of Judaism's core claims about the worth of persons.

All of this raises the question of how we imagine what it means to be a self in the first place. Some people (and some philosophers) tend to picture people as separate (or at least separable), individual units: I am a totally independent self and then I decide whether or not to enter into relationships with others. But this is not how human beings actually develop, grow, and interact in the world. As an infant, I don't decide to enter into relationships with my caretakers—I am connected to and dependent upon them long before I make a choice, or even know what a choice is. More generally, and throughout the course of life, who I am as a person is irreducibly shaped by the people I care about and who care for me, by the people whose well-being I feel responsible for and who feel responsible for mine.[39] I am my parent's child and my child's parent; I am not, and do not have, a self apart from those relationships and countless others. Total impartiality, I think, is an implausible ideal because it fails to take adequate account of what it means to be a self at all. People are not monads. A real, live human self is always already partial to certain, select others. Morality needs to take this essential fact about human selfhood into account rather than pretend to override it.

To be partial to loved ones, then, is not selfishness; it is just part of what it means to *be* a self at all.

LOVE GROWS IN AND FROM THE PARTICULAR

No one starts out loving all of humanity; we begin by loving our parents. We learn to experience love and responsibility through our connections to family[40] and friends. The notion that we can somehow bypass or transcend that on the road to universal love seems unrealistic, even fantastical. More than that, it seems self-defeating. For most of us, the consequence of claiming to love all of humanity (or all of creation, for that matter) equally is that we will end up loving no one at all. "If our first love is to some narrower group," the philosopher Andrew Oldenquist warns, "this forced shift [to impartial universal love] may render our moral concern weak and pallid. Equal moral concern for the whole of humanity or the whole of sentient nature is, for most of us, too diluted to be able to generate moral enthusiasm and too weak to outweigh narrower loyalties."[41] What this means is that "the danger in [any] attempt to eliminate partial affections is that it may remove the source of all affections."[42] If we don't allow people to care about *someone in particular*, they will likely end up caring about *no one at all*.

We've encountered two ideas that may strike some readers as

contradictory: first, that there is a hierarchy of precedence in terms of what we owe others, and second, that we are obligated to love all human beings. But in reality there is no contradiction: for Jewish ethics, the path to universal love is *through* partiality rather than around it. The goal of moral growth, in other words, should be to *expand upon* rather than replace the narrower loyalties that come more naturally to us.[43]

I want to underscore this idea of working with, rather than against, the (deep, even fierce) loyalties that come naturally to us. Evolutionary biologists have taught us that as human beings we have certain "'genetically based emotional predispositions' that give special preference to biologically related kin." Most of us recognize this from our experience of daily life. It isn't surprising, therefore, that blood ties tend to be the "strongest and most durable of bonds" (though there are obviously many exceptions).[44]

There is a Talmudic principle that "the Blessed Holy One does not deal imperiously (*be-tirunya*) with [God's] creations."[45] The word that I have translated as "imperiously," *be-tirunya*, could also be rendered as "tyrannically" or "despotically," the idea being that God does not make demands that are impossible for human beings to fulfill.[46] In the same spirit, Rabbi Meir Simhah of Dvinsk (1843–1926) observes that the Torah does not "burden the Israelite with what the body is incapable of fulfilling."[47] Jewish sources recognize the unavoidable fact that we love some more than others. Jewish law would never tell us to consider our own child as just one child among many, and evolutionary biology confirms what we've always known from experience: that it would be impossible for us to do so in any case.

It would not just be impossible for us to override or eliminate the preference we grant to those close to us, it would also be undesirable. What scientists refer to as "kinship altruism" produces moral goods. As the ethicist Stephen Pope puts it, "It is good . . . that we feel strongly about our families, take care of family members, especially the young, teach our children to love and care for theirs when the time is right, and try to work for a society in which families thrive and children are loved and respected."[48]

It is good, but it is not good *enough*.

WORKING WITH NATURE, NOT AGAINST IT

Most of us, I suspect, hold two intuitions rather strongly: first, that we have greater obligations to those close to us, and second, that both morality and religion demand that we expand our sense of obligation beyond our inner circle. Most of us know, on some level, that limiting our love to those closest to us is problematic. There may be honor among thieves but it hardly renders them moral paragons. With this intuition in mind, how do we prevent family *first* from collapsing into family *only*?[49]

We are not mere machines, programmed (or "hardwired," as some would say) to care exclusively for those we define as "our own." As the philosopher Mary Midgley explains, our instincts are "open" rather than "closed": whereas closed instincts motivate patterns of behavior that are "fixed genetically in every detail, like the bees' honey dance," open ones are more like "programs with a gap. Parts of the behavior pattern are innately determined, but others are left to be filled in by experience."[50] The openness of most human instincts means that we can work to shape how they are expressed in our lives.[51] "'Genes hold culture on a leash' . . . but apparently the leash is pretty long."[52] Although we naturally love family first, we can learn to extend our love and care beyond our kin—and doing so is a moral and religious imperative.

We do not override but instead expand upon what is given naturally. The idea I am getting at is nicely expressed by the medical ethicist Stephen Post. "Human beings," he writes, "generally learn about love concretely in special relations, and . . . true love for humanity is often . . . an expansion of this learning. Universal love for humanity is a tremendously important moral ideal, but one that for most of us must be built up step by step from what is learned in committed special relations."[53] We don't come to love humanity by ignoring our family but by allowing our love to grow outward from it.[54] Recall what we saw in chapter 4: family love is both an intrinsic good and an instrumental one—intrinsic because intimate, loving relationships are part of any plausible conception of the good life; instrumental because it is these loves that enable us to spread our love more broadly.

As Jewish ethics conceives it, moral education works with the grain of nature rather than against it. So we may—from Jewish law it seems we *must*—show preference to the near and dear, but we are forbidden from stopping there. A wonderful homily that captures this insight: according to Jewish law, birds of prey are not kosher.[55] Some commentators suggest that the law is animated by a concern lest the cruelty of such birds rub off on people, rendering them too cruel of heart.[56] One of the birds explicitly prohibited by the Torah is the stork, known in biblical Hebrew as the *hasidah* (Leviticus 11:19). A Talmudic sage is puzzled by the bird of prey's Hebrew name, which seems to be connected to the Hebrew word for righteousness, *hasidut*: What could possibly be righteous about a bird of prey? The sages answer that the *hasidah* performs charity (*hasidut*) for its "friends" (*haveiroteha*, more literally here, its fellow birds) by sharing its food with them.[57] But in that case we might wonder why a bird that displays such good qualities should be forbidden for consumption. A modern commentator offers a beautiful homiletical explanation: the stork is described as doing kindness to her friends, but as for everyone else, she gives no thought at all to their well-being. Such righteousness is not good enough, and a bird with exclusively parochial concerns is considered beyond the pale and thus not kosher.[58]

EXPANDING OUR HORIZONS

There is another way to think about why commitments to partiality and localism must be balanced with more expansive and even universal commitments. Here (as elsewhere) love has to wrestle with the demands of justice. We can—and, I've suggested, we should—embrace the idea that people should prioritize looking after their own, but we can't justly advocate for "family first" while remaining blithely indifferent to the fact that so many families have next to nothing to *prioritize with*. We have to ask: What are our moral duties in a world in which so many lack the resources to meet their loved ones' most basic needs? The philosopher Marilyn Friedman, who worries that "relationship norms" tend to be "silent about social and economic context," is an especially compelling advocate on this point. "It must matter to the partialist's stance," she writes, "that the resources for favoring loved ones are distributed in a vastly unequal manner in virtually any society—and, of course, worldwide." I may gain satisfaction from providing my children with a good education, but what about those who cannot do the same for *their* children? Surely they deserve the same (or at least a similar) opportunity for gratification as I do. The fact of the matter, Friedman writes, is that "those who cannot care for their loved ones well will not realize integrity or fulfillment through such relationships because they can do little to enhance the well-being of those they love." This reality has crucial implications for how partiality needs to meet the demands of justice. "Partiality, if practiced by all, untempered by any redistribution of wealth or resources, would appear to lead to the integrity and fulfillment of only some, and not all, persons."[59] Virtue cannot be limited to those with the means to practice it.

These are obviously difficult questions—excruciatingly difficult questions, if we confront them honestly. But the main point I want to make here is simply that (to borrow Friedman's words again) "social institutions should be structured so that partiality, as practiced in close relationships, contributes to the integrity and fulfillment of as many people as possible."[60] Love your own, in other words, but make sure that others have the resources to do the same.[61]

IMPARTIALITY MATTERS TOO

I have been arguing at length for moral partialism. But it's important to emphasize that no one who cares about justice and fairness thinks that partiality is acceptable (let alone desirable) in every circumstance. Biblical law gives voice to the need for judicial impartiality, for example. In hearing a legal dispute, a judge is forbidden to show favoritism either to the powerful or to the needy (Deuteronomy 1:17). The judge is warned not to subvert the rights of the poor person but also to avoid favoring him (Exodus 23:3, 6); rather, as Leviticus puts it, "You shall not render an unfair decision: do not favor the poor or show deference to the rich: judge your kinsman fairly" (Leviticus 19:15).

It's not just judges. All of us need some degree of commitment to impartiality lest we give in to the temptation to exempt ourselves, and those we love, from the moral rules to which we (often passionately and even indignantly) subject others. We allow our own children to break or bypass rules we would be horrified to learn others had violated; we forgive those we love for the very same flaws for which we condemn those we don't; we excuse in our community what we would rightly censure in others . . . and the list goes on. Even partialists need a good dose of impartiality to keep us honest. We should also keep in mind that we need to be impartial in our commitment to partiality: If it is okay for me to feed my child before I feed yours, it is equally okay for you to feed yours before mine. If I am entitled to my partial loves and commitments, then so too are you.

BETWEEN JUDAISM AND CHRISTIANITY

There is a stark contrast between Jewish and Christian ethics regarding these questions of partiality and impartiality. In one of the most influential books of modern Christian ethics, the philosopher Gene Outka argues that agape, or Christian love, ought to be understood as "equal regard." The primary characteristic of Christian love, according to Outka, is impartial regard for human beings "qua human existent[s]."[62] Although Outka tries to make space for personal relationships, critics have argued that his vision of agape "do[es] not sufficiently appreciate the moral significance of the kind of love that is part of ordinary human life and that, in particular, is marked by special degrees of affection, loyalty, and moral obligation."[63] Christian thinkers are divided: some see the ideal as nonpreferential equal regard, while others insist that the partial nature of love reflects the divine will.

The kind of debate we find among Christian writers is alien to Judaism. As we've seen, Jewish ethics never doubts the priority of special relations; that family, friends, and neighbors come first is never really doubted.

This is reflective, I think, of something deeper. Christian thinkers are much quicker than Jewish ones to leap to the universal. In a Christian society, it can be tempting to assume that universalism is always and everywhere superior to particularism, but in fact life is more complicated than that. Historically speaking, universalism often went—and goes—hand in hand with imperialism: we care about everyone and we will convince (force) them to live in the best possible way—that is, our way. History is littered with the corpses of universalism run amok. Jews are slower to embrace universalism, not least because we have so often been its victims; in the eyes of historical Christianity, one of the Jews' greatest sins was our stubborn adherence to our own particularity. To be sure, particularism too has its limits. Particularists sometimes limit their horizon; they focus on their own and leave other people to take care of themselves. My point is not to argue for the superiority of either particularism or universalism but to be honest about the trade-offs we are forced to make in embracing one over the other. To put the issue somewhat crudely, Judaism has always excelled at leaving other people alone, but it has sometimes tended to forget that other people matter; Christianity, in contrast, has always remembered that other people matter but it took almost two thousand years for Christianity even to consider leaving other people alone.[64] The ideal, we might say, is to combine the best of what particularism and universalism have to offer (and demand): we care about everyone but we start local and we allow other people to be who they are. This is the dialectic that Jewish ethics at its best seeks to express.

LINGERING QUESTIONS

It's probably worth spelling out just one example of what I mean in suggesting that finding a proper balance between supporting our children, say, and supporting the needy is extraordinarily difficult. We've established, I think, that if my child and yours are both malnourished, I am permitted—and, many ethicists and Jewish legal decisors would insist, required—to provide for my child first. For argument's sake, at least, let's assume more than this, namely that I am obligated to make sure my child has a good, healthy, and secure life before I begin to turn my attention outward. Just how much should I provide for my child before I begin to provide for yours, or for someone else's who lives oceans away? I need to ensure that my child is well-fed, but do I need to send her to an illustrious private school? Must I provide her with a room of her own and a nice vacation or two every year, before providing for other children's bare necessities? *May* I do so? How much luxury is a sin in a world where children die of famine every day?[65] I don't know the answer to any of these questions[66] but I do think it is crucial to wrestle with them—and most of us, I fear, would simply prefer to ignore them. If we take seriously the idea that we are obligated to love all human beings, we cannot in good conscience simply pretend that such questions do not exist.

WHICH PARTIALITIES—FAMILY, YES, BUT PEOPLE TOO?

We've encountered the ideas of Rabbi Jacob Emden, who taught that there are two obligations of interpersonal love: first, Jews must love our fellow Jews because of the mitzvah to love our neighbor as ourselves, and second, we must love all human beings because we are all God's creations. In other words, the mandate to "love your neighbor" is particularistic, but it is not the only source of our obligation to love others. A person's being created by God means that they are to be loved, whether or not they are our "neighbor."[67]

R. Emden is right about the plain sense of the biblical text: in context, the commandment to love our neighbor refers to our fellow Jews. As we saw in the previous chapter, however, the plain sense notwithstanding, there are also Jewish thinkers who maintain that the biblical mandate to love our neighbor extends not just to the Jewish people but to all of humanity. While I obviously see the appeal of the latter view,

I find myself more drawn to the former—first, as I've said, because I think it hews closer to the Bible's and Jewish tradition's own view, and second, because I think it better encapsulates Judaism's commitment both to particularism and to universalism.

Most philosophers are willing to concede that special relations with family and friends are morally acceptable, and many that they are morally desirable—although they will often disagree about precisely how and why that is the case. But they are far more divided about other kinds of attachments that, some claim, also elicit special duties.[68] How are we to make moral sense of Judaism's ethos of "love everyone, but love your fellow Jews more"? (If you prefer, you can see this as "love Jews first, but love everyone else too.")

One path we could take follows the spirit of Bernard Williams. For some of us, attachment to a broader community (or communities) is so basic, so elemental to how we understand what it means to be a human being, that the question simply doesn't have teeth. I don't try to justify why I would save my wife before I'd save yours, and in much the same way, I don't try to justify why I'd support my people before someone else's. I am not interested in having "one thought too many."

But what if I do take the moral question to heart? Can we make *moral* sense, as opposed to merely "human sense," of the idea that Jews are obligated to help other Jews before they help non-Jews—or if you prefer, of the idea that Jews have an additional obligation to love our fellow Jews over and above our love of all humanity?

In considering this, it's important to state at the outset that Jews are an anomalous group. We are a people but also a religious community; we are a religious community, but also a people. Philosophers like to think in categories but Jews defy easy categorization. The parallel is problematic in many ways, but I nevertheless find it helpful to think about special obligations to fellow Jews in light of philosophical debates on the ethics of patriotism.

The political theorist David Miller helps clarify what's at stake in questions about patriotism—and also, by extension, why they can be so difficult to answer. Probing the ethics of patriotism, Miller writes that "people . . . who defend special duties toward compatriots often find themselves in a kind of pincer movement." They compare national loyalties to familial ones, as I did in the previous chapter, only to be told by critics of nationalism (or patriotism, or some other form of special attachment that extends beyond family and local community) that nations are not in fact like families. The fact that we may morally show preference to the latter doesn't mean we may show it to the former. So defenders of such special duties try to show that families and nations can indeed be brought "under the same umbrella," and therefore that if preference is justified in the one case, it can be justified in the other too. But this in turns elicits another challenge—that at least some approaches to legitimating special duties to compatriots could also apply to racists and bigots of various stripes. To meet this objection, those who want to defend special duties to one's people (or nation, or country, or whatever) have to show how and why special duties to one's people are different from other, morally odious, group attachments.[69]

We could argue, with Miller, that in order to be morally defensible, special attachments "should not inherently involve injustice." Thus being part of a church, for example, would be different from being part of a white supremacist group—the latter, but not the former, is founded on the desire to degrade and oppress Blacks, Jews, and others. But at least some critics of nationalism and group identity are likely to demur, since they are "inclined to see nations as exclusive clubs whose very existence is premised on the exclusion of others both from membership and from the resources" the group possesses.[70] Even so, Miller says, we need to maintain a "distinction between groups founded on injustice, so to speak, and groups which contingently may act in unjust ways, but without the injustice becoming an essential part of the group's distinctive character." The second type of group, but not the first, is capable of morally grounding special duties.[71]

I am inclined to agree with the basic thrust of Miller's argument but I confess that it leaves me somewhat uneasy. The fact remains, as Miller himself acknowledges, that "any group has the potential to act in unjust ways, and so it may be hard to decide whether the injustice is inherent in the group or incidental to it."[72] It is always tempting to see injustices perpetrated by groups with which we are sympathetic as contingent rather than essential, but I worry that the distinction tends to be neater in theory than in reality. Native Americans could be permitted to wonder whether the brutal mistreatment they have endured over the course of American history is a feature of American nationalism rather than a bug; and Jews could be forgiven for questioning whether antisemitism should be seen as merely "incidental" to Christianity.

Be that as it may, a critic could grant Miller's point and still insist that ties to a people—in our case, the Jewish people—can't be compared to ties to family or friends because the former just aren't real in the same way as the latter. After all, most people who would say they love the Jewish people will likely never meet 99.9 percent of their fellow Jews. And yet this argument isn't as strong as it might at first appear, since people who see themselves as part of the Jewish people are linked, as are many other groups, by "a set of shared understandings about what it is that they are members of, and what distinguishes them from outsiders"; this, Miller maintains, is "sufficient to bind them together into a relationship that has genuine value."[73]

Skeptics may worry that accepting the notion that we can have special duties to our people or our coreligionists can only weaken our sense of duties to humanity at large. But this need not be the case; in fact, as I argue repeatedly in this book, special attachments need not conflict with, much less obliterate, more universal attachments and commitments. Just as being thoroughly rooted in a place need not lead to provincialism, so being deeply rooted in a people need not lead to parochialism. People are complicated and we can have multiple attachments; sometimes those attachments compete with, and sometimes reinforce, one another. This is, I think, part of what makes us human.[74]

Of course, what all this ought to look like in practice is complicated and elusive. In what circumstances is it legitimate for Muslims to give preference to fellow Muslims, for Jews to give preference to fellow Jews, and, moving from religious communities to national ones, for Americans to give preference to fellow Americans—and in what circumstances is it illegitimate? At minimum we can say that partiality always has limits. There are some duties we have to others that we can't set aside for our family; in much the same way, "there are some global duties that cannot be set aside in favor of local ones." Thus, to take what ought to be an obvious example, our (necessarily) partial commitments to family, friends, and people do not give us license to trample on the human rights of others.[75]

LOVING THE JEWISH PEOPLE

What should love of the Jewish people actually look like?

Ahavat yisrael, love of the Jewish people, can include pride in the Jewish people's religious heritage, passion about keeping its ethical and spiritual commitments alive, delight in its food, music, literature, etc. It is closely tied to love of the land of Israel, the place where many of the Torah's commandments can exclusively be fulfilled and the site where the Jewish people's deepest dreams and longings are one day to be fulfilled. But to return more directly to the key theme of this chapter, it must also include a sense of mutual responsibility and care for other Jews. Love of the Jewish people is, primarily, love of actual, flesh-and-blood Jews.[76] It is, first and foremost, love of individual Jews, not love of the Jewish people as an abstraction or a collective (though it may include those too).[77] As the Torah tells it, the Jewish people began as a family, and Jews have always sought to see themselves as an extended family. Accordingly, it's possible to feel responsible to and for one another, even when there is much about which we passionately disagree; that's no small part of what family *is*.

To love the Jewish people is, in part, to love its ideals; *ahavat yisrael* is not ultimately separable from *ahavat Hashem* (the love of God) and *ahavat ha-Torah* (the love of Torah). After all, as the Jewish philosopher Sa'adia Gaon (882–942) tells us, "The Jewish people is a people only by virtue of the Torah."[78] We are—or ought to be—a people in service of its ideals. The fact that love of Israel is intertwined with love of God and love of Torah means that the people are always subject to judgment from the perspective of God and Torah—which, I hasten to add, includes morality.

Ahavat yisrael is not—*cannot* be—the religious equivalent of "our country, right or wrong." First, to hold moral beliefs with any degree of seriousness is to know that all human institutions are subject to moral critique;[79] to make an exception of one's people is to walk extremely treacherous ground. Second, Judaism's sacred texts consistently subject the Jewish people to blistering moral critique; to be an heir of the prophets is to insist that one's people is unequivocally subject to the demands of morality—and, of course, to the will of God. We should also note an additional dimension to this: as we began to see in chapter 1, and as we will consider more expansively again in chapter 7, Jewish theology attempts to instill in the Jewish people a commitment to the dignity of every human being without exception; there can be no Jewish theology without a fundamental commitment to human solidarity. To adapt slightly a declaration from the philosopher Robert Audi, the only kind of group loyalty that is morally justifiable is one leavened by loyalty to the community of all people, and all peoples.[80] Concern for human beings in general means that sometimes Jews will be subjected to moral critique from other Jews for failing to live up to Judaism's own values. Adapting an oft-cited slogan advocating moderate patriotism for our purposes, we can perhaps define the ethos of *ahavat yisrael* thus: "My people, right or wrong! If right, to be kept right; and if wrong, to be set right."[81]

Love of the Jewish people, then, is not morally problematic; to be sure, like any group loyalty, it can take problematic forms, but there is nothing inherently problematic about it.[82] But is love of the Jews (or any other people, for that matter) morally salutary? Perhaps so, since, as Miller puts it, "It has yet to be demonstrated that a purely cosmopolitan ethics is viable." If you doubt that "people will be sufficiently motivated to act on duties that are likely to be very demanding in the absence of the ties of identity and solidarity" that ethnic, national, or religious

affiliations provide, then you may well conclude that the latter are morally valuable, not just unobjectionable.[83]

Even if we conclude that "wider partialist structures of interdependence"[84]—that is, groups broader than families and local communities
but narrower than the entire human race—are morally valuable, they
might still not be morally obligatory. Not everything that is (potentially)
morally *good* is morally *required*. But as for love of the Jewish people, even
if one wants to argue that it is morally neutral, it is nevertheless theologically significant. In more traditional Jewish language, *ahavat yisrael* is a
mitzvah. God's ideals as expressed in Torah are meant to be implemented
in community; more broadly, they are meant to be embodied by a people.
The Torah's command that Israel be holy because God is holy (Leviticus
19:2) is addressed to the people in the plural rather than the singular.
Judaism is not a religion for the individual seeker alone; it is a vision for
how human beings ought to live together in pursuit of the right and the
good. For that, we need ties—deep, abiding ties—that extend beyond
nuclear families.

7

HUMAN DIGNITY AND SOLIDARITY

Judaism's Other "Great Principle"

"LOVE YOUR NEIGHBOR as yourself," R. Akiva teaches, is "the great principle of the Torah." But his view does not go uncontested. Simeon ben Azzai, another prominent Talmudic sage, insists that another verse, "This is the book of the generations of Adam" (Genesis 5:1), is "an even greater principle."[1]

What is this disagreement about?

Rabbi David Frankel (1707–1762) offers a pair of provocative interpretations. He first suggests that whereas R. Akiva emphasizes love of neighbor as the core principle of Torah, ben Azzai points to the fact that we are all descended from the same person, namely Adam. The foundation of Torah, in other words, is the realization that the entire human community is one family, that we are united by our shared origins. The fact that this truth is universal, R. Frankel explains, makes it even more fundamental than the more particularistic mandate to love our neighbor.[2] Ben Azzai sees universal human relatedness as the core principle of the Torah.

R. Frankel's second suggestion is based on the conclusion of the verse that ben Azzai cites. The words "This is the book of the generations of Adam" are followed by "When God created man, God created him in the likeness of God" (Genesis 5:1). On R. Frankel's second reading, ben Azzai emphasizes not our shared biological origins but our shared metaphysical status: We are, each and every one of us, created in the image of God and therefore worthy of being treated with respect. The core principle of the Torah is thus the obligation to "be careful with other people's dignity."[3] According to this second interpretation, we could say that ben Azzai considers divinely bestowed and universally shared human dignity the core principle of the Torah.[4]

Both of R. Frankel's interpretations of the debate center on the relative priority of the particular and the universal. "Love your neighbor as yourself," we've seen, is first and foremost an obligation toward fellow members of the covenant; common descent from Adam and creation in God's likeness, on the other hand, are claims about humanity in general. Perhaps R. Akiva thinks that Jewish thought begins with the particularly Jewish, whereas ben Azzai insists that it begins with the universally human. Each sage would undoubtedly affirm what the other demands: ben Azzai would accept that we are obligated to love our fellow Jews (as the Torah itself makes clear) and R. Akiva would embrace the notion that we are obligated to treat all human beings with respect (as being created in God's image would seem to require). The issue that divides them is where we begin in thinking about our place in the world and our obligations to other people: Do we start with covenantal commitments or with shared humanity? Or perhaps we could say that R. Akiva and ben Azzai disagree about which principle implicitly contains more of the Torah in it, a universal claim about humanity or a particular demand about a more circumscribed community.[5]

GENESIS 1: WE ARE ALL ROYALTY

If we truly took the Bible seriously, I'm not sure we'd ever get past the first chapter. The claims that Genesis 1 makes about who and what we are as human beings are so potent, so stirring, so breathtaking, and ultimately so demanding that we can't just read it and move on. The chapter demands nothing less than a radical reorientation of our lives.

In ancient Near Eastern societies, it was the king who was thought of as an image of his god; it was he who was appointed to rule over his people and to mediate the god's blessings for them. This meant that from the very creation of the world, some people were destined to rule over others.[6]

Genesis 1 will have none of this. It is not (just) the king who is the image of God but each and every human being, without exception: "And God said, Let us make the human being in our image, after our likeness. They shall rule the fish of the sea, the birds of the sky, the cattle, the whole earth, and all the creeping things that creep on earth. And God created the human being in God's image; male and female [God] created them" (Genesis 1:26–27). In these verses, the whole idea of being created in God's image is radically democratized. The dramatic claim of Genesis 1 is that *we are all kings and queens*. Whatever hierarchies of status and power human societies may have developed, Genesis 1 relativizes.[7] Human beings are appointed to rule over the rest of creation, but no one human being is appointed to rule over any other.[8]

In the ancient world, the king, as an image of his god, was given vast responsibility. Ancient kings were expected to show special concern for the poor and vulnerable, to protect them and ensure their well-being. The Bible's vision of an ideal ruler is one who defends and protects his most vulnerable subjects.[9] In Genesis 1, humanity as a whole is assigned that role.[10] Since we are all kings and queens, we are all summoned to safeguard the exposed and the defenseless. Accordingly, being appointed to rule over creation is decidedly not the same thing as being given carte blanche to do as we will with the natural world:[11] as God's vice-regents on earth, human beings are "expected to care for the earth and its creatures. Such is the responsibility of royalty."[12] The fact that all human beings are created in God's image thus represents a democratization of moral responsibility. More radically, Genesis 1 insists that the poor and vulnerable are themselves royalty, bearers of the divine image in the same way and to the same extent as the monarch himself.[13]

Genesis 1 goes out of its way to observe that both male and female were created in the image of God (1:28). No matter how deeply entrenched they are in human societies, gender hierarchies are not ultimate. We are all royalty, regardless of gender.

Imagine taking this to heart. Consider the awe you may feel in the presence of a person who has great power or renown; consider the deference you may be inclined to show them. The opening chapter of the Torah invites us, *requires* us, to treat every human being this way.

COVENANT AND ROYAL STATUS

Some scholars discern a similar dynamic at play in the Torah's portrayal of the covenant between God and Israel. The covenant is modeled on ancient Near Eastern suzerainty treaties, in which a sovereign power holds supremacy over another state, which has its own ruler but which cannot act as an independent power. As a rule, suzerainty treaties were enacted between kings, not between peoples. In the Torah, God is the supreme sovereign, but who is God's vassal? The Israelites do have a leader, Moses, but he is not referred to as a king, and "nothing in the language of the covenant narratives suggests that it is Moses who is the vassal king." As the the Bible scholar Joshua Berman observes, God seems to be forming this treaty, or covenant, with the people. It is not that God is entering a suzerainty treaty with the collective body of the Israelite people; rather, "the subordinate king with whom God forms a political treaty is, in fact, the common man of Israel." The implication of this is that "every man in Israel is to view himself as having the status of a king conferred upon him." Biblically speaking, we might say that God is the King but all Israelite men are kings. Notice that any human king of Israel is demoted, stripped of any metaphysical or theological status. The covenant that is at the heart of the Torah's religious and political vision was formed between God and the people; the king is left out of the picture. All this is deliberate, the consequence of a deep-seated commitment to equality. "Only through the sublimation of the metaphysical standing of the monarchy in Israel," Berman writes, "could the biblical texts . . . achieve a reformulation of social and political thought along egalitarian lines." The "common man" is not so common after all. He is a king—a servant king, to be sure, but a king nonetheless.[14]

Consider some examples. Elsewhere in the ancient Near East the gods spoke exclusively to kings; in the Torah, in contrast, God addresses the masses. Elsewhere, the vassal king is periodically required to hear the treaty stipulations read aloud; in Deuteronomy, in contrast, that duty is incumbent upon all Israelites (Deuteronomy 31:10–13). Elsewhere, the vassal king is obligated to visit the court of the suzerain; in Israel, in contrast, every Israelite male is included in the obligation to make pilgrimage to Jerusalem. The "theological breakthrough" of the Torah is "the transformation of the status and standing of the masses, of the common person, to a new height." Part and parcel of this, as we've seen, is that the Torah "strips earthly hierarchies of their sacral legitimation."[15]

We ought to tread carefully here. The idea that the Torah elevates "the masses" and the "common person" requires some critical nuancing. As Berman acknowledges (but too quickly moves past), "The blueprint the Pentateuch lays out takes for granted women's subordination to men, excluding them from participation in many areas, including the judiciary, the cult, the military, and land ownership, to name a few."[16] Impressive—stunning—as the Torah's movement toward equality is, it nevertheless maintains a stark gender hierarchy; where gender is concerned, I think we can say, the rest of the Torah isn't quite as radical as Genesis 1. In Deuteronomy, the king is indeed demoted and the masses are indeed elevated, but the masses who are elevated are men—and not all men, for that matter, but rather heads of household.[17] The Bible scholar Saul Olyan suggests a more nuanced formulation of Berman's point: "It might be best to speak of a relative egalitarianism envisioned among heads of household . . . rather than to speak of a vision of 'a single, uniformly empowered, homogeneous class,' as Berman does."[18] The covenant between God and Israel is not egalitarian but it does contain a strong egalitarianizing thrust.

PEOPLE, NOT STATUES, REPRESENT GOD

From the Torah's perspective, since God and the world are not made of the same stuff, "there can be no man-made symbols of God." And yet, as Rabbi Abraham Joshua Heschel observes, "There is something in the world that the Bible does regard as a symbol of God. It is not a temple or a tree, it is not a statue or a star." Rather, "the symbol of God is the person, every person."[19] The words "image" (*tzelem*) and "likeness" (*demut*), which are used in the Bible to refer to forbidden idols,[20] are the very words used to describe the human being created in God's image: "And God said, 'Let us make the human being in our image (*tzalmeinu*), after our likeness (*demuteinu*)'" (Genesis 1:26). The startling implication is that "there is one way in which God is imaged in the world, and only one: humanness!"[21] God is revealed to us not through carved wood or sculpted stone but through the human being who stands before us.[22]

In other words, producing images of God is prohibited not because there may be none, but because *there may only be one*. To make a representation of God is to undermine the privileged and sacred status of the human being. Idolatry is not just a sin against God; it is also a sin against other people—*all* other people—since it undercuts the basis of their (and of *our*) infinite worth and preciousness.

Making idols is not just an attack on the dignity of humanness; it is also a refusal of the responsibility that goes with it. As images of God, we are created to reflect God; when we fashion idols, however, we abdicate our responsibility by making ourselves the reflect*ed* instead of the reflect*or*. We turn ourselves into "image-*makers*" instead of being "image-*bearers*," as God intends.[23]

In the ancient Near Eastern world that was the Bible's original context, the line between a representation and what it represents was often blurred. In other words, the representation in some sense *becomes* what it represents. The god represented in the image remains transcendent but is nevertheless present within the image. A statue of a god, then, does not remain mere wood, metal, or stone, but in some sense actually becomes "a divine being, the god it represents."[24] One of the many powerful implications of all this is that the image "functioned as a valid substitute of the referent when the referent was not physically present."[25]

In ancient Israel, as we've seen, statues of wood, metal, or stone are prohibited; human beings take their place. In the opening chapters of Genesis, "human beings are a sort of statue of God . . . Human beings are what Israelite religion has in place of divine statues."[26] The human being as the image of God is, as we've seen, God's earthly vice-regent, but more basically than that, the human being is a manifestation of God's very presence.[27] In a world where God frequently seems (or perhaps is) absent, the human being serves as a kind of "substitute" for God. The human being makes God present even in God's absence.[28]

THE ETHICAL IS THEOLOGICAL

Needless to say, all of this dramatically raises the stakes of the interpersonal realm. How we treat others is in some important sense how we treat God; God's honor and ours are inextricably intertwined. The ethical is theological.

Jews are commanded to affirm both that God is King and that human beings too are royalty. When a person dies, a midrash says, she is brought before the heavenly court and asked, "Did you make your Creator sovereign over you every morning and evening? Did you make your friend sovereign over you with pleasantness?"[29] A modern sage explains that the two questions are really one: Just as we are obligated to accept God as our sovereign, so also are we required to treat other human beings as royalty. The two commitments are interlaced because "One who shows respect to a person made in God's image in effect shows respect for God." In fact, from a theological perspective, the principle of vigilance with other people's honor flows directly from the awareness that they are created in the image of God. These two commitments, he concludes, are the very core of what is asked of us in our lives.[30]

Connecting the Hebrew word for "image" (*tzelem*, as in *tzelem Elohim*, the image of God) with the word for "shadow" (*tzel*), Rabbi

Yeruham Levovitz teaches that a human being is God's very shadow. Since a shadow cannot appear without a presence that casts it, when we see a human being, it is as if we were beholding the divine presence (*shekhinah*) itself. "Since we say that there is an image of God here, in truth there is God here too."[31] If a person stands before us, then so too, as it were, does God. To be solicitous of another person's honor is thus, in effect, to be solicitous with God's.[32] The same logic applies to negative behavior: to be less than vigilant with the honor of another person is akin to denigrating the divine presence (*shekhinah*) itself.[33]

Imagine really taking all of this to heart and orienting our lives around it: each and every human being on the face of the earth is a kind of theophany, a visible revelation of God. This is where the Bible begins and it's where Jewish ethics ought to begin too.

The principle of being solicitous with the dignity of others is, R. Levovitz writes, the fountainhead of interpersonal relations.[34] As he explains, "From being solicitous about the honor of other people all the interpersonal commandments flow."[35] The concern with human dignity is so central and so pervasive in Jewish law that one prominent twentieth-century Jewish thinker goes so far as to assert that "it is possible that all of the interpersonal commandments are based on the value of human dignity (*kevod ha-beriyot*)."[36]

A WARM (AND SINCERE) SMILE

The Talmud reports that when the sage Rabbi Eliezer fell ill, his disciples asked him for guidance in following the straight path. "Be careful with the honor of your colleagues," he responded.[37] In the same spirit, another Talmudic sage instructs: "Be the first to greet all others,"[38] and indeed, it is reported of one of the greatest of the Talmudic sages that no one ever greeted him before he greeted them.[39] In the same vein, yet another Talmudic sage teaches that if someone greets us and we do not reply, we are considered "robbers."[40] A modern Musar master warns that we should not interpret the mandate to greet people as supererogatory, something we may choose to do if we are particularly righteous;

rather, he says, it is a straightforward matter of Jewish law and thus obligatory on all of us.[41]

The Talmudic sage Shammai instructs us to "receive every person with a warm smile."[42] Another prominent sage, Rabbi Yishmael, teaches that we ought to "receive every person with joy."[43] Taking these two statements together, we again come face-to-face with Judaism's concern for integrating the internal with the external, emotion with action. Greeting another person with genuine joy reflects a higher spiritual plane than greeting them merely with a friendly countenance.[44] Crucial as it is to greet each person warmly, it is not sufficient; ideally, we must also feel genuine joy in seeing them—and this, in turn, requires caring about them. How do we get to the point of a warm countenance reflecting a warm heart? We train our hearts by setting the intention to have them follow our deeds. In other words, we smile at others with the intention of genuine human warmth emerging from us.[45]

Musar writers emphasize that respect for the dignity of others is not only a matter of how we act; rather, as we've come to expect, honoring others must be both externally manifested and internally felt. As with loving others, so with honoring them, the ideal is the full integration of the inner and the outer, motivation and action, feelings of respect and respectful actions.[46]

Note that both Shammai and Rabbi Yishmael talk about how we should engage with "every person." The mandate is not just to smile at the people we know and like; we probably don't need all that much coaxing to do that. It is to smile at everyone, even people we don't know, and even, for that matter, people we don't like. This can be a difficult practice, especially at first; one medieval sage says it takes legitimate "heroism" to fulfill it.[47] But human warmth is fundamental to what it means to take human dignity seriously, and it is elemental to what it means to be a religious person.

A medieval sage, Rabbi Asher ben Yehiel (Rosh, 1250?–1327), insists that this mitzvah of receiving people warmly applies not just to one-on-one encounters but also to the way we carry ourselves in public. "Let not your face be angry toward passersby," he says, "but receive them with a friendly countenance."[48] How we comport ourselves in the world makes an impact.

A seemingly odd Talmudic teaching tells us that smiling at someone is even greater than giving them milk to drink.[49] Whether or not we always like to acknowledge it, as human beings we need to be seen, recognized, and appreciated.[50] This is true of all of us, regardless of social status. Being seen is a spiritual-emotional need in the same way that being fed is a physical one—we can't really survive, let alone flourish, without it. As the moral philosopher Robin Dillon explains, we have the power in whether and how we look at someone (or refuse to) "to make or unmake others as persons, and the power to foster or subvert self-respect."[51]

Judaism's commitment to human dignity is so deep that it sometimes goes to seemingly radical extremes. For example, a Talmudic sage teaches that it is preferable for a person to throw herself into a fiery furnace rather than embarrass another person in public.[52] Remarkably, some of the most prominent legal decisors of the Middle Ages insist that this is not hyperbole but simple, straightforward law.[53] The prohibition on embarrassing another is one of Judaism's cardinal sins, they say, and one should sooner die than transgress it.

There is nothing generic or one-size-fits-all about such commitment to human dignity. As we've seen repeatedly, Jewish theology insists on the uniqueness and irreplaceability of each person. To live in accord with Jewish ethics therefore requires us not to respect human beings in general but to respect them in all their particularity. This has concrete ramifications in the interpersonal sphere. What one person takes as playful banter another experiences as painfully humiliating. What one person takes as an expression of concern another perceives as an invasion of privacy. What is permissible or even desirable to say to one person may be problematic or even forbidden to say to another. Among other things, this means that central to Jewish ethics as it is, law alone can never fully capture what taking dignity seriously requires. To honor human dignity rightly, we need not just law but moral wisdom, not just rules but deep attentiveness to other people's sensitivities and experiences.[54]

Asked about the highest level a person can achieve in this lifetime, Rabbi Abraham Isaiah Karelitz (Hazon Ish, 1878–1953) is purported to have responded: "To live seventy years without hurting another person."[55]

THE DIGNITY OF PEOPLE WHO ARE POOR

Jewish theology teaches that God's honor is deeply entwined with the honor of human beings, but it lays special emphasis on the honor of the poor. "He who oppresses the poor insults his Maker," says the book of Proverbs, while "he who shows pity for the needy honors [his Maker] (14:31).[56] Similarly, "He who mocks the poor insults his Maker" (17:5). As the Bible scholar Richard Clifford explains, "God is the maker of all, rich and poor, and God's honor is bound up with each person, no matter how lowly."[57] The poor person is spoken of in the singular; like anyone and everyone else, she matters to God not as a member of a class but as an individual.[58] She is not an idea but a flesh-and-blood human being with deeply felt needs, feelings, and vulnerabilities.

Note also the deliberate ambiguity of the phrase "his Maker" in the two verses: One who belittles the poor affronts the One who made both the belittler and the belittled. Subtly, the Bible's words remind us that economic status is of no metaphysical import. You may be richer, more powerful, and better connected than I, but in God's eyes you are not worth more than I. As Proverbs itself puts it, "The rich and the poor have this in common: the Lord is the maker of them all" (22:2).[59] While other ancient Near Eastern cultures also recognized a duty to be kind to the poor, the Bible is unique in tying that obligation to our shared status as God's creations.[60]

Proverbs states, "One who is generous to the poor makes a loan to the Lord" (19:17).[61] The Hebrew word used for "generous" derives from the root *h-n-n*, which means to give graciously, without thought or expectation of being repaid. As a medieval sage explains, since this is how God gives to us, it is how we ought to give to others.[62] A midrash adds in the same vein that when a person intends to give tzedakah, God considers it as if they had offered a sacrifice to God.[63] The lesson is stark: How we treat the poor is how we treat God. Honoring one is honoring the other; deriding one is deriding the other.

A contemporary Bible scholar observes: "Through the poor, the Creator of heaven and earth becomes vulnerable to our contempt! Likewise, in them God waits to be honored."[64] This idea may seem far-fetched at first, but if we take the notion of God as a parent at all seriously, it actually makes a great deal of sense. Imagine that you're a parent and someone hurts or insults your child. You love your child so deeply that you are likely to feel that they've hurt or insulted you (you may even find yourself wishing that they had actually wounded you *instead of* your child). Jewish theology suggests that that's the type of relationship that God has with all of us[65]—and that God has it with a special degree of intensity with people who are poor.

Why this special depth of feeling for the poor? Because God cares especially for those whom others tend to forget about; as we've discussed, people need to be seen, and God sees those we tend to treat as invisible.[66] That's why Hagar, an Egyptian slave mistreated and dehumanized by her mistress but acknowledged and blessed by God, proclaims, "You are the God who sees me!" (Genesis 16:13).[67] And more generally, that's why God is, according to the book of Psalms, "the father of orphans and the champion of widows" (Psalm 68:6).

To worship the God who sees those whom others neglect is to be called upon to do the same. We live in a world in which some are treated like royalty whereas others are rendered invisible and considered of no account. But recall again: we are *all* royalty, and to take Torah to heart is to strive to affirm the dignity of every last human being, even and especially those who are most often spurned or overlooked.

Jewish law gives concrete expression to God's special concern for the dignity of those who are poor. To take a biblical example, when we lend money to the poor, the book of Exodus says, we must not act as creditors toward them, and it is forbidden to charge them interest. Exodus then adds: "If you seize your neighbor's garment as collateral,[68] you must return it to him before the sun sets." Collateral that must be returned every evening is, in effect, not really collateral at all. It may well be that in this situation, the garment is "collateral more for the benefit of the feelings of the borrower than for the security of the lender."[69] Why does the Torah require the creditor to keep returning the garment? The text itself answers with great pathos: "It is his only clothing, the sole covering for his skin. In what else shall he sleep?!" (Exodus 22:24–26).[70] The rights of the creditor are subordinated to the dignity and welfare of the debtor.[71] No one deserves to spend the night naked and cold.[72] In this remarkable law, the dignity of the borrower is paradoxically protected both in the handing over of the garment as collateral *and* in its nightly return. Compassion for the poor person and her predicament trumps the ordinary ways economic affairs are conducted.[73] If we disobey and keep the garment overnight, Exodus threatens, God will be moved to act by the cries of the poor: "If he cries out to Me, I will pay heed, for I am merciful" (22:26).[74]

Following the Bible's lead, Maimonides emphasizes that we must take special care in our dealings with the widow and the orphan, not just because they are economically vulnerable but because "their spirits are very low and their feelings are depressed." (As a result of this, according to Maimonides the same rule actually applies to wealthy widows and orphans too.) Very concretely, we must "speak to them gently and treat them only with honor."[75] When we give tzedakah to a poor person, we must do so "happily" and "with a smile"; conversely, "one who gives tzedakah with an unpleasant countenance and with his face cast downward loses and destroys his merit," no matter how much money he actually gives. In giving, we must empathize and "commiserate," offering "words of sympathy and comfort."[76] Commenting on Isaiah's demand that "you offer the hungry your very self" (58:10), Rabbi Meir Leibush Weiser (Malbim) explains that beyond giving the poor person what he materially needs (58:7), we have to give our very selves: "Give him with a whole heart . . . do not give him bread only but also sate his soul with a generous spirit and comforting words."[77]

HUMAN DIGNITY AND HUMAN RIGHTS

Humanity being created in the image of God has political implications, not just interpersonal ones. To take human dignity seriously in the modern world is necessarily to be committed to human rights.

Moral philosophers and human rights theorists argue about whether or not human rights require God as their ultimate grounding.[78] Important as this question is, from a religious perspective the more pressing question is whether God needs (requires, commands) human rights.

Why should human rights matter so much? If we believe, with the book of Genesis, that human beings are royalty, then we believe that they ought to be treated with respect, and maybe even reverence. And in the modern world we've learned that, as the philosopher Nicholas Wolterstorff puts it, "Human rights are what respect for worth requires."[79] Given everything we've seen about God's impassioned concern for the dignity and worth of human beings, it makes sense that God would want us to use every available means to protect against oppression and abuse.

Why talk about rights and not just duties? Duties are about what we (must) do; rights, in contrast, are about "how we have been done unto." Accentuating the rights of the vulnerable draws our attention not just to culprits "being guilty" but also to victims "being wronged." As Wolterstorff explains, "The reason rights-language has almost always been the preferred language for social protest movements is that such language enables the oppressed to call attention to their own . . . condition." Recall that when the book of Exodus instructs us not to keep our debtor's garment in pledge overnight, it adds, "It is his only clothing, the sole covering for his sin. In what else shall he sleep?!" (22:25–26). The rhetorical question moves our attention away from ourselves and toward our potential victim. Human rights language functions similarly: It shifts our attention to what Wolterstorff calls the "recipient dimension" of our actions. We learn to focus not just on how we ourselves treat others but also on how others are treated. In talking about rights, we "decenter" ourselves morally.[80]

It's important to emphasize: I am not suggesting that we could (or should) attempt to derive the specific rights enumerated in the Universal Declaration of Human Rights (proclaimed by the United Nations in 1948) from biblical texts. That would undoubtedly be a fool's errand. To be sure, we could learn a great deal about human rights from the Bible's insistence that the poor and downtrodden can go over the head of their rulers and appeal directly to God for protection, and that the cries of the mistreated reach heaven; there are some things that the powerful simply may not do.[81] But as the Israeli scholar Gili Zivan observes, "One of the main difficulties of basing . . . human rights discourse on scriptural verses is that many biblical precepts fail to support human rights and do precisely the opposite, such as the injunctions to annihilate idol worshipers, eradicate Amalek, and wipe out the seven Canaanite nations . . ."[82] So we need to move back and forth, integrating our biblical belief in the immense dignity of the human person and our biblically motivated passion for the well-being of the abused and downtrodden, on the one hand, with an unapologetic embrace of modern enumerations of human rights, on the other.[83]

UNIVERSAL HUMAN SOLIDARITY

Recall where we started. The Talmudic sage ben Azzai points to the words "This is the book of the generations of Adam" (Genesis 5:1) as "the great principle of the Torah," and Rabbi David Frankel explains that ben Azzai wants to underscore the fact that all of us, every human being without exception, are descended from the same ancestor. We are, literally, one family.

The first chapter of the Bible emphatically makes this same point.

The Bible's account of the creation of humanity differs dramatically from other ancient Near Eastern creation stories. Whereas other creation stories culminate in the creation of the people and the culture doing the telling,[84] the Torah assigns no role to ancient Israel within the story of creation; "Israel is not primordial." Genesis 1 thus accentuates the point that all people, and not just Jews, are created in the image of God. As the Bible scholar Jon Levenson explains, Genesis 1 "serves as a powerful warrant for a Jewish doctrine of human solidarity."[85] We are all human, all created in the divine image.

In Genesis 11, the story of God's destruction of Babel, the Bible will strenuously defend human diversity and forcefully denounce totalitarian uniformity.[86] But tellingly, the Torah does not begin there. Before championing diversity, it seeks to establish a sense of shared humanity. Linguistic, cultural, and geographic diversity are a crucial part of God's hopes for human life, but the text stresses the value of diversity only after it has established that we are all, first, one human family.

As God proceeds through the work of creation, the Bible repeatedly draws our attention to the dazzling variety of what God makes. Genesis 1 reads like a hymn to biodiversity: God does not just create vegetation, God creates vegetation "of every kind" (*le-mino*, 1:11–12); God does not just create animals, God creates animals "of every kind" (1:25). Similarly with sea creatures, birds, and beasts: the Bible seems to revel in the breathtaking multifariousness of God's creation (1:21, 24–25). As we progress through the chapter, we come to expect that everything God creates will be created in stunning and multicolored diversity. When God finally creates the human being, we expect to hear that "God created the human being in God's image in all its kinds," but that final phrase is absent. The omission is striking—the Bible is perhaps suggesting that in contrast to vegetation and the (rest of the) animal kingdom, *there simply are no kinds of human beings.*[87] Our common humanity is one of the most fundamental truths about us.

What does a sense of shared humanity require of us? What does it make possible within us? To take creation in God's image seriously is to cultivate a sense of solidarity with all human beings,[88] even those whom we have never met, even those who differ from us in almost every conceivable way. Ideally this becomes second nature, part of how we perceive and experience others—and therefore of how we act toward them. When the political scientist Kristen Monroe studied people who had rescued Jews during the Holocaust, she found that the one trait that united them was their perception of themselves as strongly linked to others through shared humanity. "This perception of themselves as one with all mankind is such an intrinsic part of their cognitive orientation, of the way they define themselves," Monroe writes, "that they need not stop to make a conscious decision when someone knocks on the door or is drowning in a lake." No matter how carefully Monroe scrutinized selfless individuals, she kept arriving at this sense they had of being part of an "all-embracing mankind"; it was the one factor, she says, that "refused to go away."[89]

Human solidarity[90] is rooted, ultimately, in a refusal to see individuals as fundamentally separate, atomized, responsible only to and for ourselves. We are, as we saw in chapter 1, utterly unique; but, no less importantly, we are also inextricably interconnected. Human solidarity is thus believing and feeling that an assault on your dignity is also an assault on mine, that a diminishment of you also diminishes me. It is knowing, as deeply as we can know anything, that we are interdependent and responsible for one another. As one of Monroe's rescuers tells her, "You're part of a whole . . . I mean the human race, and . . . you should always be aware that every other person is basically you."[91]

In the Haftarah (prophetic reading) read by Jews on Yom Kippur morning, the prophet Isaiah tells the people that God wants a fast that goes far beyond ritual performance. God demands justice—"This is the fast I desire: To unlock the fetters of wickedness and untie the cords of the yoke; to let the oppressed go free; to break off every yoke"—as well as loving generosity toward the poor: "It is to share your bread with the hungry, and to take the wretched poor into your home; when you see the naked, to clothe him, and not to ignore your own flesh" (Isaiah 58:6–7).[92] This last demand, not to ignore our own flesh, has frequently been taken to refer to the care we must extend to our kin,[93] but Malbim reads the text differently. On his interpretation, the verse teaches us to share our food with the impoverished and to open our homes to them, and then adds that we must even share our very own clothes. When it comes to this last mandate, he says, the text urges us not to feel that we've lost anything by giving another person our clothing, because, after all, putting clothes on a poor person is like putting it on ourselves, since "all human beings are one flesh."[94]

Dr. Martin Luther King Jr. captures this idea with characteristic eloquence:

> As long as there is poverty in the world [, he writes,] I can never be rich, even if I have a billion dollars. As long as diseases are rampant and millions of people in this world cannot expect to live more than twenty-eight or thirty years, I can never be totally healthy even if I just got a good checkup at Mayo Clinic. I can never be what I ought to be until you are what you ought to be. This is the way our world is made. No individual or nation can stand out boasting of being independent. We are interdependent.[95]

Some thinkers who write about solidarity place great emphasis on the centrality of human rights in practicing human solidarity. This begins with not violating the human rights of others but it also includes a positive duty to promote human rights. We are thus obligated not just to refrain from abuse but also to work to ensure that others—again, even faraway others—have social and economic opportunities to flourish and thrive.[96]

We face an uphill climb. To take perhaps the most basic challenge, much of the world is trapped in dire, immiserating poverty. As of 2015, a staggering 736 million people, 10 percent of the world's population, were living on less than $1.90 a day. Fully 2.2 million people lack access to a safely managed drinking water service (located nearby, available when needed, and free from contamination). Approximately 297,000 children under five die every year from diarrheal diseases due to poor sanitation, poor hygiene, or unsafe drinking water.[97] If we mean it when we say that all human beings are created in God's image, that each and every one of us has divinely bestowed dignity and ought to be able to live accordingly, then the sheer magnitude of human suffering and vulnerability cannot but make a claim on us.

Genuine solidarity is careful to avoid paternalistic solutions to global poverty (and to other people's problems more generally). In seeking to ameliorate the living conditions of poor people, for example, we ought to privilege their perspectives and see them not as "passive recipients of help from altruistic benefactors" but instead as "agents in their own destiny."[98] True solidarity is not present unless and until those who are (comparatively) wealthy treat those who are poor with the same dignity as they themselves would expect—and demand—to be treated.

BETWEEN LOVE AND RESPECT

Recall again the debate between R. Akiva and his colleague ben Azzai about what constitutes "the great principle of the Torah." One way to understand their disagreement is about whether it is love or respect that lies at the heart of Judaism. In prioritizing love of neighbor, R. Akiva would be placing love at the center; in prioritizing creation in God's image, in contrast, ben Azzai would be placing respect there. It's worth exploring what might be at stake in the debate: How are love and respect related?

In an influential argument, Immanuel Kant suggests that while love brings us closer to one another, respect keeps us at a distance.[99] Taking issue with Kant's view, many thinkers have expressed doubt that love and respect really pull us in opposite directions. Love stands in opposition to hate and to indifference, they say, but not to respect.[100]

If respect always involves keeping our distance, then the duties of respect must be negative ones—that is, they must involve things we must not do.[101] Does Jewish ethics share this view?

To be sure, in Judaism, respect does include some negative duties; to take an example we've already seen, in Jewish law it is considered a grave crime to belittle or humiliate another person. But for Jewish ethics respect also includes positive duties, like the simple obligation we've seen to greet people and the obligation to give to the poor in ways that actively affirm their dignity.[102] And if my contention above is correct, respect for human dignity also requires us to work to protect other people's rights.

The lines in Judaism between love and respect are not at all stark. The two often go hand in hand. As a midrash imagines God saying to the Jewish people, "What do I ask of you? That you should love one another, and treat one another with respect [honor one another]."[103] I'd suggest, in fact, that there is often a slippage in Jewish thinking between what is required by respect and what is required by love. It is striking, for example, that whereas some Jewish thinkers see the obligation to greet others warmly as a manifestation of the respect we owe them, others see it as an expression of the love we should have for them.[104]

Moreover, if we take seriously the idea that loving our neighbor involves doing for them what we would want them to do for us, then treating others with respect can be seen as a form of loving them.[105] Indeed, Maimonides writes that part of what it means to love each and every Jew as we love ourselves is to protect their honor just as they themselves protect it.[106]

If both love and respect carry positive obligations, and if there is a slippage between them, then what differentiates them? We can start by saying, I think, that whatever respect requires, love requires more (love always intensifies what is expected of us). Respect may require us to greet someone but it alone does not require us to want them to have everything that we do (recall our discussion of Nahmanides on neighbor love from chapter 5). To return to a point that I made in chapter 6, one could argue that we owe respect to everyone simply because they are human but we owe love only to the smaller subset of people who form our own people and community.

Love requires more than respect—never less. In other words, love includes respect but goes beyond it; without respect, we might worry, love can be "paternalistic or otherwise invasive."[107] It may be useful to underscore that there are (at least) two different types of respect: respect for human beings as such and respect for people based on evaluative criteria.[108] I respect Sarah for being a virtuoso violinist and David for being the kindest person I know; I respect the warmhearted saint much more than I do the cold-blooded murderer. Respect of this kind might be called admiration. But it is the former type that I am concerned with here. Love without evaluative respect is possible (I can love my friend even if I have long ago stopped respecting the decisions she makes) but love without basic respect for the other's status as a person is not. In contrast, respect need not necessarily include love (I can and must respect you as a human being even if I actively dislike you).

A Kantian philosopher might worry that respect without love makes for excessive aloofness.[109] But as we've seen, a Jewish vision of respect contains significant elements of human warmth within it—we can't remain all that aloof if we take seriously the obligation to greet everyone warmly and to wear a smile on our faces. Indeed, given the slippage between love and respect we might even say that Jewish respect contains glimmers of love within it.[110] If that is right, then perhaps we can say that love intensifies what is already there in less developed form in respect.

THE VIRTUE OF CARING ABOUT DIGNITY

The philosopher Adam Pelser has introduced the idea that respect for human dignity is its own distinctive virtue; as he explains it, "A deep concern for and appreciation of . . . the value of human persons as such . . . lies at the heart of the virtue of respect for human dignity."[111] I am sympathetic to Pelser's view, and as I hope this chapter has shown, I think one can make a good case that Jewish sources agree. To have the virtue of respect for dignity, I would argue, is to care about human dignity with every fiber of one's being, to strive to affirm it in ways both large and small. To take Jewish ethics seriously is to understand that holding the door for the person behind you and advocating for human rights for people far away are on the same spectrum; both are ways of enacting the truth of human dignity in a world in which it is so often trodden and trampled upon.

Just as I have argued that love and compassion in their ideal forms include an affective, emotional dimension, I would make much the same point about respect for dignity. Dignity, Rabbi Shlomo Wolbe writes, must be respected in both heart and deed.[112] As Pelser puts it, "The virtue of respect for human dignity will be incomplete without a disposition to *feel* respect for all who are worthy of it"[113]—and as I've argued, all human beings are worthy of it simply by dint of being human. When we have the virtue of respect for dignity, we don't just cognitively judge that the other person is worthy of respect; we actively see, perceive, and experience the person as worthy both of the emotion of respect and of respectful treatment. Respect for human dignity shapes the way we see and experience the world and all human beings within it.[114]

Since I have written extensively about the Jewish ideal of integrating the inner and the outer, it seems worthwhile to quote Pelser at length:

> Just as we would not call a person ideally generous who gives to the needy begrudgingly or merely out of a sense of moral duty and not out of love and concern for the needy themselves, so too we should not think of a person as ideally respectful of human dignity if she treats others with respect outwardly, but feels condescension toward them or is indifferent toward their basic value as human persons. In addition to being disposed to treat others respectfully and to judge that they are worthy of respect (both emotional and behavioral), the person with the full virtue of respect for human dignity will be perceptually attuned to the dignity of others; that is, she will be disposed to perceive their dignity directly through her emotion of respect.[115]

What will a person who has this virtue be like? First, she "will be especially attuned to perceive violations of human dignity" and will be inclined to act to "protest and redress such violations." From a Jewish ethical perspective, this will include sensitivity both to the small indignities of everyday life—having the door close just as one approaches; being spoken to with unearned scorn; being seen as less than worthy of a greeting—and to the large-scale violations of basic human rights—not having enough food to eat or clean water to drink; having one's right to political representation thwarted; having one's freedom of religion stripped away. A person who has the virtue of respect for human dignity will be appalled by assaults on human dignity and will act both to ameliorate their effects and to prevent their recurrence. Conversely, as

Pelser points out, "The virtue of respect for human dignity . . . includes dispositions to experience joy, gratitude, and other positive emotions in response to victories in the cause of human dignity."[116] To attain this virtue is to place the dignity of others at the very center of our lives, our consciousness, and our commitments.

8

LOVING THE STRANGER

The Bible's Moral Revolution

ASK MANY JEWS whom the Torah commands us to love and you will likely get two answers: God and our neighbor. But the Torah in fact commands three loves: love of God (Deuteronomy 6:5), love of neighbor (Leviticus 19:18), and love of the stranger (*ger*). Strikingly, of the three loves only love of the *ger* is repeated twice (Leviticus 19:34 and Deuteronomy 10:19), seemingly for emphasis.

According to most scholars, by *ger*, commonly rendered as "stranger," "sojourner," "alien," or "foreigner," the Torah refers to a non-Israelite resident of the land who has no family or clan to look after him, and who is therefore vulnerable to social and economic exploitation.[1] Other scholars insist that a *ger* need not be a non-Israelite, and suggest that at least some of the time the term *ger* may refer to a native Israelite who has been dislocated for one reason or another; on their account the key point is that the stranger is "a vulnerable person from outside the core family."[2] Precise definitions of the *ger* are a matter of ongoing debate, but for our purposes we'll assume that at least some were in fact immigrants. If, as we've seen, loving our neighbor means loving our fellow Israelite, then love of the *ger* pushes our love outward, to the foreigner who resides among us. Loving members of our own community can be difficult enough, but we are asked for more: to love the stranger like a neighbor.

The Torah is not unique in its concern for the defenseless. All over the ancient Near East we find evidence of concern for the widow, the orphan, and the impoverished. But rarely, if ever, do we find the stranger included in such lists outside of the Torah.[3] The Torah extends our concern for the widow and the orphan, who are vulnerable members of our own society, to include the stranger, the foreigner who is similarly vulnerable.[4] Despite not being part of the kin group, and therefore of the "in group," the stranger is to be treated not only justly—itself a radical enough obligation—but also with love and solicitous concern. The mandate to love the stranger thus enacts a major moral revolution: we are commanded not to just love *our* vulnerable but to love *the* vulnerable, whether they are "our own" or not.

FROM EXODUS TO LEVITICUS TO DEUTERONOMY: RAISING THE STAKES

The book of Exodus admonishes the people: "You shall not oppress a stranger (*ger*), for you know the feelings of the stranger,[5] having yourselves been strangers in the land of Egypt" (Exodus 23:9).[6] The Torah's charge is based on an urgent demand for empathy: since *you know what it feels like* to be a stranger, you must never abuse the stranger.

Leviticus begins by reiterating the prohibition on mistreating the stranger—"When a stranger resides with you in your land, you shall not wrong him"—but it goes significantly further, laying down a positive mandate, and a stunningly radical one at that: "The stranger who resides with you shall be to you as one of your native-born; you shall love him as yourself, for you were strangers in the land of Egypt: I the Lord am your God" (Leviticus 19:33–34). Not oppressing the foreigners living among us is one thing; actively loving them is obviously a far more intense demand.

Note well: the obligation not to oppress the stranger does not actually *derive* from memory or historical experience. If it did, we could imagine someone claiming that since she has never experienced oppression, she remains free to mistreat whomever she wants—a preposterous claim on its face. Memory itself does not generate the obligation not to prey on the stranger; rather, it amplifies and intensifies obligations that are always present regardless of what has or has not happened to us (or our people) in the past.[7] The prohibition on oppressing the stranger is a basic moral obligation felt more keenly as a result of Israel's long period of vulnerability (amplification); the obligation to love and seek the well-being of the stranger, which goes beyond basic, universal moral requirements, on the other hand, grows from Israel's experience and the empathy it elicits in us (intensification).[8]

Deuteronomy subtly takes all this another step further: "For the Lord your God is God of gods and Lord of lords, the great, the mighty, and the awesome God, who shows no favor and takes no bribe, but upholds the cause of the fatherless and the widow, and loves the stranger, providing him with food and clothing. You too must love the stranger, for you were strangers in the land of Egypt" (Deuteronomy 10:17–19). The obligation to love the stranger, which we already saw in Leviticus, is repeated in Deuteronomy, but with a crucial difference: here, the obligation for Israel to love the stranger is interwoven with an affirmation that the God of Israel loves the stranger. In other words, loving the stranger is a form of "walking in God's ways," or imitating God. Just as God "loves the stranger" (10:18), so also must we (10:19). Deuteronomy presents a potent challenge. If you want to love God, love those whom God loves: love those who are vulnerable to exploitation and abuse. Deuteronomy thus gives us two distinct but intertwined reasons for this core commitment of Jewish ethics: we must love the stranger both because of who God is and because of what we ourselves have been through.

Exodus teaches us the baseline requirement: not to oppress the stranger. Leviticus magnifies the demand: not only must we not oppress the stranger, we must actively love him.[9] And Deuteronomy raises the stakes even higher: loving the stranger is a crucial form of "walking in God's ways."

Deuteronomy subtly makes another startling theological claim. We are told that God loves the stranger and "provides him with food and clothing." But how does God go about doing that? By commanding *us* to love the stranger. We are the means by which God expresses God's love for the stranger.[10] We serve as God's agents and emissaries; we serve as God's hands. "God's love, we deliver."

Immediately preceding the command to love the stranger in Deuteronomy is another charge. As part of entering into relationship with God, the people are told: "Circumcise the foreskin of your hearts and stiffen your necks no more" (10:16). For the Bible, a circumcised heart is the opposite of a stiffened neck. To circumcise our hearts is to open them, to be genuinely receptive to God, and responsive to God's command.[11] How are circumcision of the heart and love of strangers connected? They appear together, the Bible scholar Daniel Carroll suggests, because love of strangers serves as "proof of a circumcised heart."[12] How do we show that we have truly opened our hearts to God? By loving those whom God loves—by loving the vulnerable stranger who lives among us.

LEGAL PROTECTION

Love for the stranger is core to God's vision for Israelite society. And yet as important as cultivating love for the stranger is, the Torah is not content to let the fate of the stranger be contingent on the generosity of the native-born.[13] Emotions, and even existential commitments rooted in emotions, can be notoriously fleeting—we feel them strongly one day and then cannot seem to access them at all the next. Moreover, we tend to be much better at caring for those who are similar to us than for those whom we see as other. So the Torah turns to law to establish the stranger's status and ensure his protection.

As a safeguard against exploitative employers, Deuteronomy instructs that the day laborer is to be paid before sunset each day; crucially, it includes the stranger in these protections.[14] The Torah also enjoins that the stranger may partake of some of Israelite society's most important social benefits. The Israelites are expected to set aside some of the produce of trees and fields for the poverty-stricken to glean; in a similar vein, every third year the people are expected to tithe the produce of their fields for those in need. The stranger is included in both of these provisions.[15]

The stranger is also invited to participate in Israel's religious life. Provided he circumcise himself,[16] the stranger may take part in the celebration of Pesah (Passover), and even make his own sacrifice;[17] like the native-born, he must also eat no leaven on the holiday.[18] He is included in Yom Kippur.[19] And like native Israelites, he must observe the Sabbath[20] (which means, among other things, that others may not force him to work).[21]

Although my focus in this chapter is on the responsibilities of the native-born toward the stranger rather than the reverse, it's worth noting that the stranger was obligated to keep God's "laws and rules" (Leviticus 18:26)[22] and to be present when the Torah was read aloud to the whole people every seventh year (Deuteronomy 31:10–13). This means that just as the stranger was protected by the law, so also was he obligated to observe it, and to be aware of his obligations. As Carroll explains, "The law assumes that there is movement on the part of the [stranger] toward the host culture (Israel): learning its ways and its language, and respecting its laws and taboos."[23] The Torah adjures Israel to love and protect the stranger and to include him in various aspects of communal and national life, but it also expects at least some degree of assimilation on the stranger's part.

CONTEMPORARY RELEVANCE?

What about now? Does Jewish law still charge us to protect and love the vulnerable immigrant? After all, for the past two thousand years, the central meaning of *ger* in Jewish law has been a convert to Judaism, not a sojourner in a foreign land. Over the years I have been told by some critics that it is a "falsification" of the Jewish tradition not to emphasize that normatively speaking, a *ger* is a convert rather than an immigrant.

It's important to understand that Rabbinic tradition knew full well that a *ger* in the Torah is not a convert. After all, the Torah repeatedly reminds the Israelites that they were *gerim* in the land of Egypt, and they were obviously not converts to Egyptian religion during their long sojourn there. Not surprisingly, a variety of traditional Jewish Bible commentators are explicit that the contextual meaning (*peshat*) of *ger* in the Torah is "immigrant" rather than "convert."[24]

Why did the meaning of the term evolve from immigrant to convert?[25] In a time when Jews went from ruling to being ruled, the imperatives around treatment of the *ger* could easily have become a dead letter. The Jews simply did not control a land in which they could decide whether and how to welcome *gerim*. If anything, under foreign rule in antiquity, the Jews themselves *were* the vulnerable *gerim*. For the biblical mandates to carry any normative meaning at all in a radically new context, it only made sense to apply them to people who sought to join the "ethnic-religious" community of Israel rather than immigrating to a particular "geographical-political" area.[26] Thus a *ger* became a convert.[27]

That transformation took place quite a long time ago. After more than two thousand years of Jewish law in which *ger* has been understood to mean convert, should the original meaning of *ger* as stranger carry any normative weight? Consider: the Torah prohibits us from "placing a stumbling block before the blind" (Leviticus 19:14). Jewish law focuses almost exclusively on a metaphorical meaning of this verse: not to trick or take advantage of someone who is "blind" in this matter or that. But even though the metaphorical meaning becomes dominant over time, the literal meaning, one rarely discussed in Jewish legal texts, remains fully in force: one may not place a literal stumbling block before a person who literally cannot see.[28] In light of this example and others like it, Zvi Zohar, a respected historian of Jewish law, has shown that as a rule, even when Jewish law has traditionally interpreted a verse differently from what its plain sense suggests, that plain sense continues to have normative legal standing alongside the later meaning. In light of this, Zohar insists that in the modern-day State of Israel (the context in and for which he is writing), there is a biblical-level (*de'oraita*) obligation to treat the stranger-immigrant with love and concern.[29]

BUILDING A RADICAL ALTERNATIVE TO EGYPT

The memory of extreme vulnerability is at the very heart of Jewish identity. "The memory of oppression included life under a brutal legal system of a people, whose gods and religion legitimized the exploitation of immigrants and their labor."[30] Jews never tire of telling and retelling the story: we were oppressed by a tyrant and then liberated by God. The experience of enslavement followed by exodus shapes our understanding of God, and, no less, of our own responsibilities in the world. God is the champion of the oppressed, and we, having tasted the bitterness of oppression, are bidden never to become oppressors. Again and again, the Bible insists that "God's people must not show any sign that they are becoming like the Egyptians . . . in how they treat others, whether fellow Israelites or aliens living among them."[31] We are summoned to create a radical alternative to Egypt, an "anti-Egypt," if you will, a society in which the weak and defenseless are protected rather than exploited, loved rather than demeaned. The Torah as a whole can be seen as "an act of social imagination that plays out an alternative way of organizing reality."[32]

To take one of the most powerful examples in the Torah, consider the biblical law of the fugitive slave.[33] Ancient Near Eastern law codes did everything they could to hinder runaway slaves in their pursuit of freedom. When a slave ran away, he was subject to extreme penalties, sometimes including death. One who harbored a runaway slave was subject to severe punishment, and conversely, one who returned him to his master was richly rewarded. Deuteronomy turns all of this on its head: "You shall not hand over to his master a slave who seeks refuge with you from his master. He shall live with you in any place he may choose among the settlements in your midst, wherever he pleases; you must not oppress him" (Deuteronomy 23:16–17). Biblical law permits escaped slaves to settle anywhere in the land they wish and explicitly forbids Israelites from returning or extraditing them to the lands from which they have fled.

Why is the Torah so sensitive to the plight of slaves fleeing their master? The people of Israel are themselves a nation of runaway slaves worshiping a God who liberates slaves. Here again, our ethical sensibilities are to be guided both by what we've been through and by who God is. We were fugitive slaves pursued by an almost unimaginably hostile master—and God refused to return us. If we keep this in mind and at heart, "another person in bondage [becomes] a brother or sister, bound in relationship of care or protection."[34] Remembering the bitterness of slavery and the joy of liberation, we commit to siding with the slave and helping him achieve his freedom.

LEARNING EMPATHY FROM OUR PAST— AND OUR PRESENT

But the Jewish people's sense of being vulnerable strangers goes back even further than the time of their enslavement in Egypt. As the book of Genesis narrates the stories of the patriarchs, they "become in effect a continuing story of living as resident aliens in a strange land."[35] In pursuit of food in a time of famine, Abraham is forced to "sojourn" (*lagur*) in Egypt.[36] Abraham is a stranger in the land of Canaan, as are Isaac and Jacob.[37] And before he can become the leader of Israel, Moses too endures a period of being "a stranger in a strange land" (Exodus 2:22).[38]

Not content merely to portray the patriarchs as strangers, the Bible deftly evokes the precariousness of their lives in foreign lands. When Abraham arrives in Egypt, defenseless and frightened for his life, he makes the morally ambiguous decision to pass off his wife as his sister, accentuating "the ambiguity of life as a resident alien and the compromises into which such an existence may lead," even for those who are (otherwise?) considered righteous.[39] The basic ingredients of the life of a stranger are all on display here: "The necessity of immigrating in order to sustain life in the face of the exigencies of one's situation, the apparent ease with which the immigrants can be subject to the domination of the leaders of the land in which they are forced to dwell, and the tendency, which can be perceived as a necessity, to accommodate to the situation into which one is forced to go."[40] Intense vulnerability leads to impossible choices.

In a particularly poignant moment, Genesis brings us face-to-face with the unceasing sense of exclusion and peril confronted by the sojourner. Attempting to protect his houseguests from a cruel mob, Abraham's nephew Lot pleads with the people of Sodom, "I beg you, my brothers (*ahai*), do not commit such a crime" (Genesis 19:7). Utterly unmoved, the Sodomites respond with disdain: "This fellow came here as a stranger (*ger*), and already he acts the ruler!" (19:9). Lot assumes (hopes?) that the Sodomites among whom he lives see him as a brother, but he is cruelly reminded of his lowly status. Both Lot the stranger and the strangers to whom he has opened his home find themselves in grave danger.[41] Hostility raging, the people of Sodom remind him: You will never be one of us! Directing venom at the outsider may well be the defining characteristic of the biblical Sodomite.[42]

The experience of being a stranger is thus built into the very cultural DNA of the Jewish people. To be a Jew, according to these texts, is to remember what it's like to be vulnerable and susceptible to exploitation—and to strive to grow in compassion in response.

Even after the people are redeemed from slavery and brought into the land, God tells them that at the deepest level they will always remain strangers. Instructing them that the land God gives them must not be sold in perpetuity (the original owners must be given a chance to redeem the land that had belonged to their ancestors), God explains that "the Land is Mine; you are but strangers (*gerim*) and residents with Me" (Leviticus 25:23).[43] In other words, being a stranger is not just a historical memory from the past; it is an existential reality that is always also true in the present.[44] Living in the land, the people remain dependent on God's mercy and goodwill. One of the Bible's key hopes, it seems, is that an awareness of their own vulnerability and dependence on *God* will render the Israelites keenly sensitive to the needs of those who are vulnerable and dependent on *them*.[45]

THE NEED FOR MORAL IMAGINATION

The lesson—having been strangers in Egypt, the Jewish people are forbidden to oppress the stranger—is so familiar and so often cited that it's easy to miss just how radical it is. The Torah could have responded to the memory of affliction quite differently, saying, Since you were tyrannized and exploited and no one did anything to help you, you don't owe anything to anyone; how dare anyone ask anything of you? Might that not have been a natural response? But the Torah chooses the opposite path: Since you were exploited and oppressed, you must never be among those who exploit and oppress. You must remember *what it feels like* to be a stranger, and the empathy you muster must intensify your commitment to siding with the weak and vulnerable against those who would harm them.

How are we, readers living three millennia after the experiences evoked by these verses, to relate to them? To be an heir to the Jewish story, I think, is to engage in a double act of moral imagination. First, we reenact the story and make it our own. It is not (only) our forefathers who were slaves in Egypt, but we ourselves; as the Passover Haggadah puts it, "In every generation, a person is obligated to see herself as if she herself had gone out from Egypt." But making the Exodus story our own is only the beginning of the spiritual work. Once we "remember" that we ourselves were there, we must allow that memory to teach us empathy: we were sojourners, we know just how wretched that experience can be, and so we commit to not oppressing—more than that, we commit to loving—the sojourners among us.

The observance of Passover presents a powerful ethical-spiritual opportunity in this regard. At the seder(s), we reenact the journey from slavery to freedom and thereby (re)immerse ourselves and our children in the foundational story of the Jewish people. But what if we really pushed ourselves harder—what if we took time, either at the seder or during the days that follow, to ask: Yesterday we were strangers and today we are free. How would our lives be different if we took the ethical implications of that transformation seriously? How would we and our families live differently? How would our communities conduct themselves differently? The challenge is not just to celebrate Passover but to internalize its lessons.

DEMOCRATIZATION OF RESPONSIBILITY

Throughout the ancient Near East, societies expressed the expectation that the king would protect the downtrodden.[46] In places like Egypt and Mesopotamia, the king was seen as the image of the god the society worshiped and thus as that god's "representative and intermediary." If a god wanted the widow and the orphan protected from those who would abuse them, it was the king, charged with "mediat[ing] divine blessing to the earthly realm," who was tasked with being their earthly protector.[47] As we've seen, Genesis, with its dramatic insistence that each and every human being without exception is created in the image of God, represents a radical democratization of ancient Near Eastern royal ideology: it is not just *the king* who is an image of God, it is *all of us*, every last one of us. Or, to put it differently, Genesis maintains that we are, all of us, kings and queens. But democratizing royal ideology means democratizing moral responsibility too: if kings and queens must care for the vulnerable and the oppressed, and if we are all kings and queens, then the whole community is responsible for the fate of those who are vulnerable to exploitation.[48] In more contemporary terms, you and I, and not just our political leaders, are answerable for how the weakest members of our society are treated. We remain, always, responsible.[49]

What if any contemporary political implications should all this have?

I often hear some American Jews say that they "don't want to hear about politics in the synagogue." On the one hand, I understand and for the most part share their resistance to synagogue services becoming just another vehicle for partisan politics; there is something sullying about that. Yet on the other hand, the yearning to completely banish pressing political questions from our services amounts to an attempt to exile God from the synagogue. The God of the Torah demands justice and cares for the vulnerable and downtrodden—and summons us to do the same. To wrestle with God's word is to ask ourselves—even and especially when it is uncomfortable—what it is that God asks of us in the present moment. So Torah must have something important to say about contemporary issues.

So what *does* the Torah tell us about contemporary immigration policy, for example? It is difficult (and usually impossible, I'd say) to draw one-to-one correspondences between ancient texts and contemporary policies;[50] we should be highly skeptical of people who presume to do just that, whether they are on the political right or the political left. Good, well-intentioned people can and do disagree about the implications of Torah for the present day.

But there are crucial lessons that I think we can learn from the texts we've seen. Some key examples: (1) The demonization and dehumanization of immigrants and foreigners is an abomination, and an assault on biblical ethics. You cannot call yourself a religious person and hate those whom God loves. (Again: you can disagree in good faith about how best to help the defenseless but you cannot simply dismiss the mandate to assist them.) (2) Be careful about assuming that the immigrant comes with belligerent intentions. The word *ger* is connected to the Hebrew root meaning "to be hostile."[51] Yet the Torah wants us to love the *ger*, not hate him. In other words, we are taught to love the one we too easily tar as an enemy. To be absolutely clear, sometimes a perceived enemy really is an enemy and needs to be treated as such. The Torah does not preach naivete but it does challenge us to overcome prejudice and expand our circle of concern. (3) Immigrants should be cared for but also protected by law; we can't rely on empathy alone. Societies need to ensure that the vulnerable are protected even when, for whatever reason, those who are more powerful than they harbor them ill will.[52]

SHAPING THE MEMORIES THAT SHAPE US

As we've seen, we face momentous choices about what meaning to make of our suffering. This is true for the Jewish people as a whole but it is no less true for each of us as individuals.

The Torah's explicit appeal is to the Jewish people as a whole, and to our shared memory of oppression and degradation. But Jewish spiritual texts also insist that each of us should personalize the story of Exodus: we are asked to identify our own Egypts and learn to leave them behind.[53] Along similar lines, I'd suggest that we ought to personalize the biblical mandate to remember as well. Each of us is obligated to remember times when we have been "strangers," vulnerable to abuse and exploitation at the hands of those who held power over us. Such experiences are blessedly rare for some people. Tragically, they are part of the daily bread of others. From these experiences, the Torah tells us, we are to learn compassion and kindness.

Here too the mandate is far from obvious. Thinking back on the ways we have suffered, we may respond by wanting to make sure that no one else has to endure what we did, but we may just as easily feel entitled to be indifferent. If you had been through what I've been through, we hear ourselves saying, you would understand that I don't owe anybody anything. Worse yet, consciously or not, we may grant ourselves license to behave as badly as our former oppressors did. Although it may be tempting to assume that "good people" learn empathy from their afflictions, while "bad people" learn hostility and xenophobia, the truth is usually far more complicated: many of us have both responses at the same time. We all have many internal voices and are pulled in many different directions. As Leon Wieseltier once remarked, "The Holocaust enlarged our Jewish hearts, and it shrunk them." Fully aware that we may well have both impulses within us, the Torah challenges us to nurture and cultivate compassion and to prevent rage from becoming the animating principle of our lives.

The relationship between memory and ethics is extremely complex. As Miroslav Volf writes, "Memory of wrong suffered is from a moral standpoint *dangerously underdetermined* . . . It is possible to draw rather divergent, even conflicting lessons from the same experience of mistreatment."[54] What we learn will be determined not by memory itself but by "a broader set of convictions about the nature of reality and our responsibilities within it."[55] For the recently redeemed Israelites, the moral and spiritual goal was to become like the God who had liberated them rather than the Pharaoh who had enslaved them,[56] and thus to learn kindness rather than callousness from their suffering. The pivotal point is that there is nothing automatic about this process. "We are not just shaped *by* memories; we ourselves *shape* the memories that shape us."[57] Memory as the Torah understands it is anything but a passive activity. We are who we are in no small part because of how we choose to let our memories affect us.[58]

It is difficult to overstate this point: memory can be redemptive, but it can also be toxic. Even so impassioned an advocate of memory as Elie Wiesel admits that in our world, memory, which, he insists, "should be a sanctuary, has [instead] become almost an abomination." During the Bosnian War of the 1990s, he says, "it is memory that [was] a problem. It's because they remember what happened to their parents or their sister or their grandparents that they hate each other."[59] Sometimes the memories went back much further in time: during that horrific war, Serbian nationalists regularly referred to a military grudge dating back six hundred years! By tying the memory of enslavement so tightly to an ethical responsibility—you were strangers and you know what it feels like, therefore do not oppress—the Torah resists the potentially noxious side of memory: the insistence that since we were victims once, we are always and everywhere victims.[60] On the contrary, says the Torah: victims all too often become victimizers,[61] and memory not infrequently yields moral blindness instead of empathy. In the starkest possible terms—"love the stranger!"—the Torah attempts to marshal memory in the service of love and justice.

We all carry wounds—experiences of abuse, or deprivation, or vulnerability. If we do not work to heal them—for many of us, this can be the task of a lifetime—the bruises we bear can render us heedless of other people's pain; after all, we are too busy with our own. In more extreme cases, these bruises can make us hungry for revenge or lead us—consciously or not—to inflict unspeakable harm on innocent people. Think about how often parents who were abused as children inflict some version of their own suffering upon their children. I'd suggest that we hear Exodus's words, "for you know the feelings of the stranger," as a kind of mandate:[62] we have to bring our own "estrangement" to consciousness in order to weaken the impulse to do unto others what has been done unto us—or, more moderately, to soften the barriers we erect so that other people's suffering simply fails to register with us. As Albert Camus writes, "We all carry within us places of exile, our crimes, our ravages; our task is not to unleash them on the world; it is to transform them in ourselves and others."[63]

When it comes to our inner lives, the problem is that what we don't know *will* hurt us—and other people too. As a Buddhist teacher puts it, "Whatever you push away is going to bounce back at you; it is nature's law. Whatever you run from becomes your shadow,"[64] making yourself and the people around you miserable. Conversely, when we learn to open to our own suffering, it becomes much easier to open to other people's too. "When I acknowledge my own pain, I am much less squeamish about drawing nearer to yours."[65] This is why psychotherapy and meditation can—let me underscore *can*—be religious mandates: they have the potential to restore our freedom and deepen our capacity for empathy and care. This is not easy work: confronting our own suffering can be excruciating—and it can also be liberating. Moral growth often requires immense psychological courage. But trite as it may sound, being kind to ourselves and being kind to others really are inextricably linked.

I was working as a rabbi in Boston when the horrific scandal of Catholic priests sexually abusing children came fully to light. Nearly everything about that story was devastating and unbearable, but one of the most distressing (but frequently overlooked) aspects of the whole sordid affair was how many of the abusers had themselves been abused as children—often by other priests. Freudians would no doubt consider this a case of repetition compulsion. From a moral perspective, what was so excruciating was to witness the all-too-familiar tragedy of victims becoming victimizers, of those who had been prey becoming predators themselves. Unhealed traumas wrecked the lives of those priests, and of thousands of innocent children entrusted to their care. To avoid any misunderstanding: I am not in any way suggesting that their past sufferings somehow exonerate these priests from their crimes. Quite the contrary, their grotesque misconduct testifies to just how urgently necessary it is to bring our suffering to awareness. Knowing our wounds, and working to ease them, is not supererogatory (meaning that it would be nice if we did it, but we don't really have to); it is a fundamental requirement of the spiritual life, and of moral responsibility.

On both the personal and political levels, we make choices about memory; in doing so, we reclaim our freedom. People who have been oppressed—whether politically or interpersonally—often feel imprisoned by their past sufferings, so much so that those sufferings feel like they are still taking place in the present. To turn memory into empathy, to allow suffering to teach us love, is to recover our sense of agency, to insist that despite what we have been through we still possess the ability to be the authors of our own lives.[66] But we do more than that: Having endured an assault on justice, we reaffirm that a commitment to justice remains possible, indeed urgently necessary. And having been violated by hate, we insist that love is still possible.

9

MUST WE LOVE
OUR ENEMIES TOO?

THE TORAH COMMANDS us to love our neighbors as ourselves. But what about our enemies—must we love them too? Is love of enemies possible, and, for that matter, is it desirable?

The word "enemy" can conjure up many different things: a professional rival, perhaps; someone who has deeply hurt or disappointed us in a personal relationship; someone who is, or whom we perceive as, actively hostile toward us; someone who evinces disdain for a group we're a part of, whether religious, racial, ethnic, political, or what have you; or someone who is resolutely committed to harming us and the fellow members of our group. This is obviously a very broad spectrum, from a friend with whom we fell out to a malicious genocidaire. Must we love any of them? Must we love them all? *May* we love them all?

I readily confess that I find these questions almost impossibly difficult both philosophically and emotionally. On the one hand, I am keenly aware that grudges are like acid for those who hold them. As a child of European refugees, I saw how post-Holocaust anger almost consumed my mother at times; her rage took an enormous toll on her and on the people around her (myself very much included). Yet on the other hand, I can't fathom what it would mean to recommend (let alone demand) that people like my mother, whose entire worlds were destroyed in the Nazi onslaught, forgive—let alone love—their enemies. I confess that part of me finds the very thought of prescribing forgiveness in such cases presumptuous and even outrageous. I want to be clear: it's not just that I find the idea of suggesting that survivors forgive their tormentors *psychologically impossible*; I think it may also be *ethically problematic*.

Yet tempting as it is—*natural* as it is in some ways—to take Hitler as a test case, I see it as a mistake to do so. I think often about what the journalist Ron Rosenbaum refers to as the *"argumentum ad Hitlerum,"* "the resort to Hitler to end discussion on nearly everything from capital punishment ('Well, *Hitler* deserved it, didn't he?') to vegetarianism ('It didn't improve *Hitler's* character, did it?')."[1] The simple truth is that most people are not Hitler; it should hardly need saying that there is a big difference between someone we personally dislike or detest (or who dislikes or detests us) and one of history's most murderous villains. So let's think about the former without getting too distracted by the latter.

HEALING THE BREACH BETWEEN PEOPLE

"When you encounter your enemy's ox or donkey wandering," says the book of Exodus, "you must take it back to him. When you see the donkey of your enemy lying under its burden and would refrain from raising it, you must nevertheless raise it with him" (Exodus 23:4–5).[2]

It's possible to read these laws in a somewhat minimalist fashion: no matter how much you dislike someone, or how much they dislike you, these laws could be saying, you are still obligated to do the good and decent thing in your interactions with them. This may be a minimalist interpretation, but even this is not always easy to live up to; after all, we often convince ourselves that we bear no moral obligations to people we dislike.

In a closely related way, it's also possible to interpret these laws as focused on maintaining basic norms that hold the social fabric together: if you see something that obviously belongs to someone else, you have to return it to them, regardless of your personal feelings toward them, or theirs toward you; similarly, if you see that their animal is in trouble, you have to assist them, again regardless of your personal feelings toward them. Without a commitment to such behavior, society is in very real danger of falling apart.

But a third, very different interpretation is possible: if you see your enemy's animal lost or in trouble, you have an opportunity to heal the breach that has opened between you. These laws are thus aimed at restoring ruptured relationships. Whereas the first two approaches focus on ensuring that we *do the right thing*, the third one goes further, seeking also to make us *feel the right way* and thus to reestablish relations.[3]

Readers of these laws about lost or overburdened donkeys have often been bothered by the cases as presented. Given the prohibition on "hating our kin in our heart" (Leviticus 19:17), how can we have enemies at all? Some interpreters assume that these laws address those rare situations that we will look at more closely below, where, according to traditional Jewish law, it seems that we are actually obligated to hate someone.[4] Others, though, don't find the verse problematic at all. Hating other people may be prohibited, they say, but in real life it still happens. In order for law to be relevant, it must address people as we are, not (just) people as we ideally would be. Accordingly, one Talmudic sage avers that the donkey laws deal with a case in which someone has done something to hurt or upset us and has thus become a "temporary enemy."[5]

Might the Torah be concerned to mitigate our hate in such cases? The early interpretive Aramaic translation of the Bible known as Targum Onkelos seems to think so: "When you see your enemy's donkey fallen beneath its load and would withhold from taking it up, *you should let go of what is in your heart about him* and unload with him."[6] One could argue that Onkelos's concern is only that we put down our hostile feelings just long enough to do what is expected of us,[7] but it's likely that his intentions go deeper: we should take this opportunity to let go of our animosity altogether.

Of course, the biblical text does not explicitly say anything at all about letting go of the antipathy we feel for our enemy; that's what makes the first two interpretations, which focus exclusively on getting us to do what is right, both possible and plausible. Yet many interpreters follow in the path laid out by Onkelos. As the modern commentator Nehama Leibowitz (1905–1997), for example, notes, "The Targum expound[s] the spirit of the text even if [it does] not reflect its surface reading."[8] On this interpretation, although the text does not straightforwardly say so, it endeavors to reshape our inner world, to dissipate the hatred that is in our hearts.[9]

A midrash imagines a scenario where these laws achieve their goals. Two donkey drivers who detest one another are traveling along the same road, and one of the donkeys falls down. The driver whose donkey is still standing sees what has happened but does not stop to help. Yet he soon pauses to reflect: "It is written in the Torah that 'When you see the donkey of your enemy . . . you must nevertheless raise it with him.'" He immediately goes back to help the other man with the load, whereupon the latter begins to ruminate: "This man is apparently my friend, but I didn't know it." The two of them go to an inn where they eat and drink together and become genuine friends. A Talmudic sage comments, "What led them to make up? The fact that one of them looked into the Torah. This is what the book of Psalms means when, addressing God, it says that 'You have established equity, You worked justice and righteousness in Jacob [that is, in the people of Israel]'" (Psalm 99:4).[10]

The point of the story, I think, is to emphasize that the purpose of the law is not just to ensure that minimum standards of good behavior are upheld; the intent of the law, rather, is to bring wholeness (shalom) to relationships, to restore human connections that have been fractured.[11] More than that, the law aims to elicit genuine human goodness from the people it addresses. It reshapes the interactions between these two men so that they can see one another in a positive light and discover, or recall, one another's goodness.

A modern Bible scholar, Rabbi Benno Jacob (1862–1945), interprets the laws in the same spirit. "At the beginning," he says, "such a venture [of one enemy assisting another] would be done in silence, but then some exchange will be necessary for the effort to succeed; that will break the ice and finally the enemy would have to express thanks, which may very well build a bridge of friendship, so that they could leave not as enemies but as brothers. Not common need brought them together, but danger to one, which led the other to be helpful."[12] What commences in tentativeness concludes in camaraderie.

Does all this amount to a mandate to love our enemies? Rabbi Jacob, who finds in these verses "instruction in the practical aspects of love of neighbor,"[13] appears to think so. On his interpretation, the text demands that we act lovingly toward our enemy, and more, that we open ourselves to the possibility that genuine care and goodwill will emerge, or reemerge, between us.

Some interpreters agree that the donkey laws are about love of enemies, but they interpret such love more minimalistically. Thus, for example, in commenting on our verses, the Bible scholar Peter Enns declares that these laws "get close to the heart of the matter: treating all Israelites with love, whether one loves them or not."[14] Whereas Enns seems to interpret the idea of loving our neighbor as focused on action, Jacob turns our attention to the nexus of action and emotion—or, perhaps more precisely, to the ways that choosing to act in certain ways can lead to profound change in the ways we feel as well.

The divergence between these two interpretations brings us back to an issue we explored at length in chapter 5: in mandating us to love our neighbor, is the Torah concerned only with how we act toward others, or also with how we feel toward them? If, as we saw some interpreters maintain, the Torah's interest is exclusively in behavior, and love is therefore to be understood as an action, then it would seem reasonable to conclude that these laws about providing assistance do indeed push us to "love" our enemies. Yet if, as I've argued, the commandment to love our neighbor reaches beyond action to embrace emotions as well, then whether or not we take these laws about assistance to be demanding love of neighbor will depend on how we interpret them. On the first two approaches we've seen, according to which the laws are aimed at ensuring that we do the moral minimum and uphold the social fabric, the laws can be understood as demanding that we "do the right thing" and no more. Yet according to the third approach, which interprets the laws as inviting us to restore broken relationships, the laws should be understood as seeking to eliminate enmity and perhaps even elicit love—emotional love—for our enemies.

I sometimes imagine the two donkey drivers in this scene as having had a spat. Maybe they disagreed about some business matter, or perhaps one felt slighted by the other. What could have remained a tiff instead became a rift and eventually mushroomed into outright hostility. It's disconcerting to think how easily we can allow that to happen. Someone hurts us and the way we perceive them quickly changes. We start to see them as insensitive, then as bad, and utimately, perhaps, as alien and even monstrous. When the hurt feelings are mutual, the animus that develops often is too; sometimes the antagonism is intense even though we can barely remember how and why it first emerged. The story suggests that on occasion, at least, a simple gesture of kindness can deflate the balloon of mutual enmity. "You're not a horrible person," we think, "let alone a monster. You're just someone I had a disagreement with." Ill will dissipates, so that friendship, or at least cordiality, can re-emerge, which gives us a chance to fulfill a wonderful Rabbinic proverb: "Who is mighty? One who turns an enemy into a friend."[15] Heroism, it seems, consists not in willingness to start a fight but in eagerness to end one.

The laws we've been considering are paralleled in the book of Deuteronomy: "If you see your fellow's ox or sheep gone astray, do not ignore it; you must take it back to your fellow . . . If you see your fellow's donkey or ox fallen on the road, do not ignore it; you must help him raise it" (Deuteronomy 22:1, 4). The contrast between Exodus and Deuteronomy is striking: whereas the latter discusses "your fellow" (or, perhaps, "your brother"—*ahikha*), the former talks about "your enemy." Taken together, the texts can be understood to teach a powerful lesson: my enemy, too, is my brother. In coming face-to-face with him, Nahmanides (Ramban) writes, "Remember the brotherhood and forget the hatred."[16]

LETTING GO OF VENGEANCE

The book of Leviticus instructs us not "to take vengeance or bear a grudge" against one who hurts us (Leviticus 19:18), and the book of

Proverbs underscores the prohibition: "Do not say (*tomar*), 'I will requite evil'; put your hope in the Lord and [the Lord] will deliver you" (Proverbs 20:22).[17] Wounded by another, we may be tempted to retaliate—we may even feel a burning need to do so—but Proverbs recommends a different path: put aside retaliation and trust in God instead. The counsel of this proverb is not indifference to evil or injustice, but rather "trust in God's justice and . . . relinquishment of control over the timing and nature of judgment."[18] Vengeance may sometimes have its place, but "vengeance belongs to the Lord, not to the one who suffered wrong."[19] If anything, from the perspective of this verse one who takes justice into her own hands may thereby reveal a lack of faith in God's justice.[20]

Refusing retaliation is not tantamount to embracing passivity. While the verse in Proverbs does seem to affirm that ultimate justice depends on God, it does not prohibit using earthly, judicial means to redress wrongdoing.[21] Having been mistreated, we are permitted to protest and to seek justice—but we are forbidden from taking matters into our own hands.

Gersonides (Ralbag, 1288–1344) notes that the verse directs our attention to needing deliverance from our predicament, not to the fate of the one who seeks to do us harm. Gersonides insists that it is unbecoming of a person of faith to be plotting to hurt others, even (perhaps especially?) those who have hurt us. "This is not the way of a person of faith," he writes, "for he does not desire the doing of evil." Moreover, says Gersonides, we should not even ask God to harm those who harm us but pray "only that God should save [us]" because this and only this is what we truly need. Praying for others to suffer, let alone actively making them suffer, is simply not what a virtuous person does—and so it would be inappropriate at best for us to do so.[22]

Notice that the verse goes beyond prohibiting actively taking revenge and forbids even thinking or talking about doing so (the biblical Hebrew, *tomar*, "say," can just as easily be rendered "think"; we should not even think of taking vengeance). Here, then, is another example of Jewish texts reaching inward, making a claim not just on our actions but also on our inner worlds. Acts of revenge are prohibited, and revenge fantasies are problematic too.

As often in the Bible, there are countervailing voices as well. In Psalm 41, for example, the psalmist longs for the day when he can "repay" a former friend who has turned against him (Psalm 41:11). But in a remarkable display of exegetical boldness, a midrash utterly transforms the meaning of this verse to bring it into line with the proverb we have been discussing. When the psalmist says he wants to repay the evildoer, says the midrash, he means not that he wishes to repay evil with evil but rather that he wishes to repay evil with good! "Let me repay him good for the evil he did," the midrash imagines the psalmist saying, "and the Blessed Holy One will exact punishment from him."[23] The startling interpretive move is to take even verses like this one, which can be read as condoning the urge to hate and seek vengeance, and instead construe them as relinquishing those very urges.

REFUSING SCHADENFREUDE

Not only must we not exact (or dream of exacting) vengeance, several biblical verses teach, but we also must not delight in the downfall of those who have hurt us. "If your enemy falls, do not rejoice," says Proverbs; "if he trips, let your heart not exult, lest the Lord see it and be displeased, and avert His wrath from him" (Proverbs 24:17–18). It is difficult to know how to interpret this advice. On the one hand, one can interpret its second part as guided by less-than-noble motives. As the Bible scholar Kathleen Farmer explains, "The Lord might see your reaction and be displeased by it. Thus the saying as a whole is clearly self-serving. Do not gloat, because gloating might reverse your enemy's misfortune."[24] But the verse can also be understood very differently: one can interpret the second clause as insisting that "your glee may well be a more punishable sin than all the guilt of your enemy."[25] On this reading, the text emphatically rules out schadenfreude, smugness, and callous reveling in the sufferings of others. Although these verses say only that God will "avert God's wrath" from our enemy in response to our jubilation at her misfortune, they may be hinting that God will turn God's anger away from them *and toward us*.[26] After all, "gloating is what the wicked do."[27]

With the prohibition on schadenfreude, these verses reach inward to "condemn an unworthy feeling even when it does not lead to vengeance."[28] If this is right, then our verses provide still more support for my argument that Jewish ethics is focused not only on our actions but also on our emotions, and more generally, on the state of our inner world. As the Bible scholar Michael Fox observes in commenting on these verses, "Proverbs is concerned with the quality of [our] deepest and hidden thoughts and feelings, for they are the substance of character and determine deeds as well."[29]

The refusal to celebrate the downfall of our enemies, no matter how cruel, plays a significant role in the development of Jewish liturgy. It is customary on most Jewish holidays to recite the Hallel, a collection of psalms of praise and thanksgiving. Observing that during the festival of Sukkot Jews recite the entirety of the Hallel, whereas during much of the festival of Passover we recite only part of it, a midrash explains that we don't express full-throated joy on Passover "because of the death of the Egyptians . . . Why not? Because 'If your enemy falls, do not rejoice; if he trips, let your heart not exult.'"[30]

Here too some interpreters discern a "move[ment] in the direction of loving one's enemy."[31] This may well be too strong a reading: not delighting in another's suffering does not amount to loving them. What we do find in these verses, however, is a forceful denunciation of hatred and schadenfreude. It is not just that we may not act to hurt our enemies but also that we may not take (even purely internal) pleasure in their affliction.

When Job defends his character, he asks rhetorically and with great force, "Did I rejoice over my enemy's misfortune? Did I thrill because evil befell him?" (Job 31:29). The implicit answer, of course, is a resounding no, because, Job is convinced, good people do not revel in others' sufferings. But Job goes further, insisting that "I never let my palate sin by wishing his death in a curse" (31:30). Job admits that there is a certain appeal in seeing those who seek to hurt us be injured themselves; his mention of his palate "implies that the cursing of one's enemies was a dainty morsel, which Job never suffered himself to taste."[32] In other words, Job does not claim that he is untempted by schadenfreude; he insists, rather, that he is of solid enough character that he turns away from the debased pleasure it offers. Unless we are perfect saints, we may be tempted to take satisfaction in our enemy's setbacks, but some temptations are meant to be resisted. Crucially, Job declares that not only did he not rejoice in his enemy's downfall, he did not even allow himself to wish for it. Again, the biblical text turns inward, making a claim not just on how we treat other people but also on how we see and feel toward them.

Some interpreters suggest that Job "goes a step beyond" the obligation to love one's neighbor "in claiming [that] he has treated his enemy as a neighbor."[33] But treating our enemy as we would a neighbor may well represent a fulfillment of the mandate to love our neighbor rather than a reach beyond it. After all, the book of Leviticus does not say, "Love your neighbor as yourself—unless there is bad blood between you." Job may understand, in other words, that his enemy is nevertheless his neighbor.

To be sure, there are verses in the Bible that do "acknowledge and even encourage Schadenfreude by people and God—particularly when the wicked stumble."[34] Thus, for example, we learn that "when the righteous prosper the city exults; when the wicked perish there are shouts of joy"[35] (Proverbs 11:10), and that when "the wicked schemes against the righteous . . . The Lord laughs at him, for [the Lord] knows that his day will come" (Psalm 37:12–13).[36] Yet in a spirit reminiscent of the verses we've been considering, a biblical proverb emphatically declares that "one who rejoices over another's misfortune will not go unpunished" (Proverbs 17:5), and the author of Psalm 35 asserts that when those who had sought to harm him were themselves brought low, not only did he not celebrate, he actively mourned over them: "When they were ill, my dress was sackcloth, I kept a fast . . . I walked about as though it were my friend or my brother; I was bowed with gloom, like one mourning for his mother" (Psalm 35:13–14). On this issue, as on so many others, the Bible does not speak with one voice.

SHOWING KINDNESS TO ENEMIES

We've seen that taking vengeance on our enemies is forbidden, as is taking pleasure in their downfall. But the book of Proverbs goes still further, instructing us to treat our enemies with genuine kindness: "If your enemy is hungry, give him bread to eat; if he is thirsty, give him water to drink" (Proverbs 25:21). Presented with an opportunity to exercise vengeance, we are to extend kindness instead.[37] "An enemy's vulnerability is not to be made into an opportunity to settle old scores";[38] a hungry person should be fed, regardless of our personal feelings for them.

The verse suggests, according to R. Menahem Ha-Meiri, that "a person should not be cruel, but should rather be merciful toward others, even their enemies." Teachings such as this one, he concludes, are intended "to distance us from the attribute of cruelty."[39] As so often in Jewish ethics, then, these verses seek both to ensure good conduct and to instill good character.

The next verse, however, significantly complicates the picture: "You will be heaping live coals on his head, and the Lord will reward you" (25:22). Since the image is obscure, it's difficult to know what the verse intends to convey. Perhaps the coals represent the shame or humiliation that your enemy is likely to feel in the wake of your kindness; this sounds more vindictive than merciful.

The mention of burning coals notwithstanding, some interpreters maintain that our verses "tell the reader to love not only the neighbor but also one's enemy."[40] Yet are these verses really about love? Again it depends on whether we think that the biblical mandate to love is about actions, in which case these verses could indeed be said to demand love, or whether the Torah is concerned with emotions too, in which case it is quite a stretch to see our verses as requiring love. After all, the "highly admirable advice" of one verse is followed by the seemingly less-than-noble motivation in the next. If anything, our verses appear to assume that "intentions do not have to be entirely altruistic . . . in order to be judged 'good.'"[41] Giving our enemy food to eat or water to drink with impure motives may be less than ideal, but it's a start—and in any case, it represents a vast improvement over how people usually treat people they disdain.

A midrash on these verses radicalizes them in a stunning way. The Talmudic sage Rabbi Hama b. Rabbi Hanina says, "Even though [your enemy] intended to kill you, yet he arrived hungry or thirsty in your house, feed him and give him water. Why? 'For you will be heaping live coals upon his head, and the Lord will reward (*yeshalem*) you'—do not read 'will reward you' but rather 'will bring peace between him and you (*yashlimenu lakh*).'"[42] Whereas the verse itself suggests that God will reward us for showing kindness to the one who seeks to harm us, R. Hama takes it to mean that God will induce a change of heart in him so that he will no longer seek to harm us.[43] R. Hama thus shifts the meaning of the verse in two ways: first, he insists that not only must I feed my enemy in general, I must feed him *even when he comes seeking to kill me*; and second, he promises, God will see to it that a transformation takes place, both within my enemy and between my enemy and me.

This text is as elusive as it is provocative: if a violent enemy enters my home with malice in mind, am I really supposed to offer him a sandwich? This guidance would seem to go far beyond the idea of turning the other cheek. If someone intends to kill me but arrives in a weakened state, I should . . . help make him stronger again? Must I neutralize him first? *May* I neutralize him first? Does Jewish law really require me to live on the boundary between lofty idealism and reckless naivete? Given the Rabbinic principle that "we do not rely on miracles,"[44] would it not be irresponsible (and potentially prohibited by Jewish law) to follow R. Hama's advice? All of this is especially surprising given Jewish law's enshrinement of the right to self-defense: "If someone comes to kill you, rise up and kill him first."[45]

R. Hama's words are a provocation. A midrash can open a question without resolving it; midrash is not law. The law is what the law is, the midrash seems to say, but might there be situations when you need not resort to what it prescribes? If someone comes to kill you, you must kill him . . . unless you can disarm him with kindness and generosity instead. Perhaps R. Hama envisions a scenario in which your enemy expects you to meet his hatred with your own. Your good will so surprises him that it stirs something in him; perhaps your kindness reawakens his own.[46] But how can you know in advance whether or not this will occur? The truth is that you can't always know. R. Hama's guidance completely unsettles us . . . and then the text simply moves on, leaving us to grapple with its implications. The midrash is about complicating our questions, not about offering us easy answers.

Let's take stock of where we've come so far. Given free rein, hatred can totally overtake us; our feelings fester and we can come to behave in appalling ways. Tradition offers us guidance for cooling the flames of enmity: (1) When you see your enemy in need, help them. At the very least you will have behaved properly and even nobly; at most you will open the door to genuine healing and reconciliation. (2) When someone has hurt you, you may be tempted to seek vengeance. Resist that temptation because whatever satisfaction vengeance may bring, it will also corrupt your character (not to mention perpetuating a feud). Where appropriate, you can and perhaps even should pursue justice, but whatever superficial similarities they may exhibit, vengeance is not justice. (3) Sometimes when you're nursing a grudge, you may eschew the pursuit of vengeance but nevertheless delight when your enemy suffers or is brought low. Such feelings are no less base for being common; resist them. (4) When fighting your enemy seems necessary and unavoidable, pause for just a moment and ask whether that perception is fully accurate. Are there really no alternatives to violence? Might you be able to disarm your enemy with kindness? Turning an enemy into a friend is, it's worth remembering, a heroic achievement.

Are all of these instances of loving our enemy? Are any of them? As we've seen, a great deal depends on whether we take the idea of loving enemies to refer exclusively to how we act or whether it also includes how we feel. If enemy-love is about action, then all of the guidance we've seen could fall under that rubric. If it is about emotion too, then none of this guidance is unequivocally about love but at least some of it can be understood that way.

LOVE OF ENEMIES: BETWEEN JEWS AND CHRISTIANS

Christians have often insisted that whereas Judaism teaches us to love our neighbors, Jesus goes much further and instructs us to love our enemies too. Love of enemies, Christians have maintained—or taken to be self-evident—is the far superior teaching. Living as a minority in a majority Christian culture, it's easy for Jews to take such claims at face value, but the truth is more complicated. First, it's important to note that, as we've seen, an array of classical Jewish sources can be read as requiring us to love our enemies. Second, it's crucial to keep in mind that Jesus's own teachings on love of enemies are themselves stubbornly elusive. And third, I think there's good reason to doubt whether a blanket mandate to love our enemies, if that's what Jesus in fact issues, is unequivocally a good thing.

In order to better understand what's at stake here, let's briefly consider Jesus's teachings on enemy-love.

On a surface reading, at least, it would seem that Jesus himself contrasts his own command with that of the Hebrew Bible. As he says in the Sermon on the Mount, "You have heard that it was said, 'You shall love your neighbor and hate your enemy.' But I say to you, Love your enemies and pray for those who persecute you" (Matthew 5:43–44).[47]

But what is Jesus referring to when he says that his listeners have "heard it said"? Where are they supposed to have heard a mandate—or even just a granting of permission—to hate their enemies? Nowhere does the Hebrew Bible instruct us to hate our enemies; in fact, as we've already seen, Leviticus admonishes us about hating fellow Israelites.[48] In light of this simple fact, many contemporary New Testament scholars maintain that the license to hate that Jesus opposes is not the teaching of the Hebrew Bible itself but rather a mistaken interpretation thereof.[49] If anything, it would seem, Jesus's contention is that hatred of enemies is a violation of biblical law, not a consequence of it.

More plausible is the suggestion that Jesus has in mind the ancient Jewish Dead Sea Sect, who, like many sectarians, believed in loving one another ("the children of light") but hating outsiders ("the children of darkness").[50] Yet Jesus may well have something simpler and more common in mind: it is not hard to imagine everyday students of the Bible hearing that they are obligated to love their neighbor and finding ways to rationalize the notion that people they detest are somehow excluded from the category of neighbor. Perhaps it is that kind of thinking that Jesus is resisting. In any case, there is no basis for the suggestion that loving neighbors but hating enemies was the teaching of the Hebrew Bible or of most of its early Jewish interpreters.

How new is Jesus's insistence that his followers love their enemies? This is quite a difficult question. Contrasting Jesus's teaching with Proverbs 25:21, the verse we've seen about feeding our enemies, one contemporary New Testament scholar writes that "showing hospitality to an enemy is one thing; loving them is taking it to another level." And yet he almost immediately goes on to say that these verses in the Gospel of Matthew offer "guidance on conduct, not feelings or experiences." Accordingly, when Jesus speaks of loving one's enemies, he has in mind not "having warm feelings toward others, but rather . . . a certain kind of conduct or activity."[51] But if love refers to conduct rather than emotion, then what greater display of love can there be than the kind of gracious hospitality prescribed by the book of Proverbs?

The idea that Jesus's instruction to "love your enemies" refers to actions rather than emotions is actually fairly common among New Testament scholars.[52] But, if they are right, then the gap, if indeed there is one, between what the Hebrew Bible demands and what Jesus calls for is vanishingly small. Again, on their interpretation, Matthew 5 mandates concrete acts of kindness toward one's enemies, whereas Proverbs 25:21 calls for giving them food and drink. There is no daylight between these two positions.

If, on the other hand, Jesus means to demand that his followers *feel* love toward their enemies,[53] then perhaps there is a real distinction on this point between the Hebrew Bible and the New Testament. I have argued in chapter 5 that "love your neighbor" involves both emotion and action, but the word "love" is never explicitly applied to the enemy in Tanakh.* The law about the overburdened donkey acknowledges that we may not *want* to help our enemy ("and would refrain from raising it"), but insists that we are *obligated* to do so anyway. Similarly, Proverbs demands that we engage in acts of kindness for our enemy but it says nothing about how we feel toward her. And yet since the enemy spoken of in the Tanakh passages we've explored is a fellow Israelite, it may be that these verses simply assume that the obligation to love remains in effect. (Again, the Torah never says, "Love people except when you don't like them.") If that is the case, then the Hebrew Bible's view may be that we should ideally love our enemies emotionally, but in cases where that just isn't possible, we are still obligated to act lovingly toward them.

In thinking about love of enemies, it's worth noting another of Jesus's teachings: "You have heard that it was said, 'An eye for an eye and a tooth for a tooth.' But I say to you, Do not resist an evildoer. But if anyone slaps you on the right cheek, turn the other also" (Matthew 5:38–39). This, too, may at first seem like a repudiation of the law as found in Tanakh, but it isn't really clear that that's the case. Many scholars understand Jesus to be speaking about the interpersonal rather than the judicial sphere. As the New Testament scholar Dale Allison explains, "While in the Pentateuch the *lex talionis* [an eye for an eye] belongs to the judiciary process, this is not the sphere of application in Matthew. Jesus does not overthrow the principle of equivalent compensation on an institutional level—that question is just not addressed—but declares it illegitimate for his followers to apply it to their own private disputes."[54]

When I was growing up, I was taught that there is a stark dividing line between Jewish and Christian ethics: Christianity instructs its adherents to turn the other cheek, and Judaism counsels its followers to defend themselves and fight back. In the schools I attended, this was accepted almost as a truism. And yet in point of fact the Talmudic sages

---

* *Tanakh* is how Jews traditionally refer to the Hebrew Bible. It is an acronym for Torah (the Five Books of Moses), Nevi'im (the Prophets), and Ketuvim (the Writings).

celebrate "those who are insulted but do not insult, hear themselves re-
viled but do not answer"[55] and to this day, traditional Jews pray three
times a day: "To those who curse me, let my soul be silent." Although it
is surely not the only strain in Jewish tradition, an ethos of nonretaliation is deeply grounded in Jewish sources.[56]

When a person has been assailed or assaulted, she may well have the
impulse to strike back even harder—the thought that "I'll make you suffer ten times worse than you made me suffer" is hardly alien to human
nature—but the Torah wants to rein in that urge. Despite the ways it
is typically presented, the law of talion is intended to set firm limits on
retaliatory violence. "An eye for an eye," the Torah says, and not a life
for an eye; "a tooth for a tooth," and not a life for a tooth.[57]

Still, I think it is fair to say that Jesus offers a radicalized version
of what was already present in biblical tradition. Retaliation is severely
curtailed by biblical law, but it is not eliminated. If Jesus is ruling out all
forms of retaliation, then he is indeed saying something new.

Some Christian writers insist that Jesus is not just prohibiting retaliation; he is laying out an ethos that precludes violence in any form. By
their lights, Jesus is a pacifist who teaches that violence is always illicit.[58]
But others insist that a stark line should be drawn between retaliation,
on the one hand, and resistance or defense, on the other. What Jesus is
ruling out, they say, is doing bad things to people because they've done
bad things to you; nowhere does he forbid trying to prevent people from
harming us or others. "There is a world of difference," they say, "between
'wanting to do something *so that* these people can't do bad things to my
children' and 'wanting to do something bad to the attackers *because* they
have done something bad to my children'; between wanting to stop the
attackers and wanting to pay them back."[59] More generally, some scholars maintain that Jesus deals only with interpersonal relations, with the
"squabbles of day-to-day life"; on their account, Jesus says nothing here
about how to interact with "external, political enemies."[60] To leap from
a teaching about how to deal with an abusive neighbor to a conclusion
about how to engage with an invading enemy is unwarranted at best
and downright dangerous at worst. Accordingly, some interpreters insist

that Christians do have a right to self-defense,[61] and that war to defend against evil is sometimes necessary.[62]

If Jesus is speaking only of interpersonal conflicts, then one could plausibly hold that his teachings and those of the Hebrew Bible are in fact not very far apart; he is arguably taking what the Hebrew Bible sees as an ideal (nonretaliation) and rendering it obligatory for all of his followers. But if, on the other hand, he intends to renounce the use of violence in every circumstance, then he does indeed go far beyond the dominant trends in biblical and Rabbinic ethics; for the latter, there are times when violence and war become necessary, even if they always remain a tragic last resort.[63]

But what about revenge fantasies in the Hebrew Bible? Don't we read of people praying for their enemies to be brought low by God? Don't we encounter impassioned calls for vengeance? "O God, if you would only slay the wicked," prays a psalmist (Psalm 139:19); "O God, smash their teeth in their mouth," pleads another (58:7). We do indeed find such prayers in the Bible, but—and this point is frequently overlooked—we find similar appeals in the New Testament as well. "How long, Sovereign Lord, holy and true," pray the martyrs, "until you judge the inhabitants of the earth and avenge our blood?" (Revelation 6:10). In the Gospel of Luke, Jesus himself is described as promising his listeners that in time God will avenge them: "And shall not God avenge his own elect, which cry day and night unto him, though he bear long with them?" (Luke 18:7). And in the Gospel of Matthew, Jesus declares to the sinners, "Depart from me, you who are cursed, into the eternal fire" (Matthew 25:41). My interest for now is not in whether and how such perspectives can be reconciled but only to observe that, as the Christian scholar Roland Worth aptly puts it, "The problem [to the extent that there is one] is not in reconciling a punitive Old Testament with a loving New Testament, but in reconciling the punitive and loving strains found in *both* Testaments. However one explains the coexistence of these two patterns of thought in the New Testament, one simultaneously provides an explanation for their presence in the [Hebrew Bible] as well."[64]

An influential Christian scholar notes that "interpreters of Jesus are appropriately united in seeing the commandment to love one's enemy as a normative summary of the attitudes and action of Jesus."[65] This may provide another useful angle for understanding the divide between Judaism and Christianity where love of enemies is concerned: from a Jewish perspective, love of enemies is often a possibility and sometimes, perhaps, even a requirement, but it cannot serve as an encapsulation of Jewish teaching.[66] For Jewish ethics, "defend the weak, protect the widow and the orphan" are more fundamental than "love your enemy." Texts like the midrash about feeding the enemy who comes to kill you are like internal Jewish critics: Sometimes violence in self-defense is the only option, we hear ourselves say. Yes, replies the midrash, but are you sure that this is really one of those times? In a world as complex and messy as ours, we need both a readiness to fight and a willingness to call that very readiness into question.

As I've indicated, I do think that Jesus presents a radicalization of Jewish teaching, but whether or not that radicalization represents progress is an open question. For a variety of reasons, I think, Jews have historically been hesitant to embrace a global principle like "love your enemies." First, we have been somewhat skeptical about how and when it is actually possible to love those who hate us and actively seek to harm us. Second, we have wanted to stay sober about the often intractable reality of enmity in the world. When some interpreters understand Jesus to be saying that "those who love their enemies have no enemies,"[67] Jews take a deep breath and wonder whether that is really true and whether it might not be irresponsible to think so. Moreover, Jews never forget that we do not now live in the peaceable kingdom—whether we like it or not, the kingdom of God is not in fact at hand—and that there may therefore be times when taking up arms in defense of ourselves or others becomes necessary—not just permitted but required. As Ecclesiastes reminds us, there may even be a time for hate (Ecclesiastes 3:8). To be sure, opening the door to military conflict makes egregious abuses possible, but shutting the door too tight can lead to inexcusable passivity in the face of genuine evil.[68] If the first makes unjustifiable wars more likely, the second makes passivity in the face of genocide almost inevitable. It is surely telling that so many Christian thinkers have felt compelled to mitigate the literal force of Jesus's teaching.

Where have we come in comparing Jesus's teaching on enemy-love with Jewish tradition? We've seen that both the Bible and the Talmudic sages provide precedents for the idea of showing kindness to our enemy. Jesus may go beyond this, insisting that we must also have feelings of love for our enemy, but it isn't entirely clear that that's the case. Precisely what Jesus intends to teach about love of enemies is difficult to ascertain—is he offering instructions for how to act, or also for what to feel? Is he focused exclusively on interpersonal relations, or does his guidance extend further? Is violence ever permitted to Jesus's followers, and if so, under what circumstances?—and this makes it extremely difficult to be confident about whether and to what extent he differs and dissents from Rabbinic tradition. But if it's true that loving our enemies is a "normative summary" of Jesus's teachings, then I think he does in fact go beyond anything we find in Jewish tradition. In any case, I am skeptical that in confronting the reality of evil, loving our enemies is always and everywhere the highest ideal.

HATING SINNERS?

For all of Judaism's emphasis on love, some teachings appear to mandate hate. Thus, for example, in proclaiming his unwavering faithfulness to God, the psalmist declares: "O Lord, You know I hate those who hate You and loathe Your adversaries; I feel a perfect hatred toward them; I count them my enemies" (Psalm 139: 21–22). And in the same vein, one Talmudic sage argues that one may hate a fellow Jew whom one has witnessed engaged in sin, whereas another insists that one *must* hate him; as the book of Proverbs teaches, "The fear of the Lord is to hate evil" (Proverbs 8:13).[69]

The impulse to hate sinners finds its way into Jewish law as well. A prominent commentator on Maimonides's *Mishneh Torah* (his code of Jewish law), for example, maintains that one must love one's neighbor "only if he is a 'neighbor' with regard to Torah and the commandments.

However, if he is a wicked person who does not accept rebuke, it is a commandment to hate him, as it is written, 'The fear of the Lord is to hate evil.' And so too, it is written, 'You know I hate those who hate You.'"[70] This approach is based on a passage in which Maimonides himself says that one must love "one who is your brother in the Torah and the commandments"—presumably excluding those who are not.[71] Alongside its insistence that all Jews are to be loved, Jewish law also maintains—or at least appears to maintain—that some Jews are to be hated.

It is striking that for as long as texts have mandated hating sinners, other texts have effectively neutralized them. Jewish law may have required Jews to hate sinners in theory, but in practice the requirement has been radically circumscribed.

Let's take a fascinating example. Take the idea we have just seen, that we are obligated to love only those who are "our brothers in Torah and the commandments." The commentary on Maimonides we saw took this to mean that we are obligated to love only those who *observe* the Torah and its commandments. Interpreting the phrase very differently, however, others maintain that the category of "our brothers in Torah and the commandments" is not limited to those who *observe* the commandments but rather includes all those who are *obligated* by them in the first place. In other words, this is just another way of restating what we saw in chapter 5, namely that according to most interpreters, the mandate to love our neighbor applies to Jews but not to non-Jews. No one is excluded from love by reason of their nonobservance.[72]

Another approach notes that according to Jewish law one may only hate sinners after one has properly rebuked them;[73] until that time, they are to be loved exactly as other Jews are. What about those who have in fact been rebuked in the correct way? There's the rub—or, if you prefer, the solution: it is widely acknowledged by Jewish legal authorities that in this day and age, no one knows how to rebuke properly—with the proper degree of love, etc.—so that every sinner is considered as one who has not yet been properly rebuked, and the mitzvah to treat her with love thus remains in force.[74] Crucially, where rebuke is concerned, "this day and age" did not begin in the modern world; already the Talmudic sages talk about how no one knows how to properly give rebuke, no one knows how to correctly receive it, and in fact no one even knows what appropriate rebuke would look like.[75] In light of this, hatred of sinners is not a live possibility in Jewish law. Whereas the mandate to love Jews remains in force, the mandate to hate them does not.

But let's imagine a situation in which one was in fact rebuked in an appropriate way but one rebuffed the rebuke. Wouldn't there be an obligation to hate such a sinner? Perhaps, say several modern rabbinic figures, but the mandate is not to hate the sinner *instead* of loving her but rather to hate her *in addition* to loving her. In other words, one would have to love and hate the sinner at the very same time. You hate the evil they do and love the goodness found within them. Psychologically, I think, the implication of this is that we are not really hating people so much as hating the wrong they do—hating sin, in other words, but loving the sinner, who is, after all, more than just a sinner, since no one ought to be defined entirely by what they do wrong.[76]

Let me briefly mention one more approach taken by some Haredi rabbis. In a remarkable ruling, Rabbi Abraham Isaiah Karelitz says that Jewish legal rulings about "heretics" (*apikorsim*, traditionally seen as particularly egregious sinners) only applied in times when divine providence was manifest to all, when miracles abounded, and when heavenly voices could be heard. In times such as those, R. Karelitz argues, one became a heretic and a sinner out of spite, but in times like ours, when divine providence is hidden and the masses have lost faith, such rulings are not applicable at all. If anything, applied today they would do more harm than good. What is perhaps most significant about R. Karelitz's argument is his recognition that modern times are different—it's almost as if we inhabit a different reality than people did in premodern times—and that it therefore makes little sense to go on treating "heretics" the way religious people once did. Accordingly, he concludes, those who have strayed from Torah and the commandments ought to be wooed back with love, not condemned with hate.[77] In light of all this, many modern rabbis conclude that "the mitzvah to love one's fellow Jew applies to virtually all Jews today, even those who do not believe in the basic tenets of Judaism."[78] The mandate to hate may exist "on the books" but it has very little—if any—purchase in real life.

Some Jewish thinkers set the legal debate aside and take a more explicitly theological tack instead. Reminding his listeners that God loves sinners, Rabbi Israel Ba'al Shem Tov ("The Besht," 1700–1760) is reputed to have said, "God loves even the least of Israel more than a father and mother love their only child, born to them in old age."[79] He expresses the wish to have the same love for the most righteous that God has for the most wicked. Any genuinely religious person will hesitate to hate those whom God loves and, on the contrary, will strive to love those whom God loves. Not surprisingly, then, the Besht sometimes describes himself as loving the wicked and unrighteous of Israel even more than other people love their own children.[80]

Discussions of hating sinners often proceed on the assumption that there is one group of people, the righteous, who must decide how to view, and therefore how to engage with, another group (or groups), the sinners. But that very division no longer seems tenable to me. We know all too well that people can be deeply engaged in religious life—they can devotedly study religious texts and punctiliously observe ritual laws, say—while engaging in moral and interpersonal violations of every kind. Conversely, people can have cast off religion completely and nevertheless be passionately committed to moral goodness and interpersonal responsibility. Which of these groups is the righteous and which the sinners? Which one has the standing to judge and evaluate the other? Most of us accept almost as a truism that religious commitment does not necessarily correlate with moral probity; for a truly religious person, this may be self-evident but it ought also to be devastating. Before those of us who are religiously observant presume to judge those who don't observe Shabbat or keep the laws of kashrut, we ought to consider the ways in which we, no less than they, are the real sinners. Let's heal ourselves before we make bold to assess others.

And let's also keep in mind the simple (but often extremely difficult) principle expressed by an Israeli rabbi of the last century: "We must make hatred itself hated as the height of all ugliness."[81]

HATING ANTISEMITES?

Just who is the enemy we've been talking about? One gets the impression from some texts that the enemy is someone with whom we do not quite get along; perhaps a personal dispute or squabble has come between us. If you see the donkey of the person you've fallen out with, traditional texts say, put down your hostility and offer your assistance. Yet other texts seem to imagine a genuine enemy, one who seeks to harm or even kill us. Thus R. Hama's suggestion that when an enemy arrives with murder on his mind, we ought at least to consider disarming him with love.

As we've seen, the line between sinner and righteous can be blurry, but sometimes, as with committed antisemites, it is actually quite clear. How do we respond to resolute haters, adversaries who seek to destroy us—our community, our people, our nation? Jewish ethics licenses us—*obligates* us—to repel them and defend ourselves. Folk wisdom has it that we may, and perhaps must, actively hate them. That's why many Jews say *yemah shemo*, "may his name be erased," in making reference to truly evil people (for example, we might say, "Hitler, *yemah shemo*," or "Stalin, *yemah shemo*").

Needless to say, being the object of hatred or contempt can be enormously corrosive of one's sense of self; being hated by others can lead to hating oneself. On the one hand, as we saw in chapter 1, knowing that we are infinitely valuable and loved by God can help us hold strong in the face of contempt and dehumanization. Yet on the other hand, as any member of a minority group can attest, sometimes the contempt breaches our boundaries and has a real impact. The philosopher Macalester Bell makes the provocative argument that the best way to respond to racial contempt is to "marshal a defiant counter-contempt for racists—if targets of racist contempt can disengage and dismiss the racists as low, then their self-esteem is less likely to be compromised by the racists' contempt."[82] Counter-hate, in other words, can enable resilience in the face of an oppressor's "contemptuous gaze."[83]

All of this raises another complicating dimension to our discussion. Many Christian discussions of the ethics of hate take place in the context of Christian power; many Jewish discussions of hate take place in conditions of relative powerlessness. It may be that what is permitted—and perhaps even sometimes necessary—for the powerless is forbidden for the powerful. Of course, this means that when Jews have power, what is permitted and forbidden to us changes.

So may we hate our enemies—not our friend with whom we are not on speaking terms, but the raging antisemite who wants to do us harm? Must we hate them? Under what circumstances? How often, and how intensely? There are no easy answers to these questions. As I've tried to show, there may well be moments when hatred is appropriate and even salutary, but it's also crucial that we bear in mind the dangers of embracing hatred. Rabbi Yehezkel Levenstein (1885–1974) worries that since our hearts are profoundly impacted by what we do, hating others, no matter how sinful or evil, cannot but leave a deep imprint on us. If we allow ourselves to hate evildoers, he warns, we "will implant hatred deep within" ourselves, which will prevent us from "attaining the virtue of loving people, which is one of the foundations of the Torah."[84]

But is that always right? Isn't it sometimes possible to hate in targeted ways? Most people are not Hitler, but the reality is that sometimes there is a Hitler. If I hate Hitler, or Nazis more generally, will that really necessarily prevent me from loving (most) people? Will it somehow damage or impair my capacity for love? I'm honestly not sure.[85]

R. Levenstein takes his concern with eschewing hate to its logical conclusion. An oft-cited Talmudic legend has it that when the Egyptians drowned at the Sea of Reeds, the ministering angels began to sing songs of praise, but God scolded them: "The works of My hands are drowning, and you sing songs?"[86] Yes, the Egyptians were evildoers, and yes, they were being punished for the evil that they did, but nevertheless, R. Levenstein insists, "there is no place for hating them"; celebration is therefore entirely out of place. As he concludes from the midrash, "The recognition that the evildoers too are the work of God's hands must prevent us from hating them."[87]

Does this perhaps suggest that although there is no clear *ethical* argument that hatred is always forbidden, there is nevertheless a *theological* one? If human beings—even awful, murderous ones—are created in God's image, then perhaps we are forbidden—for religious reasons—from hating them. If we love God, we cannot hate what God has made.

Is this right? Again, I am not at all certain.

Religion helps us ask hard questions but it does not often offer us easy answers.

PART III

HESED:
BRINGING GOD'S LOVE
TO OTHER PEOPLE

10

IMITATING GOD

The Beginning and End of Judaism Is Love

WHAT IS JUDAISM ultimately *about*, and what is it really *for*? A Talmudic sage offers a simple but startling answer: Judaism is about love, and its goal is to make us kinder and more present for one another. This is what tradition refers to as "walking in God's ways."

Rabbi Simlai declares: "The beginning of Torah is acts of loving kindness and the end of Torah is acts of loving kindness." At the beginning of the Torah, when Adam and Eve discover their nakedness, God clothes them (Genesis 3:21); at the end, when Moses dies, God buries the body (Deuteronomy 34:6).[1] A midrash goes a step further, insisting that "the beginning of Torah is acts of loving kindness, the middle of Torah is acts of loving kindness, and the end of Torah is acts of loving kindness."[2] Not only does God clothe the first couple and bury the great prophet, God also visits Abraham when he is in need of healing (Genesis 18:1).

R. Simlai is obviously not just making a pedestrian point about the sequence of stories or ideas in the Torah; he is saying something crucial about what lies at the heart of Torah.[3] The purpose of Torah is to bring love and kindness into the world. As we've seen, at the heart of the Jewish religion is a God of love and kindness who summons God's people to live lives of love and kindness.[4]

"WALKING IN GOD'S WAYS"

In the book of Deuteronomy, after recounting the story of the people's rebelliousness, Moses turns to the people and announces: "And now, O Israel, what does the Lord your God demand of you? Only this: to fear the Lord your God, to walk in God's ways, to love God, and to serve the Lord your God with all your heart and with the whole of your being" (Deuteronomy 10:12). Notice the pattern of verbs in this verse: fear, which is an emotion; walk, which is an action; love, which is an emotion, and serve, which again is an action. The interweaving of emotion and action in this all-important verse suggests something fundamental about Judaism's vision of the good life: God asks both for our inner life and our outward deeds, for our feelings as well as our actions. Our aspiration, even if it can never be fully realized in this lifetime, is the full integration of *who we are on the inside* and of *what we do on the outside*.

Most modern academic scholars think that when Deuteronomy asks the people to "walk in God's ways," it refers to the ways God has laid out for the people to walk in—that is, the mitzvot (commandments).[5] But the Talmudic sages, and not a few modern scholars,[6] understand the phrase differently, as mandating the people to walk in the ways in which God walks.[7]

What would it mean to walk in the ways that God walks?

The prophet Joel imagines a great day when "whosoever shall be called by (*yikarei*) the name of the Lord shall be delivered" (Joel 3:5).[8] A midrash expresses perplexity: "How is it possible for a person to be called by the name of the Lord?!" Isn't God God, and humanity . . . well, *not* God? "Rather," the midrash explains, "as God is called merciful, so you too must be merciful; as the Blessed Holy One is called gracious, so you too must be gracious. As God is called righteous, so you too must be righteous; as God is called kind, so you too must be kind."[9] To be called by the name of God, then, is to embody the character traits tradition most powerfully associates with God.

If the midrash focuses on character traits, a Talmudic passage, in contrast, turns our attention to concrete actions. Rabbi Hama B. Rabbi Hanina asks what Deuteronomy could possibly mean when it charges the people to "walk after the Lord your God" (Deuteronomy 13:5); how can a human being "walk after" a God who is referred to as "a devouring fire" (4:24)?! "Rather," he explains, "the meaning is to walk after the attributes of the Blessed Holy One. As God clothes the naked, so you too must clothe the naked; the Blessed Holy One visited the sick, so you too must visit the sick. The Blessed Holy One comforted mourners, so you too must comfort mourners; the Blessed Holy One buried the dead, so you too must bury the dead."[10] To "walk after God," in other words, is to perform the same acts of kindness that the Bible tells us that God did.

Taken together, these two texts amplify the point that godliness consists of two intertwined things: the kind of person we are and the kinds of things we do. We are called both to *be loving* and to *act lovingly*.

Each of the texts corrects for possible misinterpretations of the other. If we read the midrash and are tempted to conclude that what matters most is how we *feel* about other people's suffering, the Talmud bluntly reminds us that real compassion is manifested in concrete deeds; compassion without a commitment to action is not really compassion at all. But if, in contrast, we read the Talmud and are tempted to think that what really matters is what we *do*—as long as we visit our friend who is in mourning, it makes no difference how we feel about her or her situation—the midrash points us inward, to our emotions and our character traits.[11]

The traditional Jewish words for all this are *hesed* or *gemilut hasadim*, both of which are notoriously difficult to translate. Going back to the Coverdale Bible (1535), *hesed* has often been rendered in English as lovingkindness.[12] The problem for many people is that lovingkindness sounds hopelessly archaic; it conjures up images of addressing God as Thou and pleading for "Thy tender mercies." The word begins to have more resonance, I think, when we reinsert a space (or a hyphen) between love and kindness, yielding "loving kindness." In light of what I've been arguing,

I'd suggest that we think of *hesed* in its ideal form as "love manifested in acts of kindness"[13]—that is, as an internal state concretely expressed in external action. God's call and challenge to us is to live lives of love manifested in acts of kindness. Perhaps not surprisingly, then, a Talmudic sage declares that "the reward of tzedakah depends entirely upon the extent of the kindness (*hesed*) in it."[14]

IMITATING (ONLY SOME OF) GOD'S ATTRIBUTES AND ACTIONS

Some people find the idea of walking in God's ways perplexing. How can it be, they wonder, that some divine attributes, like mercy and righteousness, are to be emulated, while others, like anger and jealousy, are not; and how can it be that some divine actions, like clothing the naked and visiting the sick, are held up as models for us to follow, while others, like flooding the world and smiting our enemies, are not? (No Jewish source anywhere tells us that "just as the biblical God sometimes gets angry and launches a plague, so too must you.") How can the sages do this? Isn't this selective reading of the most egregious kind?

The challenge can be made even stronger. Jewish texts do more than *not require* us to emulate God's jealousy, for example; they actively *prohibit* us from doing so. Indeed, a midrash lists "jealousy" and "vengeance," among others, as divine attributes that it would be "unbecoming" (*lo na'eh*) for us to emulate.[15]

But why? Why would Judaism require us to emulate God's compassion[16] but forbid us from emulating God's jealousy?

One reason is that the sages were extremely concerned with encouraging people to act from a place of freedom rather than compulsion. They imagined that even when God gets angry, God does not lose control of Godself; God always maintains the capacity to decide how to act. "I control my jealousy," a midrash pictures God saying; "my jealousy does not control me."[17] When human beings get angry, however, we quickly lose control of ourselves; we are in thrall to our anger.[18] We may not emulate God's anger or jealousy, in other words, because anger and jealousy compromise our freedom. If this sounds abstract, ask yourself: When was the last time you burned with anger and felt totally in control of yourself?

But I suspect that something deeper is also at play here: the sages make a judgment about which character traits attributed to God in the Bible are reflective of God's essential character, and which are somehow secondary.[19] As we will see at length in chapter 13, love and mercy are at the very heart of who God is, whereas anger and jealousy are not. *How* do the sages arrive at this judgment? On one level, of course, one can argue that they "simply read Scripture" and that this is the conclusion they reach. To take just one example, in Psalm 103 we learn that God "will not . . . nurse [God's] anger for all time," but that God's "steadfast love [*hesed*] is for all eternity" (Psalm 103:9, 17). In other words, whereas divine anger is fleeting, divine love is enduring and thus more fundamental to who God is.

Textual support notwithstanding, I'd like to suggest that part of what allows the sages to conclude that God's mercy is somehow more essential to who God is than is God's wrath, is that they trust their own religious intuitions. (Of course, reading Scripture can shape our intuitions and our intuitions can shape our readings in ways that can never be teased apart.) The sages are quite comfortable with the idea that some things are just more appropriate to attribute to God than others; we shouldn't need scriptural support to show that love is more fundamental than anger to who God is. That is the kind of intuition that religion should honor rather than override. To demand textual evidence that love is a higher form of perfection than hate, for example, is to betray a kind of spiritual sickness.

What so disturbs many people ought perhaps to inspire us instead: The sages' "selective reading" reflects their deep trust in their sense of what the highest good is. The Bible itself honors this too: God wants Abraham to protest against the imminent destruction of Sodom and Gomorrah not because Scripture instructs him to—Abraham predates Sinai and thus has no Scripture to turn to—but because God honors Abraham's internal moral sense. Most often, religion is not about overturning our moral intuitions so much as bolstering them and moving us to act on them.

BEING PRESENT AMID PAIN

Let's take a closer look at the list of concrete actions the Talmud mandates: clothing the naked, visiting the ill, comforting the bereaved, and burying the dead. The actions appear in the order in which God performs them in the Bible—God clothes the naked Adam and Eve (Genesis 3:21); visits the ailing Abraham (Genesis 18:1); comforts Isaac after the death of his father, Abraham (Genesis 25:11); and buries Moses upon his death (Deuteronomy 34:6). But something else is also noteworthy about the list: each situation mentioned is less open to reversal than the one before. The naked (the poor) are vulnerable, but their situation is reversible—at least in theory, any poor person can be lifted out of poverty; the sick are vulnerable, but some—though not all—who are sick can recover. Mourners have suffered an immense and permanent loss, but the way they carry their grief will often evolve and soften over time; the dead are gone, and will not be coming back.[20] It's my sense that for many of us, the less reversible a situation, the more frightening it is—a baby who does not understand what we are saying does not frighten us, whereas an Alzheimer's patient often does. And when we are afraid, we are tempted to flee.

But Judaism's message is clear: resist the urge to flee. Run *toward* the very people and places you most want to run *away* from. If you want to be a religious person, learn to be present for other people[21] when they are in pain.

In telling us that offering care and support to people in pain is "walking in God's ways"—in other words, that it is the very pinnacle a human being can achieve in this life[22]—the sages subtly alert us to the fact that it can be intensely hard work. So we are simultaneously pushed—if we are serious about the spiritual life, we have to learn to care more and more deeply about other people and to be there for them when they are in need—and gently encouraged: this is extremely important, and/but it can be very hard work. Keep at it; learning to be more and more present with people who need comfort and support is the task of a lifetime. It is the heart of the religious life. "All the rest is commentary; go and learn."[23]

BETWEEN COMPASSION AND PITY

Being present with people calls for compassion rather than pity. Although compassion and pity can superficially seem similar, they are in fact oceans apart.[24] In pity, the philosopher Lawrence Blum explains, "one holds oneself apart from the afflicted person and from their suffering, thinking of it as something that defines that person as fundamentally different from oneself." What has happened to someone else, we convince ourselves, could never happen to us. When we have compassion for someone, in contrast, we are keenly aware both of our own vulnerability and of our shared humanity. As Blum puts it, compassion "promotes the *experience* of equality, even when accompanied by an acknowledgment of actual social inequality."[25] In other words, pity is a vertical posture, whereas compassion is a horizontal one. When we pity someone, we reach *down* to them, but when we show compassion for them, we reach *across* to them, keenly aware that what connects us runs far deeper than what divides us.[26] In the first instance, we feel sorry *for* someone; in the second, we feel sorry *with* them.[27] Pity is thus entwined with condescension, while compassion is enmeshed with equality and connection.

To pity someone is ultimately to keep our distance from them; if we can't keep our physical distance from them, then we work hard to keep our psychological and existential distance. This need for distance is, most often, about fear—fear of even acknowledging, let alone reckoning with, our own vulnerability. To have compassion depends precisely on being conscious and accepting of our own vulnerability, fragility, mortality. As Blum writes, in compassion, "the other person's suffering (though not necessarily their afflicting condition) is seen as the kind of thing that could happen to anyone, including oneself insofar as one is a human being."[28] When we sit with someone who has lost a child, we are aware that, God help us, this could happen to us too; when we care for an elder beset by dementia, we are aware that this could happen to us, or to someone close to us too. For understandable reasons, for many people all this can feel like too much to bear—so they have recourse to pity instead of compassion.

Pity need not be a function of arrogance or apathy, though it certainly can be; as we've seen, it can stem from fear, most often fear of acknowledging our own vulnerability.[29] So we harbor the illusion of invulnerability to keep us "safe" (or so we think). But by dint of being human, we are, whether we like it or not (and few of us like it), always vulnerable. So in a deep sense, compassion is a more honest posture than pity. Pity does not ultimately keep us safe; it merely keeps us disconnected.

SITTING WITH FEAR

Walking in God's ways, being fully present for others when they suffer, thus depends, to a large extent, on learning to sit with fear. If we can't manage our own fears in the face of other people's suffering, we will frequently do more harm than good. Let me share a personal example, one of the more surreal moments I have ever experienced. I was visiting a friend whose younger brother—healthy, vibrant, and still only in his thirties—had just died of a heart attack. As we sat and talked, one of my friend's mother's friends walked into the shiva home, sat down with the two of us, and declared (yes, this really happened): "Dave,[30] this must be an extremely rough moment for you. I mean, one can only assume that it was genetic." My first reaction was to wonder whether I was hallucinating—could it really be that this woman had just said something so dumb and so hurtful? My second reaction was to get irritated—I actually had the urge to escort the woman out of the apartment and yell at her about what is and isn't appropriate to say. And then it hit me: she had said what she did because she has children the same age as my friend and his now-deceased brother. She was insisting that the cause of death was ultimately genetic because it was the only way she could manage her fear that one of her children could meet the same tragic fate. This could not happen in *my* family, she seemed desperate to assert—and convince herself. As soon as I realized this, I felt compassion for her. Her fear was understandable, and only human. But what situations like these call for is being conscious of our fears and having the wisdom and the self-control not to act on them.[31]

I want to underscore this point: The goal is not to be fearless. The goal is to learn to sit with our fears. If we learn to comfort ourselves when we are afraid, we can disarm our fears and thus free ourselves from the compulsive need to try to relieve them or make them disappear. Certain things may understandably scare us, but we can learn to stop being governed by fear. The aspiration to walk in God's ways requires us to engage in this often intense spiritual-psychological work. The work can be hard and exhausting, but it can also be liberating and profoundly enlivening.

STAYING PRESENT EVEN WHEN WE CAN'T "FIX" THINGS

We've been focused on the challenges that fear poses to compassion. But it is not only the fear of a similar fate befalling us or someone we love that leads many of us to flee hospitals or shiva homes. For several years, I took groups of young adults (mostly recent college graduates) to visit Alzheimer's patients on a weekly basis. One day soon after we started paying visits, one of the students declared, with a combination of exasperation and sadness, "I don't understand why we come here. I mean, it's not like we can actually *do anything* for the residents." When I probed a little to get at what was really bothering him, it became clear that many of the students found it extremely difficult to tolerate the feelings of powerlessness the visits were eliciting in them. After all, as successful, ambitious young adults, they'd been told time and again that there was nothing they couldn't do if they just set their minds to it. Yet here they were, asked to sit with people who had lost so much— people who had in many ways *lost themselves*—and it seemed that there was nothing at all my students could do for them. Nothing, I reminded them, except being present with people who often have no one to keep them company. It was true, they could not *fix* what ailed the patients; but they could simply be with them.[32] In order to give the gift of presence, we sometimes have to let go of the urge to be fixers or saviors.[33] For many students, this was a long journey—learning to sit and be present, without needing to be "productive" or "effective," was a new skill, and at first a highly uncomfortable challenge.[34] But most of them learned it, and many began to understand on a visceral and emotional level what it takes to "walk in God's ways."

PROVIDING ASSISTANCE AND PRESENCE

What is it that we are asked to provide? On the one hand, where appropriate, we are asked to grant concrete assistance. As a modern Jewish code of law puts it, "The core of the commandment of visiting the sick is to look into what the patient needs, and to do for them whatever is necessary."[35] But where practical help is not needed, or not possible, we can still give the gift of our own presence. When we visit people who are sick, for example, we are charged not with ending their suffering, but only with ameliorating it to the extent possible. And sometimes the extent possible involves rendering the patient's experience less lonely and isolating,[36] and thereby reminding them that they are still very much part of the community, and part of our lives.

It should go without saying that the list the Talmud presents— clothing the naked, visiting the sick, comforting the mourners, burying the dead—is meant to be illustrative rather than exhaustive. As important as the concrete examples like visiting the sick and comforting mourners are in themselves, they are also emblematic of a broader commitment to a life oriented around love and kindness.[37] Imagine a friend who calls you in crisis, lamenting that her husband of several decades has just abandoned her for a much younger woman, leaving her devastated and alone with four young children. A certain crude way of reading texts might imagine that since your friend is not poor, or ill, or in mourning over the death of a loved one (though she may well be in mourning over the death of something very precious to her), you are not obligated to attend to her. But this is thoroughly (and almost comically) misguided. Just as no legal code can cover our obligations in every concrete circumstance, so also can no list of vulnerable situations include every circumstance in which we are called upon to respond. *Hesed* is an ethos and an orientation, a commitment to a certain way of being and responding in the world. If a person is suffering, their pain makes a claim on us; we are called to offer them both assistance and presence.

THE NEED FOR WISDOM AND DISCERNMENT

The kind of assistance and presence we offer will vary with circumstance because genuine compassion is not generic. It responds not to categories but to persons, to individuals with unique needs, circumstances, and emotional makeups.[38] Words that may comfort one mourner may alienate another; sentiments that would buoy one patient may grate on another. The philosopher Heather Battaly explains that "the virtues are not canned responses." To have the virtue of compassion, then, is "to do and feel what is appropriate to the context."[39] Compassion, in other words, requires attention and discernment, a commitment to understanding as robustly as possible both the person in need and the situation in which they find themselves and to acting accordingly.[40] As Rabbi Chaim Friedlander (1923–1986) points out, this is *hesed* at its best and its deepest, "that a person should sense the [unique] needs of the other and do the work of giving accordingly."[41]

Hesed also requires discernment of another kind: while compassion may lead us to want to help, we need practical wisdom to help us discern how best to do so. What initially strikes us as the compassionate response in a given situation may actually be unhelpful, or even actively destructive. Imagine you get to know someone in your neighborhood who is homeless. Filled with compassion, you regularly offer money for food and shelter. Over time, though, you see firsthand that they are addicted to drugs and alcohol. The next time they ask you for money, you find yourself torn: Should I give them money as I have in the past, or

might I actually be enabling them on their path to self-destruction? Giving money in this kind of a situation may well be a moral error, in Jewish
legal terms a violation of the prohibition on "placing a stumbling block
before the blind" (Leviticus 19:14). In this particular circumstance, you
have other options: you can give food instead of money, for example,
or you can provide information on where they can receive assistance
with what ails them. Compassion alone cannot always tell you what to
do—and sometimes what it tells you will be unreliable, or even dangerous. You also need what Aristotle calls "phronesis," or practical wisdom,
which guides the compassionate (or courageous, or virtuous in whatever
way) person on the best course of concrete action to take.[42]

BEYOND RECIPROCITY (SOMETIMES)

Reciprocity in relationships can be important; there is no virtue in being a doormat. And yet when we fully give ourselves over to *hesed*, to
love manifested in acts of kindness, at moments at least we put aside
questions about whether and what we will get in return, or of whether
the person in need would do for us what we are doing for them.[43] The
person and her present needs capture and dominate our attention.[44] This
is why the mitzvah of burying the dead is referred to in Rabbinic literature as *hesed shel emet*, true *hesed*:[45] when we care for a dead body,
there is no chance that the person will do anything at all to pay back
the kindness. Our focus remains centered on the other and on how we
can be of service.

Hesed shel emet, giving with no thought of reciprocity, is arguably
the loftiest peak on the already elevated ground of walking in God's
ways. God's grace elicits moments of grace from us. Just as God gives
generously, without receiving anything in return, an influential Musar
teacher suggests, so too are we capable of giving generously, without any
thought of being recompensed.[46]

Important—imperative—as it can sometimes be, the call to transcend reciprocity can be dangerous. Men have often constructed ethical
theories that valorize women's self-sacrifice; on these accounts the mean-

ing of women's lives consists primarily—and sometimes exclusively—in serving others, usually men. As feminist writers have taught us, the relentless insistence on women's self-sacrifice has deprived many women of any sense of self at all. Needless to say, there is something profoundly problematic about this. As the political philosopher Jean Hampton observes, care for others that is totally self-effacing "cannot be moral because it is born of self-abnegation rather than self-worth . . . A genuine moral agent has to have a good sense of her own moral claims if she is going to be a person at all and thus a real partner in a morally sound relationship."[47]

One of the characters in Charlotte Brontë's novel *Shirley* gives powerful voice to the realization that all is not well when women are put on a pedestal for their selfless giving:

> I perceive that certain sets of human beings are very apt to maintain that other sets should give up their lives to them and their service, and then they requite them by praise: they call them devoted and virtuous. Is this enough? Is it to live? Is there not a terrible hollowness, mockery, want, craving, in that existence which is given away to others, for want of something of your own to bestow it on? I suspect there is. Does virtue lie in abnegation of self? I do not believe it. Undue humility makes tyranny.[48]

How should we respond to this challenge? Sacrifice *is* an important part of ethics, as most parents intuitively know.[49] But crucially, sacrifice cannot be expected of women only; if there is (sometimes) a virtue in sacrificing our own desires for the good of others, it must be expected of men as well as women. And sacrifice cannot be turned into the whole of women's interpersonal experience. Women exist for more than just serving others.[50]

How can we understand all this in theological terms? First, we need to remember that as human beings created in the image of God we all have intrinsic worth. Because God so values us, we have to value ourselves. We cannot treat ourselves, or allow others to treat us, as mere

means to other people's ends. The philosopher Ruth Groenhout is helpful on this point: "If a theory [or a theology] has strong grounds for
asserting the equal value, or equal sanctity, of each individual, then
it cannot call for unrestrained self-sacrifice. The self should be valued
as are others, and this places limits on the place of self-sacrifice in the
theory [or theology]."[51] Affirming our own worth, and thus setting limits on self-sacrifice, are theological imperatives.

Moreover, as we saw in chapter 1 in the Mishnah's focus on human
uniqueness, we do not make our way in the world and serve God as generic examples of the human species. We live, and serve, with all of our
individuality—our strengths, our interests, and our passions (and also
our weaknesses, shortcomings, and limitations). As individual images of
God, we have a right—I am tempted to say an obligation—to nurture
our own development and attend to our own needs. Having a self is a
religious value; we cannot simply abnegate what God loves.

I'd like to propose another potentially helpful way of thinking about
this. In order to forget ourselves, we first need to *have* a self; we cannot
forget what we have never known. Self-transcendence, the realization
that our ego is not the center of the universe and the commitment to
act accordingly, depends on having a self to transcend. When people do
nothing but give, when they feel that they are *required* to do nothing
but give, we may be permitted to wonder whether they have a self at all.

So yes, transcending reciprocity is at times integral to the moral and
religious life. But it must be understood and experienced as part of a
broader picture in which giving is a *human* privilege and responsibility,
not merely a "feminine" one, and in which the giver is a self who matters
no less than the receiver.[52]

LOVING GOD LEADS TO LOVING OTHERS

Just how central is *hesed* to a life genuinely committed to Torah?[53] Consider this Rabbinic pronouncement: "Expounders of *aggadah* [that is, of
the stories and nonlegal dimensions of the Jewish tradition] say: 'Is it
your desire to know [or perhaps: be intimate with] the One who spoke

and the world came into being? Study *aggadah*, for, through doing so, you will come to know the One who spoke and the world came into being, and will cleave to God's ways.'"[54] Note what happens in this short passage: the text asks whether one wants to achieve closeness with God and suggests that if so, one should study a curriculum broader than law (halakha) alone. The midrash could have simply stopped there—after all, the initial question has seemingly been answered—but instead it adds what it anticipates (hopes?) will happen ineluctably (ideally?) to one who studies Torah in the hopes of knowing God: such a person will "cleave to God's ways." In other words, the person who studies these texts will grow in compassion, presence, and kindness.[55]

How is the study of *aggadah* supposed to bring us to lead kinder, more compassionate lives? This text seems to express the *hope* that the study of religious narrative will deepen our focus on God, and that this focus, in turn, will deepen our commitment to love. The idea of knowing God that the text presents is fascinating: if we really come to know God, it seems to say, we will become more like God. Love a loving God, it promises, and you'll work to become more loving yourself. This of course raises the question every religious person ought to ask: Is the God we love loving enough? Or have we cut God down to our own size, so that God loves whomever we love, and hates whomever we hate? The problem is that that god is not God at all; it's just an inflated version of ourselves, or, in more traditional terms, an idol.

Here we see why Jewish spirituality can never be divorced from Jewish ethics: love God, the midrash suggests, and you'll love people more. It's as if we say to God, "I love you," and God responds, "There are people suffering. Go love them too because that's a major part of what it means to love me." Implicit in all this is a simple but revolutionary claim: acts of loving kindness are not diversions or distractions from what really matters; they are the very heart and culmination of the spiritual life.

There is a spiritual litmus test implied in this remarkable statement: if we study Torah and it does not render us kinder and more willing to be present with people facing crisis, sorrow, or loss, then it is not Torah that we have studied. Perhaps it is Jewish culture, or academic Jewish studies; but it is not Torah. Torah leads to love, the midrash implies, or it is not Torah at all.

I am making a normative claim, not a descriptive one. In other words, I am advocating for how I believe religion *should* function, not portraying how it always *does* function. Plenty of people engage with religious matters on a regular or even a constant basis, and do not grow kinder or more compassionate—and many do not even aspire to. I do not mean to open the door to evasions of responsibility, as when people say that those who act violently or cruelly in the name of a religious tradition are not really practitioners of that tradition. My goal is to make life harder for believers, not easier: make sure your religious life in general, and your religious study in particular, makes you kinder and more present, because after all, *that's ultimately what it's all about.*

As we've just seen, the study of *aggadah* is supposed to lead us to lives of *hesed.* But strikingly, according to another midrash, the study of law (halakha) is supposed to take us to the same place. The Talmudic sage Rabbi Judah the Prince observes that the verse containing the commandment to "love the Lord your God with all your heart" (Deuteronomy 6:5) does not specify how it is to be fulfilled. But the next verse, "These words which I command you this day shall be upon your heart" (6:6), can serve as an explanation: "Take these words to heart," the verse is understood to be saying, "for, through doing so, you will come to know the One who spoke and the world came into being, and will cleave to God's ways."[56] Taken together, these two teachings convey an essential lesson: no matter which aspect of the Jewish tradition most draws us, the ultimate outcome of our study should be the same—a heightened capacity for, and a deeper commitment to, love and compassion.

CLEAVING TO GOD('S LOVE)

Embodying God's love is a profound—arguably the profoundest—expression of closeness to God. A biblical verse recited three times a day in traditional Jewish liturgy declares that "the Lord is good to all, and

[God's] mercy is upon all [God's] works." (Psalm 145:9). The two halves of the verse are usually taken to point in the same direction, to the vast expansiveness of God's goodness and mercy: God is good and merciful to all of God's creatures. But a Talmudic sage explains it differently. "Rabbi Joshua of Sikhnin says in the name of Rabbi Levi: 'The Lord is good to all, and God gives of God's mercy to God's creatures.'"[57] In other words, people have the capacity to partake of God's compassion and bestow it upon others. In bringing God's love to people who are suffering, we thus become God's partners and emissaries.[58]

Jewish tradition imagines that those who bestow love manifested as kindness dwell in the very presence of God.[59] I confess that my skeptical side is tempted to hear this as a flowery but empty exhortation. And yet I also find great hope and comfort in it. In a world in which God so often seems utterly absent, moments of interpersonal kindness—whether we are bestowing or receiving—are the closest many of us will get to intimations of God's presence. To commit to a life of love manifested as kindness is to dwell in the only place many of us will ever find God.

Jewish spirituality holds up the ideal of *devekut*, of cleaving to God. Some emphasize that *devekut* can be achieved through prayer, others through study. But the older I get, the more moved (and challenged) I am by Jewish thinkers who insist that the most authentic form of cleaving to God is holding fast to God's compassion. Rabbi Yehezkel Levenstein observes that "the whole purpose of the human being is only to delight in the divine presence."[60] But contrary to popular impression, R. Levenstein notes, "basking in the divine presence is not limited to the next world"; rather, "the righteous merit basking in the divine presence even in this world." When and how is it possible to dwell in the presence of God? "When the righteous merit the attribute of *hesed*—an attribute that is one of God's own attributes—in its wholeness, then they are basking in the divine presence in this world, in that they merit God's own attributes."[61] The converse is also true, another Musar figure adds: "One who is lacking in doing *hesed*—this is not a lack in *hesed* only. Such a person also lacks connection (*devekut*) to God, or even closeness to God."[62]

I believe this claim about the spiritual life lies at the very core of Judaism's vision of the world. If we are not committed to becoming kinder, then we are not on anything Judaism would recognize as a spiritual path. As the Talmudic sage Rav Huna puts it, "One who occupies himself only with the study of the Torah [and not with *hesed*] is as if he had no God."[63] Knowing God leads to love, he suggests, or it is not actually God we know.

BEYOND BEING "A GOOD PERSON"

When I teach some of the texts we've been discussing, on occasion someone reacts dismissively, even condescendingly: "So what you're really saying," they'll insist, "is that I should be a good person." I find this response extremely frustrating, not least because it suggests that they haven't really heard—or been willing to listen to—what's being said. If "being a nice person" means saying "please" and "thank you," being reasonably polite, and not committing any egregious interpersonal crimes, then no, that's not at all what these texts are speaking about. Commenting on the prophet Micah's declaration, "He has told you, O mortal, what is good and what the Lord requires of you: only to do justice, to love kindness (*ahavat hesed*), and to walk humbly with your God" (Micah 6:8),[64] the Bible scholar Kathleen O'Connor explains: "Micah's understanding of kindness requires a way of living that does not simply do kindness. For Micah, the people must 'love' kindness, be devoted to kindness. To love kindness (*hesed*) is to make it a priority, to live committed to it, to act from it fully."[65] The texts we have been considering call for far, far more than a superficial performance of niceness; they ask us to orient our lives around love, to embrace compassion with the whole of our being, and to be fully present in the face of profound suffering.

Micah's words make clear that the obligation to "love kindness" is closely entwined with the mandate to "walk humbly with your God." True kindness does not show off or call attention to itself;[66] there is a reason that most of us find people who do an act of kindness and call a press conference so off-putting. On the one hand, Micah implies what we've already seen: kindness can bring us into the presence of God. Yet on the other hand, he also reminds us that love and kindness are unpretentious:[67] one can perform an act of kindness in a self-promoting way, but in that case one is not yet walking with God. Walking in God's ways and being in God's presence require us to couple sincere goodness with genuine humility.[68]

AUTHENTICALLY BUT NOT EXCLUSIVELY JEWISH

Every once in a while, when I give a class or a lecture about *hesed* in a Jewish setting, someone will object, "But a commitment to acts of kindness is not uniquely Jewish!" My response is pretty much always the same: the fact that a commitment to loving kindness is not uniquely Jewish is an extremely good thing, since there are very few Jews and a tremendous amount of suffering in the world. The more communities and worldviews that advocate and inculcate love manifested as kindness, the better. But more than that: something does not need to be *uniquely* Jewish in order to be *authentically* Jewish. After all, Muslims too believe passionately in one God; is affirming the oneness of God rendered somehow less Jewish by that fact?

Kindness is at the very core of Judaism's vision of the good life. If only we taught and embodied that message with everything we have, and if other religious (and secular) communities did the same, our world would be a lot less broken as a result.

That said, Judaism represents a vision of integrating universal values with particularist practices: we raise our children to be kind, and also to observe Shabbat; we inculcate the value of compassion and also of eating and praying as a Jew. This is the only way for Judaism qua Judaism to flourish, and it's also the only way for it to survive. Any religious tradition that wants to survive has to teach more than universal values. In other words, we can't have Judaism without a commitment to love and compassion lying at its very core; but we also can't have Judaism if all we teach is love and compassion. Jews need to teach our children about *hesed* but we also need to teach them about how to mark time (Shabbat, holidays, etc.) as a Jew, how to internalize the laws and stories that make Jews . . . well, Jewish. A Judaism that isn't about compassion is bankrupt, but a Judaism that is only about compassion is self-liquidating.

TAKING THE CENTRALITY OF COMPASSION TO HEART

What would Jewish communities and institutions look like if we truly took all of this to heart?

Jewish schools should be animated by the principle that love and kindness are the very heart of what Judaism is about and what it is for. Both students and their teachers must understand that feeding the homeless, visiting the sick, and comforting mourners are not extracurricular activities or oppressive burdens to get through so that they can get back as quickly as possible to what truly matters—like science, or Talmud, or basketball. *Hesed* is what matters most. No *hesed*, no Judaism. In places where these values are internalized, we have Jewish schools, and not just schools for Jews.

Let students be given the unequivocal message: how kind you are and how much *hesed* you do are far more important than which colleges do and don't accept you. We must impart these values both cognitively and emotionally, so that students come to think and feel differently about the world and about their place and role within it. Many Jewish communities need to reevaluate what we mean when we say that we want our children to be successful. It is perfectly fine to be successful in conventional American terms—be proud of your child being a doctor, or a lawyer, or whatever. But be prouder of the fact that your child makes the time to visit a homebound old woman, to serve dinner to the poor, or to help a struggling child learn to read—or relate.

One of my main dreams for Jewish communities is really very simple. People should be able to look at any Jewish school, synagogue, community center, or Hillel the way they already look at some, and say: That's a Jewish institution; it must be a bastion of love and goodness. It's simply amazing how much kindness they do.

LOVE AND JUSTICE

On one level, love—or its close sister mercy—stands in some tension with justice. As any judge will tell you, it can be difficult to know when to apply strict judgment and when to temper justice with mercy—or, for that matter, when to choose mercy instead of justice. An oft-cited Talmudic image suggests that even God finds the proper balance between judgment and mercy elusive; on the Days of Awe, we're taught, God struggles to decide whether to sit on the Throne of Judgment or the Throne of Mercy.[69]

Yet on another level, love and justice can sometimes walk hand in hand. It's one thing when we show compassion to someone who's just endured a painful loss—a woman loses her spouse after decades of marriage, for example; or even a tragic one—a child grieves for a father who suffered from a congenital heart defect and suddenly died in the prime of life. But there are also countless situations when caring for those who have suffered loss leads ineluctably—or ought to—to questions about justice. When we "clothe the naked," for example, at a certain point we have to ask why they are mired in poverty in the first place; when we visit some ailing patients, we have to ask what social factors make some people more likely to fall ill than others. In other words, compassion for those who are suffering often raises questions of justice and equity. Such questions are frequently difficult and usually controversial (preach about feeding the poor and you'll be considered a saint; ask why they are poor in the first place and you'll be labeled a troublemaker, or a Communist, or some other derisive epithet).

The God of Judaism is a God of love *and* justice. To speak of justice without compassion is to miss out on love, and potentially to forget the crucial urgency of being present with people in their suffering. But to speak of compassion without justice is to focus on people who are suffering without ever stopping to ask *why* they are suffering. To be sure, some suffering—a great deal of suffering, actually—results from our finitude and mortality. But some suffering—more than many of us are willing to admit—stems from injustice. Some people get sick, for example, because of problematic genes, but some become ill because they are relatively powerless and are forced to endure conditions that would make the powerful rebel.

The struggle for justice derives its energy from love. We care about the world so deeply that we are willing to fight for it; we care about other people, and especially widows and orphans, so deeply, that we work to prevent their being mistreated and exploited.[70]

But there's another dimension to justice where love matters a great deal. It is one thing to show compassion for victims; it's quite another to show compassion for their victimizers. In my view, the former is more important and more urgent than the latter, but the latter is significant too, not least because the best hope we have of changing people's behaviors is by stirring their hearts. What can beget humility and compassion on their part is humility and compassion on ours. When confronting people whom we think are guilty of injustice, it is easy to succumb to hatred or self-righteousness. But the people we confront are also images of God, and as such are loved and infinitely precious.

This approach may not always be possible. Sometimes, in confronting evil, the best we can hope for is to resist the temptation to dehumanize our opponents. But sometimes, and probably more often than we think, we are called to do more than that: to struggle for justice with love.

11

LOVE IN THE RUINS

Responding to Devastation

IMAGINE LIVING IN a world that seems fundamentally coherent and meaningful. You know that God cares about you and you know where God's presence can be found. You know what your obligations and commitments are, and when you fall short of them, you know where to go and what to do in order to make things whole again.

According to the book of Exodus, God commands the people to build a tabernacle (*mishkan*) because God wants to dwell among them; the presence of the tabernacle in turn enables the people to be confident that God is with them.[1] The Temple in Jerusalem serves a similar role: when the Temple is dedicated, it is filled by a cloud of glory in which the presence of God abides.[2] For the Bible, the Temple is nothing less than God's abode and dwelling place.[3] In a psalm recited regularly by Jews to this day, the psalmist gives voice to his longing to "live in the house of the Lord" where he knows intimacy and closeness with God can be found (Psalm 27:4). Rabbinic texts make clear that for Jews in ancient times Jerusalem was the center of the world, and the Temple was the center of the center.[4] As the historian Shaye Cohen explains, "The [T]emple was more than a building and more than the home of the sacrificial cult. It was the sacred center of the cosmos, the place where heaven and earth meet, the visible symbol of God's love for Israel."[5]

When the Temple was destroyed by the Romans in 70 CE, all of that disappeared. The trauma must have been immense, almost unfathomable. It may be hard for many of us, living as we all do in an at least somewhat disenchanted world, to fully imagine the sense of loss the people must have felt. The center of the world had been . . . razed to the ground. Listen to how Jewish historians describe the event and what it meant. The Destruction, one writes, was "one of the most cataclysmic crises in Jewish history";[6] "no longer," another explains, "did Judaism have a sacred center, a temple, a priesthood, and a sacrificial cult."[7] With the Temple gone, a third declares, "much of Jewish life lay shattered."[8]

For many Jews, the world without the Temple was but a pale shadow of the world with it. As a midrash describes it, "So long as the Temple service is maintained, the world is a blessing to its inhabitants and the rains come down in season . . . But when the Temple service is not maintained the world is not a blessing to its inhabitants and the rains do not come down in season."[9] The Temple was nothing less than a source of life and sustenance; without it, the world was an emptier, less fertile place.

Adding to the misery, many of the old theological explanations fell flat. The prophets had taught that disasters befell Israel because of its sins; traditional Jews still give voice to this idea in the traditional Musaf prayer, in which we declare that "because of our sins we were exiled from our land." Although some scholars maintain that Jews for the most part interpreted the Destruction of the Second Temple along these lines[10]— God had meted out just punishment for Israel's sins—others seriously question that. As one scholar puts it, the Talmudic sages "had inherited from the days of the prophets a clear, morally coherent account of why Israel suffers disaster, but [many of them] could not bring themselves to apply it to the troubles of their own day." Part of the tragedy they faced was rooted in the fact that "they knew the implied accusation was not just, but not how to explain things otherwise."[11] The world as they had known it no longer made sense.

Jews responded in a variety of ways—with grief, and mourning, and lament, but also with a relentless commitment to rebuilding, reconstituting, and where necessary reimagining Jewish life.

While an exploration of the diverse ways Jews found and made meaning (and preserved Judaism) in the wake of the Destruction is beyond the scope of this book, it's important for us to pay close attention to one crucial aspect of Judaism's response to the devastation.

RESPONDING TO DESTRUCTION . . . WITH LOVE

Among the Temple's many functions was that those who had transgressed could go there and atone for their sins. In a world without the Temple, was atonement no longer available and reconciliation with God no longer possible? An oft-cited story offers a startling response:

> Once as Rabban Yohanan ben Zakkai was coming forth from Jerusalem, Rabbi Joshua followed after him and beheld the Temple in ruins. "Woe unto us!" cried R. Joshua, "that this place, the place where the iniquities of Israel were atoned for, is laid waste!" "My son," R. Yohanan said to him, "be not grieved; we have another atonement that is like it (*kemotah*). And what is it? It is acts of lovingkindness (*hesed*), as it said, 'For I desire lovingkindness and not sacrifice'" (Hosea 6:6).[12]

Atonement through sacrifice may no longer be possible, says R. Yohanan, but another, equally powerful means of atonement is available: acts of love and kindness can play the same role in the present that sacrifice had played in the past.[13] Later Talmudic passages go further, suggesting that lovingkindness is not *equal* to sacrifice but *superior* to it: *hesed* can achieve what sacrifice cannot.[14] As a midrash imagines God telling the people: "The lovingkindness you do for one another is more precious to me than any sacrifice that Solomon offered before Me."[15]

Why would the sages argue that lovingkindness can take the place of sacrifice? On one level, I think, the answer is that Jewish tradition had long held that the world rests on three pillars: on the Torah, on the Temple service, and on deeds of lovingkindness.[16] When one of the three was effectively taken away, the other two were relied upon to take its place. In a world where Temple service had become impossible, the study of Torah and deeds of lovingkindness would serve as means of effecting atonement.[17]

But I'd like to suggest another possibility too. We saw in chapter 7 that for both biblical and Rabbinic theology, how we treat others *is* in a sense how we treat God. Recall, for example, how the book of Proverbs declares that "one who is generous to the poor makes a loan to the Lord" (Proverbs 19:17). In some sense, sacrifice and acts of lovingkindness are structurally parallel: both are about giving something to God. Since, in the absence of the Temple, we can't give something to God directly, we give something to God indirectly, by giving to God's creations. Perhaps not surprisingly, then, a midrash explicitly affirms that when a person gives tzedakah, God considers it as if they had offered a sacrifice to God.[18]

THE HAPPIEST DAY: CELEBRATING LOVE

As a mishnah makes clear, the ninth day of the Hebrew month of Av is a national day of catastrophe, a time set aside to mourn the various disasters that have befallen the Jewish people during our history. On the Ninth of Av, we are told, the generation of the Exodus learned that they would not enter the Promised Land; both the First Temple and the Second were destroyed (in the years 586 BCE and 70 CE); and the revolt against Rome was effectively defeated (circa 136 CE).[19] The biblical reading for the day is the book of Lamentations, which is understood as an "eternal lament for all Jewish catastrophes, past, present, and future."[20] The Ninth of Av is a day of intense grief and sustained mourning. "When the month of Av begins," the mishnah says, "we limit our rejoicing."[21]

Recall what we've seen about just how much was lost when the Temple was twice destroyed. To this day, on the Ninth of Av the sense of anguish and bereavement is acute and palpable. "Remember, O Lord, what has befallen us," we plead; "behold, and see our disgrace" (Lamentations 5:1).

And yet, just a few days later, the Jewish calendar makes a dizzying transition. A Talmudic sage declares that "there were no happier days for Israel than the Fifteenth of Av and the Day of Atonement (Yom Kippur)." The reason why is critical: on those days, young women would go out and dance in the vineyards, and women and men would meet one another.[22]

Now, let's think about this for a moment. The Temple has been destroyed and we are in mourning; the traditional seven days of mourning (*shiva*) have not yet been completed—and suddenly we are thrust into one of the most joyous days of the year. What is going on here?

The tradition implicitly makes a stunning claim. In the wake of destruction and devastation, we should respond with . . . more love. Grief and lament have their place but they cannot, must not, be given the final word. When everything seems lost, the Mishnah subtly reminds us, set about reaffirming life and rediscovering love.

Trauma can lead us to retreat into ourselves, to withdraw from community and companionship, to feel so defeated that we grow incapable of intimacy and connection; few things can be as isolating as intense loss. In the face of all this, the mishnah responds by inviting us, by summoning us, to insist upon love, to find hope and take inspiration in one another.

But let's not fool ourselves. Love is not the only response to desolation, and it's often not even the first. There is a place for grief and, as we've seen in chapter 3, for protest and lamentation. And often, there are concrete tasks that need attending to: rebuilding in the wake of destruction can consist of endless seemingly quotidian tasks. Yet the mishnah resolutely adjures us: to heal from loss, choose love.

There is another dimension of this that is worth considering. According to an extremely influential Talmudic teaching, the Second Temple was destroyed because "baseless hatred" was pervasive among the people. Baseless hatred, the Talmud teaches, is as grave a transgression as Judaism's three cardinal sins—idolatry, sexual immorality, and murder—put together![23] Later Jewish writers add that the exile is ongoing because this sin is so enduring.[24]

In light of this, the logic of the Jewish calendar comes into focus: If hatred is what caused the Temple to be destroyed, then perhaps love is what will one day enable it to be restored. So from the very midst of the desolation, we emerge into a holiday celebrating love.

But romantic love will not suffice: Finding a spouse to love is not enough, since the love between spouses in and of itself does nothing to overcome social strife. People can love their spouses and hate just about everyone else. We've all met couples who are kind to one another and apathetic or even hostile toward others. Like a unit of one, a grouping of two can be governed by selfishness. Our mishnah responds to this danger by adding another striking detail about the celebration of the Fifteenth of Av: when the young women would go dancing in the vineyards, all of them, including the wealthiest among them, would do so while wearing borrowed white garments, "so as not to embarrass the one who had none."[25] Precisely in the moment when people are going to couple off, to form new, cohesive (and potentially selfish) family units, they (we) are reminded to keep the experiences and needs of others firmly in mind and at heart. The Fifteenth of Av celebrates the love between spouses . . . and insists, at the very same time, on compassion and generosity toward those who are not our spouses, those who may in fact be complete strangers. In place of baseless hatred comes Judaism's prescription: compassion for all.

RESPONDING INSTEAD OF EXPLAINING

How ought we to respond when faced with destruction and devastation in our own time? What does confronting suffering require of us?

I often come back to an argument made by Rabbi Joseph Soloveitchik about what he sees as Judaism's approach to the problem of evil. The ideal Jewish response to evil and suffering, he says, is not metaphysical but practical. "We do not inquire about the hidden ways of the Almighty," R. Soloveitchik writes, "but, rather, about the path wherein a person shall walk when suffering strikes. We ask neither about the cause of evil nor about its purpose, but rather, about how it might be mended and elevated. How shall a person act in a time of trouble? What ought a person to do so that they not perish in their afflictions?"[26] We cannot know why a good God permits so much excruciating suffering but, often at least, we can decide how to respond. From my perspective this is where Judaism's emphasis on love, and specifically on kindness and compassion, comes into play. We will never know why the parent in front of us was widowed at such a young age, but we can offer them concrete assistance as well as an open heart and a listening ear; we cannot know why we have been beleaguered by lifelong illness but we can work to grow in empathy and compassion as a result.[27]

On one level, R. Soloveitchik's argument could be heard as something of an evasion. We don't have an answer, so we change the question. There may be some truth to that charge. But on another level R. Soloveitchik is obviously right: we will never know why the world works as it does, but we do have the capacity to exercise agency even in the face of unimaginable pain, our own and others'. Remember: the sages don't mandate that we explain why some are hungry, but that we feed them; they don't ask us to explain illness, but to heal it, and to comfort those who are beset by it; and so on. (Let me avoid misunderstanding: we do need social, economic, and political explanations for why some are impoverished; without such analyses, we cannot work for a more just world. It is metaphysical explanations that we don't need in order to respond. In any case, much as we might yearn to have such explanations, they elude us.)

The deepest response to the problem of evil is to walk in God's ways, to be a vehicle for God's mercy. In discussing the love that the Torah mandates us to have for the stranger, we encountered the idea that we must be the ones to deliver God's love to others. I take the same idea here: faced with suffering, we must respond with love.

In his classic *I and Thou*, Martin Buber imagines a religious person reciting the Lord's Prayer. "Thy will be done," she says, but, Buber adds, "the truth goes on to say for her: 'through me whom you need.'"[28] At the end of the day, for me the only response to the problem of evil and suffering that really matters is this: whether or not we help God bring love and compassion to places of darkness and affliction.

12

WAITING FOR GOD

JUDAISM IS BUILT on a dream.

Judaism dreams of a world in which human dignity is real and the presence of God is manifest. Yet the world in which we live all too often makes a mockery of that dream.

As we've seen, Jewish theology tells us that we are created in the image of God, and that we are therefore infinitely valuable and loved by God. This claim is so radical and so powerful as to be breathtaking. Every human being everywhere is infinitely valuable; there are no exceptions.

How seriously does Jewish theology take human dignity? It asks us to instill a commitment to the incalculable worth of every person deep in our consciousness, and it mandates that we live each day accordingly. As the Talmudic sage Rabbi Joshua ben Levi teaches: "When a person walks on his or her way, a procession of angels walks before them and says, 'Make way for an image of the Blessed Holy One.'"[1]

But to take this to heart is to live with an often excruciating tension. On the one hand, Judaism tells us that every human being matters, and matters in an ultimate way. Yet on the other hand, we are forced to live with the reality that human dignity is trodden and trampled upon in countless ways every day—by cruelty and callousness, by illness and disease, by deprivation and desperation, and by pervasive hunger, poverty, oppression, and loneliness. If we open our eyes to it, the extent of human suffering threatens to reduce our belief that human beings are created in the image of God to just so much Pollyannaish nonsense.

We cannot but confront the fact that everyday life—not to mention world history—often seems to give the lie to our most deeply held beliefs. The ongoing degradation of human beings calls everything sacred into question: do human beings really matter, or is that just a pious platitude, words we speak but could not possibly mean?

We dream of a world in which human dignity is real, yet so often, in so many ways, human dignity seems decidedly un-real.

It is sometimes tempting to choose. We want to hold on to our religious beliefs, so we look away from the intense brokenness that surrounds us everywhere. Or we stare into the abyss and decide that those religious beliefs are untenable at best and absurd at worst. I have a great deal of sympathy for both of these options. Many days I feel an urge to make the same excruciating choice: keep the Bible and stop reading *The New York Times*, or keep *The New York Times* and realize that the Bible's dreams must be jettisoned for their hopeless naivete.

But Judaism bids us to embrace a third alternative: the dream *and* the reality, the Bible *and The New York Times*. To live with the faith that each and every human being—whether neighbor, stranger, or even enemy—is infinitely valuable and to face the world that debases and devalues human life with our eyes and our hearts wide open.

The fact that human dignity is under constant assault contributes (mightily) to the sense that God is hidden, or absent, or maybe just nonexistent.

How can we go on talking about a God who loves when brutality and bloodshed are everywhere, when the fate of so many is to suffer in unimaginably horrific ways? How can we believe in a God who cares when the world is overrun by so much pointless, gratuitous, unredeemed misery?

We yearn for a world in which God's presence is manifest—and yet, all the way back to the Bible, people have asked—they have lamented and protested: In a world like this, where could that God possibly be?

To take Judaism to heart is to live with the enormous chasm between what we affirm—that there is a God and that God loves us—and what we experience each day—that perhaps there is no God and we do not really matter in any ultimate way. To take Judaism to heart is to live with that gap, to live *in* the vast chasm between our theology and our daily experience.

But what does living in the chasm look like?

LIVING IN THE "NOT YET"

On the face of it, the ending of the Torah is somewhat baffling. It is so familiar to so many of us that we often miss just how strange and surprising it is—or ought to be.[2]

The Torah is, in large part, about a journey to the Promised Land, and about the massive difficulties involved in getting there. The book of Deuteronomy goes to great lengths to prepare the Israelites for arrival in the land—it offers them inspiration to remember and love God, warns them of the consequences of forgetting God and being hard-hearted with one another, and grants them righteous laws (Deuteronomy 4:8) to help them build a good, decent, and just society, and to guide them in thanking and serving God.

And then, with the people on the border of the land, the book simply ends. Imagine reading a long and gripping drama and then discovering that the author simply decided to forgo a conclusion. Studying the Torah is in a way like that. The story seems to end in mid-sentence, giving it "the character of an unfinished symphony."[3]

The Pesah (Passover) Haggadah mimics the Torah. In the book of Exodus, having heard the "moaning" of the Israelites as they endure Egyptian bondage, God makes five promises: "I am the Lord. (1) I will take you out from under the burdens of Egypt and (2) I will rescue you from their bondage. (3) I will redeem you with an outstretched arm and through extraordinary chastisements. And (4) I will take you to be My people, and I will be your God. And you shall know that I, the Lord, am your God who took you out from under the burdens of Egypt. (5) I will bring you into the land . . ." (Exodus 6:6–8). There are five crucial terms here, suggestive of five stages of divine redemption. These verses are crucial to Pesah, and yet at the Seder we drink *four* cups of wine, which are said to correspond to the *four*-staged redemption promised by God. This pivotal biblical text has been truncated and the last stage of redemption, arrival in the land, has seemingly been totally erased. What has happened to the long-awaited destination?

People who believe have no choice but to live in a long and often excruciating period of "not yet."[4] We dream of a world in which human dignity is real and the presence of God is manifest. But for the time being, we are forced to live in a world in which, to put it mildly, that dream has not yet been realized.

It's worth noting that many academic Bible scholars suggest that what is now the Pentateuch (the Five Books of Moses, or the Torah) was originally a Hexateuch.[5] In other words, the "original Torah" contained six books rather than five, and ended with the book of Joshua, which reports on the Israelites' conquest of the land. At a certain point, the sixth book—the conquest of the land—was lopped off, leaving our current, "incomplete" text. We should not let ourselves be derailed here by a discussion of biblical criticism and the origins of the text. I mention the Hexateuch theory only to emphasize how jarring the ending of the Torah is and to underscore the message I think this (non)conclusion is intended to convey. As the Bible scholar Clinton McCann explains, "By making the canonical division after Deuteronomy and before Joshua, the effect is to leave the people of God perpetually outside the land, thus perpetually unsettled. The book of Deuteronomy ends with the people of God . . . still waiting to enter the land . . . This canonical shaping . . . [is] very important. The unsettledness has the effect of leaving the people of God perpetually in a position of waiting."[6] What McCann calls "the position of waiting" is what I mean by living in the "not yet."

Why is all of this so significant? Judaism is not just a set of abstract propositions about what *is* true; it is also—and arguably primarily—about a set of dreams for what will one day *become* true. Time and again traditional Jewish liturgy suggests, startlingly, that God will only be fully

God when God is universally recognized as such—and so, on some level, in the present moment God is not yet God. Near the end of every prayer service, Jews invoke the prophet Zechariah's dream of a "day when there shall be one Lord with one Name" (Zechariah 14:9).[7] A crucial piece of what faith is, then, is the capacity to wait and to live in the "not yet."

The Bible gives voice to the particularistic messianic dream of the Jewish people being restored to its land, able to live sovereignly and peacefully in the presence of God. Yet coupled with that vision there is a universal messianic dream of a reality utterly transformed.[8] Needless to say, a world in which human dignity is real and the presence of God is manifest would represent a radical transformation—a re-creation, really—of the world we presently inhabit.

WAITING FOR GOD

To live a life of faith, then, is to wait for God. As the Talmudic sage Abba Saul puts it, "The King has a retinue? What must it do? Wait (*mehakah*) for the King."[9]

But what does waiting consist of?

The Talmudic sage Rava teaches that when a person dies and is brought before the Heavenly Court, he is asked a series of questions aimed at assessing and evaluating the life he has led. For example: "Did you conduct your affairs with integrity?" "Did you set aside fixed times for studying Torah?" One of the questions Rava imagines the Court asking is, "Did you wait for redemption" (*tzipita lishu'ah*)?[10] I find this last question arresting: when we die, we are asked whether or not we waited for redemption—a better translation might be "whether or not we anticipated redemption."

What does this mean? What does waiting for redemption look like?

There is one possibility that we can dispense with right away. Imagine that a friend walks into your home on a Sunday afternoon and finds you, feet on the table, potato chips in hand, watching football. She asks, "What are you doing?" and you reply, "What does it look like I'm doing? I'm waiting for redemption."

There is something patently absurd about this response. We sense that waiting for redemption does not mean—*cannot* mean—silent, passive waiting. So what *does* it mean?

I think that what it means is this: when we die, each of us is asked, Did you create moments of redemption even in the midst of this impossibly broken, thoroughly unredeemed world? Did you create pockets of holiness even in the midst of this so often totally profane and degraded world? Did you create a home, or a school, or a classroom, or a work environment, or a city block, in which human dignity was real and the presence of God was manifest? With the way you carried yourself, did you strive to build those things? Or, to return to the imagery of the Torah: Did you catch glimmers of the Promised Land even as you had no choice but to live in the wilderness? Did you *create* glimmers of the Promised Land even as you had no choice but to live in the wilderness?

Human beings are not capable of redeeming the world. The world is stubborn, recalcitrant, and indescribably complex. So often we try to resolve one problem and end up, despite ourselves, creating another. The brokenness is so deep, the problems so intractable, that for a fully redeemed world we have no choice but to wait for God.

But in the face of that, Rava teaches us something inspiring and daunting in equal measure: we cannot redeem the world, but we can—and must—anticipate its redemption. We can catch glimpses of what a redeemed world would look like; we can create glimpses for others of what a redeemed world would look like.

We've already encountered Abba Saul's seemingly simple teaching: "The king has a retinue. What must it do? Wait (*mehakah*, with the Hebrew letter *kaf*) for the king." But fascinatingly, the better manuscripts of Midrash Sifre, from which this line is taken, differ by one letter. "The King has a retinue? What must it do? Imitate (*mehaqah,* with the Hebrew letter *kuf*) the King."

The King's retinue—that is, we—should imitate the King. What does imitation consist of? Abba Saul himself tells us elsewhere. Expounding upon the biblical image of human beings "glorifying" God (Exodus 15:2), the sage explains: "'I will glorify God.' Be similar to God. Just as

God is merciful and compassionate, so should you be."[11] We are commanded, in other words, to walk in God's ways.

So which one is it—do we wait for God or imitate God? The answer, I think, is both: we wait by imitating. We wait for God by manifesting love and kindness and compassion in the world. We wait for God by conducting our lives as if human dignity were a fact rather than an ever-deferred dream. We wait for God, I'd venture to say, by making it seem less crazy and less implausible to believe in God.

To live in the chasm, to wait for God, is to catch glimpses, to *create* glimpses, of a world in which human dignity is real and the presence of God is manifest.

In a world suffused with suffering, we are called to clothe the naked and visit the sick, to comfort the mourners and bury the dead. In a world plagued by indifference, we are commanded to care about and for our neighbors; in a world overrun by cruelty, we are challenged to embody kindness, even and especially toward those the world ignores or demeans. In a world preoccupied with wealth and possessions, we are bidden to lead lives of openhearted generosity. In a world drowning in hatred and hostility, we are summoned to stand for love.

PART IV

THEOLOGY OF
A LOVING GOD

13

THE GOD OF JUDAISM
(AND OF THE "OLD TESTAMENT")
IS A GOD OF LOVE

WHAT MAKES GOD God? What is it that makes God unmistakably ultimate and worthy of worship? Some would say that God's power is what makes God God. God is infinitely more powerful than any created being; God can do anything God chooses. Others might say that God's knowledge is what makes God God. God knows everything there is to know about everybody and everything; human knowledge utterly pales in comparison with its divine counterpart. There is truth in both of these claims: God's omnipotence and omniscience mean that God is radically unlike anything else we can imagine.

But Jewish sources offer another, very different answer too. What makes God God is that God's love is unfathomably vast, vaster and greater than anything human beings can imagine, let alone embody. What makes God God, in other words, is the depth, steadfastness, and extent of God's love.

THE DEPTHS OF GOD'S LOVE

The first part of the book of Isaiah (chapters 1–39) ends with a sense of impending doom. Having rebelled against God, the people will be driven into exile; everything in the king's palace will be taken to Babylonia, where the king's own sons will serve the emperor as eunuchs (Isaiah 39:6–7). But the next part of the book (chapters 40–55) shifts dramatically and looks toward a glorious future. Having endured humiliating exile at the hands of an oppressive enemy, the people are now promised a triumphant return to the Promised Land. The Babylonian Empire may be powerful, but God is more so, and God will alter Israel's destiny.

The people have sinned mightily and borne the consequences, but if they only repent, the prophet assures them, God will forgive them. In a passage chanted as part of the liturgy for public fast days, Isaiah calls the people to "seek the Lord" and explains just what this challenge entails: "Let the wicked give up his ways, the sinful person his plans; let him turn back to the Lord, and [the Lord] will pardon him, to our God for [God] forgives abundantly" (55:6–7). The prophet continues: "For My plans are not your plans, nor are My ways your ways—declares the Lord. But as the heavens are high above the earth, so are My ways above your ways" (55:8–9).

Interpreters have long struggled to understand these last words. What does the prophet intend to convey in asserting that God's thoughts and ways are so utterly different from those of human beings? Are Isaiah's words intended to make a general point, that God's "plans and purpose . . . differ in kind from those of human beings as greatly as that distance dividing heaven and earth"?[1] Along similar lines, are they intended, perhaps, to emphasize that "the ways and thoughts of God are incomprehensible to [human beings]," such that "even though God reveal them to [us, we] cannot fully understand them"?[2] Or, instead, is the prophet referring concretely to the here and now: though the people are "weary" and have resigned themselves to staying in Babylonia, God's very different plans are to redeem them and bring them home?[3] Alternatively, does Isaiah want to remind a skeptical and skittish people that though plans that *they* make may be thwarted, plans that *God* makes always come to fruition?[4]

All of these are possibilities, but there is an additional one that I find particularly compelling: perhaps the people doubt the power of repentance. Given the depth of their wrongdoing, they find it hard to believe that God will forgive them; it seems more likely that God will remain eternally angry. After all, *they* would not be quick to forgive grave crimes committed against *them*. Perhaps, several traditional commentators suggest, what makes God unique from Isaiah's perspective is God's wondrous capacity for, and commitment to, genuine forgiveness. Rabbi David Kimhi (Radak) explains that "if a person sins against his fellow, his fellow will take revenge upon him and will not forgive him. And even if he appears to forgive him, he will bear a grudge in his heart."[5] In her lustrous novel *Gilead*, Marilynne Robinson speaks of two characters, father and son, who "had buried their differences." But she quickly adds: "It must be said, however, that they buried them not very deeply, and perhaps more as one would bank a fire than smother it."[6]

God doesn't merely bank fires, says Radak; God smothers them. Radak imagines God saying, in effect, "Unlike you, I am greatly forgiving, and when I forgive, I forgive truly, and nothing of the sin remains with me."[7] Through Isaiah's prophecy, Rabbi Isaac Abravanel (1437–1508) writes, God makes clear that "I don't take revenge or bear grudges against those who offend Me, as a person would." In human relations, even when the offender apologizes, the aggrieved party often still bears the offender ill will. But "that is not the case with My thoughts, because I forgive the one who repents and bear him no hatred or ill-will."[8]

What makes God unique, according to these sages, what makes God *God* rather than a human being, is God's forgiveness—or perhaps better, God's forgivingness. God's "Godness" is inextricably bound up with God's goodness.

In one of the most exquisite chapters in the Hebrew Bible, the prophet Hosea imagines God struggling with how to respond to a recalcitrant people. So exasperated and hurt is God by the people's constant backsliding that God considers walking away from them altogether. But Hosea discovers that God just can't do that.

The premise of the chapter is simple: God loves Israel. Everything that God feels, thinks, and says stems from that basic commitment.[9] "When Israel was a child," God recalls, "I loved him, and out of Egypt I called my son" (11:1). God has loved Israel, the prophet says, since it was a small, helpless child.[10] Nothing about Israel's character is offered as an explanation or justification of God's love. The people have not done anything to earn God's love; God's love is grace. God's love comes first, before any divine command or expectation.

But the people have repeatedly turned their back on God. Hosea portrays God as a loving parent[11] who is distraught over the stubborn waywardness of her children; here, God appears to struggle with sadness rather than anger. The more God calls the people, the more they turn away (Hosea 11:2).[12] With great tenderness, God recalls times when Israel was a small child and God provided nurture and succor: "It was I who taught Ephraim [i.e., the people of the northern kingdom of Israel] to walk, I took them up in my arms . . . I led them with cords of human kindness, with bands of love. I was to them like those who lift infants to their cheeks.[13] I bent down to them and fed them" (11: 3–4). But things have since turned sour. Time and again Israel has betrayed and rejected God. God is tempted to withdraw from the relationship and "return to God's place" (5:15), but somehow God cannot bring Godself to do that. So deep is God's love for God's children that God will not let their relationship come to an end.

The prophet daringly portrays God as internally tormented: "How can I give you up, O Ephraim? How surrender you, O Israel?[14] How can I make you like Admah, render you like Zevoiim?" (11:8). (Admah and Zevoiim were cities destroyed with Sodom and Gomorrah;[15] if you've never heard of them, that may be the point: God cannot tolerate the thought of a world without Israel.) Implicit within all of God's "How can I?" questions is an answer: God can't.[16]

Sure enough, we soon hear—three times—that God will not act on God's anger and frustration any further (11:9). As the Bible scholar Marvin Sweeney explains, God "gives in to the emotional bonds of mother and child, and reverts to the traditional promise of protection for Israel."[17] Although the people will be exiled for their sins (11:5–7), God will not completely and permanently reject them. Israel's disloyalty notwithstanding, God's love has the final word: "I have had a change of heart,[18] My compassion[19] grows warm. I will not act on My wrath, will not turn to destroy Ephraim" (11:8–9).

What stops God from acting on God's anger? "For I am God, not man, the Holy One in your midst" (11:9). It may seem odd to find Hosea, of all people, insisting on God's radical otherness. After all, as any reader of Hosea can attest, "anthropomorphism is Hosea's stock-in-trade"; Hosea's God is nothing if not personal. Yet Hosea wants to be clear that metaphors for God are precisely that—metaphors and not "essential definitions."[20] That's how metaphors work: they tell us that *x* is *y*, but they also "contain the whisper, 'it is *and it is not*.'"[21] God is *like* a human parent (11:1–4), but God is not, in fact, a human parent (11:9).

Human parents, even good human parents, have limits. Sometimes a child grows so wild, so wayward, that the parents feel they have no choice but to sever ties, at least for a time. God does not. Unlike human parents, says Hosea, God will never truly give up on God's child.[22] What makes God so different from us, what makes God *God*, is that God's love is inexhaustible.

Think about how radical this is. Imagine hearing someone say that God loves us like a mother loves her children. Now imagine that they add, "But keep in mind: God is *like* a person but God is not *actually* a person." You might be tempted to think: "Okay, since God is God and not a person, then God doesn't really love us. After all, that's anthropomorphism, attributing human characteristics to God. People love, but God doesn't, and to say that God loves is just a figure of speech." But Hosea argues precisely the opposite: The fact that God is God and not a person means that God can love in a much deeper and more enduring way than we can even begin to fathom, let alone embody ourselves. We are reminded that God is God not so that we remember that God doesn't really love us, but on the contrary, so that we understand that God's love for us far outstrips anything we could possibly imagine.[23]

HUMAN LOVE AS "THEOMORPHISM"

But isn't there still a problem here? At the end of the day, aren't we still attributing human emotions to God? If this is how we imagine God, wouldn't we be guilty of worshiping little more than a glorified version of ourselves?

Only, I think, if we assume that love is somehow an exclusively human capacity, such that any talk of nonhuman love must be guilty of attributing irreducibly human qualities to that which is not human. Here, I think, an insight from Rabbi Abraham Joshua Heschel may be helpful. The prophets took it as a given, R. Heschel claims, that "the human could never be regarded as divine," and therefore "there was no danger that the language of [emotions applied to God] would distort the difference between God and [humanity]."[24] God is God, and we are not; accordingly, God's love and our love are related, but they are decidedly not the same thing. When biblical texts talk about God's love, then, the point is not to "project human traits into the divinity" but rather to offer "genuine insight into God's relatedness to [humanity]."[25]

If we accept the Bible's claim that God loves in ways that are deeper and more enduring than the ways we do, then to talk about both divine love and human love is not necessarily to project human emotions onto God. On the contrary, it may be a way of saying that our love is a (pale) imitation of God's much more powerful love. As R. Heschel writes in a slightly different context, "The idea of the divine pathos [that is, the idea that God *feels*] combining absolute selflessness with supreme concern for the poor and the exploited can hardly be regarded as the attribution of human characteristics [to God]. Where is the [human being] endowed with such characteristics?"[26] In a similar vein, to talk about a God who loves the Jewish people and all of humanity, a God who loves every human being on the face of the earth, and who has especial love for the poor and downtrodden, is emphatically not to describe God in human terms, for no human being has ever, or could ever, wholly embody that kind of love. To borrow another term from R. Heschel, to talk about God's love is not anthropomorphism; on the contrary, human love is "theomorphic"[27]—we attribute to human beings something that belongs most fundamentally and fully to God.

GOD'S SELF-DESCRIPTION:
GOD OF MERCY (AND JUDGMENT)

In the wake of the people's apostasy at the Golden Calf, Moses pleads with God to forgive them their grievous sin. In response to Moses's requests to be shown "God's ways" (Exodus 33:13)—which, recall, Isaiah insists are not like our own—and to behold "God's presence" (33:18), God passes before him and declares: "[v. 6] The Lord,[28] The Lord, a God merciful and gracious, slow to anger,[29] abounding in steadfast love (*hesed*) and faithfulness, [v. 7] extending steadfast love to the thousandth generation, forgiving iniquity, transgression, and sin; yet [the Lord] surely does not clear the guilty, but visits the iniquity of parents upon children and children's children, upon the third and fourth generations" (34:6–7). God's self-description in these words, which have come to be known in Judaism as "the thirteen attributes of God,"[30] plays a significant role in Jewish liturgy: it is recited on festivals and holidays when the ark is opened for the taking out of the Torah, and forms the heart of *selihot*, or Jewish penitential prayers.[31]

The first verse of God's self-description describes God's character, or *who God is*; the second describes God's actions, or *what God does*. Only one word is repeated in both verses, thus underscoring its immense significance: *hesed*, steadfast love.[32] Whatever else God may be, these verses teach, God is a God of love. More precisely, it's essential that we notice that in Exodus 34:6, which describes *who God is*, no mention whatsoever is made of anger; God's anger is introduced only in verse 7, which portrays *what God does*. The implication of this is crucial for a proper understanding of Jewish theology: anger is not essential to who God is in the way that love is. God *gets* angry, but God *is* loving.[33]

The text emphasizes that God forgives "iniquity, transgression, and sin." As a recent commentary on Exodus puts it, the text "seems to search the Hebrew lexicon exhaustively to make sure to miss no 'sin' family word."[34] To put the point starkly, there is no misdeed that is beyond the reach of God's forgiveness.[35]

And yet God's self-description does not simply end with its dramatic declaration of God's commitment to forgiveness. Despite God's love, or *perhaps because of it*, God takes human wrongdoing seriously. The forgiveness God offers is "never to be mistaken for winking at or condoning, let alone colluding in, the iniquity that humankind is capable of."[36] Love does not rub out the need for consequences. Accordingly, for the Bible there is no contradiction between forgiveness and punishment. God's forgiveness *mitigates* punishment but does not *eliminate* it.[37]

There is obviously a tension in these verses between God's love and mercy, on the one hand, and God's justice, on the other.[38] And yet one side of the scale significantly outweighs the other: "The merciful attributes are given preeminence, while the wrathful attributes are second in both number and place. Ancient Israel believed the chief characteristic [of God] to be mercy, rather than wrath."[39] This point is brought home by the fact that whereas punishment is extended for three or four generations, divine love is extended even to the thousandth generation.[40]

The truly amazing thing about God's self-revelation as a God of love and mercy is that it happens precisely when God feels most profoundly betrayed. Commanding the Israelites not to worship images or idols, God had said: "You shall not bow to them or serve them, for I the Lord your God am an impassioned[41] God, visiting the iniquity of the parents upon the children, upon the third and upon the fourth generations of those who reject[42] Me, but showing steadfast love to the thousandth generation of those who love Me and keep My commandments" (Exodus 20:5–6). Following the logic of these verses, in the wake of the Golden Calf we would expect God to lead with anger; after all, the people are guilty of the very type of treachery that God had warned against. But instead God leads with love, even now, when we would least expect it.[43] There, in the Ten Commandments, God had characterized Godself as a punishing God whose anger is tempered by mercy; here, after witnessing apostasy, God characterizes Godself as a merciful God whose forgiveness is tempered by anger.[44] Faced with a sinful people, in other words, God "changes the whole tenor" of God's relationship with them.[45] There, God had described Godself as an impassioned (*kana*, often rendered as "jealous") God; here, that characterization is entirely absent.

In warning the people against worshiping idols, God had promised to show love to those who love God. Here, on the heels of betrayal, God makes the promise of steadfast love effectively unconditional.[46] In Exodus 34, God moves from "I love those who love Me" to "I love." The heart of God's self-revelation is a radicalization of God's grace, love, mercy, and forgiveness.

When Jews recite the thirteen attributes in prayer, we display a remarkable degree of chutzpah. Lopping off the end of the credo, we recite: "The Lord, The Lord, a God merciful and gracious, slow to anger, abounding in steadfast love (*hesed*) and faithfulness, extending steadfast love to the thousandth generation, forgiving iniquity, transgression, and sin, and clearing (*nakeh*)"—instead of acknowledging that God "surely does not clear the guilty" (*nakeh lo yenakeh*), we quote only part of the Hebrew phrase, effectively turning it on its head and declaring that God does indeed "clear the guilty" (*nakeh*). This is made possible by a creative misreading offered by the Talmudic sage Rabbi Elazar. In biblical Hebrew, the emphatic is conveyed by what is known as the infinitive absolute: if we want to say that God assuredly does not clear the guilty, we say that God "clear does not clear" (*nakeh lo yenakeh*). The presence of the infinitive ("clear") only amplifies the negation ("surely does not clear"). But R. Elazar imagines that there is a contradiction in this phrase: How can the Torah declare both that God clears the guilty and that God does not clear them? The answer, he suggests, is that God clears the guilt of those who repent, and does not clear the guilt of those who do not repent.[47] Now, since those reciting penitential prayers in synagogue are presumably penitents, it stands to reason that "clears the guilty" applies to us whereas "does not clear the guilty" does not. We who are sincere in our remorse can be confident that God will clear our guilt—and yet, as we'll see, we are not permitted to take it for granted.

Bold and beautiful though this is, this interpretation of the verse significantly changes its accent. Whereas R. Elazar's point is that God reliably forgives the penitent, the thrust of the biblical verse itself is that God forgives *even those who are not penitents*. In the aftermath of the Golden Calf episode, it is Moses who pleads with God; the people remain completely in the background. Nothing in the story itself suggests that penitence on their part is what elicits God's mercy. In other words, in the biblical text God's mercy is a function of God's grace.

Both the biblical and the Rabbinic approaches have their appeal—as well as attendant dangers. The biblical emphasis on divine grace reveals God's love and beneficence in all their majestic color, but it also runs the risk of devaluing human effort and responsibility. Conversely, R. Elazar's focus on human penitence places human moral responsibility front and center, but it runs the risk of forgetting that God's unfathomably vast love means that God sometimes goes beyond what is "required" of God. God wants penitence but God's love is such that God sometimes forgives even when penitence is absent.

PUNISHING CHILDREN FOR THEIR PARENTS' SINS?

Returning to the verses in Exodus: many (probably most) readers find the idea of God punishing to the third and fourth generations deeply disturbing. The whole idea of intergenerational punishment offends against our sense of fairness.[48] Why, after all, should our children and grandchildren suffer the consequences of *our* actions?

It's worth noting, first, that some scholars see the text as ambiguous. When God describes Godself as "visiting the iniquity of parents upon children and children's children, upon the third and fourth generations" (34:7), the message seems clear: God punishes descendants for the crimes of their forebears.[49] Yet the description in the Ten Commandments seems to sound a somewhat different note: "Visiting the iniquity of the parents upon the children, upon the third and upon the fourth generations *of those who reject me*" (20:5). In other words, according to this passage God punishes descendants for the sins of their forebears only if they follow in their waywardness.[50] This may still be unsettling to modern readers—it makes sense to insist that we bear the consequences of our own misdeeds, but why should our burden grow because of who our parents and grandparents were?—but it does seem to soften the idea somewhat.

The Bible itself struggles with the problem of intergenerational punishment. After the First Temple is destroyed, the people bemoan the unfairness of their situation: "Our fathers sinned and are no more, and we must bear their guilt" (Lamentations 5:7).[51] The prophet Jeremiah looks forward to a future time when people "will no longer say, 'Parents have eaten sour grapes and children's teeth are blunted.' But every one shall die for his own sins; whoever eats sour grapes, his teeth [and no one else's] shall be blunted" (Jeremiah 31:29–30); and the prophet Ezekiel forcefully rejects the notion of intergenerational punishment *now*: "The person who sins, only he shall die. A child shall not share the burden of a parent's guilt, nor shall a parent share the burden of a child's guilt; the righteousness of the righteous shall be accounted to him alone, and the wickedness of the wicked shall be accounted to him alone" (Ezekiel 18:20).[52] As a Talmudic passage explains, Moses taught one thing but Ezekiel came along and "revoked it."[53]

Many modern scholars take it for granted that the focus on the individual in passages like the ones we've just seen from Jeremiah and Ezekiel represents progress over purportedly older, more "primitive" notions of corporate identity found in other biblical texts.[54] But an individualized conception of identity is not unambiguously superior to a community-based one. To my mind the move (if that's what it really is)[55] from the latter to the former is more complex than a simple story of progress and improvement.

An individual-centered theology doesn't run afoul of our sense of fairness. More than that, an individualized conception of identity helps make ideas like nonnegotiable individual human rights more plausible. But it runs the risk of embracing a simplistic and unpersuasive understanding of what it means to be a person. At the very core of Jewish tradition is the idea that we are responsible for one another[56]—and more than that, that we are implicated in one another's deeds.[57] Fundamentally, there is no self that is fully prior to, or independent of, human relationships. We are not isolated monads but ever-connected members of families and communities. I am my parent's child and my child's parent before I am "my own person."[58] Given those assumptions, the idea that actions have intergenerational consequences begins to make some sense. Disturbing as it can be—and it can be very disturbing indeed—the notion of corporate responsibility reflects something true, and crucial, about human selfhood.

More concretely, the insistence that people only suffer the consequences of their own actions rubs up against the (often extremely painful) reality of our experience. As the Bible scholar Klaus Koch observes, "It may seem right and just that each individual alone should bear the fruits of what he does; but nonetheless, general human experience tells us that children also have to suffer when their parents suffer. The ties between the generations, and collective liability, cannot be entirely abrogated, even in a nation."[59] When parents commit a crime, the consequences often reverberate within the family for generations. And when a nation goes astray, the consequences can affect its members for generations. For all the appeal of an individualized conception of moral responsibility, "if one takes this theology to its extreme, it no longer speaks to our experience."[60]

It may be empirically true that the sins of parents impact profoundly upon the lives of their children, but that does not make it fair, or just. And the fact that children often feel the *effects* of their parents' actions does not entail that they bear *moral responsibility* for those parental deeds.[61] But the main point I am making is that there is something true to our experience, even if also disturbing and unsettling, about the biblical idea that our actions have intergenerational consequences. More than that, for all its strengths, the turn to extreme individualism has been a decidedly mixed blessing in Western history.

ULTIMATELY, MERCY WINS

These verses characterizing God have a robust afterlife; within the biblical corpus itself no verses are cited more frequently.[62] As the verses are quoted and reworked, greater and greater emphasis is placed on God's love and mercy.[63]

Later in the biblical world, in periods of desolation and despair, the thirteen attributes served as a beacon of hope and possibility.

The prophet Joel warns a wayward people of imminent devastation. "The Day of the Lord has come," he says; it is "a day of darkness and gloom." A plague of locusts is on its way, and the nation is in danger of complete annihilation. The scene Joel paints is bleak, even harrowing: "Nothing like it has ever happened, and it shall never happen again through the years and ages" (Joel 2:1–2).

Yet like so many prophets before and after him, Joel cannot seem to let judgment have the last word. The very survival of the people is in question. "Yet even now" they are invited, in Joel's memorable words, "to rend [their] hearts rather than [their] garments and turn back to God." How is hope still possible even at this late date, with doom and destruction approaching? Like Moses before him, Joel remembers what God had said in the wake of the apostasy at the Golden Calf: "For [God] is merciful and compassionate, slow to anger,[64] abounding in steadfast love, and relents from sending calamity." The prophet adds: "Who knows? Perhaps [God] may return and relent, and leave a blessing behind . . ." (2:12–14).

Following the lead of Exodus 34, Joel mentions God's mercy, slowness to anger, and abundant love. But what Joel does *not* mention is as suggestive as what he does. The tension between God's mercy and God's judgment, so central in Exodus 34, is entirely elided here; Joel simply excises the part about God's wrath.[65] One could argue that the prophet fails to invoke God's anger and judgment because he has no need to; the people are, after all, already experiencing God's retribution.[66] Yet even so, the transformation of God's self-description remains highly significant: as a rule, when these verses are cited in the prophets and

the writings, the pole of God's mercy is much more heavily accentu-
ated than the pole of God's judgment. In the same vein, the text never
mentions God's punishment to the third and fourth generations, and as
we've seen, at least two of the prophets (Jeremiah and Ezekiel) explicitly
repudiate the very idea of intergenerational punishment.

Joel's recitation of these words serves as the book's "fulcrum": what
began as anger and destruction gives way to renewed hope and possibility.[67] God will send grain, wine, and oil, Joel proclaims, and "you shall
have them in abundance" (2:19); Israel will no longer be humiliated by
other peoples, and its connection to God will be revitalized and deepened. With astonishing audacity, Joel declares that what aroused God's
mercy is that God was "jealous (vayekanei) for [God's] land" (2:19).
God's jealous, impassioned nature, which had constituted a threat in the
Ten Commandments, now becomes the very ground of God's forgiveness and mercy. "The result of God's passion for the people is that the
destructive impact of God's wrath will be reversed."[68]

But note Joel's crucial words, "Who knows?" The prophet walks
a fine line. On the one hand, he wants to reassure the people: God's
love and mercy mean that repentance and return remain eternally possible. Yet on the other hand, he wants to discourage overconfidence
and complacency. As the Bible scholar Walter Moberly explains, Joel
wants the people to understand that although God's mercy "can be
relied upon, it should not be presumed upon. God's mercy remains
[God's] to give, and [God] interacts sovereignly and relationally but not
mechanically."[69] In other words, God can be moved by repentance but
"God cannot be controlled or manipulated."[70] God is loving, but God
remains, always, God.

What we've seen so far is that according to the Bible, God is loving and merciful by nature, and that God is committed to manifesting mercy in God's relationship with the people—even, and perhaps
especially, when their commitment to God has faltered. In all of the
cases we've seen, the context is covenantal—that is, it's about how God
relates to Israel, with whom God has entered into a unique relationship
grounded in mutual love and obligation. But what about the rest of the

world? Are God's love and mercy reserved exclusively for Israel or are they available to the rest of humanity too?

GOD'S MERCY EXTENDS TO ALL, EVEN TO ISRAEL'S ENEMIES

A psalm Jews traditionally recite three times a day[71] offers a resounding answer to that question: "[v. 8] The Lord is gracious and merciful, slow to anger and abounding in steadfast love. [v. 9] The Lord is good to all and [the Lord's] mercy is upon all that [the Lord] has made" (Psalm 145:8–9). Whereas the first verse cites God's now-familiar self-description in Exodus 34:6–7, the second moves these words from a covenantal context to a creational one. In other words, God shows mercy and grace not just to the Israelites but to "all that [God] has made"; God's generosity and kindness "extend to everyone or everything, to all creation."[72] (The word *kol*, "all," appears in the psalm no fewer than sixteen times!)[73] The psalmist begins with his own pledge to bless God (Psalm 145:1, 2), moves to a declaration that all God's faithful will bless God (Psalm 145:10), and tellingly concludes with the hope that "all flesh will bless God's holy name forever and ever" (Psalm 145:21).[74] As Robert Alter explains, the psalmist's theological point is that "God's beneficent dominion extends over all living creatures,[75] and [consequently] 'all flesh' (verse 21) praises [God]."[76] Note well: As this psalmist imagines it, God's reign as ruler of the whole world[77] is tied to God's loving and merciful nature, not to God's wrath or punishment.[78] Those aspects of God simply go unmentioned.

God's love and mercy, then, extend not just to Israel but to all of creation. But what about Israel's enemies, or the wicked more broadly? Are they too beneficiaries of God's love and mercy? As we saw in chapter 9, the question of whether human beings ought to love their enemies is complicated and elusive; are things any different for God?

On the surface at least, the book of Jonah is the rarest of treasures, a story of a biblical prophet whose prophecy is successful in eliciting repentance and transformation. But rather than take satisfaction in what he has accomplished, Jonah is dejected,[79] and finally, as the book nears its conclusion, we learn why he sought to evade God's summons in the first place: "O Lord!," he cries out, "isn't this just what I said when I was still in my own country? That is why I fled . . . for I know that You are a gracious and merciful God, slow to anger, abounding in steadfast love, and relent[ing] from sending calamity." Jonah is so despondent over Nineveh's repentance and God's forgiveness that he implores God to take his life (Jonah 4:2–4).

Like Joel, Jonah cites the words of Exodus 34, and like Joel, he simply avoids any mention of God's wrath. But Jonah's omitting any mention of divine anger is particularly striking given that divine anger is precisely what he *wants* God to display.[80] Jonah quotes God's description of God's own nature . . . only so that he can complain about it![81] God is forgiving but Jonah thinks that (in this situation at least) God ought to be strict in judgment.

Why is Jonah so disconsolate? What is it about God's nature that sends him into such despair?

Among some Christian scholars there is a disturbing tendency to accuse Jonah of a crude ethnic chauvinism.[82] On their account, Jonah wants God to show mercy to Israel but harshness to everyone else. As one such scholar puts it, "For Jonah . . . foreigners deserved only hate, Israel only love."[83] But the problem with interpretations along these lines is that there is nothing at all in the text to support them.

In biblical times,[84] Nineveh was symbolic of the Assyrian Empire and its brutality; it was, in the words of the prophet Nahum, a "city of blood" (*ir damim*) (Nahum 3:1) and a bastion of "endless cruelty" (3:19).[85] In order to understand what so disheartens Jonah, "the reader must bear in mind that Nineveh or Assyria would one day destroy Jonah's homeland and carry its people off into exile."[86] Moreover, "it was the Assyrian Empire that first carried out a systematic policy of deporting captured peoples and of replacing them with foreigners, a policy that led to the disappearance from history of the ten northern tribes of Israel when they were defeated by Assyria in 721 BCE."[87] In Jonah's eyes, Assyria represented the epitome of inhumanity.

Jonah is bothered by God's display of mercy toward Nineveh not because Nineveh is filled with non-Israelites but because in Jonah's mind it is the very embodiment of cruelty and callousness. The issue that so vexes Jonah, in other words, is not that God shows mercy to *non-Israelites* but that God shows mercy to *evildoers*.

God's response to Jonah's protest is stunning. God provides Jonah with a plant to protect him from the unforgiving sun, which greatly pleases Jonah. But the next day God sends a worm that attacks the plant, causing it to wither and die. God sends a "sultry east wind" and the sun beats down on the miserable prophet, leading him to grow faint. When Jonah again asks to die, God asks him whether he is really so deeply grieved over the death of the plant. Jonah replies that he is, so much so that he prefers death to life. God then explains to the exasperated prophet: "You cared about the plant, which you did not work for and which you did not grow, which appeared overnight and perished overnight. And should I not care about Nineveh, that great city, in which there are more than a hundred and twenty thousand persons . . . and many beasts as well" (Jonah 4:10–11).

What Jonah does not understand—what he perhaps *refuses* to understand—is that though the Ninevites may have committed great evil, they are still God's creatures. "They are evil," Jonah protests; "Perhaps," God in effect responds, "but I made them. Do you really expect Me to hate them the same way you do? Would you not show mercy to something or someone that you had created, even if they had strayed from the path you had set for them?" The Bible does not explicitly call the Ninevites "God's children" because in the Bible that term is exclusively covenantal, but Jonah comes extremely close to doing just that. As Marvin Sweeney explains, "The Ninevites were understood to be a people that only a parent could love in biblical tradition . . . Nevertheless, [God] is their creator"[88] and therefore God cares about and takes mercy on them—whether Jonah likes it or not.

It is here that the real battle lines between Jonah and God are drawn: God loves God's creatures, even if Israel (legitimately?) detests them. Jonah cannot abide God's love for those Jonah himself hates—for those Jonah believes with all his heart that *God too should hate*.

This text makes a momentous and deeply unsettling claim: we are never entitled to assume that God shares our attitude toward other people, no matter how wicked they are. God does not hate all the same people we do; God's openness to forgiving potentially extends even to "the whole sinful wicked world of violence and wrong."[89] On the one hand, it's pivotal to notice that it is only when the Ninevites repent that God forgives them; God's love is not a blank check. But on the other hand, it is not human beings who decide whether God may accept people's repentance. That prerogative belongs to God and God alone—and as we've repeatedly seen, God is more loving and merciful than we human beings can possibly fathom.

DIVINE ANGER AND DIVINE JUDGMENT

A strong case can be made that the God of Tanakh is a God of love. The biblical verses most often cited within the Bible itself, which play such a central role in Jewish liturgical experience, are a breathtaking declaration of God's love—and of just how profoundly God's love outweighs God's anger.

And yet the God of Tanakh sometimes behaves in ways that seem less than loving. God gets vehemently angry; God is violent; and God allows the righteous to suffer, sometimes seemingly abandoning them just when they are most desperately in need of rescue.

Biblically speaking, divine anger is deeply entwined with divine judgment. Just as we don't tell our children, "I love you and I don't care how you conduct yourself," so God doesn't say, "I love you and I grant you unlimited license to do what you will." On the contrary, one of the foundations of Jewish theology is the insistence that God has expectations of us. As we saw in chapter 1, genuine love comes *with* expectations but *without* conditions. God does not stop loving us when we sin, but God does judge us for it.

So we can't (or at any rate, we shouldn't) talk about God's love without also talking about God's judgment. A God who is all love and no judgment quickly becomes a god of saccharine sentimentality, but a God who is all judgment and no love is a merciless tyrant. In biblical theology, and in Jewish theology more broadly, God both loves *and* judges.

The tension between love and judgment—or, more precisely, between mercy and judgment—runs deep. A striking midrash imagines that on Rosh HaShanah, the holiday marking the beginning of the Jewish year, God ascends to the throne of judgment, intending to render strict justice in assessing human beings and their behavior. But when God hears the blast of the shofar, the ram's horn, God gets up from the throne of judgment and sits instead on the throne of mercy. God may set out to render strict judgment, but upon hearing the plaintive wail of the shofar, God acts from mercy instead.[90] The dramatic claim of the midrash, I think, is that deciding between justice and mercy is so hard that even God struggles with it. From a religious perspective, there is no more powerful way to express the depths of this tension than to imagine that even the Creator of the world is vexed by it.

But despite the dramatic picture it paints, perhaps the midrash misses something by presenting the choice between judgment and mercy as a zero-sum game. Perhaps on some level, love—or mercy—and justice go hand in hand. Can't a passion for justice be animated by love and compassion? If, for example, you care deeply about people who have nowhere to live, no way to dress their children for the cold, no net to protect their children from malaria, you will eventually be confronted by questions of distributive justice, of who is entitled to what across the world.

In the end, something similar can be said, I think, in considering the relationship between God's love and God's judgment. We may be tempted to set the two attributes in opposition to one another, as if the task of each is to balance or moderate the other. As the midrash we've just seen indicates, there is undoubtedly some truth to this, but I don't think the midrash tells the whole story, because ideally love involves respect—and therefore expectations—meaning that love is ideally enmeshed with judgment. So, God's love can, ultimately, necessitate God's judgment. God's judgment can ultimately flow from God's love.[91]

The next step is challenging: How does divine judgment relate to divine anger?

Before we address the challenge of divine anger head-on, let's dispense with the pernicious anti-Judaic idea (sadly internalized by many Jews) that divine anger is unique to the so-called "Old Testament." Consider just a few examples from the New Testament. What is so striking about New Testament passages that give voice to divine wrath is how continuous they are with the declarations of the Hebrew prophets. Just as the prophets warn continuously that turning away from God leads to calamitous consequences, including the utter destruction and desolation of Jerusalem, so Luke warns of the day of God's vengeance that those trapped in Jerusalem will find themselves unable to escape the devastation. "Woe to those who are pregnant and to those who are nursing infants in those days! For there will be great distress on the land and wrath against this people."[92]

In a similar vein, the Gospel of John declares that "whoever believes in the Son has eternal life; whoever disobeys the Son will not see life, but must endure God's wrath."[93] So far from sweetness and light, this Gospel insists that the anger of God abides on the disbeliever. In speaking of "the wrath to come," John too echoes the words of the prophets. Isaiah, for example, had warned that "the day of the Lord is coming with pitiless fury and wrath, to make the earth a desolation, to wipe out the sinners upon it" (Isaiah 13:9). In John's perspective, the threat of retribution for those who stubbornly refuse to obey God's will by following Christ is intense and imminent.

As a contemporary Christian writer puts it, in the New Testament Jesus is "both friend to sinners and righteous judge, extending both mercy and wrath."[94] To the extent that divine anger is a problem, it's a problem that bedevils both the "Old Testament" and the New; it is not an Old Testament problem that the New easily solves. As the Christian theologian Alastair Campbell forthrightly puts it, "Not all the 'darkness' is to be found in the Old Testament and not all the 'light' in the New."[95]

Divine anger is thus a challenge for both Jews and Christians. What can we make of it?

Divine anger, I'd suggest, is the emotional aspect of divine judgment. When it comes to judging people, God is not a neutral arbiter emotionally untouched by the cases at hand; God is, rather, like a parent who evaluates her child's behavior—and that kind of evaluation involves both thought and feeling. God gets angry because God cares deeply.

In contrast to that of other ancient Near Eastern deities, God's wrath is not arbitrary. In the Atrahasis Epic (eighteenth century BCE), for example, the god Enlil grows irritated that the noise made by human beings disturbs his sleep, so he sends a flood to wipe out the human race. The biblical flood, in contrast, is initiated when the world is overrun by evil and lawlessness—not because humanity is a noisy neighbor. God's anger may be fierce, but it is not random.

God's anger is also temporary. The prophet Isaiah, for example, declares that God's anger lasts "but a little moment" (Isaiah 54:8). And Psalm 103 explicitly contrasts the temporality of God's anger with the eternality of God's love. "[God] will not contend forever, or nurse His anger for all time," the psalm says, yet "The Lord's steadfast love is for all eternity toward those who hold Him in awe" (Psalm 103: 9, 17). In other words, whereas God's anger is "limited," God's love "knows no boundaries."[96]

As we've seen, God's anger—in contrast to God's love—is not essential to who God is. The Bible scholar Terence Fretheim explains, "Anger is a divine response not a divine attribute; if there were no sin, there would be no anger."[97]

MIGHT GOD'S ANGER BE A GOOD THING?

God's ire is most frequently elicited by injustice, and particularly by the exploitation of the weak. In Exodus, after commanding the people not to mistreat any widow or orphan, God warns, "If you do mistreat them, I will heed their outcry as soon as they cry out to Me, and My anger shall blaze forth and I will put you to the sword, and your own wives shall become widows and your children orphans" (Exodus 22:22–23). God's anger is involved in liberating the Israelite slaves from Egypt (Exodus 15:7); in saving the righteous from their enemies (Psalm 7:7–12); and in rescuing Israel from its foes (Isaiah 30:27–33).[98] As R. Heschel writes, "Divine sympathy for the victims of human cruelty is the motive of anger."[99]

God's concern about the weak and vulnerable stands in stark and dramatic contrast to pervasive human indifference: Where human beings may remain apathetic in the face of cruelty and brutality, God is always "personally affected" by how people treat one another. I find R. Heschel helpful here. Divine anger, he says, signifies "the end of indifference!" As he arrestingly puts it, "To a generation afflicted by the fury of cruel men . . . no condemnation is too harrowing . . . The message of wrath is frightful, indeed. But for those who have been driven to the brink of despair by the sight of what malice and ruthlessness can do, comfort will be found in the thought that evil is not the end, that evil is not the climax of history."[100] In a world overrun by savagery, in a world in which children are burned alive while the world callously goes about its business, divine anger can be a blessing. It means that somewhere, someone (Someone) truly cares about the victims.[101]

Following R. Heschel we can say that Jews should not be embarrassed by the Bible's depictions of God's anger; on the contrary, we should recognize that in a world like ours, a God who *does not* get angry is an inadequate God. God's anger renders God *more* praiseworthy rather than less. God is the One who cares when no one else does.

In a similar vein, the Bible scholar Erich Zenger provocatively suggests that a God who never gets angry would be little more than "a spectator uninterested in the world." Such a God would be otiose, Zenger maintains, "lacking in every kind of social-critical potential." When we speak about the divine wrath, we say something critical "about the violent and wretched state of society and the world" and we insist that "this situation is not created by God, nor can it be legitimated or tolerated as something God-given."[102]

There is another important dimension to divine anger in the face of injustice: God gets angry because God takes us seriously as moral agents. As we saw in chapter 3, taking people seriously has a cognitive aspect—we judge their actions negatively when they fall short; a behavioral aspect—we cause them to suffer the consequences of their actions; and, at least according to some philosophers, an emotional aspect too—we get angry at people when they fail precisely because we respect them as moral agents (we might not get angry at those from whom we wouldn't expect any better). Legitimate moral anger can be a sign of profound respect. Thus Israel disappoints and angers God when it mistreats the defenseless—not only because God cares for the down-trodden but also because God shows moral respect for their oppressors. God wants and expects better of them.

But it's important to realize and admit that God's anger in the Bible is not directed only at injustice. As the Ten Commandments make clear, God's anger also blazes when Israel turns to other gods.[103] God gets angry when the people turn prideful and forget about God (Deuteronomy 6:10–15); and when they betray insufficient reverence for the sacred.[104] If God's anger is *not* always about injustice, it *is* always about violations of the covenant—which, of course, include injustice prominently among them. God's anger responds to faithlessness in the relationship God so passionately seeks.

In light of all this, we might be tempted to conclude that divine anger per se is not a theological problem at all. On the contrary, an indifferent God would constitute a much more serious problem than an angry one. If this were correct, then the real problem with divine anger as depicted in the Bible would be its frequent fierceness and ferocity, which often manifest themselves in terrifying violence. The real problem with divine wrath in the Hebrew Bible, we might be inclined to say, is overkill.

There is undoubtedly some truth to this. Yet overkill is hardly a minor problem; the portrayal of a God who "gets carried away" in unleashing devastation is obviously extremely troubling. The possible responses available to us in confronting this problem will depend, to a great extent, on (whether and) how we think of the Bible as a revealed text. Some, who maintain that the Bible is just a human effort—or better, a series of human efforts—to grasp something about the divine will argue that while it contains powerful and even revolutionary insights, it also reflects the limitations of human understanding. Others, for whom a robust theory of revelation precludes this type of stance, are forced to try to make sense of how an "accurate" picture of God could be so perplexing—or to seek ways of denying that it is perplexing at all. My own view is that God does communicate with us through revealed texts, but that these texts reflect both *God's* revelation and *our* perception. What we hear when God speaks is profoundly affected by our own capacities and, crucially, by our shortcomings too. As R. Heschel writes, "In a sense, prophecy consists of a revelation of God and *a co-revelation of man*. The share of the prophet manifested itself not only in what he was able to give but also in what he was unable to receive."[105] Accordingly, although for reasons of space I cannot explore this here, I think we should remain open to possible gaps between God as rendered in the text and God beyond the text, God as God is in Godself.

DIVINE ANGER AS THE FLIP SIDE OF DIVINE LOVE

Let's probe a little more deeply: Why, ultimately, does God get angry?

A God who cares is a God who is not, who *cannot be*, indifferent about what takes place in human affairs. As we've seen, God is a personal God who seeks genuine relationship with human beings. The ways in which we respond to God—or fail to—make a profound difference to God. God cares enough to be affected—pleased, delighted, hurt, offended, and even enraged—by human behavior. As R. Heschel puts it, "God is not only the Judge, Guardian, and Lawgiver, but also the loving Father Who is intimately affected" by what people do.[106] If we care about people, we are impacted by how they act—and if biblical theology affirms anything, it is that God cares about people. Thus, when Israel turns its back on God, for example, God is wounded, and God reacts.[107]

Divine anger is thus arguably the flip side of divine love. In fact, divine anger most often *stems from* divine love; anger is, in a sense, thwarted love.[108] So, for example, when the people worship the Golden Calf, God is infuriated and wants to let God's anger blaze forth against the people to destroy them (Exodus 32:10). Just days after the revelation at Sinai, God suffers the fate of the jilted lover—and God is none too pleased. Later, Psalm 78 tells us, the people "vexed" God by praying in forbidden places and "incensed" God with their idols. "God heard it and was enraged"; in response, God "gave God's people over to the sword";

indeed, God "was enraged by God's very own" (Psalm 78:58–59, 62). As the Bible sees it, God's rage is a function of God having been repeatedly rejected and abandoned.

While I find this way of thinking about divine anger as portrayed in the Bible fruitful, I readily admit that I also find it unsettling. At times, God seems to say, in effect, "I am sorry that you made Me do this . . . I am hurting you because I love you"—and that, quite frankly, sounds like something an abusive spouse would say. So I think we need to be extremely cautious about this type of explanation of divine wrath. Sometimes the problem with God's anger is overkill, but other times something much more dangerous is depicted: a God imaged as male burns in anger and perpetrates horrific (and highly gendered) violence against God's people, pictured as female.[109] As I've noted, I think the notion of divine anger can be positive and salutary for the religious life. But if we wish to take divine anger seriously as part of our theology, we also have to wrestle with the disturbing—"terrifying" might be the better word—dimensions of the Bible's portrayals.[110] Again, our approach to divine revelation will play a critical role in shaping our response.

A VIOLENT GOD?

The second chapter of the book of Lamentations, written in the wake of the destruction of Jerusalem and its Temple, describes God in almost savage terms. The chapter begins and ends with references to the "day of God's rage" (Lamentations 2:1, 21), suggesting that God's anger is "all-encompassing."[111] The text is relentless in describing the damage that God has done and the suffering that God has inflicted: "The Lord has laid waste without pity all the habitations of Jacob . . . [the Lord] has ravaged Jacob like flaming fire, consuming on all sides . . . Babes and sucklings languish in the squares of the city" (2:2, 3, 11). These verses accuse God of "overseeing, catalyzing, and executing atrocities" against the city and its inhabitants; the Bible scholar Kathleen O'Connor argues that the God portrayed here is simply "out of control."[112]

Even if we can make our peace with God's anger in general—and we've seen that there are ways to make sense of, and even to value, the idea that God sometimes gets angry—verses such as these are still hard to live with.

One thing I find strangely comforting in reading Lamentations is that the narrator shares our revulsion at the extent of the violence and horror. The same haunting questions unsettles both us and the narrator: Why would God act in this way? How could God perpetrate such cruelty on those whom God loves?

Here again, the problem is not unique to the "Old Testament"; the same issues emerge front and center in the New. Consider just a few verses from the book of Revelation: "From his mouth comes a sharp sword with which to strike down the nations, and he will rule them with a rod of iron; he will tread the winepress of the fury of the wrath of God the Almighty." Revelation imagines "the kings of the earth and the magnates and the generals and the rich and the powerful, and everyone, slave and free" all hiding from "the wrath of the Lamb"—that is, Jesus.[113] Nor is it just Revelation. John places these words in the mouth of Jesus: "Whoever does not abide in me is thrown away like a branch and withers; such branches are gathered, thrown into the fire, and burned" (John 13:1–6). And Mark's picture of the end-times is no less distressing: "How dreadful it will be in those days for pregnant women and nursing mothers! Pray that this will not take place in winter, because those will be days of distress unequaled from the beginning, when God created the world, until now—and never to be equaled again."[114] In light of examples like these, the Christian Bible scholar Brent Strawn comments: "It doesn't seem to be going too far to say the violence in the New Testament, especially in eschatological scenarios . . . *rivals if not surpasses* anything found in the Old Testament."[115]

THE BOOK OF JOSHUA: A GOD WHO COMMANDS VIOLENCE?

According to the book of Joshua, at God's command, and with God at their back, the Israelites conquer the land of Israel and slaughter its inhabitants en masse.

Some scholars argue that there is a vast gap between what the text describes and what actually happened. Historically speaking, they say, there was no conquest of the kind described in the Bible. Some readers may find that idea hard to accept (if the text is divine revelation, how can it report something that never happened?[116]) but even if we do accept it, I am not sure it solves the problem. In Israelite memory, even if not in actual history, Israel conquered the land through a series of actions that amount to genocide. The text is problematic even if the actual history isn't. In more theological terms, a God I have characterized as a God of love is presented as mandating the annihilation of the entire indigenous population of Canaan.[117] How can we possibly make sense of this? How can the God of the Bible order genocide?

The answer, I think, is that God doesn't.

In Deuteronomy the people are instructed that when God brings them to the land, they must doom the seven nations that inhabit it to destruction.[118] "Grant them no terms," they are told, "and give them no quarter" (Deuteronomy 7:1–2).[119] In Joshua—or in parts thereof, at least—those instructions appear to be carried out. Describing the battle of Jericho, for example, the book of Joshua states that the Israelites "exterminated everything in the city with the sword: man and woman, young and old, ox and sheep and ass" (Joshua 6:21). God commands mass killing, and the people do as they are told.

Yet a deeper look at the book of Joshua paints a far more complex picture. The book of Joshua works to "mitigate and reinterpret" the Israelites' gruesome conquest.[120] It's as if the book itself feels uncomfortable with the story it's telling. As Joshua describes it, several of Israel's most violent campaigns take place only as a result of aggression against Israel; hostilities are initiated not by the Israelites but by the Canaanite kings.[121] These battles are thus understood as a "defensive reaction" to the belligerence of others rather than as an unprovoked war of aggression.[122]

In addition, the text of Joshua also makes it seem that Joshua defeated the armies of the Canaanite cities but that he left the inhabitants of the cities unmolested. Thus, for example, on the one hand we're told that the Israelites defeated Gezer, yet on the other hand we hear that the Israelites failed to dispossess the Canaanites who lived there. The same pattern occurs with other cities, such as Jerusalem. Of all the cities mentioned in Joshua, only three are explicitly described as having been utterly eradicated: Jericho, Ai, and Hazor. Most of the other battles describe confrontations of armies against armies, and not Israelite invasion and annihilation.[123] What is presented, in other words, is war, not genocide.

Joshua also subtly implies a more radical claim. Joshua was at war with the Canaanite kings, we are told, because "not a single city made terms with the Israelites." As the Bible scholar Lawson Stone explains, "The text comes close to suggesting that war would not have been necessary had the Canaanite response been more cooperative."[124] Juxtapose the aggression of the kings with the peace-seeking of the Gibeonites, with whom the Israelites establish—and keep—a covenant (9), and it seems that "had other Canaanites taken the latter approach, they, too, would have survived." The text thus implies that it was the nations' own hostility that led to their deaths.[125] Interpreting Joshua along these lines may help soften the portrayal of the Israelite conquest somewhat, but it can also sound to modern ears like a disturbing example of blaming the victim for their suffering.

The book of Joshua complicates the notion that all Canaanites without exception were wiped out and undermines the idea that there was an impregnable wall separating insiders (Israelites) and outsiders (Canaanites). The Canaanite prostitute Rahab, who provides safe harbor to two Israelite spies sent to scout the land and who readily acknowledges that God is "the only God in heaven above and on earth below" (Joshua 2:11), receives a promise of protection for her and her family. Remarkably, in a scene reminiscent of the Israelites spreading blood on their lintels on the night of the Exodus, the spies tell Rahab to hang a crimson cord from her window so that she can be saved from the violence of the conquest (2:17–19). Rahab goes through her own exodus; her experience mirrors Israel's. The reader is left to wonder whether other Canaanites who responded to God as Rahab did would have similarly been spared.[126]

On the other hand, in the wake of Israel's defeat of Jericho, an Israelite named Akhan defies God's command that the entire city be desig-
nated as *herem*—that is, that it be consecrated for destruction. Eliciting
God's fury, Akhan's violation causes God to withdraw protection from
the people, who suffer military defeat as a consequence. Akhan is eventually found out and stoned to death by the entire community. Subtly,
I think, the text suggests that Akhan has effectively become a kind of
Canaanite. He is buried in much the same way as is the Canaanite king
of Ai (7:26 and 8:29), and the place of his interment, we are told, is
known as the Valley of Achor "to the present day," a phrase that ironically contrasts his fate with those of Rahab and the Gibeonites, who live
among the Israelites "to the present day" (6:25 and 9:27).[127]

The violence of Akhan's story is understandably disturbing to modern ears. Some of its assumptions about consecration to destruction may
strike some readers as archaic. But taken together, the stories of Rahab
and Akhan temper the otherwise sharp distinctions between insider and
outsider, Israelite and non-Israelite. As the Bible scholar Lori Rowlett
explains, "Rahab was transformed from the quintessential Other into
an insider deemed worthy of protection (and life)." Akhan, on the other
hand, was "the exemplary insider"[128] who effectively wrote himself out
of the community by refusing to accept God's authority.[129]

The process begun in the Bible continues in Talmudic tradition—
and it's important to understand that Judaism as we know it understands biblical stories more through the lens of rabbinic interpretation
than through reading the biblical text alone. As the Talmudic sages
read the conquest story, it is both softened and rendered nonprecedential. The story is softened in that a Talmudic sage insists that Joshua sued
for peace before entering into battle: "He published an edict in every
place he came to conquer wherein it was written, 'Whoever desires to
go, let him go; whoever desires to make peace, let him make peace; and
whoever desires to make war, let him make war.'"[130] And it is rendered
nonprecedential in that the Talmudic sages interpret the commandment to wipe out the land's inhabitants as a one-time-only event now
relegated to the past; the story told in the book of Joshua cannot be le-

gitimately invoked to justify violent conquest in later times.[131] As Rabbi Moshe Greenberg (1928–2010) explains, "Had there been any inclination [among the Talmudic sages] to generalize this law, it would have been easy for [them] to perform an appropriate hermeneutical enterprise to that end."[132] Tellingly, the sages do not do so.

Remarkably, as the Bible progresses the figure of Joshua all but completely fades away. After the opening chapters of the book of Judges, Joshua is mentioned only three times in the entire rest of the Bible.[133] Several recountings of Israel's early history completely ignore the conquest, while others contain broad and fairly vague statements about how God "drove out" the Canaanites or brought Israel to the land;[134] according to the Bible scholar Robert Hubbard, only three later biblical texts describe Israel violently dispossessing the nations in war.[135] The Hebrew Bible "rarely recalls the violent conquest, never glories in its goriness, and never promotes it as policy for the future."[136] We are left to consider the possibility that Joshua's eclipse reflects later biblical writers' desire "to move beyond the violent era of Joshua or the fact that they already had."[137]

Yet I began with a more radical claim, that the God of the Bible does not actually command the genocide of the Canaanites. What do I mean by that?

THE BOOK OF JOSHUA: A BOOK THAT SUBVERTS ITSELF

Strikingly, the book of Joshua consistently subverts and undermines its own claims. It boldly makes one claim, only to deconstruct it just a few verses later.

Consider: Joshua 11 ends with an announcement that Joshua successfully conquered the whole land of Israel: "Thus Joshua conquered the whole country, just as the Lord had promised Moses; and Joshua assigned it to Israel to share according to their tribal divisions. And the land had rest from war" (11:23). Yet just two chapters later, the narrator tells us that "Joshua was now old, advanced in years. The Lord said to him, 'You have grown old, you are advanced in years; and very much of the land still remains to be taken possession of'" (13:1). We've just been told that the other nations have been vanquished and that there is no more need for war, and now we hear that on the contrary, much of the land remains unconquered and further battles are necessary. As the book progresses, we again hear both of total victory—"The Lord gave to Israel all the land that He had sworn to give to their ancestors, and they possessed it and dwelt in it. The Lord gave them rest on every side" (21:43)—and of conquests only partial. We learn of multiple peoples whom the Israelites fail to dispossess and who live among the Israelites "to this day"—the Geshurites and the Maacathites (13:13); the Jebusites from Jerusalem (15:63); Canaanites who dwelled in Gezer (16:10); and Canaanites who dwelled near the Manassites (17:12).[138] The litany continues in the book of Judges, where we hear of more peoples who were undefeated and who therefore remained in the land (Judges 1:21, 29–30, 33).[139] Reading Joshua we are left somewhat bewildered: Did Israel conquer the whole land, as some verses suggest, or did it not, as others say?

And just what had God commanded Joshua to do, anyway? According to Joshua 10, Joshua "conquered the whole country . . . he left no one remaining, but utterly destroyed all that breathed, as the Lord God of Israel commanded" (10:40).[140] And yet when the book of Judges—which follows on the heels of, and is generally considered to be part of the same broader narrative as, the book of Joshua—summarizes God's command, God declares that God will "drive out" the peoples of the land, making no mention of killing them. Israel's responsibility, in turn, is to refrain from making covenants with the inhabitants of the land and to tear down their altars (Judges 2:3–4).[141] So which one was it—were the native peoples to be killed, as Joshua suggests, or driven out, as Judges does?

What are we to make of the fact that the book of Joshua is rife with "tensions and contradictions"? The philosopher Nicholas Wolterstorff draws our attention to the "formulaic literary conventions" repeatedly found in Joshua; again and again we are told, for example, that Joshua struck down all the inhabitants of a city with the edge of a sword. Wolterstorff suggests that "the repetition makes it unmistakable that we are dealing here with a formulaic literary convention.[142]

The prevalence of such conventions suggests that they are not meant to be taken literally. What we have in Joshua is a "highly stylized, exaggerated account of events designed to teach theological and moral points rather than to describe in detail what *literally* happened."[143]

The key point, I think, is this: if reports of the fulfillment of God's promises are to be taken as hyperbolic, then so too should the command itself be understood as hyperbolic.[144]

WHAT IS COMMANDED IN DEUTERONOMY?

When the people enter the land and conquer it, they are told, they should doom the nations they find there to destruction. Wolterstorff wisely suggests that the way we've interpreted Joshua "forces a back-interpretation of Deuteronomy."[145] Just as the fulfillment in Joshua is to be understood in hyperbolic terms, so too should the original command in Deuteronomy.

The text of Deuteronomy may well contain an internal hint of this. Right after they are ostensibly commanded to wipe out the inhabitants of the land, the people are instructed, oddly: "You shall not intermarry with them: do not give your daughters to their sons or take their daughters for your sons" (Deuteronomy 7:3). Presumably, if you kill people, you will not intermarry with them; if you've already commanded the former, the latter seems gratuitous at best. It's possible to understand the prohibition on intermarriage as a rationale for the mandate to wipe out the land's inhabitants: kill them, lest you intermarry with them and become corrupted by their worship of other gods (7:1–5),[146] but I am skeptical that this is the correct explanation of the flow of these verses. More likely, I think, the warning about intermarriage serves as a kind of wink: of course you aren't literally going to *kill* every last one of them, so be careful not to intermarry with them. In other words, like much of what we've seen in Joshua, the command in Deuteronomy to doom every last inhabitant of the seven nations to destruction is hyperbolic, not meant to be taken literally.[147]

In attempting to understand the violent language of Deuteronomy and Joshua, Wolterstorff offers a clever contemporary analogy: "When a high school basketball player says his team slaughtered the other team last night, what is he asserting? Not easy to tell. That they scored a decisive victory? Maybe. But suppose they just hardly eked out a win? Was he lying? Maybe not. Maybe he was speaking with a wink-of-the-eye hyperbole."[148]

According to Wolterstorff, what we have in Joshua are exaggerated references to actual skirmishes and battles. Israel did emerge victorious in battle with the Canaanites, but the formulaic speech means that we can't know just how decisive those victories were.

Yet even this may be too literal an interpretation. More likely, the account in Joshua is both hyperbolic *and metaphorical*. As Ellen Davis puts it, "Joshua is a story that seeks to engender within Israel the courage to resist and overcome the ever-present threat of religious apostasy and assimilation to the dominant culture."[149] *Herem*, says Walter Moberly, is "a metaphor for unqualified allegiance to YHWH." According to Deuteronomy, the people must reject intermarriage and the presence of foreign religious symbols within the land of Israel. "Deuteronomy uses the language and imagery of warfare for Israel vis-a-vis the 'seven nations of Canaan' in a metaphorical mode, so as to depict the real conflicts over identity and allegiance that confront Israel in engagement with its immediate neighbors."[150] What Deuteronomy asks for is not genocide but single-minded dedication to God.

Even if this hyperbolic-metaphoric interpretation of Joshua doesn't persuade everyone, I am convinced that the text cannot be responsibly read in flat, literalistic ways. It gives us too many hints that a literal reading, in this instance, is a wrongheaded one.

THE BOOK OF JOSHUA: A DANGEROUS TEXT

Still, Joshua remains a dangerous text;[151] with good reason Davis refers to it as "the hardest book of the Bible to live with."[152] Part of the problem is that the metaphor of annihilation is a dead one—and, frankly, a revolting one—for most modern readers. We may speak of the Yankees murdering (or even butchering) the Red Sox, yet genocide as a controlling metaphor in the religious life strikes us as jarring at best and abhorrent at worst. To be honest, I wish the Bible had chosen a different metaphor, one that would be at once more resonant and less dangerous. But I am comforted that the text of Joshua rebels against itself and that subsequent Jewish tradition consistently sought ways to eliminate its normative sting.

My suggestion that Deuteronomy and Joshua wanted us to understand *herem* metaphorically may diverge from some of the Jewish tradition's more literal reading of the text. But elsewhere the tradition itself mitigated the potentially violent implications of the text. The Talmudic sage R. Joshua, for example, insists that since an ancient Assyrian emperor had "mingled all the nations" through forced population transfers, we simply cannot discern people's national origins with any accuracy.[153] Since we can't know whether anyone is an actual Canaanite, *the biblical laws cannot possibly be applied and hence are effectively moot.*

It's important to notice what tradition does and does not do in confronting the moral challenge. Jewish sources do not declare that the law is immoral and therefore not binding, or the law is immoral and therefore could not have been commanded by God. (While I understand and to some degree even sympathize with the impulse behind such a posture, I worry that Scripture loses its status as Scripture once we adopt this kind of critical stand toward it.)[154] Instead, as we've seen, the problem is solved practically, by making it impossible to treat the text as precedent legitimating contemporary violence.

The biblical corpus as we've encountered it so far is highly complex. On the one hand, we've unearthed the centrality of God's love in biblical theology and discovered the radical reach of that love. And we've seen how divine anger can be a kind of tonic in a world awash in indifference. Yet on the other hand, we've investigated the undersides of divine anger as portrayed in the Bible—the problems of overkill and of gendered violence. And we've confronted the complicated legacy of the book of

Joshua, which, on the surface at least, presents God as commanding the annihilation of the Canaanites. We've judged that this horrifying command is hyperbolic and metaphorical, but we've also observed that, with its fantasies of blotting out entire peoples, Joshua remains an extremely troubling text.

In the face of all this, it's worth noticing another, very different dimension of God's love as depicted in the biblical canon: a God of uncontrolling love whose love for us depends on making space for us to be truly other than God, and whose desire to be loved in turn depends on granting us genuinely robust freedom to make choices of our own.

A THEOLOGY OF LOVE AND SELF-RESTRAINT

What would a contemporary Jewish theology of divine love look like?

Recall R. Isaac Luria's conception of *tzimtzum*, or contraction: In order for something finite to exist, the infinite must first withdraw or retreat into itself.[155] God "withdraws from Godself into Godself," thus making room for the world (Kabbalists would likely say worlds) to be. Before creating the world, in other words, God contracts into Godself to create a space that is not-God. This is what makes a world that is other-than-God possible.

Let's take the idea of divine self-contraction or self-limitation further. As we saw in chapter 4, genuine relationship depends on otherness; it's precisely the other person being separate from me that makes it possible for me to enter into relationship with them. Remember Martin Buber's insistence that there must be a "primal setting at a distance" that precedes our "entering into relation"; when we want to be in relationship with someone, we first must allow them to be "an independent opposite."[156]

The God of Judaism is nothing if not relational; God wants to be in relationship, *wants to love*.[157] God wants to love persons who can respond to God, commune with God, and *reciprocate God's love*. In order to make this possible, God chooses to create human beings who are separate from God—who think, feel, and make decisions for themselves. In order to love, God creates persons who are free.

In creating the world and the human beings within it, God engages in a *tzimtzum*, a dramatic act of self-limitation. God is and remains omnipotent but, moved by both love and respect for human beings, God chooses not to exercise the full extent of God's power.[158] As the Chrisrtian theologian Clark Pinnock argues, "Unlimited power fosters subservience, not fellowship, and is not what God wants . . . God wants covenant partners, not slaves."[159] Restrained omnipotence is the price of relationship.[160]

Tzimtzum in the sense that I am using it does not signify complete withdrawal. Rather, God limits Godself precisely in order to be more relationally present. God is, paradoxically, less manifest but more deeply present.

Love requires allowing the other to be *truly other*. Yet this is profoundly risky: love can be ignored, refused, or violated. Few experiences are more painful—and often humiliating—than unrequited or betrayed love. So in creating human beings with the capacity to ignore, refuse, or violate God's love, God takes an enormous risk. The cost of God seeking relationship is that God can be hurt. In order to be relational, God must be vulnerable.

Genuine freedom also means that the future is open; God doesn't know how we will choose to act—or, more precisely, God *can't* know how we will choose because we have not chosen yet. God is omniscient but I don't think that omniscience can include foreknowledge. Just as omnipotence means that God can do everything that is logically possible but God cannot do what is logically impossible, like make a square circle or a married bachelor, so omniscience means that God knows everything that is logically knowable—and the future is not one of those things. "If future free decisions do not become real, or do not exist, until they occur, . . . [then] prior to their occurrence there is nothing there to know."[161] This is not an attenuated view of omniscience: God still knows everything there is to know.

If we want to build a theology in which love and self-limitation are intertwined, we can do no better than to start with the opening chapters of the Torah.

THE POWER-SHARING AND (THEREFORE) VULNERABLE GOD OF THE BIBLE

From its very first pages, the Torah emphasizes that God makes space for human effort and initiative, actively encouraging human agency.[162] According to a variety of ancient myths, human culture and civilization were gifts of the gods; as these stories had it, "humanity did not develop any aspect of human culture."[163] In ancient Mesopotamia, for example, "every aspect of human society was decreed by the gods . . . Everything in the universe, material or immaterial, human or divine, was laid down by decree."[164] The Torah understands the world very differently. Cain, we're told, built the first city (Genesis 4:17); three generations later, three brothers, descendants of Cain, also made significant contributions to civilization: one was the first to herd livestock, another invented music, and the third invented metallurgy (4:20–22). Noah, we soon learn, planted the first vineyard (9:20), while Nimrod became the first hunter and empire builder (10:8–10). In contrast to the ancient world in which it emerged, in the Torah "the human being, a creature created by God, is the initiator and creator of its own culture."[165]

The refrain from Genesis 1 is likely familiar. Again and again, God looks at what God has made and finds it "good"; looking at the whole of creation at the end of the sixth day, God finds it "very good." But good, even very good, is still not perfect. When God creates human beings, God instructs them to "subdue" the earth, which suggests that for all of creation's goodness, there is still work to do to move it toward perfection.[166]

The text subtly underscores that divine effort alone will not bring the world closer to perfection.

Genesis 1 says something that is as crucial as it is easy to miss. On the third day, when God wants vegetation to emerge, God does not create it on God's own. Rather, God assigns that task to the earth itself: "Let the earth sprout vegetation: seed-bearing plants, fruit trees of every kind . . ." And indeed, that's what happens: the earth brings forth vegetation—plants, trees, etc. (1:11–12). Then, on the fifth day,

God invites the waters to "bring forth swarms of living creatures, and birds that fly above the earth across the expanse of the sky"; and on the sixth day, the earth is invited to "bring forth every kind of living creature: cattle, creeping things, and wild beasts of every kind" (1:20, 24). God wants creation to continue to unfold, but God does not want to do it alone. Terence Fretheim describes what happens in Genesis 1 as "mediate rather than immediate creative activity." God works not unilaterally but multilaterally; "God recruits assistance from the creatures in creating."[167]

When God creates the sun and the moon on the fourth day, one of the explanations given of their purpose is that the sun will "govern" the day and the moon will "govern" the night (Genesis 1:16). This correlates with another of their purposes, to "separate" the day and the night (1:14, 18). Governing and separating are "paradigmatically divine acts" both in the ancient Near East in general and in Genesis 1 in particular, where God spends the first three days of creation separating the major realms of the created order from one another. In addition, God gives the firmament the "god-like function" of separating the waters above from the waters below (1:6), "in imitation of God's own separation of light and darkness on day 1."[168]

Once created, animals are called to "be fruitful and multiply" (Genesis 1:22). And then, of course, human beings are given the same blessing, and then some: in addition to being fruitful and multiplying, they are assigned to "fill the earth and subdue [or perhaps, master] it" and to rule over the rest of creation (1:28). Creating human beings in God's own image, God delegates a tremendous amount of authority to them. As we saw in chapter 7, human beings are to be God's vice-regents, ruling the earth on God's behalf. Fretheim observes that "God gives the human being certain tasks and responsibilities and, necessarily, the power with which to do them . . . God chooses not to be the only one who has creative power and the capacity, indeed the obligation, to exercise it."[169] God shares power rather than hoarding it.[170]

The Bible insists that God does not want to build this world alone. Genesis 2 tells us that in the early days of creation "no shrub of the field was yet on earth and no grass of the field had yet sprouted because the Lord God had not sent rain upon the earth and there was no person to till the soil" (2:5). Remarkably, "the presence of the human being to till the ground is . . . indispensable for the development of the creation."[171]

According to texts such as these, human beings are dependent on God but in some fundamental way the reverse is also true: God is dependent on human beings for the achievement of God's aims in the world. This is obviously asymmetrical: people cannot but depend on God, whereas *God chooses to be dependent on people.* But the Biblical narrative shows God making this choice and committing to it: "God gives over power and responsibility to the human . . . in such a way that results in divine dependence."[172] More generally, as we've seen, God entrusts the created order itself with further developing God's world.

What all this means is that "God's creation is a dynamic reality and is going somewhere; it is a long-term project, ever in the process of becoming."[173] Even as God orders the world, some degree of disorder persists. In a painstaking rhetorical analysis of Genesis 1, the Bible scholar Richard Middleton demonstrates both that the text is carefully patterned and that the pattern plays itself out somewhat loosely. For example, on the first day God declares by fiat "let there be" and then there is a summary execution report, "and it was so"; only later, after an evaluation report ("and God saw that it was good"), do we find an extended execution report in which God's specific creative act is described. Yet on the second day, immediately after the initial "let there be" we find an extended execution report, and only then a summary execution report; there is no evaluation report. And so on with an array of variations on each day. "There is a discernible pattern to each of God's creative acts," Middleton explains, "[but] this pattern is by no means simple, obvious, or predictable." What this suggests, he argues, is that "whereas the world rhetorically depicted in Genesis 1 is certainly ordered, patterned, and purposive . . . this world is not mechanistically determined, as if it were governed by ineluctable ironclad Newtonian laws." On the contrary, the existence of a pattern with variations suggests that "creation is neither random . . . nor strictly predictable. There is a certain (if I might dare to say it) incipient subjectivity or freedom granted to the cosmos by God, by which it is allowed, in response to the Creator's call, to find its own patterns."[174] The world will continue to evolve. Precisely what it will become is left somewhat open; the created world as a whole, and human beings in particular, have extensive roles to play in the unfolding of God's world. We—and by the logic of Genesis 1, creation as a whole—are, to borrow a term from Rabbinic literature, "partners of the Blessed Holy One in the work of Creation."

The culmination of all this, arguably, is a surprising absence in the text. At the end of each of the first six days, we hear that "there was evening, there was morning, the x day." But with the seventh day that formula disappears. Perhaps this is meant to convey that God purposefully left the final day "open-ended and unfinished . . . God continues to 'rest' from creating, having entrusted care of the earth to human beings."[175] Yet I do not think we should take this idea too far. God delegates a substantial amount of responsibility to humanity but God's active involvement in the development and unfolding of the world continues.[176]

THE NATURAL COURSE OF THINGS

God's allowing the world to run its own course means, Fretheim explains, that the world is not a "tightly woven system" and that "it does not run like a machine; some randomness . . . ambiguity, disorder, and unpredictability characterize its complex life." This means that people are vulnerable to being hurt by nature's ongoing processes. Consider Job, the Bible's paradigmatic sufferer: much of this suffering is inflicted by what we tend to refer to as "natural disasters"—windstorm, lightning and other fires, and disease (Job 1–2). In a provocative interpretation of God's famous speech from within the whirlwind, Fretheim argues that God is directly responding to Job's questions about why he suffers. What God is saying, according to Fretheim, is that "human suffering may occur in God's world because of the way God's world has been created and the way in which God lets the creation be and become." In other words, God has elected not to be an all-controlling sovereign and "one effect of that divine decision regarding governance is that human beings are not protected from the wiles of the wicked or the disorderly workings of the natural world." This is the painful (at least where human suffering is concerned) truth: "The world that God has created is not (and never has been) a risk-free place, and God has not provided danger-free zones for righteous people."[177]

In trying to make sense of life in such a world, Fretheim turns us to Ecclesiastes, who declares that "again I saw that under the sun the race is not to the swift, nor the battle to the strong, nor bread to the wise, nor riches to the intelligent, nor favor to the skillful, but *time and chance happen to them all*" (Ecclesiastes 9:11). As part of how the world works, chance is a significant factor in all of our lives and it can sometimes have calamitous consequences.[178]

HUMAN FREEDOM AND ITS IMPLICATIONS

Human beings are hurt by the world, but they are also hurt by one another. The early chapters of Genesis insistently draw our attention to the underside of human freedom. People are summoned to do God's work, but God does not coerce them to obey. We can heed God's call or we can flout it; we can further God's ends or we can thwart them. Genesis tells a depressing story. Given both permission and encouragement to enjoy the fruit of God's Garden, Adam and Eve partake of the one fruit forbidden to them (Genesis 3:6). When God confronts Adam, he tries to pass the blame onto his wife, and indirectly onto God, who had created her for him (3:12). Disappointed by God's accepting Abel's sacrifice rather than his, Cain murders his brother, and then brazenly refuses to acknowledge his ghastly deed (4:8–9). Things only get more violent from there, as Cain's descendant Lemekh positively revels in his own violence (4:23–24). And soon enough, the world as a whole falls apart, becoming mired in unrestrained violence and lawlessness. This is not what God had planned. Indeed, as Genesis describes it, God is heartbroken and regrets having created human beings at all (6:6).

As Genesis indicates, a God who shares power and takes risks is a God who may be sorely disappointed, hurt—and angered. In the pages of the Bible, we are very far removed from the Aristotelian Unmoved Mover; instead, we encounter a relational God whose care and concern for creation mean that God can suffer.[179] The Bible scholar Bruce Birch makes the striking observation that God is in fact the first character in the Bible who experiences "woundedness in relationship."[180] The freedom granted to creation—both to people and to nature's own processes—means that the God of the Bible is vulnerable. God suffers *because of* people who reject God (think back to God's grief and regret in response to the generation of the flood); and God suffers *with* people when they are downtrodden (e.g., Isaiah 63:9; Psalm 91:15). This latter idea is especially emphasized by the Talmudic sages; as Rabbi Joshua puts it, "When Israel went down to Egypt, the Blessed Holy One went down with them."[181] It is not only human beings who lament when they are in pain; in the book of Jeremiah, at least, God does the same (Jeremiah 2–3, 8–9). God is affected by what happens in the world and has promised, in the wake of the flood, not to destroy it, so God may continue to be hurt again and again. As Fretheim puts it, "The divine decision to go with a wicked world, come what may, means for God a *continuing* grieving of the heart."[182]

GOD AND AN OPEN FUTURE

The fact of freedom in the world—the fact that the world is free to run according to its own processes, coupled with the fact that human beings are free to make our own choices and decisions—means that the future has not yet been determined. As the physicist-theologian John Polkinghorne writes, "The play of life is not the performance of a predetermined script, but a self-improvisatory performance by the actors themselves . . . God shares the unfolding course of creation with creatures, who have their divinely allowed, but not divinely dictated, roles to play in its fruitful becoming."[183] To continue the image, God cannot know the future because it remains to be acted out.

If God is a vulnerable God who does not know the future in all its details, then God experiences reality as it unfolds. In that regard, I think it makes sense to say that God changes; but God's character and God's purposes for creation do not.[184] God's love, and God's yearning to be loved, remain steadfast.

To return to where we started, all this talk about divine love may strike some readers as . . . well, unJewish. And, that's precisely why I've written this book: to help us overcome impoverished and distorted understandings of the Jewish tradition. Judaism tells us of a God of love who summons us to lead lives of love; we are called both to feel love and to act lovingly. Jewish law, ritual, and practice are intended to give concrete expression to our love, both for one another and for God.

The loving God will not force us to love; God is too invested in our freedom for that. God does not determine what we feel or how we act—but God waits on our love. We saw in chapter 12 that part of what it means to live a religious life is to wait for God. If I may be so bold, I'd add that a significant part of what it means to be God is to wait for us.

14

ENGAGING CHOSENNESS

What It Does and Doesn't Mean

IN HIS CLASSIC work on Jewish theology, the Reform scholar and thinker Rabbi Kaufmann Kohler (1843–1926) declared that "the central point of Jewish theology and the key to an understanding of the nature of Judaism is the doctrine 'God chose Israel as His people.'"[1] It is an idea many regard as scandalous: that God, Creator of heaven and earth, is passionately in love with a particular people. This idea—the chosenness, or election, of Israel—has more than its share of critics. Thus, for example, one writer complains that "the biblical idea of election is the ultimate anti-humanistic idea,"[2] and a renowned Christian Bible scholar, warning that chosenness is an "immensely problematic" notion, urges his readers to "choose against chosenness."[3]

But just what does divine election mean, and does it deserve all the opprobrium that is assigned to it?

GOD'S SPECIAL LOVE FOR ISRAEL

In one of his best-known teachings, the Talmudic sage Rabbi Akiva declares that each and every human being is precious in God's eyes.

"Beloved is the human being," he says, "for s/he was created in the image of God." R. Akiva adds that not only are we beloved, we are *told* that we are beloved, which is a sign of just how beloved we are: "Even more beloved is [the human being], for it was made known to him that he was created in the image of God, as scripture says, 'For in God's image did God make the human being' [Genesis 9:6]."[4]

As fundamental as God's universal love is to Jewish thinking, R. Akiva does not stop there. He goes on to proclaim that though all human beings are loved by God, the Jewish people are even more so. "Beloved are Israel," he says, "for they were called children of God. Even more beloved are they, for it was made known to them that they are called children of God, as scripture says, 'You are children of the Lord your God' [Deuteronomy 14:1]."[5] Although God's love is universal, Israel enjoys a special degree of intimacy with God.

R. Akiva continues: As God's children, the Jewish people have been given God's Torah as a special gift. "Beloved are Israel, for a precious vessel was given to them. Even more beloved are they, for it was made known to them that this precious vessel, with which the world was created, was given to them, as it is said: 'For I give you good instruction; do not forsake my teaching' [Proverbs 4:2]."[6]

Unsettling as it may be for some, it's important to understand the structure of R. Akiva's teaching. Only human beings—and not other creatures—are created in God's image, he maintains, and only Israel—and not other nations—are called God's children and given the gift of Torah.

In contrast to—and perhaps in response to—Christian insistence that God had abandoned the Jews (based on an unnuanced reading of Paul[7] and the Gospels, and promulgated through millennia of preaching and teaching), R. Akiva's student Rabbi Meir emphasizes that God's special love for the Jewish people is unconditional. Even if the people sin, they remain, always, God's children.[8] As we've seen before, God's love comes *with* expectations, but *without* conditions.

LOVE AND GRACE
(PREVENTING SELF-CONGRATULATION)

The point cannot be underscored enough: the election of Israel is first and foremost about love. According to the Bible, God chose the Jewish people because God fell in love with them. That idea, that election is rooted in divine love, is inextricably linked with another: that Israel did nothing to earn its special status and hence it has no basis for thinking itself superior to others.

Every theology that takes divine election seriously is confronted with an unavoidable trade-off. Explain what it is about the elect that led to their election and you risk eliciting a superiority complex ("God loves us because we're better than everyone else"); insist that their election was pure grace—that is, that the elect did nothing at all to earn it—and you risk making God's choice seem capricious, and even arbitrary ("God loves us because, well, God loves us").[9] No matter which path you take, you pay a real price.

In the book of Genesis, God's election of Abram (later to be called Abraham) comes as "a bolt from the blue."[10] Nothing about Abram has distinguished him from his peers, and yet God chooses to shower him with blessings—he will have bountiful offspring and they will inherit the land. Genesis, it seems, is willing to take the risk of making God's choice seem almost random, as long as it protects Abram and his descendants from triumphalism and self-glorification.

Perhaps not surprisingly, from the earliest days biblical interpreters attempted to fill in the gap.[11] Surely, interpreters assumed, there must have been *something* about Abram that merited God's fateful choice. And so we begin to hear stories that become familiar to every Jewishly educated child: Abram shattered his father's idols and exposed the shame of idolatry; Abram saw the world overrun by chaos and cried out in bewilderment and protest.[12] And God in effect rewarded him for his virtuousness. But popular assumptions notwithstanding, none of these stories are in the Bible itself. As a result, we might say that while the Bible implicitly insists that Abram did nothing to earn divine election,[13] the history of interpretation maintains otherwise. Abram was different from those around him and, on some level, he earned what he received.

The point Genesis makes implicitly Deuteronomy makes explicitly: "It is not because you are the most numerous of people that the Lord took a passion to[14] you and chose you," the Israelites are told; "indeed, you are the smallest of peoples; but it was because the Lord loved you and kept the oath He made to your fathers that the Lord freed you with a mighty hand and rescued you from the house of bondage, from the power of Pharaoh king of Egypt" (Deuteronomy 7:7–8).[15] God chose you, the Jewish people, Deuteronomy boldly proclaims, because (a) God loves you and (b) God will keep the oath that God made to your ancestors. In these verses, "any notion of inherent character, beauty, or merit leading to the Lord's desire and choice of Israel is explicitly rejected."[16]

In the same spirit, the people are soon told that they will dispossess the nations and inherit the land not because of their "righteousness" or "uprightness of heart" but rather because of the "wickedness" of the nations who presently inhabit the land and because of the oath God made to their ancestors (which, recall, their ancestors had done nothing to earn). If anything, Deuteronomy adds, the people's character speaks against them, since they are not virtuous but "stiff-necked" (9:4–6). To be sure, Israel must obey God's commands going forward but this obedience is not the reason why God chooses to give them the land in the first place.[17] Commandments come after election, not before.

The point of all this is to eliminate (or at least dramatically mitigate) the possibility of complacency or self-congratulation on Israel's part. You are who you are, and you have what you have, the Torah tells the people time and again, not because of anything you did but because of God's grace and love. Gratitude, not arrogance, is the appropriate religious response.[18]

In this context, it's worth briefly considering the patriarch Jacob, whose name is changed to Israel and who is thus the very namesake of the Israelites. As the Bible portrays him, Jacob is a complex figure, but one thing he is decidedly not is a saint. As the prophet Jeremiah warns in a play on Jacob's Hebrew name, Ya'akov, "Do not trust any of your brothers, because every brother is a deceiver (*akov ya'akov*)" (Jeremiah 9:3).

To take just the most troubling example, Jacob famously tricks his father into giving him the blessing the latter intends to give to his brother Esau (Genesis 27). The situation is complicated—Isaac wants to bless Esau but God (like Rebecca) wants the blessings to go to Jacob—yet the Bible forcefully expresses its disapproval of Jacob's deception. Jacob is repeatedly punished *for* deception *by means of* deception. His father-in-law Laban tricks him into marrying Leah, whom he does not love, instead of her younger sister, Rachel, whom he adores (Genesis 29). Tellingly, the root of the word used to describe Laban's actions toward Jacob, *r-m-h*, is the same root used to describe Jacob's own actions toward Isaac.[19] And the fact that Laban uses nighttime darkness to enact his scheme recalls Jacob's taking advantage of his father's dimmed vision. In addition, just as Jacob deceives his father, so too do his sons deceive him, conspiring to have him believe that his beloved son Joseph is dead. At the heart of Jacob's life, in other words, is a moral violation[20] for which he pays for the rest of his life.[21] And yet he is loved.

A PASSIONATE MARRIAGE

Assessing the canon of Rabbinic literature, Rabbi Solomon Schechter (1847–1915) declares: "There is not a single endearing epithet in the language such as brother, sister, bride, mother, lamb, or eye which is not, according to the [R]abbis, applied by Scripture to the intimate relation between God and [God's] people."[22] Two images in particular matter most: God and Israel as husband and wife, and God and Israel as father and son.[23]

One of the Jewish tradition's favorite ways of imagining the relationship between God and Israel is as a marriage.[24] The prophet Jeremiah hears God wistfully recall the early days of God's love affair with Israel: "I remember the devotion of your youth, how as a bride you loved Me" (Jeremiah 2:2);[25] and the prophet Hosea imagines God renewing God's covenant-marriage with the people: "I will betroth you forever; I will betroth you with justice and with righteousness, and with love and with mercy; I will betroth you with faithfulness, and you shall know the Lord" (Hosea 2:21–22). The Talmudic sages portray the revelation at Sinai as a wedding between God and Israel,[26] and they see the Torah as the *ketubah*, or wedding contract, that concretizes the love and commitment between God and Israel.[27] Before fulfilling a commandment, Jews traditionally recite a blessing that begins, "Blessed are You, Lord, Ruler of the universe, who has sanctified us with [God's] commandments"— but the Hebrew word for "sanctified us," *kideshanu*, can also mean "betrothed us." As we are about to perform a mitzvah, we acknowledge it as an expression of the eternal marriage between God and the Jewish people.

The love God feels for Israel is not abstract and Platonic. On the contrary, Jewish tradition imagines God as Israel's passionate lover. As Deuteronomy tells it, God didn't just love (*ahav*) the people, God rather "took a passion to" (*hashak*) on the people (the Hebrew word *hashak* conjures eros and passion). In a striking teaching, the Talmudic sage Rabbi Katina imagines that when the Jewish people would come to Jerusalem for the pilgrimage festivals, the priests would roll up the curtain that usually covered the ark and show them the two cherubs, winged figures that were placed above the ark. Seeing the cherubs entwined with one another, the people would be told, "See how you are beloved before God, like the love of a male and female [like the love between lovers]."[28] Covenant love is passionate love.

PARENT AND CHILD

But marriage is not the only metaphor the Bible invokes to convey the intimacy between God and Israel. Early on in his mission of helping God liberate the people, Moses is instructed to say to Pharaoh: "Israel is My firstborn son" (Exodus 4:22).[29] To be considered God's firstborn son is a sign of special divine favor; the firstborn son is "preeminent . . . first in rank."[30] For the Bible, all firstborn sons are holy, consecrated to

God.[31] This means that as God's children we belong to God and are meant to serve God.

Being considered God's son has another pivotal dimension. According to the Bible, covenants establish familial relations and responsibilities; to be God's son is to be God's very own family.[32] At Sinai, God and Israel become a family.[33] God does what a parent naturally does—God nurtures and guides the people; and Israel does what a child does—to borrow a phrase from a modern Bible scholar, it seeks to live "according to the father's heart."[34]

INTIMACY, JOY, AND THE COMMANDMENTS

What does chosenness require of the chosen?[35]

God expresses God's love for the people by giving them the Torah; we reciprocate our love by keeping the commandments. As Jewish liturgy demonstrates, the election of Israel is closely entwined with the revelation of the Torah at Mount Sinai. Consider the blessing recited daily before studying Torah (and upon being called to the Torah in the synagogue): "Blessed are You, Lord our God, Ruler of the universe, who has chosen us from among all the peoples and given us His Torah. Blessed are You, Lord, Giver of the Torah." According to this prayer, God gives expression to God's election of Israel by giving them the Torah.[36] In turn, another key prayer, recited (in different versions) twice a day, acknowledges that the Torah has been given in love, and expresses our commitment to studying the Torah and observing its commandments. Each evening we declare: "With everlasting love have You loved Your people, the house of Israel. You have taught us Torah and commandments, decrees and laws of justice. Therefore, Lord our God, when we lie down and when we rise up we will speak of your decrees, rejoicing in the words of Your Torah and your commandments forever." The primary way we give expression to our intimacy with God is through our faithful and loving observance of the commandments.[37]

The idea of intimacy conveyed through commandments—both God's giving them and our receiving and observing them—may strike some readers (especially Christian ones) as strange. This is perhaps the legacy of Christianity in general, and of Martin Luther in particular. According to Luther, "The Law is a taskmaster; it demands that we work and that we give. In short, it wants to have something from us. The Gospel, on the contrary, does not demand; it grants freely; it commands us to hold out our hands and to receive what is being offered. Now demanding and granting, receiving and offering, are exact opposites and cannot exist together."[38] Luther's words would strike most observant Jews as utterly alien; needless to say, they would not recognize their Judaism in Luther's complaints about "the Law." So far from seeing law as a burden that brings us up against our own inadequacy, Jews traditionally experience it as a delight that reflects God's concern for our well-being and respect for our agency. Accordingly, a core part of Jewish spirituality is "the joy of the commandments" (*simhah shel mitzvah*).

The joy Jews take in the commandments has a variety of aspects: enthusiasm in fulfilling God's will and delight in doing things for the right reasons (*lishmah*), without thought of benefit or reward.[39] But bound up with these is another crucial, arguably even more fundamental dimension of joy: God's issuing commands to us suggests that God cares about what we do, that God takes us and our capacity to impact the world seriously.[40] Commandedness is a sign of God's love and respect—and that is a reason for joy and celebration. We should therefore think of *simhah shel mitzvah* not simply as the joy of fulfilling a commandment but also, and even more fundamentally, as the joy of being commanded.

Deuteronomy nicely captures this sense that love and commandment are deeply intertwined. "For what great nation is there," it asks, "that has its gods so close at hand, as is the Lord our God whenever we call upon God? Or what great nation has laws and rules as righteous (*tzaddikim*) as all this Teaching that I set before you this day?" (Deuteronomy 4:7–8). Again, some readers may find the connection between these two rhetorical questions elusive, but from a biblical perspective the link is natural, even obvious: God's presence is manifest to us in part through the commandments and laws that God has given us.[41]

Among the Torah's many commandments, Shabbat has a special

place in expressing the covenantal love between God and Israel. It is, according to the book of Exodus, "a covenant for all time" and "a sign for all time" of Israel's recognition of God as Creator of heaven and earth (Exodus 31:16–17). To turn to liturgy again, in reciting the Kiddush (the liturgical sanctification of Shabbat) on Friday evening, we recite: "For You chose us and sanctified us from all the peoples, and in love and favor gave us Your holy Shabbat as a heritage." And during the afternoon prayers we speak of the community partaking of a "rest of love and generosity" (*menuhat ahavah u-nedavah*) on the seventh day, which a medieval commentator explains means that we observe Shabbat out of feelings of love.[42] God gives us Shabbat as an expression of God's love and we in turn observe it as an expression of ours.

MORAL GOODNESS AND INTEGRITY

If the chosen people are both obligated and inspired to keep the commandments, they are especially called to live lives of moral goodness and integrity. (Another way of saying this is that moral integrity and goodness are at the very heart of Torah and the commandments.)

When God hears the cries of the victims of Sodom and is considering what to do in response, God makes the startling decision to confer with Abraham. God does this, Genesis tells us, "Since Abraham is to become a great and populous nation and all the nations of the earth are to be blessed through him." The purpose of God's blessing the progenitor of Israel is made explicit: "For I have chosen him, that he may instruct his children and his posterity to keep the way of the Lord by doing what is just and right (*tzedakah u-mishpat*) . . ." (Genesis 18:18–19). Abraham and his descendants have been chosen, in other words, so that they can pursue the good. Crucially, the mandate does not apply to Abraham alone but to him and all the generations that will follow him. To be an heir of Abraham is to pursue justice and righteousness.

Precisely what is meant by justice and righteousness? The prophet Ezekiel explains via illustration. "If a person is righteous and does what is just and right . . . If he has not . . . raised his eyes to the idols of Israel;

if he has not wronged anyone; if he has returned his debtor's pledge to him and has taken nothing by robbery;[43] if he has given bread to the hungry and clothed the naked . . . if he has abstained from wrongdoing and executed true justice between people; if he has followed My decrees and kept My laws and acted honestly—he is righteous" (Ezekiel 18:5–9). Ezekiel places special emphasis on being economically upstanding and openhanded. In sum, Abraham and his descendants are charged to worship God alone, and in the interpersonal sphere, negatively, to "avoid sin"; and positively, to "do good to [their] neighbors."[44] They are to embody human goodness in all its forms. This is, the book of Proverbs makes clear, more precious to God than the traditional trappings of religious life (Proverbs 21:3).

It is undoubtedly significant that God speaks of Abraham and his descendants in this way just as God is about to deal with Sodom. If Sodom is a bastion of cruelty and injustice,[45] Abraham and his descendants must exemplify the radical alternatives of justice and kindness. The summons of covenant is to be ethically upright, even and especially when surrounded by heartlessness and corruption.

The Talmudic sages take the word "tzedakah" as used in Genesis to refer specifically to acts of lovingkindness. As a midrash explains, "tzedakah" refers to "providing a meal to the mourners" and "visiting the sick."[46] Indeed, from this verse about tzedakah, the Talmud concludes that performing acts of lovingkindness is (or should be) a distinguishing characteristic of the Jewish people.[47] Although the plain sense of the verse in Genesis may suggest that Abraham and his descendants are first and foremost charged with doing justice, Rabbinic tradition hears the verse as prescribing lives of love and kindness.[48] Abraham and those who follow him were chosen by God *in* love[49] so that they would in turn live lives animated *by* love.

A PLACE FOR GOD TO DWELL

One of the most audacious claims that the Bible makes is its insistence that Israel can play host to God, that it can create a space on earth where

God's presence can dwell. As Exodus describes it, God's longing is to find a home in and with Israel;[50] God therefore commands, "Let them make Me a sanctuary that I may dwell among them" (Exodus 25:8). One passage goes so far as to suggest that this, rather than bringing them to the Promised Land, is God's purpose in redeeming the people from Egypt: "I will dwell among the Israelites, and I will be their God. And they shall know that I the Lord am their God, who brought them out from the land of Egypt that I might dwell among them, I the Lord their God" (Exodus 29:45–46).

Yet this is no small undertaking because, as Leviticus emphasizes, God is holy and we are sinful. The Bible scholar Ellen Davis explains that "holiness is, at its fullest intensity, almost too much for ordinary human beings to bear. Reciprocally, ordinary human sinfulness is, over time, almost too much for God to bear."[51] Still, the Bible insists that we can help make God welcome, or, tragically, that we can chase God away.

Near the end of Leviticus the Bible gives voice to a powerful yearning. God promises that if Israel obeys God's laws, "I will establish My abode in your midst, and I will not spurn you. I will walk to and fro in your midst: I will be your God, and you shall be My people" (Leviticus 26:12).[52] The divine promise recalls Eden, where God was described as "walking to and fro in the garden" (Genesis 3:8). That is the longing at the heart of Leviticus: to turn the land of Israel into a new Eden—at peace, and filled with the presence of God.

As Exodus portrays it, God's presence will be localized. Israel will build a house for God, as it were, and God will contract God's presence (as later commentaries would put it) and dwell there.[53] But Leviticus imagines something more radical. God will dwell not (only) in the sanctuary but everywhere in the land: "My glory will be seen wherever you will be."[54]

Consider how much power Israel has. In Leviticus, God is awesome and sometimes terrifying, and yet God is also . . . vulnerable. Israel builds a home for God, but Israel can also effectively drive God away. To take what is perhaps the most powerful and dramatic example, Numbers warns the people not to take murder lightly, not to make peace with it as an unavoidable part of human life. Should the people treat the deaths of innocents lightly, the land will become "defiled" and God will no longer be willing (able?) to abide in their midst (Numbers 35:34). As a midrash comments, "Bloodshed pollutes the land and causes the divine presence (*shekhinah*) to depart."[55] Where God dwells—and doesn't—depends to no small extent on us.[56]

ELECTION AND HOLINESS

The call that lies at the heart of Leviticus is for Israel to embody holiness: "You shall be holy (*kedoshim*), for I, the Lord your God, am holy" (Leviticus 19:2). The fact of election and the mandate to holiness are intrinsically linked: "For you are a people holy (*kadosh*) to the Lord your God; the Lord your God chose you from among all other peoples on earth to be His treasured people" (*am segullah*) (Deuteronomy 14:2). There is obviously an enormous amount one could say about the meaning(s) of holiness in the Bible, but in this context I will make only three brief observations to help orient us: First, different biblical texts accentuate different aspects of holiness. Whereas, for example, some texts stress ritual purity, others accentuate social justice, and still others emphasize personal moral integrity. A biblical vision of holiness, let alone a more expansively Jewish one, will thus necessarily be multidimensional.

Second, although the Bible never actually defines holiness, the Hebrew word for holy, *kadosh*, literally means "separate from." Permitting myself some homiletical license, I often think of this as a mandate for the Jews to be countercultural in the deepest sense—in a culture of materialism, to be animated by the life of the spirit; in a culture of greed, to embody generosity; in a culture of selfishness, to decenter the ego; in a culture permeated by oppression, to pursue justice; in a culture overrun by inhumanity, to strive for righteousness; in a culture obsessed with self-promotion and "branding," to orient our lives around service (of God and of one another).

Third and finally, holiness is inextricably linked to love. It is surely no coincidence that the same chapter that is headed by the call to holiness includes within it the commandments to love our neighbor and the stranger (Leviticus 19:2, 18, 33–34). Holiness is also tied to compassionate concern for the weak and downtrodden. Consider Moses's first encounter with God. When God appears to Moses at the burning bush, God instructs him, "Remove your sandals from your feet, for the place on which you stand is holy ground" (Exodus 3:5). There is nothing intrinsically holy about the place where Moses is standing; rather, God's presence there renders it holy. What follows immediately is God's attentiveness to the cries of God's enslaved people—"I have seen the misery of my people . . . and I have heard their cry . . . I know [that is, I am concerned about] their sufferings" (3:7)—and, accordingly, God's plans to liberate them. It is perhaps not too much of a stretch to wonder whether for this passage God's attention to the plight of the persecuted stems from God's holiness.[57] Compassion and mercy surely do not exhaust the meaning of holiness but there can be no holiness without them. In seeking to be holy because God is holy, we are charged to cultivate love and compassionate concern.

THE MANDATE TO HOLINESS

To be in covenant with God, then, requires the people to observe the mitzvot, to pursue justice and righteousness, to sanctify God's name, to strive for holiness, and to live in such a way that enables the transcendent God to be immanent too. Should the people be faithful, their status will be elevated even more. "Now then," says the book of Exodus, "if you will obey Me faithfully and keep My covenant, you shall be My treasured possession (*segullah*) among all the peoples. Indeed, all the earth is mine, but you shall be to Me a kingdom of priests (*mamlekhet kohanim*) and a holy nation (*goy kadosh*)" (19:5–6).

It's important that we understand the "if" here.[58] Israel's status as a kingdom of priests and a holy nation is contingent upon its faithfulness but its status as God's elect is not.[59] I hear in Exodus's words both a challenge and a promise: Israel must strive for holiness (the challenge); if and presumably only if it does, it will be a kingdom of priests and a holy nation (the promise). To put this differently, Israel's status as chosen is irrevocable, but whether its chosenness reaches its fullest possible fruition remains in *its* hands.[60]

The mandate to holiness helps ward off the temptation to complacency and self-satisfaction. In Genesis, Abraham is promised that he will have vast numbers of progeny and thus become a "great nation" (*goy gadol*) (Genesis 12:2).[61] Here in Exodus, a challenge is attached to the promise: the great nation is charged to become a holy one too.[62] Covenant is not just a promise; it is also a task.

SET APART TO SERVE GOD

What does it mean for a people to be a "kingdom of priests and a holy nation"?

In my view, the idea of being a kingdom of priests and a holy nation is primarily focused on the Jewish people's relationship with God, not on its relationship with the broader world.

Many interpreters, especially—but not exclusively[63]—Christian ones, see the role of a priest as mediating between God and other people. For Israel to be a kingdom of priests, therefore, means that they are to serve as a bridge of sorts between God and the rest of the nations. To take just one example, the Bible scholar A. H. McNeile explains that a kingdom of priests is "a kingdom whose citizens are all priests to bring other nations to the worship of God, and to teach them [God's] will."[64] Since priests in ancient Israel were (among other roles) teachers,[65] Israel as a nation of priests must offer instruction to the broader world. As one scholar puts it, "God's call for Israel as a people to be his priest *may*, even *must*, be understood as Israel, now corporately God's people, called to function as teacher about God to the nations of the world."[66] On this interpretation of the verse, a nation of priests is essentially a nation of missionary teachers.

I am skeptical that this is what these verses have in mind. Their focus seems to be on observance of the commandments, not outward-facing preaching and teaching.[67]

More likely, I think, is that just as the priests form a distinct group, governed by laws and obligations that are unique to them, so also is Israel a distinct people, governed by laws and obligations that are unique to them.[68] Moreover, just as priests are specially set apart to serve their gods, so will Israel be utterly dedicated to serving God. What the people are told here, in effect, is that *if* they "obey [God] faithfully," *then* they will be a "kingdom of priests"; their priestly status—but again, not their election—is contingent upon their observance of the commandments.[69] The holiness of the people, a midrash observes, is "the holiness of commandments . . . Each time the Blessed Holy One adds another commandment to Israel, God [thereby] adds to their holiness."[70]

Another, related dimension of this connects these verses to the ones we've seen from Leviticus: to be a holy nation is to "experience the privilege of having God dwell among them."[71] But again, this depends on their faithfulness to God. Whether or not God has a home on earth will depend on Israel's choices.

If one wants to insist that these verses do look beyond the boundaries of Israel itself, then what they imagine, I think, is not mission but leadership by example. Covenanted to God, Israel is summoned to embody holiness. As the Bible scholar John Durham explains, the people of Israel "are to be a people set apart, different from all other people on what they are and are becoming—a display-people, a showcase to the world of how being in covenant with God changes a people."[72] A nation of priests is a nation of exemplars.[73]

Let's stay with the idea of being set apart for another moment. Should we interpret the challenge of being a "kingdom of priests and a holy nation" as mandating separatism? Judaism's answer, I think, is dialectical. The Jewish people are to be both separate—passionately devoted to the unique intimacy with God made possible by a robust commitment to Torah and the commandments—and fully integrated—actively participating in common human struggles and pursuits and, as we saw in chapter 7, ardently embodying universal human solidarity and the demands it makes. In a sense, Israel is to be separate as God is separate—God is distinct from the world but ever-present within it.[74] Another way of saying this, perhaps, is that Israel is religiously other but humanly the same. We pray separately but we can and must pursue justice, righteousness, and moral goodness together.

DO JEWS HAVE A UNIVERSAL MISSION?

I've suggested that the focal point of being a kingdom of priests and a holy nation is Jewish people's relationship with God; it's not primarily an outward-facing notion and does not necessarily imply a mission to the non-Jewish world. But do other biblical texts suggest that the Jewish people have a mission to spread God's word (and/or to teach morality)?

In one of the most oft-cited but least understood passages in Tanakh, the prophet Isaiah hears God telling the people: "I the Lord, in My grace, have summoned you, and I have grasped you by the hand. I created you and appointed you, a covenant-people[75] (*berit am*), a light of nations (*or goyim*), to open eyes that are blind" (Isaiah 42:6). Oceans of ink have been spilled arguing over the meaning of Israel's being "a light of nations."[76] Here again, as in Exodus, some scholars take the words in question to mean that God assigns the Jews a mission to bring the word of God to the rest of the nations. Such interpretations are especially popular among Christian scholars, who often see in Isaiah's words an anticipation of the apostle Paul's commitment to spreading the word of God to the Gentiles. Imagining that the prophet wanted the chosen people to become "a nation of world-traversing missionaries,"[77] some go so far as to refer to Isaiah as "the missionary prophet of the Old Testament."[78]

But others flatly reject the idea that Isaiah imagines ancient Israelites becoming missionaries. Insisting that Isaiah is barely interested in foreigners at all, they argue that the only role non-Israelites play in the prophet's vision is that they will acknowledge God's sovereignty over the world. The prophet's focus, however, is unabashedly particularistic.

Unfortunately, the seemingly all-important phrases "*berit am*" and "*or goyim*" are hopelessly obscure. Although Isaiah's words are probably ambiguous enough to permit either of the approaches I've described, my sense from the broader context of the book of Isaiah is that the prophet's vision is about the restoration of Israel and the exaltation of its God.[79] The prophet *is* a kind of universalist in that he envisions the whole world ultimately acknowledging the one God, but this does not necessarily translate into a mandate to missionize. This is one of the key ways that Jewish love has traditionally differed from Christian: Jews do not assume that loving people requires us to convert them. In any case, when it comes to the nations, Isaiah's eye is on what *God* will do, not what the people will do. As the Bible scholar Robert Martin-Achard explains, "The encounter of the [nations] and YHWH . . . depends upon divine initiative alone . . . Israel has no other mission to the [nations] than to be the chosen people."[80]

To the extent that we wish to focus on the people's responsibility, we can say that Israel is charged to become a good and holy people, not to crisscross the world in search of converts. As the Jewish philosopher Raphael Jospe nicely puts it, "Isaiah's vision neither negates separate Jewish nationhood, nor does it send the Jews out to enlighten the non-Jews. It calls for Jewish national life to be exemplary."[81]

"UNIVERSALISM?": BETWEEN CHRISTIANITY AND JUDAISM

There is a great deal at stake in this debate over Isaiah's words, because the insistence that Isaiah puts forward a mandate to missionize the non-Jewish world has often gone hand in hand with Christian supersessionist claims. Since Jews were supposed to spread God's word but refused to, the argument goes, God turned instead to the church as the New Israel and, fulfilling God's wishes, it in turn set about seeking converts.[82]

This supersessionism, in turn, is bound up with a broader polemical claim—that whereas Judaism is particularistic and therefore benighted, Christianity is universalistic and therefore enlightened.[83] This type of assumption is so common and widespread that we rarely pause to examine it.

Is Christianity really universalistic? It depends on how we understand universalism. On one level, Christianity clearly is universalistic in that it seeks to bring what it takes to be the word of God to the farthest reaches of the earth. On another level, though, it isn't universalistic at all, since the real debate between Jews and Christians in antiquity was not over particularism versus universalism but over who, precisely, could and could not claim Israelite identity. As the Bible scholar Jon Levenson explains, "Whether one is heir to Abraham's promise still means everything to Paul; although he specifies a different rite of passage from that of the [R]abbis, like them, he still assumes that whether one is of Israel or not is of supreme importance."[84] If you prefer, we can say: Christianity, like Judaism, has insiders and outsiders. In this crucial sense, both are particularistic religions. In this sense, in fact, *all* religions are—necessarily—particularistic religions.

But for argument's sake, let's concede the point that Christianity really is universalistic where Judaism is not. Is that unambiguously a good thing? In the history of religions, universalism has rarely yielded tolerance, let alone embrace, of the other. On the contrary, universalism has often had precisely the opposite effect: an insistence that everyone must worship the One God the same way right now and an attendant unwillingness to tolerate the other's religious otherness.[85] Consider the Christian Bible scholar Herbert May's definition of "theological universalism": "This may briefly be defined as belief in one God who is to be worshiped by all peoples, Jew and Gentile alike." So far, perhaps, so good. But May continues: "It comprehends a single world religion and a common religious culture; it implies a single cultus."[86] Betraying no hint of self-consciousness about it, May effectively presents intolerance not as an implication of universalism, but as part of its very definition. Universalism demands uniformity. Not surprisingly, then, universalism has often been conjoined with imperialism.[87] To put it crudely, "We have the truth and we will bring it to you. Should you resist, you will be coerced to conform—for your own good."

To return to a point we saw in chapter 6, theological universalism often fails at the seemingly simple task of leaving other people alone. It refuses to allow the religious other to be just that—religiously other.

It is no exaggeration to say that human (and Jewish) history are littered with the corpses of those who resisted other people's universalist passions.

Is particularism as dreadfully primitive as it is sometimes made out to be? Although Rabbinic tradition is vast and contains many conflicting voices, the dominant thrust of Jewish thought is that righteous Gentiles have a share in the world-to-come[88]—that is, that they are potentially (to coin a phrase) "good with God." One of the reasons Jews have never warmed to missionizing is that they have not seen mission as necessary. As Levenson observes, "Those who think outsiders can have a proper relationship with God as they are will feel less of an impulse to make them into insiders."[89] Jews have therefore tended to allow others to remain other. As the Talmud scholar Daniel Boyarin wonderfully puts it, "The genius of Christianity is its concern for all the peoples of the world; the genius of rabbinic Judaism is its ability to leave other people alone."[90]

In other words: surprising as some may find it, as we saw in chapter 6, the fact is that particularisms can often be more tolerant of others in their otherness than universalisms tend to be.

To be sure, particularisms have their undersides: they can take chauvinistic forms, whereby God loves the in-group but is indifferent—or even actively hostile—to everyone else. And universalisms have their strengths: they can boldly affirm that as Creator of all, God cares for every human being everywhere, without exception. But as we've seen, they have dangerous and potentially violent undersides too: they are frequently drawn to coerce others to conform to their vision of the truth.[91]

Ultimately, terms like "particularism" and "universalism" confuse more than they clarify. As the Bible scholar Ellen Birnbaum points out, since both terms are "value laden" and "hard to define," they "in fact obscure what we wish to learn—namely, in what specific ways are religious traditions, practices, and concepts open to others and in what specific ways are they not?"[92] In reality, Judaism is not less universalistic than Christianity; it is differently universalistic. If we take universalism to require toleration of others in their otherness, Judaism is in fact far more universalistic.

IS GOD'S ELECTION OF THE JEWS INSTRUMENTAL?

The insistent prioritization of the universal over the particular frequently causes non-Jews seeking to understand God's covenant with Israel to go astray. There is a troubling tendency among some thinkers to interpret the election of Israel in purely instrumental terms. Take the example of Christopher Wright, a prominent evangelical Christian Bible scholar. Wright maintains that "Israel came into existence as a people with a mission entrusted from God for the sake of the rest of the nations. *All that Israel was*, or was supposed to be—all that YHWH their God did in them, for them, and through them—was ultimately linked to this wider purpose of God for the nations."[93] No less starkly, he declares that "the people of Israel . . . were called and brought into existence *only* because of God's missionary purpose for the blessing of the nations."[94] On Wright's account, God chooses Israel *only* so that Israel can benefit the rest of the world.

But the biblical picture is more complex. Take God's initial summons to Abram in the book of Genesis: "The Lord said to Abram, Go forth from your native land and from your father's house to the land that I will show you. I will make of you a great nation, and I will bless you; I will make your name great, and you shall be a blessing. I will bless those who bless you and curse him that curses you." What comes next is notoriously difficult to translate. The Hebrew words *ve-nivrekhu vekha kol mishpehot ha-adamah* can mean either "all of the families of the earth shall be blessed through you" or "all of the families of the earth shall bless themselves by you" (Genesis 12:1–3). Whereas the first possibility seems to suggest some sort of active role on Abram's part in bringing blessing to the nations, the second seems to envision something more passive: Abram's greatness will be such that other people(s) will invoke his name in blessing others. But let's assume, for argument's sake, with Wright and many others, that the first translation is the better one. Abram is somehow implicated in causing blessing to flow to the broader world—though precisely how, it should be said, is not specified. Does this mean that the whole series of blessings Abram receives are all ultimately in the service of this one? In my estimation, scholars like Wright confuse an "and" for a "so that." According to these verses, God chooses Abram *and* this choosing is to redound to the benefit of all humanity, but nowhere does the text say that God chooses Israel only *so that* benefit will redound to all. As we've seen, election is first and foremost about God's love for Israel and God's desire to live in a mutually loving relationship with the people. To put it differently, God's election of Israel may *also* be instrumental, but it is not *only* or even primarily instrumental. So obvious is it to some that the universal is somehow more valuable than the particular that they simply assume that any divine embrace of the particular must ultimately be in service of the universal.

This is a very odd way of thinking about love. When we fall in love with someone and commit to marriage, we don't fall in love with them in order to benefit other people—let alone *only* in order to benefit other people. We may hope that the love we share with our spouse radiates outward to the broader world; we may even commit to ensuring that this happens—but this hardly exhausts the meaning and purpose of our marriage. We love our spouse *and* we hope that our love will redound to the benefit of others, but we do not love our spouse *so that* our love will redound to the benefit of others. "Love relationships are not best conceived in instrumental terms."[95]

IS GOD INDIFFERENT TO THE NON-ELECT?

If election means that God falls in love with Israel, what does that mean for other people? Does election imply, as some worry, that God loves Israel and is indifferent to everyone else?

One of the Bible's central theological claims is that God has given (the Hebrew root is *n-t-n*) the land of Israel to the people of Israel. But as they journey toward the Promised Land, the people are warned not to provoke the Edomites because God "has given (*n-t-n*) the hill country of Seir as a possession to Esau" (Deuteronomy 2:5); again, they are admonished not to harass the Moabites, since God "has given (*n-t-n*) Ar as a possession to the descendants of Lot" (2:9); and yet again, they are enjoined not to harass or provoke the Ammonites because God "has given (*n-t-n*) [the land of the Ammonites] as a possession to the descendants of Lot" (2:19). The geographical details of the story need not concern us; what matters is Deuteronomy's insistence that other peoples besides Israel have been given a home by God.

As the Israelites are about to enter the land, they learn that there are giants ("Anakites") in the land, people about whom it is said, "Who can stand up to the children of Anak?" Yet they are bidden not to fear, since God, who is "crossing at [their] head," will defeat their opponents (9:2–3). Now, there are no Anakites in the lands to be captured by the Edomites, the Moabites, and the Ammonites, but Deuteronomy goes out of its way to inform us that the inhabitants these nations were forced to confront were "like the Anakites" (2:10–12). These inhabitants were a frightening formidable obstacle standing between these peoples and the lands that had been promised them. Sure enough, we are told that just as God will destroy the enemies Israel faces, God has already destroyed the enemies these other nations faced (2:21–22). In a striking passage, we are told that the Edomites did just "as Israel did in the land they were to possess, which the Lord had given (*n-t-n*) them" (2:12). Edom's experience thus directly corresponds to Israel's, and the blessings it receives come from God, just as Israel's do. As the Bible scholar Patrick Miller observes, in Deuteronomy's telling "the stories of God's involvement with these other peoples parallel in every way the story of God's dealing with Israel."[96]

It's crucial that we understand what the Bible is doing in these passages. No biblical book is more focused on the election of Israel than Deuteronomy. Yet as Miller notes, the book—perhaps for that very reason—"vigorously resists a misreading" of election. Lest we think that election suggests exclusivity, that Israel alone is to be the recipient of God's gifts, Deuteronomy starkly reminds us otherwise. In being told that "others have benefitted in the same fashion from the Lord's power and grace, Israel . . . hears that its story is not the only one going on."[97] The implication of all this should be clear: God cares about, and provides for, nations other than the Jewish people. From a biblical perspective,

God may be concerned about Israel *most* but God is assuredly not concerned with Israel *only*.

Important (and as often overlooked) as all these passages are, they do not in fact make the case that God cares about *all* peoples. What all the nations mentioned in Deuteronomy share in common is that they are descended from Abraham; as Deuteronomy tells it, they are all "brothers" or "kin" to Israel (1:8).[98] Deuteronomy establishes that God cares about, and is at work in the lives of, all of Abraham's offspring.

Yet the prophet Amos goes further. Amos seeks to dismantle the complacency, stubbornness, and self-satisfaction of the people. Apparently convinced that their election by God renders them immune to divine judgment, the people have rejected the prophet's warnings of imminent doom. Amos undermines their misplaced confidence by teaching them a powerful and subversive theological lesson: "To Me, O Israelites, you are just like the Cushites—declares the Lord. True, I brought Israel up from the land of Egypt, but also the Philistines from Caphtor and the Arameans from Kir" (Amos 9:7). The Cushites were geographically far removed from the Israelites; indeed, Cush is sometimes invoked in the Bible as a prime example of a remote place.[99] Moreover, Cushites are sometimes mentioned in the Bible as servants and eunuchs.[100] And in the book of Numbers, Miriam and Aaron express opposition to Moses's choice of a wife because she is a Cushite.[101] One can imagine that Amos's listeners were seriously aggrieved at his comparison. As the Bible scholar Daniel Simundson explains, "To equate Israel with people they considered obscure and subservient would be . . . a serious affront to their self-satisfied pride in their special status in God's eyes."[102] But that is precisely the prophet's point. Israel is not alone in being cared for by God; God's attention and concern extend even to the most far-flung nations.[103]

As for the Philistines and the Arameans, they were not "brothers" of Israel but adversaries. If the Cushites were obscure to the Israelites, the Philistines and Arameans were well-known—and frankly loathed. The people were perhaps tempted to think that God would condemn these nations or, at the very least, want nothing to do with them. But

Amos tells them just the opposite. God is active in the history of these enemy nations. As Miller writes, Amos wants the Israelites to understand that God "has similar stories of deliverance and guidance with other peoples, in this case *not just with kinfolk, but with enemies.*"[104] Again the pivotal point is that Israel is not alone in being cared for and saved by God.[105] "God is the God of all peoples, acting decisively in the stories of non-chosen nations,"[106] even when those nations are in conflict with the chosen people.

In another pivotal verse, Amos insists that election doesn't entail moral license. "You alone have I singled out of all the families of the earth," the prophet hears God say to the people; "Therefore I will call you to account for all your sins" (Amos 3:2). God has established a covenant uniquely with Israel ("singling out" is covenant language).[107] Yet covenant is not a blank check; it does not lessen the covenant partner's moral responsibility but rather amplifies it: Amos unequivocally affirms the uniqueness of Israel's relationship with God—but he argues that this very uniqueness entails *more* accountability rather than less. Having a special relationship to God "exposes [the people] to judgment rather than exempting them from it."[108] The phrase translated as "therefore" (*al ken*) in the verse is crucial. As Simundson explains, "One might expect that to be in such a relationship with God would lead to privileges, immunities, favoritism, security. After all, 'we are God's chosen people.' The word 'therefore' turns that way of thinking upside down."[109] To be clear, Amos believes that God holds other nations to account for their failings too; in fact, the book opens with a devastating indictment of the nations, enumerating both their sins and the consequences they will face (1:1–2:3). But Israel's status as God's elect means that more is expected of it. Intimacy accentuates accountability.

DIVINE CARE FOR A LOWLY SLAVE

God's loving concern extends not only to other peoples but also to other individual persons—even persons who find themselves in conflict with God's elect family.[110]

Distressed by not having had children, the matriarch Sarai (later to be called Sarah) devises a plan. She wants her husband Abram (soon to be called Abraham) to sleep with her Egyptian maid Hagar; perhaps, she hopes, she will have a son through her. Abram does as Sarai wishes—without enthusiasm, it seems;[111] Hagar conceives, and then trouble begins.[112] "When [Hagar] saw that she had conceived, her mistress was lowered in her esteem." One can surely understand why Hagar may see Sarai negatively. Hagar has, after all, been treated as little more than a "womb with legs,"[113] an object rather than a person with a will of her own. Affronted by the disrespect, however, Sarai directs her ire at Abram. Wanting no part of the conflict, Abram responds by telling Sarai, "Your maid is in your hands. Deal with her as you see fit" (Genesis 16:1–6).

Sarai "oppresses" Hagar and the latter flees from her. The word "oppresses" (va-te'anaha), laden with meaning, is the same one that will be employed later, to describe the Egyptians' "oppression" of Israel (e.g., Exodus 1:11–12). Some traditional commentators pick up on the remarkable choice of words and condemn Sarai (and by extension Abram) for "sinning" in their treatment of Hagar.[114]

Subtly, the text shows the reader that Abram and Sarai do not see Hagar as fully human. Sarai refers to her only as "my maid" (Genesis 16:2, 5), Abram as "your maid" (16:6). It is as if the woman has no name, no identity of her own. Strikingly, when an angel finds her in the wilderness, the first word he speaks is her name, "Hagar" (16:7). Abram and Sarai may not see Hagar's humanity, the text seems to say, but God surely does.[115]

The angel asks Hagar where she is coming from and where she is going, but Hagar, seemingly bereft and dejected, replies only about her past: "I am running away from my mistress Sarai" (Genesis 16:7–8). She is only too keenly aware of the miseries of her past; perhaps she is uncertain about having any future at all. And yet the narrator informs us that the angel finds Hagar at "the spring on the road to Shur," which is close to Egypt, so the reader is perhaps intended to assume that she is on the road back home to Egypt.[116] Hagar is lost, but not completely lost.

What happens next is odd—and, on the surface at least, deeply troubling. The angel instructs Hagar to "go back to [her] mistress and submit to her oppression" (Genesis 16:9).[117] If the angel (and by extension, God) wishes to affirm Hagar's humanity, why does he send her back to the place where she will undoubtedly undergo further misery and hardship?

Strikingly, the angel's actions directly contradict the law as laid out in Deuteronomy. As we saw in chapter 8, in sharp contrast to other ancient cultures in which one was forbidden to harbor fugitive slaves, according to Deuteronomy one is *obligated* to harbor them and forbidden to return them to their master (Deuteronomy 23:16–17).[118] So how can the angel of God send a slave back to her (abusive) master?

We will return to this, but first let's consider the rest of the angel's words. "And the angel of the Lord said to her, I will greatly increase your offspring, and they shall be too many to count." He announces that Hagar is pregnant and instructs her to name her son Ishmael—which means "God hears"—because "the Lord has heard your suffering." The angel then offers what may seem like a strange prediction about the son to be born: "He shall be a wild donkey of a man, his hand against everyone, and everyone's hand against him; he shall live at odds[119] with his kin" (Genesis 16:10–12). Is giving birth to a combative fighter really such a blessing? The point, I think, is that Ishmael will be strong and not easily subjugated.[120] As Jon Levenson puts it, "The fierce independence of the Ishmaelites will vindicate the humiliating thralldom of their matriarch's life."[121] Though Hagar has been, and will continue to be, forced to endure slavery, she is assured that her son will be spared the same fate.

In one of the most moving moments in the Hebrew Bible, when God sees Hagar (*really* sees her) and promises her a son in the short-term and innumerable offspring in the long-, Hagar responds by naming God—she is the only character in the Bible to give God a name—"You are the God who sees me" (*El-Ro'i*)[122] (16:13).

The person God sees, and reveals Godself to, is, in Israelite terms, a foreigner and an outsider. God's promise to Hagar indicates that God is concerned with, and active in the life of, people—and peoples—beyond Israel. God cares for those who are not Israel, especially for those who are vulnerable and downtrodden.

Now we're ready to return to the disturbing question: Why does the angel send Hagar back to suffer oppression at Sarai's hands?

Some scholars describe the unsettling scene as "the most pointed counterexample to the misleading overgeneralization . . . that the biblical God is on the side of the impoverished and the oppressed." Yet even they acknowledge that the blessings the angel bestows upon Hagar do seem to imply something similar to what liberation theologians refers to as the "preferential option for the poor,"[123] which is the claim that the Bible consistently gives special preference to the poor and marginalized. To be sure, God doesn't emancipate the slave, but God does shower her with blessings. Strikingly, though all three of Israel's patriarchs hear such words of blessing from God, Hagar is the only woman to receive them.

Let's carefully consider: Why does the angel of God instruct Hagar to return and endure further oppression at Sarai's hands?[124] In order to understand what's really at play in this story, it's crucial that we note the parallels between Hagar's abuse at Sarai's hands and Israel's later torment at Egypt's. In Egypt, Israel will endure enslavement and oppression, and will be alien, strangers in a strange land (Genesis 15); in this story, Hagar (the Egyptian!) endures enslavement and oppression, and her name sounds very much like *ha-ger*, meaning "the stranger."[125] In each case, the stronger (Pharaoh, Sarai) "oppresses" the weaker (Israel, Hagar) and "banishes" them. In each instance, God sees the affliction of the victim and, encountering them in the wilderness, God blesses them and transforms them into a great nation.[126]

Hagar's oppression parallels Israel's and so too do her blessings parallel Israel's. Recall that when the angel finds Hagar after she flees from Sarah, he declares: "I will greatly increase your offspring, and they shall be too many to count" (Sarai, 16:10); later, when God encounters her again after she is banished, God instructs her to lift up her son Ishmael and hold his hand, "for I will make a great nation of him" (21:18). The divine promises made to Hagar are starkly reminiscent of the promises made to Israel.

We can learn a great deal by juxtaposing Genesis 16 with the chapter that immediately precedes it. In Genesis 15, God tells Abram that God will multiply his descendants but that they will be strangers in a foreign land where they will be enslaved and oppressed for four hundred years; only then will God bring them out and give them the land. In Genesis 16, "God's angel tells Hagar to return to be exploited; afterward she will have a child who cannot be exploited, and God will multiply her progeny." In critical ways, Hagar's story mirrors—and anticipates—Israel's. As the Bible scholar Tikva Frymer-Kensky puts it, "The story of Hagar parallels the story of Israel; she is the archetype."[127]

We can ask why Hagar has to endure such suffering before she can experience the blessings that God promises. That question parallels another, equally difficult one: Why must Abram's descendants endure generations of slavery before they can experience the blessings that God promises? Frymer-Kensky offers an explanation that is as disturbing as it is insightful: "The pattern of Hagar and Abram and of later Israel shows that the way to God's reward is through the margins of society and the depths of degradation . . . This pattern," Frymer-Kensky adds, "offers hope to the oppressed, but it remains an unexplained aspect of God's behavior in the world."[128]

I don't pretend to have an explanation, let alone a justification, for why the road to blessing is so often paved with suffering. But I do know that there is a deep truth evident here: often the deepest blessings emerge from great pain or even desolation.[129]

The story of Sarah (as Sarai is by now called) and Hagar continues several chapters later. God blesses Sarah with the child she has longed for and Abraham names him Isaac (Yitzhak). Giving voice to her wonderment and delight, Sarah plays on the boy's name and proclaims, "God has brought me laughter (*tzehok*); everyone who hears will laugh (*yitzhak*) with me" (Genesis 21:6). The boy is circumcised and eventually weaned. Abraham (as Abram is by now called) holds a great feast on the day that Isaac is weaned—and then things take a very ugly turn: "Sarah saw the son of Hagar the Egyptian playing [*metzahek*, another play on Isaac's name]." It isn't clear precisely what Ishmael has been doing—the midrash raises the possibility that he was engaged in idolatry or that he was abusing or molesting Isaac,[130] but the plain sense of the text may be that he was simply enjoying himself or playing with his brother; in any case, it enrages Sarah, who demands that Abraham "cast out that slave-woman[131] and her son, for the son of that slave shall not share in the inheritance with my son Isaac" (21:9–10). Sarah does not accord either Hagar or Ishmael the dignity of being named;[132] all they are is foreign and lowly, and most important of all, a perceived threat to her beloved Isaac.

The contrast between Sarah's feelings about the boy and Abraham's is poignantly drawn. The text tells us that "the matter greatly distressed Abraham, for it concerned his son" (21:11). To Sarah, Ishmael is no more than "the son of that slave" but to Abraham he is his *very own* son.[133]

To the reader's surprise (and consternation), God appears to side with Sarah: "But God said to Abraham, Do not be distressed over the boy or your slave; whatever Sarah tells you, do as she says, for it is through Isaac that offspring shall be continued for you. And as for the son of the slave-woman, I will make a nation of him, too, for he is your seed" (21:12–13).[134] Disturbingly, God echoes Sarah's pejorative language for Hagar and Ishmael—they are the slave and the son of the slave, not flesh-and-blood human beings. Or perhaps God speaks this way in order to lessen the pain Abraham feels at what he is being asked to do.

In this second story, too, God's actions raise questions. Why, when Abraham hesitates to send Hagar and Ishmael away, does God bid him do as Sarah says? The Bible scholar Phyllis Trible worries that "the deity identifies here not with the suffering slave but with her oppressors."[135] (Why) does God side with the powerful against the powerless?

I am not sure that God does. Frymer-Kensky again offers a powerful perspective on what transpires here. "We should note," she writes, "that in a world in which slavery is accepted, Hagar and Ishmael are not sold: they are freed. Hagar and Ishmael leave Abraham's household as emancipated slaves."[136] Where Trible sees exile, Frymer-Kensky sees exodus.[137] To be sure, the path before Hagar is filled with uncertainty and danger, but as the text itself makes clear, God is with the mother and her son; when their water runs out, God shows them to a well.

Note how Hagar's experience again parallels and prefigures Israel's. After Abraham sends her away, Hagar wanders thirsty through the desert until God provides her with water—just as Israel will wander thirsty through the desert until God provides them with water. "In slavery and in freedom," Frymer-Kensky writes, "Hagar is Israel."[138] Hagar is not in fact Israel, and that is the point: God's concern for Israel and God's care for non-Israel directly mirror one another.[139]

BETWEEN BIBLICAL CHOSENNESS
AND CHRISTIAN SALVATION

From a biblical perspective, God's election of Israel decidedly doesn't entail rejection of those who are not Israel. So why do some writers insist that "the problem of election . . . is the problem of scarcity, the sense that there is not enough to go around" and that "for those who regard themselves as elect, their particular identity tends to become an exclusive identity—salvation only on their terms?"[140] Treating divine love as a finite resource, they misrepresent the Bible's own logic.

Consciously or not, the biblical idea of chosenness has frequently been conflated with later Christian understandings of salvation. But the distinction between chosen and unchosen does not overlap with the distinction between saved and damned (or, for that matter, with the distinction between good and bad).[141] "The Hebrew Bible did not endorse the notion that election meant that the non-elect were either damned or out of the purview of God's blessings, nor does it claim that the elect escaped all hardship."[142] If we want to understand biblical notions of chosenness, we must not imagine that to be non-elect is to be hated or permanently rejected by God.

In laying out Tanakh's vision of election, the Bible scholar Joel Kaminsky helpfully distinguishes among three categories of peoples, which he labels the elect, the non-elect, and the anti-elect. The anti-elect are groups like the Canaanites and Amalekites, who are condemned as enemies of God and whom the Israelites are commanded to annihilate. (For people who take the Bible seriously as Scripture, the very existence of the category of anti-elect should be profoundly unsettling and disturbing. This, much more so than chosenness itself, seems to me to represent an immense problem and challenge.) But the overwhelming majority of non-Israelites are part of the non-elect, not the anti-elect. The non-elect, Kaminsky explains, were seen as included under the umbrella of God's concern, and, in fact, "Israel was to work out her destiny in relation to them, even if in separation from them." More than that, the non-elect sometimes serve as moral models for ancient Israel to emulate and learn from, and even "articulate God's saving actions to the sometimes erratic and unfaithful Israelites." As Kaminsky convincingly argues, "The failure by certain . . . scholars to distinguish between the non-elect and the anti-elect leads them to misunderstand and ultimately to reject the notion of election on false grounds."[143] The scope of God's concern extends far beyond the boundaries of Israel. God is not Israel's exclusive possession.

ELECTION: A DOUBLE-EDGED SWORD

Modern Jews have often found the notion that Israel is chosen troubling. No Jewish thinker more forcefully argues for jettisoning the idea of Jewish chosenness than Rabbi Mordecai Kaplan (1881–1983), founder of Judaism's Reconstructionist movement. According to R. Kaplan, to believe ourselves chosen is to be guilty of "self-infatuation," to hold a "romanticized and glamorized" conception of ourselves, and to make an "invidious assumption of superiority" in comparison with other peoples. To maintain the idea of chosenness in this day and age, R. Kaplan insists, is simply "unethical."[144] (R. Kaplan advocates for speaking instead of Jewish "vocation," which, he insisted, "carries with it no implication of superiority.")[145]

R. Kaplan's condemnation of chosenness is less than nuanced. He maintains, for example, that chosenness necessarily means that "the 'Chosen People' is accepted and others rejected,"[146] but as we've seen from the allotment of lands to other peoples, for example, God's choosing of Israel does not imply neglect of other people—and peoples. R. Kaplan also holds that election is about "privileged status," part of a universe in which "privilege is bestowed and does not have to be earned."[147] There is undoubtedly some privilege attached to chosenness (the gifts of land and progeny that we hear about time and again in Genesis, for example), but here too the picture is more complex. As we've learned from the prophet Amos, chosenness also comes with immense—and frankly frightening—responsibility. Biblically speaking, chosenness makes people more accountable, not less.

R. Kaplan writes as if God's choosing of one people entails God's rejection of all others, but as we've seen, the Bible consistently eschews this type of zero-sum thinking. God chooses Israel and still engages with and cares for other peoples. My point is not to delegitimize all criticisms of chosenness—far from it. But R. Kaplan consistently fails to do justice to the Bible's own picture(s) of chosenness.

And yet it is critical to acknowledge that the idea of election can be a double-edged sword: it can prod a people to strive for goodness and holiness and it can inspire it to serve goals and ideals beyond itself. No less important, confidence in being God's chosen helped enable Jews to withstand centuries of persecution and degradation. In the eyes of the world the Jews were cast off and downtrodden, but in their own eyes they mattered . . . and mattered ultimately.

And yet believing in chosenness can be extremely dangerous, and at times downright poisonous (this is, no doubt, part of what so troubled R. Kaplan about it). The prophets were constantly forced to fight against interpretations of election that guaranteed the people impunity and rendered them impervious to critique. Not a few Jews in history (and today) have thought, consciously or not, that chosenness is bound up with special entitlement. Yet reading the prophet Amos, one quickly realizes that denunciation of destructive understandings of chosenness is part of the idea of chosenness itself. In other words, chosenness itself requires vigilance against toxic notions of chosenness.

I have focused primarily on the Bible, where Jewish belief in chosenness is rooted. But it is critical to admit that later Jewish discussions of chosenness can frequently sound more chauvinistic than biblical ones do (at least to my ears). Thus, for example, in the Middle Ages one can find conceptions of chosenness that maintain that Jews are ontologically different from non-Jews, that there is something hardwired in them that renders them distinctive in relation to all other human beings.[148] Now, one can point out that such ideas arose and grew in prominence in times and places when Jews suffered acute persecution,[149] that such ideas served as consolation of sorts for a people that knew its share of far-more-powerful enemies. There is a great deal of truth in this, and yet we should not allow apologetics to have the final word. Ideas that are comforting to people when they are powerless are potentially noxious when they grow powerful.

This means that we must be responsible heirs and interpreters of tradition. To say that "God loves us and is more or less indifferent to everyone else" may be unfortunate but also understandable in a persecuted culture; the very same idea is pernicious and unconscionable in a context where one wields power and is afforded dignity. So as always, we need to decide which voices to accentuate in contemporary Jewish life.

Let me present just one example of the kind of choice I am envisioning. As we've seen, in Exodus 19 God offers the people the opportunity to become God's "treasured possession among all the peoples"; God immediately adds that "indeed, all the earth is mine" (Exodus 19:5). The reader is left to wonder about the relationship between the whole earth belonging to God, on the one hand, and the Jewish people being God's special treasure, on the other. One traditional commentator, Rashi, imagines that God is saying, in effect, "You, Israel, are my special treasure and even though the whole earth is mine, in My eyes [the other nations] are as naught." Israel, and Israel alone, matters to God. But another traditional commentator, Rabbi Obadiah Seforno (ca. 1475–1550), hears God's words very differently. On his account, God declares, in effect, "All of the nations are Mine, and the whole human race is precious to me, but nevertheless you, Israel, will be a kingdom of priests and a holy nation."[150] On some level, there is a choice here: we can understand chosenness in a way that actively belittles others (literally treats them "as naught") or through a lens that insists on the utter preciousness of all human beings.

WHAT KIND OF GOD CHOOSES?

In obvious ways, the question of chosenness raises the question of God. If God is merely an idea or some sort of impersonal being, then obviously God does not enter into relationships. But as we've seen, one of the Bible's central claims is that God does choose to form relationships with human beings. And so we need to ask: What kind of God makes a covenant?[151]

First, such a God must be a Subject, must have will and consciousness, must, in other words, be able to say "I." Second, such a God must value relationship, must want to love someone other than Godself—even if, as Jewish theology affirms, God must first create the other to whom God will relate. Third, a God who covenants must be willing to be vulnerable, since to relate to another is always to risk the possibility of rejection and disappointment; a God who covenants can be hurt.[152]

An Aristotelian Perfect Being, contemplating itself for all eternity, cannot enter into a covenant. That kind of God exists entirely outside of time and therefore entirely outside of earthly human affairs.[153] And a purely naturalistic God—a God who simply is nature, or is an impersonal force within nature—cannot enter into a covenant either. Such a God lacks the will and consciousness (not to mention the personlikeness) that makes relationships possible.

Rabbi Mordecai Kaplan rejects election not just for ethical reasons but also for metaphysical and theological ones. He is a thoroughgoing naturalist—for him, nature is all there is—and he rightly realizes that the idea of election is "rooted in supernaturalism"[154]—that is, in a God who is beyond nature. Chosenness implies that there is a Divine Chooser, and only a transcendent God who has both will and consciousness can make a choice. For R. Kaplan, a transcendent ("supernatural")

God is a nonstarter, part of a thought-world he insists is outdated and obsolete—and so, too, therefore is chosenness.[155]

But if one doesn't embrace R. Kaplan's naturalism, one needn't accept its implications. I think it is very much still possible to talk about a transcendent God, and about a God who enters into relationships—and therefore I think it is still possible to talk seriously about a God who makes covenant(s) with human beings.

In a classic essay, the Jewish thinker Will Herberg (1901–1977) maintained that opposition to the idea of chosenness was ultimately rooted in an overly abstract (and therefore faulty) conception of God. "A truly rational and universal God," opponents of chosenness aver, "could not do anything so arbitrary as to 'choose' one particular group out of mankind as a whole. It is, indeed, 'odd of God to choose the Jews,'" they hold, "because it is odd of God to 'choose' anybody." Herberg is impatient with arguments like these. "To be scandalized by the universal God acting in and through particularities of time, place, and history," he writes, "is to conceive the divine in essentially impersonal intellectual terms." But Judaism (and Christianity, for that matter) have never been focused primarily on universal truths and eternal ideas; they are centered on a relationship, and "truly personal relations are never universal; they are always concrete and particular." God does not love us merely as examples of the human species; God loves us as *us*, in all our particularity. As Herberg argues, "Within the framework of Jewish faith . . . the doctrine of 'chosenness' constitutes no incongruity; it is only to abstract . . . human reason that it constitutes a scandal and offense." For Herberg, the logic of chosenness is entirely consistent with Judaism's foundational theological commitments; in his words, "The insistence on historical particularity contained in the notion of 'chosenness' is . . . part of the Biblical-[R]abbinic affirmation of the '*living*' God, who meets [people] in personal encounter in the context of life and history."[156]

A choosing God, then, is a living and personal God.

And yet still: Can't God love people (and peoples, for that matter) in all their particularity without having favorites?

The Jewish theologian Michael Wyschogrod (1928–2015), an

impassioned champion of the idea of election, offers a provocative response. "As a father," Wyschogrod writes, "God loves his children and knows each one as who he is with his strengths and weaknesses, his virtues and vices." Like a good human parent's, God's love is not generic. So far, so good. But Wyschogrod continues: "Because a father is not an impartial judge but a loving parent and because a human father is a human being with his own personality, it is inevitable that he will find himself more compatible with some of his children than others and, to speak very plainly, love some more than others."[157] In my estimation, there are (at least) two significant problems here. First, it is one thing to affirm that God is personal and another to speak of God as if He—and God is always, in such arguments, a He—were just another person with the same predilections and (frankly) weaknesses as we humans have. For if it is true that some parents love some of their children more than others, this seems to me that this is something of a failure on their part. And this brings us to the second problem. Because fathers are indeed human beings with their own personalities, it is inevitable that there will be times when they feel more connected with one child than another, but if my own experience is any indication, the intensity of connections ebbs and flows—sometimes one is more connected to this child, and other times to that one. I know of almost no fathers who would be untroubled by loving one child more than the rest, with no caveats or qualifications. To my mind, Wyschogrod's defense of God's knowing us in variegated ways is compelling, but his insistence that God loves some more than others—just as we purportedly do—just doesn't hold water.

So there remains something unsettling about the idea that God, who could "love every single person there is without that love being remote and abstract in the least,"[158] would love some more than others.

This question brings me all the way back to where we started, to Rabbi Akiva's teaching about God's love for human beings, and about God's unique love for Israel. Recall what R. Akiva proclaims: "Beloved is the human being," he says, "for s/he was created in the image of God." The Talmudic sage speaks in the singular: each and every human being on the face of the earth is loved by God. Continuing, R. Akiva declares:

"Beloved are Israel, for they were called children of God." In speaking of God's extra love for Israel, the sage speaks in the plural. The contrast between the reference to human beings in the singular and Israel in the plural is extremely suggestive, even if it is almost never remarked upon. Perhaps R. Akiva's point is that God loves all humanity but God has especial love for one particular collective, the Jewish people. It is not that God loves this Jew or that more than everyone else; it is, rather, that God has entered into a unique relationship with the people of Israel qua the people of Israel.

In the end, any covenant theology will necessarily have both insiders and outsiders. We can soften the edges around that fact but we can't sidestep it altogether—and I'm not sure we should want to. Covenants, like religions in general—like identities in general, for that matter—are inherently particular; what matters from a moral perspective is not whether or not they have outsiders but how they imagine and interact with those outsiders.

COULD GOD HAVE MULTIPLE "WIVES"?

To be sure, this idea raises its own questions—could not God have entered into multiple relationships with multiple peoples?

This leads me to another possibility that I share only with great hesitancy, both because it strays further from tradition than is usual for me, and because I am uncomfortable with the patriarchal assumptions embedded within it.

In biblical times, men could marry more than one woman, though a woman could be married to only one man. As we've seen, Jewish tradition imagined the relationship between God and Israel as a marriage, with God as the groom and Israel as God's bride. Israel was not permitted other husbands and, as the Bible tells it, it often incurred God's ire when it strayed and cavorted with other gods. The striking thing, though, is that the Bible never describes God taking—or even considering taking—another wife (=people) in addition to Israel. In a culture that permitted polygamy, God demonstrates God's faithfulness by . . . going beyond the letter of the law and staying utterly faithful to God's one and only beloved spouse (we might say that in this sense God resembles monogamous Isaac more than polygamous Abraham and Jacob).

But what if we take what the law permitted seriously? What if we think of ourselves as God's beloved, monogamously committed to God, but not necessarily as God's only love? We positively revel in the love we share with God but we do not discount the possibility that perhaps God has other enduring relationships too. Whether we talk about multiple covenants, or about prophecy in varied settings, or about some other way of interpreting God's committed presence beyond the boundaries of the Jewish people, we should be careful not to hold God on a leash of our own making.

I offer this inchoate, underdeveloped possibility only in the most tentative of ways. What I am after is a way of making sense of God loving persons and peoples in concrete, nonabstract ways, but also of recognizing that God's love is greater and wider-reaching than any merely human love could ever be.[159]

I have made the best case I can for the theological and ethical viability of election. Yet, as I have implied, I remain somewhat uneasy. It is one thing to talk about a God who cares about each of us uniquely and accordingly enters into distinctive relationships with us; it is quite another to insist that God chooses some over others, indeed loves some more than others.

I am sometimes tempted to think of chosenness in mostly phenomenological terms, as a description of what it feels like to be loved, summoned, and commanded by God. By this logic, when we talk about God choosing us from among all the nations, perhaps what we are doing is describing our experience of God's transformative love, not making definitive claims about the nature and boundaries of God's own love. When we are surrounded by God's love, we feel we are the only ones (even if we are not). But this solution seems inadequate to me too, since I am a theological realist, meaning that I believe that God exists independently of human beings, and that the things we say when we talk about God can be more or less true (or false). Thus, when I talk about God, I mean to talk about *God* (however ham-handed and inadequate all human talk of God must inevitably be) and not just my/our own experience thereof.

To the extent that we regard the biblical and Rabbinic canons as authoritative, it is difficult to imagine a coherent Jewish theology that eliminates chosenness altogether.[160] In being called to the Torah in the synagogue, some Jews speak of God having "brought us close to [God's] service" instead of having "chosen us from among the peoples" . . . but they then proceed to chant from the Torah that time and again affirms the election of the Jewish people. As Joel Kaminsky observes, "As long as the Torah remains central to the Jewish liturgy, all other efforts at eliminating claims of Jewish election will simply create a rather odd incoherence in the liturgy, but will not succeed in excising the idea of Jewish chosenness."[161] The idea of election is fundamental to the Jewish tradition. To maintain fidelity to and continuity with the past, we should hold on to this idea, and at the same time we should remain ever conscious of our responsibility as heirs of tradition to interpret what is handed down to us. For that we need to be at once textually literate, morally sensitive, conscious of God's vast love, and honest with ourselves about what we can and can't believe (or yearn to believe). That task of keeping tradition alive is—always—ongoing.

15

LOVING A LOVING GOD

JEWISH LITURGY CASTS the relationship between God and Israel as a love story. In many liturgical traditions, every morning we acknowledge God's "abounding love" (*ahavah rabbah*) and every evening God's "everlasting love" (*ahavat olam*);[1] each time, our recognition of God's love is immediately followed by a call for us to reciprocate: "And you shall love the Lord your God with all of your heart,[2] and with all your being, and with all your might" (Deuteronomy 6:5). In this, Jewish liturgy hews to the logic of Deuteronomy itself, where we are told that God "took a passion to [us]" (7:7) and are exhorted to love God in return.

In speaking of God's everlasting love, we echo the prophet Jeremiah, who had heard God proclaim to the people: "I have loved you with an everlasting love (*ahavat olam*); I have drawn you with unfailing kindness (*hesed*)" (Jeremiah 31:3). Incorporating these prophetic words into our liturgy, we readily acknowledge God's enduring love for us.[3] Acknowledgment is the first step toward requital. Given how frequently the Bible describes Israel being faithless and disloyal to its Divine Lover, this first step is arguably a momentous one.

The version of the prayer recited in the morning speaks also of the "great and extraordinary tenderness (*hemlah gedolah v'iteirah*)"[4] God shows us. As we've seen, some traditional texts depict God's love as fierce and zealous, but this prayer presents a much gentler picture, God as steady and steadfast lover.

In discussing the idea of divine election in the previous chapter, we encountered the image of God as spouse and as parent. But this prayer is animated by a different image of divine love, God as a devoted pedagogue who teaches "laws of life." In the version of the prayer recited in the morning, we implore God to give us guidance for good living, just as God did for our ancestors. As a contemporary scholar of Jewish liturgy explains, in this prayer "the Torah is epitomized as rules for living, the teaching of which is evidence of God's love. Apparently, the greater the love, the greater the desire to impart counsel on how to live."[5]

In the version of the prayer recited in the evening, emphasis is placed on the idea that God "has loved [God's] people with everlasting love" and that God therefore "taught us Torah and commandments, statutes and laws." The point is critical: God's love for us is expressed in the giving of the commandments in love; our love for God, in turn, is expressed in the keeping of those commandments in love. God's love and God's commandments are inextricably intertwined.

The point cannot be emphasized enough, since so much anti-Judaism depends on denying or distorting it: In Judaism, law is a manifestation of love.[6] Even now, Jewish thinkers insist, the Torah keeps God close to us. As Rabbi Joseph Soloveitchik declares, "We all believe that the One who gave us the Torah has never deserted the Torah. [God] simply walks and accompanies the Torah wherever the Torah has, let us say, a rendezvous, an appointment or date, with somebody. The Giver of the Torah is there!"[7]

As we've seen, Deuteronomy hints at a similar idea. "For what great nation is there," it asks, "that has a god so close at hand, as is the Lord our God whenever we call upon Him? Or what great nation has laws and rules as perfect as all this Teaching that I set before you this day?" (Deuteronomy 4:7–8). The pairing of these two rhetorical questions suggests that God's presence is made manifest through the commandments that God gives us.[8]

Strikingly, (in the morning) we ask God for the grace that will enable us to grasp God's Torah. In this, the liturgy follows the book of Psalms. "Open my eyes, that I may perceive the wonders of Your Torah,"[9] the psalmist says; "Give me understanding that I may know Your commandments" (Psalm 119: 18, 73).[10] As the liturgy imagines it, God's love and grace are involved both in giving us the Torah and in granting us the ability to understand it. In our own time, focused as we often are on autonomous human achievement, this is a countercultural posture, a recognition that the minds with which we perceive and understand are themselves gifts we did nothing to earn. As a psalm beautifully puts it, "By Your [i.e., God's] light do we see light" (Psalm 36:10).

Our prayer for God's grace in understanding God's teaching culminates in a yearning not just to fulfill God's commandments, but to fulfill them "out of love" (be-ahavah). The significance of this should not be overlooked: the aspiration underlying this whole liturgical unit is for our worship to be animated and driven by love. As important as keeping the commandments is in Jewish life, it is not enough; the ideal is for us to keep the commandments *out of love*. God gives the commandments in love and we, in turn, strive to observe them in love. As we've seen time and again in this book, motives matter; emotions are crucial; and inwardness is key to Judaism's vision of the good life. Just as we are commanded to perform acts out of kindness (*gemilut hasadim*) for others from a place of love for them, so are we commanded to perform God's commandments from a place of love for God.

PERFORMING THE COMMANDMENTS OUT OF LOVE

What does performing mitzvot out of love look like?

Jewish tradition offers two connected answers: first, to perform mitzvot joyfully, and second, to perform them with neither hope of reward nor fear of punishment (*lishmah*).

Joyfully: a psalm invites the people to "worship the Lord joyfully, [to] come before [the Lord] with shouts of gladness" (Psalm 100:2). Commenting on the verse, Rabbi David Kimhi (Radak) writes that "the service of God should not be a burden but rather undertaken with joy and gladness."[11] Another authority instructs, "Do the good because it is good; choose the true because it is true."[12]

And without thought of reward: Psalm 112 declares, "Happy is the one . . . who finds great delight in God's commands" (Psalm 112:1). A Talmudic sage underscores: happy is the one who delights in God's *commands*, not in their *reward*. Tying the idea of performing the commandments from joy with putting aside any thought of reward or punishment, the Talmud cites a well-known dictum attributed to an early Sage: "Do not be like the servants who serve the master on the condition of receiving a reward; rather, be like the servants who serve the master not on the condition that they receive a reward."[13] One who serves God in hopes of receiving a reward or avoiding a punishment, a medieval sage declares, ultimately worships not God but herself.[14]

Living as we do in a time when God seems hidden and when so many Jews have understandably lost the belief that God actively rewards good and punishes evil, we have a unique opportunity to fulfill the commandments *lishmah*, for the sake of serving God, and without thought of recompense. Ironically, then, it is precisely the hiddenness of God that makes deeper piety and commitment possible.

LOVE FOR GOD IS EMOTIONAL

For traditional Jewish thought, love of God and observance of the commandments are interwoven.[15] But it's essential to emphasize something that ought to be obvious but often isn't: love and observance aren't the same thing.

Bible scholars frequently assert that the love commanded in Deuteronomy is about action rather than emotion. The Torah's commandment to "love the Lord your God with all your heart," they insist, is a mandate to loyalty and obedience, not to an affective response to God.[16]

Yet such interpretations are ultimately inadequate. For Deuteronomy, love *includes* obedience but it is not *limited* to it. Scholars too often lose sight of a crucial aspect of the story that Deuteronomy is telling.

God has fallen in love with (*hashak*, perhaps better rendered as "took a passion to")[17] Israel and God summons Israel to reciprocate. It seems odd to imagine that God's love for Israel is emotional, passionate, even erotic, as the Hebrew verb *hashak* would suggest, whereas "Israel's love for God is a code word for obedience and bears no trace of desire" or passion.[18] Given the focus on divine-human mutuality and reciprocity, it would make sense that the love Israel is asked for would in some way reflect God's own love for us. If God loves Israel emotionally, then presumably Israel's attempt to reciprocate ought to be emotional in tenor too. Accordingly, it makes sense to conclude that the love command in Deuteronomy "involves human emotions in a significant way and is not simply constituted by actions borne of obedience."[19]

In order to understand Deuteronomy's conception of love more clearly, it's important to recall that before the Romantics (in the early nineteenth century), emotions were rarely if ever understood as "purely internal"; in the biblical world, the line between an internal feeling and an external action was much less stark than it is for many moderns. As the Bible scholar Jacqueline Lapsley puts it, research into the history of love suggests that "the categories of feeling and action . . . are distinctly modern ones that may well not apply to the biblical texts."[20] In other words, if we ask whether by love the Bible means emotion *or* action, the correct answer will be that it includes *both*, and that the two were regarded and experienced as inseparable. Affective love and observance of the commandments are not the same thing but they may be two aspects of one thing (biblical "love"). When Deuteronomy commands the people to love God, then, it may well be summoning them to obedience (love as action) at the same time as it is making a claim upon their inner world (love as emotion).

My sense is that different readers need to hear this point differently. Some, whose conception of love tends toward the sentimental, need to be reminded that biblical love includes concrete expression in deeds. Others, whose conception of love is all about deeds ("Of course I love you, I do x, y, and z for you"), need to be reminded that love is about affect as well as action.

Those who insist that love in Deuteronomy refers exclusively (or almost exclusively) to obedience sometimes seem motivated at least in part by a sense that affective love cannot be commanded, but we have dealt with this issue before: True, emotions cannot simply be switched on or off at will, but they can be cultivated. In fact, love for God can be cultivated precisely through the performance of mitzvot. In any case, as the Bible scholar Jeffrey Tigay writes, "The idea of commanding a feeling is not foreign to the Torah, which assumes that people can cultivate proper attitudes"[21]—and for Deuteronomy, I think we can say, there is no more proper attitude than love of God.

THE INTERLACING OF LOVE AND OBSERVANCE

It's worth pausing for a moment to ask why love and observance are so intertwined in Jewish thought. On one level, part of the logic of love is that it is expressed in action. As a modern philosopher puts it, "Love is always outgoing. It must express itself in activity or it is not love but admiration."[22] When we love someone, we want to fulfill their wishes and meet their expectations.

On another level, Judaism seeks to prevent lofty ideals from devolving into empty platitudes. Or, to put it positively, Judaism is eager for high ideals to find concrete expression in the real day-to-day world. If we say we love humanity but never lift a finger to help anyone, then we have accomplished little besides cheapening the language of love. If we say we love God but nothing about our lives in the world gives expression to that claim, then again, we have uttered lifeless words.

Ideally, loving God and keeping the commandments form a virtuous circle. Keeping the commandments helps us grow in love of God, which in turn deepens our commitment to observing the commandments. Commenting on the words "And you shall love," a midrash says, "Act [that is, serve God] from love!"[23] Another midrash imagines God declaring, "All that you do, do only from love!"[24] If observing the commandments leads to love, so too does love lead to observing the commandments. Love is both a consequence and a cause of mitzvah-observance.[25]

Love of God and observance of the commandments are interlaced but they are not synonymous. Thus the Israeli philosopher Yeshayahu Leibowitz (1903–1994) is mistaken in insisting that in Judaism "the acceptance of yoke of Torah and Mitzvoth *is* the love of God";[26] as the midrashim we've been discussing make clear, love is ideally intended to serve as the *motivation* for observance of the commandments ("All that you do, do only from love!") but the former is not simply reducible to the latter. To suggest that love and mitzvah-observance are essentially the same thing is to rob the Jewish tradition of its consistent concern with inwardness and motivation.

OBSERVANCE AND INTIMACY

Performing mitzvot gives expression to love for God, but according to some Jewish thinkers, it also makes genuine intimacy with God possible. The word "mitzvah" is derived from the Hebrew root meaning "command." A mitzvah is a commandment (note: not a "good deed,"[27] though performing good deeds is commanded). But the Hasidic masters connected the word "mitzvah" to an Aramaic word, *tzavta*, meaning "togetherness."[28] A mitzvah is an opportunity for togetherness with God.

Other schools of thought also connect observance of the commandments with intimacy with God. Thus, for example, the Musar master Rabbi Yeruham Levovitz teaches that "the very foundation of mitzvot is attachment and cleaving to God." As he observes, "A mitzvah is attachment and cleaving and love . . . when we perform a mitzvah, we are cleaved to the Blessed Holy One." As he sees it, every mitzvah we perform is itself love and can lead to deeper love.[29]

Mitzvot in general are a mode of togetherness with God, but for me—and, I suspect, for many observant Jews—Talmud (i.e., learning) Torah is an especially powerful path to intimacy with God.

Consider the flow of Deuteronomy 6.[30] We are commanded, "You shall love the Lord your God with all your heart, and with all your being, and with all your might"; and immediately thereafter we are told, "These instructions with which I charge you this day shall be upon your heart"

(Deuteronomy 6:5–6). For Judaism, loving God and poring over God's words are inextricably intertwined. It may be useful to note here that the biblical Hebrew word *lev*, usually rendered as "heart," also includes what we moderns refer to as "mind." In Deuteronomy, we are commanded to love God with both emotion and intellect—and needless to say, with action too.[31]

Jews traditionally understand Torah as a gift from God; some Talmudic sages go so far as to describe it as a series of kisses from God.[32] As such, it is experienced as a source of profound joy. "I delight in Your laws," says the psalmist; for him, life without Torah would be no life at all. "Were not Your teaching my delight," he proclaims, "I would have perished in my affliction" (Psalm 119:16, 92). In just this one short verse, the psalmist evokes the powerful sense many Jews have that Torah is both the rarest treasure and an elemental necessity; we simply cannot imagine life without it. This unshakable connection to Torah is enacted in Jewish ritual life: the practice of reading from the Torah every Monday, Thursday, and Saturday flows from the sense that just as we become ill if we do not drink water for three days, so also do we begin to wither spiritually if we fail to engage with words of Torah for that amount of time.[33]

In the spirit of Torah as delight, we pray each morning that God make the words of Torah sweet in our mouths. We don't just study Torah; we positively revel in it.

In Jewish thought, there are two modes of studying Torah. In the first, we study so that we know what to do; this kind of Torah study is essentially instrumental in that its purpose is to prepare us to fulfill other mitzvot. In the second, we study not to prepare for anything else but because Torah study is a significant mitzvah in its own right. Thus, even if one were expert in every aspect of Torah (if that is imaginable), one would still have an obligation to study.[34]

Each morning, when we recite blessings over Torah study, we speak of being commanded *la'asok* in words of Torah, which means not (merely) to study but to labor in them. "What is envisioned is clearly not merely an act, or even a series of acts, but an enterprise." Talmud Torah is less a discrete mitzvah and more a "calling" and a "vocation"—and that requires both "aspiration and commitment."[35]

Arrestingly, the Talmudic sages imagine the Jewish people as "betrothed to Torah." I'd suggest that in crucial ways marriage to Torah is like marriage to another person. We can have transformative moments with texts no matter what our background or level of commitment—we encounter a text and through it come to see the world, and ourselves within it, with different eyes. Such moments have their place but they are not ultimately enough to sustain a relationship with Torah. For that we need steadfastness, discipline, and a commitment to coming back day after day after day, even during times when the fire goes out of the learning. There are no shortcuts in the spiritual life; the project of making Torah our own is the task of a lifetime.

INTIMACY THROUGH LEARNING

What do I mean when I speak of a sense of togetherness with God through learning?

It is something of a cliché in some Jewish circles that "when I pray, I talk to God, but when I study Torah, God talks to me." For me, the experience is less of God talking to me—and in any case I am wary of the implications of saying that God speaks to me given that my interpretations could always be mistaken—than of God being present with me as I study. As a Talmudic sage teaches, if ten sit together and occupy themselves with Torah, the *shekhinah* is present with them; this is true, he goes on to say, even if five sit together, even if two do, and even if only one does.[36] Note that the sage doesn't say that God *speaks to* us, but he does insist that God is *present with* us when we study. It's almost as if we learn Torah as an expression of our love for God and God, as it were, appears from time to time[37] to reciprocate that love. In a deeper sense, it is a virtuous circle: God's love is always already found in the Torah that God has given; we study in an attempt to reciprocate God's love; and God appears (subtly, to be sure), to reciprocate our reciprocation.[38]

Learning Torah is an experience of togetherness with God, but it also constitutes an additional form of connection and togetherness. In poring over the same texts that our ancestors studied—in studying God's words as well as theirs—it is as if generations upon generations of devoted Jews come and study together in the same room. Time bends as we talk to the Talmudic sage Rabbi Akiva about the meaning of the Shema; with Maimonides about what we can and can't legitimately say about God; with Rabbi Joseph Caro (1488–1575) about arcane matters of Jewish law; with Rabbi Israel Ba'al Shem Tov (the Besht, 1700–1760); about praying with passion; with Rabbi Israel Salanter (1810–1883) about Torah and the ethical personality; and so on. Sometimes we talk, and even argue, with our ancestors; sometimes we just listen; always we marvel at the privilege of taking part in a conversation that spans millennia.[39] In those moments, it doesn't matter that centuries and oceans separate us; they and we are partners in a quest to understand what God wants and expects from us, and in a commitment to enacting God's will. Talking Torah together, multiple generations come to love God together.

There is another critical aspect of divine-human companionship that is expressed in Talmud Torah. In studying Torah, we are not passive receptacles but active cocreators. God and we are, as it were, co-authors of Torah—God reveals Torah and we constantly discover new dimensions in it. Playing with a verse from Ecclesiastes that describes the words of Torah as "well planted" (Ecclesiastes 12:11), the sages declare that "just as a plant grows and increases, so also the words of Torah grow and increase."[40] Similarly, when we recite the daily blessings over studying Torah, we note that God has "planted" eternal life within (or among) us, which is taken to refer to the Oral Torah, which sprouts—through human interpretation—from the seeds that God plants.[41] In some fundamental sense, then, Torah is a collaborative venture involving both God and us. "The Blessed Holy One gave the Torah to Israel," a midrash says, "as wheat to extract flour from it and as flax to make into a garment."[42] God actively seeks this collaboration and validates our role as coauthors.

LOVE FOR GOD IN ALL THAT WE DO

Ultimately, love of God extends beyond the performance of mitzvot to any and all actions we undertake. Part of what it means to love God, I think, is to maintain a sense of God's presence wherever we go and whatever we do. A Talmudic teaching drives home this point: "Bar Kappara expounded: What short text is there upon which all the essential principles of the Torah depend? 'In all your ways know God, and God will make your paths smooth' (Proverbs 3:6)."[43]

But what does it mean to know God in all our ways?

In our massively distracted world, it can sometimes seem that we are never fully present anywhere. We're praying, but we're thinking about baseball; we're studying, but we're thinking about the stock market; we're taking care of a friend in need, but we're thinking about how much work we still need to do today; and so on, seemingly forever.

Even when we're ostensibly focused on God, we may still find our attention divided. We're praying, but we're thinking about learning Torah. We're learning Torah, but we're thinking about our struggles with prayer; we're helping a friend in need, but we're thinking about what we've been learning. One mitzvah distracts us from another, and so we are never fully present in and for the mitzvah we're engaged in.

Rabbi Abraham Isaac Kook emphasizes the word "in" in the phrase "in all your ways know God." "One must seek the Blessed Holy One," he says, "in the midst of the ways one acts," and that means that we should be fully immersed in whatever it is that we are doing. Thus, when we pray we should be focused only on prayer; "one should not seek to know God through other matters, because since one is engaged in this service-worship (*avodah*), God is, as it were, present at one's side in this mode of service specifically, and there one will find God—and not in some other place." God is to be found "in" our prayer—and nowhere else. Similarly, when we study Torah, our attention should be entirely directed to study. During times of study, one should seek God only "in God's Torah, and not in any other manner, because at that time God is revealed in that mode of service." In the same way, when we are engaged in acts of loving kindness, we should "seek the Blessed Holy One only through deeper thought on the way to benefit one's friend in a great, upright, and enduring way."[44]

Prayer, Torah study, and acts of loving kindness are, religiously speaking, the "pillars of the world."[45] What about the other things we do? Are they only means to an end, tasks to be endured more or less impatiently, until we can get back to what "really matters"? According to R. Kook, "The truth is that there is nothing in the world that is not for the honor of the Blessed Holy One, hence everything one does will be according to God's commandment and will—and in each action one should search for God."[46] Our eating can be holy—and not just because it keeps us healthy enough to pray or study; shopping for groceries, or talking to our children, or any one of a myriad of other things we have to do in a given day—all of these activities can be holy, R. Kook insists, provided that we're fully present as we do them.

The verse from Proverbs actually offers two interwoven teachings: first, that we can know God in *all* our ways, and second, that we can know God *in* all our ways. Crucially, "all our ways" includes not obviously or explicitly religious ones. How one engages with them can make them moments of piety and devotion.

There are two levels to R. Kook's teaching. The first is about training our minds and our hearts to be fully present in the moment before us. This is what we nowadays refer to as mindfulness. But there is a second level, too, and it is about training our minds and our hearts to be fully present to the possibility of *serving God* in the present moment. R. Kook's remarkable insight is that whether a given activity at a particular moment is holy depends not just on *what* we do, but also on *how* we do it—with what quality of presence and awareness.

It's critical that we not misunderstand R. Kook's words. There are still better and worse things to do with our time, and better and worse things we can do with our lives; there are still, for those privileged to have such choices, better and worse career paths, and better and worse ways to spend our leisure time. R. Kook's point is about being present in whatever moment we find ourselves in, and knowing that it, too, can be elevated to the realm of divine service. To love God is to (strive to) be in God's presence always and everywhere.

LOVING WITH GOD

As we've seen, feeling love, observing the commandments, and knowing God in all our ways are all crucial expressions of love for God. But let's turn our attention to another, arguably more radical path of love for God.

In our exploration of the love of the stranger in chapter 8, we saw that Deuteronomy makes a subtle but powerful claim about what it means to love God. One verse tells us that God loves the stranger, and the following one instructs us that we too must love the stranger (Deuteronomy 10:18–19). Love of the stranger is thus elevated to a form of *imitatio Dei*, of walking in God's ways.

But an even more fundamental point comes through too: If you want to love God, Israel is implicitly told, you must love those whom God loves.[47] (And so the most important theological question in many ways becomes: Whom does your God love?) If, as we've seen, God loves all human beings, then to love God is to strive to do the same. There is both a prescriptive and a descriptive point here: if we want to love God, we must commit to growing our love for flesh-and-blood human beings; if we truly love God, we will inevitably come to love what God has created.

The Musar master Rabbi Chaim Shmuelevitz (1902–1979) writes that "love of God and love of neighbor are the root upon which all the commandments and the whole Torah depend."[48] Note that the two commandments are described not as two separate roots but as one; they are thoroughly enmeshed with one another. Love of God leads to love of neighbor, Jewish thinkers argue, and—this is perhaps a more difficult claim for many modern readers—love of neighbor leads to love of God.[49] Conversely, says Rabbi Hayyim Vital, one who hates his fellow as it were hates God for creating them."[50]

Let's focus on how love of God flows into love of neighbor.

When we love someone, when we wish the best for them, we usually want their children to flourish too; after all, the well-being of a person's children is to a significant degree determinative of their own. The same applies to God: when we truly love God, we will love God's children too.[51] If we love God and hate God's children, then it isn't God we love but an idol of our own making; as Rabbi Judah Loew (Maharal) writes, "If one hates people, it is impossible for him to love God, who created them."[52]

The goal, some thinkers argue, is to come to see others through God's eyes. God loves those whom God creates, and if we truly love God, then so also will we; God sees God's creatures with a generous eye (*ayin tovah*), and if we truly love God, then so too will we.[53]

Although God loves all human beings, I think it's fair to say that according to the Bible, God shows particular love and concern for the widow, the orphan, and (as our verses from Deuteronomy indicate) the stranger. Psalm 68 describes God as "the father of orphans [and] the champion of widows" (Psalm 68:6); and Psalm 146, part of the daily liturgy, declares that "the Lord watches over the stranger, [the Lord] gives courage to the orphan and the widow" (146:9). One of the things the Bible itself seems to marvel at is the idea that God, the transcendent Creator of heaven and earth, is passionately concerned with the plight of the lowly and defenseless. As the prophet Isaiah hears God say, "I dwell on high, in holiness; yet with the broken[54] and lowly in spirit" (Isaiah 57:15); in other words, even though God dwells in the heights of heaven, God is nevertheless present with those who are crushed underfoot.[55] As the psalmist says quite simply, "High though the Lord is, [the Lord] sees the lowly" (Psalm 138:6).[56] If we are commanded to love those whom God loves, then we are especially mandated to love the persecuted and oppressed. If God is not too exalted to attend to the afflicted and abused, then neither, certainly, are we.

LOVING CREATION

God's tender care extends beyond humanity toward creation as a whole. As we saw in chapter 7, Genesis 1 positively revels in the diversity of creation. God creates fruit trees "of every kind"; seed-bearing plants "of every kind"; birds "of every kind," wild beasts "of every kind"; cattle "of every kind"; and creeping things "of every kind" (Genesis 1: 11–12, 21, 24–25). God looks at the work of each day and pronounces it "good" (separate from and before human beings come on the scene) and God bestows blessings of fertility upon the animals. The very first chapter of the Bible is like a joyous hymn to biodiversity.

If Genesis 1 pictures God creating and then resting, Psalm 104 instead pictures a God who is engaged full-time in sustaining and nurturing every aspect of creation. God "waters the mountains from [God's] lofts" and God "sates the earth from the fruit of [God's] work"; God provides sustenance for each creature—grass for cattle, water for trees, adequate drink for all the wild beasts. The world imagined in the psalm is fundamentally harmonious—lions go hunting for food by night, human beings by day. All of God's creatures share an elemental dependence on God, who willingly provides: "All of them look to you to give them their food when it is time." God "opens [God's] hand," and all of God's creatures are "well-satisfied." If the text does not explicitly speak of God's love, a sense of God's merciful and attentive care is nevertheless pervasive. God loves the natural world and wants it to flourish—actively *helps* it flourish. If we are to love what God loves, care for what God cares for, then our love and care must extend beyond humanity to the rest of creation.[57]

BECOMING GOD'S HANDS

Returning to the love of the stranger, in chapter 8 we also encountered another interpretation. In one verse, we learn that God loves the stranger, and that God manifests that love by providing the stranger with food and clothing. Perhaps we will wonder: Just how does God do that? The following verse provides an answer: in being commanded to love the stranger, we become the vessels and vehicles of God's love. In loving God, we become God's hands (Deuteronomy 10:18–19). To love God, then, is to serve as a vehicle of God's love.[58] God loves human beings and depends on us to make that love concrete.

Another, somewhat more mystical way of saying this is that to love God is, in a sense, to participate in God's love, mercy, and goodness.[59] That, I would argue, is the deepest meaning of *devekut*, or cleaving to God. When Deuteronomy instructs us to "hold fast" (*tidbakun,* from the same root as *devekut*) to God, Rashi explains that the commandment is to hold fast to God's ways, to "bestow kindness, bury the dead, and visit the sick, just as the Blessed Holy One did."[60] To hold fast to God, says the Musar master Rabbi Yehezkel Levenstein, is to hold fast to God's attributes—and that means to be utterly devoted to the well-being of others. This, he insists, is what it means to bask in the divine presence.[61]

Rabbi Aharon Kotler wonders how this can be. How can being thoroughly enmeshed in mundane, worldly matters by trying to help someone bring us closer to God than, say, wearing a tallit (a prayer shawl) and praying from the heart? Wouldn't attempting to connect with God directly (e.g., through prayer) bring us closer than connecting indirectly (through interpersonal kindness)? The answer R. Kotler offers is stunning: The whole point of creation, he says, is to bestow *hesed*, love; everything that God does, from creating the world and onward, has that end in mind. To give generously and to bestow love and kindness are thus the very essence of what it means to hold fast to God. To live in this way is to bring being created in the image of God to its fullest realization.[62]

Recall the midrash that we saw in chapter 10. One verse bids us to love God and the next tells us to keep God's words upon our hearts—that is, to study them (Deuteronomy 6:5–6). The midrash explains that if we do so, we will come to "recognize the One who spoke and the world came into being"—but refusing to stop there, it adds, "And you will cleave to [God's] ways." (As we saw there, cleaving to God's ways refers to compassion and mercy and kindness.) I wonder about the relationship between the two clauses—recognizing God and cleaving to God's ways. If recognizing God is a stand-in for loving God, is cleaving to God's ways being presented as a consequence of loving God or as a definition of it? I don't think it's clear. But what is clear is that for the midrash, loving God is inextricably bound up with showing kindness and compassion to others.

This capacity for compassion is, at least in part, a divine gift we all share. As a contemporary ethicist nicely puts it, "Since God is the Creator of all that is, God's loving nature cannot be totally alien to—much less contradictory of—creatures, especially those made in God's image."[63] To love God is to actualize that in-born divine capacity in our day-to-day lives.

For Judaism, ethics and spirituality are inseparable. There simply is no greater act of religious devotion than caring for another person.

LOVE OF GOD CAN'T BE REDUCED TO LOVE OF NEIGHBOR

We've seen that love of God and love of neighbor—indeed, love of God and love of all humanity—are inextricably linked. Some thinkers take this one step further and effectively equate love of God with love of neighbor, thus effectively reducing the former to the latter.

The idea that one can love God directly, says Kierkegaard, is delusory. As he sees it, the gap between humanity and God is just too wide: "God is too exalted," he says, "to be able to receive a person's love directly."[64] In fact, one of his interpreters explains, "We can only love God indirectly by loving other people and, specifically, by loving the people we see."[65]

For thinkers like Kierkegaard, there is no other way to love God than by loving the neighbor; loving the neighbor simply *is* loving God. But why should this be so? Loving the neighbor is undoubtedly an essential aspect of loving God, but can't one cleave to God through prayer, for example, or devote one's heart and mind to God through learning Torah? Can't mitzvot that Jews traditionally categorize as "between a person and God" (dwelling in a sukkah on Sukkot; eating matzah on Passover; eating only kosher food, etc.) be paths to genuine intimacy and closeness with God?

There is something odd about arguing that God loves us and that our only possible response is . . . to love God's children. If I declare my love for my wife and she responds by promising to take care of our children, something is amiss in her words. Loving our children may be part of how my wife loves me, but it cannot be the whole story. Presumably, my wife would want to spend time with me, not only with our children; she would want to have moments of intimacy with me and her life would include gestures of love aimed directly at me. Loving our children is not a substitute for loving me. The same logic applies to our relationship with God. Loving human beings is part—an *integral* part, arguably even the *most important* part—of how we love God, but the former is not the entirety of the latter. Loving God involves moments of intimacy between us and God, without other people as necessary third parties to the relationship.[66]

As for Kierkegaard's worry that God is too exalted to receive our love, the Bible insists that the transcendent God is also immanent, that the Creator of heaven and earth is also passionately concerned with human flourishing. If God is not too exalted to love us, then neither is God too exalted to receive our love in return.

One of Kierkegaard's interpreters writes that "self-love, the giving of human love, and the receiving of human love, are all equivalent to loving God."[67] But that is not quite right: self-love, the giving of human love, and the receiving of human love are all *entwined* with loving God, but they are not *equivalent* to it.[68]

More abstractly, the point I am making is that while ethics is at the heart of religion, the latter should not be reduced to the former. There can be no religion without ethics, but there is more to religion than just ethics. Indeed, the total reduction of religion to ethics often spells the end of religion.

MAKING GOD LOVED

A midrash understands the obligation to love God in a somewhat surprising way: "And you shall love (*ve-ahavta*) the Lord your God" is interpreted to mean "And you shall cause the Lord your God to be loved (*ahaveihu*) among people."[69] To love God entails—or, according to this midrash, perhaps simply *equals*—endearing God to others. But how does one do that?

Jewish tradition hears this idea in two very different ways. According to one, the commandment to lead others to love God is a mandate to proselytize. Just as, Rabbinic tradition imagines, Abraham and Sarah "converted [others] and brought them under the wings of the divine presence (*shekhinah*)," so too must we.[70]

The second approach is subtler and, I think, more powerful. In a passage similar to one I alluded to in chapter 14, the Talmudic sage Abaye teaches that when a person who studies Torah and spends time with sages conducts his affairs with integrity and speaks to others pleasantly,[71] people proclaim, "Fortunate is he who learned Torah; fortunate are the parents[72] who taught him Torah; fortunate is his teacher who taught him Torah. Woe to the people who have not studied Torah. So-and-so, who learned Torah,[73] see how pleasant are his ways, how correct are his deeds." God's name is thus glorified through the behavior of such a person.[74]

So often, religious adherents give religion a bad name. Religious people (just like everyone else) can be smug rather than humble, cruel rather than compassionate, callous rather than caring, indifferent rather than empathetic. Religious leaders often stoke hatred instead of inspiring their followers to love; they often model self-satisfaction rather than generosity, hypocrisy rather than integrity. According to Abaye, such people, too, elicit a reaction from others, who proclaim, "Woe to him who learned Torah; woe to his teacher who taught him Torah. So-and-so who studied Torah, see how destructive are his deeds, and how ugly are his ways."[75] God's name is debased through the behavior of such a person.[76]

If the first approach (proselytization) instructs us to increase love for God by seeking converts, a position that has rarely been popular among Jews, the second (modeling integrity) challenges us to do so by living principled, virtuous lives. Others should see the way we conduct our lives and think, "If that's what religion is, count me in." We make God loved by living in ways that give God a good name.

BUILDING A HOME FOR GOD

Part of what it means to love God, I think, is to try to build a dwelling place for God. God creates a place for us to live and we, in turn, attempt to return the favor.

A midrash offers a striking image of God's own yearning. "When the Blessed Holy One created the world," it says, "God longed to have an abode below just as God had on high." But things don't always go as planned, even for God. When Adam disobeyed God's command in the Garden, the midrash tells us, God "removed God's presence up to the firmament"; when Cain killed his brother Abel, God moved up from the first firmament to the second; and when the generation of Enoch began worshiping idols, God moved up from the second firmament to the third. When the generation of the flood became morally corrupt and pushed God away, God ascended to the fourth firmament; when the builders of the Tower of Babel came along, God ascended to the fifth; when the "evil" and "sinful" Sodomites committed all three of Judaism's cardinal sins—sexual impropriety, idolatry, and bloodshed—God ascended to the sixth; when the Philistines angered God, God ascended to the seventh and highest firmament. God began to feel desperate: God was now as high as God could go, yet the world was still sinning.

So God raised up Abraham. When Abraham began to perform good deeds (*ma'asim tovim*), God "immediately" descended from the seventh firmament to the sixth; the midrash's use of the word "immediately" suggests just how eager God remained to find a dwelling place on earth. When Isaac arose, God descended to the fifth firmament; and when Jacob arose, God descended to the fourth. When Jacob's son Levi arose, God came down to the third firmament; when Kohath (Levi's son and Moses's grandfather) arose, God came down to the second; when Amram (Moses's father) arose, God came down to the first. When Moses arose and built the *mishkan* (tabernacle), "he brought the divine presence down to earth." What God had once had—a place on earth where God could dwell—God now had again.[77]

Two connected claims animate this midrash: first, God desires a dwelling place on earth, and second, whether God has such a dwelling place depends on us. The transcendent God wants to be immanent but does not force the issue; the transcendent God is vulnerable. God may remain homeless on account of our failings.

This idea of bringing God down into the world, of helping the transcendent God become immanent, is a major theme in several of the most important Jewish thinkers in modern times.

Judaism is not a spiritual path that removes us from the world, or elevates us above it (whatever that might mean). Rather, as R. Soloveitchik teaches, Judaism embraces this world and seeks to draw the divine presence down into it. Holiness is thus not separation from the world but rather "the descent of divinity into the midst of our created world."[78]

Religion should not tempt us to leave the world behind. We won't succeed even if we try, R. Soloveitchik argues, but even more importantly, a longing to leave the world behind leads to ethical blindness. As R. Soloveitchik puts it, those who "yearned to break through the bounds of concrete reality and escape to the sphere of eternity [became] so intoxicated by their dreams of an exalted supernal existence that they failed to hear . . . the sighs of orphans, the groans of the destitute."[79] To withdraw from the world is to abandon the vulnerable to their fate.

Early in his career, Martin Buber had been taken with ecstatic religious experiences that lifted him out of ordinary life, but over time he came to reject the aspiration to "exaltation" and ecstasy and began to focus instead on the everyday.[80] Buber's goal was no longer to be lifted out of the quotidian but, on the contrary, to be fully present within it.

If in his younger days Buber concentrated on mystical union with God, in his more mature writings he focused instead on otherness, on the "elementary, life-claiming and life-determining experience of the *other*, the otherness, as of something coming to meet one and acting toward one."[81] Buber left mysticism behind and embraced dialogue instead. It was in genuine dialogue between people, Buber believed, that God's presence could be sensed and "realized." As he put it, the Divine

> attains its earthly fullness only where . . . individual beings open
> themselves to one another, disclose themselves to one another and
> help one another; where immediacy is established between one per-
> son and another; where the sublime stronghold of the individual is
> unbolted, and a person breaks free to meet another person . . . True
> community is that relationship in which the Divine comes to its
> realization between person and person.[82]

According to Buber, the Jewish people could be holy by showing the world that "the realization of the Divine on earth is fulfilled not *within* persons but *between* them, and that, though this does indeed have its beginning in the life of the individual person, it is consummated only in the life of true community."[83]

For Rabbi Abraham Joshua Heschel, "God is ensconced in mystery, hidden in the depths. Prayer is pleading with God to come out of the depths."[84] The image of human beings pleading with God makes it seem that the situation is entirely in God's hands, but R. Heschel sometimes sounds a more radical note—God, he says, has been exiled as a result of our actions. "To pray," R. Heschel writes, "is to open a door, where both God and soul may enter."[85] If God is homeless, seeking a dwelling place in our world, then for R. Heschel "our task is . . . to enable [God] to enter our moments, to be at home in our time." To pray, in other words, is "to overcome distance, to shatter screens . . . to heal the break between God and the world."

"To pray," R. Heschel writes, "means to bring God back into the world, to establish [God's] kingship for a second at least. To pray means to expand [God's] presence . . . To worship . . . means to make God im-manent, to make [God] present. [God's] being immanent in the world depends on us."[86] While I am not sure that we can make God immanent

(God is after all, free), I do think we can make it possible for God to be immanent. We open a door; God decides whether to walk through it.

In a startling formulation, R. Heschel declares that a mitzvah is "a prayer in the form of a deed."[87] If a mitzvah is a prayer and prayer is an invitation to immanence, then I think we can say that anytime we perform a mitzvah, we open a door to divine immanence.

There are different points of emphasis in R. Soloveitchik, Buber, and R. Heschel. Where R. Soloveitchik places great weight on the enacting of Jewish law in the world, Buber on interpersonal dialogue and community, and R. Heschel on opening to God in prayer and deed, there are obviously also profound points of overlap. (Halakha requires deep attentiveness to the needs of the other, for example; and we can't open to God without at the same time opening to the person who stands before us.) Yet all three of these giants of Jewish thought champion an insistently this-worldly picture of Judaism.[88] To love God is to provide God with an earthly home. To love God is to live with a passion for the ethical and an openness to the sacred and thus to invite God back into our world.

RECIPROCATED LOVE—AT LONG LAST

We began with images of divine-human mutuality and reciprocity. Yet so much of the Bible is about God's hopes and dreams being thwarted by human recalcitrance. God loves Israel and wants the people to love God back. But the people repeatedly stray, turning to other gods, abandoning the covenant and the commandments. The love between God and Israel endures more than its share of crisis and disappointment. The Bible is overrun with moments in which God feels let down by Israel, and Jewish history has known many excruciating experiences when Israel has felt let down by God.

The Song of Songs is a biblical text that vividly speaks of love—but what is the nature of this love?

For many centuries, Jews understood the Song primarily in allegorical[89] terms[90]—what seemed on the surface an earthy love song (or series of love songs) was interpreted as a meditation on the love shared between

God and the Jewish people (or between God and the individual soul). Many, perhaps most, pious Jews still interpret the Song in these terms.

Most modern scholars see the Song for what it appears to be at first glance—a song (or series of songs) giving voice to the passionate and often highly erotic love shared by two young lovers. These scholars tend to be skeptical of allegorical readings and sometimes even scornful of them.[91]

But recently, some scholars have argued that the two possibilities— the Song as a poem about human love in all its dimensions and the Song as a poem about divine-human love—need not be mutually exclusive. On the contrary, on their reading, the Song "glides and skips among . . . different levels of reference."[92] It is, they say, about *both* the love between two human beings and about the love between God and Israel.

The Song is saturated with references and allusions to other biblical texts, many of which seem to point beyond the earthly lovers to the love between God and Israel. Thus, for example, the Bible scholar Ellen Davis writes that "the Song is thick with words and images drawn from earlier books. By means of this 'recycled' language, the poet places this love song firmly in the context of God's passionate and troubled relationship with humanity (or, more particularly, with Israel), which is the story the rest of the Bible tells."[93]

Let's consider just a few examples.

As the book opens and the young woman sings her lover's praises, she announces, "Let us delight and rejoice (*nagilah ve-nismehah*) in your love" (Song of Songs 1:4). Yet this pair of words, "delight" and "rejoice," is elsewhere used repeatedly to express praise of God. Thus, for example, in reciting the Hallel prayer, Jews proclaim, with Psalm 118: "This is the day that the Lord has made—let us delight and rejoice (*nagilah ve-nismehah*) in it" (Psalm 118:24). And expressing the confidence that ensues from knowing that God is with him, another psalmist declares that his heart "rejoices," and his whole being "delights" (16:9).[94]

Coincidence? Possibly, but consider: In the third chapter of the Song, one of the characters asks, "Who is she that comes up from the desert like columns of smoke, in clouds of myrrh and frankincense, of all the powders of the merchant?" (Song of Songs 3:6).[95] First, it's worth observing that the image of the woman being led by a cloud may be an allusion to the Israelites entering the Promised Land led by a cloud.[96] In any case, there is something anomalous, as Davis notes, about this image of the young woman coming forth from the desert, since the poem tends to place the lovers either in the streets and houses of Jerusalem or in the fields that surround it. When they frolic or search for one another in nature, we find them in a garden or a forest, not in the wilderness. In light of this, Davis suggests that our verse "resounds deeply with the biblical tradition of Israel entering into the Promised Land after forty years in the wilderness." So the woman in question may well (also) be the bride Israel, who is remembered as having honeymooned with God in the wilderness (Jeremiah 2:2).

More tellingly, it is strange that the woman is described as perfumed in frankincense, since the latter was not used as a cosmetic, but was, instead, reserved for use in the Temple, to accompany sacrifices and create a pleasant odor for God (e.g., Leviticus 6:15). Perhaps, then, as Davis suggests, "the poet is picturing Israel as itself a sacrificial offering to its God." Again, the text can be read on two levels simultaneously; we needn't choose. On one level, it is about a young woman coming forth from the wilderness to meet her human lover; but on another level, it is about Israel, God's bride, coming forth from the wilderness to meet her divine lover in the latter's holy temple.[97]

There is a range of other possible allusions in the Song. A particularly suggestive one: The young woman time and again refers to her lover as "the one whom my being loves" (*et she-ahavah nafshi*).[98] Noting that this phrase is a potent allusion to the all-important command in Deuteronomy: "And you shall love the Lord . . . with all your being" (*ve-ahavta . . . be-khol nafshekha*), Davis writes that "the repeated echo of the weightiest verse in the [Hebrew Bible] confirms—in my judgment, beyond reasonable doubt—that at one level of the poet's meaning, the one who is loved and sought after so intently is God."[99]

All this leads to the moment I've hinted at above. The most powerful allusion in the Song is one that may seem somewhat obscure at first but that is pregnant with meaning. The phrase *hamu mei'ai*, which we can translate as "my innards churned," appears only three times in Tanakh. In a verse that has become part of the Rosh HaShanah liturgy, God longs for the people who have disappointed God time and time again: "Truly, Ephraim [a reference to the Northern Kingdom of ancient Israel] is a dear son to Me, a child that is dandled! Whenever I have turned against him, my thoughts would dwell on him still. That is why My innards churn (*hamu mei'ai*) for him; I will receive him back in love— declares the Lord" (Jeremiah 31:20).[100] The words are repeated in the Song, when the woman declares that her beloved "took his hand off the latch, and my innards churned (*mei'ai hamu*) for him" (Song 5:4).

Consider what is being played out here. For so long God has loved Israel and yearned for that love to be reciprocated; time and again in Tanakh, God has been forced into the role of jilted lover. But here, finally, something changes. God loves Israel and Israel, it seems . . . loves God back. As Davis writes, "When this poignant scene is read intertextually, it seems that God's passion is at last reciprocated by its object, Israel."[101]

The relationship the Song describes is hardly smooth or blissful. Even the scene in which the female lover/Israel's innards churn is a complex one: despite her arousal and her lover's desire to be intimate with her, in a moment of torpor she sends him away (Song 5:3). Perhaps she is just flirting and plans to let him in—the Song is brilliant in its ambiguity and elusiveness, so it is difficult to know—but even if that is the case, he seems to take her words seriously and leaves. She finally rises to let him in but he is gone; she goes out into the streets to search for him but fails to find him. The city watchmen, however, find *her* and abuse her. This is hardly a beatific vision of love fully realized.

I mention this because even in portraying a moment of intense mutuality (God loves Israel and Israel loves God), the Song makes ample space for the reality that the love between God and Israel is always aspirational and never consummated once and for all; the love between God and Israel is constantly forced to reckon with "the transience of the lovers' availability to each other."[102] For God to live with human beings is for God to face stubbornness and intransigence and just plain indifference; for Israel to live with God is to face moments of silence and absence and the sense of having been abandoned. And yet . . . as the Song hints, there are also moments when the love is mutual and powerful, so real that one can almost touch it. Such moments are worth everything, and we seek to live by their light even and especially when the world, and the presence of God within it, seem to go dark.[103]

CONCLUSION:
JUDAISM IS ABOUT LOVE

DEUTERONOMY DESCRIBES GOD as a "faithful God" (*El emunah*) (Deuteronomy 32:4). Playing with the fact that the Hebrew word *emunah* can mean either faith or faithfulness, a midrash interprets the verse as alluding not to God's faithfulness but to God's faith: "'A faithful God'—[God] believed in the world and created it."[1]

Sometimes these words strike me as hopelessly naive. If God has faith in this world, then God must not be paying attention. Or perhaps we should take the past tense seriously. God had faith when God created the world, but by now God has undoubtedly seen enough to know better.

But at other times I find these words tremendously moving. God knows who we are—knows of the cruelty and callousness of which we are capable; knows how trapped many of us are within the prisons of our own egos; knows how far we often stray from the divine ideals of love and compassion and the pursuit of justice—and yet, in the face of all that, *God believes in us.* God believes in our capacity for love.

As we've seen, Kierkegaard says that part of what it means for a human being to love someone is to believe that they are capable of love. Believing in the other person's capacity for love helps draw out their love. In Kierkegaard's memorable formulation, love "loves forth love."[2]

It would be the height of arrogance, Kierkegaard warns, to think ourselves capable of implanting love in someone else. We do not create love in another person; rather, we "presuppose that love is in the other person's heart and by this very presupposition build up love in them."[3]

God, in contrast, does not merely presuppose our capacity for love. God actively implants it within us. So God *knows* that we are capable of love. To be sure, we are capable of other things too, like hatred, and brutality, and indifference to the suffering of others. I hear the midrash about God believing in the world and creating it as suggesting that God has faith in our capacity for love, and even that God has faith that we will—at least some of the time—manifest and express that love.

But God will not force us to love. God implants a capacity for love within us, but God does not determine whether and how we exercise that capacity. For God to do so would be self-defeating, since coerced love is not really love at all. More fundamentally, as we have seen, God is invested in our freedom and willingly takes on the risks that granting us agency requires. God wants us to love, but we can, and often do, choose to hate—or to remain indifferent—instead.

God's command that we love our neighbor as ourselves provides additional evidence of God's faith in us. This Jewish understanding of the commandment is not the only possible one. Some Christian readers even suggest that the purpose of the commandment is to bring us up against the fact that we are *not* capable of fulfilling it. The law, they say, "aims to make one aware of, and destroy, the egocentric in human nature. This is achieved by inculcating the realization that one cannot observe this commandment."[4] We can't actually obey God's law; we can only discover how mired we are in our own egos. But this is a very far cry from how Jews understand the commandment.

I see no evidence that the Torah issues commands that it assumes we cannot fulfill. In fact, Deuteronomy explicitly states the opposite: "Surely the instruction (Torah) which I enjoin upon you this day is not too baffling for you, nor is it beyond reach . . . No, the thing is very close to you, in your mouth and in your heart, *to observe it*" (Deuteronomy

30:11, 14). What we are commanded to do, we are capable of doing.[5] It may not be easy, but it is nevertheless possible.

How does the commandment to love our neighbor function? As we saw in chapter 5, according to Nahmanides the commandment is that we wish for others to have everything we have to the same extent as we do. This is a daunting demand, but not an impossible one. Rather than see the law as intended to bring us up against our limits, we should understand it as reminding us of our potential. In general, I think, Jewish ethics encourages us to realize that we are capable of more than we might think—more, even, than we often want to think. We may not be able to love our neighbor perfectly at all times, but we can grow toward loving them, and at moments at least, we can fully observe the commandment. As for how emotions can be commanded, we've seen repeatedly that though emotions cannot simply be turned on and off, they can be cultivated. With effort and steadfast commitment, we can grow closer to the Torah's ideal of love. The God of love insists that we too are capable of love.

The Torah's opening chapters subtly highlight God's abiding faith in us. To be created in the image of God is to be appointed God's vice-regent, to rule on God's behalf—even though, as any reader of Genesis discovers, God's plans are thwarted from the very beginning. Disobeying God's command, Adam and Eve eat from the fruit of the garden (Genesis 3:6); unable to manage his feelings of rejection, Cain murders his brother (4:8); far from learning from his ancestor's mistake, Cain's descendant Lemekh positively exults in his own brutality (4:23–24). We might have expected that, in the wake of all this, God would realize that human beings are not what God had hoped and that God would therefore strip us of our privileged status. But no, the very next chapter after the stories of Cain and Lemekh begins by reiterating that people are created in the image of God (5:1). Having given us our status and our assignment, God will not revoke them.

Things soon get worse, as violence and lawlessness overrun the earth, so much so that God does begin to regret having created us (Genesis 6:7). God brings the flood, of which Noah and his family are the only human survivors. And yet when the waters subside, God immediately blesses Noah and his family, reiterating the blessing-command from Genesis 1 that humanity should be fruitful and multiply (9:1). Just a few verses later, we are again reminded that human beings are created in the image of God (9:6). The status and the mission remain in effect; time and again we fail, and time and again God insists that we are capable of success.

The reason God had brought the flood was that God had seen "how great was humanity's wickedness on earth, and how every plan devised by humanity's mind was nothing but evil all the time" (6:5). In the aftermath of the flood, God commits never to destroy the world again because "the devisings of humanity's mind are evil from their youth" (8:21). This is extremely strange: the very reason that God had brought devastation now becomes the basis of God's commitment never to do so again. God, it seems, decides to see us through the lens of mercy rather than judgment and therefore to stick with us even when we least deserve it.[6]

In other words, it's not just that God has faith in us. It's that God takes mercy on us too. God's need to take mercy makes it clear that it isn't easy to have faith in humanity, even (and perhaps especially) for God. But God has decided to remain faithful to us, come what may.

THE AMBITIOUSNESS OF JEWISH ETHICS

God's faith in us is one reason why Jewish ethics is so ambitious and demanding. Beyond telling us what we may or may not do, Jewish ethics prescribes goals for who and how we must be. Despite the excuses and exceptions we often make for ourselves, it tells us, we are capable of living lives animated by love, mercy, compassion, and generosity. Considering this, we can readily understand why Jewish ethics is about more than what the philosopher Annette Baier refers to as "workable traffic rules for self-assertors."[7]

Jewish ethics is about counting our blessings and sharing our bounty (chapter 2), and it's about combating injustice and standing with the downtrodden (chapter 3). It's about building families that are "schools of love" and teaching our children to care (chapter 4); it's about wishing others well and seeing them with loving eyes (chapter 5); and it's about caring both for those in our immediate orbit and for those on the other side of the world (chapter 6). It's about seeing and struggling for the dignity of all humanity and of every human being we encounter (chapter 7); it's about welcoming the stranger and learning empathy from our suffering (chapter 8); and it's about healing broken relationships and refusing schadenfreude (chapter 9). It's about being present with those who are impoverished, or ill, or grieving (chapter 10), and it's about loving, even and especially in the face of destruction and devastation (chapter 11). It's about showing kindness and compassion, even and especially in life's hardest moments and the world's darkest places, and it's about creating moments of redemption in the midst of an excruciatingly unredeemed world (chapter 12).

It's not *only* about these things. It's also about striving for intimacy with God; it's about worship and ritual; it's about observing the commandments—and not just the interpersonal ones. Ethics, no matter how radical, is not all there is to Judaism—and as I've suggested, a Judaism that is only about ethics will quickly disappear—but a passionate concern for the well-being of others is absolutely central to what Judaism is.

HOW SHOULD WE SEE OURSELVES?

In light of everything we've learned, then, how should we see ourselves?

We are created with love, for love.

We are created, given a gift of life that we did not earn, and thus our lives are (or ought to be) oriented around gratitude. Genuine gratitude includes both generosity and responsiveness—to God and to the needs of others.

With love. Loved into being, we are always already loved; we don't earn God's love, we strive to live up to it.

For love. Loved, we strive to be lovers ourselves. God's love is both a gift and a challenge: a gift, in that it is unearned and unconditional; a challenge, in that it comes with hopes and expectations for who and how we can be, and for what we can do in the world. To be(come) human is to grow in love, love for friends, family, and community; love for all humanity, and especially the vulnerable and downtrodden; and love, ultimately, for all creation.

We are relational beings all the way down. Created in the image of a relational God, we are built for—and always in need of—relationships. Long before we know our own name, our lives are interwoven with the lives of others. There is no self that is not already in relationship.

We need one another. As the philosopher Mary Midgley puts it, "We are not self-contained and self-sufficient, either as a species or as individuals, but live naturally in deep mutual dependence."[8] We share joy and sorrow, achievements and disappointments. Not surprisingly, Judaism's highest ideal is that we bring compassionate presence to those who are suffering.

Although it moves on to champion human diversity,[9] Genesis begins by establishing our shared origins: descended from Adam, we are all one family. Too often the idea that when one person is hurt all are wounded, and that what we do to one person we effectively do to all, is uttered as a mere platitude, but it contains a deep truth that we should aspire to make real in our own lives. Other people matter to us—even those who differ from us in countless ways. "They" are in fact part of "us." We are, to borrow a wonderful phrase from Midgley, "members of one another."[10]

Yet we are also individuals. As we saw in chapter 1, God created Adam singly, so that we would understand the incalculable worth of every human being, without exception. This means, among other things, that we are responsible to think for ourselves and, when the situation requires, to pursue the good, even if those around us do not, or will not, or cannot. Our relationships shape us, form us, in a sense even create us, and yet they do not completely control us. "Everybody's doing it" is the last refuge of scoundrels. Part of what it means to be individual images of God is that we are capable of resisting social conformity. As the philosopher Stephen Evans explains, "If we believe that human beings were created by God and intended by God to have a relation to God, this allows us to understand how the self can be fundamentally relational and yet possess a limited, although real, capacity to transcend human social relations." In other words, we can have "relative autonomy" even as we are "thoroughly relational."[11]

On one level, being human is a gift; we are created in the image of God and are therefore both loved and infinitely precious. On another level, though, being human is a call and a summons.[12] We are created with a capacity for love, but we have other countervailing impulses too. Unhealed hurts and unprocessed fears can lead to baneful traits and brutal behaviors. Being human—or perhaps better, becoming human—is about actualizing the potential for love that is ever-present within us. Created with love, for love, we are tasked with embodying love.

Genesis 1 tells us that just as God was about to create Adam, God declared, "Let us make a human being in our image, after our likeness." The words for "image" (*tzelem*) and "likeness" (*demut*) are usually taken as synonyms, but one commentator, Rabbi Reuven Hoschke Ha-Kohen (d. 1673), reads the verse differently. God creates human beings in God's image, he writes, but whether or not we become God's likeness is left in our own hands.[13] It is through growing in love, I am suggesting, that we become more like God.[14]

HOW SHOULD WE SEE GOD?

We are created in the image of a God of immeasurable love. At its best, Jewish theology stretches beyond conventional religious thinking; it refuses to domesticate God or to cut God down to our own size. It imagines God's love and mercy as endlessly vast, extending beyond any boundaries that we might be inclined to set for them. God loves those near to us and those far from us; God loves even those whom we're convinced that we have good reason to hate. God's love is not subject to human control or limitation (chapter 13).

The God we worship is a power-sharing God. God restrains Godself and refrains from using all of God's power. God delegates to us, appointing us as vice-regents and charging us with "tilling and tending" the earth (Genesis 2:15). And God bids us to establish justice on earth (Genesis 9:6).

To put this differently, God has chosen to need us. God wants partners—partners in love and partners in world-building. God wants us to reciprocate God's love and God wants us to be the means whereby God's love for others is concretely expressed. As we saw in chapter 8, God loves the stranger in part by commanding us to love the stranger; we serve as God's hands, the means by which God accomplishes God's ends.

Yet God grants us genuine freedom; we are persons, not puppets. We can contribute to the fulfillment of God's hopes and plans, or we can choose to thwart them instead. The decisions we make are immensely consequential. God does not clean up the messes we make.

Nor does God micromanage the natural world. As we saw in chapter 13, to a significant degree God allows the world to make itself. Nature runs its own course. Both humanity and the (rest of the) natural world are given the freedom of being other than God.

A God who loves and grants freedom is, unavoidably, a vulnerable God. To love is to take the risk of being hurt and disappointed. Like any parent, God takes risks; there are no guarantees for how our children will turn out.

There is both beauty and tragedy in this picture. God knows full well the good and the bad of which we are capable, and God chooses to believe in us. God's love is stubborn, persistent, faithful. There are moments when God's faith is richly rewarded and there are moments when God's faith in us seems like a divine delusion. Looking down on human life, sometimes the heavens shriek with disappointment. And yet divine love is *hesed*, one of the central meanings of which is "steadfast love."

In Jewish experience, the Torah and its teachings keep God near. R. Abraham Joshua Heschel writes: "The way to faith in the 'Torah from Heaven' is the preparation of the heart to perceive the heavenly in the Torah. Such a perception may be momentary; it may happen in the blink of an eye. But all of life is scarcely worth that momentary gift of heaven."[15] Two things especially stand out in R. Heschel's observation. First, that the perception of religious truths requires preparation of the heart;[16] without an attunement to the truths of religion, we will inevitably miss them. And second, that the perception may come and go, may appear and then disappear like a flash of lightning. The religious life is lived in light of those precious, sacred, and rare moments.

Sometimes it seems as if we live in a godless world. God can seem hidden, absent, perhaps even nonexistent. For me, as for many Jews, Torah is a deep comfort in those moments, because even when God is not available, God's teachings are. For many of us, the textual cord uniting heaven and earth is a precious lifeline in moments of spiritual darkness and aridity. Our task is to make Torah so deeply our own that it, and therefore God, are always with us. As the psalmist puts it, "Your Torah is in my very innards" (Psalm 40:9); the Torah is an essential part of our very being.

God's Torah is both a gift and a challenge. On one level, it is a gift, a concrete manifestation of God's love. Yet on another level it is a challenge, a set of prescriptions and ideals that prod us to live good, loving, and holy lives; to create good, loving, and holy communities; to work toward a good, loving, and holy world. It asks us to be more and to do more than we might otherwise be inclined to do or to be.

HOW SHOULD WE SEE THE WORLD?

The world is a gift; as we've seen, its very existence is grace. And yet it is also a summons and an invitation in that it's unfinished, incomplete, and open-ended. The kind of world we inhabit depends to a great extent on the decisions that we and other people make.

At every moment, we create worlds and shape the course of history. This takes place on a vast scale—we can, for example, contribute to creating a society that takes the dignity of the downtrodden seriously and that seeks healing and justice for those who have endured oppression and mistreatment, or the opposite; and on a small scale too—we can pay attention when an acquaintance is lonely and overrun with sorrows and we can work to assuage their pain, or we can ignore them. The secret of human relations is that in reality there is no small scale. We are always dealing with images of God and something infinitely precious is therefore always at stake. The decisions we make in each moment are written into eternity.

The world is God's. God loves the world and accordingly, so must we. To love God is to love *with* God, to love what God loves. We are invited to shape the world and to improve life within it, but not to exploit or consume it. The world is vulnerable to our power, just as we are vulnerable to its. I have spoken of the world as a gift but perhaps it would be more accurate to think of it as a loan—a loan that must be returned to the lender in the same condition as or better condition than when we borrowed (entered into) it. We are permitted to use the world's resources, but not to use them up. In a culture of unbridled consumerism, to see and treat the world as a gift-loan is an act of counterculture and resistance—and an urgent obligation.

In a world that can often seem godless, we wait, and we hope for God. We wait and hope for a world in which human dignity is real and the presence of God is manifest. But waiting and hoping are active, not passive. What separates hoping from mere wishing is our commitment to acting.

ONE LAST TIME: WHAT IS TORAH FOR?

The book of Ruth tells the story of a family in major crisis. Amid famine, a family from Bethlehem—a man named Elimelekh, his wife, Naomi, and their two sons, Mahlon and Chilion—move to neighboring Moab. Elimelekh dies, leaving Naomi alone with her two sons. The two marry Moabite women and then die themselves, leaving a bereft Naomi with her two widowed daughters-in-law. Naomi is, both practically and psychologically, a shattered woman. This rich and moving tale holds up Ruth, one of the daughters-in-law, as a paragon of *hesed*, of faithful and steadfast love, and in this instance of love that goes far beyond the call of duty or legal obligation.[17] Out of deep love for, and devotion to, Naomi,

Ruth works to restore her fortunes and to help her overcome her bitterness and dejection. In a very real sense, Ruth loves Naomi back to life.

I'd like to note two things about the book of Ruth and its place in Jewish life. First, in what is probably the most often-cited Rabbinic teaching about Ruth, the sage Rabbi Zeira proclaims that the book was written "to teach how great is the reward of those who do deeds of kindness."[18] It's possible that R. Zeira meant to be making a simple claim, that Ruth is the paragon of *hesed*, who therefore merits being the progenitor of King David, Israel's most storied ruler (Ruth 4:18–22). But I prefer to read him as making a much more fundamental point: the book of Ruth is not just about people doing acts of *hesed*, it is also about the kinds of healing, transformation, and redemption that lives of *hesed* make possible.

Ruth is read on the festival of Shavuot, which is traditionally understood to commemorate the giving of the Torah on Mount Sinai. What's the connection between Ruth and revelation? The book of Ruth is all about love and kindness, and, tempted as we may sometimes be to forget it, so too is Torah as a whole: "The beginning and end of Torah is lovingkindness."[19] As an eleventh-century sage explains, "This scroll [Ruth] is all *hesed*, and the Torah is all *hesed* . . . and it was given on Shavuot."[20] Reading Ruth on Shavuot, we are reminded through powerful example about the kind of life Torah intends for us to live: lives animated by love manifested in concrete acts of kindness and generosity.

Second, the book of Ruth opens by situating the story in dark times: "In the days when the chieftains [or judges, *shoftim*] ruled . . ." (Ruth 1:1). The time of the biblical chieftains was a time of moral decay and social unraveling; unrestrained by fear of God or legal authorities, people did whatever they pleased (Judges 21:25). Ruth's story reminds us that we are capable of deep, transformative love even (and sometimes especially) in the grimmest times and the bleakest places.

A midrash tells us that when the people gathered at Sinai, they stood "as one person, with one heart."[21] How, asks R. Shmuelevitz, was it possible for six hundred thousand people with a long history of conflict and combativeness to be of one heart? When they arrived at the mountain, he explains, they began to take care of one another's needs; concretely assisting others, in turn, taught them to love one another, thus fulfilling and embodying the mandate to "love your neighbor as yourself."[22] For that brief moment at least, the people achieved a foretaste of what Torah demands and makes possible: a community centered on love and mutual care. It is a window into that kind of living—motivated by love and kindness, ever aware of their transformative and redemptive potential, even in times of crisis—that the book of Ruth provides us each year.

We embrace the Torah and it leads us into love.

NOTES

Introduction

1. David Nirenberg and Leonardo Capezzone, "Religions of Love: Judaism, Christianity, Islam," in Adam J. Silverstein and Guy G. Stroumsa, *The Oxford Handbook of the Abrahamic Religions* (Oxford: Oxford University Press, 2015), 519.

2. Another misconception, this one arguably the most pervasive: because Christianity places such great weight on what happens after we die, generations of Jewish children have been taught that Judaism has no notion of an afterlife. Where classical Jewish sources are concerned, this is totally false, almost comically so.

3. David Hume, *An Enquiry Concerning the Principles of Morals* (Oxford: Oxford University Press, 2014; originally published in 1751), section 9, part 1, p. 64.

4. Thus Rabbi Leo Baeck's (1873–1956) contention that "Judaism is the religion of ethical optimism" requires nuancing. I'd prefer: "Judaism is the religion of ethical possibilism." Leo Baeck, *The Essence of Judaism* (New York: Schocken, 1948), 84.

5. Maimonides, *Guide of the Perplexed*, 3:53. The Christian theologian Michael Jinkins wonderfully refers to creation as "that which God loves into existence from moment to moment." Michael Jinkins, *In the House of the Lord: Inhabiting the Psalms of Lament* (Collegeville, MN: Liturgical Press, 1998), 28. For the idea that the heavens, and even the divine throne, depend on *hesed*, see Midrash Tehillim 89:2; and for an elaboration upon the midrash, see Rabbi Israel Meir Kagan (The Hafetz Hayyim), *Sefer Ahavat Hesed*, part 2, ch. 1.

6. Some thinkers accordingly suggest that we speak not of *creatio ex nihilo* but rather of *creatio ex amore*. For one example, see James H. Olthuis, "Creatio Ex Amore," in *Transforming Philosophy and Religion: Love's Wisdom*, ed. Norman Wirzba and Bruce Ellis Benson (Bloomington: Indiana University Press, 2008),

155–70. It's worth noting that interpreting creation as an act of grace and love is largely postbiblical. The Bible itself says nothing, or almost nothing, about God's motivation in creating the world. On this, see John Goldingay, *Old Testament Theology*, vol. 1, *Israel's Gospel* (Downers Grove, IL: IVP Academic, 2003), 57. Goldingay sees Psalm 33 as an important exception to this rule.

7. Rabbi Shimon Shkop (1860–1939), *Sha'arei Yosher*, introduction, opening sentence. For an additional example of a similar view, see R. Aharon Kotler, *Mishnat Rabbi Aharon*, vol. 1, p. 150.

8. God creates the world, says Rabbi Joseph Soloveitchik, "in order to care, to sustain, and to love." Rabbi Joseph B. Soloveitchik, *Family Redeemed: Essays on Family Relationships* (Jersey City, NJ: Ktav, 2000), 39.

9. Norman Wirzba, *Way of Love: Recovering the Heart of Christianity* (New York: HarperOne, 2016), 159. Wirzba adds: "Life is not simply lived *with* or *alongside* others. It is lived *through* others and *by means of* them."

10. As the Christian ethicist Timothy Jackson nicely puts it, "If the most fundamental virtue is that which is most indispensable to the growth of moral persons . . . it seems clear that . . . love is prior to justice. For moral persons only evolve over time and with a good deal of 'parental' care that is not premised on the reciprocity characteristic of justice. Our adult capacity for balancing competing interests and for keeping valid contracts comes only after unconditional nurturance by others while we are weak and dependent children, incapable of either stating our interests or entering into binding agreements." Timothy Jackson, *The Priority of Love: Christian Charity and Social Justice* (Princeton, NJ: Princeton University Press, 2003), 7. I am indebted to Jackson's writing for helping give greater shape and expression to what had been merely an inchoate intuition for me.

11. Genesis Rabbah 8:5, based on a creative reading of Psalm 85:11–12. But compare Genesis Rabbah 12:15.

12. R. Zalman Sorotzkin, *Oznayim La-Torah* to Leviticus 19:18. In the same vein, R. Ryan Dulkin writes that midrashic stories like this one "proclaim that human beings should conduct themselves, broadly speaking, with dispositions tilted toward mercy and kindness, and should begin their decision-making processes in discerning ethical choices from this vantage point, all things being equal, for it is upon the basis of divine mercy that humanity was created in its beginning. If competing rational and justifiable arguments may be made on an ethical dilemma, these exegetical stories suggest that the 'right' choice should be the one that errs toward the side of mercy, for without mercy, no human being capable of making ethical decisions would have come to be." Ryan S. Dulkin, "The Triumph of Mercy: An Ethical-Critical Reading of Rabbinic Expansions on the Narrative of Humanity's Creation in Genesis Rabbah 8," *Journal of the Society of Christian Ethics* 33, no. 1 (Spring/Summer 2013): 148.

13. For some examples, see Rabbi Eliyahu Dessler, *Mikhtav Me-Eliyahu*, vol. 1, p. 32; R. Shimon Shkop, *Sha'arei Yosher*, introduction, opening sentence; R. Aharon Kotler, *Mishnat Rabbi Aharon*, vol. 1, p. 151.

14. R. Aharon Kotler, *Mishnat Rabbi Aharon*, vol. 1, p. 150.

15. Hichem Naar, "Love as a Disposition," in *The Oxford Handbook of Philosophy of Love*, ed. Christopher Grau and Aaron Smuts, online ed. (Oxford: Oxford Academic, 2017), 5. "The challenge," as Naar explains it, is "to have an account [of love] that is able to accommodate the temporal differences between love and ordinary emotions while preserving the thought that love is affective in some way" (6).

16. Naar, "Love as a Disposition," 14.

17. On this, see Jacqueline Lapsley, "Feeling Our Way: Love for God in Deuteronomy," *Catholic Biblical Quarterly* 65, no. 3 (July 2003): 350–69; see especially 354–55, 365.

18. For the idea that there is no isolated, purely internal realm of emotions in the Bible, see especially Françoise Mirguet, "What Is an 'Emotion' in the Hebrew Bible? An Experience That Exceeds Most Contemporary Concepts," *Biblical Interpretation* 24, no. 4–5 (November 2016): 443. Note also Mirguet's discussion of hate, in which she shows that the same Hebrew word can refer to what we think of as the emotion of hate, to experiences of physical repulsion, to concrete actions, and even to relationships. The key point is that the Bible makes no sharp differentiation between these distinct realms of human experience (450).

19. On actions that lead to emotion, see Gary A. Anderson, *A Time to Mourn, a Time to Dance: The Expression of Grief and Joy in Israelite Religion* (University Park, PA: Penn State University Press, 1991), 95–97.

20. The concept of "walking in God's ways" is biblical (see, for example, Deuteronomy 10:12), but the idea that this refers specifically to compassionate feeling and action is Rabbinic. For an extended discussion, see chapter 10.

21. Babylonian Talmud (BT), Sukkah 49b.

22. R. Chaim Friedlander, *Siftei Hayyim: Middot ve-Avodat Hashem*, vol. 1, p. 318.

23. For a remarkable legal responsum to this effect, see Rabbi Yehiel Yakov Weinberg (1884–1966), *Responsa Seridei Eish* 1:61.

24. BT, Pesahim 50b.

25. For the idea of love as an asymptote, see James Kellenberger, *The Asymptote of Love: From Mundane to Religious to God's Love* (Albany, NY: SUNY Press, 2018).

26. BT, Sanhedrin 106b.

27. I am grateful to Rabbi Joel Roth and to Professor David Marcus for our exchange on this point.

28. Robert C. Roberts, "What an Emotion Is: A Sketch." *Philosophical Review* 97, no. 2 (April 1988): 203.

29. Robert C. Roberts, *Recovering Christian Character: The Psychological Wisdom of Søren Kierkegaard* (Grand Rapids, MI: Eerdmans, 2022), 268.

30. This paragraph is indebted to Norman Wirzba, "The Primacy of Love," in Wirzba and Benson, *Transforming Philosophy and Religion*, 16. In this context, it may also be worth noting the philosopher Kristján Kristjánsson's observation

that "we have good reason to doubt that love possesses the required specificity to constitute an emotion . . . It seems more appropriate to think of love as an umbrella term covering a range of different—if interrelated—emotions, dispositions, desires and behaviors." Kristján Kristjánsson, "The Trouble with Ambivalent Emotions," *Philosophy* 85, no. 4 (October 2010): 491–92. See also Roberts, "What an Emotion Is," 203.

31. I borrow this formulation from Tomáš Halík, *I Want You to Be: On the God of Love* (Notre Dame, IN: Notre Dame Press, 2016).

32. For the idea that turning to Scripture in particular "stands in the way of our solipsism," see Timothy Gorringe, "Learning to Live Within a Tradition," in *Theologians on Scripture*, ed. Angus Paddison (London: Bloomsbury, 2016), 73.

33. The Jewish concern with proper attribution is also worth noting here. As the Talmudic sage R. Hanina declares, "Whoever reports a statement in the name of the one who said it brings redemption to the world." BT, Megillah 15a. See also Tanhuma Buber, Numbers 27.

34. Michael Marmur, "Why Jews Quote," *Oral Tradition* 29, no. 1 (March 2014): 13.

35. Simon Rawidowicz, "On Interpretation," *Proceedings of the American Academy for Jewish Research* 26 (1957): 83. To be clear, Rawidowicz expresses significant misgivings about this characterization of Jewish intellectual history. It needs to be "revised," he says, so that we draw important distinctions between different types of commentary and the goals each has, and so that we do not overestimate the gap between "creating," on the one hand, and "interpreting," on the other (45–46). I accept Rawidowicz's point (and highly recommend his powerful essay) but I still find this initial formulation helpful for situating my work and describing the place I hope it has within Jewish tradition. It goes without saying, from my perspective, that all commentary is interpretation and thus simultaneously an act of both fidelity and creativity.

36. A canon, Delwin Brown writes, is "inherently polyphonic and plurivocal . . . A canon is a context of varied visions and voices. Its diversity may not be infinite, but it is expansive and substantial . . . A canon is not an answer, a point of view, a truth, a way of life. It is many answers, points of view, claims to truth, and ways of life." A canon, in other words, is a "multilith" rather than a monolith. Delwin Brown, *Boundaries of Our Habitations: Tradition and Theological Construction* (Albany, NY: SUNY Press, 1994), 72, 74, 80.

37. Maimonides, *Introduction to the Eight Chapters* (introduction to Mishnah Avot).

38. Walker Percy, *Lost in the Cosmos: The Last Self-Help Book* (New York: Farrar, Straus and Giroux, 1983), 187.

1. We Are Loved

1. Mishnah Avot 3:14. Here in the opening chapter I focus on God's love for human beings as such. I will deal with God's special love for Israel at length in chapter 14.

2. This is undoubtedly the reason why R. Akiva cites Genesis 9:6 as opposed to Genesis 1:27 or 5:1. Whereas in the other two instances, it is the narrator who informs us that God created humanity in God's image, in 9:6 God tells Noah and his sons directly. Here in 9:6, only, is it made known to human beings that they are created in God's image. See R. Judah Loew of Prague (Maharal), *Derekh Hayyim* to Avot 3:14. Maharal adds that R. Akiva goes on to cite Deuteronomy 14:1 rather than Exodus 4:22 for the same reason: whereas in the latter verse God speaks *about* Israel, in the former God speaks *to* them.

3. Maimonides, *Commentary to the Mishnah*, Avot 3:14.

4. R. Judah Loew of Prague (Maharal), *Derekh Hayyim* to Avot 3:14.

5. Depending on which liturgical tradition you recite, the blessing before the Shema begins either with "With vast love have You loved us" (*ahavah rabbah ahavtanu*) or with "With abiding love have you loved us" (*ahavat olam ahavtanu*), and the line immediately after it bids us to "love the Lord your God with all your heart, and with all your being, and with all your might" (Deuteronomy 6:5).

6. Some scholars see Hosea 11 as describing God as the "Divine Father." See, e.g., James Luther Mays, *Hosea: A Commentary* (Philadelphia: Westminster, 1969), 150–59. Yet it is striking that many of the images of parenting evoked in the chapter are ones traditionally associated with motherhood. God's maternal role in this chapter is emphasized, for example, by Marvin A. Sweeney, *The Twelve Prophets*, vol. 1 (Collegeville, MN: Liturgical, 2000), 112–16. See also Daniel Simundson, *Hosea-Joel-Amos-Obadiah-Jonah-Micah* (Nashville: Abingdon, 2005), 85.

7. This paragraph is adapted slightly from my essay "God's Unfathomable Love," in *The Heart of Torah: Essays on the Weekly Torah Portion*, vol. 2 (Philadelphia: Jewish Publication Society, 2017), 84.

8. Simundson, *Hosea-Joel-Amos-Obadiah-Jonah-Micah*, 84.

9. R. Israel Meir Kagan, *Shemirat Ha-lashon, sha'ar ha-zekhirah*, ch. 2.

10. My interpretation of the mishnah significantly expands upon (and at some small points diverges from) Rabbi Greenberg's.

11. Rabbi Eliyahu Lopian (1876–1970) wonders whether perhaps it would have been better for God to begin with twenty thousand people, which would have made it easier for human beings to work and cultivate the earth. Yet had God done so, he says, people would have mistakenly concluded that "it was worth creating such a vast world for twenty thousand people, but for one single person—it would not have been worthwhile." Therefore, Lopian concludes, God decided to begin with one person, to teach us that "all of the worlds, those above and those below, were worth creating for one single person," because each was created in the image of God. Eliyahu Lopian, *Lev Eliyahu* (2005 ed.) (Hebrew), vol. 3, p. 375. I leave aside here Lopian's strongly anthropocentric view that the whole world was created *for* human beings; my interests here are elsewhere. Compare, for a very different, nonanthropocentric approach, Maimonides, *Guide of the Perplexed*, 3:13.

12. Mishnah Sanhedrin 4:5. The Hebrew *nefesh* is often translated as "soul," but I assume that here it retains its older, biblical meaning, "life." Strikingly, the same teaching appears in the Koran 5:32.

13. This seems to be the logic of the flow of the mishnah itself: immediately before the section we are discussing, the mishnah teaches that when God tells Cain that his "brother's blood(s) [Hebrew *demei*, which can be read as 'bloods' rather than "blood"] cries out to [God] from the ground" (Genesis 4:10), God is referring to Abel's blood and to "the blood of his posterity" as well. Thus in killing Abel, Cain had effectively killed many. See the commentary of Rabbi Obadiah of Bertinoro to Sanhedrin 4:5, s.v. *lefikhakh nivra yehidi*.

14. I borrow this phrase from Immanuel Kant, *Grounding for the Metaphysics of Morals*, trans. James W. Ellington (Indianapolis, IN: Hackett, 1981), 40 (Ellington renders the German *über allen Preiß* as "above all price"). I invoke Kant here not because I agree with him that human dignity is inextricably bound up with moral autonomy but because I find his linkage of dignity with pricelessness extremely resonant.

15. It's worth noting that Jewish law does make monetary assessments of human life for purposes of dedicating such amounts to the Temple (see Leviticus 17:1–8 and Mishnah Arakhin chapters 1–6). Such assessments are symbolic and should not be taken to suggest that a human life has a cash value. Nevertheless, the very existence of such a discourse is unsettling.

16. In this regard, see also the first explanation given by Rabbi David Frankel to the Talmudic sage ben Azzai's maintaining that "this is the book of the generations of Adam" (Genesis 5:1) is "the great principle of the Torah." *Korban Ha-Edah* to PT, Nedarim 9:4. The same interpretation is also offered by Rabbi Aharon Ibn Hayyim (1545–1632), *Korban Aharon* to Sifra Kedoshim 4:12. I will discuss this interpretation at some length in chapter 7.

17. I would say that the Mishnah's emphasis is on equality of origins rather than on equality per se, but I don't think it's a big stretch to get from there to R. Greenberg's somewhat broader claim.

18. Jewish texts too, especially Kabbalistic ones, often fall into the trap of positing ontological distinctions between Jews and non-Jews. There is something ironic about thinkers who aspire to perceive the inner unity of all things (one of the central premises of Kabbalah), also insisting on the metaphysical superiority of Jews over non-Jews. For a useful discussion (and some painful documentation), see Jerome Gellman, "Jewish Mysticism and Morality: Kabbalah and Its Ontological Dualities," *Archiv für Religionsgeschichte* 9 (2007): 23–35. Similar ontological essentialist tendencies may be found in Yehudah Halevi's (1075–1141) classic *Kuzari*; see, for some examples, I: 27, 96, 103, and 115. Among classical Jewish thinkers, it was Maimonides who most vigorously opposed such dangerous distinctions. For important discussions, see Menachem Kellner, *Maimonides on Judaism and the Jewish People* (Albany, NY: SUNY Press, 1991), and Kellner, *Gam Heim Keruyim Adam: Ha-Nokhri Be-Einei Ha-Rambam* (Ramat Gan: Bar-Ilan, 2016).

19. Ephraim Urbach, "If Anyone Saves a Single Soul" (Hebrew), *Tarbitz* 40 (1971): 268–84.

20. Unfortunately, it has not always been heard this way. See, for example, Maimonides, *Mishneh Torah*, Laws of Murderers and Protection of Life, 1:16 (and note also 1:1).

21. The psychiatrist Rabbi Abraham Twerski is thus imprecise when he writes that as a human being, "I am *entitled* to regard myself as having value and worth because I was created by God, and endowed with a Godly soul" (emphasis mine). According to our mishnah, I am not entitled but *obligated* (*hayyav*) to so regard myself. See Abraham Twerski, *Ten Steps to Being Your Best: A Practical Handbook to Enhance Your Life in Every Way* (Brooklyn, NY: Shaar Press, 2004), 57.

22. As R. Twerski puts it, "I have unconditional value and intrinsic worth just by 'being,' independent of doing and accomplishing." Twerski, *Ten Steps*, 57.

23. Of course the opposite can also be true. Some people spend an inordinate amount of their time comparing themselves negatively to others, thereby deepening their self-doubt and self-loathing. Needless to say, such comparisons are no less problematic than their more "positive" cousins. Knowing that we are created in the image of God and are thus both loved and infinitely valuable means that comparisons, whether they demean or purport to elevate us, are unnecessary and out of place.

24. For a similar approach from a Christian perspective, see Robert C. Roberts, *Spiritual Emotions: A Psychology of Christian Virtues* (Grand Rapids, MI: Eerdmans, 2007), 89.

25. Kohelet (Ecclesiastes) complains that he has noted that "all labor and skillful enterprise come from men's envy of each other" and dubs this kind of competitiveness (like so much else) "futility (*hevel*) and pursuit of wind" (Ecclesiastes 4:4). Commenting on the verse, the Bible scholar Craig Bartholemew helpfully distinguishes between "the God-given desire to excel," on the one hand, and "a distorted desire to be better than one's neighbor," on the other. It is the latter that is so injurious and that is condemned by Ecclesiastes. Craig G. Bartholomew, *Ecclesiastes* (Grand Rapids, MI: Baker, 2009), 195.

26. I am focused here on the psychological and the interpersonal realms, but the need for a healthy sense of self-worth is also critically important in the political realm, since "hatred of the self is all too often projected outward onto vulnerable others." All decent societies thus need to "keep at bay" the common human "tendency to protect the fragile self by denigrating and subordinating others." Martha C. Nussbaum, *Political Emotions: Why Love Matters for Justice* (Cambridge, MA: Harvard University Press, 2013), 21, 3.

27. I use "worthful" here to mean full of intrinsic worth. See David K. Clark, "Philosophical Reflections on Self-Worth and Self-Love," *Journal of Psychology and Theology* 13, no. 1 (1985): 5.

28. The Talmudic sage Ben Zoma teaches, "Who is honored? One who honors others" (Mishnah Avot 4:1). This is usually taken to mean that one who treats others with respect will herself be treated similarly. But some take Ben Zoma's words

to imply that only one who respects herself is capable of truly respecting others. "One who does not respect herself will find it difficult to respect others—a person does not give to another what she herself does not have." Yoel Schwartz and Meir Landsman, *Sefer Ha-Kavod He-Amiti*, in *Sefer Ha-Kavod He-Atzmi He-Hadash Ve-Sefer Ha-Kavod He-Amiti* (Jerusalem: Devar Yerushalayim, 2005), 42. See also Moshe Don Kestenbaum, *Run After (the Right) Kavod: Changing the World—and Yourself!—Through Proper Use of Respect, Self-Esteem, and Honor* (Brookline, MA: Israel Bookshop Publications, 2011), 45.

29. Maimonides, *Mishneh Torah*, Hilkhot De'ot 2:3. (A note to readers: Because translating the word *de'ot* as Maimonides uses it is difficult and controversial, I leave the title of this section of the *Mishneh Torah* untranslated. Something like "Laws of Character Traits" would probably be appropriate.)

30. I am grateful to Arthur Egendorf for a conversation nearly two decades ago that spurred my thinking in this direction. Authentic humility entails neither understating nor underestimating our worth. Rather, "humility is a function of the attitude a person has toward certain facts and of the significance he attaches to them." George N. Schlesinger, "Humility," *Tradition* 27, no. 3 (1993): 8. See also R. Eliyahu Lopian, "Shevivei Lev," in *Lev Eliyahu*, vol. 1, pp. 237–38. For some useful sources on this theme presented in English, see Abraham Twerski, *Angels Don't Leave Footprints: Discovering What's Right with Yourself* (Brooklyn, NY: Shaar Press, 2001), 46–48.

31. Maimonides, *Commentary to the Mishnah*, Avot 2:18.

32. See Rashi to Sanhedrin 37a, s.v. *bishivili nivra ha-olam*. Much more expansively, see R. Chaim Shmuelevitz, *Sihot Musar* (2016 ed.), no. 28, pp. 116–22. "Nobility" in this sentence is my best attempt to capture the sense of R. Shmuelevitz's untranslatable "*nikhbadut*"—nobility, dignity, honorability.

33. In a similar vein, Rabbi Sol Roth (b. 1927) writes that a person is "obligated to experience a profound sense of self-importance in virtue of his location in the scheme of creation . . . This sense of self-importance is required." Crucially, though, Roth maintains, it must be balanced by a sense of one's own insignificance in comparison with God. Sol Roth, *The Jewish Idea of Ethics and Morality: A Covenantal Perspective* (Jersey City, NJ: Ktav, 2007), 158.

34. Lit. "afterward" (*ahar kakh*). For R. Tzadok, believing in oneself is derivative of believing in God.

35. R. Zadok Ha-Kohen of Lublin, *Tzidkat Ha-Tzaddik*, no. 154.

36. R. Abraham Isaac Kook, *Orot Ha-Kodesh*, vol. 3, p. 65; and *Orot*, p. 169 (*Shemonah Kevatzim*, I, 860). See also A. I. Kook, *Middot Ha-Ra'ayah*, Anavah, no. 8. Of course, R. Kook's statement potentially complicates matters somewhat by implying that we do affect our worth through our self-perception.

37. R. Shlomo Wolbe, *Alei Shur* (2014 ed.), vol. 1, p. 168. R. Wolbe is emphatic: There are not two approaches to the "greatness of man" in Jewish thought, one side accepting and the other rejecting it. Human greatness, he insists, is one of the most fundamental Torah teachings (*gufei Torah*), with which there is no room to disagree (170).

38. R. Shlomo Wolbe, *Alei Shur*, vol. 1, p. 169.

39. Teshuvah (repentance/return), according to this line of thought, is less about castigating ourselves or enumerating our manifold sins than it is about remembering what we are capable of and taking stock of what we still need to do in order to live in a way that reflects God's love and our worth. Moreover, teshuvah requires us to consider not only our potential but also our successes. As Rabbi Elyakim Krumbein notes (in the name of Rabbi Joseph Soloveitchik), "Any confession of sin must include, in order to be meaningful, the realization that one is a spiritual being with spiritual achievements." Elyakim Krumbein, "On the 'Humility' Dilemma and Its Solution," *Tradition* 39, no. 1 (Spring 2005): 54.

40. Dale S. Ryan, "Self-Esteem: An Operational Definition and Ethical Analysis," *Journal of Psychology and Theology* 11, no. 4 (December 1983): 298. Ryan also notes that arrogance and low self-esteem are both "motivated by anxiety"; in each case, "this anxiety leads to a self-reference dominated by comparison to other persons." Krumbein goes further, actually equating arrogance and low self-esteem. His approach goes too far, I think, but the general thrust is the same. Krumbein, "The 'Humility' Dilemma," 49–50.

41. Clark, "Philosophical Reflections on Self-Worth and Self-Love," 9.

42. See also Schlesinger, "Humility," 12.

43. Cited in Everett L. Worthington, "Humility: The Quiet Virtue," *Journal of Psychology and Christianity* 27, no. 3 (Fall 2008): 271. In the same vein, see Robert C. Roberts, "The Vice of Pride," *Faith and Philosophy* 26, no. 2 (April 2009): 129.

44. To be clear, abuse and assault can and often do undermine our subjective sense of dignity and worth, but Jewish teachings insist that objectively speaking, our dignity and worth always remain intact. An insistent awareness of this can sometimes help us strip abusers and assaulters of the outsize power they seem to hold over us; it can also help us reclaim our sense of dignity and worth in the aftermath of mistreatment. Abusers can wound us but they cannot define us.

45. See also, in the same spirit, Miroslav Volf, *The End of Memory: Remembering Rightly in a Violent World* (Grand Rapids, MI: Eerdmans, 2006), 79–80.

46. NJPS. More literally, "from the presence of the Lord" or "from before the Lord's face."

47. I am grateful to Dan Libenson for first prodding my thinking in this direction more than two decades ago.

48. And yet that homeless shepherd had also had the experience of being adopted by a king's daughter and raised in a royal household. Perhaps the two experiences together—his experience of intimate access to the powerful, on the one hand, and his status as a hunted refugee, on the other—are what prepare Moses to confront Pharaoh on behalf of an abused and downtrodden people. I am grateful to Professor Lawrence Kaplan for helping me think this point through.

49. Walter Brueggemann, "Exodus," *The New Interpreter's Bible*, vol. 1 (Nashville, TN: Abingdon, 1994), 713.

50. Abraham J. Heschel, *Who Is Man?* (Stanford, CA: Stanford University Press, 1965), 119.

51. Joseph Soloveitchik, "*Shelihut*," in *Yemei Zikaron* (Jerusalem: WZO, 1996), 9–27.

52. Mishnah Berakhot 5:5.

53. Soloveitchik, "*Shelihut*," 10–11. R. Soloveitchik seems to invert the principle of *sheluho shel adam kemoto* (an agent is likened to his sender) to *kemoto shel adam sheluho* (one who is like her sender becomes her agent).

54. Soloveitchik, "*Shelihut*," 11.

55. Soloveitchik, "*Shelihut*," 12.

56. Soloveitchik, "*Shelihut*," 12.

57. See Schwartz and Landsman, *Sefer Ha-Kavod He-Amiti*, 17–18; Kestenbaum, *Run After (the Right) Kavod*, 53–54; and Abraham J. Heschel, *The Insecurity of Freedom* (Philadelphia: Jewish Publication Society, 1966), 155.

58. The Talmud attributes this prayer to Rava (BT, Berakhot 17a). Presumably part of his daily prayers, in our liturgy it has become part of the Yom Kippur services.

59. Abraham Isaac Kook, *Olat Re'iyah*, vol. 2 (Jerusalem: Mossad HaRav Kook, 1963), 356. See also Shlomo Wolbe, *Alei Shur*, vol. 1, p. 168.

60. See Isaiah 6:8.

61. Worth comparing here is Rabbi Joseph Soloveitchik's contrast between what he calls "species man," on the one hand, and the true individual, on the other. See Rabbi Joseph B. Soloveitchik, *Halakhic Man*, trans. Lawrence Kaplan (Philadelphia: Jewish Publication Society, 1983), 123–28.

62. Timothy Jackson writes that "God's gracious bestowal of value on individuals makes possible their bestowal of value on others. Human beings love because they are first loved by others and the Holy Other." Timothy Jackson, *Love Disconsoled: Meditations on Christian Charity* (Cambridge: Cambridge University Press, 1999), 65. Jackson describes this as the perspective of Christianity, but it is no less so the perspective of Judaism

2. The Gifts of God Flow Through You

1. Genesis Rabbah 100:1, following the *ketib* of Psalm 100:3: "[God] created us, and not we ourselves." Perhaps not surprisingly, according to the book of Ezekiel, Pharaoh, the great biblical villain, brazenly declares that he did indeed create himself—see Ezekiel 29:3. (The Hebrew *ani asitini* can be rendered either as "I created it [the Nile] for myself" or as "I created myself.") See also Augustine, *Confessions*, book ix, ch. 10.

2. All of this assumes that having been created is a good thing. For the classic Jewish discussion, see BT, Eruvin 13b.

3. At first glance, the most pertinent Jewish source for this claim is Maimonides, *Guide of the Perplexed*, book 3, ch. 53. There, Maimonides interprets the key theological term *hesed* to mean "grace," and maintains that God's bringing the whole of reality into existence was pure grace. He takes the phrase "*olam hesed yibaneh*" (Psalm 89:3) to mean "the world is built on grace." (More literally, "*olam hesed yibaneh*" might be rendered as "Your steadfast love is confirmed forever" [NJPS translation].) Maimonides was preceded in this interpretation

by Sa'adia Gaon, *Introduction to the Book of Job*, ed. Joseph Kafih, p. 11; for an English translation, see Sa'adia ben Joseph, *The Book of Theodicy: Translation and Commentary on the Book of Job*, translated with commentary by L. E. Goodman (New Haven, CT: Yale University Press, 1988), 124. Sa'adia Gaon makes explicit that both the existence of the world, and our existence within it, are unearned gifts from God, hence my statement above that "my life in this world is a gift within a gift."

The potential problem with invoking this passage from Maimonides in the context of exploring the connection between grace and gratitude is that the God of Maimonides is beneficent (in creating the world, God causes good to come to us) but not benevolent (in creating the world, God does not *intend* to cause good to us), and there is a strong case to be made that gratitude is due only to one who *intends* to benefit you. This position goes back as far as the Stoic philosopher Seneca (c. 4 BCE–65 CE), who maintains that gratitude is due to a benefactor because of the benefactor's goodwill. Seneca, *On Benefits*, book I, ch. 5, section 2. Some philosophers disagree, and think that benefit rather than intention is determinative of whether gratitude is owed. See, for example, A. D. M. Walker, "Gratefulness and Gratitude," *Proceedings of the Aristotelian Society*, New Series, vol. 81 (1980–1981): 39–55, especially at 43–44. Such thinkers would therefore insist that it does make sense to be grateful for beneficence, even when no benevolence is present. By their lights, gratitude to the beneficent God of Maimonides would thus not be problematic. For a recent discussion of both sides of this debate, see Liz Guilford et al., "Recent Work on the Concept of Gratitude in Philosophy and Psychology," *Journal of Value Inquiry* 47, no. 3 (2013): 302–305. In any case, Sa'adia Gaon's benevolent God offers a less ambiguous case than Maimonides does.

4. Along similar lines, see Kenneth L. Schmitz, *The Gift: Creation* (Milwaukee, WI: Marquette, 1982), 33; and see also Edward Collins Vacek, SJ, "God's Gifts and Our Moral Lives," in *Method and Catholic Moral Theology: The Ongoing Reconstruction*, ed. Todd A. Salzman (Omaha, NE: Creighton, 1999), 110.

5. Soloveitchik, *Family Redeemed*, 39.

6. Eugene Borowitz, *Renewing the Covenant: A Theology for the Postmodern Jew* (Philadelphia: Jewish Publication Society, 1996), 141.

7. This is how Quentin Lauer describes G. K. Chesterton in *G. K. Chesterton: Philosopher Without Portfolio* (New York: Fordham University Press, 2004), 16.

8. Genesis Rabbah 14:9.

9. The prayer, by the Kabbalist Rabbi Moshe Ibn Machir (sixteenth century), first appeared in 1599. I am grateful to Rabbi Elie Kaunfer for helping me track down this information.

10. I am grateful to Rabbi Michael Marmur for this wonderful formulation.

11. Paul F. Camenisch, "Gift and Gratitude in Ethics," *Journal of Religious Ethics* 9, no. 1 (Spring 1981): 23.

12. I develop this idea in "Can We Be Grateful and Disappointed at the Same Time? Or, What Leah Learned," in *The Heart of Torah*, vol. 1, pp. 60–63.

13. Or, to borrow language from Aristotle, perhaps we can say that our focus is on gratitude as a fixed disposition.

14. Robert Roberts describes virtues (and vices) as "pronenesses." "The virtue of gratitude," he writes, "is a readiness or predisposition to respond to the actions of others by seeing the goodness and benevolence in them, and consequently desiring to return acknowledging tokens of benefit." Robert C. Roberts, "The Blessings of Gratitude: A Conceptual Analysis," in *The Psychology of Gratitude*, ed. Robert A. Emmons and Michael E. McCullough (Oxford: Oxford University Press, 2004), 68.

15. See the passages from Sa'adia Gaon and Ibn Bahya cited in the next note, and see also the declaration of Rabbi Eliyahu Lopian that "the whole demand for *yirat shamayim* (lit. fear of God or holding God in awe) stems from gratitude." Eliyahu Lopian, *Lev Eliyahu*, vol. 3, p. 334. Note also Mekhilta de-Rabbi Ishmael to Exodus 20:2, where the people's willingness to serve God is bound up with their experiences of God's liberation, care, and protection.

16. See Sa'adia Gaon, *Book of Beliefs and Opinions*, III: 1, trans. Samuel Rosenblatt (New Haven, CT: Yale University Press, 1948), 139; and note Diana Lobel, *A Sufi-Jewish Dialogue: Philosophy and Mysticism in Bahya Ibn Paqūda's Duties of the Heart* (Philadelphia: University of Pennsylvania Press, 2007), 201; and Bahya Ibn Paquda, *Hovot Ha-Levavot*, section 3, introduction. Among more modern thinkers, see, for example, R. Eliyahu Lopian, *Lev Eliyahu*, vol. 3, p. 334; and Louis E. Newman, *Past Imperatives: Studies in the History and Theory of Jewish Ethics* (Albany, NY: SUNY Press, 1998), 68–69.

17. Genesis Rabbah 6:5, where Torah is described as one of three gifts; the others are the sun and the moon, and the rain. For parallels, see Exodus Rabbah 41:2, Leviticus Rabbah 35:8, and Midrash Tehillim 18:28. And compare R. Simeon b. Yohai's statement in BT, Berakhot 5a.

18. Byron L. Sherwin, "Law and Love in Jewish Theology," *Anglican Theological Review* 64, no. 4 (October 1982): 471.

19. Exodus Rabbah 33:6.

20. Midrash Tehillim to Psalm 119:97. Slightly edited and condensed. The midrash echoes a verse that proclaims, "Your laws are a song to me, wherever I may dwell" (Psalm 119:54). See also Rabbi Bibi's comments in *Pesikta de-Rab Kahana, Ha-Hodesh* 5:9, but compare the sharply dissonant view of Rava, BT, Sotah 35a. Abraham Joshua Heschel suggests that sages of the Land of Israel tended to speak of the Torah as a song, whereas their Babylonian counterparts deemed such language insufficiently respectful. Abraham Joshua Heschel, *Torah Min Ha-Shamayim Ba-Aspaklaryah Shel Ha-Dorot*, vol. 1 (London: Soncino, 1960), xvii.

21. BT, Megillah 32a. But compare the different interpretation offered by Tosafot there, s.v. *ve-ha-shoneh be-lo zimrah*.

22. We could even say that in some ways gratitude is the paradigmatic religious posture in that it so thoroughly interweaves duty and desire (or obligation and freedom).

23. A more precise parallel with the gift of life (if one is really possible) would be an instance in which you didn't necessarily want something, didn't know you needed it, and then someone gave it to you and you realized what an immense good and a precious gift it was. I am grateful to Dr. Sydney Levine for this observation.

24. In the same vein, Robert Roberts describes gratitude as "a mirror reflection of generosity, an inverted reduplication of the generous action." Robert C. Roberts, "Generosity and Gratitude" (forthcoming).

25. Roberts, "Generosity and Gratitude."

26. On the point I make in this paragraph and the next, see, more expansively, my "No Leftovers: The Meaning of the Thanksgiving Offering," in *The Heart of Torah*, vol. 2, 15–19.

27. Along these lines, I'd maintain that some of what passes for gratitude in our culture is counterfeit gratitude in that it allows the purportedly grateful person to focus only on herself. There is much truth in the American writer Barbara Ehrenreich's caustic assessment that "it's possible to achieve the recommended levels [recommended by various self-help gurus] of gratitude without spending a penny or uttering a word. All you have to do is to generate, within yourself, the good feelings associated with gratitude, and then bask in its warm, comforting glow. If there is any loving involved in this, it is self-love, and the current hoopla around gratitude is a celebration of onanism." Barbara Ehrenreich, "The Selfish Side of Gratitude," *The New York Times*, December 31, 2015, https://www.nytimes.com/2016/01/03/opinion/sunday/the-selfish-side-of-gratitude.html. I part ways from Ehrenreich in my insistence that we separate out genuine gratitude from its impoverished imitators. As A. D. M. Walker (see the passage cited below, in note 31) would point out, what Ehrenreich describes is actually gladness (and fairly narcissistic gladness at that), not gratitude.

28. See also Maimonides, *Mishneh Torah*, Laws of the Hagigah 2:14. The same ethos is also expressed, for example, in Psalm 22:27, where a person whose prayer has been answered by God declares, "Let the lowly eat and be satisfied."

29. See Maimonides, *Mishneh Torah*, Laws of Yom Tov, 6:18.

30. R. Israel Meir Kagan, *Mishnah Berurah*, 529:17.

31. A. D. M. Walker, "Gratefulness and Gratitude," 49: "Pleasure at being favored, however undiluted, does not amount to gratefulness in the absence of any desire to make a return . . . What distinguishes being grateful from being (merely) pleased or glad is the grateful person's desire to make a return. More precisely, he wants to favor another because he has been favored himself." For a critical response to this aspect of Walker's interpretation of gratitude, see Sean McAleer, "Propositional Gratitude," *American Philosophical Quarterly* 49, no. 1 (January 2012): 56, 61. Edward Vacek emphasizes that the transition from grateful receiving to generous giving is far from automatic. Edward C. Vacek, SJ, "Gifts, God, Generosity, and Gratitude," in *Spirituality and Moral Theology: Essays from a Pastoral Perspective*, ed. James Keating (Mahwah, NJ: Paulist, 2000), 109. And Norman Wirzba writes: "It is easy to say that life is a gift. It is another

matter to understand that the acknowledgement of life as a gift entails living in the world in particular sorts of ways. More specifically, it means that we need to reposition ourselves as persons who do not *possess* and *control* life, but continually *receive* and *share* it." Wirzba, *Way of Love*, 117.

32. R. Yitzhak Hutner, *Pahad Yitzhak*, Rosh HaShanah, no. 3, pp. 45–46. See also Tikva Frymer-Kensky, unpublished essay, cited in Tamara Cohn Eskenazi and Tikva Frymer-Kensky, *Ruth: The Traditional Hebrew Text with the New JPS Translation* (Philadelphia: Jewish Publication Society, 2011), xlix.

33. R. Judah Loew of Prague (Maharal), *Netivot Olam, Netiv Ha-Tzedakah*, ch. 2. See also, for example, R. Chaim Friedlander, *Siftei Hayyim: Middot Ve-Avodat Hashem*, vol. 1, p. 282 (though the notion expressed there, that we receive "only" so that we may pass on the divine flow, strikes me as problematic. To reverse what I've said above, we are not only intermediaries, we are also beneficiaries).

34. Lewis Hyde, *The Gift: Creativity and the Artist in the Modern World* (New York: Vintage, 1983), 4, 9.

35. For these terms, I am indebted to Scott N. Dolff, "The Obligation to Give: A Reply to Tanner," *Modern Theology* 21, no. 1 (January 2005): 133.

36. Dolff, "The Obligation to Give," 133.

37. See, for example, the statement of Rav Hizkiah in PT, Kiddushin 4:12, as well as the discussion of the Nazirite's "sinfulness" in BT, Nedarim 10a.

38. On this, see, for example, R. Chaim Friedlander, *Siftei Hayyim: Middot Ve-Avodat Hashem*, vol. 1, p. 282 .

39. Sifre Deuteronomy, Ekev 49.

40. See Camenisch, "Gift and Gratitude," 29. I take Camenisch's observations about gratitude in general and apply them specifically to gratitude to God.

41. R. Eliyahu Dessler, *Mikhtav Me-Eliyahu*, vol. 1, p. 32. Note also R. David Hartman's characterization of the spirituality of Maimonides in David Hartman, *Maimonides: Torah and Philosophic Quest* (Philadelphia: Jewish Publication Society, 1976), 204–205; see also 94–95. Yet keep in mind the caveats I raise above, in note 3.

42. Miroslav Volf, *Free of Charge: Giving and Forgiving in a Culture Stripped of Grace* (Grand Rapids, MI: Zondervan, 2005), 60.

43. The Talmud cites an odd teaching according to which "a poor person is accounted as dead" (BT, Nedarim 64b). R. Shmuelevitz explains beautifully that the reason for this is not that the poor person lacks for himself but that he lacks the ability to give anything to another. R. Shmuelevitz, *Sihot Musar*, no. 3, p. 270. Perhaps this is part of why Jewish law requires even the poor who are dependent on tzedakah to give tzedakah themselves. See the statement of Mar Zutra, BT, Gittin 7b.

3. Sacred Indignation

1. Portions of this chapter are adapted from Shai Held, "Wonder and Indignation: Abraham's Uneasy Faith," *Jewish Review of Books* (winter 2013), and "In Praise of Protest: Or, Who's Teaching Whom?," in *The Heart of Torah*, vol. 1, pp. 35–39;

a few sentences are taken from "Standing Tall: Serving God with Dignity," in *Heart of Torah*, vol. 2, pp. 86–89.

2. Genesis Rabbah 38:13.

3. Genesis Rabbah 39:1.

4. Commentary of Pseudo-Rashi to Genesis Rabbah 39:1.

5. R. David Luria, *Hiddushei Ha-Radal* to Genesis Rabbah 39:1.

6. The experience of protest is arguably an example of what the sociologist Peter Berger refers to as "signals of transcendence." See Peter L. Berger, *A Rumor of Angels: Modern Society and the Rediscovery of the Supernatural* (Garden City, NY: Anchor, 1969), 52–75; and note especially what Berger terms the "argument from damnation," 65–69.

7. For a fascinating scholarly perspective on this midrash, which yields a powerful new interpretation thereof, see Paul Mandel, "The Call of Abraham: A Midrash Revisited," *Prooftexts* 14, no. 3 (September 1994): 267–84.

8. Miroslav Volf, *Against the Tide: Love in a Time of Petty Dreams and Persistent Enmities* (Grand Rapids, MI: Eerdmans, 2010), 36.

9. In a related vein, the philosopher Peter Byrne points out that, paradoxically, the problem of evil can be used to make arguments *against* the existence of God, but it can also be used to make arguments *for* it. See Peter Byrne, *The Moral Interpretation of Religion* (Edinburgh: Edinburgh University Press, 1998), 15–16. "The intuition from protest" I describe here is related to the moral argument because it is rooted in the sense that there is a moral order underneath (or beyond) the seemingly purely natural and amoral order.

10. Volf, *Against the Tide*, 36.

11. Jonathan Sacks, *A Letter in the Scroll: Understanding Our Jewish Identity and Exploring the Legacy of the World's Oldest Religion* (New York: Free Press, 2004), 57.

12. R. Zev Wolf Einhorn, *Peirush Maharzu* to Genesis Rabbah 39:1.

13. Sacks, *A Letter in the Scroll*, 57.

14. G. K. Chesterton, *Orthodoxy* (New York: John Lane, 1909), 130.

15. For a more expansive account of how this story is driven by God's desire to elicit protest from Abraham, see Shai Held, "In Praise of Protest."

16. Or perhaps, "all the nations of the earth are to bless themselves by him." Scholars disagree over whether the verb *ve-nivrekhu* is reflexive (they will bless themselves by you) or passive (they will be blessed by, or because of, you). The interpretation I am about to share, based on the scholarship of Joel Kaminsky, is more convincing if the verb is passive rather than reflexive.

17. Or perhaps promised Abraham that he would be a blessing.

18. Joel S. Kaminsky, *Yet I Loved Jacob: Reclaiming the Biblical Concept of Election* (Nashville: Abingdon, 2007), 39; see also 83–84.

19. BT, Pesahim 66a.

20. BT, Shabbat 54b.

21. R. Menahem Ha-Meiri, *Beit Ha-Behirah* to BT, Shabbat 54b. Note also Rashi's very different interpretation of the passage: whereas the former holds that "anyone" who can protest must do so, the latter maintains that the text has "a king

or a patriarch" in mind because their words are likely to be obeyed. See Rashi, Commentary to BT, Shabbat 54b, s.v. *be-khol ha-olam kulo*. It's worth remembering that Rashi lived in a feudal society. As Rabbi Aryeh Cohen notes, it's important to consider how things might differ in a democracy, "where seemingly it is the citizens whose decrees must be fulfilled." See Aryeh Cohen, *Justice in the City: An Argument from the Sources of Rabbinic Judaism* (Brighton, MA: Academic Studies, 2012), 145.

22. R. Abraham Ibn Ezra, Shorter Commentary to Exodus 22:21–23. Also relevant here is the Talmudic understanding of Leviticus 19:16, not standing by the blood of one's fellow (BT, Sanhedrin 73a). For a very brief but useful survey of the different ways this verse has been understood, both by traditional commentators and by modern scholars, see Baruch A. Levine, *Leviticus* (Philadelphia: Jewish Publication Society, 1989), 129.

23. In this context, it is also worth noting the fascinating findings of the psychologist Solomon Asch, who discovered that despite the depressing human tendency to succumb to peer pressure and therefore to conform to the perceptions of the majority, even one dissenting voice can lead others to resist the pressure to conform to positions they know to be wrong. See, for example, Solomon E. Asch, "Opinions and Social Pressure," *Scientific American* 193, no. 5 (November 1955): 2–6.

24. Søren Kierkegaard, *Fear and Trembling*, ed. C. Stephen Evans and Sylvia Walsh (Cambridge: Cambridge University Press, 2006; originally published in 1843).

25. Robert Gordis, "The Faith of Abraham: A Note on Kierkegaard's 'Teleological Suspension of the Ethical,'" *Judaism* 25, no. 4 (Fall 1976): 417–18.

26. See, for example, Leviticus 20:2–5 and Jeremiah 19:3–6.

27. See Exodus 22:28–29. (A note to Christian readers: the Hebrew numbering system can sometimes differ from the English. In most Christian translations, these verses are Exodus 22:29–30.)

28. See Exodus 12:1–28 and Numbers 3:40–51, respectively. Numbers 3 is actually somewhat more complicated. A Levite is consecrated for service of God in place of each firstborn (and the cattle of the Levites in place of every firstborn cattle among the Israelite people). It is only for the Israelites who exceed the number of Levites that a monetary payment is made.

29. See Jon D. Levenson, "Abusing Abraham: Traditions, Religious Histories, and Modern Misinterpretations," *Judaism* 47, no. 3 (Summer 1998): 271. Much more expansively, see Jon D. Levenson, *The Death and Resurrection of the Beloved Son: The Transformation of Child Sacrifice in Judaism and Christianity* (New Haven, CT: Yale University Press, 1993), 3–52.

30. Rabbi Ethan Tucker, "Redeeming the Akeidah, Halakhah, and Ourselves" (2016), 23, online at www.hadar.org. R. Tucker adds that "the process of halakhah can never end in a place where God and morality are in conflict, and the job of the learner—and certainly the posek [halakhic decisor]—is to understand how apparent conflicts are merely incomplete understandings."

31. Moshe Halbertal, *On Sacrifice* (Princeton, NJ: Princeton University Press, 2012), 73.

32. In this context, see also R. Abraham Isaac Kook, *Orot Ha-Kodesh*, vol. 3, introduction, no. 11, p. 27.

33. For an analysis of Jewish thinkers grappling with the ethics of Moses's action, see Avi Sagi, *Yahadut: Bein Dat Le-Musar* (Tel-Aviv: HaKibbutz Ha-Me'uhad, 1998), 182–98.

34. Commenting on these verses, the Bible scholar Jeffrey Tigay writes that Moses's "passion for justice makes no distinctions between nations." Jeffrey H. Tigay, "Exodus," in *Jewish Study Bible*, ed. Adele Berlin and Marc Zvi Brettler (New York: Oxford University Press, 2004), 109. See also Shai Held, "Why Moses? Or, What Makes A Leader?," in *The Heart of Torah*, vol. 1, 123–24; as well as Shai Held, "Solidarity Ethnic and Human: Moses and Moral Responsibility," in *More Than Managing: The Relentless Pursuit of Effective Jewish Leadership*, ed. Lawrence Hoffman (Nashville: Jewish Lights Publishing, 2016), 86–89.

35. Robert Alter, *The Five Books of Moses: A Translation with Commentary* (New York: W. W. Norton, 2004), 314.

36. It's worth noting that Moses, too, gets a lesson in protest from God. See Shai Held, "In Praise of Protest," 38; and Pamela Tamarkin Reis, "Numbers XI: Seeing Moses Plain," *Vetus Testamentum* 55, no. 2 (January 2005): 213.

37. This paragraph summarizes, and in a couple of sentences directly quotes from, Shai Held, "Why Moses?," 124.

38. B. Keith Putt, "Indignation Toward Evil: Ricoeur and Caputo on a Theodicy of Protest," *Philosophy Today* 41 (Fall 1997): 465.

39. Richard Elliot Friedman, *Commentary on the Torah* (New York: HarperOne, 2001), 175.

40. Walter Brueggemann, "Exodus," 707.

41. John Goldingay observes that in biblical theology, although God "may be sovereign in the world . . . it is not simply [God's] sovereignty that initiates events in the world. [God] waits upon people's cry." John Goldingay, *Old Testament Theology*, vol 1, p. 301. See also Walter Brueggemann, *Theology of the Old Testament: Testimony, Dispute, Advocacy* (Minneapolis, MN: Fortress, 1997), 414, n5.

42. Rabbi Yehudah Leib Alter of Ger, *Sefas Emes*, Shemot, 1796.

43. Walter Brueggemann, *Old Testament Theology: Essays on Structure, Theme, and Text*, ed. Patrick D. Miller (Minneapolis, MN: Fortress, 1992), 47.

44. For a fascinating analysis of the slaves' movement from numb silence to "loud protest" and ultimately to "the word," see Rabbi Joseph B. Soloveitchik, "Redemption, Prayer, Talmud Torah," *Tradition* 17, no. 2 (Spring 1978): 57–60.

45. Brueggemann, "Exodus," 706. But compare John Goldingay, *Old Testament Theology*, vol 1, p. 299, who writes that the slaves evince "no awareness that not only is their condition unreasonable, but . . . it might also be changed."

46. Brueggemann goes so far as to insist that the mere act of noticing one's pain can be a powerful source of hope. "Those who are incapable of noticing their hurt," he writes, "the ones numbed to despair and resigned to conforming docility, do not hope. When human pain is noticed, however, it is noticed

as unnatural and abnormal, and finally as unacceptable." Brueggemann, *Old Testament Theology*, 51.

47. See, for example, Terence E. Fretheim, *Exodus* (Louisville, KY: Westminster John Knox Press, 1991), 48; and Victor P. Hamilton, *Exodus: An Exegetical Commentary* (Grand Rapids, MI: Baker, 2011), 41; and note also Brueggemann, "Exodus," 706, who describes Israel's cries as "neither God-induced nor God-directed." But compare Numbers 20:16 and Deuteronomy 26:7, and, for a dissenting interpretation, see John I. Durham, *Exodus* (Waco, TX: Thomas Nelson, 1987), 26.

48. Brueggemann, *Old Testament Theology*, 47. God's attentiveness to cries is subtly but powerfully brought home by the fourfold repetition of God's name in these verses—"God heard . . . God remembered . . . God looked upon . . . God took notice"—which matches one-for-one Israel's fourfold cry. On this, see J. Gerald Janzen, *Exodus* (Louisville, KY: Westminster John Knox Press, 1997), 26. The idea that God hears the cries of the oppressed is expressed not just in biblical narrative but also in biblical law. See, for example, Exodus 22:21–23.

49. Brueggemann aptly notes that "the hope articulated in ancient Israel is not a vague optimism or a generic good idea about the future but a precise and concrete confidence in and expectation for the future that is rooted explicitly in YHWH's promises to Israel." Walter Brueggemann, *Reverberations of Faith: A Theological Handbook of Old Testament Themes* (Louisville, KY: Westminster John Knox Press, 2002), 100. Even more forcefully, Brueggemann characterizes biblical hope as the conviction that "God has not quit, God will make it right. God will yet do what God has already done." Walter Brueggemann, "Suffering Produces Hope," *Biblical Theology Bulletin* 28, no. 3 (August 1998): 98. It is precisely here where many modern people, very much including people who think of themselves as believers, struggle so deeply.

50. I say that faith in a transcendent God *ought to* relativize every status quo because (even in the Bible itself) it can sometimes be used for the very opposite—to legitimate and provide ultimate sanction for one political order or another. On this, see Brueggemann, *Old Testament Theology*, 16–17, 20. The God of Exodus, Brueggemann avers, is radically different from "the structure-legitimating gods of the empire . . . As there is conflict among social systems, so there is also conflict between the gods, between those who legitimate the structures of repression and denial and the One who forms new history around the reality of pain" (20).

51. Walter Brueggemann, "A New Creation—After the Sigh," *Currents in Theology and Mission* 11, no. 2 (April 1984): 86.

52. Claus Westermann, "The Role of the Lament in the Theology of the Old Testament," *Interpretation* 28, no. 1 (January 1974): 24–25.

53. Westermann, "The Role of Lament," 25. The one biblical text that seems to explicitly oppose lobbing challenges at God is Isaiah 45:9–10: "Shame on him who argues with his Maker, though naught but a potsherd of earth! Shall the clay say to the potter, 'What are you doing?'" On this see Dov Weiss, *Pious Irreverence: Confronting God in Rabbinic Literature* (Philadelphia: University of Pennsylvania, 2017), 5.

54. BT, Ta'anit 21a. Note also Rabbi Joseph Caro, *Shukhan Arukh, Orah Hayyim*, 230:5: "A person should be in the habit of saying, 'Whatever God does God does for the good.'"

55. Scott A. Ellington, *Risking Truth: Reshaping the World Through Prayers of Lament* (Eugene, OR: Pickwick, 2008), 21.

56. On this see especially Jon Douglas Levenson, *Creation and the Persistence of Evil: The Jewish Drama of Divine Omnipotence* (San Francisco: Harper and Row, 1988).

57. Brueggemann worries that "covenant minus lament is finally a practice of denial, cover-up, and pretense" and argues that such religion leads to "bad faith which is based in fear and guilt . . . The absence of lament [, he writes,] makes a religion of coercive obedience the only possibility." Walter Brueggemann, "The Costly Loss of Lament," *Journal for the Study of the Old Testament* 11, no. 36 (October 1986): 60–61.

58. For a useful and accessible survey of protest in Judaism, see Anson Laytner, *Arguing with God: A Jewish Tradition* (Northvale, NJ: Jason Aronson, 1990).

59. As one marker of the book's complexity, compare God's support of Job's speech in 42:7 with God's condemnation of it in 38:2.

60. See Ellington, *Risking Truth*, 104–105, building upon David Penchansky, *The Betrayal of God: Ideological Conflict in Job* (Louisville, KY: Westminster John Knox, 1990).

61. See Ellington, *Risking Truth*, 115, building upon Gustavo Gutiérrez, *On Job: God-Talk and the Suffering of the Innocent* (Maryknoll, NY: Orbis, 1987), 29–30.

62. Judaism is often described as unique among monotheistic traditions in making room for theological protest. See, for example, Bernard Schweitzer, *Hating God: The Untold Story of Misotheism* (Oxford: Oxford University Press, 2011), 168. And yet as the Rabbinics scholar Dov Weiss shows, in postbiblical Judaism, at least, the picture is not monolithic. "In rabbinic Judaism," he explains, "the idea of debating God was itself a matter of debate." While some Talmudic sages embraced this mode of religious expression, others rejected it. Weiss, *Pious Irreverence*, 10. One can readily understand their ambivalence. On the one hand, as we've seen, real relationship requires honesty; yet on the other hand, there does seem to be something rather presumptuous about "hurling words heavenward" (for this Rabbinic phrase, *lehatiah devarim kelapei ma'alah*, see, for example, BT, Berakhot 32a) especially when most of us are hardly above moral reproach ourselves. As in the Bible, in Rabbinic tradition we do encounter an audacious willingness to cry out not just *to* God but also *at* God—but we also find very different, more conventionally pious voices as well.

63. Brueggemann, "The Costly Loss of Lament," 62, 63.

64. Brueggemann, "The Costly Loss of Lament," 64.

65. See Ellen F. Davis, *Getting Involved with God: Rediscovering the Old Testament* (Lanham, MD: Rowman and Littlefield, 2001), 16.

66. Ellington, *Risking Truth*, 29.

67. Westermann, "The Role of Lament," 31.

68. Soloveitchik, "Redemption, Prayer, Talmud Torah," 56.

69. Coming at this from another angle, laments bind us to God even as we express disappointment with God; in a sense, protesting God's absence paradoxically makes God present.

70. In this vein, see Maureen Whitebrook, "Love and Anger as Political Virtues," in *The Politics of Compassion*, ed. Michael Ure and Mervyn Frost (New York: Routledge, 2014), 21–36, especially at 28.

71. William Neblett, "Indignation: A Case Study in the Role of Feelings in Morals," *Metaphilosophy* 10, no. 2 (April 1979): 140. For an example of a philosopher who seems to hold up indignation at injustice as a paradigmatic moral emotion, see Edward Sankowski, "Love and Moral Obligation," *Journal of Value Inquiry* 12 (1978): 104.

72. I borrow this encapsulation of Strawson's position from Antti Kauppinen, "Valuing Anger," in *The Moral Psychology of Anger*, ed. Myisha Cherry and Owen Flanagan (London: Rowan and Littlefield, 2018), 35. For Strawson's extremely influential argument, see Peter Strawson, "Freedom and Resentment," in *Freedom and Resentment and Other Essays* (New York: Routledge, 2008; originally published 1962), 1–28. For Strawson, moral indignation is best understood as "resentment on behalf of another" (Strawson, 15). In a related vein, note also Beverly Harrison's observation that "anger directly expressed is a mode of taking the other seriously." Beverly W. Harrison, "The Power of Anger in the Work of Love," *Union Seminary Quarterly Review*, vol. xxxvi (1981): 50. Yet note, in contrast, William Neblett's insistence that "feelings of indignation are ordinarily condescending feelings, feelings of disdainful regard for those persons negatively judged." Neblett, "Indignation," 150.

73. Kauppinen, "Valuing Anger," 37.

74. See Kauppinen, "Valuing Anger," 38–39.

75. On this, see Céline Leboeuf, "Anger as a Political Emotion: A Phenomenological Perspective," in *The Moral Psychology of Anger*, 15–29, especially at 24. Along the same lines, James Jasper argues that "the ability to feel and display the emotions associated with political agency—anger, indignation, pride, and so on—represents a kind of emotional liberation." James M. Jasper, *The Emotions of Protest* (Chicago: Chicago University Press, 2018), 150.

76. On this, see Emily McRae, "Anger and the Oppressed: Indo-Tibetan Buddhist Perspectives," in *The Moral Psychology of Anger*, 106.

77. Beverly W. Harrison, "The Power of Anger in the Work of Love," 49. (Harrison overstates the case, however, when she adds that "all serious human moral activity, especially action for social change, takes its bearings from the rising power of human anger.") In the same vein, see also Lee A. McBride III, "Anger and Approbation," in *The Moral Psychology of Anger*, 1. Note also Amartya Sen's observation that "resistance to injustice typically draws on both indignation and argument" and that the former is needed for "motivation." Amartya Sen, *The Idea of Justice* (Cambridge, MA: Harvard University Press, 2011), 390.

78. The Christian theologian Oliver O'Donovan writes that passions "involve an

energy which supports action—ill-considered action sometimes, perhaps, but not necessarily so, and, if not ill-considered, the more effective for being energetic." Oliver O'Donovan, *Finding and Seeking* (Grand Rapids, MI: Eerdmans, 2014), 66.

79. Owen Flanagan, "The Moral Psychology of Anger," in *The Moral Psychology of Anger*, xxvi. In this context, note also Andrew Lester's concern that "the inability to get angry at events that would normally be threatening" is a "common symptom of hopelessness." Andrew D. Lester, *The Angry Christian: A Theology for Care and Counseling* (Louisville, KY: Westminster John Knox Press, 2003), 191.

80. John Kiess, *Hannah Arendt and Theology* (London: Bloomsbury, 2016), 125.

81. It is worth noting, though, that it takes Jacob quite some time until he finally does so. I treat this story at length in "Underreacting and Overreacting: Dinah's Family in Crisis," in Shai Held, *The Heart of Torah*, vol. 1, 114–19.

82. Genesis Rabbah 49:8; see also Mekhilta de-Rabbi Ishmael, Bahodesh 6 (to Exodus 20:5).

83. In her recent work on anger, Martha Nussbaum worries that "the idea of payback or retribution—in some form, however subtle—is a conceptual part of anger." In other words, it's not that the urge to pay someone back for the harm they have inflicted is what sometimes *results* from anger; it is, rather, *constitutive* of what it means to be angry. Martha C. Nussbaum, *Anger and Forgiveness: Resentment, Generosity, Justice* (Oxford: Oxford University Press, 2016), 15. Leaving aside the question of whether the urge for retribution is always and everywhere a bad thing, I'm not convinced that anger always contains such an urge. As Nussbaum recognizes, sometimes the content of anger is merely "How outrageous. Something should be done about that." Nussbaum, *Anger and Forgiveness*, 6 and elsewhere. (Nussbaum hedges about whether this form of anger, which she dubs "Transition-Anger," is really a form of anger at all. Nussbaum, *Anger and Forgiveness*, 36.) It's thus possible to have a sense of outrage and indignation in the face of injustice or oppression without being focused on payback. As the feminist writer Rebecca Traister notes, "Not all political anger is about a drive to get even . . . it can stem from a straightforward objection to injustice, a desire to free those who have been unjustly constrained or harmed." Rebecca Traister, *Good and Mad: The Revolutionary Power of Women's Anger* (New York: Simon and Schuster, 2018), xxii. Among philosophers, see Flanagan, "The Moral Psychology of Anger," xvi (whose disagreement with Nussbaum is implicit); and McBride, "Anger and Approbation" (whose disagreement is impassioned and explicit). Given the potential benefits of anger (which we'll discuss below), it's worth adding that even when the impulse to retaliate is present, it need not be actualized in a concrete act of retaliation. See Leboeuf, "Anger as a Political Emotion," 28, n43. We can have that impulse, and choose to direct its energy in another, more constructive direction. On this last point Emily McRae speaks of "metabolized anger," which she defines as "the virtuous channeling of the power and energy of anger without the desire to harm or pass pain." Emily McRae, "Anger and the Oppressed," 113.

84. As the Stoic philosopher Seneca puts it, "The wise man will never cease to be angry, once he begins, so full is every place of vices and crimes." Seneca, *De Ira*, II.9.

85. See McRae, "Anger and the Oppressed," 108.

86. Jackson, *Love Disconsoled*, 150.

87. Kathleen M. O'Connor, "Reflections on Kindness as Fierce Tenderness," *Journal for Preachers* 39, no. 4 (Pentecost 2016): 36.

88. Lester, *The Angry Christian*, 13.

89. As Scott Ellington puts it, "The anguish of lament is that of violated trust. Without a history of relatedness and of love, there is no trust to be violated." Ellington, *Risking Truth*, 57.

90. Thus, although I have great admiration for the honesty and courage of Rabbi David Blumenthal's Jewish theology of protest, I worry that there is not enough expression of goodness to hold the protest and make sense of it. David R. Blumenthal, *Facing the Abusing God: A Theology of Protest* (Louisville, KY: Westminster John Knox Press, 1993). For a response to "theologies of protest" that is similar to my own, see William Hasker, *The Triumph of God Over Evil: Theodicy for a World of Suffering* (Downers Grove, IL: IVP Academic, 2008), 40.

4. Learning to Love and Be Loved

1. The Hebrew *ezer ke-negdo* can be translated variously. NJPS, cited in the text, renders "a fitting helper for him"; NRSV offers "a helper as his partner"; NIV, "a helper suitable for him"; and Robert Alter, "a sustainer beside him." The King James, famously, has "an help meet for him." Some readers may be tempted to assume that labeling the woman Adam's "helper" suggests that she is inferior to him but note the use of *ezer* to refer to God in, e.g., Psalm 121:1, and the description of God as *neged* the person in Psalm 16:8. The influential feminist Bible scholar Phyllis Trible notes that *neged* implies that the *ezer* connotes equality. Thus *ezer ke-negdo* is "a helper who is a counterpart." Phyllis Trible, "Depatriarchalizing in Biblical Interpretation," *Journal of the American Academy of Religion* 41, no. 1 (March 1973): p. 36. Needless to say, this is not how the verse has always been heard.

2. See Terence E. Fretheim, "Creator, Creature, and Co-Creation in Genesis 1–2," in *What Kind of God? Collected Essays of Terence E. Fretheim*, ed. Michael J. Chan and Brent A. Strawn (Winona Lake, IN: Eisenbrauns, 2015) 201. Fretheim explicates the argument made in Walter Brueggemann, *Genesis* (Atlanta: Westminster John Knox Press, 1982), 47.

3. Gordon J. Wenham, *Genesis 1–15* (Nashville: Thomas Nelson,1987), 71.

4. Bruce K. Waltke with Cathi J. Fredricks, *Genesis: A Commentary* (Grand Rapids, MI: Zondervan, 2001), 90. In this context, note also the classic debate between Rashi, who sees the verse as alluding to the progeny a couple can have, and Nahmanides (Ramban), who sees it as referring to the enduring sexual union between them. See their respective commentaries to Genesis 2:24.

5. Nahum M. Sarna, *Genesis* (Philadelphia: Jewish Publication Society, 2001), 23. Sarna offers a different interpretation of the paradox than the one I offer here.

6. Ilham Dilman, *Love and Human Separateness* (Oxford: Basil Blackwell, 1987), 105–106.

7. Dilman, *Love and Human Separateness*, 106.

8. Here issues of ethics (treating the other as a dignified other, a person in their own right) and issues of emotional maturity (being confident enough to let the other be, and remain, other) are inextricably intertwined. Worth noting in this context is the philosopher John Hardwig's insistence that "personal relationships between adults . . . are to be entered into and continued out of a sense of strength, fullness, and vitality, both in yourself and in the other, not out of a sense of weakness, need, emptiness, or incapacity . . . If I see myself as a being in need, I will be too focused on myself and my needs. I will then tend to depersonalize you into a someone who can meet my needs." John Hardwig, "In Search of an Ethics of Personal Relationships," in John Hardwig, *Is There a Duty to Die? And Other Essays in Bioethics* (New York, Routledge, 2000), 21–22. I am grateful to Jana Loeb for introducing me to Hardwig's important essay. And note also Anthony Giddens's observation that "in any addictive relationship the self tends to become merged with the other because the addiction is a prime source of ontological security." Anthony Giddens, *The Transformation of Intimacy: Sexuality, Love, and Eroticism in Modern Societies* (Stanford, CA: Stanford University Press, 1992), 92.

9. Martin Buber, "The Question to the Single One," in *Between Man and Man*, trans. Ronald Gregor Smith (London: Routledge, 1947), 72, 71. It's worth noting, if only briefly, that the same logic applies to close friendship too. Appealing to the history of philosophy, we can observe that while Montaigne held that friends almost become one person, or as he put it, "one soul in two bodies," other philosophers strongly—and in my view rightly—demurred. Nietzsche, for example, insisted that friends always remain "other" to one another. As the philosopher Mark Vernon explains, "The joy of . . . friendship is not the collapse of all boundaries between the individuals." See the brief but informative discussion in Mark Vernon, *The Philosophy of Friendship* (Hampshire, UK: Palgrave, 2005), 59.

10. This paragraph and the several that follow are taken, with very minor modifications, from Shai Held, "Being Present While Making Space: Or, Two Meanings of Tzimtzum," in *The Heart of Torah*, vol. 1, pp. 184–88.

11. Pesikta de-Rav Kahana, 2:10. Note also the version in Exodus Rabbah 34:1, according to which God contracts the divine presence even more intensely, into one small square cubit.

12. Gershom G. Scholem, *Major Trends in Jewish Mysticism* (Jerusalem: Schocken, 1941), 260. My presentation of the contrast between the Rabbinic conception and the Kabbalistic one is deeply indebted to Scholem's classic work. To complicate Scholem's portrayal of *tzimtzum* somewhat, see Moshe Idel, "On the Concept of Tzimtzum in Kabbalah and in Scholarship" (Hebrew), *Jerusalem Studies in Jewish Thought* 10 (1992): 92–100.

13. Martin Buber, *I and Thou* (1923), trans. Walter Kaufmann (New York: Scribner, 1970), 69, 78.

14. Martin Buber, "Distance and Relation" (1950), in *The Martin Buber Reader: Essential Writings*, ed. Asher Biemann (New York: Palgrave, 2002), 207.

15. Ruth Calderon, *A Talmudic Alphabet: A Private Collection* (Hebrew) (Tel-Aviv: Yediot Aharonot, 2014), 80. Calderon adds: "I think this is the most beautiful name [for sex] that I have ever heard."

16. Maimonides, for example, writes that "the sense of touch is a shame to us." Maimonides, *Guide of the Perplexed*, 2:36 and 3:8; see also 3:49. Maimonides here appeals to Aristotle; see Aristotle, *Nicomachean Ethics* iii.10.1118b2.

17. For an erudite but remarkably accessible survey of Jewish approaches to (and ambivalences toward) marital sexuality, see Noam Sachs Zion, *Sanctified Sex? The Two-Thousand Year Jewish Debate on Marital Intimacy* (Philadelphia: Jewish Publication Society, 2021).

18. Soloveitchik, *Family Redeemed*, 50. R. Soloveitchik adds: "The ethic of marriage is hedonistic, not monastic."

19. BT, Sotah 17a.

20. Genesis Rabbah 20:3. According to the midrash snakes and fish also have sex face-to-face. While the language of the text is heteronormative in obvious ways, I don't think the point needs to be.

21. R. Zadok Ha-Kohen of Lublin, *Tzidkat Ha-Tzaddik*, no. 200. I borrow the English translation from Norman Lamm, *The Religious Thought of Hasidism: Text and Commentary* (New York: Yeshiva University, 1999), 129. The passage is far richer and more complex than I can attempt to convey here; I merely focus on one key point in R. Zadok's presentation. For a brief, accessible analysis of the passage, see Norman Lamm, *The Shema: Spirituality and Law in Judaism* (Philadelphia: Jewish Publication Society, 1998), 101–103.

22. William Shakespeare, Sonnet 116. For readers who prefer the much drier language of moral philosophy, Philip Pettit gets at a similar notion of enduring love: "What I cherish in cherishing your love has to be a disposition to provide care that is resilient enough to survive situational shifts in the inclinations of pressures that affect you . . . In order to give me the good of love, you must provide me with . . . care . . . across certain possible variations on actual circumstances." Philip Pettit, *The Robust Demands of the Good: Ethics with Attachment, Virtue, and Respect* (New York: Oxford University Press, 2015), 24, 28.

23. *Tzidkat Ha-Tzaddik*, no. 200. Lamm, *Religious Thought*, 129. R. Lamm suggests that R. Zadok's analysis may contain a subtle but significant wordplay. Kabbalists use the Hebrew word for "everlasting," *olam*, to evoke the idea of *he'elem*, meaning "hiddenness" or "concealment." *Ahavat olam* (everlasting love) is more hidden and concealed than *ahavah rabbah* (abounding love); the former is, in Lamm's words, "of a far lower emotional temperature" than the latter. Lamm, *The Shema*, 202–203, n2.

24. Bemidbar Rabbah 3:6; see also BT, Sotah 2a; and for a fascinating discussion of this image, see R. Judah Loew of Prague (Maharal), *Be'er HaGolah*, 4:17.

25. BT, Sanhedrin 7a. That is why, the Talmud goes on to say, when relations were strong between God and Israel, God could fit into the tight confines of the

Tabernacle, but when the relationship fell on hard times, even the vast Temple that Solomon built could not contain God's presence.

26. BT, Gittin 90b.

27. Abraham ben Natan, *Sefer Ha-Manhig, Hilkhot Eirusin Ve-Nisuin* (Laws of Betrothal and Marriage), 540.

28. There is another potential meaning of getting married under an open-walled huppah: it can serve to remind us that we don't need to get everything we need in life in and from our marriage. There are, and should continue to be, other parts of our lives, and other friendships that also nurture and sustain us. In this context, note Mark Vernon's dismissal of the myth of modern love, which, he says, is based on "a totalisation of life in other," and his observation that this myth wrongheadedly denigrates friends as "incidental—pleasant but nonessential adornments to the lover's (sic) life together." Vernon, *The Philosophy of Friendship*, 49

29. Genesis Rabbah 48:9 (see the statements of Rabbi Abbahu and Rabbi Yudan there). The text speaks only of Abraham but it does not seem like much of a stretch to include Sarah in the description as well.

30. Mishnah Avot 1:5. For the connection between Yosi ben Yohanan's teaching and Abraham's example, see, for example, the commentary of Rabbi Obadiah of Bertinoro to Avot 1:5.

31. On family life in biblical times, see Arthur J. Keefer, "Family and Everyday Life," in *The Biblical World*, ed. Katharine J. Dell, 2nd ed. (London: Routledge, 2021), 666. I am indebted to Samuel Brody for a fruitful exchange on this topic.

32. This expansiveness extends outward beyond the single household as well. Taken together the homes of an extended family formed a *bet av* (literally, "father's house"); when in turn several extended families came together to form a village, they constituted a *mishpahah* (clan). Anthony Giddens observes that in modern times the spread of ideals of romantic love was a key factor "tending to disentangle the marital bond from wider kinship ties and give it an especial significance." In modern times, he writes, kinship relations have been "largely destroyed," which means that the nuclear family has been left standing in "splendid isolation." Giddens, *Transformation of Intimacy*, 26, 96. There is something nettlesome here: on the one hand, few of us, I suspect, would want to abandon the ideals of romantic love as a core foundation of marriage; on the other hand, the sense of "ontological rootlessness" that many people suffer in the absence of deep attachment to place and to extended family and the malaise that it often brings in its wake need to be confronted. For the concept of "ontological rootlessness," I am indebted to Judith M. Green, *Deep Democracy: Community, Diversity, and Transformation* (Lanham, MD: Rowman and Littlefield, 1999), vii. I am grateful to Akiva Mattenson for introducing me to Green's work.

33. It is also, I should note, an opening to thinking in more inclusive ways about families by choice that don't consist of kin in any conventional sense. I am grateful to Samuel Brody for forcefully making this point to me.

34. Wirzba, *Way of Love*, 113.

35. On this, see Soloveitchik, *Family Redeemed*, 37–39.

36. After I completed work on this chapter, I was delighted to discover that the philosopher Laurence Thomas makes much the same point. See Laurence Thomas, *The Family and the Political Self* (Cambridge: Cambridge University Press, 2006), 40–41.

37. On this see Paul Tournier, *The Meaning of Gifts* (Richmond, VA: Westminster John Knox Press, 1963), 23–24.

38. In a closely related vein, the philosopher Natalia Marandiuc observes from a theological perspective that "our lives are permeated by a longing not only to love God and our fellow human beings, but also to experience the reception of love, both in human and divine forms." Natalia Marandiuc, *The Goodness of Home: Human and Divine Love and the Making of the Self* (Oxford: Oxford University Press, 2018), 13. The point I am adding is that without experiences of human love, we are unlikely to be capable of receiving God's love. Put differently, it is not just that we need God's love and also our parents' love; it is that God's love is mediated and experienced through the love shown to us by human caregivers. We only sense what God's love is because we have experienced human love, however limited and imperfect that love may have been.

39. Mishnah Avot 5:16.

40. The philosopher Michael Austin helpfully distinguishes between "unconditional parental acceptance and love," on the one hand, and "unconditional parental approval," on the other. It is the former, and not the latter, that parents ideally offer to their children. Michael W. Austin, *Conceptions of Parenthood: Ethics and the Family* (Burlington, VT: Ashgate, 2007), 115–16.

41. It's worth noting the way the book of Kings explains King David's son Adonijah's bad behavior: "His father had never scolded him: 'Why did you do that?'" (1 Kings 1:6).

42. Robert C. Roberts, "Unconditional Love and Spiritual Virtues," in *The Wisdom of the Christian Faith*, ed. Michael T. McFall and Paul K. Moser (Cambridge: Cambridge University Press, 2013), 158. Of course, there is a point at which imperfect love ceases to be genuine love at all, even if that exact point can be difficult to identify. As Roberts writes, "Many of the conditions that love often carries within it undermine its status as love. For example, to the extent that parental love is conditional on the beauty, good behavior, or outstanding performance of the child, parental love is not love but only 'love'" (169).

43. Christopher Cordner, "Unconditional Love?," *Cogent Arts and Humanities* 3, no. 1 (December 2016): 3.

44. Cordner, "Unconditional Love?," 3–4.

45. It's probably worth saying here that this attunement requires—and teaches—parents to overcome self-absorption. On this see Claire Elise Katz, "'For Love is as Strong as Death': Taking Another Look at Levinas on Love," *Philosophy Today* 45 (2001): 129.

46. BT, Berakhot 58a and Mishnah Sanhedrin 4:5. For a beautiful description of Abraham praying to be inherited by a son who will be his own person rather

than a slave who will merely imitate his master, see Rabbi Kalonymus Kalman Epstein (1753–1823), *Ma'or Va-Shemesh*, Parashat Lekh Lekha, s.v. *vayomer mah titen li.*

47. Mara H. Benjamin, *The Obligated Self: Maternal Subjectivity and Jewish Thought* (Bloomington: Indiana University Press, 2018), 87, 8. Note also Benjamin's critique of much modern Jewish thought as concerned with an abstract as opposed to a concrete other (13). For our purposes, and borrowing from the philosophy of Emmanuel Levinas, we can take "command" in this context to refer to the idea that the other person—in this case, my child—makes a claim on me from an "ethical height," that is, as my superior and not merely as my equal. The needs of the concrete other shatter any illusion of autonomy I might have; my obligations stem not from my own will but from the needs of the other. In the moment that the other "summons me, calls for me, begs me," I am not autonomous but *responsive.* I borrow the phrase cited from Emmanuel Levinas, "Ethics as First Philosophy," in *The Levinas Reader*, trans. Sean Hand (Oxford: Blackwell, 1989), 83. The philosopher Roger Burggraeve describes the claim a child's need makes on us as "the ultimate heteronomous experience." Roger Burggraeve, "The Ethical Voice of the Child: Plea for a Chiastic Responsibility in the Footsteps of Levinas," in *Children's Voices: Children's Perspectives in Ethics, Theology, and Religious Education*, ed. Annemie Dillen and Didier Pollefeyt (Leuven: Peeters, 2010), 278. My point here is not to embrace Levinas's ethics writ large but only to underscore, with Benjamin, the uniqueness of the command that each child "speaks."

48. On this point note Exodus Rabbah's portrayal of King David as a shepherd who responds to the needs of individual sheep rather than seeing and treating the whole flock as one indistinguishable mass. Exodus Rabbah 2:2; and see the comments thereon in R. Chaim Friedlander, *Siftei Hayyim: Middot Ve-Avodat Hashem*, vol. 1, p. 366.

49. R. Samson Raphael Hirsch, *Yesodot Ha-Hinnukh: Sihot Pedagogiyot* (Tel-Aviv: Netzah, 1957), 53. And note also in this context R. Hirsch's critical assessment of Isaac and Rebecca's parenting of Jacob and Esau. R. Samson Raphael Hirsch, Commentary to Genesis 25:27, and, more expansively, "Lessons from Jacob and Esau," in Samson Raphael Hirsch, *The Collected Writings, Volume VII: Jewish Education* (New York; Feldheim, 1992), 319–31.

50. R. Meir Leibush Weiser (Malbim), commentary to Proverbs 22:6.

51. Rita Nakshima Brock, *Journeys By Heart: A Christology of Erotic Power* (New York: Crossroad, 1988), 9.

52. Monique Wonderly, "Early Relationships, Pathologies of Attachment, and the Capacity to Love," in *The Routledge Handbook of Love in Philosophy*, ed. Adrienne M. Martin (New York: Routledge, 2019), 28, 29. Wonderly helpfully encapsulates much of the salient research on attachment and our capacity for love on p. 30.

53. Brock, *Journeys*, 4, 7, 4.

54. Søren Kierkegaard, *Works of Love*, ed. and trans. by Howard V. Hong and Edna H. Hong (Princeton, NJ: Princeton University Press, 1995; originally published in 1847), 12.

55. Marandiuc, *The Goodness of Home*, 99. According to Marandiuc, human and divine love "co-participate in the making of the self" (12). Marandiuc is speaking of Kierkegaard's views but these words describe her own approach as well.

56. See, similarly, in Marandiuc, *The Goodness of Home*, 7.

57. BT, Berakhot 55a.

58. Moshe Odes, *Sefer Da Et Yaldekha: Pirkei Hadrakhah Le-Horim Be-Vinyan Rigshi U-Mahshavti Shel Ha-Yeled* (Jerusalem, 2008), 20–21. I owe the idea of taking the dispute between Moses and Bezalel as a parable about education to Odes, though whereas he takes the tabernacle to refer to the love between parent and child, I take it to refer to the child who has developed a robust sense of being loved. (I am not honestly sure whether this makes a meaningful difference.)

59. Cited in Noach Orlowek, *Mishma'at Mi-tokh Ahavah: Bein Horim Le-Yaldehem* (Jerusalem: Feldheim, 1996), 30.

60. Benjamin, *The Obligated Self*, 59.

61. Daniel Engster, *The Heart of Justice: Care Ethics and Political Theory* (Oxford: Oxford University Press, 2007), 209.

62. Engster, *The Heart of Justice*, 218.

63. Engster, *The Heart of Justice*, 221; and note bibliographical references there. For a good introduction to some of the core questions about caring, gender, and families, see there, at pp. 216–26. For an early, influential engagement (from a psychoanalytic lens) with many of these questions, see Nancy Chodorow, *The Reproduction of Mothering: Psychoanalysis and the Sociology of Gender* (Berkeley: University of California Press, 1978); and for a useful discussion of the critical literature on Chodorow's approach, see Engster, *The Heart of Justice*, 216–23.

64. See further Mishnah Kiddushin 4:14 (including what appears to be a dissenting voice there).

65. BT, Kiddushin 29a.

66. Mara Benjamin notes that "the Talmud contains nothing comparable to the . . . list of paternal obligations found in [the Talmud] for the obligations that mothers owe their children; neither can we find a comparable normative statement on what daughters should be given or taught by parents of either gender." Benjamin, *The Obligated Self*, 72, n12.

67. Although the interpretations I offer diverge in places from his, what follows is heavily influenced by the analysis offered by Rabbi David Hartman in *Joy and Responsibility: Israel, Modernity, and the Renewal of Judaism* (Jerusalem: Ben-Zvi-Posner, 1978), 78–92. It should be noted that exegetically speaking, R. Hartman's essay is not particularly strong; he stretches the Talmudic text to make the points about parenting he deems important. But the points he makes about parenting are indeed foundational to a Jewish theology of child-rearing, and I follow many of them in what follows.

68. Rabbi Joseph Soloveitchik declares, provocatively, that part of raising children is "befriending [them] with [their] Maker." Soloveitchik, *Family Redeemed*, 57.

69. This is one of the central thrusts of the Torah, as we will see in chapter 8. But

NOTES TO PAGES 97–100

note for now Exodus 23:9: "You shall not oppress the stranger, for you know *the feelings* of the stranger (*nefesh ha-ger*)."

70. On widows and orphans see, for example, Psalm 68:6; on strangers, see Deuteronomy 10:18.

71. Hartman, *Joy and Responsibility*, 84.

72. Hartman, *Joy and Responsibility*, 87.

73. See Hartman, *Joy and Responsibility*, 87.

74. There is a fascinating implicit debate between the Babylonian Talmud (BT, Kiddushin 29a) and the Palestinian (PT, Kiddushin 1:7) over which should come first, economic sufficiency or marriage. Whereas the former speaks of marriage and then learning a trade, the latter speaks of learning a trade first and then marrying. For an influential endorsement of the latter view, see Maimonides, *Mishneh Torah, Hilkhot De'ot*, 5:11.

75. See Rashi's comments to BT, Kiddushin 29a, s.v. *af le-hashito la-mayyim*.

76. Hartman, *Joy and Responsibility*, 87.

77. Maria Konnikova, "How People Learn to Become Resilient," *The New Yorker*, February 11, 2016, describing the work of the psychologist Emmy Werner. Resilience is, Konnikova writes, "a set of skills that can be taught."

78. For a biblical example of this, consider how, in the book of Ruth, Naomi first prays that her daughter-in-law Ruth find "security" (*menuhah*) in the house of a husband (Ruth 1:9) and then sets out to find such "security" (*mano'ah*) for her (3:1).

79. Martha C. Nussbaum, *The Monarchy of Fear: A Philosopher Looks at Our Political Crisis* (New York: Simon & Schuster, 2018), 31.

80. In a related vein, Søren Kierkegaard memorably writes, "When it is a duty in loving to love the people we see, then in loving the actual individual person it is important that one does not substitute an imaginary idea of how we think or could wish that this person should be. The one who does this does not love the person he sees but again something unseen, his own idea or something similar." Kierkegaard, *Works of Love*, 164. Using children as a means to some end is, Barbara Miller-McLemore writes, "the most serious act of violence with which all parents struggle." Barbara Miller-McLemore, "Feminism, Children, and Mothering: Three Books and Three Children Later," *Journal of Childhood and Religion* 2, no. 1 (January 2011): 25. There are undoubtedly more serious acts of violence at least some parents commit, but the thrust of Miller-McLemore's point is important.

81. On this, see Wirzba, *Way of Love*, 98.

82. Cecil Day-Lewis, "Walking Away," from *The Gate and Other Poems* (London: Jonathan Cape, 1962), 21.

83. In some cases, the pain can stem from the realization that at the end of the day, we can't force our children to be kind or to care about others. Ideally, we teach, we model, and we create opportunities . . . but there are no guarantees. Sara Ruddick reminds us that parents can "neither predict nor control the intellectual skills, moods, tastes, ambitions, friendships, sexuality, politics, or morality

of [our] children." Sara Ruddick, *Maternal Thinking: Toward a Politics of Peace* (Boston: Beacon, 1989), 34.

84. Ruddick, *Maternal Thinking*, 68, 70. In the same spirit, Mara Benjamin speaks of the "emotional whiplash" often experienced by parents. Benjamin, *The Obligated Self*, 24. The question of whether to speak of "mothering" or "parenting" (and thus of "motherhood" or "parenthood") is vexing and complicated. On the one hand, to speak exclusively of "mothering" risks reinforcing the patriarchal idea that all the work of child-rearing should fall on mothers; yet on the other hand, as Benjamin notes, "if used without qualification, the contemporary, gender-neutral term 'parent' risks whitewashing a reality that still bears a strongly gendered aspect." Benjamin, *Obligated Self*, xvii. Interestingly, Ruddick maintains that "a mother is a person who takes on responsibility for children's lives and for whom providing child care is a significant part of her or his working life." Note the "her or his": on Ruddick's account, fathers too can be "mothers" (*Maternal Thinking*, 40–41). In line with Benjamin and others, I speak both of motherhood and of parenthood.

85. Adrienne Rich, *Of Woman Born: Motherhood as Experience and Institution* (New York: W. W. Norton, 1976), 33. But note how Rich attributes at least some of this to "the patriarchal institution of motherhood" (34).

86. Ruddick speaks of mothering as "an activity governed by a *commitment* that perseveres through feeling and structures the activity." Ruddick, *Maternal Thinking*, 70; emphasis hers. For an interpretation of fatherhood rooted in the philosopher Gabriel Marcel's vision of "creative fidelity," see Stephen Joseph Mattern, "The Heart of the Merciful Father," in *Fatherhood: The Dao of Daddy*, ed. Lon S. Nease and Michael W. Austin (Malden, MA: Wiley-Blackwell, 2010), 130–41.

87. Deena Aranoff, "The Biblical Root *'mn*: Retrieval of a Term and Its Household Context," in *Mothers in the Jewish Cultural Imagination*, ed. Marjorie Lehman, Jane L. Kanarek, and Simon J. Broner (Liverpool: Littman, 2017), 327–41.

88. Aranoff writes that "the mother became invisible while her metonym flourished as a designation for the abstract notion of fidelity." Aranoff, "The Biblical Root," 330.

89. As Stephen Post nicely puts it, "Familialism ought never to provide an excuse for apathy to the fate of strangers." Stephen G. Post, "Conclusion to Part V," in *Altruism and Altruistic Love: Science, Philosophy, and Religion in Dialogue*, ed. Stephen G. Post, Lynn G. Underwood, Jeffrey P. Schloss, and William B. Hurlbut (New York: Oxford University Press, 2002), 377. Post condemns what he refers to as "insular familialism." Although I wouldn't want to overstate this point, I find Reinhold Niebuhr's observation sobering: "The family is still essentially selfish, and many a man is beguiled from ideal ventures by a false sense of obligation to his family." Reinhold Niebuhr, *Leaves from the Notebook of a Tamed Cynic* (Hamden, CT: Shoe String Press, 1956), 158.

90. Eva Feder Kittay, *Love's Labor: Essays on Women, Equality, and Dependency*, 2nd ed. (New York: Routledge, 2020). The theme of all of us being "some mother's

child" runs throughout the book; on the implications of this idea for conceptions of human equality, see especially pp. 29–30, 71–72. A major emphasis for Kittay is on the need for individuals and for society as a whole to take seriously the ways that those involved in the labors of care are themselves also "some mother's child" and thus entitled to concern and equal treatment.

91. Benjamin, *The Obligated Self,* 117. See also Ruddick, *Maternal Thinking,* 57.

92. See Numbers 39, and note the reference in the same unit to God's blessing the *kohanim,* which may be in the back of R. Luntschitz's mind as he constructs his interpretation of the ritual (see next note, and notice R. Luntschitz's interpretation of Genesis 12:3 therein, which proceeds along these same lines).

93. R. Shlomo Ephraim Luntschitz, *Keli Yakar* to Numbers 6:23, s.v. *amor lahem.* But for a very different approach, according to which it is God rather than the *kohanim* who blesses Israel, see, for example, Maimonides, *Mishneh Torah,* Laws of Prayer, 15:7.

5. Loving Our Neighbor

1. *Kelal gadol ba-torah.* Sifra Kedoshim 2:4; PT, Nedarim 9:4; Genesis Rabbah 24:7. The Jewish philosopher Franz Rosenzweig (1886–1929) refers to the command as the *Urgebot,* or "arch-commandment," of the Torah. See Franz Rosenzweig, *The Star of Redemption,* trans. William Hallo (New York: Holt, Rinehart & Winston, 1973), 205.

2. Jacob Milgrom, *Leviticus 17–22* (New York: Doubleday, 2000), 1656.

3. Samuel E. Balentine, *Leviticus* (Louisville, KY: Westminster John Knox Press, 2002), 166.

4. For the idea that being commanded to do what is beyond our capacity to do is incoherent, see Maimonides, *Mishneh Torah,* Laws of Repentance 5:4. (The focus there is on the incompatibility of determinism and commandedness, but the point transfers to our context as well.)

5. An even fuller analysis of the verse would also need to consider why the verse concludes as it does: "I am the Lord." Rabbi Isaac Abravanel makes the beautiful suggestion that the verse wants to make us aware that loving our neighbor— and in particular having only love and no hate for our neighbor—is a form of *imitatio Dei.* R. Isaac Abravanel, commentary to Leviticus 19:18.

6. Immanuel Kant, *Grounding for the Metaphysics of Morals,* trans. James W. Ellington (Indianapolis, IN: Hackett, 1981), 399, 312.

7. Immanuel Kant, *The Metaphysics of Morals,* part II, The Metaphysical Principles of Virtue, I The Elements of Ethics, second part: Concerning Ethical Duties to Others, 449, in *Immanuel Kant: Ethical Philosophy,* trans. James W. Ellington (Indianapolis, IN: Hackett, 1983), 113. Kant writes: "Love is a matter of feeling, not of willing, and I cannot love because I will to, still less because I ought to (I cannot be constrained to love); so a duty to love is an absurdity." Immanuel Kant, *The Metaphysics of Morals,* trans. Mary Gregor (New York: Cambridge, 1991), 402, 203 (For ease of reading, I have mixed and matched translations of Kant's *Metaphysics.*) On the other hand, practi-

cal love "resides in the will and not in the propensities of feeling, in principles of action and not in tender sympathy." Kant, *Grounding for the Metaphysics of Morals*, 399, 312.

8. Beneficence is doing or producing good for others. The term implies nothing about the motivations of the doer or producer. It seems clear that beneficence alone is not love, but whether benevolence (doing or producing good for others *with the intention* of benefiting them) should be considered a species of love is a more difficult question. The Catholic ethicist Edward Vacek bundles beneficence and benevolence together, since he assumes that neither implies caring about those we help. Edward Vacek, SJ, "A Catholic Theology of Philanthropy," in *Religious Giving: For Love of God*, ed. David H. Smith (Bloomington: Indiana University Press, 2010), 103. But others maintain that benevolence implies "emotional engagement" and "ever-attentive commitment." and thus consider it a form of love. Timothy Jackson, *The Priority of Love: Christian Charity and Social Justice* (Princeton, NJ: Princeton University Press, 2003), 2, n4. I am inclined toward the latter view but a robust analysis of the relationship between benevolence and love would require a clear definition of what attitudes and emotions we see as characteristic of benevolence. This is something many philosophical and theological discussions of benevolence lack; one gets the impression that different thinkers use the term differently and thus talk past one another. The benevolence that I think is close to love and may even be a version of love is the desire to do good for others coupled with sympathetic concern for them.

9. James Kellenberger, *The Asymptote of Love: From Mundane to Religious to God's Love* (Albany, NY: SUNY Press, 2018) 7, 16. As Kellenberger nicely puts it, "The exterior dimension without the inner side of love is not fully love" (85).

10. This is so even if we assume that legal systems will sanction and punish people according to the ways they behave and generally not do so where "emotion, taken by itself" is in question. See Edward Sankowski, "Responsibility of Persons for Their Emotions," *Canadian Journal of Philosophy* 7, no. 4 (December 1977): 830–31.

11. As further evidence for this, Nancy Sherman points to "moments of self-reproach" in which the presence of certain emotions within us yields shame and a sense of disappointment in ourselves. Nancy Sherman, "Taking Responsibility for Our Emotions," *Social Philosophy and Policy* 16, no. 2 (Summer 1999): 298–99.

12. As Sankowski puts it, "It is a man's very hatred or affection which we deem reprehensible or commendable sometimes; we do not confine ourselves entirely to behavior expressive of those emotions." Sankowski, "Responsibility of Persons for Their Emotions," 830. See also Sherman, "Taking Responsibility for Our Emotions," 294.

13. Sherman, "Taking Responsibility for Our Emotions," 294–95.

14. Sherman, "Taking Responsibility for Our Emotions," 294, 295–96.

15. See, similarly, Sankowski, "Responsibility of Persons for Their Emotions," 834–35. Presumably, someone so emotionally damaged that they are incapable

of exercising any control over their emotions could not be considered responsible for them. In halakhic categories, one might consider this a case of internal psychological coercion, or *ones*.

16. Sherman, "Taking Responsibility for Our Emotions," 296. For a similar approach in the context of the mandate to love our neighbor, Rabbi She'ar-Yashuv Cohen (1927–2016) writes (in the name of his grandfather), "You can't be certain that a feeling of love for your fellow will emerge [lit. be formed] within you in the short-term, but you must do everything in your power in order for such a feeling to emerge. In other words, you must create in your heart and your mind as well as in your deeds all of the conditions that make for devotion and love, and thus will you merit to fulfill the commandment of love." She'ar-Yashuv Cohen, "*Mitzvat Ahavat Yisrael—Ba-Halakhah u-va-Aggadah*," *Torah She-Be-Al-Peh* 36 (1995), 50 (translation mine).

17. Louis Jacobs, *The Book of Jewish Values* (Chappaqua, NY: Rossel, 1960), 119–20. Oddly, in later writings Jacobs retreats to the view that Leviticus is focused on behavior rather than feeling. See, for example, Louis Jacobs, *Religion and the Individual: A Jewish Perspective* (Cambridge: Cambridge University Press, 1992), 25–26.

18. Sherman, "Taking Responsibility for Our Emotions," 301.

19. Hence, despite its deep learning, the essay on Jewish approaches to love by the Jewish historian Lawrence Schiffman operates from a faulty premise (and by extension, with a faulty title): "Commandment or Emotion?" The answer to that question is, in a word, yes. See Lawrence Schiffman, "Commandment or Emotion?," in *Love—Ideal and Real—in the Jewish Tradition from the Hebrew Bible to Modern Times*, ed. Leonard J. Greenspoon, Ronald A. Simkins, and Jean A. Cahan (Omaha, NE: Creighton, 2008), 1–19.

20. Rabbeinu Yonah Gerondi (1200–1263), *Shaarei Teshuvah*, 3:36 (see also 3:35). In the same extended passage, Deuteronomy 15:10 exhorts the people to "give generously to him [i.e., the poor person] and without a grudging heart, for because of this the Lord your God will bless you in all your efforts and in all your undertakings." In a creative reading of the verse, the philosopher Rabbi Joseph Albo (c. 1380–1444) suggests that "because of this" refers not to the giving itself, but to our lack of a grudging heart when giving. A reward is promised not for the fact of giving but for the openheartedness we bring to the giving. R. Joseph Albo, *Sefer Ha-Ikkarim*, 3:33.

21. C. Stephen Evans, *Kierkegaard's Ethic of Love: Divine Commands and Moral Obligations* (Oxford: Oxford University Press, 2004), 195, 197.

22. Kierkegaard, *Works of Love*, 32. See also the discussion of this in Roberts, *Recovering Christian Character*, 270–72. Another potential challenge: in Kenneth Seeskin's words, "If the person loves you, a command is unnecessary; if the person does not love you, [the command] will not accomplish anything." The Jewish philosopher Franz Rosenzweig insists that love can indeed be commanded, but only by love itself. In other words, it is only God, who loves us, who can command us to reciprocate that love. For a lucid introduction to Rosenzweig

on love, see Kenneth Seeskin, "Philosophical Issues: Survey," in *Modern Judaism: An Oxford Guide*, ed. Nicholas de Lange and Miri Freud-Kandel (Oxford: Oxford University Press, 2005), 308–309.

23. See, for example, Rabbi Eliyahu Aryeh Fridman, *Kuntres Ve-Ahavta Le-Rei'akha Kamokha* (Brooklyn: Moriah Offset Company, c. 1994), 7–8. But note that Fridman himself seems to hold a different view (see at p. 41). For the organization and flow of this section, I am indebted to R. Fridman's work.

24. BT, Bava Metzia 62a, based on an interpretation of Leviticus 25:36.

25. For two examples of this approach, see the commentaries of Rabbi Shmuel Eidels (Maharsha, 1555–1631) and Rabbi Zvi Hirsch Chajes (Maharatz Chajes, 1805–1855) on BT, Shabbat 31a.

26. BT, Shabbat 31a.

27. Targum Pseudo-Jonathan to Leviticus 19:18. (The origin and date of the Targum are disputed, but it was available to and cited by many medieval rabbinic figures.) See also Maharsha and Maharatz Chajes to Shabbat 31a, as well as Rabbi Isaac Aboab (fourteenth century), *Menorat Ha-Ma'or*, 6:1, introduction (313); 6:2, 2 (326). For a recent affirmation of this approach, see R. Zalman Sorotzkin, *Oznayim LaTorah* to Leviticus 19:18. For an extensive bibliography on this connection (which brings different sources from the ones I have mentioned), see David Novak, *Jewish Social Ethics* (Oxford: Oxford University Press, 1992), 182, n30. For this school of thought, the association between the verse and Hillel's dictum is so strong that a midrash attributes Hillel's teaching to Rabbi Akiva, who had taught that "love your neighbor as yourself" is "the great principle of the Torah," instead. Avot de-Rabbi Natan, Version B, ch. 26. In support of a negative interpretation of our verse, R. Fridman notes that Leviticus 19 consists largely of prohibitions. Fridman, *Kuntres Ve-Ahavta*, 11–12. And see, similarly, R. Eliyahu Bakshi-Doron, "*Ve-Ahavta le-Rei'akha Kamokha le-Halakhah u-le-Ma'aseh*," *Torah She-Be-Al-Peh* 36 (1995), 34.

28. And yet we should be careful not to overstate the point. One could after all argue that the negative formulation can effectively demand the same as the positive one: Just as you would not wish to be abandoned in your time of need, so also must you not abandon others in theirs. On this, see, for example, the very brief comments in Shubert Spero, *Morality, Halakha, and the Jewish Tradition* (New York: Ktav, 1983), 208.

29. Franz Rosenzweig characterizes this actional prohibition as merely the "lower negative limit" of the command. Rosenzweig, *Star of Redemption*, 239.

30. Maimonides, *Mishneh Torah*, Laws of Mourning 14:1. See also Laws of Gifts to the Poor, 8:10. In the same vein, see the commentary of Rabbi Hezekiah ben Manoah (Hizkuni, thirteenth century) to Leviticus 19:18.

31. I am grateful to Professor Bernard Septimus for this insight.

32. R. Yaakov Tzvi Mecklenburg, *HaKetav Ve-ha-Kabbalah* to Leviticus 19:18.

33. I am grateful to Shani Tzoref for our exchange on this point. This is a significant theme in care ethics, which emphasizes the obligation to care for the other in all their particularity. Stephanie Collins notes that "empathetic aware-

ness . . . requires listening to the other person and attempting to see the world as they see it from *their* perspective—not to see the world as the sympathizer would see it, were the sympathizer occupying the other person's perspective." Stephanie Collins, *The Core of Care Ethics* (New York: Palgrave, 2015), 24. In this context, note also Robin Dillon, "Respect and Care: Toward Moral Integration," *Canadian Journal of Philosophy* 22, no. 1 (March 1992): 126. Although I obviously cannot prove this, I suspect that at least to some extent, R. Mecklenburg would take this as a "friendly amendment" to his approach. To couch what I've been arguing in R. Mecklenburg's own terms, just as I would want and expect my neighbor to ask me what I need, so also am I obligated to ask her what she needs.

34. For an argument that Rabbi Akiva interpreted the mandate to love the neighbor in emotional terms, see She'ar-Yashuv Cohen, "*Mitzvat Ahavat Yisrael*," 47–48. For R. Cohen, "the essence is the thought that is in the heart; speech or action come only to reveal the thought that is in the heart."

35. Nahmanides, commentary to Leviticus 19:18. The same approach is adopted by Rabbi Abraham Ibn Ezra in his commentary to Leviticus 19:18; a similar but not identical approach is taken by Rabbi Obadiah Seforno in his commentary to the verse.

36. Shmuel Goldin, *Unlocking the Torah Text: An In-Depth Journey into the Weekly Parsha*, vol. 3, Leviticus (New York: Gefen, 2010), 179.

37. Maimonides, *Sefer Ha-Mitzvot*, Positive Commandment No. 206.

38. For love of neighbor explicitly defined as an ethical disposition, see Maimonides, *Sefer Ha-Mitzvot*, Root 9. I am grateful to Professor Bernard Septimus for our exchange on this point.

39. Balentine, *Leviticus*, 165.

40. Maimonides, *Mishneh Torah*, Laws of Character Traits 6:3. Professor Lawrence Kaplan points out that in this formulation of Maimonides's, speech functions as a kind of intermediate level between emotion and action (private exchange, January 2022).

41. For another influential interpretation of "love your neighbor" that emphasizes both emotional and actional dimensions of the commandment, see the anonymous *Sefer HaHinnukh* (written sometime in the late thirteenth century), Positive Commandment No. 243.

42. Rabbi Eliezer in Mishnah Avot 2:9. See also the statement in Avot 5:19 that a "good eye" is one of the three characteristics that make one a "disciple of Our Father Abraham." In light of Rabbi Eliezer's assertion, Hananel Elran concludes that a good eye is "literally the basis of our lives, the basis of Jewish life." Hananel Elran, *Ahavat Olam Ahavtikh*, 68.

43. For a good eye as "contentment" (*histapkut*), see, for example, Maimonides, *Commentary to the Mishnah*, Avot 2:9; and Rabbi Obadiah of Bertinoro, *Commentary to the Mishnah*, Avot 2:9. For "rejoicing in what one has" (*samei'ah be-helko*), a phrase borrowed from Avot 4:1, see, for example, Rabbeinu Yonah Gerondi, Commentary to Avot 2:9.

44. Raphael Sappan, *The Israeli Slang Dictionary* (Hebrew) (Jerusalem: Kiryat Sefer, 1965).

45. For a much earlier connection of "love your neighbor as yourself" with the tenth commandment, the prohibition on coveting, see the comments of Rabbi Levi in Leviticus Rabbah 24:5, and note the commentaries of Rabbi David Luria (Radal) and Rabbi Zev Wolf Einhorn (Maharzu) there.

46. Rabbeinu Yonah Gerondi, Commentary to Avot 2:9 (*nedivut*). Contrast the approach of Rabbi Judah Loew of Prague (Maharal), who distinguishes between a "good eye," which is the desire for others to have good, and a "good heart" (*lev tov*), which is the desire to bestow good upon others oneself. Maharal, *Netivot Olam, Netiv Ayin Tov*, ch. 1.

47. What I refer to as envy is often colloquially spoken of as jealousy. But jealousy is usually understood by psychologists and philosophers as the fear of losing something or someone we possess (or think we possess) to a threatening third party. In other words, envy is dyadic, whereas jealousy is triadic. For an example of this distinction explained and defended, see W. Gerrod Parrott and Richard H. Smith, "Distinguishing the Experiences of Envy and Jealousy," *Journal of Personality and Social Psychology* 64 (1993): 906–20. For some reservations about this commonly accepted distinction, see Kristján Kristjánsson, "A Philosophical Critique of Psychological Studies of Emotion: The Example of Jealousy," *Philosophical Explorations* 19, no. 3 (2016): 244–45.

48. See Mishnah Avot 2:10. In his commentary to Mishnah Avot 5:19, Rashi, in fact, defines a "good eye" as one devoid of envy.

49. See, perhaps most famously, the way the students of R. Akiva are described as having been ungenerous ("of narrow eye") with one another. Genesis Rabbah 61:3. Employing the same image, the Christian writer Mary Louise Bringle notes that "envious people look on their rivals with a narrowed and withering gaze." Mary Louise Bringle, *Envy: Exposing A Secret Sin* (Louisville, KY: Westminster John Knox Press, 2016), 115.

50. I follow the NIV translation. It should be noted that not all commentators agree that *kin'ah* in this verse means "envy." Both the NJPS and NRSV translations render "passion." R. Menahem Ha-Meiri and Rabbi David Altschuler (eighteenth century), *Metzudat Tziyon*, take *kin'ah* in our verse to refer to anger (for *kin'ah* connected to anger, see, for example, Deuteronomy 32:21).

51. For the idea that *kin'ah* inflicts suffering on those around us, see Rashi's commentary to Proverbs 14:30; for the notion that it destroys envious people themselves, see R. David Altschuler, *Metzudat David* to Proverbs 14:30 (though note again that according to *Metzudat David*, *kin'ah* in this verse has the valence of anger more than jealousy).

52. John Rawls, *A Theory of Justice* (Cambridge, MA: Harvard University Press 1999), 533.

53. Mishnah Avot 4:21. As Rabbi Moshe Alsheikh (1508–1593) explains, envy almost inevitably brings its "friends," like hatred, a lust for gossip, and a hunger for revenge, in its wake. R. Moshe Alsheikh, *Yarim Moshe* to Pirkei Avot 4:21.

Martha Nussbaum points out that "people like to moralize their envy, and very often what begins as pure envy slides over to, *They are bad people, they don't deserve what they have*." Nussbaum, *The Monarchy of Fear*, 145.

54. Robert C. Roberts, "The Blessings of Gratitude: A Conceptual Analysis," 75.

55. For some brief but important observations on how a similar dynamic plays out between groups in society, where shaming others brings "psychological relief," see Martha Nussbaum, *Political Emotions*, 360.

56. Rebecca Konyndyk DeYoung, *Glittering Vices: A New Look at the Seven Deadly Sins and Their Remedies* (Grand Rapids, MI: Brazos, 2009), 44–45. DeYoung cites Francis Bacon's observation that "envy is ever joined to the comparing of a man's self; and where there is no comparison, no envy." Bacon, "Of Envy," cited on p. 45. DeYoung powerfully insists that "hatred of the rival is an elaborate cover-up, ultimately, for the envier's sense of rejection and unworthiness—his own self-hatred. The commandment is to love your *neighbor* as you love *yourself*. The envier can do neither" (51).

57. Robert C. Roberts, "What Is Wrong with Wicked Emotions?," *American Philosophical Quarterly* 28, no. 1 (January 1991): 16.

58. Roberts, "Wicked Emotions," 18.

59. In a more secular context, John Rawls notes that one of the "main psychological root[s] of the liability to envy is a lack of self-confidence in our own worth." Rawls, *Theory of Justice*, 535.

   Some traditional Jewish thinkers see envy as a manifestation of distrust in God for other reasons as well, namely that it suggests discontent with what God has decreed for us. See, for example, Rabbi Eliyahu de Vidas (1518–1587), *Reishit Hokhmah, Sha'ar Ha-Anavah*, chapter 7. This argument does not resonate with me because I do not share its assumptions about divine providence (I don't believe in divine micromanagement of the world). Moreover, as we saw in chapter 3, expressions of dissatisfaction with and even indignation about one's situation can themselves be manifestations of deep faith and connection to God.

60. Not surprisingly, Jewish sources speak harshly about those who "seek honor at their fellow's expense" (*ha-mitkabed biklon haveiro*). See, for example, PT, Hagigah 2:1; BT, Megillah 28a; and Maimonides, *Mishneh Torah, Hilkhot De'ot* 6:3 and Laws of Repentance 4:4.

61. Roberts, "Wicked Emotions," 16, 17. Roberts adds that when we see our friend as "an enemy of our self-esteem," we violate the terms of our friendship because to view another person as "an enemy of anything as fundamental to [us] as [our] self-esteem is to view [her] significantly as an enemy" (17). As DeYoung adds, "The fundamental attitude of the envious is directly opposed to love. To love is to seek others' good and rejoice when they have it . . . Envy directly undercuts love of our neighbor." DeYoung, *Glittering Vices*, 51.

62. As DeYoung points out, "Envy's view of the world is essentially antagonistic: it's me-versus-you, my good *or* your good—never both." *Glittering Vices*, 46. In other words, envy is the antithesis of *firgun*, which we discussed above.

63. Mishnah Avot 1:6. For the argument that judging favorably is constitutive of

having a "good eye," see Yehudah Moriel, *Be-Derekh Tovim: Mitzvot She-bein Adam La-Havero Le-Or Ha-Mekorot Ba-Mikra U-Va-Halakha* (Jerusalem: World Zionist Organization, 1975), 21.

64. Rabbi Abraham Saba, *Tzror Ha-Mor* to Parashat Kedoshim, s.v. *ahar kakh tzivah al he-aniyim*.

65. Maimonides, *Sefer Ha-Mitzvot*, Positive Commandment No. 177; see also, for example, R. Yonah Gerondi, *The Gates of Repentance*, 3:218; and note also BT, Shevuot 30a re: Deuteronomy 19:15.

66. *Sefer Ha-Hinnukh*, no. 235. See also Yoel Schvarts, *Ish Ve-Rei'eihu: Yalkut Hadrakhah Be-Inyenei Hitnahagut Ha-Adam Im Zulato, U-Ve-Sofo Kuntres Dinei Mitzvot Bein Adam La-Havero* (Jerusalem: Ha-Mosad le-Idud Limud Ha-Torah, 1995), 140.

67. See R. Elijah de Vidas, *Reishit Hokhmah*, *Sha'ar HaAnavah*, ch. 4.

68. R. Chaim Friedlander, *Siftei Hayyim, Middot Ve-Avodat Hashem*, vol. 1, p. 301. A "good heart," R. Friedlander maintains, is dependent on first developing a "good eye."

69. In the same spirit, the philosopher James Kellenberger writes of love that "a change in feeling correlates so closely with a change in perception that they are indistinguishable, so that they are two aspects of the same change in consciousness." Kellenberger, *The Asymptote of Love*, 125.

70. Mishnah Avot 1:5.

71. I am thinking here, for example, of sexual predators and domestic abusers, about whom see below.

72. Mishnah Avot 2:4.

73. R. Israel Meir Kagan, *Shemirat Ha-Lashon, Sha'ar Ha-Tevunah*, ch. 6. For the idea that the ending of Leviticus 19:18, "I am the Lord," suggests that loving our neighbor is a form of *imitatio Dei*, see R. Isaac Abravanel, commentary to Leviticus 19:18 (mentioned above, n5).

74. In the same vein, Rabbi Abraham Isaac Kook writes that we should strive "to remove anger from the heart entirely, and to see everything with a good eye (*ayin yafah*), with limitless loving compassion, and thus to become like the Eye above." R. Abraham Isaac Kook, *Orot Ha-Kodesh*, vol. 3, p. 326 (Ha-Ayin Ha-Elyonah).

75. Gordon Marino, *The Existentialist's Survival Guide: How to Live Authentically in an Inauthentic Age* (San Francisco: HarperOne, 2018), 207.

76. Rebbe Nahman of Bratzlav, *Likkutei Moharan*, no. 282 (1992 ed.), 894.

77. Charles Taylor, "The Politics of Recognition," in *Multiculturalism: Examining the Politics of Recognition*, ed. Amy Guttman (Princeton, NJ: Princeton University Press, 1994), 25. For a modern Jewish thinker who worries that seeing people with a begrudging, hostile eye (*ayin ra'ah*, literally a "bad eye") can have adverse consequences upon them, see R. Eliyahu Dessler, *Mikhtav Me-Eliyahu*, vol. 4, p. 506; but see also vol. 3, p. 314.

78. On being "maimed" by how others see us, see Natalia Marandiuc, *The Goodness of Home*, 55. Marandiuc speaks powerfully of "outer recognition" as "an ingredient in human selfhood" (56).

79. BT, Shabbat 97a.

80. R. Obadiah of Bertinoro, *Commentary to the Mishnah*, Avot 1:6. See also Maimonides, *Commentary to the Mishnah*, Avot 1:6, s.v. *ve-hevei dan.*

81. I am grateful to Dr. Elana Stein Hain for forcefully making this point in response to an earlier version of this chapter.

82. Derekh Eretz Rabbah, ch. 5.

83. An awareness of this trap is implicit in the commentary of Rabbi Abraham Saba, *Tzror Ha-Mor* to Parashat Kedoshim, s.v. *ahar kakh tzivah al he-aniyim.*

84. Maimonides, *Mishneh Torah*, Laws of Repentance, 2:9.

85. Maimonides, *Mishneh Torah, Hilkhot De'ot*, 6:6.

86. For useful perspectives on the dynamics between understanding and forgiveness, see Jerome Neu, "To Understand All Is to Forgive All—Or Is It?," in *Before Forgiving: Cautionary Views of Forgiveness in Psychotherapy*, ed. Sharon Lamb and Jeffrie G. Murphy (Oxford: Oxford University Press, 2002), 17–38; and Glen Pettigrove, "Understanding, Excusing, Forgiving," *Philosophy and Phenomenological Research* 74, no. 1 (January 2007): 156–75.

87. Robert C. Roberts, "Forgivingness," *American Philosophical Quarterly* 32, no. 4 (October 1995): 292, 293, 296. Roberts writes: "It is this vision of the other as properly alien on grounds of guilty offense that, it seems to . . . me, is characteristically overcome in forgiveness" (292).

88. R. Natan Gestetner, *Lehorot Natan: Pirkei Avot*, to Avot 1:6, p 60.

89. Gestetner, *Lehorot Natan: Pirkei Avot*, 60. See also Rebbe Nahman of Bratzlav, *Likkutei Moharan*, no. 282.

90. Nel Noddings, *Caring: A Relational Approach to Ethics and Moral Education*, 2nd ed. (Berkeley: University of California Press, 2013; first edition, 1984), 112.

91. Nel Noddings. *Starting at Home: Caring and Social Policy* (Berkeley: University of California Press, 2002), 22. Some readers might find it helpful to think of caring-for as "personal caring" and caring-about, in contrast, as "humanitarian caring." On this, see Michael Slote, "Caring Versus the Philosophers," in Michael Slote, *Selected Essays* (Oxford: Oxford University Press, 2010), 262. Also relevant in this context is Tove Pettersen's distinction between thick care and thin care, the former carried out toward those with whom we have established relations, the latter toward those with whom we do not have such relations and of whom we thus have only "generalized knowledge." The distinction is pervasive in the second half of Tove Pettersen, *Comprehending Care: Problems and Possibilities in the Ethics of Care* (Lanhan, MD: Lexington, 2008).

92. For a more recent feminist philosophical argument that we can indeed care *for* distant others, and not just care *about* them, based not surprisingly, on a reimagining of how we should understand what caring-for looks like, see Lisa Cassidy, "'Starving Children in Africa': Who Cares?," *Journal of International Women's Studies* 7, no. 1 (2005): 91–94, especially 93–94. Note also the implicit disagreement with Noddings in Danuel Engster, *The Heart of Justice*, 35–36.

93. In a recent publication, the Bible scholar John Goldingay argues that the mandate to love our neighbor means "caring for, not just caring about." John

Goldingay, *Old Testament Ethics: A Guided Tour* (Downers Grove, IL: IVP Academic, 2019), 119. But Goldingay uses these terms very differently from the way Noddings does (and by extension, from the way I do). For Goldingay, caring-for refers to action, and caring-about to emotion; the point of his statement is that the Bible is interested not only in emotion but also (and, on his account, primarily) in action. In other words, there is nothing in his statement that contradicts what I've said here.

94. Elimelekh Bar-Shaul, *Mitzvah Va-Lev*, vol. 2 (Tel-Aviv: Avraham Tziyoni Publishers, 1957), 175–77; passage cited is at p. 176.

95. Insisting otherwise, some interpreters have taken the mandate of loving the neighbor to be universal. Among traditional commentators, see, for example, Rabbi David Zvi Hoffmann (1843–1921), commentary to Leviticus 19:17–18; and Rabbi Yaakov Tzvi Mecklenburg, *Ha-Ketav Ve-Ha-Kabbalah* to Leviticus 19:18 (whatever good deeds one would want someone else to do for him, "he should do for his neighbor [*rei'eihu*], *who is every human being*"); among classical sources, Avot de-Rabbi Natan, ch. 16 (see Goldin edition, 86), can be interpreted this way; and see Rabbi Isaac Aboab, *Menorat Ha-Ma'or*, ch. 17 ("*Ahavat Haveirim*"), 305, who appears to interpret similarly. For additional sources that interpret the verse in the same spirit, see Rabbi Menaham Kasher, *Torah Sheleimah*, Milu'im to Parashat Yitro, no. 20, section 1, pp. 261–63. Among modern interpreters, see, for example, Hermann Cohen, *Der Nächste: vier abhandlungen über das verhalten von mensch zu mensch nach der lehre des judentums, mit einer vorbemerkung* (Berlin; Schocken, 1935), 15–16, cited in Yehudah Moriel, *Be-Derekh Tovim*, 25–26; Nehama Leibowitz, *New Studies in Vayikra*, trans. Rafael Fisch and Avner Tomaschoff (Jerusalem: WZO, 1993), 366–67; Meir Paran, *Olam Ha-Tanakh: Shemot*, 134 (in both cases appealing to Exodus 11:2); Richard Elliott Friedman, *The Exodus: How it Happened and Why It Matters* (New York: HarperOne, 2017), 199–216; and Lenn Evan Goodman, "Love in the Jewish Tradition," in *The Routledge Handbook of Love in Philosophy*, ed. Adrienne Martin (New York: Routledge, 2019), 386 (based on Genesis 11:3; 38:30; and Exodus 11:2). That the verse refers to fellow Israelites is affirmed, for example, by Milgrom, *Leviticus 17–22*, 1647; Jay Sklar, *Leviticus* (Downers Grove, IL: InterVarsity Press, 2014), 246; and seemingly Frank H. Gorman, *Leviticus: Divine Presence and Community* (Grand Rapids, MI: Eerdmans, 1997), 114; and see also Ellen F. Davis, "Critical Traditioning: Seeking an Inner Biblical Hermeneutic," *Anglican Theological Review* 82, no. 4 (Fall 2000): 746. Among traditional Jewish thinkers, see, for example, Maimonides, *Mishneh Torah*, Laws of Mourning, 14:1, and the sources cited in *Entziklopedia Talmudit*, vol. 1, s.v. *ahavat yisrael*. In general, the Bible scholar Deena Grant observes, "early rabbinic traditions converged around the view that 'your neighbor' (Leviticus 19:18) refers to a fellow Jew." Deena Grant, "How to Love God: Deuteronomy, Early Rabbinic Literature, and Gospel Texts," *The Journal of Interreligious Studies* 26 (March 2019): 71. See also Reinhard Neudecker, "'And You Shall Love Your Neighbor as Yourself—I am the Lord' (Lev 19.18) in Jew-

ish Interpretation," *Biblica* 73 (1992): 499–503; and Ernst Simon, "The Neighbor (Re'a) Whom We Must Love," in *Modern Jewish Ethics: Theory and Practice*, ed. Marvin Fox (Columbus: Ohio State University Press, 1975), 33–45. See also Louis Jacobs, *Religion and the Individual*, 26. For a comprehensive argument insisting that in the history of Jewish law, the word *rei'a* refers to fellow Jews only, see Rabbi Shlomo Schneider, *Divrei Shlomo*, no. 121.

Some interpreters take the Hebrew *kamokha*, as "yourself," as adjectival rather than adverbial—that is, they think the verse should read not as "Love your neighbor as [you love] yourself" but rather as "Love your neighbor [who is] as yourself." This, they propose, would yield a universalistic interpretation: love your neighbor who is, after all, a human being like yourself. See, for example, Naphtali Herz Wessely (1725–1805), *Biur* to Leviticus 19:18. But it should be said, first, that this is not a persuasive reading of the Hebrew (especially in light of Leviticus 19:34); and second, that the phrase "[who is] as yourself" can be taken to suggest a limiting of the commandment rather than a universalization of it: "Love your neighbor [when he is] as yourself." In other words, the verse could still refer only to other Jews ("Love your neighbor [if he is a Jew] as yourself"), or even only to other Jews who are observant of mitzvot like yourself. That is how Maimonides seems to interpret the verse in *Mishneh Torah*, Laws of Mourning, 14:1; so also Rabbi Moshe of Coucy, *Sefer Mitzvot Gadol*, Positive Commandment No. 9. And see also, for example, Rabbi Samuel ben Meir (Rashbam, 1085–1158), commentary to Leviticus 19:18. And note the discussion of this in Simon, "The Neighbor Whom We Shall Love," 38–39.

96. In a similar vein, see Joel S. Kaminsky, "Loving One's (Israelite) Neighbor: Election and Commandment in Leviticus 19, *Interpretation: A Journal of Bible and Theology* 62, no. 2 (April 2008): 132. For an example of reading the Bible, and the Jewish tradition more broadly, along these lines, see Harold Fisch, "A Response to Ernst Simon," *Modern Jewish Ethics*, 57–61, especially at 58. Kaminsky maintains that in contrast to the radical ethics articulated by Jesus, Leviticus upholds a "much more realistic ethic"; on his account, "Much of the brilliance of the Hebrew Bible's theology is its keen awareness of working within the real limitations we humans have" (128, 132). The extraordinary standards of behavior demanded by both Jesus and Paul, in contrast, are a function of their belief that the end-time was near (128).

97. Commenting on the command to love our neighbor, Kaminsky writes: "My own suspicion is that we remain hypnotized by a universalistic ideal even though few assume that treating everyone the same way is a good idea. Most would acknowledge that it is normal and even positive to relate more intimately with one's own family than with others. Few believe that we bear no additional responsibility toward our closest relatives than we do to any other human being." Kaminsky, "Loving One's (Israelite) Neighbor," 128.

98. Noting how the mandate to love the stranger echoes the mandate to love the neighbor, Ellen Davis writes: "The effect of that echo is to force wide the scope of the love commandment. Through the proximity of these two verses, the resi-

dent alien [the *ger*, which I have rendered as "stranger"] has been redefined as a neighbor, to whom is due the covenant obligation of love." Davis, "Critical Traditioning," 746. I am not sure that it's quite right to say that the resident alien has been "redefined" as a neighbor; rather, I think our obligations to the neighbor now extend beyond the neighbor to include the stranger too. The difference between Davis's interpretation and my own may ultimately come down to semantics—I am honestly not sure—but my point is that the boundaries between insider and outsider are stretched, but not eliminated, by the verse: even in the face of this radical new command, the stranger remains a separate category (an "other," if you will) in biblical thinking.

99. To take one clear example, the intellectual historian Paul Mendes-Flohr writes that according to Leviticus 19, "I am to love both my fellow Jews *and* the stranger, that is, my fellow human beings." Paul Mendes-Flohr, *Love, Accusative and Dative: The B. G. Rudolph Lectures in Jewish Studies* (Syracuse, NY: Syracuse University Press, 2007), 16. It is that last clause, the leap from "the stranger" to "my fellow human beings," that is exegetically problematic. To repeat, I am sympathetic to the impulse but skeptical of the exegesis. See, similarly and more expansively, Friedman, *The Exodus*, 199–216. For a rejection of this approach, more in line with my own, see Kaminsky, "Loving One's (Israelite) Neighbor," 123–24.

100. As examples, Levenson cites Genesis 25:28 and 29:30; and Malachi 1:2–3.

101. Jon Levenson, personal communication, March 25, 2020.

102. Radak, commentary to Psalm 15:3. For an English translation of the text, from which I have borrowed here, see Moshe Greenberg, "On the Political Use of the Bible in Modern Israel: An Engaged Critique," in *Pomegranates and Golden Bells: Studies in Biblical, Jewish, and Near Eastern Ritual, Law, and Literature in Honor of Jacob Milgrom*, ed. David P. Wright, David Noel Freedman, and Avi Hurvitz (Winona Lake, IN: Eisenbrauns, 1995), 468.

103. And yet this fails to deal with the question of the *nokhri*, the non-Jew who is not a stranger. On this see chapter 8.

104. Louis Jacobs, *The Book of Jewish Values*, 122. Somewhat surprisingly, Jacobs makes no mention of Radak, who appears to provide historical precedent for his approach.

105. Rabbi Jacob Emden, *Migdal Oz*, *Aliyat Ha-Ahavah*, 12:4 (and note the influence of BT, Berakhot 10a). In a similar vein, see Rabbi Judah Loew of Prague (Maharal), *Netivot Olam*, *Sha'ar Ahavat Ha-Rei'a*, ch. 1, beginning. On this see also Rabbi Raphael Stohl, *Sefer Torat Ha-Kavod* (Hollywood, FL: Raphael Stohl, 2018), 206–10.

106. This is clear from the juxtaposition of *Aliyat Ha-Ahavah* 12:4 and 12;5, where only the love of one's fellow Jews is placed under the umbrella of love of neighbor.

107. Of course, the analogy has its limits. There are, after all, wonderful parents who have toxic and insufferable children. Though loving the parents may mean that we must not share our views of their children with them, it does not seem to entail that we actively love such children. I am grateful to Professor Lawrence Kaplan for our exchange on this point.

108. For a powerful and impassioned—though also controversial—insistence that the mandate to love our neighbor includes non-Jews within it, see Rabbi Pinhas Eliyahu Hurwitz (1765–1821), *Sefer Ha-Berit*, 2:13 ("*Ahavat Rei'im*"). As we've seen, many reject this view. See, for just one example, Rabbi Shmaryahu Yosef Chaim Kanievsky (1928–2022), *Siah Ha-Sadeh*, 6th ed. (Benei Brak), part 1, to *Orhot Hayyim Le-Yom Aleph*, p. 5a, n12.

109. Rabbi Hayyim Vital, *Sha'arei Kedushah*, 1:5. See also, crucially, the logic of Maimonides, *Mishneh Torah*, Laws of Slaves 9:11, and note the uses to which Maimonides puts Job 31:13, 15 and Psalm 145:9. In the spirit of Maimonides, we can say that if and when we are truly virtuous, our commitment to mercy extends beyond ethnic and religious boundaries.

110. R. Abraham Isaac Kook, *Middot Ha-Ra'ayah*, "*Ahavah*," no. 1, 3, 5, 6, 10, 10–11. Translations are taken either from Don Seeman's as-yet-unpublished translation and commentary on Middot HaRa'ayah or from Ben Zion Bokser, ed., *Abraham Isaac Kook: The Lights of Penitence, Lights of Holiness, the Moral Principles, Essays, Letters, and Poems* (Mahwah, NJ: Paulist, 1978), 135–39. I am grateful to Professor Seeman for sharing his work with me. For another modern voice passionately insistent on love of all God's creatures rather than just fellow Jews, it is worth exploring the writings of Rabbi Simhah Zissel Ziv (1824–1898). See, for example, his *Hokhmah U-Musar* 2, no. 6, p. 8; for a careful study of his thought, see Geoffrey D. Claussen, *Sharing the Burden: Rabbi Simhah Zissel Ziv and the Path of Musar* (Albany, NY: SUNY Press, 2015).

111. Rabbi Shlomo Goren (1917–1994) makes the provocative suggestion that the classic debate between R. Akiva and ben Azzai over what constitutes "the great principle of the Torah" is actually an argument about whether particular or universal love is the most essential foundation of the Torah. For R. Akiva, who maintains that love of neighbor is the great principle, love of the Jewish people is the most essential foundation; for ben Azzai, in contrast, who maintains (at least according to the most common interpretation of his words) that humanity having been created in the image of God is the great principle, "universal brotherhood" is the most essential foundation. R. Goren insists, though, that even according to ben Azzai, love of Israel is the first stage, and that universal love can only unfold in stages. R. Shlomo Goren, "*Ahavat Yisrael Le-Or Ha-Halakhah*," *Or Ha-Mizrah* 1 (1954): 10. For the debate between R. Akiva and ben Azzai, see Sifra Kedoshim 2; PT, Nedarim 9:4; and Genesis Rabbah 24:7; and for some different interpretations thereof, see the opening of chapter 7.

6. Loving Our Own, and Everyone Else Too

1. BT, Bava Metzia 71a. For the biblical derivation of the obligation to support the poor of other cities, see Bava Metzia 31b re: Deuteronomy 15:8.

2. R. Menahem Ha-Meiri, *Beit Ha-Behirah* to BT, Bava Metzia 71a, s.v. *Yisrael ve-Goy*.

3. Tanna de-Be Eliyahu, chapter 27. For an earlier, more authoritative Rabbinic midrash about tzedakah that proceeds along similar lines, see Sifre Deuter-

onomy 116. I cite Tanna de-Be Eliyahu in the text because its expansiveness is instructive.

4. For loan-giving, see *Shulkhan Arukh, Hoshen Mishpat* 97:1; for almsgiving, see *Shulkhan Arukh, Yoreh Deah* 251:3.

5. The Stoic philosopher Hierocles (second century CE) imagines people in a series of concentric circles and speaks of drawing the various circles in toward the center. I am not sure there is any practical difference between imagining our commitments spreading out, on the one hand, and imagining pulling outer circles inward, on the other. The key aspiration is that "we should think of nobody as a stranger, outside our sphere of concern or obligation." Martha C. Nussbaum, *The Cosmopolitan Tradition: A Noble but Flawed Ideal* (Cambridge, MA: Harvard University Press, 2019), 78.

    I've been developing the idea that Jewish ethics imagines our obligations to others as a series of expanding concentric circles—family first, then friends, then community, then the Jewish people as a whole, then humanity, and ultimately all of creation. But I ought to issue an important qualification to this model. In a world as complex and interconnected as our own, I'm not sure that it quite makes sense to view our commitments and obligations as merely one set of concentric circles. We may have a heterogeneous set of inner circles that may or may not overlap in various ways—our friends, our local Jewish community, our colleagues at work, the neighbors who live on our block, a group of activists with whom we work to provide assistance to the homeless, those with whom we share a vision of a just society, the community with whom we share a passion for music and the arts, and so on. This more variegated picture no doubt complicates the work of prioritization, but the world is a complicated place and the task of setting priorities is nothing if not formidable. Needless to say, more work needs to be done to flesh out this idea and its implications. I am grateful to Akiva Mattenson for pushing me to better formulate what had been an inchoate notion.

6. R. Jacob Emden, *Migdal Oz, Birat Ha-Ahavah*, ch. 12, beginning.

7. Sifre Deuteronomy 116.

8. For a potentially relevant precedent of prioritizing a neighbor over a brother, see BT, Bava Metzia 108b and Ketubot 85b, as well as the explanation given by Rabbi Asher ben Yehiel (Rosh), Ketubot 9:9. For a text that maintains that where tzedakah is concerned a neighbor "whom we care about" takes precedence over a relative with whom we are distant, see Rabbi Aharon ben Jacob Ha-Kohen (thirteenth–fourteenth century), *Orhot Hayyim*, part 2, *Din Tzedakah*, section 1; and for a modern legal authority arguing similarly, see, for example, R. Shmaryahu Yosef Chaim Kanievsky, *Derekh Emunah* (commentary to Maimonides, *Mishneh Torah*), Laws of Gifts to the Poor, 7:13, s.v. *aniyei veito*; but for a different view compare Rabbi Abraham Danzig (1748–1820), *Hokhmat Adam, Sha'ar Mishpetei Tzedek*, no. 145. For a broader Jewish legal argument that the category of "neighbor" in texts dealing with tzedakah refers not to geographical proximity but to interpersonal closeness, see Rabbi Yehudah

Zoldan, "*Sidrei Kedimut be-Matan Tzedakah Be-Yameinu*," *Tzohar* 37 (2015), 37–50. In the same vein, R. Zoldan argues that "city" in texts about tzedakah refers not to a geographical location but to a community (*kehillah*). For precedent for that view, see Rabbi Chaim Benveniste (1603–1673), *Shayarei Knesset Ha-Gedolah* to *Tur, Yoreh Deah* 151, *Hagahot Tur*, no. 3. In general, R. Zoldan writes, "a person is interested in giving to and assisting institutions that are close to his heart, and oftentimes the local poor and local institutions are less close to his heart" (43). This is undoubtedly true but the discussion cannot simply be left there. There are many additional factors beyond where a person's heart is drawn that merit consideration in thinking through obligations of tzedakah—and interpersonal obligations more generally. It is one thing to weigh personal interest, but it is quite another to (always? everywhere?) give it the final word.

9. Maimonides, *Guide of the Perplexed*, 3:42. Translation modified very slightly from Pines, 569.

10. R. Ozer Glickman, "Think Local, Act Global: Tzedaka in a Global Society," in *Toward a Renewed Ethic of Jewish Philanthropy*, ed. Yossi Prager (New York: Yeshiva University Press, 2010), 277. This is not an approach Rabbi Glickman advocates or embraces. In this context, I find it extremely striking that the author of the Gospel of John, living as part of an embattled community enduring both hatred and persecution (John 15:19–21), seems to interpret the commandment to love the neighbor in narrow terms: the charge Jesus gives to his disciples, as John presents it, is "Love one another as I have loved you" (John 15:12). Commenting on Jesus's words, the New Testament scholar Johannes Nissen writes: "The injunction to love one another reflects the condition of the Johannine community drawn together into communal solidarity in the face of the hostility of the . . . world." Johannes Nissen, "The Distinctive Character of the New Testament Love Command in Relation to Hellenistic Judaism: Historical and Hermeneutical Reflections," in *New Testament and Hellenistic Judaism*, ed. Peder Borgen and Søren Giversen (Aarhus, Denmark: Aarhus, 1995), 143.

11. Maimonides, *Sefer Ha-Mitzvot*, Positive Commandment No. 195. I leave the questions of how best to translate Leviticus 25:35 and how the verse has traditionally been understood for another day.

12. Glickman, "Think Local, Act Global," 279.

13. For this reason, R. Glickman notes, "Writing a check to a conglomerate . . . does not evoke the same sense of fulfilling a mitzvah that working in a soup kitchen or handing cash to an indigent street person does." Glickman, "Think Local, Act Global," 288.

14. Some readers might find it helpful to think of caring-for as "personal caring" and caring-about, in contrast, as "humanitarian caring." I borrow these terms from Michael Slote, "Caring Versus the Philosophers," in Michael Slote, *Selected Essays*, 262.

15. Noddings, *Starting at Home*, 23–24.

16. The ethos of tzedakah would thus endorse the insistence of the political philosopher Daniel Engster that "we should aim to care for distant others whenever

possible by enabling them to care for themselves and their immediate dependents as well as other individuals in their immediate social milieu . . . We should shift the actual delivery of care whenever possible to the most local and personal levels." Engster, *The Heart of Justice*, 58.

17. For harsh words directed at one who gives alms to others while his family goes hungry, see Judah ben Samuel of Regensburg (Yehudah He-Hasid, 1150–1217), *Sefer Hasidim*, no. 145 and no. 530; and see also no. 324.

18. See John Kekes, "Morality and Impartiality," *American Philosophical Quarterly* 18, no. 4 (October 1981): 301. To be clear, Kekes is fiercely opposed to impartiality as a moral ideal that should apply in every circumstance. John Cottingham, also an opponent of impartialism, explains that "the intuition underlying impartialism is that 'ethical' considerations are opposed to 'self-interested' ones." John Cottingham, "Ethics and Impartiality," *Philosophical Studies* 43, no. 1 (January 1983): 84.

19. Kurt Baier, *The Moral Point of View: A Rational Basis of Ethics* (Ithaca, NY: Cornell University Press, 1958), 201.

20. I borrow the phrasing from Kekes, "Morality and Impartiality," 295.

21. For the idea of an "impartial spectator," see Adam Smith, *The Theory of Moral Sentiments* (1759); for the purposes of this discussion, see especially part III, ch. 3.

22. Peter Singer, *Practical Ethics*, 2nd ed. (Cambridge: Cambridge University Press, 1993), 12, 13.

23. Singer, *Practical Ethics*, 233.

24. To be fair, many (most) impartialists take a far more nuanced view of special relations than Singer does. They tend to argue that impartiality is required for *justifying moral principles* but not for *deliberating about moral decisions* in everyday life. For a powerful example of this type of approach (from a Kantian philosopher), see Marcia Baron, "Impartiality and Friendship," *Ethics* 101, no. 4 (July 1991): 836–57. We do well to keep in mind Gene Outka's observation that in modern discussions, "impartiality is not one determinate view, but a class of views." Gene Outka, "Universal Love and Impartiality," in *The Love Commandments: Essays in Christian Ethics and Moral Philosophy*, ed. Edmund Santurri and William Werpehowski (Washington, D.C.: Georgetown University Press, 1992), 74. I nevertheless cite Singer here both because of the wide reach of his views and because the contrast allows me to more clearly draw out the perspective(s) I find in Jewish ethics.

25. John Cottingham, "Partiality, Favouritism, and Morality," *The Philosophical Quarterly* 36, no. 144 (July 1986): 357–58.

26. Cottingham, "Partiality, Favoritism, and Morality," 357. For an argument similar to Cottingham's, see Andrew Oldenquist, "Loyalties," *The Journal of Philosophy* 79, no. 4 (April 1982): 186–87. The case Cottingham describes is about people stuck in a burning building, only one of whom we can save. It is thus a parallel case to Singer's, though their arguments are diametrically opposed.

27. Bernard Williams, "Persons, Character, and Morality," in *Moral Luck: Philo-*

sophical Papers 1973–1980 (Cambridge: Cambridge University Press, 1981); passage cited is on p. 14.

28. In the same vein, John Cottingham writes that "if each day I was to consider how each moment could best be spent furthering, for example, global utility, without according any special priority to the fact that certain projects are the ones in which *I* am involved, it seems that I would disintegrate as an individual. For I would be obliged to drop any activity or project in which I was engaged whenever another project presented itself whose contribution to the general utility was marginally greater." Cottingham, "Partiality, Favouritism, and Morality," 365.

29. This argument would be available to rule-utilitarians, at least. Of course, true partialists would deem rule-utilitarian justifications of (some) partiality too weak, because such utilitarians arguably see the value of family primarily in instrumental terms, thus reducing what partialists view as an intrinsic good to a merely pragmatic device through which one goes about fulfilling what are at bottom universal duties.

30. Williams, "Persons, Character, and Morality," 18. Marilyn Friedman encapsulates Williams's position thus: "A self who is too heavily encumbered with impartialist moral responsibilities to treat everyone with equal consideration will be alienated from close others and from her own self because she won't have time for her most fundamental, integrity-conferring relationships and projects." Marilyn Friedman, "The Social Self and the Partiality Debates," in *Feminist Ethics*, ed. Claudia Card (Lawrence: University Press of Kansas, 1991), 166. It's worth noting that the same philosophers who criticize Singer's approach to ethics for demanding too much of us sometimes also criticize Williams's for demanding too little. See, for example, Michael Slote, *Morals from Motives* (Oxford: Oxford University Press, 2001), 73.

31. My interpretation of Williams's argument is heavily influenced by Susan Wolf, "'One Thought Too Many': Love, Morality, and the Ordering of Commitment," in *The Variety of Values: Essays on Morality, Meaning, and Love* (Oxford: Oxford University Press, 2015), 143–62. This is of a piece with Wolf's influential—but controversial—argument that the good life and the moral life are not identical, that is, that a good life is committed to the realization of nonmoral values in addition to—and sometimes over against—moral ones. See Susan Wolf, "Moral Saints," in *The Variety of Values*, 11–29.

32. For criticism of Williams (and others) for not allowing adequate space for partiality and particularism as essential to morality itself, see, for example, Lawrence Blum, *Moral Perception and Particularity* (Cambridge: Cambridge University Press, 1994), 16.

33. As Friedman explains, "Close relationships call . . . for personal concern, loyalty, interest, passion, and responsiveness to the uniqueness of loved ones, to their specific needs, interests, history, and so on. In a word, personal relationships call for partiality rather than impartiality." M. Friedman, "The Social Self and the Partiality Debates," 163.

34. Cottingham, "Partiality, Favoritism, and Morality," 369.

35. Cottingham, "Ethics and Impartiality," 90. More fully: "A world in which I accorded everyone at large the same sort of consideration which I accord to myself, my children and my friends would not be 'one big happy family'; it would be a world in which affection no longer existed because the sense of 'specialness' had been eliminated. It would [thus] be a world where much of what gives human life preciousness and significance had disappeared."

36. In this context, it is worth noting the bioethicist John Hardwig's powerful observation that almost all ethical theories depersonalize personal relationships and thus "do violence to what these relationships are; to what is characteristically and normatively going on in them; and to the intentions, desires, and hopes we have in becoming involved in them." Hardwig, "In Search of an Ethics of Personal Relationships," 15–16.

37. Mishnah Sanhedrin 4:5.

38. Williams, "Persons, Character, and Morality," 15.

39. Feminist theorists have been particularly insistent upon the irreducibly social or relational constitution of the self. To take just one example, Nel Noddings writes that "the self is a relation. It is constituted in encounters with other selves and with objects and events in the world." Noddings, *Starting at Home*, 116.

40. As Stephen Post writes, parental love is "at the very center of any adequate ethics because the memories of caring, comfort, and sustenance are carried by the child throughout life, and without these memories there is little hope for the moral life." Stephen G. Post, *Spheres of Love: Toward a New Ethics of the Family* (Dallas: Southern Methodist University Press, 1994), 18.

41. Oldenquist, "Loyalties," 181.

42. John Benson, "Duty and the Beast," *Philosophy* 53, no. 206 (October 1978): 536.

43. And yet we should be honest about how rare a genuine balance between particularistic commitments and obligations, on the one hand, and universal, cosmopolitan concerns, on the other, really is. On this see also Martha Nussbaum on the challenge that Stoicism poses, in Nussbaum, *Cosmopolitanism*, 94.

44. Stephen J. Pope, "The Order of Love and Recent Catholic Ethics: A Constructive Proposal," *Theological Studies* 52, no. 2 (June 1991): 269, 275.

45. BT, Avodah Zarah 3a.

46. Yet see Rabbi Yosef Engel (1859–1920), *Atvan De-Oraita*, Principle (Kelal) 13, who maintains that this principle only applies to mitzvot between a person and God. As for interpersonal mitzvot, an obligation can stand whether or not people are able to fulfill it. It is worth exploring whether R. Engel would hold this view in a case where human nature itself makes something impossible as opposed to one in which a particular person is unable to fulfill an obligation because her individual circumstances render that impossible (*ones*). I am grateful to Akiva Mattenson for the reference.

47. R. Meir Simhah of Dvinsk, *Meshekh Hokhmah* to Genesis 9:7.

48. Pope, "The Order of Love," 278.

49. Needless to say, what's true of family is often true of friends too: friends first can also easily devolve into friends only.

50. Mary Midgley, "The Concept of Beastliness," *Philosophy* 48, no. 184 (April 1973): 125.

51. Mary Midgley, *Beast and Man: The Roots of Human Nature* (Ithaca, NY: Cornell University Press, 1978), 51–57, 331–44.

52. Pope, "The Order of Love," 277. Pope's formulation is based on a famous declaration by E. O. Wilson to the same effect.

53. Post, *Spheres of Love*, 12.

54. As the ethicist Don Browning nicely puts it, "Love for the remote other entails . . . building on, not repressing, natural kin affections." Don Browning, "Altruism and Christian Love," *Zygon* 27, no. 4 (December 1992): 434.

55. BT, Hullin 61a.

56. Nahmanides, commentary to Leviticus 11:13.

57. BT, Hullin 63a.

58. Bunim Ye'ushson, *Me-Otzareinu Ha-Yashan*, vol. 2, Shemot and Vayikra (Tel-Aviv: Mofet, 1977), 281.

59. Marilyn Friedman, "The Practice of Partiality," *Ethics* 101 (July 1991): 829. It's striking that this particular argument of Friedman's is focused on justice for potential givers rather than potential recipients.

60. M. Friedman, "The Practice of Partiality," 830.

61. Although I will not elaborate upon this here, it seems clear to me that our obligations to distant others run even deeper. We are tied to other, faraway people not just because of shared humanity but also through what one writer refers to as "the interdependence of contemporary global economic, social and political institutions." Marian Barnes, *Care in Everyday Life: An Ethic of Care in Practice* (Chicago: Policy Press, 2012), 108. Some would argue that our duties extend still deeper, since, they maintain, the suffering of many distant others is caused, or at least exacerbated, by choices made by people in prosperous industrialized nations. "By shaping and enforcing the social conditions that, foreseeably and avoidably, cause the monumental suffering of global poverty," one political philosopher writes, "we are *harming* the global poor." Thomas Pogge, "A Cosmopolitan Perspective on the Global Economic Order," in *The Political Philosophy of Cosmopolitanism*, ed. Gillian Brock and Harry Brighouse (Cambridge: Cambridge University Press, 2005), 93.

62. Gene Outka, *Agape: An Ethical Analysis* (New Haven, CT: Yale University Press, 1972). The comment about regard for people "qua human existent[s]" is at p. 9.

63. Stephen J. Pope, "The Moral Centrality of Natural Priorities: A Thomistic Alternative to 'Equal Regard,'" *The Annual of the Society of Christian Ethics* 10 (1990): 110. But Pope appears to take a somewhat more nuanced, less critical view of Outka's ethics in Stephen J. Pope, "'Equal Regard' Versus 'Special Relations? Reaffirming the Inclusiveness of Agape," *The Journal of Religion* 77, no. 3 (July 1997): 353–79. In this latter essay, Pope finds significant "convergence" between advocates and critics of equal regard.

64. On this see Daniel Boyarin, *A Radical Jew: Paul and the Politics of Jewish Identity* (Berkeley: University of California Press, 1997), 232–33, and Shai Held,

"A Torah for All? Universalism and Its Dangers," in *The Heart of Torah*, vol. 2, pp. 98–102. We will return to this in chapter 14.

65. The moral philosopher Virginia Held writes: "Though the hunger of our own children comes before the hunger of children we do not know, the hunger of children in Africa ought to come before some of the expensive amusements we may feel like providing for our own children." Virginia Held, *Feminist Morality: Transforming Culture, Society, and Politics* (Chicago: University of Chicago Press, 1993), 74. More generally, Stephen Post writes: "A problem of injustice arises when special relations sap our resources and energies at the cost of huge distributional inequalities between the haves and the have-nots . . . Justice requires a considerable degree of impartiality." Post, *Spheres of Love*, 137.

66. I'm sad to say that John Hardwig's frank admission that "the issues about the extent to which one can legitimately favor those to whom one is personally related are, for me, deeply troubling and almost impenetrable to my ethical insight" resonates deeply with me. Hardwig, *Is There a Duty to Die?*, 26. But let me emphasize again: the difficulty of the question is not an excuse for hiding from it altogether.

67. Other modern rabbinic thinkers posit something similar. To take one example, Rabbi Shlomo Schneider argues both that "love your neighbor" refers to fellow Jews and that there is also an obligation to love all human beings because this is simply what ethics (*musar*) requires. In terms similar to R. Emden's, R. Schneider explains the Talmudic teaching that Jews are obligated to live in a way that is "pleasing to all human beings," by saying that "all human beings are the work of God's hands and each of them is created in the image of God." Although R. Schneider's distinction calls for more conceptual elaboration than he offers, he argues that love of non-Jews is an obligation, even though it is not a distinct biblical commandment. Rabbi Shlomo Schneider, *Divrei Shlomo*, no. 121.

68. This despite the fact that, as Andrew Oldenquist observes, "It is likely that loyalties ground more of the principled, self-sacrificing, and other kinds of non-selfish behavior in which people engage than do moral principles and ideals." The implication of this, Oldenquist says, is that "Anglo-American philosophy has ignored an important area of the normative." Oldenquist, "Loyalties," 173.

69. David Miller, "Reasonable Partiality Towards Compatriots," *Ethical Theory and Moral Practice* 8, no. 1–2 (January 2005): 64–65.

70. In a similar vein, Oldenquist writes that "racism is usually dependent on the ignorance of the nature of race differences and on hostile, false claims about other races. Family, community, and civic loyalties seldom have those features . . ." Oldenquist, "Loyalties," 176–77. The believer can insist that religious loyalties are in this sense akin to family, community, and civic loyalties, but the skeptic will point out that the history of religion positively overflows with examples of ignorance of, and hostile, false claims about, other people of other religions, and of no religion.

71. D. Miller, "Reasonable Partiality Towards Compatriots," 66–67. To critics who say that patriotism is beyond the moral pale because it involves "differen-

tial treatment of insiders and outsiders—people who are part of the nation [or people, or even community] get benefits that are not provided to foreigners [or others more generally]," Miller responds that the objection is question-begging, since "what is at stake is precisely whether we can legitimately owe special duties to compatriots." If we can, then giving preference to some (Jews, say) over others (non-Jews) is no more problematic than giving preference to some (relatives) over others (strangers). See D. Miller, "Reasonable Partiality Towards Compatriots," 70.

72. D. Miller, "Reasonable Partiality Towards Compatriots," 66.

73. D. Miller, "Reasonable Partiality Towards Compatriots," 68.

74. See, along very similar lines, D. Miller, "Reasonable Partiality Towards Compatriots," 69.

75. D. Miller, "Reasonable Partiality Towards Compatriots," 72–73. For an attempt to tease out how people might establish priorities between (different types of) human rights claims and more local duties, see pp. 72–77. Whether and how this discussion would be relevant to a religious-ethnic group like Jews as opposed to members of a distinct political nation-state is a difficult question best left for another day.

76. And yet I'd insist that morally speaking, it is more difficult to defend pure ethnic priority than it is group loyalty based on common purpose and shared ideals. A comment from Andrew Oldenquist is perhaps helpful in clarifying my point: "A loyalty defines a moral community in terms of a conception of a common good and a special commitment to the members of the group who share this good." Oldenquist, "Loyalties," 177.

77. Shira Kupfer and Asaf Turgeman argue convincingly that in classical Jewish sources *ahavat yisrael* refers to love of Jews rather than "the Jewish people." Shira Kupfer and Asaf Turgeman, "The Secularization of the Idea of Ahavat Israel and Its Illumination of the Scholem-Arendt Correspondence on Eichmann in Jerusalem," *Modern Judaism* 34, no. 2 (May 2014): 188–209; see especially 190–94. I am grateful to Raphael Magarik for bringing this study to my attention. Note especially how Maimonides formulates the commandment in *Mishneh Torah, Hilkhot De'ot*, 6:3, and note also the version presented in Alter Hilavitz, *Lilshonot Ha-Rambam: Mehkarim U-Verurim* (Jerusalem: Mossad Ha-Rav Kook, 1970), 24, where Maimonides speaks of love of "*haveiro*," his friend, rather than "*Yisrael*," Israel.

78. Sa'adia Gaon, *The Book of Beliefs and Opinions*, III:7.

79. On this see Igor Primoratz, "Patriotism and Morality: Mapping the Terrain," in *Patriotism: Philosophical and Political Perspectives*, ed. Igor Primoratz and Aleksandar Pavković (Aldershot, England: Ashgate, 2005), 20. It's also worth noting Albert Camus's words, written to a former friend who had become a devoted Nazi: "If at times we seemed to prefer justice to our country, this is because we simply wanted to love our country in justice, as we wanted to love her in truth and in hope." Albert Camus, "Letters to a German Friend," in *Resistance, Rebellion, and Death*, trans. Justin O'Brien (New York: Knopf, 1961), 10. I am

grateful to Professor Lawrence Kaplan for directing me to Camus's extraordinary letters.

80. Compare the concluding sentence of Robert Audi, "Nationalism, Patriotism, and Cosmopolitanism in an Age of Globalization," *Journal of Ethics* 13, no. 4 (October 2009): 365–81: "The only kind of patriotism that is morally justifiable is one leavened by loyalty to the community of all peoples" (380).

81. Cited, for example, in Primoratz, "Patriotism and Morality," 25. The saying is attributed to the German American politician Carl Schurz (1829–1906), in a speech in the US Senate in 1872.

82. What the political theorist Stephen Macedo says about patriotism can be extended to all group loyalties: "The dangers of patriotism make it highly tempting to, and could justify simply denying, that patriotism is ever a virtue. [Yet] ordinary people can see that there is something to be said for patriotism. The best and safest course is to acknowledge the truth that there can be a just patriotism, while also recognizing its inherent dangers, and to seek to elicit greater awareness of both its dangers and the stringent conditions that must be met before it can be warranted." Stephen Macedo, "Just Patriotism?," *Philosophy and Social Criticism* 37, no. 4 (May 2011), 414. For an example of just such a patriotism, articulated and defended in real time, see Camus, "Letters to a German Friend." Camus writes movingly on his yearning to "debase nothing for [his country's] sake" (10).

83. D. Miller, "Reasonable Partiality Towards Compatriots," 79. Martha Nussbaum's comments about nationalism are also potentially helpful here. "Most people," she writes, "tend toward narrowness of sympathy. They can easily become immured in narcissistic projects and forget about the needs of those outside their narrow circle. Emotions directed at the nation and its goals are frequently of great help in getting people to think larger thoughts and recommit themselves to a larger common good." For Nussbaum, national sentiment is a "fulcrum . . . on which we leverage universal love of humanity." Nussbaum, *Political Emotions*, 3, 69. It's critical to note, though, that Nussbaum warns against the danger of grounding the nation on "a racial or ethnic identity" (69).

84. I borrow this phrase from Cottingham, "Partiality, Favouritism, and Morality," 372.

7. Human Dignity and Solidarity

1. Sifra Kedoshim 2; PT, Nedarim 9:4; and Genesis Rabbah 24:7.

2. David Frankel, *Korban Ha-Edah* to PT, Nedarim 9:4.

3. David Frankel, *Korban Ha-Edah* to PT, Nedarim 9:4.

4. Philosophers tend to speak of dignity in two very different ways. There are "aristocratic" or "comparative" conceptions of human dignity, on the one hand, and "egalitarian and non-comparative" conceptions, on the other. According to the first conception, some people have more dignity than others on the basis of their unique talents, excellences, or what have you. According to the second conception, in contrast, all human beings have equal dignity, regardless of what

talents or excellences they may or may not have. As the philosopher Adam Pelser explains, on the egalitarian conception, "Human dignity is understood as a kind of inherent value or worthiness of respect that is a property of all people, not in virtue of their comparative social status, but rather in virtue of their moral status as persons." See Adam Pelser, "Respect for Human Dignity as an Emotion and Virtue," *Res Philosophica* 92, no. 4 (October 2015): 744. In the same vein, note also Stephen Darwall's classic distinction between "recognition respect" (owed equally to all), on the one hand, and "appraisal respect" (variable), on the other. Stephen Darwall, "Two Kinds of Respect," *Ethics* 88, no. 1 (October 1977): 36–49. And note also Gilbert Meilaender, "Human Dignity: Exploring and Explicating the Council's Vision," in *Human Dignity and Bioethics: Essays Commissioned by the President's Council on Bioethics*, ed. Edmund D. Pellegrino, Adam Schulman, and Thomas W. Merrill (Notre Dame, IN: Notre Dame Press, 2009), 253–77. It is with egalitarian, noncomparative dignity that I am concerned in this chapter.

5. For an influential modern probing of the nature of the debate between these two eminent sages, see Leon Roth, "Moralization and Demoralization in Jewish Ethics," in Leon Roth, *Is There a Jewish Philosophy: Rethinking Fundamentals* (Oxford: Littman, 1999), 133–36. Roth's essay goes in a different direction than the one I pursue here.

6. For a very useful discussion of kings as images of gods in the ancient Near East, see Bernard F. Batto, "The Divine Sovereign: The Image of God in the Priestly Creation Account," in *David and Zion: Biblical Studies in Honor of J. J. M. Roberts*, ed. Bernard F. Batto and Kathryn L. Roberts (Winona Lake, IN: Eisenbrauns, 2004), 143–86.

7. See J. Richard Middleton, *The Liberating Image: The Imago Dei in Genesis 1* (Grand Rapids, MI: Brazos, 2005), 205. Some scholars interpret the democratization of the image of God idea as suggesting full and universal human equality. For one example, see Robert K. Gnuse, "An Overlooked Message: The Critique of Kings and Affirmation of Equality in the Primeval History," *Biblical Theology Bulletin* 36 (Winter 2006): 146–53 (see especially p. 147). Though I am sympathetic to such readings, I am not sure that they are quite right. After all, the Bible does recognize that there are greater and lesser kings in the world. More cautiously, I think we can say that the democratization of *tzelem Elohim* takes a highly significant step toward human equality (and even that the next step toward full equality is not in fact such a large one) but is not yet an argument for full equality. For discussions on this point over the years, I am grateful to Richard Middleton, Benjamin Sommer, and Jon Levenson.

8. This is the theology of Genesis 1; it is not the theology of the royal psalms, for example, which celebrate God's appointment of King David to rule over Israel. See, for example, Psalms 2, 89, and 110, and contrast Psalm 8, which echoes and develops the theology of Genesis 1; and see the discussion in Batto, "The Divine Sovereign," 183–85.

9. See especially Psalm 72 for a vision of what is expected of royalty, and

Ezekiel 34 for vehement condemnation of kings who fail to live up to their obligations.

10. The point I am making is that solicitous concern for the vulnerable is central to what it means to be appointed God's vice-regent on earth, not that it is the entirety of what the appointment means. Human beings are also supposed to make the world habitable for themselves. The challenge, of course, is how to do that without running roughshod over the rest of creation.

11. For an extended discussion, see Shai Held, "Created in God's Image: Ruling for God," in *The Heart of Torah*, vol. 1, pp. 7–11. And see R. Abraham Ibn Ezra, commentary to Psalm 115:16.

12. James Limburg, "Who Cares for the Earth? Psalm Eight and the Environment," in *All Things New: Essays in Honor of Roy A. Harrisville*, ed. Arland J. Hultgren, Donald H. Juel, and Jack D. Kingsbury (St. Paul, MN: Word and World, Luther Northwestern Theological Seminary, 1992), 50.

13. Richard Lints, *Identity and Idolatry: The Image of God and Its Inversion* (Downers Grove, IL: InterVarsity Press, 2015), 70–71.

14. Joshua A. Berman, *Created Equal: How the Bible Broke with Ancient Political Thought* (Oxford: Oxford University Press, 2008), 41, 47, 49. In contemporary parlance, the word "egalitarian" often connotes equality among genders. Berman uses it in the more general sense of suggesting equality among people. For the problems with describing the Torah as egalitarian precisely from the perspective of gender analysis, see below.

15. Joshua A. Berman, "*Created Equal*: Main Claims and Methodological Assumptions," *Journal of Hebrew Scriptures* 10 (2010): 8, 7.

16. Berman, "*Created Equal*," 13.

17. See the sources cited in Saul M. Olyan, "Equality and Inequality in the Socio-Political Visions of the Pentateuch's Sources," *Journal of Hebrew Scriptures* 10 (2010): 40.

18. Saul M. Olyan, "Equality and Inequality," 40. Olyan writes that "there is a greater degree of inequality and privilege manifest in Deuteronomy's social and religious vision than Berman acknowledges. Women, resident aliens, and others, though part of the covenant community, have a distinctly inferior status to that of the male head of household as indicated by the privileges the text assigns to him." The Bible scholar Susan Ackerman puts it more acidly: "In Israel, it turns out, only men—indeed . . . only some men—are created equal." Susan Ackerman, "Only Men Are Created Equal," *Journal of Hebrew Scriptures* 10 (2010): 16. Ackerman's point is well-taken, but in light of the gender egalitarian nature of Genesis 1, we might wish to say that for the Torah, all humans are created equal (or almost equal—see note 7, above) and that the covenant contains an egalitarianizing thrust even as it upholds strict gender hierarchies. This is less lapidary, I acknowledge, but also more accurate in my assessment. For Berman's response to gender-based critique of his work, see Joshua A. Berman, "A Response: Three Points of Methodology," *Journal of Hebrew Scriptures* 10 (2010): 48–49. For critiques of Berman's thesis along historical-critical lines,

see Olyan, "Equality and Inequality," 36–37; and Bernard M. Levinson, "The Bible's Break with Ancient Political Thought to Promote Equality—'It Ain't Necessarily So,'" *The Journal of Theological Studies* 61, no. 2 (October 2010): 685–94.

19. Abraham Joshua Heschel, "Religion and Race," in *The Insecurity of Freedom*, 95. I have changed the word "man" to "the person."

20. For "image" (*tzelem*), see, e.g., Numbers 33:52; 2 Kings 11:18; Amos 5:26; Ezekiel 7:20; and 2 Chronicles 23:17; for "likeness" (*demut*), see Isaiah 40:18.

21. Walter Brueggemann, *Genesis* (Atlanta: Westminster John Knox Press, 1982), 32. See also Henri Blocher, *In the Beginning: The Opening Chapters of Genesis*, trans. David G. Preston (Downers Grove, IL: InterVarsity Press, 1984), 86; and Lints, *Identity and Idolatry*, 82.

22. The Semitic philologist Mayer Gruber argues that the correct translation of *tzelem Elohim*, usually rendered as "image of God," is in fact "statue of God." Mayer I. Gruber, "Tzelem Elohim—What Is It?" (Hebrew), in *Teshurah Li-Shmuel: Mehkarim Be-Olam Ha-Mikra*, ed. Tsiporah Ṭalshir, Shamir Yonah, and Daniel Siyan (Beer-Sheba: Ben-Gurion University, 2001), 81–87, especially 83, 86. Thus Genesis 1:27 would read: "And God created the human being as [God's] statue, as God's statue God created him, male and female God created them."

23. See Lints, *Image and Identity*, especially 76–77, 82.

24. Thorkild Jacobsen, "The Graven Image," in *Ancient Israelite Religion: Essays in Honor of Frank Moore Cross*, ed. Patrick Miller, Paul D. Hanson, and S. Dean McBride (Philadelphia: Fortress, 1987), 23. Jacobsen warns that we should not think of "a vessel filled with a different content" or "a body with a god incarnate in it." Rather, he argues, "we must think . . . in terms of a purely mystic unity, the statue mystically becoming what it represents, the god, without, however, in any way limiting the god, who remains transcendent" (22). Of course, a good definition of precisely what Jacobsen means by "mystic" would be helpful. But perhaps the elusiveness and mysteriousness of precisely what takes place here is constitutive of the phenomenon in question.

25. Stephen L. Herring, *Divine Substitution: Humanity as the Manifestation of Deity in the Hebrew Bible and the Ancient Near East* (Gottingen: Vandenhoeck and Ruprecht, 2013), 117.

26. Benjamin D. Sommer, *The Bodies of God and the World of Ancient Israel* (Cambridge: Cambridge University Press, 2009), 70.

27. Herring, *Divine Substitution*, 95.

28. Historically speaking, one of the most crucial ramifications of all this is that it likely enabled the people to hold on to the presence of God even in exile. Scholars argue that the idea of humanity being created in the image of God was not a particular point of emphasis in Jewish theology during the period when the Second Temple stood. Perhaps the people didn't need that belief in quite the same way when there was a concrete edifice that was believed to house God's presence. But in the wake of the Second Temple's destruction, the idea of humanity

created in God's image took pride of place in Jewish theology and ethics. For the early Talmudic sages, the human being was considered an "icon" of God, and thus, as in Genesis 1 itself, was seen as containing God within. God was understood to be present within the icon that represented God—that is, within the human being. God was seen as transcendent but also immanent—and not just immanent *around* us but also immanent *within* us. See Yair Lorberbaum, "From Temple to Person: Changes in the Locus of Holiness in Rabbinic Literature" (Hebrew), *Da'at* 86 (2018): 377–98. On the Rabbinic theology of the icon in its ancient context, see Yair Lorberbaum, *In God's Image: Myth, Theology, and Law in Classical Judaism* (Cambridge: Cambridge University Press, 2015), especially 156–94 (and throughout). For the relative unimportance of the idea in Second Temple times, see Lorberbaum, "From Temple to Person," 388–91.

29. The original source of this midrash, cited often in Musar literature, is to the best of my knowledge unknown. This midrash is, the Musar leader Rabbi Yehezkel Levenstein writes, "the singular foundation of the entire Torah." R. Yehezkel Levenstein, *Or Yehezkel* (1988 ed.), vol. 4, p. 113. For two different approaches to what it meant by "with pleasantness" (*be-nahat ruah*), see, on the one hand, Rabbi Eliyahu Dessler, *Mikhtav Mi-Eliyahu*, vol. 5, p. 236 (the one who crowns does so wholeheartedly and without ambivalence, and therefore "with pleasantness"), and Rabbi Elijah of Vilna (Gra, 1720–1797), *Iggeret Ha-Gra*, on the other (one who crowns the other brings him joy, or "pleasantness"). For a brief discussion of these sources, see n.a., *Hovat Ha-Adam Be-Olamo, vol. 8, Hadrakhot Ma'asiyot Le-Tikkun Middat Ha-Kavod* (n.p., c. 2000), 131–32.

30. Levenstein, *Or Yehezkel*, vol. 4, pp. 118–19, 172. Stressing both the centrality and the intensity of the demand, R. Yeruham Levovitz writes that the question of whether we treat others like kings is meant literally (*devarim kifshutan mamash*): "'Did you make your friend sovereign over you with pleasantness?' is literally to make him a king, to stand before him as one would before a king. There is no hyperbole here . . ." R. Yeruham Levovitz, *Da'at Hokhmah U-Musar*, vol. 2, p. 35.

31. R. Yeruham Levovitz, *Da'at Hokhmah U-Musar*, vol. 1, pp. 195–96. In a very different vein, the notion of image as shadow can also be used to emphasize our radical dependence on God, since "the shadow itself is nothing without its connection to what lies behind it." See David Novak, *Natural Law in Judaism* (Cambridge: Cambridge University Press, 2008), 171. In truth, the same idea could be derived from the word "image" itself. As the French theologian Henri Blocher points out, "An image is only an image. It is not the original, nor is it anything without the original. Mankind's being an image stresses the radical nature of his dependence." Blocher, *In the Beginning*, 82.

32. See, for example, Rabbi Hayyim of Volozhin, *Ruah Hayyim* to Avot 4:1.

33. R. Eliyahu Lopian, *Lev Eliyahu*, vol. 2, p. 215.

34. R. Yeruham Levovitz, *Da'at Hokhmah U-Musar*, vol. 1, p. 260. In a similar vein, Rabbi Judah Loew of Prague (Maharal) writes that "treating others with

respect is the very essence of life." Maharal, *Hiddushei Aggadot* to Yevamot 62b, s.v. *ve-khulan meitu.*

35. R. Yeruham Levovitz, *Da'at Hokhmah U-Musar*, vol. 1, p. 260.

36. Rabbi Joseph B. Soloveitchik, *Yemei Zikaron*, 9.

37. BT, Berakhot 28b. He also used to instruct his students to "let the honor of your fellow be as precious to you as your own" (Avot 2:10).

38. Mishnah, Avot 4:15.

39. BT, Berakhot 17a, about Rabbi Yohanan ben Zakkai.

40. BT, Berakhot 6b. The proof text cited in the Talmud is Isaiah 3:14, which specifically mentions robbing the poor. Rashi, s.v. *gezeilat ha-ani*, explains that not greeting people who have so little is particularly egregious—and, perhaps we should add, particularly common. Rabbi Eliyahu Dessler poignantly observes that "the poor person has nothing left save his self-respect, and if you take that from him by showing contempt for his feelings, there is no greater robbery than that." *Mikhtav Me-Eliyahu*, vol. 4, p. 247.

41. R. Elyahu Dessler, *Mikhtav Me-Eliyahu*, vol. 4, p. 246.

42. Mishnah, Avot 1:15.

43. Mishnah, Avot 3:12.

44. Rabbi Baruch Ha-Levi Epstein (1860–1941), *Barukh She-Amar* to *Pirkei Avot* (Tel-Aviv: Am Olam, 1930) 3:12, pp. 117–19.

45. For an example of an approach such as this one, see Rabbi Moshe Hayyim Luzzatto (1707–1746), *Mesilat Yesharim*, ch. 7 and 23.

46. R. Chaim Shmuelevitz, *Sihot Musar*, no. 37, p. 157.

47. See the commentary of Rabbi Obadiah of Bertinoro to Mishnah, Avot 1:15.

48. R. Asher ben Yehiel, *Orhot Hayyim Le-Ha-Rosh*, no. 57. See also R. Chaim Friedlander, *Siftei Hayyim: Middot Ve-Avodat HaShem*, vol. 1, p. 314.

49. BT, Ketubot 111b.

50. As R. Friedlander puts it, "Attention is our greatest need." R. Chaim Friedlander, *Siftei Hayyim: Middot Ve-Avodat HaShem*, vol. 1, p. 315.

51. Dillon, "Respect and Care," 128.

52. BT, Bava Metzia 59a. Commenting on this, Rabbi Eliyahu Dessler notes that Rabbi Yohanan, the sage in question, was a major scholar and the leader of the generation, yet even though he was undoubtedly burdened by many thoughts and worries, he never failed to greet others. Busyness and hurriedness do not exempt us from the obligation. R. Eliyahu Dessler, *Mikhtav Me-Eliyahu*, vol. 4, p. 246.

53. See, for example, Rabbi Isaac Alfasi (Rif, 1013–1103) commentary to BT, Bava Metzia 59a; Tosafot to BT, Sotah 10b, s.v. *noah*; and Rabbeinu Yonah Gerondi, *The Gates of Repentance*, 3:139.

54. What the philosopher Allen Wood writes about Immanuel Kant's ethics could just as well have been written about Jewish ethics: "Proper expression of respect . . . surely is a contextual matter; it is not evident that it could be reduced to any set of rules or generalizations . . . It might instead be something that has to be apprehended in each set of particular circumstances, perhaps by a sort of

educated moral perception." Allen Wood, *Kant's Ethical Thought* (Cambridge: Cambridge University Press, 1999), 150–51. The striking implication of Wood's argument is that Kant should be understood as a moral particularist (151).

Karen Stohr explains that "for Aristotle the exercise of virtue is a complex skill, involving both appropriate emotional attunement (the job of the moral virtues) and correct judgment honed through experience (the job of practical wisdom)." Karen Stohr, "Feminist Virtue Ethics," in *The Routledge Companion to Virtue Ethics*, ed. Lorraine L. Besser and Michael Slote (New York, Routledge, 2015), 276. Jonathan Jacobs asserts that in contrast to Aristotle, Maimonides does not recognize practical wisdom as a virtue. On his account, the role phronesis plays for Aristotle is played for Maimonides by the divinely revealed Law. Jonathan Jacobs, "The Ethics of Perfection and the Perfection of Ethics," *American Catholic Philosophical Quarterly* 76, no. 1 (2002): 149–52. In making this case, Jacobs has been preceded by Marvin Fox (whom he does not mention). See Martin Fox, *Interpreting Maimonides: Studies in Methodology, Metaphysics, and Moral Philosophy* (Chicago: University of Chicago Press, 1990), 115–18. This approach is mistaken, because it advocates for an implausible view of what law (even divine law) can do, a view that Maimonides himself explicitly rejects. See *Guide of the Perplexed*, 3:34. Much more convincing on this issue is Lawrence Kaplan, "An Introduction to Maimonides's 'Eight Chapters,'" *Edah Journal* 2, no. 2 (2002): 11–17. I am grateful to Professor Kaplan for our exchange on this point.

55. Tzvi Yavrov, *Ma'seh Ish: Toldot Hayyav Ve-Hanhagotav Shel Ha-Adam Ha-Gadol Ba-Anakim Rabban shel Yisrael Ha-Gaon He-Hasid Meran Rabbeinu Avraham Yeshayahu Karelitz* (Bnei Brak: n.p., 1999), 166.

56. Commenting on the verse, Rabbi Meir Leibush Weiser (Malbim) writes that God has created the world in such a way that the wealthy are intended, and expected, to help support the destitute. When they refuse that role, they create the mistaken impression that God has created the poor but then abandoned them to their fate. Conversely, one who gives to the impoverished honors God by living up to the divine expectation that the rich will support the poor. Malbim, Commentary to Proverbs 14:31.

57. Richard J. Clifford, *Proverbs: A Commentary* (Louisville, KY: Westminster John Knox Press, 1999), 147. It's possible to suggest that the disrespect shown to God is in flouting God's command. See Mordecai Zer-Kavod and Yehudah Kil, *Sefer Mishlei* (Jerusalem: Mosad HaRav Kook, 1983), 89. But I think Clifford's interpretation is more convincing.

58. On this see R. N. Whybray, *Proverbs* (London: Marshall Pickering, 1994), 223.

59. More literally, the verse could be translated as "rich and poor meet (*nifgashu*); the Lord is Maker of them all." But the text likely means to suggest that rich and poor meet "in a figurative sense, as equals in the sight of God." R. N. Whybray, *Wealth and Poverty in the Book of Proverbs* (Sheffield: Sheffield Academic Press, 1990), 41. In the same vein, see also Proverbs 29:13: "The poor and the oppressor have this in common: the Lord gives light to the eyes of both." The implication of the two verses (Proverbs 22:2 and 29:13) is that not only are we

equal in some ultimate sense, we are also equally vulnerable. The wealthy, no less than the impoverished, are "contingent beings who wholly depend on God for life and livelihood." Duane A. Garrett, *Proverbs, Ecclesiastes, Songs of Songs* (Nashville: B&H, 1993), 186. An awareness of shared vulnerability shatters any illusions of superiority—or ought to.

60. R. N. Whybray, *The Book of Proverbs* (Cambridge: Cambridge University Press, 1972), 85. Bruce Waltke observes that in Proverbs, "the creation of humankind functions as the philosophical basis for social ethics." Bruce K. Waltke, *The Book of Proverbs: Chapters 1–15* (Grand Rapids, MI: Eerdmans, 2004), 607. See also Ellen F. Davis, *Proverbs, Ecclesiastes, and Song of Songs* (Louisville, KY: Westminster John Knox Press, 2000), 95.

61. The verse concludes: "[God] will repay his due." See the statement of Rabbi Yohanan in BT, Bava Batra 10a. The point here is not to suggest a quid pro quo, as if one should assist the poor so that one will be rewarded; rather, "the underlying thought is that generosity is a characteristic of a person who is righteous . . . [and that] righteousness is, and ought to be, materially rewarded." Whybray, *Proverbs*, 282.

62. Rabbeinu Bahya ben Asher (1255–1340), commentary to Proverbs 19:17, based on Sifre Deuteronomy, Ekev 49.

63. Midrash Tehillim to Psalm 50:8. See also Midrash Tannaim to Deuteronomy 15:9 (D. Z. Hoffman edition), 83.

64. Davis, *Proverbs, Ecclesiastes, and Song of Songs*, 95.

65. Rabbinic tradition continues in much the same vein. The Talmud recounts a disturbing story about the sage Rabbi Elazar b. Rabbi Simeon, who was riding his donkey when he passed a man the Talmud describes as "exceedingly ugly." The man greets R. Elazar, but rather than reciprocate the greeting, the sage responds, "Empty One, how ugly you are! Are all your fellow citizens as ugly as you are?" The man replies, "I do not know, but go and tell the Craftsman who made me, 'How ugly is the vessel You have made.'" Realizing how poorly he has behaved, R. Elazar prostrates himself before the man and begs him for forgiveness. The man demurs, insisting that he will not forgive the sage until he goes to God and declares, "How ugly is the vessel You have made." BT, Ta'anit 20a–20b. To insult a person is to sin against and offend their Maker. In a more particularistic mode, the Talmudic sage Rabbi Hanina declares that "one who smacks an Israelite on the jaw, is as though she had assaulted the *shekhinah* [divine presence]." BT, Sanhedrin 58b, based on a homiletical interpretation of Proverbs 20:25.

66. See Isaiah 57:15: "For thus said He who high aloft forever dwells, whose name is holy: 'I dwell on high, in holiness; yet with the contrite and the lowly in spirit—reviving the spirits of the lowly, reviving the hearts of the contrite." And see also Rashi there, and R. Eliyahu Lopian, *Lev Eliyahu*, vol. 2, p. 220.

67. Translating this phrase, and the verse as a whole, is difficult—Hagar might be saying "You are the God of seeing," but the effect is the same in either case.

68. For this translation, see Rashi to Exodus 22:25, s.v. *im havol tahbol*; and Tigay, "Exodus," 157.

69. Durham, *Exodus*, 329. Walter Brueggemann, in contrast, sees this law as intended "to make the daily pick up and return of collateral so inconvenient that the need for collateral is waived." Walter Brueggemann, *Deuteronomy* (Nashville: Abingdon, 2001), 238.

70. See also Deuteronomy 24:12–13.

71. Tigay, "Exodus," 157.

72. That the Israelites did not always live up to these norms is made explicit by the prophet Amos, who lambastes the wealthy for "reclining . . . on garments taken as collateral" (Amos 2:8).

73. Speaking of Deuteronomy as a whole, the Bible scholar Patrick Miller observes that "the subordination of economic proprieties to the protection of basic need is . . . deemed to be an explicit indicator of righteousness before God on the part of members of the community" (see Deuteronomy 24:13). Patrick D. Miller, *Deuteronomy* (Louisville, KY: Westminster John Knox Press, 1990), 173.

74. Of course, the Torah's appeal to the poor person's power to elicit God's response arguably only underscores her lack of concrete political and economic power.

75. Maimonides, *Mishneh Torah, Hilkhot De'ot*, 6:10.

76. Maimonides, *Mishneh Torah*, Laws of Gifts to the Poor, 10:4, expanding upon Avot DeRabbi Natan 13:4. In the same spirit, see Rabbi Isaac's comments about speaking kindly to the poor in BT, Bava Batra 9b.

77. R. Meir Leibush Weiser (Malbim), commentary to Isaiah 58:10. See also, in a similar vein, Gary V. Smith, *Isaiah 40–66* (Nashville: B&H, 2009), 582.

78. For arguments that human rights need God as a foundation, among human rights theorists see Michael J. Perry, *The Idea of Human Rights: Four Inquiries* (New York: Oxford University Press, 2000), 11–41; among philosophers, see especially Nicholas Wolterstorff, *Justice: Rights and Wrongs* (Princeton, NJ: Princeton University Press, 2008), especially part III; for a much shorter presentation of many of the most salient points in Wolterstorff's arguments, see Nicholas Wolterstorff, "Can Human Rights Survive Secularization?," *Villanova Law Review* 54, no. 3 (2009): 411–20; and for a much more popular, accessible presentation, see Nicholas P. Wolterstorff, *Journey Toward Justice: Personal Encounters in the Global South* (Grand Rapids, MI: Baker, 2013), especially chapters 6–12; among Christian apologists, see Paul Copan, "Grounding Human Rights: Naturalism's Failure and Biblical Theism's Success," in *Legitimizing Human Rights: Secular and Religious Perspectives*, ed. Angus J. L. Menuge (Burlington, VT: Ashgate, 2013), 11–31; and among theologians, see Max L. Stackhouse, "Why Human Rights Need God: A Christian Perspective," in *Does Human Rights Need God?*, ed. Elizabeth M. Bucar and Barbra Barnett (Grand Rapids, MI: Eerdmans, 2005), 25–40.

79. Wolterstorff, *Justice: Rights and Wrongs*, 360.

80. Wolterstorff, *Journey Toward Justice*, 55, 54, 55.

81. David Novak makes a similar point in David Novak, "God and Human Rights in a Secular Society: A Biblical-Talmudic Perspective," in *Does Human Rights Need God?*, 50–54.

82. Gili Zivan, "'Have You Murdered and Also Taken Possession?!' (1 Kings 21:19): The Gains and Losses of Basing Human Rights Discourse in the Bible," in *Religion and the Discourse of Human Rights*, ed. Hanoch Dagan, Shahar Lifshitz, and Yedidia Z. Stern (Jerusalem: Israel Democracy Institute, 2014), 306. Of course, the Talmud softens many of the harder edges of biblical law, but as Zivan notes, "Even in the Talmud, in spite of greater leniency, there are still halakhic concepts that contradict the most basic intuitions of human rights discourse, such as the attitude toward women, minors, the deaf, and those with mental disabilities" (307).

83. For a richer and more sophisticated account than I have space for here of how this integration-negotiation might take place, see Zivan, "Have You Murdered?"

84. In the Babylonian Enuma Elish, for example, the god Marduk concludes creation by constructing the city of Babylon and its temple. See Alexander Heidel, *The Babylonian Genesis*, 2nd ed. (Chicago: University of Chicago Press, 1951), 48.

85. Jon D. Levenson, "The Universal Horizon of Biblical Particularism," in *Ethnicity and the Bible*, ed. Mark G. Brett (Leiden: Brill, 1996), 147. Levenson adds that Genesis 1 serves as "a formidable obstacle to any attempt to mix Judaism and racism."

86. I have developed an interpretation of Genesis 11 along these lines in "People Have Names: The Torah's Takedown of Totalitarianism," in *The Heart of Torah*, vol. 1, pp. 16–20. For an important modern commentator who interprets similarly (and whose commentary serves as the basis of "People Have Names"), see Rabbi Naftali Tzvi Yehudah Berlin (Netziv, 1816–1893), *Ha'amek Davar* to Genesis 11.

87. See Heschel, "Religion and Race," 86–87; and Sarna, *Genesis*, 13.

88. In an important essay, the philosopher David Wiggins writes about "the solidarity of the human qua human" and describes it as prereflective and preethical, a "primitive prohibitive aversion" to cruelty and inhumanity. This kind of solidarity, he argues, is the phenomenological root of concern for human rights. See David Wiggins, "Solidarity and the Root of the Ethical," *Tijdschrift voor Filosofie* 71, no. 2 (2009): 239–69. For specific references, see pp. 241, 247, 241, n1, and 262, n30. The notion of solidarity I develop here goes somewhat further, incorporating more positive obligations to achieve human rights and create the possibility of flourishing for all (for Wiggins, the "demands of human solidarity" are "mostly prohibitive" [264]). Hence my talk of "cultivating" solidarity. What I have in mind might be described as deepening and expanding upon what Wiggins insists is primally present in all of us.

89. Kristen Renwick Monroe, "John Donne's People: Explaining Differences Between Rational Actors and Altruists Through Cognitive Frameworks," *Journal of Politics* 53, no. 2 (May 1991): 427, 428.

90. Or at least human solidarity in the sense that I intend. As Wiggins and many others observe, the term has been used extremely widely to signify a vast variety of phenomena. See Wiggins, "Solidarity," 242–43.

91. Monroe, "John Donne's People," 427.

92. On sharing food with the poor, see, in the same vein, Job 31:16–17.

93. See, for example, Rashi's commentary to Isaiah 58:7, s.v. *u-mi-besarkha*.

94. R. Meir Leibush Weiser (Malbim), commentary to Isaiah 58:7.

95. Martin Luther King Jr., *The Measure of a Man* (Minneapolis, MN: Fortress, 1988), 48–49.

96. This paragraph is heavily indebted to Meghan Clark, "Anatomy of a Social Virtue: Solidarity and Corresponding Vices," *Political Theology* 15, no. 1 (January 2014): 36. I realize, of course, that I have not offered detailed guidance as to precisely what solidarity—or even a commitment to human rights more generally—requires of us. How much tzedakah, political activism, etc., are we obligated to engage in? The truth is that I am honestly not sure. I have more confidence about the thrust of human solidarity than I do about its concrete manifestations. I hope to return to this question, and I hope that I will learn from my readers.

97. Statistics in this paragraph are taken from "11 Facts About Global Poverty," DoSomething, https://www.dosomething.org/us/facts/11-facts-about-global-poverty, accessed 10/17/21.

98. Daniel G. Groody, CSC, "Globalizing Solidarity: Christian Anthropology and the Challenge of Human Liberation," *Theological Studies* 69 (June 2008): 255, presenting the perspective of the liberation theologian Ignacio Ellacuria. See also Clark, "Anatomy of a Social Virtue," 30. Genuine altruism is also humble, and we must be cautious that proposed solutions to entrenched problems do not inadvertently do more harm than good.

99. Immanuel Kant, *The Doctrine of Virtue*, trans. Mary Gregor (Philadelphia: Penn State University, 1964), 116. For reasons of space, I cannot get into this here, but Kant appears to be talking not about our feelings but about the maxims of our actions. The maxim of benevolence (which Kant considers love) draws us near, whereas the maxim of respect calls for distance. On this see Marcia W. Baron, "Love and Respect in the Doctrine of Virtue," *The Southern Journal of Philosophy* 36 (1997): 32.

100. See, most influentially, Baron, "Love and Respect in the Doctrine of Virtue," 29.

101. For an argument along similar lines based in Jewish legal sources, see Rabbi Raphael Reuven Stohl, *Sefer Torat Ha-Kavod* (n.p., 2019), 156. But compare the discussion beginning at p. 177.

102. For a nice description of this, see the commentary of R. Moshe Alsheikh to Leviticus 19:9. In addition, Jewish law contains a series of positive obligations we have in tending to dead bodies (and Jewish law treats the dignity of the dead, *kevod ha-met*, as a branch of human dignity more generally).

103. Tanna de-Be Eliyahu, ch. 28, end.

104. For an example of a thinker understanding the mandate as fundamentally about respect, see R. Jacob Emden (Yaavetz), *Birat Migdal Oz*, *Derekh Eretz*, ch. 3. For an eloquent voice interpreting it as a category of love, see R. Chaim Friedlander, *Siftei Hayyim: Middot Ve-Avodat HaShem*, 314–19. R. Friedlander writes that greeting people with a warm smile is not "some derivative branch of the attribute of hesed, but is rather the essence of the obligation of hesed" (315).

In a related vein, the philosopher Marcia Baron argues that one of the problems with Kant's presentation of love and respect as opposing forces is that in fact (at least as Baron sees it) love and respect are not "all that different in what they call for." Baron, "Love and Respect," 32.

105. On this see n.a., *Hovat Ha-Adam Be-Olamo, vol. 8: Hadrakhot Ma'asiyot Le-Hitkadmut Be-Midat Kevod Atzmo U-khvod Havero*, 2nd ed. (no publication information), 24.

106. Maimonides (Rambam), *Mishneh Torah, Hilkhot De'ot* 6:3.

107. Baron, "Love and Respect," 42. Note also Daniel Engster's observation about how respect is a virtue of care. By respect he means "the recognition that others are worthy of our attention and responsiveness, are presumed capable of understanding and expressing their needs, and are not lesser beings just because they have needs they cannot meet on their own." Daniel Engster, *The Heart of Justice* 31.

108. See above, n4, for a brief discussion of this critical distinction.

109. See, for example, Baron, "Love and Respect," 42.

110. It would be interesting to compare the conception of respect I begin to develop here with the philosopher Robin Dillon's provocative attempt to wed respect and care into something she calls "care respect." Care, on Dillon's conception, is "one kind of respect rather than a disparate rival for our moral allegiance." See Dillon, "Respect and Care," 107.

111. Pelser, "Respect for Human Dignity as an Emotion and Virtue," 745.

112. R. Shlomo Wolbe, *Alei Shur*, vol. 1, p. 118.

113. Pelser, "Respect for Human Dignity," 746.

114. Robin Dillon describes respect as most centrally a "mode of apprehending something . . . perception is the core of respect." "A person who respects something," she writes, "perceives it quite differently from one who does not respect it and responds to it in light of that perception." Dillon, "Respect and Care," 108.

115. Pelser, "Respect for Human Dignity as an Emotion and Virtue," 746–47.

116. Pelser, "Respect for Human Dignity as an Emotion and Virtue," 757.

8. Loving the Stranger

1. In his commentary to Exodus 22:20, Rashi defines a *ger* as "a person who was not born in a particular land, but rather came from another land to live there" (Rashi to Exodus 22:20). It's important to point out, if only in passing, that not all non-Israelites who find themselves in the land are considered *gerim*. Some, for example, are considered *nokhrim* ("foreigners"), who are not afforded the same kind of solicitous treatment as are *gerim*. Compare, for example, the different approaches to charging interest in Leviticus 25:35–37 (*ger*), on the one hand, and Deuteronomy 15:3 (*nokhri*), on the other. Scholars suggest that whereas the *ger* sees the land where he is sojourning as his new home for an extended period of time, the *nokhri* does not. See, for example, James K. Hoffmeier, *The Immigration Crisis: Immigrants, Aliens, and the Bible* (Wheaton, IL: Crossway, 2009), 50. The *nokhri* may well be a trader or merchant who is in the land for the purposes of business; in no sense is he making it his home. It is permissible to charge him

(but not the *ger*) interest, since "if [he] borrow[s], it [is] for business and not to survive poverty." Tigay, "Exodus," 157. On the difficulty of interpreting Leviticus 25:35, see Rolf Rendtorff, "The Ger in the Priestly Laws of the Pentateuch," in *Ethnicity and the Bible*, ed. Mark G. Brett (Boston: Brill, 2002), 80, n6.

2. Mark R. Glanville, *Adopting the Stranger as Kindred in Deuteronomy* (Atlanta: SBL Press, 2018), 250.

3. This is widely accepted among Bible scholars. See, for example, Milgrom, *Leviticus 17–22*, 1627; Tigay, "Exodus," 157; M. Daniel Carroll R., *Christians at the Border: Immigration, the Church, and the Bible* (Grand Rapids, MI: Baker Academic, 2008), 102; and Hans-Georg Wuench, "The Stranger in God's Land—Foreigner, Stranger, Guest: What Can We Learn from Israel's Attitude Towards Strangers," *Old Testament Essays* 27, no. 3 (January 2014): pp. 1129–54 (see pp. 1136–37 for a comparison to Assyria). For the dissenting view that "the laws protecting and providing for the sojourner were not unique to Israel," see Patrick D. Miller, "Israel as Host to Strangers," in Patrick D. Miller, *Israelite Religion and Biblical Theology: Collected Essays* (Sheffield: Sheffield Academic Press, 2000), 562. Unfortunately, Miller does not offer evidence for his claim. For a possible exception, see the Hittite example cited in Moshe Weinfeld, *Deuteronomy 1–11: A New Translation with Introduction and Commentary* (New York: Doubleday, 1991), 439.

4. Georges Chawkat Moucarry suggests that the word *ger* is often coupled with a verb from the same root (e.g., "*vekhi* yagur *itkha* ger," "if a sojourner sojourns with you"—Exodus 12:48) in order to "emphasize the nature of the foreigner's life in Israel" in all its precariousness and vulnerability. Georges Chawkat Moucarry, "The Alien According to the Torah," *Themelios* 14, no. 1 (October/November 1988): 17. For additional examples of the coupling, see Leviticus 16:29; 17:8, 10, 12; 18:26, and the verses cited in Moucarry, 20, n5.

5. "The feelings of the stranger" is the NJPS rendering of "*nefesh ha-ger*." *Nefesh* here likely does not mean "soul," as in later Rabbinic Hebrew, but something more like "life" or "being"—Israel is told that "you know the life of the stranger," hence NJPS's more idiomatic "feelings." NIV translates similarly: "Do not oppress a foreigner; you yourselves know how it feels to be foreigners, because you were foreigners in Egypt."

6. See also Exodus 22:20: "You shall not wrong a stranger or oppress him, for you were strangers in the land of Egypt."

7. See Rabbi Eliyahu Mizrahi (c. 1455–c. 1525), commentary to Exodus 22:20: "Your having been strangers is not the reason that you may not wrong or oppress the stranger." The Jewish philosopher Lenn Goodman writes that "God lets historic memory do the work abstraction might have missed." Lenn Evan Goodman, *Judaism: A Contemporary Philosophical Investigation* (New York: Routledge, 2017), 21. Note also Martha Nussbaum's observation that "good public emotions [like empathy] . . . embody general principles, but they clothe them in the garb of concrete narrative history." Nussbaum, *Political Emotions*, 201; see also p. 10.

8. But see R. Mizrahi to Deuteronomy 10:18 and R. Judah Loew of Prague (Maharal), *Gur Aryeh* to Deuteronomy 10:19, who insist that the mandate to love the

stranger also does not derive from Israel's experience of having been strangers in Egypt.

9. Interestingly, the Bible scholar Markus Zehnder notes that "the noun *ger* is not attested in the feminine, and is never explicitly used to refer to a woman." What this means is not really clear. As Zehnder notes, the absence of the feminine noun "does not exclude the possibility that there might have been women included in the category of *ger* . . . The matter is difficult to decide." Markus Zehnder, *The Bible and Immigration: A Critical and Empirical Reassessment* (Eugene, OR: Pickwick, 2021), 32. For speculation that women may have at times constituted the majority of *gerim*, see Glanville, *Adopting the Stranger as Kindred*, 230. Taking a cautious approach, I will use male pronouns to describe the *ger* in this chapter. In the modern world, in any case, whatever lessons we think we can take from the biblical approach to *gerim* would of course apply to people regardless of gender.

10. On this see M. Daniel Carroll R., "Welcoming the Stranger: Toward a Theology of Immigration in Deuteronomy," in *For Our Good Always: Studies on the Message and Influence of Deuteronomy in Honor of Daniel I. Block*, ed. Jason S. DeRouchie et al. (Winona Lake, IN: Eisenbrauns, 2013), 451.

11. I discuss circumcision of the heart in Shai Held, "Will and Grace, Or: Who Will Circumcise Our Hearts" in *The Heart of Torah*, vol. 2, pp. 220–24.

12. Carroll, "Welcoming the Stranger," 151.

13. I allude in this sentence to Elaine Scarry's contention that "the problem with discussions of 'the other' is that they characteristically emphasize generous imaginings [that is, the powerful seeing the powerless in generous ways], and thus allow the fate of another person to be contingent on the generosity and wisdom of the imaginer." Scarry emphasizes that generous imaginings of the foreigner must be coupled with "constitutional solutions." Elaine Scarry, "The Difficulty in Imagining Other People," in Martha Nussbaum et al., *For Love of Country: Debating the Limits of Patriotism* (Boston: Beacon, 1996), 99, 106.

14. Deuteronomy 24:14–15.

15. Gleanings: Leviticus 19:9–10, 23:22; Deuteronomy 24:19–22. Tithes: Deuteronomy 26:12.

16. Wuench argues that in circumcising himself, the stranger "voluntarily cross[es] the line separating [him] from the people of Israel." Wuench, "The Stranger in God's Land," 1146. This may help explain how it was possible for the term *ger* to evolve from meaning "stranger" or "sojourner" to meaning "proselyte" or "convert." For the question of whether the *ger*'s circumcision constitutes his conversion, see the brief discussion in Wuench, "The Stranger in God's Land," 1146, n62. When I first began to write this chapter, I considered translating *ger* somewhat colloquially as "outsider." But as my research deepened and I considered just how hard the Torah works to integrate the *ger* into Israelite society, I realized that this was not an appropriate rendering. If anything, I think *ger* might be better rendered as "partial insider" or some such. A similar approach is taken by Israel Knohl, "The Election and Sanctity of Israel in the Hebrew Bible," in *Judaism's Challenge: Election, Divine Love, and Human Enmity*, ed. Alon Goshen-Gottstein (Boston: Academic Studies Press, 2020), 9–12.

17. Exodus 12:48. Wuench notes that *gerim* being permitted to make their own sacrifice "shows that they are not only viewed as a person who is dependent on an Israelite, but may also have a household of their own." Wuench, "The Stranger in God's Land," 1146.

18. Exodus 12:19.

19. Leviticus 16: 29–30.

20. Exodus 20:8–11; Deuteronomy 5:12–15. For an accessible presentation of these and other laws aimed at including and protecting the *ger*, see Hoffmeier, *The Immigration Crisis*, 84–96.

21. In characterizing the inclusion of the stranger in Israelite society, appeal is sometimes made to Exodus 12:49: "There should be one law for the native-born and for the stranger who dwells among you." (See also Leviticus 24:22; Numbers 9:14; 15:14–16, 29.) But as Jeffrey Tigay points out, "In each of these instances strangers and Israelites follow the same specific procedure; it is not a general rule covering all cases." That said, "in later halakhic exegesis, when '*ger*' is understood as proselyte [more on this below], this verse is understood as prescribing equality between proselytes and born Jews with respect to all the laws of the Torah." Tigay, "Exodus," 131. See Mekhilta, Pisha 15 (not 14, as cited in Tigay), end.

22. There are exceptions. For example, as the laws of the Passover sacrifice, mentioned in the previous paragraph, indicate, there were some religious laws that pertained only to those strangers who chose to partake in them. (Yet according to Exodus 12:19, the stranger must obey the prohibition on eating leavened bread [*hametz*] on Passover regardless of whether he brings a Passover sacrifice.) In addition, there were some religious laws from which strangers were exempt (see, for example, Deuteronomy 14:21, but compare Leviticus 17:15–16).

23. Carroll, *Christians at the Border*, 111. More strongly, Markus Zehnder speaks of the *ger*'s "willingness to assimilate on all levels." Zehnder, *The Bible and Immigration*, 21.

24. For some examples of traditional Bible commentators who were quite clear that the plain sense of *ger* is not a convert, see Rabbi Abraham Ibn Ezra, commentary to Exodus 22:18–23, and Rabbi Abraham Maimonides (Avraham ben Ha-Rambam, 1186–1237) to Exodus 22:20. See also Rabbi Israel Meir (Ha-Kohen) Kagan (The Hafetz Hayyim), *Sefer Ha-Mitzvot HaKatzar*, cited in Zvi Zohar, "You Shall Not Oppress the *Ger*—To Whom Does This Norm Apply Today Under Jewish Law?" (Hebrew) (unpublished paper), 24, accessed at https://www.academia.edu/31992998/You_Shall_Not_Oppress_the_Ger_%E2%80%94_To_Whom_Does_This_Norm_Apply_Today_Under_Jewish_Law. Accessed 10/17/21.

25. For the question of *when* the biblical term *ger* began to refer to a convert, see the concise but useful discussion in Zohar, "You Shall Not Oppress," 10–12.

26. Zohar, "You Shall Not Oppress," 12.

27. The fact that, as we've seen, the *ger* was historically included in Israelite religious ceremonies presumably made this transition in meaning from "stranger" to "convert" more possible and plausible.

28. See the commentaries of Rabbi Abraham Ibn Ezra and Rabbi Isaac Abravanel to Leviticus 19:14; as well as Rabbi Meir Simhah Ha-Kohen of Dvinsk, *Meshekh Hokhmah* to Leviticus 19:14, and Rabbi Baruch Ha-Levi Epstein, *Torah Temimah* to Leviticus 19:14, no. 80; and the additional sources marshaled by Zohar, "You Shall Not Oppress," 28, n99. All the sources cited in this note are brought in Zohar's highly illuminating study.

29. For an additional halakhic example where the literal meaning of a biblical verse retains halakhic validity alongside its more common metaphorical interpretation, see the discussion of "not eating any living thing in its blood" (Leviticus 19:26) in Zohar, "You Shall Not Oppress," 28–29.

30. Carroll, "Theology of Immigration," 450.

31. Peter Enns, *Exodus* (Grand Rapids, MI: Zondervan, 2000), 452.

32. Walter Brueggemann, "A New Creation—After the Sigh," 91. See pp. 91–92 for a beautiful illustration of some of what this "anti-Egypt" (my term, not Brueggemann's) is intended to look like.

33. I explore this law and its implications in great detail in "Let Him Live Wherever He Chooses, Or: Why Runaway Slaves Are Like God," in *The Heart of Torah*, volume 2, pp. 250–54. This paragraph and the next are adapted from there.

34. Patrick D. Miller, *Deuteronomy* (Louisville: Westminster John Knox Press, 1990), 172.

35. P. D. Miller, "Israel as Host," 553.

36. Genesis 12:10–20. See also 17:8; 20:1; 21:34; 23:4.

37. Isaac: 35:27; 37:1; Jacob: 28:4; 32:5. Jacob's sons, too, are strangers—in Egypt (Genesis 47:4). The book of Psalms remembers a time when all three of Israel's patriarchs—Abraham, Isaac, and Jacob—were "strangers" wandering the land of Canaan long before their descendants took possession of it (Psalm 105:12–13).

38. Scholars disagree about what Moses is referring to when, living in Midian, he speaks of his sojourn in a strange land. Is he referring to his time in Egypt or to his current residence in Midian? Or might the text be "purposely ambiguous, both Midian and Egypt"? For the first view (Egypt), see Durham, *Exodus*, 24; for the second (Midian), see Hamilton, *Exodus*, 38–39, as well as the commentary of Rabbi Hezekiah ben Manoah (Hizkuni) to Exodus 2:22; for the third (conscious ambiguity), see Fretheim, *Exodus*, 42.

39. P. D. Miller, "Israel as Host," 553.

40. P. D Miller, "Israel as Host," 554.

41. P. D. Miller, "Israel as Host," 556.

42. The brutal inhospitality of the Sodomites (chapter 19) is set in stark and deliberate contrast with the gracious hospitality of Abraham (Genesis 18).

43. For subjective, first-person evocations of being a stranger before God, see also 1 Chronicles 29:15; Psalm 39:13; and Psalm 119:19 (as well as the comments of Rabbi David Kimhi [Radak] to this verse). The stranger could not own land in Israel; since Israel also could not in any ultimate sense own land either, it too is a kind of stranger. See Wuench, "The Stranger in God's Land," 1148; and Rendtorff, "The Ger in the Priestly Laws," 79.

44. As the Israeli philosopher Avi Sagi nicely puts it, existentially, being a *ger* "is not necessarily preempted by being an *ezrah* [a native-born person]." Avi Sagi, *Reflections on Identity: The Jewish Case*, trans. Batya Stein (Brighton, MA: Academic Studies Press, 2016), 154.

45. The Bible scholar Jay Sklar explains what is at stake in these verses: "The Lord was going to give land to each of the tribes (Joshua 13–21). The danger, however, was that prospering tribes would buy more and more land and cause economic disparity among the Lord's people. [God] therefore prohibits the permanent sale of land (v. 23); the Israelites were always to have the right to redeem the land at any time (v. 24). If they could not afford to do so, the land would still return to its owner in the jubilee (v. 28), giving a fresh start to those who had suffered financially." Sklar, *Leviticus*, 303. In other words, the people are reminded of their own dependence on God precisely in the context of laws being laid down to aid those who have become destitute and dependent. Know your own vulnerability, the text hopes, and you will be committed to kindness to the vulnerable.

46. See F. Charles Fensham, "Widow, Orphan, and the Poor in Ancient Near Eastern Legal and Wisdom Literature," *Journal of Near Eastern Studies* 21, no. 2 (April 1962): 129–39. For parallels in Tanakh, see, for example, Ezekiel 34 and Psalm 72.

47. Middleton, *The Liberating Image*, 121, 27.

48. See what I have written about responsibility for the widow and the orphan in "Hearing the Cries of the Defenseless, Or: We Are All Responsible," in *The Heart of Torah*, vol. 1, pp. 179–83; and see especially the shorter commentary of R. Abraham Ibn Ezra to Exodus 22:21–23.

49. Judaism, the philosopher Emmanuel Levinas writes, is "a consciousness of irremissible responsibilities." Emmanuel Levinas, *Beyond the Verse: Talmudic Readings and Lectures* (Bloomington: University Press, 1984), 9.

50. Take a fascinating contemporary example: Two devoutly Christian Bible scholars have recently written books that attempt to discern what a biblical approach to contemporary immigration issues might look like. The main thrust of one book is that the biblical *ger* is a legal immigrant, "a person who entered Israel and followed legal procedures to obtain recognized standing as a resident alien"; a *ger*, it is said, "might be likened in America to the holder of a green card." By this logic, under no circumstances does an illegal immigrant qualify as a *ger*. Hoffmeier, *The Immigration Crisis*, 52, 57. The advice of the other book is that we focus not on the legal status of the immigrant but on her status as a "disadvantaged person." Carroll, "Welcoming the Stranger," 457, encapsulating one key assumption of his *Christians at the Border*. Both books are somewhat problematic in my view. Hoffmeier does not wrestle with the question of unjust laws, does not evince much compassion for those fleeing dire circumstances in their homelands, and does not give any thought at all to possible differences, say, between immigrants seeking economic opportunity and refugees escaping a genocide. Carroll, on the other hand, dismisses the evidence Hoffmeier presents without meaningfully grappling with whether illegal immigrants should

be treated differently from legal ones. In the same spirit as Hoffmeier, see also Zehnder, *The Bible and Immigration*.

51. See Frank Spina, "Israelites as *Gerim*, 'Sojourners,' in Social and Historical Context," in *The Word of the Lord Shall Go Forth: Essays in Honor of David Noel Freedman in Celebration of His Sixtieth Birthday*, ed. Carol L. Meyers and M. O'Connor (Winona Lake, IN: Eisenbrauns,1983), 325; and Francis Brown, with S. R. Driver and Charles A. Briggs, *The Brown-Driver-Briggs Hebrew and English Lexicon* (BDB) (n.p.: Hendrickson, 2010; originally published 1906), 158 (*gur* II). There are cognates in Aramaic and Ugaritic. I am grateful to Professor Ed Greenstein for our exchange on this point.

52. Again, my focus in this chapter is on how the native-born ought to treat the immigrant. From the other side, we could talk about a willingness to integrate and even assimilate, as I discuss above.

53. This idea is key to Hasidic understandings of Passover.

54. Volf, *The End of Memory*, 34, 89.

55. Volf, *The End of Memory*, 31.

56. See, similarly, Volf, *The End of Memory*, 105.

57. Volf, *The End of Memory*, 25.

58. As Volf writes, "If salvation lies in memory of wrong suffered, it must lie more in what we do with those memories than in the memories themselves." Volf, *End of Memory*, 26.

59. Elie Wiesel and Richard D. Heffner, *Conversations with Elie Wiesel*, ed. Thomas J. Vincigoerra (New York: Schocken, 2001), 144–45, cited in Volf, *The End of Memory*, 34. It is also worth remembering that, as the historian Jacques LeGoff notes, "the commemoration of the past was carried to new heights in Nazi Germany and fascist Italy." Jacques LeGoff, cited in Tzvetan Todorov, "The Uses and Abuses of Memory," trans. Lucy Golsan, in Howard Marchitello, *What Happens to History? The Renewal of Ethics in Contemporary Thought* (New York: Routledge, 2001), 14.

60. Or, for that matter, that since someone else was our enemy once, he or she must remain our enemy forever. One of the most disturbing ideas in the Torah is the insistence that Amalek, having attacked the stragglers in Israel's camp as they wandered through the wilderness, is to be considered an eternal enemy of God, and wiped out as a result (see Exodus 17:8–16 and Deuteronomy 25:17–19). It is one thing to abhor Amalek's inhumanity; it is quite another to condemn all Amalekites, present and future, as eternal enemies of God. This is, needless to say, a very different—and very troubling—use of memory. I have offered some tentative reflections on how a variety of voices within the Jewish tradition have coped with these difficult texts in "Combating Cruelty: Amalek Within and Without," *The Heart of Torah*, vol. 2, pp. 255–59.

61. Consider that Abraham and Sarah, who, as we've seen, had been vulnerable strangers in Egypt (Genesis 12), soon find themselves oppressing an Egyptian maidservant by the name of Hagar—a woman whose very name seems to mean "the stranger" (*ha-ger*) (Genesis 16).

62. More generally, Rabbi Eliyahu Lopian underscores how critical it is for a religious

person to know their own heart. R. Lopian admits that deep knowledge of our own hearts is rare, but he warns: "Don't delude yourself that if you hide from your heart, damage will not ensue." R. Eliyahu Lopian, *Lev Eliyahu*, vol. 2, pp. 53–54.

63. Albert Camus, *The Rebel: An Essay on Man in Revolt*, trans. Anthony Bower (New York: Knopf, 1956), 301. I am reminded of the philosopher John Cottingham's observation that "given the pervasive opacity of the passions—the way in which they so often mislead us . . . any recipe for the good life that fails to find room for systematic self-scrutiny and reflective analysis . . . will be bound to be seriously impoverished." John Cottingham, *The Spiritual Dimension: Religion, Philosophy, and Human Value* (Cambridge: Cambridge University Press, 2005), 74.

64. Christina Feldman, *Compassion: Listening to the Cries of the World* (Berkeley: Rodmell, 2005), 28.

65. Marc Ian Barasch, *The Compassionate Life: Walking the Path of Kindness* (San Francisco: Berrett-Koehler Publishers, 2014), 7.

66. Along similar lines, see Volf, *The End of Memory*, 25.

9. Must We Love Our Enemies Too?

1. Ron Rosenbaum, *Explaining Hitler* (New York: HarperPerennial, 1998), xii.

2. Seeing an enemy in need, we may be tempted to turn away. So concerned is Jewish law with making sure that we do not succumb to this temptation (see Sifrei Deuteronomy, Tetze, 222 and 225) that it insists that helping our enemy with her animal takes precedence over helping our friend with hers. See BT, Bava Metzia 32b, and see also, for example, the commentary of Rabbi Yosef Bekhor Shor (twelfth century) to Exodus 23:4, and the sources gathered in Rabbi Menahem Kasher, *Torah Sheleimah* to Exodus 23:4, no. 47.

3. It's worth noting a fourth possibility, namely that the law's concern is to prevent the unnecessary suffering of animals (*tza'ar ba'alei hayyim*). See BT, Bava Metzia 32a–32b. Among modern commentators, see, for example, Robert Alter, *The Five Books of Moses: A Translation with Commentary* (New York: W. W. Norton, 2004), 449. The well-being of the animal may well be *part* of the Torah's concern, but I very much doubt that it is the Torah's *central* (let alone exclusive) concern in this instance. Note Nahum Sarna, who argues that "this case [Exodus 23:5] involves [both] humanitarian considerations and the prevention of cruelty to animals." Nahum M. Sarna, *Exodus* (Philadelphia: Jewish Publication Society, 1989), 142. The Jewish philosopher Lenn Goodman dismisses the idea that concern for animal welfare is in view here; the subject of these laws, he writes, is "love, not animal husbandry." Lenn E. Goodman, *Love Thy Neighbor as Thyself* (Oxford: Oxford University Press, 2008), 27. But Samuel David Luzzatto (Shadal, 1800–1865) bolsters the idea that the well-being of animals is at least partially at issue by noting that in the first case, which does not seem to involve animal suffering, one must intervene only when one "encounters" an enemy's ox, whereas in the second, where the animal is suffering, one must intervene even if one only "sees" the enemy's ox. Samuel David Luzzatto, commentary to Exodus 23:5.

4. See, for example, the interpretations offered by R. Eliezer, R. Yitzhak, and R. Yoshiyah in Mekhilta de-Rabbi Ishmael, Mishpatim 20; and note also Targum Yonatan (Pseudo-Jonathan) to Exodus 23:5, who assumes that the verse describes a case where one person and one person only has witnessed a fellow Israelite committing a grave sin. In all four such cases, there is (or appears to be) a mandate to hate the sinner.

5. In Mekhilta de-Rabbi Ishmael, Mishpatim 20, Rabbi Natan says that "Scripture speaks of a normal Jew [that is, someone you are not commanded to hate but are on the contrary commanded to love]. So what does it mean by 'your enemy'? Rather, if one hits your child, or one who starts a fight with your people, they become a temporary enemy."

6. Targum Onkelos to Exodus 23:5. Emphasis added. See also Targum Yonatan to Exodus 23:5. And see Midrash Lekah Tov, Rabbi Yosef Bekhor Shor, and Hadar Zekeinim on the verse as well.

7. The ambiguity I am pointing to is wonderfully encapsulated in Targum Yonatan: "At that moment you surely must let go of the hatred in your heart for him." The Aramaic phrase used for "at that moment," *be-ha-hih sha'ata*, could in fact mean either "at that moment" or "for that moment." The former interpretation is obviously much more ambitious and ethically and emotionally demanding.

8. Nehama Leibowitz, *New Studies in Shemot (Exodus), Part II: Mishpatim—Pekudei*, trans. Aryeh Newman (Jerusalem: WZO, 1993), 432.

9. R. Yosef Bekhor Shor imagines God addressing the Israelite: "Allow the love you have for Me to triumph over the hate that you have for [your enemy] and help him because of your love for Me." R. Yosef Bekhor Shor, commentary to Leviticus 19:18. Although R. Bekhor Shor does not quite spell this out, it seems that love for God is supposed to elicit good treatment even of those we don't like (God loves them too!), and that peace is then likely to ensue.

10. Midrash Tanhuma (Buber), Mishpatim 1.

11. See Rashi's commentary to Psalm 99:4, where, based on the midrash we have just seen, he notes that God establishes "compromise and the making of peace" among the people of Israel.

12. Benno Jacob, *The Second Book of the Bible: Exodus*, trans. Walter Jacob with Yaakov Elman (Hoboken, NJ: Ktav, 1992), 714–15.

13. Jacob, *Exodus*, 715

14. Enns, *Exodus*, 455.

15. Avot de-Rabbi Natan, Version A, ch. 23.

16. Nahmanides (Ramban), Commentary to Deuteronomy 22:4.

17. The connection between Leviticus 19:18 and Proverbs 20:22 is emphasized in the commentary of Rabbi Menahem Ha-Meiri to Proverbs 20:22. In the same vein as 20:22, see also Proverbs 24:29. These verses represent a kind of Golden Rule in reverse: don't do unto others what they have done unto you. On this see Roland H. Worth Jr., *The Sermon on the Mount: Its Old Testament Roots* (New York: Paulist Press, 1997), 241.

18. Christine Roy Yoder, *Proverbs* (Nashville: Abingdon, 2009), 214.

19. Bruce K. Waltke, *The Book of Proverbs: Chapters 15–31* (Grand Rapids, MI: Eerdmans, 2005), 153. See also Deuteronomy 32:35.

20. See Michael V. Fox, *Proverbs 10–31: A New Translation with Introduction and Commentary* (New York: Doubleday, 2009), 673; and Waltke, *Proverbs*, 153.

21. This is assumed, for example, in the commentary of Rabbeinu Yonah Gerondi to Proverbs 20:22. See also Raymond Van Leeuwen, "The Book of Proverbs: Introduction, Commentary, and Reflections," in *The New Interpreter's Bible*, vol. 5 (Nashville: Abingdon, 1997), 187.

22. Gersonides, Commentary to Proverbs 20:22. See also R. Moshe Alsheikh, Commentary to Proverbs 20:22.

23. Midrash Tehillim, 41:8 Note also that in Exodus Rabbah 26:2, the Talmudic sage Rabbi Meir characterizes repaying evil with good as a form of *imitatio Dei*.

24. Kathleen Anne Farmer, *Who Knows What Is Good? A Commentary on the Books of Proverbs and Ecclesiastes* (Grand Rapids, MI: Eerdmans, 1991), 114.

25. Derek Kidner, *Proverbs* (London: Tyndale, 1964), 155.

26. See R. Menahem Ha-Meiri, Commentary to Proverbs 24:18.

27. Van Leeuwen, "Proverbs," 211. For a medieval Jewish thinker arguing that rejoicing in the suffering of others is "an extremely base character trait," see R. Menahem Ha-Meiri, Commentary to Proverbs 24:18.

28. Fox, *Proverbs 10–31*, 750. See also Worth, *The Sermon on the Mount*, 119. But compare Richard Clifford, who assumes that "the verbs of rejoicing" employed in these verses "imply public displays of joy." Clifford, *Proverbs*, 215.

29. Fox, *Proverbs 10–31*, 750.

30. Yalkut Shimoni, Emor 654; also found in Pesikta de-Rav Kahana, *Naspahim*, appendix 2. See also Yalkut Shimoni, Proverbs 960, which imagines God saying that the Egyptians were indeed God's enemies, and yet God had decreed that "if your enemy falls, do not rejoice." In the context of Kings David and Saul, see Midrash Tehillim, 7.

31. Van Leeuwen, "Proverbs," 211.

32. H. H. Rowley, *Job* (London: Nelson, 1970), 203.

33. David J. A. Clines, *Job 21–37* (Nashville: Thomas Nelson, 2006), 1027.

34. Yoder, *Proverbs*, 241.

35. And yet I wonder whether this verse is meant to be read descriptively, as a characterization of what often *does* happen, in contrast to 24:17–18, which teach what *ought to* happen. For examples of traditional commentators reading 11:10 descriptively, see the commentaries of Rabbi Abraham Ibn Ezra (pseudo-Ibn Ezra) and Gersonides (Ralbag) to the verse.

36. See also, for example, Psalm 52:7–9; 58:11–12; and Job 22:19–20.

37. As the Bible scholar Victor Hamilton nicely notes, "It is one thing to ask God to prepare a table for you in the presence of your enemies (Psalm 23:5). It is another to ask God to give you enough grace to prepare a table for your enemies." Hamilton, *Exodus*, 425.

38. Clifford, *Proverbs*, 126. In this context, see the comments of Rabbi David Kimhi (Radak) to Genesis 16:6, where he condemns Sarah for using the power she wields to strike back at the vulnerable Hagar.

39. R. Menahem Ha-Meiri, commentary to Proverbs 25:22.

40. Van Leeuwen, "Proverbs," p. 220. See also Yoder, *Proverbs*, 252.

41. Farmer, *Who Knows What Is Good?*, 75.

42. Midrash Mishlei (Buber), 25:21–22.

43. Some manuscripts of the midrash, including the one used by Solomon Buber, read "and God will repay him" ("*yeshalemenu lakh*")—that is, punish—him for you. If this is the correct version of the text (which I doubt), then Rabbi Hama envisions God saying, in effect, "You treat him with kindness and I will sentence him later." In light of BT, Sukkah 52a, however where *yeshalem lakh* is read not as *yeshalemenu*, will repay him, but as *yashlimenu*, will cause him to be at peace with you, my sense is that the version I discuss is the correct one.

44. PT, Yoma 1:4, based on Deuteronomy 6:16.

45. BT, Sanhedrin 72a.

46. Reading this passage I am reminded of words written by Coretta Scott King about her husband Dr. Martin Luther King Jr.'s approach to activism. For Dr. King, she writes, nonviolent resistance was "a means of stirring and awakening moral truths in one's opponents, of evoking the humanity that, Martin believed, existed in each of us." Coretta Scott King, "Foreword" to Martin Luther King Jr., *Strength to Love* (Minneapolis, MN: Fortress, 2010; originally published 1963; preface originally published 1981), x.

47. It's worth noting, if only in passing, an interesting parallel between the New Testament and the Talmud. Jesus explains that in loving their enemies, his followers will be "children of your Father in heaven. He causes his sun to rise on the evil and the good, and sends rain on the righteous and the unrighteous." In other words, the extent of God's benevolence is expressed in God's indiscriminate generosity. In the same vein, the Talmudic sage Rabbi Abbahu declares that "the day when rain falls is greater than the day of the Revival of the Dead, for the Revival of the Dead is for the righteous only whereas rain is both for the righteous and for the wicked" (BT, Ta'anit 7a). And note also R. Zadok's characterization of God in Mekhilta de-Rabbi Ishmael, Amalek 1.

48. As D. A. Carson nicely puts it, "The people may have heard . . . [but] they were hearing falsely. The Old Testament Scriptures say, 'Love your neighbor,' but nowhere 'Hate your enemy.'" D. A. Carson, *The Sermon on the Mount: An Evangelical Exposition of Matthew 5–7* (Grand Rapids, MI: Baker, 1978), 52.

49. See, for example, Hans Dieter Betz, *The Sermon on the Mount: A Commentary on the Sermon on the Mount, Including the Sermon on the Plain (Matthew 5:3–7:27 and Luke 6:20–49)* (Minneapolis, MN: Fortress, 1995), 304; and Craig A. Evans, *Matthew* (New York: Cambridge University Press, 2012), 133. Rabbi Meir Soloveichik is thus likely mistaken in asserting that with these words Jesus was "break[ing] with Jewish tradition." Meir Y. Soloveichik, "The Virtue of Hate," *First Things* 130 (February 2003): 42–43.

50. See Dead Sea Scrolls, 1QS 1:3–4, 9–10; 9:21–22. And see, for example, W. D. Davies, *The Sermon on the Mount* (Cambridge: Cambridge University Press, 1966), 146. For an interpretation rejecting this approach, see, for example, Worth, *The Sermon on the Mount*, 124.

51. Ben Witherington III, *Matthew* (Macon, GA: Smyth and Helwys, 2006), 138, 139.

52. See, for example, Dale C. Allison, *Matthew: A Shorter Commentary* (London: T&T Clark, 2004), 84; Worth, *The Sermon on the Mount*, 120; and James L. Bailey, *Contrast Community: Practicing the Sermon on the Mount* (Eugene, OR: Wipf and Stock, 2013), 73. Note also Carl G. Vaught, *The Sermon on the Mount* (Albany, NY: SUNY Press, 1986), 109–110, who writes that what is required is "an act of will, no matter what the affective state of our psyche might be." See also Donald Alfred Hagner, *Matthew*, vol. 2 (Dallas: Thomas Nelson, 1985), 136.

53. "To love one's enemy," writes the Christian philosopher Robert Roberts, is "to cherish him and wish him well . . . from the heart." Roberts, "Unconditional Love and Spiritual Virtues," 162.

54. Allison, *Matthew: A Shorter Commentary*, 82. See also, for example, Hagner, *Matthew*, 131, who writes that "what [Jesus] presents is ethics directed more to conduct at the personal, rather than the societal, level. These directives are for the recipients of the kingdom, not for governmental legislation."

55. BT, Shabbat 88b.

56. The image of turning the other cheek also finds precedent in Isaiah 50:6 and Lamentations 3:30.

57. See, at greater length, my essay "What Can Human Beings Do, and What Can't They? Or, Does the Torah Believe in Progress?," in *The Heart of Torah*, vol. 1, pp. 3–6. As a modern scholar nicely puts it, "In the world in which Israel lived, vengeance was the rule of the day. Here [Israel was] being told that they could exact *nothing more than* justice." Robert L. Cate, *Old Testament Roots for New Testament Faith* (Nashville: Broadman, 1982), 43. But compare Deuteronomy 19:15–21, where the principle of talion seems to have a positive, prescriptive function: just punishment for offenders. I borrow some of the language here from Richard B. Hays, *The Moral Vision of the New Testament: Community, Cross, New Creation* (San Francisco: HarperSanFrancisco, 1986), 325. I had not recognized this challenge in my earlier essay.

    Taking the trajectory of the law further, Rabbinic tradition insists on monetary compensation instead of physical retaliation, and some modern scholars maintain that this was the original intent of the biblical law itself. See BT, Bava Kamma 83b–84a, and Sarna, *Exodus*, 126–27. See also Hamilton, *Exodus*, 386, about how most parts of the law were likely "never enforced."

58. See, perhaps most influentially, John Howard Yoder, *The Politics of Jesus* (Grand Rapids, MI: Eerdmans, 1972). See also Hays, *The Moral Vision*, 317–46.

59. Anna Wierzbicka, *What Did Jesus Mean? Explaining the Sermon on the Mount and the Parables in Simple and Universal Human Concepts* (Oxford: Oxford University Press, 2001), 107.

60. Perhaps most influentially, see Richard A. Horsley, "Ethics and Exegesis: 'Love Your Enemies' and the Doctrine of Non-Violence," *Journal of the American Academy of Religion* 54, no. 1 (Spring 1986): 3–31. For an attempt to rebut Horsley's approach, see Hays, *The Moral Vision*, 328.

61. See, for just one example, Jack R. Lundbom, *Jesus' Sermon on the Mount: Mandating a Better Righteousness* (Minneapolis, MN: Fortress, 2015), 178. For an intriguing argument, according to which Jesus is repudiating violence only in cases where one is humiliated rather than injured, see Worth, *The Sermon on the Mount*, 242. Worth's argument, one shared by many interpreters, is based in part on the fact that the verse deals with an enemy who "slaps" one, a way of humiliating someone rather than seriously wounding them. For slaps as acts of humiliation, see also Mishnah Bava Kamma 8:6.

62. See, for example, Nigel Biggar, *In Defence of War* (Oxford: Oxford University Press, 2013). For an insightful exploration of the issues, see Lisa Sowle Cahill, *Love Your Enemies: Discipleship, Pacifism, and Just War Theory* (Minneapolis, MN: Fortress, 1994). And yet it remains difficult to see just how a doctrine of just war can be reconciled with an absolute mandate to love one's enemies. On this, see Laurie Johnston, "'Love Your Enemies'—Even in the Age of Terrorism?," *Political Theology* 6, no. 1 (January 2005): 87–106, especially at 93.

63. For a fascinating outlying voice, the Hebrew reader may wish to consult the writings of Rabbi Aharon Shmuel Tamares (1869–1931), an impassioned pacifist. A good place to start is Aharon Shmuel Tamares, *Patsifizm le-or Ha-Torah*, ed. Ehud Luz (Jerusalem: Dinur Center, 1992). On violence as a sometimes tragic necessity, see Shai Held, "The Fear of Killing: Jacob's Ethical Legacy," in *The Heart of Torah*, vol. 1, pp. 69–73.

64. Worth, *The Sermon on the Mount*, 122. For all of his attempts to show continuity between the Hebrew Bible and the New Testament, Worth is unable to let go of some extremely derisive stereotypes of the Pharisees. See 55–57.

65. William Klassen, "Love (NT and Early Jewish Literature)," in *The Anchor Bible Dictionary* (New York: Doubleday, 1992), vol. 4, p. 386. In the same vein, the Jewish historian David Flusser characterizes the commandment to love one's enemies as Jesus's "definitive characteristic." David Flusser, *Jesus* (Jerusalem: Magnes, 1997), 88.

66. I agree both with Johannes Nissen's assertion that ample examples of enemy love can be found in Hellenistic Judaism and with his contention that "there is no real parallel [in Jewish sources] to [Jesus's] uncompromising and unconditional message: to be told to love your enemy *as* such, without qualification, goes beyond any known Jewish maxim." Johannes Nissen, "The Distinctive Character of the The New Testament Love Command," 138–40. But in contrast to Nissen and as I have said, I am not sure that Jesus's view represents progress.

67. Robert Funk et al., *The Five Gospels: The Search for the Authentic Words of Jesus* (New York: MacMillan, 1993), 147, cited in Wierzbicka, *What Did Jesus Mean?*, 114. I confess to being somewhat mystified by the Christian writer Jim Forest's statement that "if only we knew our enemies not just for what we think they believe but for who they are, Jesus' commandment to love them would be much easier." Forest, *Loving Our Enemies*, 2. Is this really so? If we really knew who Bashar Assad, or Saddam Hussein, or some other murderous dictator was,

would we really find loving them easier? At a certain point, such people are not separable from the evils they commit; to obfuscate that point is a perilous choice.

68. Note Dietrich Bonhoeffer's observation that "if we took the precept of non-resistance as an ethical blueprint for general application, we should indeed be indulging in idealistic dreams; we should be dreaming of a utopia with laws which the world would never obey." Dietrich Bonhoeffer, *The Cost of Discipleship* (New York: Simon and Schuster, 1995), 144.

69. BT, Pesahim 113b. For a modern rabbinic thinker grappling with this notion that there is a mitzvah to hate sinners and accentuating how much more fundamental love is to Jewish ethics than hate, see Rabbi Moshe Avigdor Amiel (1883–1946), *LiNvukhei Ha-Tekufah*, 3:15.

70. Rabbi Meir Ha-Kohen (thirteenth century), *Hagahot Maimuniyot* to Maimonides, *Mishneh Torah, Hilkhot De'ot*, 6:3.

71. Maimonides, *Mishneh Torah*, Laws of Mourning, 14:1. For one additional example, see Rabbi Samuel ben Meir's (Rashbam) comments on Leviticus 19:18: "If he is your neighbor—that is, if he is good, but [not] if he is wicked, as it is written, 'The fear of the Lord is to hate evil.'"

72. For some examples of modern interpreters who support this approach, see Elimelekh Bar-Shaul, *Mitzvah Va-Lev*, vol. 1 (Tel-Aviv: Avraham Tziyoni Publishers, 1957), 172, n20; Yehudah Moriel, *Be-Derekh Tovim*, 27; and Norman Lamm, "Loving and Hating Jews as Halakhic Categories," *Tradition* 24, no. 2 (Winter 1989): 104–105. In support of this approach, note that from the mandate to "love your neighbor as yourself," the Talmudic sage Rabbah bar Avuha derives an obligation to find as easy a death as possible for someone being put to death by a court for sin. In other words, even a sinner whose sin is so great that he is liable to the death penalty appears to be among those whom we are obligated to love (BT, Sanhedrin 52b; and see Rabbi Meir Abulafia [1170–1244], *Yad Ramah* to Sanhedrin 52b, s.v. *u-makshinan*). And yet to defend this approach fully, one would need to grapple with Rabbinic texts that do seem to declare some people beyond the pale as a result of their behavior. See, for example, the idea that the prohibition on "cursing a chieftain of your people" (Exodus 22:27) applies only when the chieftain "acts in a way befitting of your people" (*oseh ma'aseh amkha*). For some examples, see Avot DeRabbi Natan, chapter 16; BT, Bava Metzia 48b and Bava Batra 4a.

73. See, for example, Maimonides, *Mishneh Torah*, Laws of Murder, 13:14.

74. See the teaching of Rabbi Meir Lublin (Maharam Mi-Lublin, 1558–1616), cited in Rabbi Israel Meir Kagan (The Hafetz Hayyim), *Ahavat Hesed*, end; and see also Rabbi Isser Yehuda Unterman (1886–1976), "*Gidrei Ahavah Ve-Sin'ah Be-Inyanei Halakha U-Ve-Musar Ha-Yahadut*," *Shevilin* 20 (1968), 16.

75. Sifra Kedoshim 4:9; BT, Arakhin 16b. And see also R. Meir Leibush Weiser (Malbim), *Ha-Torah Ve-Ha-Mitzvah* to Sifra Kedoshim 4:9. But compare Maimonides, *Mishneh Torah, Hilkhot De'ot*, ch. 6.

76. For this approach, see most famously, Rabbi Shneur Zalman of Liady (1745–

1812), *Tanya*, ch. 32. See also, for example, Elimelekh Bar-Shaul, *Mitzvah Va-Lev*, vol. 1, p. 173; and Lamm, "Loving and Hating Jews," 106.

77. Rabbi Abraham Isaiah Karelitz, *Hazon Ish* to *Shulkhan Arukh, Yoreh Deah* 13:16.

78. Lamm, "Loving and Hating Jews," 110. The one possible exception would be someone who actively seeks to convert fellow Jews to idolatry, on which see Sifre Devarim, Re'eh 89; and Maimonides, *Mishneh Torah*, Laws of Idolatry, 5:4; as well as the discussion in Lamm, "Loving and Hating Jews," 105–106. For the question of whether and how to reconcile Maimonides's position in the *Mishneh Torah* with the one he espouses in his *Commentary to the Mishnah*, see Lamm, 106–109.

79. Cited in Hananel Elran, *Ahavat Olam Ahavtikh*, 52, 89. Note also the way the Talmudic sage Rabbi Meir describes the *shekhinah*'s (the divine presence) agony at the suffering of one who has been sentenced to death. Mishnah Sanhedrin 6:5.

80. Rabbi Aaron (Arele) Roth (1894–1947), *Shomer Emunim, Ma'amar Ha-Emunah*, ch. 3.

81. Elimelekh Bar-Shaul, *Mitzvah Va-Lev*, vol. 2, p. 19.

82. Bell, *Hard Feelings*, 206.

83. Brogaard, *Hatred*, 101. And yet we need to be extremely careful here, because one danger of allowing us to hate our enemies is that we run the risk of becoming just like those we hate for their hatred.

84. R. Yehezkel Levenstein, *Or Yehezkel*, vol. 4, p. 145.

85. The philosopher Jeffrie Murphy, a defender of anger in certain circumstances, writes: "If I may be permitted a bit of autobiography, let me note that I am on occasion given to hatred—at the time of this writing hating those who exploit, either out of conviction or political opportunism, the vicious racial hatred always present in segments of American society, sometimes hiding like a troll under the bridge but eager to be set loose. I do not, however, think that I am being self-deceptive in my belief that I have been successful in compartmentalizing those and the rest of my hatreds—not letting them take over my whole self and never acting in immoral or illegal ways because of them." Jeffrie G. Murphy, "A Word on Behalf of Good Haters," *Hedgehog Review* 18, no. 2 (Summer 2016): 95.

86. BT, Megillah 10b and Sanhedrin 39b.

87. R. Yehezkel Levenstein, *Or Yehezkel*, vol. 4, p. 147.

10. Imitating God

1. BT, Sotah 14a.

2. Midrash Tanhuma, Vayishla<u>h</u> 10.

3. In a similar vein, Rabbi Yitzhak Isaac Breisch writes that the phrase "beginning and end" refers to "the foundation of the matter, its essence and its purpose." Rabbi Yitzhak Breisch, *MiShemanei HaAretz*, Sotah (1995), 69. Along the same lines, Rabbi Daniel Feldman characterizes Rabbi Simlai's statement as a "dramatic declaration of the underpinnings of the Torah in its totality." Daniel

Z. Feldman, *Divine Footsteps: Chesed and the Jewish Soul* (New York: Yeshiva University, 2008), 2. See also Rabbi Judah Loew of Prague (Maharal), *Tiferet Yisrael*, ch. 20; and R. Chaim Friedlander, *Siftei Hayyim: Middot Ve-Avodat Hashem*, vol. 1., p. 274.

4. Rabbi Jack Spiro interprets a Rabbinic dictum according to which "acts of lovingkindness (*gemilut hasadim*) are considered equal (*shekulah*) to all other mitzvot (commandments)" (PT, Peah 1:1) as sharing the same thrust: "The [R] abbis imply that the very heart of Torah—the spirit of God's law and will—is encompassed by the value of *gemilut hasadim*. It gives a moral and spiritual texture to all the laws of the Torah. This, perhaps, is the meaning of *shekulah*: equal in *qualitative* weight to all other mitzvot." Jack Spiro, "An Exploration of *Gemilut Hasadim*," *Judaism* 33, no. 4 (Fall 1984): 449.

5. See, for example, P. D. Miller, *Deuteronomy*, 125; and Richard D. Nelson, *Deuteronomy*, 136.

6. See, for example, Christopher J. H. Wright, *Deuteronomy* (Grand Rapids, MI: Baker, 1996), 145; and Eryl W. Davies, "Walking in God's Ways: The Concept of *Imitatio Dei* in the Old Testament," in *In Search of True Wisdom: Essays in Old Testament Interpretation in Honour of Ronald Clements*, ed. Edward Ball (Sheffield: Sheffield Academic Press, 1999), 103.

7. The same ambiguity can be found elsewhere in the Bible as well. When, in Psalm 51, King David looks forward to God's wiping away his sins and fashioning a new heart for him, he promises to "teach transgressors Your ways" (*derakhekha*) (Psalm 51:15). It is not entirely clear whether David is promising to instruct others in the ways that God has laid down for Israel or in the ways in which God Godself walks, as evidenced in the great mercy God has shown him. For a brief discussion, see John Goldingay, *Psalms, Volume 2: Psalms 42–89* (Grand Rapids, MI: Baker, 2007), 136. All of this said, whether or not the phrase "walking in God's ways" is meant to suggest the imitation of God (*imitatio Dei*), the latter idea is undoubtedly already attested in the Hebrew Bible. To take just two examples, one well-known and one less so, the people of Israel are commanded to rest on Shabbat because that is what God does (Exodus 20:8–11 and, even more explicitly, Exodus 31:16–17); and they are commanded to help give the liberated slave a fresh economic start because (this is not quite explicit but is hinted at) that is what God did for them as they left Egypt (Deuteronomy 15:12–15). See Peter C. Craigie, *The Book of Deuteronomy* (Grand Rapids, MI: Eerdmans, 1976), 239, and Shai Held, "Opening Our Hearts and Our Hands," in *The Heart of Torah*, vol. 2, p. 233.

8. Actually, the Masoretic text of the Bible reads "whosoever shall call (*yikra*) the name of the Lord shall be delivered," which makes more intuitive sense than the version cited in the midrash. I think it unlikely that the Talmudic sages were working from a different version of the text. Instead, their interpretation depends on a certain homiletical license (what we might call an "implicit *al tikre*"). I am grateful to Jon Levenson for a discussion of this point many years ago. For a moving interpretation of the play of *yikra* (will call) and *yikarei* (will be called) in

the midrash, see Eliezer Berkovits, *Prayer* (New York: Yeshiva University, 1962), 80–81.

9. Midrash Sifre, Ekev 49.

10. BT, Sotah 14a. Gregg Gardner argues that in the earlier, Tannaitic strata of Rabbinic literature *gemilut hasadim* was understood as a "broad ethical category, including as yet unspecified acts." See, for example Tosefta Pe'ah 4:19. In the later, Amoraic literature, such as the passage from BT, Sotah discussed here, in contrast, the term is concretized as referring to actions like visiting the sick, comforting the mourners, etc. See Gregg E. Gardner, "From the General to the Specific: A Genealogy of 'Acts of Reciprocal Kindness' (*Gemilut Hasadim*) in Rabbinic Literature," in Elizabeth Shanks Alexander and Beth A. Berkowitz, eds., *Religious Studies and Rabbinics: A Conversation* (New York: Routledge, 2018), 215–17.

11. "Without certain affections," writes the Catholic ethicist Edward Vacek, "we can *act* generously, but not *be* generous." Edward Vacek, *Love, Human and Divine: The Heart of Christian Ethics* (Washington, D.C.: Georgetown University Press, 1994), 10; emphasis added. Note Maimonides, *Sefer Ha-Mitzvot*, Positive Commandment No. 8, according to which we are commanded to emulate both God's "good deeds" and God's "exalted attributes."

12. A note for historically minded readers: The Rabbinics scholar Tzvi Novick has shown that at least in the early, Tannaitic strata of Rabbinic literature reciprocation was understood as integral to the concept of *gemilut hasadim* (more on this at n43, below). Accordingly, Gregg Gardner argues that translating *gemilut hasadim* as "loving kindness," again at least for Tannaitic texts, is misleading because the English term is suggestive of a kind of "altruism" and "selflessness" that the Hebrew term did not originally convey. But Gardner maintains that the term eventually (in the later, Amoraic literature) comes to suggest "something done out of selflessness and . . . grace." See Tzvi Novick, "Charity and Reciprocity: Structures of Benevolence in Rabbinic Literature," *Harvard Theological Review* 105, no. 1 (December 2011): 33–52; and Gardner, "From the General to the Specific," 213.

13. With this in mind, depending on context I will render in this chapter *hesed* as "love," as "kindness," and as "loving kindness."

14. R. Elazar, BT, Sukkah 49b, based on Hosea 10:12: "Sow tzedakah for yourselves, but reap the rewards of *hesed*."

15. See Midrash Ha-Gadol to Genesis 37, beginning. For a very different approach, according to which it is indeed sometimes required that we emulate God's anger, see R. Moshe Troyesh, *Orah Meisharim* (1878) 3:10, n7. (*Orah Meisharim* makes no mention of the midrash we have been discussing.)

16. Compare Maimonides, *Mishneh Torah, Hilkhot De'ot*, 1:6, where other qualities besides compassion are held up for imitation too. And see also *Guide of the Perplexed* 1:54, which seems to suggest that God's judgment is also to be imitated.

17. Mekhilta de-Rabbi Ishmael, BaHodesh, 6 (to Exodus 20:5).

18. See Genesis Rabbah 49:8, commenting on Nahum 1:2. In a similar vein, see R. Norman Lamm, "Notes on the Concept of *Imitatio Dei*," in Leo Landman, ed., *Rabbi Joseph H. Lookstein Memorial Volume* (New York: Ktav, 1980), 228, n20.

19. Rabbi Norman Lamm argues similarly in "Notes on the Concept of *Imitatio Dei*," 227–28. Rabbi Judah Loew of Prague (Maharal) states that only loving kindness is considered walking in God's ways "because with this attribute you do kindness and good, and God, may God be blessed, is the Supreme Good." See *Hiddushei Aggadot* to Sotah 14a.

20. For an interpretation along similar lines (according to which the list is presented in order of "progressive helplessness"), see Warren Zev Harvey, "Love: The Beginning and the End of Torah," *Tradition* 15, no. 4 (Spring 1976): 12.

21. It's worth noting that some traditional thinkers maintain that the mandate to *hesed* extends beyond human beings to all living creatures. R. Chaim Friedlander, for example, suggests that Noah's sojourn in the ark was intended to teach him—and by extension, all of us—about the necessity of extending loving kindness to all living things; the ark, he says, was "a school for acts of loving kindness." *Siftei Hayyim: Middot Ve-Avodat Hashem*, vol. 1, pp. 278–79. For some further examples, see Rabbi Elimelekh Bar-Shaul, *Mitzvah Va-Lev*, 2nd ed., vol. 1 (Tel-Aviv: Abraham Zioni, 1987), 195–96; n.a., *Hovat Ha-Adam Be-Olamo*, vol. 7, pp. 126–28; and Rabbi Shlomo Aviner, *Vehalakhta BiDerakhav: Binyan Ha-Middot* (Beit-El: Sifriyat Hayah, 2009), 222. For the Talmudic mandate not to impose unnecessary suffering on animals, see BT, Bava Metzia 32a–32b. And see also the poignant story of R. Judah the Patriarch in BT, Bava Metzia 85a.

22. See Maimonides, *Guide of the Perplexed*, 1:54.

23. "All the rest is commentary; go and learn" is an allusion to the story of Hillel and the convert, BT, Shabbat 31a. Several sentences in this paragraph are taken, with minor modifications, from my "Why First Responders Are Jewish Heroes," *Tablet*, April 16, 2013, http://www.tabletmag.com/scroll/129737/why-first-responders-are-jewish-heroes. Accessed 3/21/18.

24. Buddhists consider pity the "near enemy" of compassion; it is superficially similar to, but is in fact very different from, compassion. Cruelty, in contrast, would be compassion's "far enemy." See Patrick Boleyn-Fitzgerald, "Care and the Problem of Pity," *Bioethics* 17, no. 1 (February 2003): 1–20; relevant passage is on p. 11.

25. Lawrence Blum, "Compassion," in *Explaining Emotions*, ed. Amélie Oksenberg Rorty (Berkeley: University of California Press, 1980), 512. For a Jewish thinker developing and expanding upon Blum's insights on the differences between compassion and pity, see Avi Sagi, *Etgar Ha-Shivah El Ha-Masoret* (Jerusalem: Shalom Hartman Institute, 2003), 476–88.

26. See Shai Held, "Returning to Sinai Every Seventh Year: Equality, Vulnerability, and the Making of Community," in *The Heart of Torah*, vol. 2, pp. 275–79. And note this description of Rabbi Chaim Soloveitchik (R. Chaim of Brisk,

1853–1918): "He shared in the sorrows and woes of everyone, not like a great man helping someone inferior to him, but like a brother to a brother." Hananel Elran, *Ahavat Olam Ahavtikh*, 130. See also Tanhuma Mishpatim 15; Rashi to Exodus 22:24, s.v. *et he-ani imakh*; and n.a., *Hovat Ha-Adam Be-Olamo*, vol. 7, *Hadrakhot Ma'asiyot le-Tikkun Midat Nosei Be-Ol* (n.p., c. 2000), 57, for an important discussion of giving tzedakah without pity.

27. I borrow this formulation from Ayya Khema, *Being Nobody, Going Nowhere: Meditations on the Buddhist Path* (Somerville, MA: Wisdom Publications, 1987), cited in Boleyn-Fitzgerald, "Care and the Problem of Pity," 10. Boleyn-Fitzgerald notes, acidly, that "to be pitied is to be judged as pitiful" (13).

28. Blum, "Compassion," 511.

29. Christina Feldman puts this nicely: "Pity is the visible face of fear and resistance." Feldman, *Compassion*, 50. In an insightful discussion, Patrick Boleyn-Fitzgerald distinguishes between "fearful pity," on the one hand, and "aloof pity," on the other. My sense is that in real day-to-day life, the two are often intermingled. Boleyn-Fitzgerald, "Care and the Problem of Pity," especially p. 15.

30. I've changed my friend's name in order to protect his privacy.

31. The story I've shared may shed light on Jewish law's insistence that those who visit a shiva home may not speak first but instead speak only when first spoken to by the mourner. Rabbi Joseph Caro, *Shulkhan Arukh, Yoreh De'ah* 376:1. Fear and anxiety sometimes lead us to say foolish and decidedly unhelpful things. Knowing that, tradition asks us to keep quiet and offer the mourner our presence before we offer our words. As the Talmudic sage Rav Pappa declares, "The reward for [visiting] a house of mourning is for the silence." BT, Berakhot 6b.

32. On presence as *imitatio Dei*, see Martin Buber, "Imitatio Dei," in Martin Buber, *Israel and the World: Essays in a Time of Crisis* (New York: Schocken, 1963), 66–77; and see especially Lawrence Kaplan's brilliant analysis of Buber's difficult essay in Lawrence Kaplan, "Martin Buber on the Imitation of God," *Da'at* 56 (Summer 2005): v–xxi.

33. For a brief but important discussion of this, see Feldman, *Compassion*, 118–19.

34. On the kind of equanimity that can be helpful in accepting the real and often dramatic limits on our power in such situations, see Boleyn-Fitzgerald, "Care and the Problem of Pity," 8–9. Boleyn-Fitzgerald defines equanimity in this context as "accept[ance of] suffering that one cannot—or might not be able to—relieve." Such equanimity, he maintains, has both cognitive and affective components.

35. Yehiel Michel Epstein (1829–1908), *Arukh Ha-Shulkhan* 335:3.

36. The author of Psalm 38 poignantly laments that "my friends and companions stand back from my affliction; my kinsmen stand far off" (Psalm 38:12). The experience of suffering is exacerbated and amplified by the feeling of having been abandoned by one's friends.

37. Interestingly, Maimonides at one point suggests that all interpersonal mitzvot fall under the umbrella of *gemilut hasadim*, acts of loving kindness. See Maimonides, *Commentary to the Mishnah*, Pe'ah 1:1.

38. The right response in any given circumstances is also presumably shaped in part by the capacities (or lack thereof) of the person responding. In a similar vein, see R. Vidal of Tolosa (fourteenth century), *Maggid Mishneh* to *Mishneh Torah*, Laws of Neighbors, 14:5.

39. Heather Battaly, *Virtue* (Malden, MA: Polity, 2015), 66. In context, Battaly is describing Aristotle's approach to virtue ethics. See also Battaly's characterization of the contemporary philosopher Michael Slote's approach to virtue: "Caring just enough about others to try to help them is not sufficient for *genuinely* caring about them . . . People who genuinely care about others will make every effort to determine how best to act" (80). For Slote's own articulation of this, see Slote, *Morals from Motives*, 105.

40. Lawrence Blum argues that the moral quality of an action depends upon the quality of the apprehension of the situation that must come first. See Lawrence A. Blum, *Friendship, Altruism, and Morality* (London: Routledge, 1980), 117–39. The influence of Iris Murdoch's moral philosophy is evident here: morality, Murdoch taught, is not just about the decisions we make but also about how attentive we are and how we see what lies before us. Also relevant here is the philosopher John McDowell's observation that "a kind person has a reliable sensitivity to a certain sort of requirement which situations impose on behavior . . . The sensitivity is, we might say, a sort of perceptual capacity . . . The knowledge constituted by the reliable sensitivity is a necessary condition for possession of the virtue." John McDowell, "Virtue and Reason," *The Monist* 62, no. 3 (July 1979): 331–32.

41. R. Chaim Friedlander, *Siftei Hayyim: Middot Ve-Avodat Hashem*, vol. 1, p. 280. See also R. Shlomo Aviner, *VeHalakhta BiDerakhav*, 214–15.

42. Rabbi Abraham Isaac Kook speaks of the need for "great wisdom . . . in order to know how to express [the desire to be good to all] in all its aspects." R. Abraham Isaac Kook, *Orot Yisrael*, 1:4. There is also the question of what to do when the urge to compassion seems to butt heads with another pressing value, like the pursuit of justice. In such situations, needless to say, wisdom and discernment are needed. Along similar lines, see the brief discussion in R. Shlomo Aviner, *VeHalakhta BiDerakhav*, 228 ("Sometimes it is *hesed* to withhold *hesed*"). For a different perspective, see also R. Yehezkel Levenstein, *Or Yehezkel*, vol. 4, pp. 164–65.

43. Some scholars suggest that altruism and lack of attention to reward or reciprocity is intrinsic to the Rabbinic conception of *gemilut hasadim*. See, for example, W. E. Nunnally, "G'meelut Chasadim: Deeds of Kindness," in *The Wiley-Blackwell Companion to Religion and Social Justice*, ed. Michael D. Palmer and Stanley M. Burgess (Chichester, West Sussex, UK: Wiley-Blackwell, 2012), 295. This does not seem correct, at least for the earliest strata of Rabbinic literature; see, for example, Midrash Sifra, Dibbura de-Hovah, Parashah 12, and the discussion thereof in Gardner, "From the General to the Specific," 212. On the contrary, as we saw above in n12, the idea of reciprocal kindness may have been fundamental to the Tannaitic conception of *gemilut hasadim*; see, for example,

Mishnah Bava Batra 9:4. Tzvi Novick goes so far as to translate *gemilut hasadim* as "reciprocation of kindness," which he fruitfully contrasts with the purer giving of charity (tzedakah); the former, he shows, but not the latter, "occasions indebtedness." Significantly, in biblical Hebrew the root *g-m-l*, from which the word *gemilut* comes, "carries the connotation of interchange, or of a background relationship between the actor and the acted-upon, against which the immediate action acquires meaning." For a biblical example, see, for example, Obadiah 1:15. For a rich discussion of the centrality of reciprocation in early conceptions of *gemilut hasadim*, see Novick, "Charity and Reciprocity"; passages cited are on pp. 38, 42. The idea of *gemilut hasadim* as "a preeminent act of altruism" (Gardner, 213) develops only in later (Talmudic) Rabbinic texts.

44. In a very different register, Maimonides seems to think of a *hasid* (a person who embodies *hesed*) as someone who, in R. David Hartman's words, has "completely transcended the idea of reciprocity." For Maimonides, the realization that the ongoing existence of the world is *hesed* (*Guide of the Perplexed* 3:53; and note our discussion of this passage in chapter 2) inspires the *hasid* to act with *hesed* toward all, without thought of recompense. This is, in effect, the highest form of *imitatio Dei*. For an insightful discussion of this, see Hartman, *Maimonides*, especially at pp. 96, 204–205; citation is from p. 96. For a different presentation of *hesed* without thought of reciprocity as the highest Jewish spiritual ideal, see R. Eliyahu Dessler, *Mikhtav Me-Eliyahu*, vol. 1, p. 32.

45. See Genesis Rabbah 96:5, and the comments of Moshe Aryeh Mirkin in his edition of the text: *Midrash Rabbah*, vol. 4 (Tel-Aviv: Yavneh, 1958), 172, s.v. "*ve-khi yesh*." See also Tanhuma, Vayehi 3; and Tanhuma Buber, Vayehi 5. The connection between *hesed* and caring for the dead grows so strong that the term *ligmol hesed*, to perform acts of loving kindness, can sometimes serve as a metonym for caring for the dead. See, for example, Genesis Rabbah 58:7 and 62:5, as noted, for example, in Novick, "Charity and Reciprocity," 45–46.

46. R. Eliyahu Dessler, *Mikhtav Me-Eliyahu*, vol. 1, p. 32. As we saw in chapter 2, R. Dessler argues that this is what it means to be created in God's image: we are created with the capacity, like God, to be gracious givers.

47. Jean Hampton, "Feminist Contractarianism," in Jean Hampton, *The Intrinsic Worth of Persons: Contractarianism in Moral and Political Philosophy*, ed. Daniel Farnham (Cambridge: Cambridge University Press, 2007), 6, 7.

48. Charlotte Brontë, *Shirley* (London: Penguin, 2006; originally published, 1849), 169. I was led to Brontë's novel by Hampton's essay cited in the previous note.

49. I am sympathetic to the ethicist Stephen Post's observation that "self-sacrifice is the *sine qua non* of all meaningful love, and that no stable bonds can endure without it." Post, *Spheres of Love*, 11.

50. Ruth Groenhout observes that living with an entirely self-sacrificing parent can actively impede the moral and psychological development of a child: "Self-sacrifice can be destructive of others' ability to have a realistic conception of their own place in the universe. Children who believe that their mother's life should revolve around them ceaselessly are being trained to be selfish autocrats."

This is not healthy. It is only when children are raised to reciprocate the care they receive that they can grow up into healthy adults, capable of fully ethical relationships with others." Ruth Groenhout, "I Can't Say No: Self-Sacrifice and an Ethics of Care," in *Philosophy, Feminism, and Faith*, ed. Ruth Groenhout and Marya Bower (Bloomington: Indiana University Press, 2003), 168.

51. Groenhout, "I Can't Say No," 160.

52. One implication of all this is that healthy love relationships need to make space both for mutuality and for self-sacrifice. For a brief but potent discussion of the dangers of holding up mutuality as an exclusive relational ideal, see Darlene Fozard Weaver, *Self-Love and Christian Ethics* (Cambridge: Cambridge University Press, 2002), 70–71.

53. Parts of this paragraph and the next are taken, with very minor modifications, from Shai Held, "The Beginning and End of Torah," in *The Heart of Torah*, vol. 2, pp. 295–98.

54. Sifre Deuteronomy, Ekev 49.

55. The structure of this statement is thus reminiscent of the structure of Jeremiah 9:22–23: "Thus said the Lord: 'Let not the wise man glory in his wisdom; let not the strong man glory in his strength; let not the rich man glory in his riches. But only in this should one glory: that he knows and understands Me, for I Lord act with love, justice, and righteousness in the world.'" And then the arguably unexpected conclusion/demand: "'For in these I delight,' declares the Lord."

56. Sifre Deuteronomy, Va-ethanan 33.

57. Genesis Rabbah 33:3. For an analysis of a fascinating midrashic story connected to this verse, see my essay "The Power of Compassion, Or: Why Rachel's Cries Pierce the Heavens, " in *The Heart of Torah*, vol. 1, pp. 74–78.

58. See Rabbi Elijah Ha-Kohen from Izmir (d. 1729), *Shevet Musar*, ch. 30.

59. See Ruth Rabbah 5:4 and Yalkut Shimoni, Ruth, 602; PT, Ta'anit 4:2 and Yalkut Shimoni BeShallah, 251; and Midrash Ha-Gadol to Genesis 18:19.

60. R. Levenstein is commenting and expanding upon an oft-cited teaching of R. Moshe Hayyim Luzzatto (Ramhal). See Luzzatto, *Mesilat Yesharim* (*The Path of the Righteous*), ch. 1.

61. R. Yehezkel Levenstein, *Or Yehezkel*, vol. 4, p. 155; see also p. 157: "One who merits the attribute of *hesed* merits being attached to the radiance of the divine presence." See also p. 99. In the same vein, see Dessler, *Mikhtav Me-Eliyahu*, vol. 1, pp. 34–35. One of the interesting questions all of this raises is whether fulfillment of the mandate to "walk in God's ways" must be consciously theistic—that is, do we need to be thinking about and feeling connected to God in order to (properly) fulfill this commandment? Or, put differently, from a theological perspective, can an atheist walk in God's ways? For a short but rich discussion of this point in a Christian context see Jackson, *Love Disconsoled*, 24–26; and for a somewhat different approach, also from a Christian perspective, see Vacek, "God's Gifts and Our Moral Lives," 108; and Vacek, "A Catholic Theology of Philanthropy," 110.

62. R. Chaim Friedlander, *Siftei Hayyim: Middot Ve-Avodat Hashem*, vol. 1, p. 299. R. Friedlander goes further, suggesting that one who does not embody *hesed* will not be able to discern signs of God's *hesed* in the world. See, for example, p. 276. R. Friedlander's point, I think, is that you can't really see what you yourself do not have. Conversely, the more you yourself embody the attribute of *hesed*, the more of God's *hesed* you will perceive and understand (277). For further statements along similar lines, see also pp. 286, 294, 296–97.

63. BT, Avodah Zarah 17b.

64. I have explored Micah 6, with different emphases, in Shai Held, "Not There Yet," in *The Heart of Torah*, vol. 2, pp. 163–67.

65. Kathleen M. O'Connor, "Reflections on Kindness as Fierce Tenderness," 35. On "loving" love, see also R. Eliyahu Lopian, *Lev Eliyahu*, vol. 3, p. 374; and Hermann Cohen, *Religion of Reason out of the Sources of Judaism*, trans. Simon Kaplan (Atlanta: Scholars Press, 1995), 425.

66. See BT, Sukkah 49b. Relevant here too are instructions about giving to the poor in discreet ways; see, for example, Mishnah Shekalim 5:6, and Ecclesiastes Rabbah 12:14.

67. The book of Ruth provides a subtle but powerful illustration of this point. When hunger threatens Ruth and her mother-in-law, Naomi, Ruth decides that she should go and glean in the fields, but she first asks Naomi for permission (2:2), though she surely does not need it. In a remarkable display of kindness, Ruth acts as if Naomi would be doing her a *hesed* in letting her go, when in fact it is Ruth who is doing a *hesed* for Naomi. To give someone who is convinced that she has nothing at all to give the sense that she has nevertheless been able to be generous is itself a wonderful display of *hesed*. Ruth's quiet, understated gesture underscores the key point that real *hesed* does not call attention to itself; it is often (always?) modest and self-effacing. On this see also Yair Zakovitch, *Ruth* (Hebrew) (Tel-Aviv: Am Oved, 1990), 69.

68. See R. Chaim Shmuelevitz, *Sihot Musar*, 196.

69. See, for example, Leviticus Rabbah 29:3.

70. Perhaps this is what R. Abraham Joshua Heschel means when he writes that "the logic of justice may seem impersonal, yet the concern for justice is an act of love." Abraham Joshua Heschel, *The Prophets*, vol. 1 (New York: Harper and Row, 1969; originally published 1962), 201.

11. Love in the Ruins

1. Exodus 25:8; 29:45–46.

2. 1 Kings 8:10–11, recapitulating Exodus 40:34–35.

3. 1 Kings 8:13. See also, for example, Psalm 76:3; and Psalm 132:13–14.

4. See, for example, BT, Sanhedrin 37a; and BT, Yoma 54b.

5. Shaye J. D. Cohen, "The Destruction: From Scripture to Midrash," *Prooftexts* 2, no. 1 (January 1982): 24.

6. Moshe David Herr, "The Identity of the Jewish People Before and After the Destruction of the Second Temple: Continuity or Change?," in *Jewish Identities*

    in Antiquity: Studies in Memory of Menahem Stern, ed. Lee I. Levine and Daniel R. Schwartz (Tübingen: Mohr Siebeck, 2009), 213.

7. Cohen, "The Destruction," 18.

8. Lee I. Levine, "Judaism from the Destruction of Jerusalem to the End of the Second Jewish Revolt: 70–135 CE," in *Christianity and Rabbinic Judaism: A Parallel History of Their Origins and Early Development*, ed. Hershel Shanks (Washington, D.C.: Biblical Archaeology Society, 1992), 126. And yet Levine warns against "overstating" the effects of the year 70, noting, for example, that the exile did not begin in that year (most Jews were already living in the Diaspora before the Temple was destroyed), and that Jewish political independence in Palestine had in reality also ended earlier.

9. Avot de-Rabbi Natan, 4. Translation from *The Fathers According to Rabbi Nathan*, trans. Judah Goldin (New Haven, CT: Yale University Press, 1955), 33.

10. For one example of such an approach, see Jacob Neusner, "How Important Was the Destruction of the Second Temple in the Formation of Rabbinic Judaism? Some Reconsiderations," in *The Words of a Wise Man's Mouth Are Gracious (Qoh 10:12): Festschrift for Gunter Stemberger on the Occasion of His 65th Birthday*, ed. Mauro Perani (Berlin: De Gruyter, 2005), 77–93.

11. Robert Goldenberg, "Early Rabbinic Explanations of the Destruction of Jerusalem," *Journal of Jewish Studies* 33, no. 1–2 (Spring-Autumn 1982): 523. I substitute "many of them" where Goldenberg has "they" both because this seems more plausible to me (the sages were hardly monolithic in their theology and their approach to disaster) and because this seems to be Goldenberg's own position as expressed later in his essay: "Early rabbis inherited the prophetic understanding of Jewish history, and . . . some tried quite seriously to apply that understanding to the events of the first and second centuries. Others, however, seem to have turned away from this approach, apparently because they could not ascribe to the generations in question the profound guilt which such a view of history implies" (525). To be sure, the sages do list transgressions that Israel may have committed (see, for example, BT, Shabbat 119b; and BT, Yoma 9b), but the gravity of the punishment seems to far outstrip the nature of the crimes. Goldenberg's description of sins like bearing grudges and treating one another with disrespect as "trivialit[ies]" (521) seems overstated to me, but the broader point he makes seems convincing.

12. Avot de-Rabbi Natan, version A, 4 (Schechter edition, p. 21). Translation adapted very slightly from *The Fathers According to Rabbi Natan*, trans. Judah Goldin, p. 34. Goldin's rendering of the Hebrew *kemotah* is "as effective as this." It is worth noting, even if only in passing, that the midrash dramatically transforms the meaning of Hosea 6:6. In context, by *hesed* Hosea seems to mean loyalty and faithfulness to God; the prophet's point is that "the first commitment [ought to be] to the love and knowledge of God; sacrificial worship, rightly understood, plays a supporting role in the first commitment." J. Andrew Dearman, *The Book of Hosea* (Grand Rapids, MI: Eerdmans, 2010), 197. In other words, Hosea's critique is of sacrifice devoid of a larger commit-

ment to the covenant and its norms. In the Rabbinic use of the verse, however, *hesed* has a very different meaning, namely acts of lovingkindness that people do for one another.

13. Another version of the same story makes the role of lovingkindess as replacement for sacrifice even more explicit: "R. Yohanan said to him, 'Be not grieved, for we have a means of atonement *in its stead*' (*tahteha*)." Avot de-Rabbi Natan, version B, 8. And see the discussion in Eric Ottenheim, "The Consolation of Rabban Yohanan ben Zakkai," *Nederlands Theologisch Tijdschrift* 66 (2012), 55–56. Anthony Saldarini labels the idea that lovingkindness, and not just Temple sacrifice, can effect atonement "one of the central theses of post-destruction Judaism." Anthony Saldarini, *The Fathers According to Rabbi Nathan (Abot de Rabbi Nathan) Version B: A Translation and Commentary* (Leiden: Brill, 1975), 75, n4. See also the discussion in Menahem Kister, *Iyunim be-Avot de-R. Natan: Nusah, Arikhah, U-farshanut* (Jerusalem: Hebrew University, 1998), 187, n355. It's worth noting that in early Rabbinic texts, *hesed* may refer to acts of piety in general, including, but not limited to, acts of lovingkindness. For an example of this, see the description of the biblical Daniel in Avot de-Rabbi Natan, A, ch. 4, and for discussion, see Judah Goldin, "The Three Pillars of Simeon the Righteous," *Proceedings of the American Academy for Jewish Research* 27 (1958), 45–47.

14. See Abaye's comments about the House of Eli in BT, Rosh HaShanah 18a (based on a creative reading of 1 Samuel 3:14). See also the statement of Rabbi Yohanan in BT, Berakhot 5b, based on Proverbs 16:6. For another Talmudic passage that sees *hesed* having powers that mere sacrifice does not, see BT, Yevamot 105a. For an enlightening discussion of the historical unfolding of Rabbinic responses to the Destruction, see Baruch M. Bokser, "Rabbinic Responses to Catastrophe: From Continuity to Discontinuity," *Proceedings of the American Academy for Jewish Research* 50 (1983): 37–61.

15. Yalkut Shimoni, Hosea 522.

16. Mishnah Avot 1:2. For an extended analysis of what these terms might mean, see Goldin, "The Three Pillars."

17. Note BT, Rosh HaShanah 18a, where Abaye and Rava appeal to Torah and *hesed* to play the role formerly played primarily by sacrifice. On Torah in relationship to sacrifice, see Avot de-Rabbi Natan, A, 4, beginning.

18. Midrash Tannaim to Deuteronomy 15:9 (ed. D. Z. Hoffman), 83. See also Midrash Tehillim to Psalm 50:8.

19. Mishnah Ta'anit 4:6.

20. Cohen, "The Destruction," p. 20.

21. Mishnah Ta'anit 4:6.

22. Mishnah Ta'anit 4:8.

23. BT, Yoma 9b.

24. See R. Hayyim Vital, *Sha'arei Kedushah* 2:4.

25. Mishnah Ta'anit 4:8.

26. Rabbi Joseph B. Soloveitchik, *Fate and Destiny: From the Holocaust to the State of Israel* (Hoboken, NJ: Ktav, 2000; originally published in Hebrew as *Kol Dodi*

Dofek), 8. For an extremely perceptive discussion of R. Soloveitchik's approach to the problem of evil, see Moshe Sokol, "Is There a 'Halakhic' Response to the Problem of Evil?," in Sokol, *Judaism Examined: Essays in Jewish Philosophy and Ethics* (New York: Touro, 2013), 67–82.

27. My argument here is in line, I think, with what R. Soloveitchik himself suggests. In a beautiful interpretation of Job, R. Soloveitchik focuses especially on the transformation that led a suffering Job to empathize with and pray for his friends. R. Soloveitchik, *Fate and Destiny*, 11–17. Suffering, R. Soloveitchik says, should "mend [a person's] unfeeling heart, [their] moral callousness" (11).

28. Buber, *I and Thou*, 131.

12. Waiting for God

1. Midrash Tehillim 17:8.
2. This and the next few paragraphs are adapted slightly from Shai Held, "The Journey and the (Elusive) Destination," in *The Heart of Torah*, vol. 1, pp. 134–38.
3. Terence E. Fretheim, *The Pentateuch* (Nashville: Abingdon, 1996), 54.
4. I am grateful to Professor Jon Levenson for a now-long-ago discussion of this point.
5. See Gerhard Von Rad, "The Problem of the Hexateuch," in *The Problem of the Hexateuch: And Other Essays* (London: Oliver and Boyd, 1966).
6. J. Clinton McCann Jr., "Waiting for God: The Psalms and Old Testament Theology," *Perspectives in Religious Studies* 44, no. 2 (Summer 2017): 163.
7. The verse is recited at the end of the second paragraph of the *Aleinu* prayer. See also Rabbi Elie Kaunfer's analysis of the Kaddish, "The Mourner's Kaddish Is Misunderstood," available at https://www.myjewishlearning.com/article/the-mourners-kaddish-is-misunderstood/.
8. See, for example, Isaiah 2 and 11.
9. Sifra Kedoshim 1.
10. BT, Shabbat 31a.
11. BT, Shabbat 133b.

13. The God of Judaism (and of the "Old Testament") Is a God of Love

1. Brevard S. Childs, *Isaiah* (Louisville, KY: Westminster John Knox Press, 2001), 437.
2. Edward J. Young, *The Book of Isaiah*, vol. 3 (Grand Rapids, MI: Eerdmans, 1972), 383. For another related possibility, see John Goldingay, *Isaiah* (Peabody, MA: Hendrickson, 2001), 314.
3. Claus Westermann, *Isaiah 40–66, A Commentary*, trans. David M. G. Stalker (Philadelphia: Westminster, 1969), 288–89.
4. This last interpretation is arguably bolstered by what follows: "For as the rain or snow drops from heaven and returns not there, but soaks the earth and makes it bring forth vegetation, yielding seed for sowing and bread for eating, so is the word that issues from My mouth; it does not come back to me unfulfilled,

but performs what I purpose, achieves what I sent it to do" (Isaiah 55:10–11). See, for example, the second explanation of the verses in Goldingay, *Isaiah*, 314; among traditional interpreters, see Rabbi Isaiah di Trani (the Younger) (thirteenth–fourteenth century), commentary to Isaiah 55:8–9. For still another possible interpretation, see John Oswalt, *The Book of Isaiah, Chapters 40–66* (Grand Rapids, MI: Eerdmans, 1998), 444–45.

5. Rabbi David Kimhi (Radak), commentary to Isaiah 55:8.

6. Marilynne Robinson, *Gilead* (New York: Farrar, Straus and Giroux, 2004), 34.

7. Radak, commentary to Isaiah 55:8.

8. R. Isaac Abravanel, commentary to Isaiah 55:8–9. See also the comments of Rabbis Abraham Ibn Ezra and Samuel David Luzzatto (Shadal) to these verses, as well as the first interpretation suggested in Amos Hakham, *Sefer Yeshayahu* (Hebrew) (Jerusalem, Mosad HaRav Kook, 1984), 592–93. And note also Ezekiel 18:25–29. Among contemporary Jewish interpreters, see Yigal Ariel, *Ha-Mevaser: Iyunim Be-Nehamot Yishayahu*, vol. 2 (Hebrew) (Beit-El, Israel, 2016), 247–48. The Bible scholar John Goldingay notes similarly that "the point of the present passage . . . is . . . that [God's] plans and ways contrast with those of human beings. They are spectacularly centered on a compassion that issues in pardon." Though this may "seem unbelievable" to Isaiah's listeners, it is what God wishes them to know, believe, and act upon. John Goldingay, *The Message of Isaiah 40–55: A Literary-Theological Commentary* (London: T&T Clark, 2005), 553.

9. See Simundson, *Hosea-Joel-Amos-Obadiah-Jonah-Micah*, 84.

10. David Allan Hubbard notes that the Hebrew *na'ar* (child) "suggests an immaturity akin to helplessness, the inability to bear the responsibilities of adulthood." See, e.g., 1 Samuel 1:24; 1 Samuel 17:33; Jeremiah 1:6. David Allan Hubbard, *Hosea: An Introduction and Commentary* (Downers Grove, IL: InterVarsity, 1989), 197.

11. Some scholars see chapter 11 as describing God as the "Divine Father." See, e.g., James Luther Mays, *Hosea*, 150ff. It is striking, though, that many of the images of parenting evoked in the chapter are ones traditionally associated with the mother. God's maternal role in this chapter is emphasized, for example, by Sweeney, *The Twelve Prophets*, vol. 1, pp. 112–16. See also the measured comments of Simundson, *Hosea-Joel-Amos-Obadiah-Jonah-Micah*, 85; and Graham I. Davies, *Hosea* (Grand Rapids, MI: Eerdmans, 1992), 254. Expressing misgivings about the idea that God is depicted as mother in this chapter, Fredrik Lundström observes, in contrast, that "several traditional motherly motifs [are] missing here, such as being taken from the womb and laid at the breast and nursed." Fredrik Lundström, "'I Am God and Not Human' (Hos 11, 9): Can Divine Compassion Overcome Our Anthropomorphisms?," *Scandinavian Journal of the Old Testament* 29, no. 1 (2015): 138.

12. The Masoretic text reads, "The more they called (*kar'u*) [Israel], the more they went away from them." Most scholars accept the version found in the Septuagint, which reads "The more I called (*karati*) [Israel], the further they went away

from me." See, e.g., Elizabeth Achtemeier, *Minor Prophets I* (Grand Rapids, MI: Baker, 2012; originally published, 1996), 94. In the Masoretic version, the "they" who called Israel would ostensibly be God's prophets. See, for some examples of this approach, the commentaries of Rashi; R. Joseph Caro; R. Eliezer of Beaugency (twelfth century); Rabbi Abraham Ibn Ezra (second interpretation); and Radak to Hosea 11:2; but compare the first interpretation offered by R. Ibn Ezra and, similarly, by Hubbard, *Hosea*, 197–98.

13. Taking the Masoretic "*ol*," seemingly meaning "yoke," as "*ul*," meaning "infant." So NIV and NRSV. NJPS renders: "I seemed to them as one who imposed a yoke upon their jaws."

14. In this passage, "Ephraim" and "Israel" seem to be employed interchangeably to refer to the entire Northern Kingdom in ancient Israel. See, e.g., Hubbard, *Hosea*, 203.

15. See Genesis 10:19; 14:2, 8; and Deuteronomy 29:22.

16. See Simundson, *Hosea-Joel-Amos-Obadiah-Jonah-Micah*, 87.

17. Sweeney, *The Twelve Prophets*, vol. 1, p. 116.

18. The Hebrew phrase *nehepakh alai libi* could perhaps be more literally rendered as "My heart is overturned within Me." It is worth noting that Deuteronomy refers to the destruction of Sodom and Gomorrah using the same Hebrew root *h-p-kh* (*mahapeikhat Sedom va-Amora*, the overturning of Sodom and Gomorrah) (Deuteronomy 29:22). Then the cities were themselves overturned; now, Israel will not be overturned because God's heart has been (instead).

19. Hebrew *nihumai*. Hubbard notes that the root *n-h-m* "suggests a desire to comfort and console." Hubbard, *Hosea*, p. 204.

20. Mays, *Hosea*, 151, 157. Mays observes that according to Hosea, God "transcends the metaphor, is different from that to which he is compared, and free of its limitations. [God] is wrathful and loving *like* man, but *as* God" (157).

21. Sallie McFague, *Metaphorical Theology: Models of God in Religious Language* (Philadelphia: Fortress, 1982), 13. Italics in original. "An ever-present danger," the theologian Vincent Brümmer warns, "is that we shall fail to hear the whisper" and thus take our metaphors (too) literally. Vincent Brümmer, *The Model of Love: A Study in Philosophical Theology* (Cambridge: Cambridge University Press, 1993), 8. See also Shai Held, "Hearing the Whisper: God and the Limits of Language," in *The Heart of Torah*, vol. 2, pp. 290–94. In the context of Hosea 11, see Samuel Balentine, "'I am a God and Not a Human Being': The Divine Dilemma in Hosea," in *Torah and Tradition: Papers Read at the Sixteenth Joint Meeting of the Society for Old Testament Study and the Oudtestamentisch Werkgezelschap, Edinburgh 2015*, ed. Klaas Spronk and Hans Barstad (Leiden: Brill, 2017), 61, n28, end.

22. See also Isaiah 49:15.

23. For reasons of space, I cannot include a discussion here of the great medieval Jewish philosopher Rabbi Hasdai Crescas (1340–1411), who placed love at the center of his systematic philosophy of Judaism. It is love, for R. Crescas, rather than rationality or intellection, that serves as the essential link between God and humanity. Most importantly for our purposes here, R. Crescas's God is not

an Unmoved Mover cognizing himself for all eternity but a boundlessly loving God who relates to the world God has created out of love. See Hasdai Crecas, *Light of the Lord* (*Or Hashem*), trans. Roslyn Weiss (Oxford: Oxford University Press, 2018). For a brief introduction to R. Crescas on love, see Weiss's introduction, at pp. 1–2; and see also Zev Harvey, *R. Hasdai Crescas* (Hebrew) (Jerusalem: Shazar Center, 2010), 97–102.

24. Abraham Joshua Heschel, *The Prophets*, vol. 2, p. 50.

25. Heschel, *The Prophets*, vol. 2, p. 51.

26. Heschel, *The Prophets*, vol. 2, p. 51. Note also Michael Knowles's observation that "it would be a serious mistake to imagine that Israel's appeal to divine graciousness, mercy, compassion, and the like were no more than a projection of their own ideals onto a metaphysical canvas; the very fact that the characteristics named in Exodus 34 [on which see at length below] reflect ideals that neither Israel nor any other nation has been able to consistently exemplify suggests something other than a purely human origin for them. It is God, and not human beings alone, who most fully and definitively fills them with meaning." Michael P. Knowles, *The Unfolding Mystery of the Divine Name: The God of Sinai in Our Midst* (Downers Grove, IL: InterVarsity, 2012), 44.

27. Heschel, *The Prophets*, vol. 2, pp. 52–52. See also pp. 40, 99.

28. Punctuating the verse somewhat differently, Maimonides (Rambam), following Sa'adia Gaon (892–942) before him, takes the first "the Lord" to be a reference to the Speaker rather than the beginning of what is said. In other words, instead of "the Lord passed before him and proclaimed: 'The Lord, the Lord, a God merciful and gracious . . .'" Maimonides interprets: "The Lord passed before him and the Lord proclaimed: 'The Lord, a God merciful and gracious . . .'" See Sa'adia Gaon's commentary to Exodus 34:6; and Maimonides, *Teshuvot Ha-Rambam*, vol. 2, ed. Joshua Blau (1957), no. 267, pp. 505–509. Maimonides's interpretation is bolstered (and perhaps motivated) by Numbers 14:17–18.

29. For the traditional insistence, based on an extremely creative reading of this phrase (*erekh apayim*, literally "long of nostrils"), that God is patient and long-suffering with righteous and wicked alike, see BT, Eruvin 22a. And see also the fascinating imagined exchange between God and Moses in BT, Sanhedrin 111a–111b.

30. For an extremely useful survey of the variety of ways traditional commentators have calculated thirteen divine attributes in these verses, see the commentary of Samuel David Luzzatto (Shadal) to Exodus 34:6. For an earlier debate about whether these verses enumerate ten, eleven, or thirteen attributes, see Midrash Tehillim to Psalm 93:5.

31. I have explored these verses and their afterlife in much briefer and less developed form in Shai Held "God's Expansive Mercy: Moses's Praise and Jonah's Fury," *The Heart of Torah*, vol. 1, pp. 207–12.

32. See, for example, Judith A. Kates, "Women at the Center: Ruth and Shavuot," in Judith A. Kates and Gail Twersky Reimer, *Reading Ruth: Contemporary Women Reclaim a Sacred Story* (New York: Ballantine, 1994), 190.

33. Terence Fretheim writes in the same vein that "wrath is not a continuous

aspect of the nature of God but a particular response to a historical situation." Fretheim, *Exodus*, 302.

34. Victor P. Hamilton, *Exodus*, 576. See also Moshe David (Umberto) Cassutto, *Peirush Al Sefer Shemot*, 2nd ed. (Jerusalem: Magnes, 1954), 307. Note, in this regard, the way the three terms for sin are used by the prophet Micah to connect God's incomparable greatness with God's radical forgiveness (Micah 7:18–20).

35. The Bible scholar Thomas Raitt labels Exodus 34:6–7 "the most important statement of forgiveness in the Old Testament." Thomas Raitt, "Why Does God Forgive?," *Horizons in Biblical Theology* 13 (January 1991): 45. But note the very different tenor of the Talmudic sage Rabbi Yossi's comment in Tosefta Yoma 4:13.

36. Janzen, *Exodus*, 252.

37. On this see Mark J. Boda, *The Heartbeat of Old Testament Theology: Three Creedal Expressions* (Grand Rapids, MI: Baker, 2017), 41. Boda observes that the Bible "regularly employs the word 'forgiveness' in contexts where punishment is also carried out"; see his discussion of Numbers 14 in this context. See also, more expansively, Jay Sklar, "Sin and Atonement: Lessons from the Pentateuch," *Bulletin for Biblical Research* 22, no. 3 (2012): 488–90. Note also that every Friday evening during the Kabbalat Shabbat service, Jews recite Psalm 99, which declares: "You were a forgiving God for [our ancestors], but You exacted retribution for their misdeeds" (99:8).

38. Thomas Raitt writes that "the rigor of juxtaposing a forgiving pole with a punishing one is echoed but never put more strongly elsewhere in the Old Testament." Raitt, "Why Does God Forgive?," 45. In contrast, Mark Boda insists that "God's anger should not be placed in conflict with his gracious and merciful character. God's anger toward injustice is designed to express mercy, grace, and loyalty to those who are experiencing that injustice." Boda, *Heartbeat of Old Testament Theology*, 43–44. I agree that "conflict" is too strong a word— the text conveys tension rather than contradiction—but Boda's argument is problematic. In the story of the Golden Calf, it is not injustice but idolatry that makes God angry. To be sure, many biblical texts assume that idolatry is bound up with immorality, but what angers God here is Israel's unfaithfulness to God, not its moral failure. At the other extreme from Boda, Walter Brueggemann speaks of "a profound, unacknowledged, and unresolved contradiction" between these two poles in God; there is, he says, an "open-ended, unresolved two-sidedness" to the God of these verses. Brueggemann, "Exodus," 947, 951. This, too, strikes me as an overstatement.

39. Nathan C. Lane, *The Compassionate but Punishing God: A Canonical Analysis of Exodus 34:6–7* (Eugene, OR: Pickwick, 2010), 27.

40. This is noted and emphasized by the sages in Mekhilta de-Rabbi Ishmael, Bahodesh, 6 (to Exodus 20:5). See also Tanhuma (Buber) Beshallah 21, where it is creatively demonstrated that in our verses mercy outweighs anger by five hundred to one. Commenting on these verses, Brent Strawn observes that the tension between God's merciful and punitive sides notwithstanding, the thrust of

the text is that God is "overwhelmingly predisposed" toward forgiveness; divine mercy, he says, "overwhelms" divine wrath. Brent A. Strawn, "YHWH's Poesie: The *Gnadenformel* (Exodus 34:6b–7), the Book of Exodus, and Beyond," in *Biblical Poetry and the Art of Close Reading*, ed. J. Blake Couey and Elaine T. James (Cambridge: Cambridge University Press, 2018), 253, 255. This resonates with other fundamental statements about God we encounter in the Bible. See, for example, Psalm 103:9, 17. For Rabbinic amplification of this emphasis, see, e.g., PT, Kiddushin 1:9 and BT, Shabbat 32a.

41. Or perhaps, "a jealous God" (*El kana*). In light of Numbers 5:14 and Proverbs 6:34, it seems we should understand idolatry here as a form of adultery—that is, relational unfaithfulness. See also Hamilton, *Exodus*, 332.

42. Or perhaps, "those who hate me" (*son'ai*). Compare Malakhi 1:3, where again the translator must choose between "reject" and "hate."

43. As Walter Brueggemann nicely puts it, "It is crucial and precisely characteristic of this God that the statement of self-disclosure is given [precisely] in the moment when God is most deeply offended and Israel is most profoundly in jeopardy." Brueggemann, "Exodus," 947. Noticing the ways that mercy and graciousness follow immediately upon God's name (YHWH, rendered here as "the Lord"), the sages conclude that "whenever scripture says YHWH, it refers to [God's] quality of mercy," whereas the divine name Elohim refers to God's quality of judgment/justice. Sifre Deuteronomy, Va-ethanan 26.

44. For a useful discussion of this point, see Lane, *The Compassionate but Punishing God*, 41.

45. Lane, *The Compassionate but Punishing God*, 47. See also Michael Widmer, *Moses, God, and the Dynamics of Intercessory Prayer: A Study of Exodus 32–34 and Numbers 13–14* (Tübingen: Mohr Siebeck, 2004), 185.

46. Note also the comments of Rabbi Meir on Exodus 33:19 in BT, Berakhot 7a, and compare the very different approach expressed by Targum Yonatan (Pseudo-Jonathan) to the same verse.

47. BT, Yoma 86a.

48. And yet, curiously, most of us find the idea of intergenerational reward far less disturbing or unfair.

49. Some scholars think that these verses actually reflect an ancient legal practice according to which all living members of a household or family are regarded as one unit; all are therefore implicated in the guilt of any one of them. The third or fourth generation is a way of referring to all possible family members alive at any one time. See, for example, Ronald E. Clements, *Exodus* (Cambridge: Cambridge University Press, 1972), 124; and Daniel I. Block, "How Can We Bless YHWH? Wrestling with Divine Violence in Deuteronomy," in M. Daniel Carroll R. and J. Blair Wilgus, *Wrestling with the Violence of God: Soundings in the Old Testament* (Winona Lake, IN: Eisenbrauns, 2015), 48, n39. (Sounding a note of caution, Michael Knowles observes that "not a single ancient commentator understands the passage in this way." Knowles, *The Divine Name*, 175.) According to Jeffrey Tigay, the fact that God extends punishment only to generations

who could plausibly be alive at the same time as the culprit implies that "the suffering of the descendants is intended as a deterrent to, and punishment of, their ancestors, not a transfer of guilt to the descendants in their own right." Tigay, *Deuteronomy*, 66. See also Cassutto, *Shemot*, 168. Joel Kaminsky suggests that intergenerational punishment may have originally been intended as an act of mercy in which punishment was spread out over several generations. Joel S. Kaminsky, "The Sins of the Fathers: A Theological Investigation of the Biblical Tension Between Corporate and Individualized Retribution," *Judaism* 46 (1997): 326-27.

50. For classical Jewish sources, see Mekhilta de-Rabbi Ishmael, Bahodesh, 6 (to Exodus 20:5); BT, Berakhot 7a; and BT, Sanhedrin 27b. See also Sa'adia Gaon, *The Book of Theodicy* (at Job 21:19, based on Leviticus 26:39), 301. Among modern Bible scholars, see, for example, Cassutto, *Shemot*, 168; Tigay, "Exodus," 149; and Hamilton, *Exodus*, 333. See also Mark Boda's analysis of Numbers 14 in Mark J. Boda, *A Severe Mercy: Sin and Its Remedy in the Old Testament* (Winona Lake, IN: Eisenbrauns, 2009), 45, n30. For a dissenting view, according to which "those who reject me" refers to the fathers rather than the descendants, see William H. C. Propp, *Exodus 19-40: A New Translation with Introduction and Commentary* (New York: Doubleday, 2006), 173. And see also Sarna, *Exodus*, 111, who seems to think the question of whether "those who reject me" modifies "parents" or "children" is ambiguous.

51. The Bible scholar Chip Dobbs-Allsopp takes Lamentations 5:7 as a statement of both "fact" and "protest." F. W. Dobbs-Allsopp, *Lamentations* (Louisville, KY: Westminster John Knox Press, 2002), 145. Some scholars, however, think that this verse too may be ambiguous about whether the speakers see themselves as sinful or not. For a brief discussion, see Adele Berlin, *Lamentations* (Louisville, KY: Westminster John Knox Press, 2002), 120-21.

52. On the Bible's movement beyond intergenerational punishment, see, for example, Sarna, *Exodus*, 110-11; and Tigay, "Exodus," 149. But compare Hamilton, *Exodus*, 334.

53. BT, Makkot 24a. In any case, human judges are explicitly prohibited from punishing children for the crimes of their parents (Deuteronomy 24:16).

54. For a trenchant critique of this scholarly impulse, see Kaminsky, "The Sins of the Fathers." Kaminsky demonstrates the ways that in scholarly accounts like these "secularized evolutionism" is often coupled with a deeply disturbing Christian supersessionism (see especially p. 321).

55. Kaminsky shows that "there are passages within the latest strata of the Hebrew Bible supporting the idea of communal responsibility (Daniel 6:25 and Esther 9:7-10), and that this view is still alive and well into New Testament times and beyond." Among Rabbinic sources, Kaminsky points to Leviticus Rabbah 4:6; BT, Sanhedrin 43b-44a; and Tanna de-Be Eliyahu, chapter 12. There was thus "no simple linear progression from earlier corporate to later more individualized forms of retribution." Kaminsky, "The Sins of the Fathers," 323.

56. See Sifra Behukkotai 7:5 (re: Leviticus 26:37) and BT, Sanhedrin 27b.

57. See also Kaminsky, "The Sins of the Fathers," 328.

58. In other words, our identities always already have both a social and a historical dimension. I am embedded in relationships with people in the present as well as the past. As Alasdair MacIntyre notes, "The story of my life is always embedded in the story of those communities from which I derive my identity. I am born with a past; and to try to cut myself off from the past, in the individualist mode, is to deform my present relationship. The possession of an historical identity and the possession of a social identity coincide." Alasdair MacIntyre, *After Virtue*, 2nd ed. (Notre Dame, IN: Notre Dame Press, 1984), 221.

59. Klaus Koch, *The Prophets: The Babylonian and Persian Periods*, vol. 2 (Philadelphia: Fortress, 1984), 108.

60. Kaminsky, "The Sins of the Fathers," 325.

61. For brief discussions of these objections, see Kaminsky, "The Sins of the Fathers," 331–32, nn. 28–29.

62. This is a claim also made, for example, by Richard Elliott Friedman, *Commentary on the Torah*, 290. For a careful book-length study of the ways the verse is quoted and reworked in Tanakh, see Lane, *Compassionate but Punishing God*. Thomas Raitt observes that "the formula in Exod 34:6–7 is as important as it is because of repeated enactment and continual expansion or abbreviation, restructuring or reapplication." Raitt, "Why Does God Forgive?," 53. My argument here touches on the perennial scholarly debate over whether the Hebrew Bible has a "theological center." I am agnostic about this question, though I'm inclined to think that if it has any, it has several rather than one. If so, the vision of God expressed in Exodus 34:6–7 is certainly one of them. For the classic study of this question, see Gerhard F, Hasel, "The Problem of the Center in the OT Theology Debate," *Zeitschrift für die alttestamentliche Wissenschaft* 86 (1974): 65–82. For a classic Jewish reflection on the question of a theological center, including analysis of why Jews have been less inclined than Christians to search for one, see Jon D. Levenson, "Why Jews Are Not Interested in Biblical Theology," in Jon D. Levenson, *The Hebrew Bible, The Old Testament, and Historical Criticism: Jews and Christians in Biblical Studies* (Louisville, KY: Westminster John Knox Press, 1993), 33-61.

63. Over the course of Tanakh, Thomas Raitt writes, Exodus 34:6–7 is cited less to emphasize the polarity of divine mercy and divine judgment and more as "an unconditional assurance of God's mercy." Raitt, "Why Does God Forgive?," 46; see also 49–50.

64. Since Joel "edits" God's words, leaving out some (mention of the third and fourth generations or the thousandth, for example), it seems odd that he invokes God's being "slow to anger" in a context where God's anger is abundantly manifest. The Bible scholar Charles Lane suggests that perhaps "the prophet wanted to remind the ancient Israelites that [God's] wrath is not hastily given or without warning: God has punished the nation [not for no reason but] because they were unfaithful and left [God]." Lane, *The Compassionate but Punishing God*, 80.

65. See Lane, *The Compassionate but Punishing God*, 78.

66. Lane, *The Compassionate but Punishing God*, 81, following Susan Pigott, "God of Compassion and Mercy: An Analysis of the Background, Use and Theological Significance of Exodus 34:6–7" (PhD dissertation, Southwestern Baptist Theological Seminary, 1995), 141.

67. See Lane, *The Compassionate but Punishing God*, 81.

68. Lane, *The Compassionate but Punishing God*, 82.

69. R. W. L. Moberly, *Old Testament Theology: Reading the Hebrew Bible as Christian Scripture* (Grand Rapids, MI: Baker Academic, 2013), 195. Thomas Raitt explains that within the terms of covenant at Sinai, forgiveness is "never guaranteed." On the contrary, "nothing locks God into forgiving or not forgiving. God never forgives any way but as a free decision." Raitt, "Why Does God Forgive?," 47.

70. Simundson, *Hosea-Joel-Amos-Obadiah-Jonah-Micah*, 136. And see, similarly, Elizabeth Achtemeier, "Joel," *The New Interpreter's Bible*, vol. 7 (Nashville: Abingdon, 1996), 319, who writes that "repentance does not coerce God."

71. BT, Berakhot 4b.

72. John Goldingay, *Psalms, Volume 3: Psalms 90–150* (Grand Rapids, MI: Baker Academic, 2008), 700. See also Walter Brueggemann and William H. Bellinger Jr., *Psalms* (New York: Cambridge University Press, 2014), 604.

73. See James L. Mays, *Psalms* (Louisville, KY: Westminster John Knox Press, 1994), 438.

74. See Leon J. Liebreich, "Psalms 34 and 145 in the Light of Their Key Words," *Hebrew Union College Annual* 27 (1956): 187; and Reuven Kimelman, "Psalm 145: Theme, Structure, and Impact," *Journal of Biblical Literature* 113 (Spring 1994): 37–58, especially 40–41, 47.

75. The seemingly universalistic implications of Psalm 145:9 were enormously important to Maimonides in his own commitment to ethical universalism. See, for a crucial example, *Mishneh Torah*, Laws of Slaves, 9:8; and see also Laws of Kings and Their Wars, 10:12. On the latter source see Gerald J. Blidstein, "Tikkun Olam," *Tradition* 29, no. 2 (Winter 1995): 14. In the *Guide of the Perplexed* 3:12, Maimonides invokes the verse to support the idea that God's mercy extends to all living things, and not just to human beings. For Talmudic precedent for using Psalm 145:9 to invoke mercy for animals, see BT, Bava Metzia 85a.

76. Robert Alter, *The Book of Psalms* (New York: W. W. Norton, 2007), 502.

77. Note that the psalmist refers to God not as "my God, *my* King" (as in Psalm 5:3 and 84:4) but rather as "my God, *the* King" (145:1). See Lane, *The Compassionate but Punishing God*, 135.

78. See Lane, *The Compassionate but Punishing God*, 134.

79. Mayer Gruber has shown that the standard translations notwithstanding, the Hebrew *harah le* (Jonah 4:1, 4, 9) refers to depression rather than anger (*harah af*, on the other hand, does refer to anger). Mayer I. Gruber, "The Tragedy of Cain and Abel: A Case of Depression," *Jewish Quarterly Review* 69, no. 2 (October 1978): 89–97.

80. Lane, *The Compassionate but Punishing God*, 85. If we accept the conventional translation of *harah le* as denoting anger, then, ironically, Jonah is angry precisely at God's lack of anger.

81. Phillip Cary, *Jonah* (Grand Rapids, MI: Brazos, 2008), 133.

82. My point is not to accuse this scholar or that of antisemitism, but to note that (often unconscious) anti-Jewish bias runs deep in some Christian circles, sometimes even among Christians who would be sincerely horrified at the thought that they harbor prejudices against Jews and Judaism.

83. Douglas K. Stuart, *Hosea-Jonah: Word Biblical Themes* (Dallas: Word, 1989), 97. See also Peter C. Craigie, *Twelve Prophets*, vol. 1 (Philadelphia: Westminster, 1984), 233. In the same deeply problematic vein, Daniel Timmer purports to find in Jonah "a shocking antipathy toward non-Israelites and an aversion to seeing God's mercy extend to them"; he finds the alleged "incongruity between Jonah's mission and his unchanging antipathy for displays of grace to non-Israelites . . . alarming" and denounces the prophet for his "xenophobia" and the "deviant nature of [his] attitudes and beliefs." Daniel C. Timmer, *A Gracious and Compassionate God: Mission, Salvation, and Spirituality in the Book of Jonah* (Downers Grove, IL: InterVarsity, 2011), 119, 123, 124. Even otherwise nuanced Christian readers of the text frequently fall into this trap. Thus, for example, Phillip Cary correctly sees that Jonah is distraught by God showing mercy to evil enemies (more on this in a moment), but nevertheless allows himself to write that Jonah "hates the fact that the Lord abounds in a loving-kindness that extends far beyond the bounds of his covenant with Israel." Cary, *Jonah*, 133. But as we shall see, Jonah's complaint against God is that God's mercy extends to the wicked, not that it extends to non-Jews.

84. This paragraph is heavily dependent on (and in parts taken verbatim from) Shai Held, "God's Expansive Mercy," 210.

85. Note, in fact, that Nahum invokes the punitive aspects of God's self-description from Exodus 34:6–7 as a warning to the malevolent Ninevites (1:3). There is thus a striking contrast between the use of these verses in the books of Nahum (beware, Ninevites!) and Jonah (understand, Jonah, that God cares deeply for the Ninevites even if you don't). Of course, Jonah himself agrees with Nahum; it is the author of the book of Jonah who passionately disagrees with the prophet he writes about and therefore subjects him to brutal critique.

86. Sweeney, *The Twelve Prophets*, vol. 1, p. 328. See also R. Isaac Abravanel, introduction to the commentary on Jonah; Walter Moberly, *Old Testament Theology*, 199–200; and Shai Held, "God's Expansive Mercy," 211.

87. Achtemeier, *Minor Prophets I*, 257.

88. Sweeney, *The Twelve Prophets*, vol. 1, p. 332.

89. Achtemeier, *Minor Prophets I*, 282.

90. Leviticus Rabbah 29:3.

91. It's worth noting that divine judgment is a highly significant theme in the New Testament too. As one recent Christian writer puts it, "It is striking to see the constant toggling back and forth between love and judgment" in the New

Testament. Stephen K. Moroney, *God of Love and God of Judgment* (Eugene, OR: Wipf and Stock, 2009), 118. Moroney is speaking about the Gospel of Matthew in particular but it is clear that he thinks this assessment is applicable to the New Testament as a whole. To take just one example chosen more or less at random, Jesus says of the cities that have heard his message but failed to repent that "it will be more bearable for Sodom on the day of judgment than for you" (Matthew 11:24). As the conservative evangelical writer J. I. Packer writes, "The Jesus of the New Testament, who is the world's Savior, is its Judge as well." J. I. Packer, *Knowing God* (Downers Grove, IL: InterVarsity, 1993), cited in Moroney, *God of Love and God of Judgment*, 124.

92. Luke 21:23.

93. John 3:36.

94. Stephen J. Nichols, *Jesus Made in America: A Cultural History from the Puritans to the Passion of the Christ* (Downers Grove, IL: InterVarsity, 2008), 226, cited in Moroney, *God of Love and God of Judgment*, 124.

95. Alastair V. Campbell, *The Gospel of Anger* (London: SPCK, 1986), 34. In the same vein, see Christopher J. H. Wright, *The God I Don't Understand: Reflections on Tough Questions of Faith* (Grand Rapids, MI: Zondervan, 2008), 77.

96. Claus Westermann, *Elements of Old Testament Theology*, trans. Douglas W. Stott (Atlanta: Westminster John Knox Press, 1982), 139.

97. Terence E. Fretheim, *Jeremiah* (Macon, GA: Smyth and Helwys, 2002), 33. Accordingly, Brent Strawn notes, "When it comes to divine judgment and wrath, human change changes God." Brent A. Strawn, *Lies My Preacher Told Me: An Honest Look at the Old Testament* (Louisville, KY: Westminster John Knox Press, 2021), 34

98. For these three sources arranged in this way, I am indebted to Terence E. Fretheim, "Theological Reflections on the Wrath of God in the Old Testament," in *What Kind of God? Collected Essays of Terence E. Fretheim*, 157–58.

99. Heschel, *The Prophets*, vol. 2, p. 68. Yet R. Heschel's argument has its limits. In interpreting divine anger, he focuses on instances in which God responds to injustice and immorality. It is God's passionate concern for the victims that gives rise to God's anger. But God is concerned with idolatry no less than with immorality, and I don't think it's persuasive to explain every case of God's wrathful response to idolatry as ultimately animated by a concern for the immorality that the Bible so frequently associated with idolatry.

100. Heschel, *The Prophets*, vol. 2, p. 64.

101. In the same spirit as Heschel, and perhaps counterintuitively for many readers, the Christian Bible scholar Brent Strawn remarks that the idea of a God who gets angry is "in the final analysis, a benevolent, even therapeutic conception" in that it means that "God is mobilized against injustice and sin." In a deliberate provocation, Strawn suggests that "the fact that many Christians [and I'd add, Jews too] would dislike this benevolent, even therapeutic notion . . . says a great deal about them (er, I mean *us*) . . . To put a fine point on it: perhaps we don't like divine judgment and wrath, wherever we find it

in Scripture, because we—unlike God—are indifferent to evil." (Strawn adds that this may also be why, as he sees it, "so many Christians seem completely tone-deaf to the notes of divine judgment Jesus continually sounds.") Strawn may be overstating his case (deliberately, I suspect) because as we'll see one can view divine anger as a good thing and still be put off by the degree of its ferocity and violence, but he makes a powerful point worth wrestling with. Strawn, *Lies My Preacher Told Me*, 35.

102. Erich Zenger, *A God of Vengeance? Understanding the Psalms of Divine Wrath*, trans. Linda Maloney (Louisville, KY: Westminster John Knox Press, 1996), 73. In a similar vein, see Julia M. O'Brien, *Challenging Prophetic Metaphor: Theology and Ideology in the Prophets* (Louisville, KY: Westminster John Knox Press, 2008), 123.

103. Exodus 20:5; Deuteronomy 5:9. I hasten to note again that I don't think it's persuasive to explain every case of God's wrathful response to idolatry as ultimately animated by a concern for the immorality that the Bible so frequently associates with it.

104. For some examples, see Leviticus 10:1–2; Numbers 1:53; and Joshua 7:1.

105. Abraham Joshua Heschel, *God in Search of Man: A Philosophy of Judaism* (New York: Farrar, Straus and Cudahy, 1955), 260. Emphasis R. Heschel's.

106. Heschel, *The Prophets*, vol. 2, p. 73.

107. In the same vein, Terence Fretheim writes simply that "as with human anger, the divine anger is a sign that the relationship is taken seriously (apathy is not productive of anger)." Fretheim, "The Wrath of God in the Old Testament," 144. "The opposite of love," the Christian theologian Jürgen Moltmann writes, "is not wrath but indifference." Jürgen Moltmann, *The Crucified God* (Minneapolis, MN: Fortress, 1993), 272.

108. In the same vein, Moltmann speaks of divine anger as "injured love." Moltmann, *The Crucified God*, 272. "It is remarkable," the Bible scholar Th. C. Vriezen, observes, "that exactly those prophets who emphasize God's love most strongly, viz. Hosea and Jeremiah, are also most vehement in their description of the divine wrath." Theodorus Christiaan Vriezen, *An Outline of Old Testament Theology*, 2nd ed. (Oxford: Blackwell, 1970), 305.

109. See, most famously, Hosea, chapter 2.

110. For readers who wish to pursue this question of troubling gendered metaphors in prophetic texts, a good place to start is O'Brien, *Challenging Prophetic Metaphor*.

111. F. W. Dobbs-Allsopp, *Lamentations*, 80.

112. Kathleen M. O'Connor, "Lamentations," in *New Interpreter's Bible*, vol. 4 (Nashville: Abingdon, 2015), 893.

113. Revelation 19:15; 6:15–16. See also, for example, 14:20.

114. Mark 13:17–19.

115. Strawn, *Lies My Preacher Told Me*, 45 (emphasis Strawn's). Strawn is most directly referring to Revelation in general and to 2 Thessalonians 1:5–12 but his point is a more general one.

116. As Lawson Stone writes, "Readers need more than a historical-apologetic fix that actually subverts the text." Lawson G. Stone, "Ethical and Apologetic Tendencies in the Redaction of the Book of Joshua," *Catholic Biblical Quarterly* 53, no. 4 (January 1991): 26.

117. Offering the reader cold comfort, Markus Zehnder notes that the commands in Deuteronomy 20 "stand out as relatively humane" in their historical context, since outside of Israel it was common practice to kill not only men but also women, children, and other noncombatants; according to Deuteronomy, in contrast, only adult males are to be killed, whereas others are to be taken as booty. Zehnder, *The Bible and Immigration*, 38–39.

118. The Hebrew term is *herem*. Walter Moberly helpfully defines *herem* as "making something the exclusive possession of YHWH and thereby removing it from the sphere of regular human use." This could entail destruction, he maintains, but need not necessarily. Moberly proposes rendering *herem* as "ban" because, like *herem* itself, the word is opaque and hard to pin down. In a contemporary context, Moberly writes, the word "ban" "combines historic resonance with opacity." See Moberly, *Old Testament Theology*, 60–61.

119. Considerations of space make it impossible for me to consider another point that seems to make the problem of Deuteronomy 7 even greater: the mandate to wipe out the Canaanites does not stand on its own but is in fact closely entwined with the text's vision of divine election (note the *ki*, "because" or "for" that begins 7:6). On this see Moberly, *Old Testament Theology*, 55–56. On the *herem* in Deuteronomy, see also Deuteronomy 20:16.

120. Stone, "Ethical and Apologetic Tendencies," 28.

121. See Joshua 9:1–2; 10:1–5; 11:1–5.

122. Stone, "Ethical and Apologetic Tendencies," 33.

123. Hayyim J. Angel, *Creating Space Between* Peshat *and* Derash: *A Collection of Studies on Tanakh* (Jersey City, NJ: Ktav, 2011), 78. More broadly, this paragraph follows Angel, 77–78.

124. Stone, "Ethical and Apologetic Tendencies," 33.

125. Robert L. Hubbard Jr., *Joshua* (Grand Rapids, MI: Zondervan, 2009), 48.

126. Robert L. Hubbard Jr., "'What Do These Stones Mean?' Biblical Theology and a Motif in Joshua," *Bulletin for Biblical Research* 11, no. 1 (2001), 10. Given the clear instructions that God had given about the *herem*, we might have expected God to disapprove of the agreements Israel reached with Rahab and the Gibeonites. But to the contrary, each agreement is followed by a military victory and each battle is preceded by an assurance of divine assistance (Joshua 6:16 and 10:8). On this see L. Daniel Hawk, "The Problem with Pagans," in *Reading Bibles, Writing Bodies: Identity and the Book*, ed. Timothy K. Beal and David Gunn (London: Taylor and Francis, 2002), 157.

127. On this see Hawk, "The Problem with Pagans," p. 160.

128. Note, for example, Akhan's impressive pedigree (see Joshua 7:1).

129. Lori Rowlett, "Inclusion, Exclusion and Marginality in the Book of Joshua," *Journal for the Study of the Old Testament* 17, no. 55 (September 1992): 23, 20.

Rowlett offers a Foucauldian analysis of how power is exercised in the text; I have adapted her arguments for my own very different purposes. Ellen Davis notes that portraits of "admirable indigenous people" like the one Joshua offers of Rahab are nowhere to be found in parallel ancient Near Eastern conquest narratives. Davis, *Opening Israel's Scriptures*, 135.

130. R. Samuel b. Nahman in Deuteronomy Rabbah 5:14; and PT, Shevi'it 6:1. See also Tanhuma Shoftim 19; and see Nahmanides (Ramban), commentary to Deuteronomy 20:10, as well as Maimonides, *Mishneh Torah*, Laws of Kings and Their Wars, 6:1. But compare Rashi, commentary to Deuteronomy 20:10; and see Sifre Deuteronomy, 199. For an extended argument that "the Torah's 'rules of war,' as filtered through the prism of the Jewish tradition, offer a context that makes the Biblical mandate appear far less cruel than it seems from initial confrontation with the text itself," see Norman Lamm, "Amalek and the Seven Nations: A Case Study of Law vs. Morality," in *War and Peace in the Jewish Tradition*, ed. Lawrence Schiffman and Joel Wolowelsky (Jersey City, NJ: Ktav, 2007), 211. For a range of examples bolstering the argument, see the list provided at p. 212.

131. This is, it's important to be clear, also the view of the Bible itself. Robert Hubbard, for example, writes that "the Bible views Joshua's policy as limited to a very unique moment in history—YHWH's conquest of Canaan and Israel's settlement there. Once Israel settles, that purpose is achieved, the mandate expires and cannot be applied elsewhere without divine warrant." Hubbard's last three words worry and frankly frighten me, but the broader point, I trust, still stands. Robert L. Hubbard Jr., "Only A Distant Memory: Old Testament Allusions to Joshua's Days," *Ex Auditu* 16 (2000): 143. For a similar argument, see Greenberg, "On the Political Use of the Bible," 469.

132. Greenberg, "On the Political Use of the Bible," 469.

133. See Judges 2:23, after which Joshua appears only in 1 Kings 16:34, Nehemiah 8:17, and 1 Chronicles 7:27. None of these are references to his role in the conquest. For these references and for the ones in the next few notes, I am indebted to Hubbard, *Joshua*, 46–47.

134. The conquest is ignored in 1 Samuel 12:9–11; Micah 6:5; Jeremiah 2:7; and Psalm 105:43–54. Note also that mention of the conquest is omitted in Ezekiel's vision of restoration (Ezekiel 40–48). For references to God "driving out" (*g-r-sh*) the Canaanites, see Judges 6:9; Psalm 78:55; and Psalm 80:9. For God "bringing" Israel to the Promised Land, see Ezekiel 20:28.

135. See Amos 2:10; Psalm 44:3–4; and Nehemiah 9:23–25.

136. Hubbard, *Joshua*, 47.

137. Hubbard "Only A Distant Memory," 141.

138. Suggesting that the author (or editor-redactor) of Joshua worked with multiple, contradictory sources will not help us, since, as Nicholas Wolterstorff nicely puts it, "Those who edited the final version of these writings were not mindless; they could see, as well as you and I can see, the tensions and contradictions—surface or real" that are present in the text. Nicholas Wolterstorff, "Reading

Joshua," in *Divine Evil? The Moral Character of the God of Abraham*, ed. Michael Bergmann, Michael J. Murray, and Michael C. Rea (Oxford: Oxford University Press, 2011), 251.

139. Put differently, if Joshua had indeed conquered the whole land, then why does Judges begin with a battle that is said to have taken place after Joshua's death (1:1–4)? On this see Matthew Flannagan, "Did God Command the Genocide of the Canaanites?," in *Come Let Us Reason Together: New Essays in Christian Apologetics*, ed. Paul Copan and William Lane Craig (Nashville: B&H Academic, 2012), 228.

140. See also Joshua 11:20.

141. On this see Flannagan, "Did God Command?," 230–31.

142. Wolterstorff, "Reading Joshua," 251. On this see also Flannagan, "Did God Command?," 234.

143. Flannagan, "Did God Command?," 234.

144. On this see Flannagan, "Did God Command?," 231, n10.

145. Wolterstorff, "Reading Joshua," 252.

146. This is the explanation offered, for example, in Tigay, *Deuteronomy*, 85; see also J. G. McConville, *Deuteronomy* (Downers Grove, IL: InterVarsity, 2002), 153. Another possible interpretation would be that since conquering the land would likely take time, the text warns the Israelites not to intermarry in the meantime. This interpretation is mentioned, though not accepted, by Moberly, in *Old Testament Theology*, 61, n61.

147. Utilizing classic Christian terminology, Moberly writes that "careful attention to the *letter* of the text indicates that its *spirit* is in fact other than is envisaged by contemporary anxieties about divinely warranted mass murder . . . Attention to the *letter* of the text problematizes a *literalist* construal. Moberly, *Old Testament Theology*, 59. For a similar point made in a more popular vein, see Strawn, *Lies My Preacher Told Me*, 47.

   Of course, one could argue that Deuteronomy 20:16, according to which Israel "shall not let a soul remain live" in Canaanite towns, requires a literal interpretation and thus calls my reading of Deuteronomy 7 into question. But one could just as easily work the other way and suggest that a metaphorical reading of Deuteronomy 7 makes a metaphorical reading of Deuteronomy 20 more likely too. In any case, as Moberly observes, "The issue concerns the genre of the text and the register of the language." Although we can't know the genre and the register with any real certainty, "there are at least some indications in the language of Deuteronomy 7 that it may be using herem for Israel's actions vis-à-vis the 'seven nations of Canaan' in a metaphorical mode" (63–64).

148. Nicholas Wolterstorff, "Reply to Antony," in *Divine Evil?*, 263.

149. Ellen F. Davis, *Opening Israel's Scriptures* (Oxford: Oxford University Press, 2019), 138.

150. Moberly, *Old Testament Theology*, 62; see also 67–68. "I propose," writes Ellen Davis, "that Joshua is a story that seeks to engender within Israel the courage to resist and overcome the ever-present threat of religious apostasy and assimi-

lation to the dominant culture." Joshua is, she says, "a text designed to engender resistance to religious assimilation . . . and to perceive the threat as literally a matter of life and death." Davis, *Opening Israel's Scriptures*, 138. For a related recent argument that Joshua should be understood "mythically" and an insistence that the book is in reality about the "radical graciousness of Israel's God," see Frank Anthony Spina, "The Irony of Reading the Book of Joshua as Christian Scripture," in *Orthodoxy and Orthopraxis: Essays in Tribute to Paul Livermore*, ed. Douglas Cullum and J. Richard Middleton (Eugene, OR: Pickwick, 2020), 40.

151. In this regard, Walter Moberly argues that the violent rhetoric of Deuteronomy 7 should not be considered separate from the fact that it is given to Israel when it is "small and weak and facing apparently overwhelming odds." Crucially, Moberly explains that "those who use the Bible in a position of strength should not forget that meaning is relative to context, and that what is said to Israel in weakness can differ significantly from what is said to Israel in strength." Moberly, *Old Testament Theology*, 51. Invoking a biblical image, Moberly adds that "a text that envisages YHWH as enabling David to be victorious over Goliath becomes entirely different if claimed by Goliath as divine warrant for overcoming David" (60).

152. Davis, *Opening Israel's Scriptures*, 129. For an argument about the centrality of the conquest narrative in providing "political-theological rationalization via scriptural narrative (the sacralization of politics) for the project of Western imperial and racist expansion, since 1500, into the peripheries and the divinely sanctioned subjugation and extermination of native peoples across the globe," see Bill Templer, "The Political Sacralization of Imperial Genocide: Contextualizing Timothy Dwight's *The Conquest of Canaan*," *Postcolonial Studies* 9, no. 4 (December 2006): 380. Although it came to my attention only after this chapter was completed, it seems likely that Rachel Havrelock, *The Joshua Generation: Israeli Occupation and the Bible* (Princeton, NJ: Princeton University Press, 2020) would also be relevant here.

153. Mishnah, Yadayim 4:4. See also Tosafot to BT, Megillah 12b, s.v. *zil legabei Amon* and Tosafot to Yevamot 76b, s.v. *minyamin*. And see Maimonides, *Mishneh Torah, Hilkhot Issurei Bi'ah*, 12:25.

154. There is undoubtedly some truth to the Bible scholar Stephen Williams's contention that "our conflicting positions on slaughter in Joshua characteristically come down to differing views of Scripture." J. Gordon McConville and Stephen N. Williams, *Joshua* (Grand Rapids, MI: Eerdmans, 2010), 120.

155. The classic scholarly presentation of this idea may be found in Gershom G. Scholem, *Major Trends in Jewish Mysticism*, 260–64; see also Gershom Scholem, *Sabbatai Sevi: The Mystical Messiah, 1626–1676*, trans. R. J. Zwi Werblowsky (Princeton, NJ: Princeton University Press, 1973), 28–29.

156. Buber, "Distance and Relation," 207.

157. I am not the first Jewish thinker to suggest this. Rabbi Joseph Soloveitchik, for example, writes that God "retreated into transcendence in order to let a

world emerge outside of [God]." As R. Soloveitchik describes the teaching of these mystics, "the Almighty . . . sacrificed [God's] all-inclusiveness, [God's] all-consuming infinity, and withdrew from a here-and-now coordinate system and retreated into transcendence in order to let a world emerge outside of [God]." God did so, according to R. Soloveitchik, "in order to care, to sustain, and to love." Soloveitchik, *Family Redeemed*, 39; and see also p. 70.

158. This is why self-restraint is probably a more accurate term for what God does than self-limitation (though I use the latter because it is more common in theological writing). God doesn't—can't—surrender God's omnipotence so much as refrain from making use of it.

159. Clark H. Pinnock, "Constrained by Love: Divine Self-Restraint According to Open Theism," *Perspectives in Religious Studies* 34, no. 2 (Summer 2007): 150. Pinnock writes that "God, although [God] could control everything, chooses not to do so but restrains [Godself] for the sake of the freedom that love requires" (149).

160. I hasten to point out that what I am advocating here is not process theology in that the limits on God's power are a function of God's choice rather than some sort of necessary limitation on God. Yet like process theologians, according to the picture I sketch here "God, having created the world, ceases to [exercise omnipotence] in relation to that world, on pain of contradicting the divine creative intent." This is how the theologian Philip Clayton characterizes both John Polkinghorne's views and his own. But where I have added "exercise omnipotence" Clayon has "be omnipotent." I am not sure it is coherent to imagine that God can cease to *be* omnipotent, whereas it does make sense to think of God as ceasing to exercise God's omnipotence. Again, this is why I think "self-restraint" is ultimately a more helpful (and less misleading) term than "self-limitation." See Philip Clayton, "Science-and-Theology from the Standpoint of Divine Kenosis," in *God and the Scientist: Exploring the Work of John Polkinghorne*, ed. Fraser Watts and Christopher C. Knight (New York: Routledge, 2016), 250.

161. Richard Rice, *The Future of Open Theism: From Antecedents to Opportunities* (Downers Grove, IL: InterVarsity Press, 2020), 129. The medieval Jewish philosopher Gersonides provides precedent for this view, having held that "statements about future contingencies have no determinate truth-value, and hence cannot be known, even by God." See Seymour Feldman, *Gersonides: Judaism Within the Limits of Reason* (Oxford: Littman, 2010), 90; and for the original source, Gersonides, *Wars of the Lord*, 6.1.10. Feldman rightly emphasizes that this does not represent any weakness or limitation on God's part, since "if future contingencies are logically unknowable . . . then even if God is the knower in question, his not knowing these events is no real cognitive limitation" (92). It should be noted, though, that there is a vast difference between Gersonides's theology, on the one hand, and the kind of open theism I am advocating, on the other. The God of Gersonides is hardly relational; in truth, the God of Gersonides, who is above both time and space, does not even know human beings as individuals.

162. This paragraph is lightly adapted from Shai Held, "What Can Human Beings Do, and What Can't They? Or, Does the Torah Believe in Progress," in *The Heart of Torah*, vol. 1, p. 3.

163. Tikva Frymer-Kensky, *In the Wake of the Goddesses: Women, Culture, and the Biblical Transformation of Pagan Myth* (New York: Free Press, 1992), 111.

164. W. G. Lambert, "Destiny and Divine Intervention in Babylon and Israel," *Outtestamentische Studiën* 17 (1972): 65–72, 67, 70.

165. Frymer-Kensky, *In the Wake of the Goddesses*, 108

166. On this see, for example, Terence E. Fretheim, *Creation Untamed: The Bible, God, and Natural Disasters* (Grand Rapids, MI: Baker, 2010), 3, 11, 13.

167. Fretheim, *Creation Untamed*, 25. I think it's important to note, however, that there is no sense in this text that the created entities can do anything other than God wants and asks of them.

168. J. Richard Middleton, "Creation Founded in Love: Breaking Rhetorical Expectations in Genesis 1:1–2:3," in Leonard Jay Greenspoon and Bryan F. LeBeau, *Sacred Text, Secular Times: The Hebrew Bible in the Modern World* (Omaha, NE: Creighton, 2000), 62.

169. Fretheim, *Creation Untamed*, 31.

170. I allude here to Fretheim's declaration that the God of Genesis is a "power-sharing" rather than a "power-hoarding" God. Terence Fretheim, "Creator, Creature, and Co-Creation in Genesis 1–2," in *What Kind of God? Collected Essays of Terence E. Fretheim*, 199. Note also Phyllis Trible's comment on Genesis 2:19: "It shows this deity . . . not as an authoritarian controller of events but as the generous delegator of power who even forfeits the right to reverse human decisions." Phyllis Trible, *God and the Rhetoric of Sexuality* (Philadelphia: Fortress, 1978), 93.

171. Terence E. Fretheim, "Divine Dependence upon the Human: An Old Testament Perspective," in Terence E. Fretheim, *What Kind of God? Collected Essays of Terence E. Fretheim*, ed. Michael J. Chan and Brent A. Strawn (Winona Lake, IN: Eisenbrauns, 2015), 30.

172. Fretheim, "Divine Dependence," 31.

173. Fretheim, *Creation Untamed*, 14.

174. Middleton, "Creation Founded in Love," 59, 61, 61–62.

175. Middleton, "Creation Founded in Love," 65. Middleton argues against the view that for Genesis God needs rest from the labor involved in creating the world. Rather, he maintains, "God's 'rest' follows naturally on the heels of God's (royal/parental) delegation of responsible stewardship to humanity" (84, n91).

176. For Fretheim, it's worth noting, the seventh day represents "a divine move to a different sort of creating . . . Resting on God's part means giving time and space over to the creatures to be what they were created to be: God will be present and active in the world but will not be invested in the management of the creatures. God will rest and let them be and become what they were created to be, without divine interference, with all the capacities that they have been given." Fretheim, *Creation Untamed*, 26–27. In earlier writings, Fretheim had expressed skepti-

cism that God's seventh day rest represented a divine pulling back. Compare Terence E. Fretheim, "Genesis," in *New Interpreter's Bible*, vol. 1 (Nashville: Abingdon, 1994), 346. In the context of this discussion, it's perhaps useful to contrast Genesis 1 with Psalm 104. Whereas in the former, it can seem that God's creative activity took place in the past, in the latter it's clear that God is engaged in continuous creation.

177. Fretheim, *Creation Untamed*, 82, 78, 81.

178. Fretheim, *Creation Untamed*, 82. The emphasis in the verse from Ecclesiastes is mine.

179. This idea is especially amplified in the writings of Rabbi Abraham Joshua Heschel. A good place to start is R. Heschel's *The Prophets*, with its extensive discussions of the "divine pathos" displayed in the Hebrew Bible.

180. Bruce C. Birch, "Creation and the Moral Development of God in Genesis 1–11," *Word & World*, Supplement Series 5 (2006), 18. God's question to Adam, "Where are you?" (Genesis 3:9), Birch tells us, is "plaintive and puzzled."

181. Mekhilta de-Rabbi Simon b. Yohai to Exodus 3:8, p. 1; and note also the statement of Rabbi Eliezer there, on Exodus 3:7. For an important discussion of how the idea that God suffers with Israel plays out in Rabbinic literature, see Abraham Joshua Heschel, *Torah Min Ha-Shamayim*, vol. 1, pp. 65–92; for a slightly abridged English translation, see Abraham Joshua Heschel, *Heavenly Torah: As Refracted Through the Generations*, ed. and trans. Gordon Tucker with Leonard Levin (London: Continuum, 2008), 104–26. According to R. Heschel, the Talmudic sages radicalized what we find in the prophets. In his words, according to the school of the sage Rabbi Akiva "The participation of the Holy and Blessed One in the life of Israel is not merely a mental nod, a measure of compassion born of relationship to God's people. The pain of compassion amounts to pain only at a distance; it is the pain of the onlooker. But the participation of the Holy and Blessed One is that of total identification, something that touches God's very essence, God's majestic being. As it were, the afflictions of the nation inflict wounds on God." *Torah Min Ha-Shamayim*, vol. 1, pp. 65–66; *Heavenly Torah*, 106.

182. Fretheim, *Creation Untamed*, 61.

183. John Polkinghorne, "Kenotic Creation and Divine Action," in *The Work of Love: Creation as Kenosis* (Grand Rapids, MI: Eerdmans, 2001), 94. See similarly: "The history of the world [is not] the performance of a fixed score, written by God from all eternity, but may properly be understood as the unfolding of a grand improvisation in which Creator and creatures both participate." John Polkinghorne, *Science and the Trinity: The Christian Encounter with Reality* (New Haven, CT: Yale University Press, 2004), 67.

184. God thus has both eternal and temporal dimensions. God always exists but, in creating, God makes a decision to enter into the flow of time. For this idea and the meaning it has in my thinking, see for example, John Polkinghorne, *Science and Providence: God's Interaction with the World* (London: SPCK, 1989), 91–93; and John Polkinghorne and Nicholas Beale, *Questions of Truth: Fifty-One Responses to Questions About God, Science, and Belief* (Louisville, KY: Westminster

John Knox Press, 2009), 32. Also worth consulting is Keith Ward, *Rational Theology and the Creativity of God* (London: Blackwell, 1982).

14. Engaging Chosenness

1. Kaufmann Kohler, *Jewish Theology, Systematically and Historically Considered* (New York: Ktav, 1968; originally published in 1918), 323. According to the Bible scholar Walter Brueggemann, the election of Israel is "the pervasive, governing premise of faith in the Old Testament." Walter Brueggemann, *Reverberations of Faith*, 61.

2. Jeremy Cott, "The Biblical Problem of Election," *Journal of Ecumenical Studies* 21, no. 2 (Spring 1984): 204.

3. Walter Brueggemann, *Tenacious Solidarity: Biblical Provocations on Race, Religion, Climate, and the Economy*, ed. David Hankins (Minneapolis, MN: Fortress, 2018), 135, 119 ("Choosing Against Chosenness" is the title of the essay).

4. Mishnah Avot 3:14.

5. Mishnah Avot 3:14.

6. Mishnah Avot 3:14.

7. As the past few decades of scholarship on Paul have shown, there may well have been a significant gap between what Paul himself intended to teach and what centuries of interpreters took him to be saying. The scholarly literature on Paul's views of God's covenant with Israel is enormous. For a succinct introduction to the discussion, one good place to start is Magnus Zetterholm, "Paul Within Judaism: The State of the Questions," in *Paul Within Judaism: Restoring the First-Century Context to the Apostle*, ed. Mark D. Nanos and Magnus Zetterholm (Minneapolis, MN: Fortress, 2015), 31–51.

8. BT, Kiddushin 36a. (Compare the contrasting perspective offered by R. Judah there.) On the unconditionality of God's choice, see also R. Judah Loew of Prague (Maharal), *Netzah Yisrael*, ch. 11.

9. It's worth adding that to imagine God choosing for no discernible reason creates the risk not just of making God seem inscrutable but of intensifying the feeling among those who are not chosen that God is fundamentally unfair.

10. Jon Levenson, "Genesis," in *Jewish Study Bible*, ed. Adele Berlin and Marc Zvi Brettler (New York: Oxford University Press, 2004), 30.

11. For an accessible discussion of the earliest interpretations of Abraham's election, see James L. Kugel, *The Bible as It Was* (Cambridge, MA: Harvard University Press, 1997), 133–48.

12. For the classic Jewish tellings of these two stories, see Genesis Rabbah 38:13 and 39:1.

13. Yet notice Genesis 22:15–18, on which see R. W. L. Moberly, "The Earliest Commentary on the Akedah," *Vetus Testamentum* 38, no. 3 (January 1988): 320–21.

14. I borrow this rendering of Deuteronomy 7:7 from Jon D. Levenson, *The Love of God: Divine Gift, Human Gratitude, and Mutual Faithfulness in Judaism* (Princeton, NJ: Princeton University Press, 2016), 41.

15. Compare ancient Israel's small size with the vastness of neighboring Egypt,

Babylon, Assyria, and Aram, and the point about being tiny is well-taken. On this see P. D. Miller, *Deuteronomy*, 112.

16. P. D. Miller, *Deuteronomy*, 113. Philosophers debate whether at bottom love *appraises* its object or *bestows* something upon it. Appraisal love is based on reasons derived from the valuable properties of the beloved; bestowal love, in contrast, is not based on such reasons—it bestows value on the beloved rather than discovering it there. I will not enter this vast discussion here but simply observe that the Bible presents God's love for Israel as a form of bestowal love. A good place to get acquainted with the contours of the philosophical discussion (although it is invested in making an argument rather than offering an introductory survey) is Dwayne Moore, "Subject-Centred Reasons and Bestowal Love," *Philosophical Explorations* 22, no. 1 (2019): 62–77.

17. On this see Jeffrey H. Tigay, *Deuteronomy* (Philadelphia: Jewish Publication Society, 1996), 97

18. For a similar concern about the potentially deleterious consequences of Israel being materially blessed in the land, see Deuteronomy 8:7–18.

19. Genesis and 27:35 and 29:25. Note also the sting in Laban's response to Jacob: "It is not the practice in our place to marry off the younger before the older" (29:26). And see also Genesis Rabbah 70:19 and Tanhuma Buber Vayetze s.v. *davar aher: vayar Hashem ki snu'ah Leah*.

20. As I've already mentioned, the words of Jacob's father, Isaac, condemn him for his actions: "Your brother came *deceitfully* (*be-mirmah*) and took your blessing" (Genesis 27:35, NIV translation, emphasis added; the NJPS rendering of *be-mirmah* as "with guile" strikes me as inexact and somewhat apologetic in tone). Of course, one could make a claim that the narrator may have a different view of Jacob's actions than Issac does but I don't see any hint or indication of that in the text.

21. Frederick Greenspahn writes of Jacob that "he is not a very positive figure. Indeed, unlike David or Moses, there is not even much evidence of hidden virtue with which his selection might be vindicated." Frederick E. Greenspahn, *When Brothers Dwell Together: The Preeminence of Younger Siblings in the Hebrew Bible* (Oxford: Oxford University Press, 1994), 130. In general, Greenspahn writes, "Israel portrayed herself as a deeply flawed culture, with repeated biblical references to sinfulness, despite her election" (131).

22. Solomon Schechter, *Some Aspects of Rabbinic Theology* (New York: Macmillan, 1923), 46–47.

23. I want to acknowledge but leave for another context the important challenges raised by feminism and broader commitments to gender equality for the imagery of God as (male) father.

24. For marriage as a covenant in biblical thinking, see especially Malachi 2:14; and for an influential study, see Gordon P. Hugenburger, *Marriage as a Covenant: Biblical Law and Ethics as Developed from Malachi* (Grand Rapids, MI: Baker, 1998). For covenant as a marriage, see, in addition to the passages cited in the body of the text, Isaiah 54:5; Jeremiah 3:14, 20, and 31:32; Ezekiel 16:8.

25. For a Rabbinic declaration that God refers to Israel as God's bride no fewer than ten times in the Bible, see the statement attributed to R. Berekhia in Deuteronomy Rabbah 2:37.

26. See BT, Ta'anit 26b; Numbers Rabbah 12:8, end; Song of Songs Rabbah 3:21 (on 3:11); and Exodus Rabbah 52:5.

27. See, for example, Tanhuma Be-Midbar 5; and Deuteronomy Rabbah 3:12.

28. BT, Yoma 54a.

29. See also Deuteronomy 14:1 and Hosea 11:1.

30. See Walter Kaiser, *Toward an Old Testament Theology* (Grand Rapids, MI: Zondervan, 1978), 102.

31. See Exodus 13:2, 11–16; and 22:28–29; and see William H. C. Propp, *Exodus 19–40: A New Translation with Introduction and Commentary* (New York: Doubleday, 2006), 159. See also Martin Buber's discussion of Jeremiah 2:3 in Buber, *On the Bible: Eighteen Studies*, ed. Nahum Glatzer (New York: Schocken, 1982), 84–85.

32. To clarify potential misunderstanding, the Bible scholar Denis McCarthy writes: "We are accustomed to make a clear distinction between a contractual group and the family group . . . Not so ancient Israel: the result of the contract, the covenant, was thought of as a kind of familial relationship." Denis McCarthy, "Israel, My First-Born Son," *The Way* 5 (July 1965): 186.

33. McCarthy explains: "The proof that the Sinai covenant was familial is simple: the rites by which it was ratified. Blood was shared [see Exodus 24:5–8], a sign which is universally recognized among the more primitive peoples as making strangers one family because symbolically they share one blood." McCarthy, "Israel, My First-Born Son," 187.

34. McCarthy, "Israel, My First-Born Son," 188.

35. I don't pretend that what follows is in any way exhaustive; in any case, from a religious perspective I am not sure one could ever construct an exhaustive list of what one owes to God. What follows is a set of images and ideas that I find provocative and that I think are central to the Jewish tradition writ large.

36. Meir Bar-Ilan argues that the two phrases "who has chosen us from among all the people" and "given us His Torah" are appositives—that is, that according to this text, "the election of Israel is the giving of the Torah and the giving of the Torah is the election of Israel." I have interpreted somewhat more cautiously—that the giving of the Torah is an *expression* of the election of Israel but is not simply synonymous with it. Meir Bar-Ilan, "The Idea of Election in Jewish Prayer" (Hebrew), in *The Idea of Election in Israel and Among the Nations: Collected Essays*, ed. Shmuel Almog and Michael Heyd (Jerusalem: Zalman Shazar Center, 1991), 130.

37. This is likely why some Talmudic sages objected to non-Jews studying Torah: a loving couple does not welcome strangers into its most private, intimate moments. See the opinion of R. Yohanan in BT, Sanhedrin 59a; but note also the contrary opinion of R. Meir cited there.

38. Martin Luther (1483–1546), *Lectures on Galatians*, *Luther's Works*, vol. 26–27,

p. 208. *Either* law *or* grace, says Luther; we cannot have it both ways. The legal historian Joseph David explains that for Luther "legalism, or being 'under the law,' . . . [is] the most colossal religious mistake against which Christianity appeared to redeem humanity." Joseph David, "Love, Law, and the Judeo-Christian Separation-Individuation," in *Law, Religion, and Love: Seeking Ecumenical Justice for the Other*, ed. Paul Babie and Vanja-Ivan Savić (London: Routledge, 2018), 156. For a very different Protestant interpretation of the law (though still obviously a very far cry from a Jewish one), it is worth consulting the works of John Wesley (1703–1791). For a useful introduction, see William M. Arnett, "John Wesley and the Law," *The Asbury Seminarian*, 35, no. 4 (1980): 22–31.

39. R. Solomon Schechter influentially connects the notion of *simhah shel mitzvah* with the commitment to doing things for their proper purpose (*lishmah*)—or as he puts it, "for the sake of him who wrought (commanded) it, excluding all worldly intentions. Schechter, *Some Aspects of Rabbinic Theology*, 148–69, especially 159–67; passage cited is at 159–60.

40. I wonder whether this may be part of what R. Schechter has in mind when he translates *simhah shel mitzvah* as "the joy experienced by the Rabbinic Jew *in being commanded* to fulfill the Law." Schechter, *Some Aspects of Rabbinic Theology*, 148; emphasis added.

41. On this see P. D. Miller, *Deuteronomy*, 56–57; and Shai Held, "A God So Close, and Laws So Righteous: Moses's Challenge (and Promise), in *The Heart of Torah*, vol. 2, pp. 215–19.

42. R. Eliezer b. Nathan (1090?–1170), *Peirush Ha-Ra'avan* to the Siddur. I am grateful to R. Elie Kaunfer for helping me locate this source.

43. The Bible scholar Marvin Sweeney explains that "robbery" (*gezelah*) refers to "any dishonest economic action." Marvin A. Sweeney, *Reading Ezekiel: A Literary and Theological Commentary* (Macon, GA: Smyth and Helwys, 2013), 95.

44. Gordon Wenham, *Genesis 1–15*, 170. Wenham writes about a tzaddik, a just or righteous person. I have modified his words slightly to describe tzedakah, justice or righteousness, as a quality instead.

45. See, for example, Ezekiel 16:49 and Pirkei de-Rabbi Eliezer, ch. 25:5–8.

46. Genesis Rabbah 49.4.

47. "There are three distinguishing marks of this nation: They are merciful, they are bashful, and they perform acts of kindness . . . Whoever has these three distinguishing marks is fit to cleave to this nation." BT, Yevamot 79a. "Bashful" (*bayshanim*, which could also be rendered "shame-faced") likely means feeling shame at committing sin. On this see Avraham Kariv, *Mi-Sod Hakhamim: BiNtivei Aggadot Hazal* (Jerusalem: Mosad Ha-Rav Kook, 1976), 141.

48. Note also R. Samuel David Luzzatto's (Shadal) explanation of tzedakah: "doing more than the law requires out of love for humanity" (commentary to Ezekiel 18:5).

49. See Rashi, commentary to Genesis 18:19, s.v. *ki yedativ*.

50. For a beautiful midrashic passage describing how from the first moments of

creation God has longed to find a home on earth, and how people's behavior has alternatively caused God either to ascend upward away from our world or to descend downward toward it, see Tanhuma Buber, Naso 24.

51. Ellen Davis, *Opening Israel's Scriptures*, 64.

52. See also Deuteronomy 23:15. Kaminsky writes that in Leviticus, Israel is charged with "creating an environment in which the Deity will become manifest" and with "maintaining a fit environment in which God could manifest himself and through his presence on earth radiate blessing to the whole terrestrial world." Kaminsky, *Yet I Loved Jacob*, 96–97.

53. See Exodus Rabbah 34:1; and Pesikta de-Rav Kahana 2:10.

54. Rabbi Obadiah Seforno, commentary to Leviticus 26:12. See also Jacob Milgrom, *Leviticus 23–27* (New Haven, CT: Yale University Press, 2001), 2299–301, on how the Hebrew *mishkani* ("My abode") in v. 11 cannot refer to the *mishkan* but refers instead to God's more portable presence. For the view that the verse has *both* the *mishkan and* a more general presence in mind, see John E. Hartley, *Leviticus* (Nashville: Thomas Nelson, 1992), 463; and S. Tamar Kamionkowski, *Leviticus* (Collegeville, MN: Liturgical, 2018), 282.

55. Sifre BeMidbar 161. For more on this, see Shai Held, "Do Not Murder! Shedding Innocent Blood and Polluting the Land," in *The Heart of Torah*, vol. 2, pp. 191–95. The last two sentences of this paragraph are taken almost verbatim from p. 195.

56. Space prevents me from considering another crucial requirement of those who are chosen—to testify against contemporary idolatries in both word and deed. See especially Will Herberg, "The 'Chosenness' of Israel and the Jew of Today," in Arthur A. Cohen, *Arguments and Doctrines: A Reader in Jewish Thinking in the Aftermath of the Holocaust* (New York; Harper and Row, 1970), 270–83.

57. For this reading of Exodus 3, I am indebted to James E. Robson, "Forgotten Dimensions of Holiness," *Horizons in Biblical Theology* 33, no. 2 (January 2011): 132–34. I find Robson's reading religiously compelling even as I remain unsure that it is entirely textually convincing.

58. I am aware, of course, of the scholarly discussion of conditional and unconditional covenants in the Hebrew Bible. What I am attempting here is a canonical reading, by which the narrative of the Torah as we have had can be understood as one coherent whole.

59. For similar but not-quite-identical interpretations to the one I offer here, see, for example, Kaiser, *Toward an Old Testament Theology*, 111; and Fretheim, *Exodus*, 213.

60. In a related but again not-quite-identical vein, John Kessler writes that whereas election is unconditional, "the blessings of the covenant" are conditional. See John Kessler, *Old Testament Theology: Divine Call and Human Response* (Waco, TX: Baylor University Press, 2013), 267.

61. Note also Genesis 18:18; 35:11; and 46:3.

62. In a similar vein, R. Meir Leibush Weiser (Malbim) observes that the people are already an *am segullah*, a cherished people, and now they are called upon to

become a *goy kadosh*, a holy people. Malbim, commentary to Exodus 19:5, s.v. *vihyitem li segullah*.

63. See, for example, Rabbi Abraham Maimonides (1186–1237), commentary to Exodus 19:6, in the name of his father, Moses Maimonides; and see also Rabbi Obadiah Seforno, Commentary to Exodus 19:6, s.v. *ve-atem tihiyu li mamlekhet kohanim*. Note also, for example, R. Seforno's commentary to Exodus 12:2, s.v. *ve-heyeh berakhah*. For a fruitful analysis of R. Seforno's vision of Israel's status as a "kingdom of priests," see Alon Goshen-Gottstein, "A Kingdom of Priests and a Holy Nation," in *Judaism's Challenge: Election, Divine Love, and Human Enmity* (Boston: Academic Studies Press, 2020), 18–23. Note also Rabbi Samson Raphael Hirsch's explanation-justification of Jewish exile "in order to bring to the world, which had lapsed into polytheism, violence, immorality, and in-humanity, the tidings of the existence of the All-One and of the brotherhood of man and his superiority to the beast, and to proclaim the deliverance of man-kind from the bondage of wealth-and-lust worship." Samson Raphael Hirsch, *The Nineteen Letters of Ben Uziel: Being a Spiritual Presentation of the Principles of Judaism*, trans. Bernard Drachman (New York: Funk and Wagnalls, 1899), 81. Contrast, for example, the vision of Rabbi Zalman Sorotzkin, who sees the verse as mandating Israel to build a model society in the Promised Land. R. Zalman Sorotzkin, *Oznayim La-Torah* to Exodus 19:6, s.v. *ve-atem tihiyu li* (no. 2). A contemporary Jewish thinker, Rabbi Eugene Korn, argues that the Jewish people have two distinct outward-looking theological obligations: to spread knowledge of God and to teach the world about "divine moral values that are fundamental to human welfare." Eugene Korn, "The Covenant and Its Theology," *Meorot* 9 (Tishrei 5772), 7.

64. A. H. McNeile, *The Book of Exodus: With Introduction and Notes*, 2nd ed. (London: Methuen, 2017), 111.

65. See, for example, Malachi 2:7.

66. Elmer A. Martens, "The People of God," in *Central Themes in Biblical Theology; Mapping Unity in Diversity*, ed. Scott J. Hafeman and Paul R. House (Grand Rapids, MI: Baker Academic, 2007), 249

67. Cornelis Houtman writes similarly that the focus of the verses is on "the unique, privileged position of the priesthood and the obligation to careful observance of the precepts laid down." Cornelis Houtman, *Exodus*, vol. 2 (Leuven: Peeters, 1996), 446.

68. See Houtman, *Exodus*, 445.

69. In the same spirit, the Bible scholar Jo Bailey Wells writes that "holiness fo-cuses, primarily, on faithful adherence to God's covenant in all aspects of wor-ship and life." Jo Bailey Wells, *God's Holy People: A Theme in Biblical Theology* (Sheffield: Sheffield Academic, 2000), 14.

70. Midrash Ha-Gadol to Exodus 19:6. For earlier precedent for tying the mandate to holiness to keeping the commandments, see the statement attributed to Issi b. Yehudah in Mekhilta to Exodus 22:30 (Masekhta de-Kaspa, parashah 20) as well as Sifrei Numbers 115:1 (to Numbers 15:40) and note the work this passage

does in Maimonides, Introduction to *Sefer Ha-Mitzvot*, Fourth Introductory Principle.

71. T. Desmond Alexander, *Exodus* (Grand Rapids, MI: Baker Books, 2016), 97.

72. Durham, *Exodus*, 263.

73. On this see the commentary of Rabbi Abraham Maimonides to Exodus 19:6, s.v. *ve-atem tihiyu li*. But note the openness to coercion he sees enabled by the invocation of kingship.

74. See, somewhat similarly, Buber, *On the Bible*, 89.

75. Or perhaps, "a covenant for the people," or "a covenant for the peoples." How one translates the phrase has repercussions for whether one understands it more in particularistic or in universalistic tones.

76. For a very brief and clear introduction to the parameters of the debate in the world of academic biblical scholarship, see Andrew Wilson, *The Nations in Deutero-Isaiah: A Study on Composition and Structure* (Lewiston, NY: Edwin Mellen Press, 1986), 1–10. Much more expansively, see Michael A. Grisanti, "Israel's Mission to the Nations in Isaiah 40–55: An Update," *The Master's Seminary Journal* 9, no. 1 (Spring 1998): 39–61.

77. T. K. Cheyne, *Introduction to the Book of Isaiah* (London: Adam and Charles Black, 1895), 244, cited in Grisanti, "Israel's Mission," 43.

78. Edmond Jacob, *Theology of the Old Testament*, trans. Arthur W. Heathcote and Philip. J. Allcock (New York: Harper and Row, 1958), 220.

79. Here I closely follow Joel Kaminsky and Anne Stewart, "God of All the World: Universalism and Developing Monotheism in Isaiah 40–66," *Harvard Theological Review* 99, no. 2 (April 2006): 139–63.

80. Robert Martin-Achard, *A Light to the Nations: A Study of the Old Testament Conception of Israel's Mission to the World*, trans. John Penney Smith (Edinburgh: Oliver and Boyd, 1962), 75.

81. Raphael Jospe, "Chosenness in Judaism: Exclusivity vs. Inclusivity," in *Covenant and Chosenness in Judaism and Mormonism*, ed. Raphael Jospe, Truman Madsen, and Seth Ward (Madison, NJ: Fairleigh Dickinson University Press, 2001), 186.

82. See, most prominently, H. H. Rowley, *The Biblical Doctrine of Election* (London: Lutterworth, 1953), 165. On this see Kaminsky, *Yet I Loved Jacob*, 153.

83. Until recently such characterizations of Judaism, and such purported contrasts with Christianity, were routine even in scholarly analyses on the ancient world. On this, and on the way it is both "unfair and tendentious," see Terence L. Donaldson, *Judaism and the Gentiles: Jewish Patterns of Universalism (to 135 CE)* (Waco, TX: Baylor University Press, 2007), 1.

84. Levenson, "The Universal Horizon," 166. See also Joel S. Kaminsky, "The Concept of Election and Second Isaiah: Recent Literature," *Biblical Theology Bulletin* 31, no. 4 (Winter 2001): 136

85. For the often inverse relationship between inclusiveness and tolerance within the Pentateuch itself, see Joel S. Kaminsky, "Election Theology and the Problem of Universalism," *Horizons in Biblical Theology* 33, no. 1 (January 2011): 35–36.

86. Herbert Gordon May, "Theological Universalism in the Old Testament," *Journal of Bible and Religion* 16, no. 2 (April 1948): 100.

87. For an important historical example, see Henry Chadwick, "Christian and Roman Universalism in the Fourth Century," in *Christian Faith and Greek Philosophy in Late Antiquity*, ed. Lionel R. Wickham and Caroline P. Bammel (Leiden: Brill, 1993), 26–42; see especially at 41.

88. For the classic statement of this position, see Tosefta Sanhedrin 13:2; and see also Midrash Mishlei 19:1. For a useful survey of relevant sources, see Gilbert S. Rosenthal, "Hasidei Umot Ha-Olam: A Remarkable Concept," *Journal of Ecumenical Studies* 48, no. 4 (Fall 2013): 467–90. Raphael Jospe encapsulates the point nicely: for the Talmudic sages, "wicked Jews are denied, and righteous Gentiles are granted, a portion in the world to come." Raphael Jospe, "The Concept of the Chosen People: An Interpretation," *Judaism* 43, no. 2 (1994): 130. But compare, for a sober assessment of "the presumption of distrust and alienation as the normal state of Jewish-gentile relations" during the Talmudic period, Robert Goldenberg, *The Nations That Know Thee Not: Ancient Jewish Attitudes Toward Other Religions* (New York: NYU Press, 1998), 84–85. For Rabbinic skepticism about the nations' ability to abide by the seven Noahide commandments and, accordingly, about their share in the world to come, see BT, Avodah Zarah 2b–3a.

89. Levenson, "The Universal Horizon," 148.

90. Boyarin, *A Radical Jew*, 232–33.

91. For "coercion to conform" as a dangerous aspect in the apostle Paul's universalism, see Boyarin, *A Radical Jew*, 235.

92. Ellen Birnbaum, "Some Particulars About Universalism," in *Crossing Boundaries in Early Judaism and Christianity: Ambiguities, Complexities, and Half-Forgotten Adversaries: Essays in Honor of Alan F. Segal*, ed. Kimberley Stratton and Andrea Lieber (Leiden: Brill, 2016), 118.

93. Christopher J. H. Wright, "Truth with a Mission: Reading All Scripture Missiologically," *The Southern Baptist Journal of Theology* 15, no. 2 (Summer 2011): 9; emphasis added.

94. Christopher J. H. Wright, "The Old Testament and Christian Mission," *Evangel* 14 (Summer 1996): 39; emphasis Wright's. Even as subtle a reader of the Bible as Martin Buber interprets election in terms that are overly instrumental: "You shall establish my kingdom over you," Buber imagines God telling the Isrealites, "but as my messengers and helpers—in order thus to begin the preparation of humanity for my kingdom." Buber, *On the Bible*, 89. As I will argue presently, this "in order" is too simple and reductive.

95. Kaminsky, *Yet I Loved Jacob*, 156.

96. Patrick D. Miller Jr., "The Wilderness Journey in Deuteronomy: Style, Structure, and Theology in Deuteronomy 1–3," in *To Hear and to Obey: Essays in Honor of Frederick Carlson Holmgren*, ed. Paul E. Koptak and Bradley J. Bergfalk (Chicago: Covenant Publications, 1997), 58.

97. P. D. Miller, "The Wilderness Journey in Deuteronomy," 57.

98. Note also Deuteronomy 23:8: "You shall not abhor an Edomite, for he is your kinsman (*ahikha*)." More precisely, of the three nations in question only Edom is explicitly described as kin in Deuteronomy. But as Miller explains, although "the word does not appear in the accounts of moving peacefully through the territory of the Moabites and the Ammonites . . . the relational connection is clearly indicated there also, as both groups are specifically referred to as 'the descendants of [Abraham's nephew] Lot' (1:9, 19), even as the Edomites are referred to as [Abraham's grandson] 'Esau' (1:5) and 'the descendants of Esau' (2:8, 12)." P. D. Miller, "The Wilderness Journey in Deuteronomy," 56.

99. See Isaiah 18:1 and Esther 1:1; 8:9. Robert Martin-Achard is quick to explain that "there is here [in Amos 9:7] not a single note either of depreciation or of racism in the prophet's words, simply a statement that would appear extraordinary and even unacceptable to his hearers, that their God was equally interested in those strange far away peoples . . ." Robert Martin-Achard, "The End of the People of God: A Commentary on the Book of Amos," in R. Martin-Achard and S. Paul Re'mi, *God's People in Crisis* (Grand Rapids, MI: Eerdmans, 1984), 65.

100. See, for example, 2 Samuel 18:21 and Jeremiah 38:7.

101. Numbers 12:1.

102. Simundson, *Hosea-Joel-Amos-Obadiah-Jonah-Micah*, 234.

103. On this point, see Mordecai Cogan and Shalom Paul, *Joel and Amos* (Hebrew) (Tel-Aviv: Am-Oved, 1994), 141–42. (The commentary on Amos is by Paul.)

104. P. D. Miller, "The Wilderness Journey in Deuteronomy," 59. Emphasis added. Paul goes so far as to say that from Amos's perspective, "Israel's exodus from Egypt is in no way unique." Cogan and Paul, *Joel and Amos*, 142. Somewhat more expansively, see Bruce C. Birch, *Hosea, Joel, and Amos* (Louisville, KY: Westminster John Knox Press, 1997), 252–53.

105. As Miller writes, in Amos 9:7 "the hubris of the Israelites is condemned, precisely at the point of their assumption of an exclusive salvific relation with the Lord." P. D. Miller, "The Wilderness Journey in Deuteronomy," 59.

106. Terence E. Fretheim, *Reading Hosea-Micah: A Literary and Theological Commentary* (Macon, GA: Smyth and Helwys, 2013), 155. Birch writes: "The exodus experience is not unique. God is at work bringing new possibilities for life even in the histories of Israel's enemies" (Birch, *Hosea, Joel, and Amos*, 253).

107. See Birch, *Hosea, Joel, and Amos*, 191; and Cogan and Paul, *Joel and Amos*, 57. For "singling out" (more literally, "knowing," *yadati*) as covenant language, see, for example, Genesis 18:19.

108. David Allan Hubbard, *Joel & Amos: An Introduction and Commentary* (Downers Grove, IL: InterVarsity Press, 1989), 147

109. Simundson, *Hosea-Joel-Amos-Obadiah-Jonah-Micah*, 181.

110. The discussion of Hagar that follows appeared previously in slightly different form as "Hagar: An Egyptian Maidservant's Suffering Is Seen by YHWH," at TheTorah.com, https://www.thetorah.com/article/hagar-an-egyptian-maid servants-suffering-is-seen-by-yhwh.

111. I say "without enthusiasm" because the text seems to go out of its way to emphasize that Abram and Hagar are brought together by Sarah. It is she who "takes" Hagar and gives her to Abram rather than Abram himself "taking" Hagar as a wife (or concubine) (see Genesis 16:2–3).

112. Although this is not our main concern here, the Bible scholar Kathleen O'Connor is undoubtedly right that although using slaves to have children was legally accepted in the ancient world, "the chapter depicts deep family tensions that act as a critique of these arrangements." Kathleen M. O'Connor, *Genesis 1–25a* (Macon, GA: Smyth and Helwys, 2018), 236–37. We might also say that although the text accepts patriarchy and its implications as the way of the world, it does not hesitate to shine a light on the suffering it causes—both to women and to men.

113. Tikva Frymer-Kensky, *Reading the Women of the Bible: A New Interpretation of Their Stories* (New York: Schocken, 2002), 228.

114. See the comments of Nahmanides (Ramban) and Rabbi David Kimhi (Radak) to Genesis 16:6. Ramban includes Abraham in his condemnation; Radak, in contrast, seems to exonerate him.

115. And yet, as Phyllis Trible notes, the angel does not refer to her simply as Hagar but as "Hagar, maid of Sarai" (Genesis 16:8). Even as the angel "acknowledges . . . the personhood of this woman," Trible writes, "the appositive, 'maid of Sarai,' tempers the recognition, for Hagar remains a servant in the vocabulary of the divine." Phyllis Trible, *Texts of Terror: Literary-Feminist Readings of Biblical Narratives* (Philadelphia: Fortress, 1984), 15.

116. See Sarna, *Genesis*, 120.

117. Here, Hagar's story reflects Israel's. Just as Israel goes into slavery having been told that this will be their fate (see God's words to Abram in Genesis 15:13), so too now Hagar is sent (back) into slavery, knowing full well what awaits her. See Frymer-Kensky, *Reading the Women of the Bible*, 233.

118. I have explored this law in depth in Shai Held, "Let Him Live Wherever He Chooses: Or, Why Runaway Slaves Are Like God," in *The Heart of Torah*, vol. 2, pp. 250–54.

119. Or perhaps, "in opposition to."

120. This, of course, contrasts with Hagar's being given no choice but to live under Sarai's *hand*—recall Abram's declaration to Sarai that "your maid is in your *hand*" and note that a more literal rendering of the angel's instructions is that Hagar must "suffer oppression under her *hand*." As Trible insightfully notes, "If Hagar lives under the hand of Sarai, the hand of Ishmael will engage in ceaseless strife against such power." Trible, *Texts of Terror*, 17. See also Frymer-Kensky, *Reading the Women of the Bible*, 230–31.

121. Levenson, *The Death and Resurrection of the Beloved Son*, 95; and see also the commentary of Rabbi Abraham Ibn Ezra to Genesis 16:12.

122. It is also possible to take *El-Ro'i* as "God of sight," which, as John Goldingay notes, "nicely covers both 'God who sees' and 'God whom I see.'" John Goldingay, *Genesis* (Grand Rapids, MI: Baker, 2020), 269.

123. Levenson, *The Death and Resurrection of the Beloved Son*, 93–95.

124. For some interpretations that differ from the one I offer here, see, for example, Renita Weems, *Just A Sister Away: A Womanist Vision of Women's Relationships in the Bible* (San Diego, CA: LuraMedia, 1988), 1–19, especially at 13; Wilma Ann Bailey, "Hagar: A Model of an Anabaptist Feminist?," *The Mennonite Quarterly Review* 68, no. 2 (April 1994): 219–28, especially at 223; and Levenson, "Genesis," 37.

125. In the same vein, Phyllis Trible refers to Hagar as "the precursor of Israel's plight under Pharaoh." Trible, *Texts of Terror*, 13.

126. Moreover, as Trible notes, in encountering God after she has fled her oppressor, Hagar parallels Moses (see Exodus 3:1–2). Trible, *Texts of Terror*, 14.

127. Frymer-Kensky, *Reading the Women of the Bible*, 233.

128. Frymer-Kensky, *Reading the Women of the Bible*, 233–34. Uriel Simon begins to gesture in a similar direction when he observes that for both Isaac and Ishmael, the vastness of the blessings bestowed corresponds to the intensity of the dangers endured. Uriel Simon, *Bakesh Shalom Ve-Rodfeihu: She'elot Ha-Sha'ah Be-Or Ha-Mikra, She'elot Ha-Mikra Be-Or Ha-Sha'ah* (Tel-Aviv: Yediot, 2002), 55.

129. The Talmudic sage R. Shimon b. Yohai declares: "The Blessed Holy One gave Israel three precious gifts, all of which were given only by means of suffering: Torah, The Land of Israel, and the World-to-Come." BT, Berakhot 5a. Note also Psalm 22, with its dramatic transition from extravagant lament to extravagant call to praise. I am grateful to Ellen Davis for suggesting this connection to me.

130. Genesis Rabbah 53:11. Notice also the third, rather extreme, possibility raised there, that Ishmael was engaged in murder.

131. Scholars are divided as to whether Sarah's shift from calling Hagar a maidservant (*shifhah*) in chapter 16 to calling her a slave-woman (*amah*) here is meaningful, and if so, precisely what it means. As John Goldingay notes, "Scholars who think one of the words suggests a higher status than the other are not agreed on which one is which." Goldingay, *Genesis*, 327, n5.

132. Nor does she consider Abraham's feelings: to Abram, Ishmael is "his son"; to Sarah, he is merely "the son of that slave" (Genesis 21:10–11).

133. Note also Genesis 17:18, which may retroactively explain some of the anger Sarah feels at Abraham.

134. Trible writes that "when Pharaoh cast out (*g-r-s*) the Hebrew slaves to save the life of the firstborn, God was on their side to bring salvation from expulsion. By contrast, the deity identifies here not with the suffering slave but with her oppressors. Hagar knows banishment rather than liberation." Moreover, when Pharaoh sends away (*sh-l-h*) the Hebrew slaves, the phrase connotes freedom, whereas when Abraham does the same to Hagar, it spells banishment and great danger. Trible, *Texts of Terror*, 22–23.

135. Trible, *Texts of Terror*, 22.

136. Frymer-Kensky, *Reading the Women of the Bible*, 235.

137. The Bible scholar Tammi Schneider points out that the fact that Hagar is allowed to find a wife for Ishmael, which would usually be the job of the boy's father, suggests that she is free at this point in the story. Tammi J. Schneider, *Mothers of Promise: Women in the Book of Genesis* (Grand Rapids, MI: Baker, 2008), 113.

138. Frymer-Kensky, *Reading the Women of the Bible*, 235–36. But as a counterpoint, note the emphasis that Trible places on the fact that Hagar "wanders about" (*vateita*) in the wilderness, something the Israelites are never described as doing. On her account, this indicates that Hagar undergoes "a wilderness experience different from [Israel's]." For Trible, for all that Hagar prefigures Israel, she experiences "exodus without liberation, revelation without salvation, wilderness without covenant, wanderings without land, promise without fulfillment, and unmerited exile without return." Trible, *Texts of Terror*, 23, 28.

139. There are also a number of significant parallels between Ishmael's being sent away in Genesis 21 and Isaac's being bound on the altar in Genesis 22, which I must leave aside for reasons of space. For analyses of the connections between the two stories, see Robert Alter, *The Art of Biblical Narrative* (New York: Basic Books, 1981), 181–82; Trible, *Texts of Terror*, 34–35, n11; Curt Leviant, "Parallel Lives: The Trials and Traumas of Isaac and Ishmael," *Bible Review* (April 1999): 20–25, 47; Uriel Simon, "The Banishment of Ishmael—The Akedah That Preceded the Akedah of Isaac" (Hebrew), in Simon, *Bakesh Shalom Ve-Rodfeihu*, 54–57; David W. Cotter, OSB, *Genesis* (Collegeville, MN: Liturgical, 2003), 145–51; and L. Daniel Hawk, "Cast Out and Cast Off: Hagar, Leah, and the God Who Sees," *Priscilla Papers* 25, no. 1 (Winter 2011): 9–13. See also Yehuda Gil'ad, *Et Kolkha Shamati: Pirkei Bereishit Be-Derekh Ha-Peshat U-Midrasho* (Ma'ale Gilboa, Israel: Yeshivat Ma'ale Gilboa, 2013), 94–97.

140. Cott, "The Problem of Election," 224. Cott goes so far as to declare that "if one believes oneself to be elect one also believes (if just unconsciously) that everyone else is *not* elect and must therefore be done away with" (202). This is, needless to say, totally false.

141. On this see especially Levenson, "The Universal Horizon," 158–59.

142. Kaminsky, *Yet I Loved*, 34.

143. Kaminsky, *Yet I Loved*, 121, 125, 109. For examples of the non-elect as articulating God's saving actions, see the stories of Jethro (Exodus 18:10–11); Rahab (Joshua 2:9–11); and Naaman (2 Kings 5:15).

144. Mordecai M. Kaplan, *The Future of the American Jew* (New York: Macmillan, 1948), 211; and Mordecai M. Kaplan, *Questions Jews Ask: Reconstructionist Answers* (New York: Reconstructionist Press, 1956), 451, 207.

145. Kaplan, *Questions Jews Ask*, 501.

146. Kaplan, *Questions Jews Ask*, 501.

147. Mordecai M. Kaplan, *Know How to Answer: A Guide to Reconstructionism* (New York: Jewish Reconstructionist Foundation, 1951), 82.

148. See, for example, Yehudah Halevi, *Kuzari*, 4:3 (see also 1:96, 111; and for how

Halevi thinks about converts given his ontological conception of Jewishness, see 1:27 and 1:115; for possible Talmudic precedent, see the statement of Rabba b. R. Huna in BT, Kiddushin 70b). On this aspect of Halevi's thought see Lipman Bodoff, "Was Yehudah Halevi Racist?," *Judaism* 38, no. 2 (Spring 1989): 174–84; and especially Daniel J. Lasker, "Proselyte Judaism, Christianity, and Islam in the Thought of Judah Halevi," *Jewish Quarterly Review* 81, no. 1–2 (July/October 1990): 79–91. For a grotesque example, see R. Yaakov Moshe Charlap (1882–1951), *Mei Marom*, vol. 6 (Jerusalem: Bet Zevul, 1977), 33.

149. It is worth remembering the subtitle Halevi gave his classic Kuzari: "The Book of Refutation and Proof on Behalf of the Most Despised Religion." And Menachem Kellner reminds us that "Halevi flourished in a place and time in which conflicting national and religious groupings each advanced its own claims to nobility and belittled the character of its opponents." Kellner, *Maimonides on Judaism and the Jewish People*, 110, n16.

150. Rashi, commentary to Exodus 19:5, s.v. *ki li kol ha-aretz*; and R. Obadiah Seforno, commentary to Exodus 19:5, s.v. *vihyitem li*.

151. There is some convergence between the ideas I present in the next two paragraphs and those presented in Robert W. Jenson, "What Kind of God Can Make a Covenant?," in Robert W. Jenson and Eugene B. Korn, *Covenant and Hope: Christian and Jewish Reflections* (Grand Rapids, MI: Eerdmans, 2012), 3–18. Also worth comparing is Joshua Golding, "Jewish Identity and the Teaching of Chosenness," in *Jewish Identity in the Postmodern Age*, ed. Charles Selengut (St. Paul, MN: Paragon House, 1999), 93.

152. This last point is one of the central thrusts in the theology of Rabbi Abraham Joshua Heschel and his notion of the "divine pathos." See Heschel, *The Prophets*.

153. This is why the word *berit*, or "covenant," plays so little role in the theology of Moses Maimonides.

154. Mordecai M. Kaplan. *Judaism Without Supernaturalism: The Only Alternative to Orthodoxy and Secularism* (New York: Reconstructionist Press, 1958), 22.

155. In the interests of space, I leave aside here another critical dimension of Kaplan's rejection of chosenness, namely his conviction that it was ultimately incompatible with citizenship and participation in a modern democratic state. On this see especially Mordecai M. Kaplan, *Judaism as A Civilization: Toward a Reconstruction of American-Jewish Life* (Philadelphia: Jewish Publication Society, 1981; originally published 1934), 22–25.

156. Herberg, "The 'Chosenness' of Israel and the Jew of Today," 281.

157. Michael Wyschogrod, *The Body of Faith: God in the People Israel* (Northvale, NJ: Jason Aronson, 1993; originally published 1986), 64–65.

158. Jerome Gellman, "Halevi, Wyschogrod, and the Chosen People," in *Jewish Philosophy Past and Present : Contemporary Responses to Classical Sources*, ed. Daniel Frank and Aaron Segal (New York: Routledge, 2017), 196

159. In light of my analysis and critique of Wyschogrod above, there is also more to be said about the possibility of developing a model in which Israel is only one of

God's children, even if also the "eldest" (Exodus 4:22). I hope to return to this in future writing.

160. I am in (ambivalent) agreement with Joel Kaminsky, who writes, with regard to both Judaism and Christianity, "I do not think that either tradition can side-step, marginalize, or jettison election theology without severing its connections to its biblical roots, a move that would greatly impoverish or perhaps even destroy both of these venerable faith traditions." Kaminsky, *Yet I Loved Jacob*, 10.

161. Joel S. Kaminsky, "Attempting the Impossible: Eliminating Election from the Jewish Liturgy," *Midstream* 51, no. 1 (January-February 2005): 24.

15. Loving a Loving God

1. For whether one version (speaking of "abounding" or "everlasting" love) is preferable to the other, see Reuven Kimelman, " 'We Love the God Who Loved Us First': The Second Blessing of the Shema Liturgy," in *Bridging Between Sister Religions: Studies of Jewish and Christian Scriptures Offered in Honor of Prof. John T. Townsend*, ed. Isaac Kalimi (Leiden: Brill, 2016), p. 245, n23. As the notes will make clear, the argument and flow of this and the next few pages are heavily indebted to Kimelman's study.

2. Some scholars suggest that the biblical Hebrew *lev*, "heart," actually refers to the seat of thought, or what we call the mind. Far more persuasive, I think, are those like Jack Lundbom who maintain that "the heart in Hebrew thought is the preeminent metaphor for the inner being of a person, the seat of intelligence; the seat of emotions; and the seat of volition, i.e., the will." Jack R. Lundbom, *Deuteronomy: A Commentary* (Grand Rapids, MI: Eerdmans, 2013), 391.

3. On this see Kimelman, " 'We Love the God Who Loved Us First,' " 245.

4. For taking *hemlah* specifically as "tenderness" rather than the more usual "compassion," see Malachi 3:17 and Kimelman, " 'We Love the God Who Loved Us First,' " 242, n4.

5. Kimelman, " 'We Love the God Who Loved Us First,' " 246.

6. Another pair of sources worth noting in this regard: A Talmudic passage describes God as having kept a precious treasure (the Torah) hidden in God's storehouse for 974 generations before the world was created, and desiring to give it to "God's children," the people of Israel. BT, Zevahim 116a. (For an explanation of the number 974, see Rashi there, s.v *tesha meot ve-shiv'im ve-arba'ah dorot*.) And a Talmudic dictum declares, "Beloved are Israel, for the Blessed Holy One surrounded them with commandments: tefillin on their heads, tefillin on their arms, ritual fringes on their garments, and *mezuzot* on their doorposts" (BT, Menahot 43b).

7. Aaron Rakeffet-Rothkoff, *The Rav: The World of Rabbi Joseph B. Soloveitchik*, vol. 2 (Hoboken, NJ: Ktav, 1999), 202.

8. On this see P. D. Miller, *Deuteronomy*, 56–57, and Shai Held, "A God So Close, and Laws So Righteous: Moses's Challenge (and Promise), in *The Heart of Torah*, vol. 2, pp. 215–19.

9. Were I translating the biblical verse itself, I would probably render Torah as "teaching" (the psalm may well refer to God's teachings in general rather than

to some fixed text, or set of texts, of Torah), but in this context I have kept the word "Torah," since for the liturgy, I suspect, it already has this more concrete and specific meaning. NJPS has "teaching," whereas NIV and NRSV have the highly misleading "law"—"Torah" means "teaching" or "instruction," not "law." I translate here as Kimelman does. See Kimelman, "'We Love the God Who Loved Us First,'" 247.

10. For connecting this theme in the liturgy to these verses from Psalms, I am indebted to Kimelman, "'We Love the God Who Loved Us First,'" 247. Kimelman also points to Psalm 119:125: "Give me understanding, that I might know your decrees." In the same spirit, Deuteronomy envisions a time when "the Lord your God will circumcise your heart and the hearts of your offspring to love the Lord your God with all your heart and all your being" (Deuteronomy 30:6).

11. Rabbi David Kimhi (Radak), commentary to Psalm 100:2, s.v. *ivdu et Hashem be-simhah*; see also Deuteronomy 28:47, which Radak alludes to in his commentary to Psalms.

12. R. Vidal of Tolosa, *Maggid Mishneh* to Maimonides, *Mishneh Torah*, Laws of Lulav 8:15.

13. BT, Avodah Zarah 19a, and see also Rashi there, s.v. *ve-lo biskhar* and *al menat she-lo lekabel peras*. The citation is of Antigonos of Sokho, found in Mishnah Avot 1:3. See also, for example, the statement of R. Yossi in Avot 2:12; the baraita in BT, Nedarim 62a; Rabbeinu Asher ben Yehiel (Rosh), *Orhot Hayyim Le-Ha-Rosh*, 52; and Maimonides, *Mishneh Torah*, Laws of Repentance 10:2. (Note, though, that Antigonos's statement in the Mishnah is followed by another one: "And let the fear of Heaven be upon you." On Antigonos's account, then, those who serve God are supposed to put the thought of reward aside but at the same time to be aware that their actions have consequences. On this, see Levenson, *The Love of God*, 66.)

14. *Sha'arei Ha-Avodah*, (controversially) attributed to R. Yonah Gerondi, chapter 26 (2015 ed., 74). A midrash teaches: "You might say, 'I am going to study Torah in order to become rich,' or 'in order to be called Rabbi,' or 'in order to receive a reward in the world-to-come'; therefore Scripture says, 'To love the Lord your God' (Deut. 11:13)—all that you do, do only from love" (Sifre Deuteronomy, 41).

15. Indeed, according to many Jewish thinkers, there can be no love of God without observance of the commandments. See, for two examples chosen almost completely at random, the anonymous *Orhot Tzaddikim* 5:51; and R. Yaakov Tzvi Mecklenburg, *Ha-Ketav Ve-Ha-Kabbalah* to Exodus 20:5.

16. See, most famously, William L. Moran, "The Ancient Near Eastern Background of the Love of God in Deuteronomy," *Catholic Biblical Quarterly* 25, no. 1 (January 1963): 77–87. In the interest of brevity, I omit any discussion of the basis of Moran's argument, namely his understanding of the ways that the covenant between God and Israel mirror and reflect ancient Near Eastern suzerainty treaties. Just as in the latter, he thinks, love is a way of talking about obedience, so also in the former.

17. See Deuteronomy 7:7 and 10:15.

18. Lapsley, "Feeling Our Way: Love for God in Deuteronomy," 360. To be clear, Lapsley is arguing against this view; my own understanding of Deuteronomy is deeply indebted to hers. Especially worth noting is Deuteronomy 10, in which, as Lapsley observes, the commandment for Israel to love God (v. 12) is almost immediately followed by an evocation of God's love for Israel (v. 15), which is an "evidently emotional attachment." Given the ways that God's love and ours are intertwined in context, it would be extremely odd to argue that the type of love God shows for Israel is utterly different from the type of love of Israel is to show for God (361). One could appeal to the fact that different Hebrew roots are used to describe God's love (h-sh-k) and Israel's (a-h-v) to argue for a difference between the loves, but the fact is that the root a-h-v also frequently has affective dimensions. Elsewhere Lapsley writes: "While obedience to the commandments is a central manifestation of . . . love [for God], Israel is also to mirror the kind of love that propels God toward Israel, and that is at root an inexplicable emotion . . . Obedience is obligatory to the covenantal life and entails its own beauty, but only when the Israelites deepen and nurture their emotional bond of love do they reflect back to God the kind of love they have received." Jacqueline E. Lapsley, "Friends with God? Moses and the Possibility of Covenantal Friendship," *Interpretation* 58, no. 2 (April 2004): 126.

19. Lapsley, "Feeling Our Way," 355. Thomas Dozeman writes that "love usually requires some form of action, but the word is rooted in emotion and affection." Describing love of God in Deuteronomy, he notes that "love is not simply a law to be fulfilled through actions that lack proper motivation. Love is affection, stemming from the heart of humans, which finds expression in obedience to Torah." Thomas Dozeman, "Love," in *Westminster Theological Wordbook of the Bible*, ed. Donald E. Gowan (Louisville, KY: Westminster John Knox Press, 2003), 306, 308.

20. Lapsley, "Feeling Our Way," 354.

21. Tigay, *Deuteronomy*, 76–77.

22. Vernon H. Kooy, "The Fear and Love of God in Deuteronomy," in *Grace Upon Grace: Essays in Honor of Lester J. Kuyper*, ed. James I. Cook (Grand Rapids, MI: Eerdmans, 1975), 111.

23. Sifre Deuteronomy 32.

24. Sifre Deuteronomy 41. Interestingly, Jon Levenson maintains that "in rabbinic literature the question of motivation, the *subjective* dimension to the observance of objective laws, is a matter of much greater importance and much more explicit attention than it is in the Bible." Levenson, *The Love of God*, 63; emphasis Levenson's. Since I am attempting a synthetic interpretation of the tradition as a whole, I leave aside this possible historical development here.

25. Speaking of love and obedience in Deuteronomy, Lapsley nicely writes that "obedience and feeling are interdependent; obedience follows feeling and feeling follows obedience in an endless circuit of faithfulness." Lapsley, "Friends with God?," 127.

26. Yeshayau Leibowitz, *Judaism, Human Values, and the Jewish State*, ed. Eliezer

Goldman (Cambridge, MA: Harvard University Press, 1992), 44. Certain formulations found in Rabbi Louis Jacobs, *The Book of Jewish Values*, 56–58, also strike me as problematic. According to R. Jacobs, "certain deeds [namely, mitzvot] . . . in themselves constitute the love of God" (58). Yet as I have been arguing, such deeds express the love of God, and may even be a part of what love of God consists of, but for the sages love cannot simply be reduced to deed. R. Jacobs rightly observes that people regularly do concrete things to fulfill their lovers' desires. But this does not mean that fulfilling those desires in and of itself is what *constitutes* the love they share. He takes the same approach in Louis Jacobs, *A Jewish Theology* (West Orange, NJ: Behrman House, 1973), 153–54.

27. The difference between a mitzvah and a good deed is important. The former implies the centrality of the divine will in a way that the latter obviously does not. Also, and accordingly, many mitzvot are not deeds that we would conventionally regard as "good deeds"—eating matzah at the seder, not wearing mixtures of wool and linen, and dwelling in a temporary structure known as a sukkah during the Sukkot holiday, to take just three examples, are mitzvot but not "good deeds" in any conventional sense. The translation of "mitzvah" as "good deed" is both inaccurate and inherently secularizing.

28. For a slightly earlier source that connects *mitzvah* and *tzavta*, see R. Isaiah Horowitz (Shelah, 1555–1630), *Shenei Luhot Ha-Berit, Masekhet Yoma, Derekh Hayyim*, Tenai 16. I am grateful to Rabbi Arthur Green for helping me locate this source. In Hasidic literature, the idea can be found, for example, in R. Menachem Nahum of Chernobyl (1730–1797), *Me'or Einayim*, Parashat Beha'alotkha, s.v. *vayedaber Hashem el Moshe* and R. Moshe Hayyim Ephraim of Sudilkov (1748–1800), *Degel Mahaneh Ephraim, Likkutim*, s.v. *mitzvah*.

29. R. Yeruham Levovitz, *Da'at Hokhmah U-Musar*, vol. 1, p. 197. "A mitzvah," says R. Levovitz, is "glue (*devek*) that cleaves and attaches a person to the Creator" (201). We've encountered images of God as parent, as lover, and as teacher, but this idea of divine-human togetherness raises the question of whether human beings can be God's "friends." The appeal of the image of divine-human friendship is, obviously, that it is more horizontal and less hierarchical than, say, images of divine royalty, but the question is whether this type of image takes adequate account of *yirat Hashem*, or awe of God, which would seem to militate against the idea that we can be friends with God. To the extent that we want to embrace the idea of divine-human friendship, we will need, at minimum, to balance it with more hierarchical (and awe-affirming) conceptions. On God as friend, see Rashi's commentary to Proverbs 27:10, s.v. *rei'akha*; see also Midrash Tanhuma, Yitro 5:1, where not only is God called a friend, but Abraham is similarly described as God's friend (*rei'a*). For biblical references to Abraham as a friend of God, see Isaiah 41:8 and see 2 Chronicles 20:7. For one who learns Torah for its proper purpose (*lishmah*) being described as God's friend, see Avot 6:1 and Rashi s.v. *rei'a*; and R. Judah Loew of Prague (Maharal), *Derekh Hayyim* to Avot 6:1. For more recent writers who talk about friendship with

God, see, for example, R. Shlomo Wolbe, *Iggerot*, vol. 2, no. 378, p. 131 (based on Menahot 53a–53b): "God is our friend, and in our prayers—we turn to a friend!" (and see also R. Shlomo Wolbe, *Ma'amarei Yemei Ratzon* [Jerusalem, 2004], 3); and Rabbi Joseph Soloveitchik, "Sacred and Profane," *Jewish Thought* 3, no. 1 (Fall/Winter 1993): 63: God is "not transcendent, mysterious, and inapproachable, but our immediate Companion."

30. And recall, too, the midrash on these verses we encountered in chapter 10. Sifre Deuteronomy, Va-ethanan 33.

31. As R. Joseph Soloveitchik beautifully puts it:

> There is no doubt that the intellect plays a tremendous role in the study of Torah. However, this study is more than simply an intellectual performance. It is a total, all-encompassing, and all-embracing involvement of the mind and heart, will, and feeling—the very center of the human personality. The emotional side of man, his logical bent, the voluntaristic impulses can all be usefully employed in plumbing the depths of Torah.

Aaron Rakeffet-Rothkoff, *The Rav*, 202.

32. See, for example, R. Yohanan in Song of Songs Rabbah 1:2; see also 1:3.

33. BT, Bava Kamma 82a.

34. On this see Rabbi Joseph Soloveitchik, *Beis HaLevi*, introduction; and see also no. 6. Compare Deuteronomy 5:1 (knowing what to do), on the one hand, with Deuteronomy 6:4–9 (seemingly greater focus on study itself), on the other; and see the discussion of the two passages in Ariel Picard, *Lir'ot Et Ha-Kolot: Masoret, Yetzirah, Ve-Herut Parshanit* (Tel-Aviv: Yediot, 2016), 140–41.

35. R. Aharon Lichtenstein (1933–2015), "Reflections upon Birkot Ha-Torah," in Lichtenstein, *Varieties of Jewish Experience* (Jersey City, NJ: Ktav, 2011), 260. In the same spirit, see also Sifra Behukkotai 2 (where the discussion is of *lihiyot ameilim be-Torah*, to be laboring in Torah); and Maimonides, Teshuvot Ha-Rambam, no. 182, where Maimonides argues that the blessing "Blessed are you, Lord, who teaches Torah to [God's] people Israel" is misguided, since "God does not teach us Torah but rather has commanded us to study and to teach it." Both of these passages are discussed by R. Lichtenstein.

36. Rabbi Halafta of Kefar Hananiah, in Mishnah Avot 3:6; see also BT, Berakhot 6a. And compare the words of R. Hanania ben Teradion in Avot 3:2.

37. I say "from time to time" because a sense of God's presence is not a constant accompaniment in the process of learning (at least not for me). On the contrary, there are periods of intense dryness and aridity. God's presence comes and goes. We cannot summon it; we can only prepare ourselves to receive it when it comes.

38. In a related vein, there is also the Talmudic idea that, like us, God spends time each day studying the words of Torah. It is as if God and we share the same passion for the same sacred curriculum. See BT, Avodah Zarah 3b.

39. In the same spirit (though focused more exclusively on Talmud and halakha), Rabbi Joseph Soloveitchik writes:

> When I sit down to learn Torah, I find myself immediately in the company of the sages of the [tradition]. The relations between us are personal. The Rambam is at my right, Rabbenu Tam at my left, Rashi sits up front and interprets, Rabbenu Tam disputes him; the Rambam issues ruling, and the Rabad objects. They are all in my little room, sitting around my table. Torah study . . . is a powerful experience of becoming friends with many generations of Torah scholars, the joining of one spirit with another, the union of souls. Those who transmitted the Torah and those who received it come together in one historical way-station.

Rabbi Joseph B. Soloveitchik, *And From There You Shall Seek*, trans. Naomi Goldblum (Jersey City, NJ: Ktav, 2008), 145.

40. BT, Hagigah 3b.

41. See Rabbi Jacob ben Asher (1269?–1313?), *Arba'ah Turim, Orah Hayyim*, 139; and the comments of Rabbi Joel Sirkes (1561–1640), *Bayyit Hadash* (BaH), 139:6.

42. Seder Eliyahu Zuta 2. In a very different (and perhaps antithetical) vein, there are also Rabbinic statements that emphasize the all-encompassing nature of God's revelation, seemingly at the expense of human interpretation. For example, Rabbi Joshua b. Levi teaches that "Scripture, Mishnah, Talmud, Aggadah, and even that which a venerable student will say before his master, all was said to Moses at Sinai." Leviticus Rabbah 22:1.

43. BT, Berakhot 63a. I have previously explored this idea of knowing God in all one's ways in "Serving God in All We Do: Israel's Journeys and Resting Places," in *The Heart of Torah*, vol. 2, pp. 185–90. Several of the paragraphs that follow are adapted (and lightly edited) from there.

44. R. Abraham Isaac Kook, "*Be-Khol Derakhekha Da'ehu*," in *Musar Avikha*, 30.

45. Mishnah Avot 1:2.

46. R. Abraham Isaac Kook, "*Be-Khol Derakhekha Da'ehu*," in *Musar Avikha*, 30.

47. On this see, for just one example, Eliezer b. Nathan (Ra'avan), *Ma'amar Ha-Sechel, ma'amar* 1. Cited in Moshe Yehiel Halevi Epstein, *Esh Da*t, vol. 9 (Tel-Aviv: Zohar, 1960) 2:1, p. 255. For Ra'avan, this notion is specifically about love of one's fellow Jews.

48. R. Chaim Shmuelevitz, *Sihot Musar*, no. 6, p. 24.

49. Ideally, says R. Yehezkel Levenstein, love of God and love of people are interwoven to the extent that love of God makes deeper love of people possible and love of people likewise makes deeper love of God possible. R. Yehezkel Levenstein, *Or Yehezkel*, vol. 4, p. 123.

50. R. Hayyim Vital, *Sha'arei Kedushah* 2:4.

51. This argument is made by, among others, R. Eliyahu Lopian, *Lev Eliyahu*, vol. 3, p. 95. See also, for example, Hananel Elran, *Ahavat Olam Ahavtikh*, 76. Worth

noting in this context is R. Moshe Hayyim Luzzatto's (Ramhal) explanation for why God loves those who love God's people: "A father loves most those who truly love his children; nature testifies to this fact." Luzzatto, *Mesilat Yesharim*, ch. 19 (Kaplan edition, 181).

52. R. Judah Loew of Prague (Maharal), *Netivot Olam, Netiv Ahavat Ha-Rei'a*, ch. 1. In general, Maharal maintains, "One who loves another loves all that the work of their hands which they have made and brought about. Therefore, when a person loves God it is impossible not to love God's creations."

53. Elran, *Ahavat Olam Ahavtikh*, 76.

54. The Hebrew *daka* is often rendered in English as "contrite" (NJPS, NIV, NRSV) but the term suggests not penitence but victimhood and marginalization.

55. On this see Shalom M. Paul, *Isaiah 40–66: Translation and Commentary* (Grand Rapids, MI: Eerdmans, 2012), 475.

56. Note also the discussion of this verse at BT, Sotah 5a. See also Psalm 66:1–2; Psalm 102:20–21; Psalm 113:4–7.

57. In the future, I hope to offer a Jewish perspective on how our increasing ecological awareness—and the climate emergency that has induced it—ought to affect both our theological thinking and the daily conduct of our lives.

58. In a provocative formulation, the Catholic ethicist Edward Vacek speaks of growing in "cooperative union" with God. Vacek, "God's Gifts and Our Moral Lives," 109.

59. Writing about the theologian Dorothy Soelle's worldview, Elizabeth Johnson writes that "we can know God's love only when we become part of it ourselves." Elizabeth A. Johnson, *Quest for the Living God: Mapping Frontiers in the Theology of God* (New York: Bloomsbury, 2007), 64. The "only" requires analysis but the point is important, and well-stated.

60. Rashi, commentary to Deuteronomy 13:5, s.v. *u-vo tidbakun*. But compare Rashi's commentary to Deuteronomy 11:22, s.v. *u-le-dovkah vo*, and see the resolution offered by *Siftei Hakhamim* to Deuteronomy 11:22, s.v. *ela hidabek* (and see also *Siftei Hakhamim* to Deuteronomy 13:5, s.v. *hidabek bi-derakhav*).

61. R. Yehezkel Levenstein, *Or Yehezkel*, vol. 4, pp. 99, 157. For similar ideas, see, for example, R. Eliyahu Dessler, *Mikhtav Me-Eliyahu*, pp. 34–35; Rabbi Abraham Isaac Kook, *Orot Yisrael* 1:4; and Elran, *Ahavat Olam Ahavtikh*, p. 126. Conversely, R. Israel Meir Kagan (The Hafetz Hayyim) teaches, one who turns away from loving kindness and "wonders why [he] should bother helping someone else utterly distances himself from God." Rabbi Israel Meir Kagan, *Ahavat Hesed* 2:2 (p. 88). Also striking in this regard is a Rabbinic midrash that insists that the highest praise of God is through acts of *hesed* (actually, in a powerfully hyperbolic mode, the midrash claims that *hesed* is the only legitimate form of praising God). See Midrash Tehillim 89:1. Worth noting in this context is the idea that pursuing justice for the weak and downtrodden is what it means to cleave to God and God's attributes. See Jeremiah 22:16 and the commentaries thereon of R. David Altschuler (*Metzudat David*); and R. Meir Leibush Weiser (Malbim).

62. R. Aharon Kotler, *Mishnat Rabbi Aharon*, vol. 1, pp. 150–51.

63. Timothy P. Jackson, *The Priority of Love: Christian Charity and Social Justice* (Princeton, NJ, Princeton University Press, 2003), 8.

64. Kierkegaard, *Works of Love*, 160.

65. Natalia Marandiuc, *The Goodness of Home*, 177. A similar assumption at times animates the writings on love of the great Catholic theologian Karl Rahner. To take just one example, Rahner insists that "one can only love God who is not seen by loving one's brother who is seen." Karl Rahner, "Reflections on the Unity of the Love of Neighbor and the Love of God," *Theological Investigations*, vol. 6, trans. Cornelius Ernst (Baltimore: Helicon, 1961), 233. It is the "only" that is so problematic.

66. My argument in this paragraph is indebted to Vacek, "A Catholic Theology of Philanthropy," 101. For a nice interpretation of the two ways the sages interpret the verse "This is my God and I will glorify [God]" (Exodus 15:2), one focused on direct love of God and one on the imitation of God through interpersonal love, see David Novak, *Covenantal Rights: A Study in Jewish Political Theory* (Princeton, NJ: Princeton University Press, 2000), 147, based on BT, Shabbat 133b.

67. Marandiuc, *The Goodness of Home*, 187.

68. Closer to the mark, I think, is the Christian ethicist who posits that "love for God, self, and neighbor are distinct though mutually entailing." Since they are distinct, she adds, "there are duties proper to each." Weaver, *Self-Love and Christian Ethics*, 9.

69. Sifre Deuteronomy 32.

70. Sifre Deuteronomy 32 based on a creative interpretation of Genesis 12:5. And see also Maimonides, *Sefer Ha-Mitzvot*, Positive Commandment No. 3.

71. I follow the text as read by Rabbi Joel Sirkes.

72. The printed Vilna edition reads "fortunate is his father." The version I present follows the reading of Rabbeinu Hananel (eleventh century).

73. The text of the Vilna edition, which reads "so-and-so, who taught him Torah," would seem to be corrupt; the version I present here makes more sense. My reading follows that of R. Menahem Manish Halpern (1865–1938), *Menahem Meishiv Nefesh* to BT, Yoma 86a, s.v. *peloni she-lamad* (Brody, 1906, edition—p. 38a [75]).

74. BT, Yoma 86a.

75. BT, Yoma 86a.

76. In the same spirit, Maimonides emphasizes that the conduct of those of great religious stature who are known for their piety profoundly impacts upon how others perceive God—they can easily sanctify or desecrate the name of God. See Maimonides, *Mishneh Torah*, Laws of the Foundations of the Torah, 5:11; and see also *Hilkhot De'ot*, 5:13.

77. Midrash Tanhuma (Buber), Naso 24.

78. Joseph B. Soloveitchik, *Halakhic Man*, 108. See also 41–42. For R. Soloveitchik, the means of bringing God down into the world is Jewish law. As one of R. Soloveitchik's most insightful interpreters explains, R. Soloveitchik imagines two stages of contraction: in the first, performed by God, God contracts Godself

within halakhic concepts; in the second, performed by human beings, the person actualizes the ideal halakha in the world and thereby lowers the presence of God into the world. See Lawrence Kaplan, "Joseph Soloveitchik and Halakhic Man," in *The Cambridge Companion to Modern Jewish Philosophy*, ed. Michael L. Morgan and Peter Eli Gordon (Cambridge: Cambridge University Press, 2007), 217–18.

79. Soloveitchik, *Halakhic Man*, 41.

80. Martin Buber, *Meetings: Autobiographical Fragments* (London: Routledge, 2003), 54–55.

81. Martin Buber, *The Origin and Meaning of Hasidism*, ed. and trans. Maurice Friedman (New York: Horizon, 1960), 166; emphasis Buber's.

82. Martin Buber, "The Holy Way," in Martin Buber, *On Judaism*, ed. Nahum Glatzer (New York: Schocken, 1967), 110.

83. Buber, "The Holy Way," 113; emphasis added.

84. In a similar vein, Martin Buber characterizes prayer as "that speech of man to God which, whatever else is asked, ultimately asks for the manifestation of the divine Presence, for the Presence's becoming dialogically available." Martin Buber, *Eclipse of God: Studies in the Relation Between Religion and Philosophy* (Amherst, MA: Humanity, 1988), 126.

85. Abraham Joshua Heschel, "On Prayer," in Abraham Joshua Heschel, *Moral Grandeur and Spiritual Audacity: Essays*, ed. Susannah Heschel (New York: Farrar, Straus and Giroux, 1996), 258, 260, 259. Heschel offers a wonderfully creative (mis)reading of Psalm 130:1, "Out of the depths I call out to you, O Lord." Whereas the verse means that the pray-er is praying de profundis, from the depths, R. Heschel takes it to mean that the pray-er is calling God to come out of the depths in which God is hidden.

86. Abraham Joshua Heschel, "Prayer as Discipline," in Abraham Joshua Heschel, *The Insecurity of Freedom*, 258. I discuss these passages from R. Heschel at much greater length and with more complexity and nuance in ch. 7 of Shai Held, *Abraham Joshua Heschel: The Call of Transcendence*.

87. Heschel, "On Prayer," 258.

88. I hasten to add that Judaism's this-worldliness does not mean that it lacks an idea of the afterlife, as popular presentations (which are really gross distortions) of the tradition often suggest.

89. On whether allegory is really the right term for how the midrash reads the Song, see Levenson, *The Love of God*, 132–34, based on Daniel Boyarin, "Two Introductions to the Midrash on the Song of Songs" (Hebrew), *Tarbitz* 56, no. 4 (1987): 479–500.

90. The fact that Rabbi Akiva forcefully condemned the practice of singing the Song in wedding banquets and taverns makes clear that even in antiquity some Jews read the Song in secular terms. See Tosefta Sanhedrin 12:10 and BT, Sanhedrin 101a.

91. For a brief survey of allegorical approaches to the Song among both Jews and Christians, see J. Cheryl Exum, *Song of Songs* (Louisville, KY: Westminster John

Knox Press, 2005), 73–77. For a scornful approach, see, for example, Marvin Pope's reference to the "allegorical charade" common in interpreting the Song. Marvin Pope, *Song of Songs* (Garden City, NJ: Doubleday, 1977), 17.

92. Davis, *Proverbs, Ecclesiastes, and the Song of Songs*, 233.

93. Davis, *Proverbs, Ecclesiastes, and the Song of Songs*, 231.

94. See also Psalm 48:12 and 96:11.

95. It's important to note, however, that many interpreters take *mi zot*, which the NJPS translation I cite renders as "who is she," to mean "what is this" instead. In other words, they tie Song 3:6 to 3:7–11, a description of King Solomon's palanquin. For an introduction to the issues, and an argument that the phrase in question does indeed mean "what is this" in this context, see Exum, *Song of Songs*, 145–47; for a scholar insisting that *mi zot* has to mean "who is this," see Davis, *Proverbs, Ecclesiastes, and the Song of Songs*, 260.

96. A connection found in Rashi's commentary to the verse, for one example.

97. Davis, *Proverbs, Ecclesiastes, and the Song of Songs*, 260, 261. This reading is bolstered by the presence of the word *olah*, "comes up," in the text, which has robust associations with the temple and the sacrifices offered there. The offering burnt on the altar is called an *olah* because it "comes up" to God; and the thrice-a-year pilgrimage to the temple was called *aliyah* (from the same root as *olah*) *la-regel*. Thus, Davis concludes, "The woman who is 'coming up' . . . appears in a dual aspect, as both the one who offers sacrifice to God and the perfumed offering itself" (261).

98. See, for example, Song of Songs 1:7 and 3:1–4 (where the phrase appears once in each of the four verses).

99. Davis, *Proverbs, Ecclesiastes, and the Song of Songs*, 255.

100. The phrase appears a second time in the prophet Isaiah's reproach of God: where, he asks, is God's yearning (*hamon mei'ekha*, "the churning of Your innards") for the people while they suffer?

101. Davis, *Opening Israel's Scriptures*, 373.

102. I borrow this phrase from Levenson, *The Love of God*, 128.

103. I should note that even if we reject Davis's suggestion that the plain sense of the Song requires us to read it on two levels at once, we are forced to confront the fact that the Song's placement in the canon of the Hebrew Bible invites theological interpretation. In other words, although according to many scholars one can read the text as a "freestanding composition, disconnected from the great story of Israel," one *need not* read it that way, and the larger framework in which we encounter it works against reading it that way. As Jon Levenson asks, "Where in [the Hebrew Bible] do we find such an intense love in which the lovers are separated much of the time, the male of the two is not continually accessible, the identities of the lovers seem to shift in various situations, powerful external forces oppose and threaten the romance, and the consummation of the relationship seems to be continually, maddeningly postponed?" The answer, of course, is that the relationship between God and Israel as portrayed in the Bible is just such a love. Whether the Song was "originally" also about God

and Israel or whether it "acquired" that meaning by being placed in the biblical canon, this interpretation is deeply grounded and theologically arresting. See Levenson, *The Love of God*, 131–32.

Conclusion: Judaism Is About Love

1. Sifre Deuteronomy 307.

2. Kierkegaard, *Works of Love*, 217.

3. Kierkegaard, *Works of Love*, 216–17.

4. See Nobuyoshi Kiuchi, "Commanding an Impossibility? Reflections on the Golden Rule in Leviticus 19:18B," in *Reading the Law: Studies in Honor of Gordon J. Wenham*, ed. J. G. McConville and Karl Möller (New York: T&T Clark, 2007), 33–47; passage cited is at 47.

5. Recall also the Talmudic statement we saw in chapter 6, according to which "the Blessed Holy One does not deal imperiously (*be-tirunya*) with [God's] creations," meaning that God does not make demands that are impossible for human beings to fulfill. BT, Avodah Zarah 3a. And see also R. Eliyahu Lopian, *Lev Eliyahu*, vol. 3, pp. 112–14.

6. I have discussed these verses at greater length in "Before and After the Flood: Or, It All Depends on How You Look," in *The Heart of Torah*, vol. 1, pp. 12–15.

7. Annette Baier, *Moral Prejudices: Essays on Ethics* (Cambridge, MA: Harvard University Press, 1994), 16.

8. Mary Midgley, "Philosophical Plumbing," *Royal Institute of Philosophy Supplement* 33 (1992): 147.

9. On this, see my "People Have Names: The Torah's Takedown of Totalitarianism," in *The Heart of Torah*, vol. 1, pp. 16–20.

10. Midgley, "Philosophical Plumbing," 145.

11. C. Stephen Evans, "The Relational Self: Psychological and Theological Perspectives," in William R. Miller and Harold D. Delaney, *Judeo-Christian Perspective on Psychology: Human Nature, Motivation, and Change* (Washington, D.C: APA, 2005), 74.

12. The psychologist-philosopher James Olthuis speaks of "the fundamental gift/call structure of human life." As he sees it, "Life is one hundred percent a gift received; at the same time, it is one hundred percent a call to respond. The two belong together as two sides of the same coin. The human self is simultaneously a gift we are and a calling we become." James H. Olthuis, "Be(com)ing Humankind as Gift and Call," *Philosophia Reformata* 58, no. 2 (1993): 170–71.

13. Rabbi Reuben Hoschke Kohen, *Yalkut Reuveni* to Genesis 1:27. The natural world tends to move from potentiality to actualization; this is not a matter of choice. Human beings are the sole exception: whether or not we move toward actualization is a matter of choice. On this see Maimonides, *Guide of the Perplexed*, 1:7; and Micah Goodman, *Maimonides and the Book That Changed Judaism* (Philadelphia: Jewish Publication Society, 2015), 19. What is disturbing about Maimonides's formulation is that as he sees it, one is not fully human unless and until one actualizes one's potential. I think it is far better to insist that

we are all fully human and that our humanity comes with a challenge, or a set of challenges, built in. The philosopher John Cottingham is helpful here: "The human is unique in that it cannot glorify God, it cannot achieve the perfection of its kind, just by being a healthy specimen of the species. We need . . . to complete the work of creation: our autonomy, our rationality, inescapably require us to do something more with our lives, to grow, to learn, not just physically but intellectually and aesthetically and morally, to orient ourselves progressively and ever more closely towards the true, the beautiful, and the good." Cottingham, *The Spiritual Dimension*, 42–43.

14. It is also through love that we become more actualized as a self. As the philosopher Natalia Marandiuc puts it, "The self is an inchoate gift that God gives to living human bodies that we must actualize in time in and through love." Marandiuc, *The Goodness of Home*, 98.

15. Abraham Joshua Heschel, *Torah Min Ha-Shamayim*, vol. III, p. 30; Abraham Joshua Heschel, *Heavenly Torah*, 667.

16. On this see, for example, John Cottingham, *Why Believe?* (London: Continuum, 2009), 99–124, and especially 105.

17. Although the word *hesed* appears only three times in the book of Ruth (Ruth 1:8, 2:20, 3:10), it's no exaggeration to say that "its meaning is woven into the book's entire fabric." Eskenazi and Frymer-Kensky, *Ruth*, 1.

18. Ruth Rabbah 2:14.

19. BT, Sotah 14a.

20. Rabbi Tobiah b. Elazar, Lekah Tov to Ruth, end.

21. Mekhilta to Exodus 19:2, cited, most famously, in Rashi's commentary to the verse.

22. R. Chaim Shmuelevitz, *Sihot Musar*, no. 6, p. 25, based on his interpretation of R. Obadiah Seforno's commentary to Exodus 19:3.

ACKNOWLEDGMENTS

I HAVE AMASSED many debts over the course of writing this book, and it is my great pleasure to thank many of the people who have made it possible.

I have had the privilege of exploring many of the ideas presented in this book with thousands of students in the United States, Canada, England, and Israel. I have learned a tremendous amount from their questions, their challenges, and their openheartedness. To each and every one of you, my deep thanks.

Talia Graff, Jonathan Lopatin, and Jeffrey Wechselblatt were my first readers of each chapter and they offered helpful feedback of every kind, from the local-grammatical to the expansive-philosophical. Rabbi Yitz Greenberg, Professor Lawrence Kaplan, Professor Tom Oord, and Leon Wieseltier read an earlier draft of the book and each offered extremely fruitful responses. My sincerest thanks to all of you.

A group of former and present students read a draft and, meeting with me seminar-style, offered an array of stimulating comments and challenging suggestions. To Rabbi Tali Adler, Dr. Vincent Calabrese, Dr. Sydney Levine, Jana Loeb, David Lowenfeld, Professor Raphael Magarik, and Akiva Mattenson, my heartfelt thanks. Thanks also to Hillel Ehrenreich for our discussions of Judaism and effective altruism.

Several friends and colleagues read and commented on various iterations of chapters from the book. To Professor Samuel Brody, Professor Ellen Davis, Dr. Mona Fishbane, Dr. Elana Stein Hain, Rabbi Elie Kaunfer, Professor Richard Primus, Miriam Steinberg-Egeth, Professor Charles Taliaferro, and Rabbi Ethan Tucker, my profound thanks.

Emily Branton carefully combed through the notes, checking countless references, and also offered sage editorial advice at the very last stages of my work on the book. Thank you, Emily.

To the librarians and staff at Columbia University's Butler Library and Union Theological Seminary's Burke Library, my deep, deep thanks. (And to Professor Rebecca Kobrin, who knows why.)

Rabbis Elie Kaunfer and Ethan Tucker have been close friends, teachers, and partners in crime for more years than any of us probably cares to remember. This book, like much else, would not have been possible without their steadfast support and their belief in me and my work.

Hadar's senior leadership team—Elie, Ethan, and Rabbis Avital Hochstein, Avi Killip, and Aviva Richman—are all cherished friends, admired colleagues, inspirational teachers, and, above all else, wonderful people. The collegiality with which we dream, build, and work together is something I marvel at and am grateful for every day. For all of that, and, no less, for the immense kindness and patience with which you respond to my ongoing medical challenges, thank you from the bottom of my heart.

Elisheva Urbas has been a loyal friend and trusted sounding board as I worked on this book. As she read many of the chapters in earlier forms, she always seemed to know just when to offer support and encouragement and when to offer trenchant critique. My debt to her is enormous.

Miriam Steinberg-Egeth helps me navigate the countless obligations, requests, and demands on my time that I am forced to juggle each day. She does so with extraordinary efficiency, effectiveness, and *menschlichkeit*. I am grateful to her and for her.

To the entire Hadar team: thank you for the passion, commitment, and professionalism you bring to everything we do. It is no exaggeration to say that each of you is an inspiration to me. This book belongs to all of you.

Rabbi Yitz Greenberg has been a cherished mentor and friend for more than three decades; my life and my teaching would not be what they are without him and his Torah. Dr. Bernie Steinberg has been a dear friend, a beloved mentor, and a treasured *havruta* in philosophy, theology, and Torah for some thirty years; my debt to him is greater than I can say.

As I struggled to make my way through the world as a child and as a young man who had tragically lost his father and been left in the care of a mother without the emotional tools to raise me, several people took me in in different ways and taught me the meaning of love and kindness. The memory of Rabbi Nahum Muschel, z'l, and of Barbara and Herb Wechselblatt, z'l, and the inspiration of Rabbi Haskel Lookstein, Josh and Anna Gottlieb, Walter and Nancy Dubler, and Dr. David Elcott and Rabbi Shira Milgrom are with me every day. Thank you.

Over the years, Sam Klagsbrun, Arthur Egendorf, Nancy Napier, and Dick Schwartz taught me an immense amount about love, compassion, and presence. Though he would likely find the term alien, Dr. David Kaufman models for me what a life of walking in God's ways can look like. My thanks to you all.

I am deeply grateful for the blessing of close and caring friends. To all of you, and to our friends and community in White Plains, my deep gratitude.

At various points Steven and Tina Price, Michael and Lisa Leffell, and Walter and Nancy Dubler provided me with secluded space in which I could research, write, and think. My sincere thanks to you all.

Helen Nash, who has believed in me and my work for many years now, very generously helped make my work on this book possible. To Helen, to the Nash Family Foundation, and to Dr. Judith Ginsberg, its executive director, thank you.

This publication was made possible through the support of a grant from the John Templeton Foundation. The opinions expressed in this publication are those of the author and do not necessarily reflect the views of the John Templeton Foundation. Special thanks to John Cunningham and David Nassar for their guidance and support.

The John Templeton Foundation, the Nash Family Foundation, the Steiner family, and Harold Grinspoon have all helped Hadar spread word of this book. To all of you: thank you.

When Farrar, Straus and Giroux acquired this book and Eric Chinski agreed to be my editor, several people commented, "Oh, Eric, he's the best nonfiction editor in the business." Little did I know how right they were. Eric and I have been through a lot together. Throughout our work, I have been inspired and challenged by his probing mind, his vast learning, and his consistently good judgment. It's been a true privilege, Eric; thank you. To Sheila O'Shea, Sarita Varma, Tara Sharma, Daniel del Valle, Rose Sheehan, Brian Gittis, and the rest of the team at FSG: thank you. Many thanks also to Eve Atterman and the team at WME for their help and support.

Tina Bennett, agent extraordinaire, has been a cheerleader, tireless advocate, and wise guide over many years. There have been many times when she seemed to be clearer about what I was trying to do than I was—a remarkable gift, I have to say. I count myself lucky to have Tina in my corner, and I owe her a great deal. Thank you, Tina.

My sister, Dalith, and brother-in-law, Zeev, never waver in their love for me and my family. It means more to me than I can or often do say. To you, and to Liat and Sigal, thank you.

My in-laws, Bill and Francine Krasker, have loved my family in incredibly nourishing and dedicated ways. Thank you.

Rachel Forster Held and I have been married for more than sixteen years now. She is my partner in life, my closest confidante, my best friend, and so much else besides. (Occasionally, she even laughs at my jokes.) Watching her parent the three children with whom we have been blessed is an inspiration to me each day. It may sound cliché but it is profoundly true that none of this would be possible without her. Rachel, what's mine is very much yours.

This book is dedicated to Lev Moshe, Maya Aviva, and Yaakov (Coby) Carmel Tzvi. For your insatiable curiosity and your relentless questioning; for your gentleness and deep kindness; and for your insistent silliness and your infectious laughter, thank you. I love you more than I could ever say. This book is a very small expression of my profound love for you. I hope you find meaning, challenge, and inspiration in it.

One final note: In accordance with the spirit in which this book is written, 20 percent of all author's proceeds will go to help feed people who are hungry, both locally and internationally.

INDEX

Schechter, Solomon, 312
Schurz, Carl, 438*n81*
secularized evolutionism, 480*n54*
seeing God, 381–83
seeing ourselves, 379–81
seeing world, 383–84
Seforno, Obadiah, 340
self-affirmation, 30–32
self-assertion, 63
self-awareness: humility and, 32; parental
love and, 99
self-congratulation, 310–12
self-contraction, 82
self-control, 233
self-creation, 396*n1*
self-defense, 207–8
self-help gurus, 399*n27*
self-importance, 394*n33*
self-loathing, 31, 393*n23*; arrogance and,
33–34; forbidding, 33; problems of,
24; as vulgar, 33
self-obsession, 34
self-restraint, 299–300, 490*n158*,
490*n160*
self-sacrifice: Groenhout on, 238, 469*n50*;
Post on, 469*n49*; of women, 236–37
self-satisfaction, 365
self-worth, 24; Amidah prayer and, 38;
arrogance and, 33–34; children and,
90; confession and, 38–39; God's
image and, 25; humility and, 34;
intrinsic, 393*n22*; in political realm,
393*n26*; Ryan on, 395*n40*; threatened,
31; trap, 26; true, 30–32; Zadok
Ha-Kohen on, 33
Sen, Amartya, 406*n77*
Seneca, 407*n84*
separateness, 80; Dilman on, 81; Luria,
I., on, 82–83; mandate, 322; sexual
relations and, 84
Sermon on the Mount, 209
servitude, 39

sexual relations: Akiva on, 85;
euphemisms of, 84; separateness and,
84; Shalom on, 84; Soloveitchik on,
84–85
Shabbat, 315–16
shadow (*tzel*), 163–64
Shakespeare, William, 86
Shalom, Imma, 84
shame, 418*n11*
Shammai, 165
Shavuot, 385
Shefatiah (Rabbi), 45
shekhinah, see divine presence
Shema, 85; blessing before, 391*n5*;
God's love reciprocated through, 24;
recitation of, 3
Sherman, Nancy: on disappointment,
418*n11*; on emotions, 108–109; on
shame, 418*n11*
Shirley (Brontë), 237
shiva home laws, 467*n31*
Shmuelevitz, Chaim, 359
Shor, Yosef Bekhor, 457*n9*
shortcomings, 33
signals of transcendence, 401*n6*
silence: Brueggemann on, 69; Soloveitchik
on, 70
Simhah, Meir, 144
Simlai (Rabbi): on lovingkindness, 225;
on Torah, 225–26
Simundson, Daniel, 330; on chosenness,
331
Singer, Peter, 139–40
sinners: assumptions around, 218–19;
children of, 274–76; Davis on, 318;
hate of, 215–19; Radak on, 267
slaves, 186–87; Goldingay on, 403*n45*;
O'Connor on, 502*n112*; Soloveitchik
on, 403*n44*; *see also specific slaves*
Slote, Michael, 468*n39*
Smith, Adam, 139
Sodom, 57, 59, 317